T0305213

THE BLACKWELL ENCYCLOPEDIA OF MANAGEMENT

MANAGEMENT INFORMATION SYSTEMS

THE BLACKWELL ENCYCLOPEDIA OF MANAGEMENT

SECOND EDITION

Encyclopedia Editor: Cary L. Cooper
Advisory Editors: Chris Argyris and William H. Starbuck

THE BLACKWELL ENCYCLOPEDIA OF MANAGEMENT

SECOND EDITION

MANAGEMENT INFORMATION SYSTEMS

Edited by
Gordon B. Davis
Carlson School of Management,
University of Minnesota

Blackwell
Publishing

BLACKWELL PUBLISHING
350 Main Street, Malden, MA 02148-5020, USA
9600 Garsington Road, Oxford OX4 2DQ, UK
550 Swanston Street, Carlton, Victoria 3053, Australia

First published 1997 by Blackwell Publishers Ltd
Published in paperback in 1999 by Blackwell Publishers Ltd
Second edition published 2005 by Blackwell Publishing Ltd

2   2006

Library of Congress Cataloging-in-Publication Data

The Blackwell encyclopedia of management. Management information
systems / edited by Gordon B. Davis.
p. cm. — (The Blackwell encyclopedia of management ; v. 7)
Rev. ed. of: The Blackwell encyclopedic dictionary of management information
Systems / edited by Gordon B. Davis. c1999.
Includes bibliographical references and index.
ISBN 1-4051-0065-6 (hardcover : alk. paper)
1. Management information systems—Dictionaries. I. Davis, Gordon Bitter. II. Blackwell
encyclopedic dictionary of management information systems. III. Series.
HD30.15 .B455 2005 vol. 7
[HD30.213]
658′.003 s—dc22
[658′.4/038′011]
2004024924

ISBN for the 12-volume set 0-631-23317-2

ISBN-13: 978-1-4051-0065-6 (hardcover : alk. paper)

A catalogue record for this title is available from the British Library

Set in 9.5/11pt Ehrhardt
by Kolam Information Services Pvt. Ltd, Pondicherry, India

Contents

Preface

Information and communications technology has changed rapidly since the first edition of the *Blackwell Encyclopedia of Management*. Each wave of new technologies enables innovations in organization systems for information processing and communication. New ways of performing the transactions and management and knowledge work activities of organizations are made possible. Organization systems are no longer simple and easily constructed or modified; they are complex, depend on technology, and require significant effort to construct, implement, and modify. Managers and other knowledge workers at all levels in an organization can do their work better if they understand information systems. They can rely on technical personnel to handle the technical issues, but they need to understand the systems if they are to use them effectively and efficiently, and if they are to be able to specify improvements and innovative changes.

Information systems are vital to products, services, and management processes in an organization. A new organization function has been established to plan, implement, and manage the information technology infrastructures and systems required by an organization. The business function is justified by the size of investments in information resources and its importance to organizations. An academic discipline has also emerged to teach and research the use of information technologies in organizations and the management of information resources.

A variety of names are applied to the new organization function and academic discipline. The term, Management Information Systems or MIS, is widely used; other often-used terms are information systems and information management. The term IT or information technology may also be used because of the importance of information and communications technology in information systems.

The focus of the *Management Information Systems* volume in the *Blackwell Encyclopedia of Management* is on information systems in organizations and the management of information and information system resources. There are articles describing the concepts, processes, and tools employed in planning, building, and managing information systems and information resources. Those persons in an organization who deal with or use information systems and information resources should have a user-level understanding of systems, applications, and databases. They frequently need to understand the information and communications technology employed in the systems. They do not need to be technologists, but they need a user-level or managerial-level understanding of the technology. The emphasis of the MIS volume is on the systems, applications, and processes that are employed in planning, managing, and delivering information resources to an organization. However, there are also user-level and management-level explanations of technical terms that are relevant to dialogue about existing systems and opportunities and requirements for new applications. In other words, technologies that are important only to technologists are not included; technologies that are important to organization systems are explained. An example of a technology that is included is RADIO FREQUENCY IDENTIFICATION (RFID), a new technology that is the basis for new systems for managing inventory and tracking customer purchases.

A useful starting point for a user of the *Management Information Systems* volume is the entry on MANAGEMENT INFORMATION SYSTEMS. It defines and describes the management information system for an organization and the scope of the organization function that manages it. Underlying concepts are found in entries on INFORMATION CONCEPTS and SYSTEM CONCEPTS APPLIED TO INFORMATION SYSTEMS.

The articles and definitions in the volume have been written by academics and professional colleagues working in the field of information systems. They were instructed to make the descriptions technically correct but understandable to a reader who is not a specialist in the field. The writers come from universities and companies in a number of countries. I appreciate their work.

Gordon B. Davis

About the Editors

Editor in Chief
Cary Cooper is based at Lancaster University as Professor of Organizational Psychology. He is the author of over 80 books, is past editor of the *Journal of Organizational Behavior*, and Founding President of the British Academy of Management.

Advisory Editors
Chris Argyris is James Bryant Conant Professor of Education and Organizational Behavior at Harvard Business School.
William Haynes Starbuck is Professor of Management and Organizational Behavior at the Stern School of Business, New York University.

Volume Editor
Gordon B. Davis is the Honeywell Professor of Management Information Systems Emeritus in the Carlson School of Management, University of Minnesota. He pioneered in the academic field of information systems, beginning in 1967 with the first formal degree program in the United States. He participated in and helped form most of the academic associations related to the field. He has served as advisor, co-advisor, or committee member to over 100 doctoral students, lectured in 25 countries, held visiting professorial appointments in Europe and Asia, written 21 books, and published over 200 articles, monographs, and book chapters. His book *Management Information Systems: Conceptual Foundations, Structure, and Development* has been recognized as a classic text. He has received recognition as an ACM Fellow, AIS Fellow, and AIS LEO award (for lifetime achievement in the field of information systems). He has a doctorate from Stanford University and honorary doctorates from the University of Lyon, the University of Zurich, and the Stockholm School of Economics.

Contributors

Dennis A. Adams
Bauer College of Business, University of Houston

Gediminas Adomavicius
Carlson School of Management, University of Minnesota

Gove Allen
Freeman School of Business, Tulane University

Soon Ang
Nanyang Technological University, Singapore

Priscilla Arling
Carlson School of Management, University of Minnesota

David Bahn
Metropolitan State University of Minnesota

Nicholas L. Ball
Carlson School of Management, University of Minnesota

Robert J. Benson
The Beta Group

Paul L. Bowen
Department of Commerce, University of Queensland

Eric S. Boyles
Consultant, St. Paul, Minnesota

Susan A. Brown
Eller College of Management, University of Arizona

Glenn J. Browne
Jerry S. Rawls College of Business Administration,
Texas Tech University

William J. Caelli
Information Security Research Center, Queensland University of Technology

Christopher L. Carr
Katz Graduate School of Business, University of Pittsburgh

C. Janie Chang
San Jose University

Norman L. Chervany
Carlson School of Management, University of Minnesota

Roger H. L. Chiang
University of Cincinnati

Alina M. Chircu
McCombs School of Business, University of Texas at Austin

Mary Beth Chrissis
Software Engineering Institute, Carnegie Mellon University

Claudio U. Ciborra
London School of Economics and Political Science

Elayne Coakes
Westminster Business School, University of Westminster

Jim Coakes
Westminster Business School, University of
Westminster

Rosann Collins
University of South Florida

Wendy L. Currie
Warwick Business School, University of
Warwick

Qizhi Dai
LeBow College of Business, Drexel University

Amit Das
Nanyang Technological University, Singapore

Michael J. Davern
The University of Melbourne

Gordon B. Davis
Carlson School of Management, University of
Minnesota

Roger Debreceny
University of Hawaii

William H. DeLone
Kogod School of Business, American University

Gerardine DeSanctis
Fuqua School of Business, Duke University

Roberto Evaristo
University of Illinois, Chicago

Gordon C. Everest
Carlson School of Management, University of
Minnesota

H. Kevin Fulk
Bauer College of Business, University of
Houston

Mark A. Fuller
Washington State University

Stefano Grazioli
McIntire School of Commerce, University of
Virginia

Jungpil Hahn
Krannert Graduate School of Management,
Purdue University

Scott J. Hamilton
The Manufacturing Guild, St Paul, Minnesota

Joel R. Helgeson
Appiant, Inc., Roseville, Minnesota

Nancy K. Herther
Wilson Library, University of Minnesota

Loke Soo Hsu
University of Singapore

Blake Ives
Bauer College of Business, University of
Houston

Rodger Jamieson
University of New South Wales

Andrew P. Jansma
School of Business and Economics, Michigan
Technological University

Brian D. Janz
University of Memphis

Sirkka L. Jarvenpaa
McCombs School of Business, University of
Texas at Austin

Jesper M. Johansson
Microsoft Corporation

Julie E. Kendall
Rutgers University

Kenneth E. Kendall
Rutgers University

William R. King
Katz Graduate School of Business, University of
Pittsburgh

Barbara Klein
Management Studies, University of Michigan –
Dearborn

Christine Koh
Nanyang Technological University,
Singapore

Vlad Krotov
Bauer College of Business, University of
Houston

Frank F. Land
London School of Economics and Political
Science

Linda Levine
Software Engineering Institute, Carnegie
Mellon University

Moez Limayem
City University of Hong Kong

Donald J. McCubbrey
Daniels College of Business, University of
Denver

D. Harrison McKnight
Eli Broad College of Business, Michigan State
University

Ephraim R. McLean
Robinson College of Business, Georgia State
University

Salvatore T. March
Owen Graduate School of Management,
Vanderbilt University

Richard O. Mason
Southern Methodist University

Manjari Mehta
Bauer College of Business, University of
Houston

Tarun Mital
Bauer College of Business, University of
Houston

Eve Mitleton-Kelly
London School of Economics and Political
Science

William D. Nance
San Jose State University

J. David Naumann
Carlson School of Management, University of
Minnesota

R. Ryan Nelson
McIntire School of Commerce, University of
Virginia

Boon-Siong Neo
Nanyang Technological University,
Singapore

Kathryn Ritgerod Nickles
School of Law, Wake Forest University

Steve H. Nickles
Babcock Graduate School of Management,
Wake Forest University

Fred Niederman
John Cook School of Business, Saint Louis
University

T. William Olle
T. William Olle Associates, Surrey, England

Jinsoo Park
Korea University Business School, Seoul, South
Korea

Stacie Petter
Robinson College of Business, Georgia State
University

Theresa M. Quatrani
IBM Software Group, Philadelphia

Reagan M. Ramsower
Hankamer School of Business, Baylor
University

Sangkyu Rho
Seoul National University

Dzenan Ridjanovic
Laval University, Quebec

Frederick J. Riggins
Carlson School of Management, University of Minnesota

Thomas M. Ruwart
Digital Technology Center, University of Minnesota

Sandy Shrum
Software Engineering Institute, Carnegie Mellon University

Sandra A. Slaughter
Tepper School of Business, Carnegie Mellon University

Randy Snyder
Consultant, Wisconsin

Christina Soh
Nanyang Technological University, Singapore

Mani R. Subramani
Carlson School of Management, University of Minnesota

Nellai Subramaniam
Bauer College of Business, University of Houston

Jonathan K. Trower
Hankamer School of Business, Baylor University

Viswanath Venkatesh
Walton College of Business, University of Arkansas

Douglas R. Vogel
City University of Hong Kong

Lester A. Wanninger, Jr.
Carlson School of Management, University of Minnesota

Hugh J. Watson
Terry College of Business, University of Georgia

Ron A. G. Weber
Faculty of Information Technology, Monash University

James C. Wetherbe
Jerry S. Rawls College of Business Administration, Texas Tech University

Charles A. Wood
Mendoza College of Business, Notre Dame University

A

absorptive capacity and information technology

Susan A. Brown

Absorptive capacity is the ability to identify, assimilate, and exploit external information (Cohen and Levinthal, 1990). This ability in an organization derives from a foundation of individual knowledge and organizational mechanisms for knowledge sharing. Some overlapping knowledge among individuals is necessary to facilitate knowledge sharing; however, a diverse base of knowledge is required across individuals for the organization to recognize the value of a wide variety of new knowledge. The concept is applicable to information technology applications because the applications employ new methods and technologies introduced from outside the organization or outside a particular functional unit, thus requiring employees to recognize the value of something new. Some organizations, and functional units within them, are able to introduce radical changes in systems more rapidly than others. One explanation is the difference in their relative absorptive capacity.

Applications of absorptive capacity in information systems have focused on identification and implementation of new information technology and systems and the relationship between absorptive capacity and organizational learning/knowledge management. Research suggests that understanding how knowledge about the business and knowledge about technology overlap among employees is important in determining organizational ability to identify and implement new information technologies (e.g., Boynton, Zmud, and Jacobs, 1994). In this case, the higher the absorptive capacity, the greater the ability to incorporate new technologies. Low absorptive capacity suggests the need to improve knowledge, mechanisms for sharing knowledge, or both. One technology approach to enhancing the knowledge sharing in an organization is through the use of a knowledge management system. Thus, one benefit of a knowledge management system may be its contribution to the absorptive capacity of the organization.

Bibliography

Boynton, A., Zmud, R., and Jacobs, G. (1994). The influence of IT management practice on IT use in large organizations. *MIS Quarterly*, 18, 299–320.

Cohen, W. M. and Levinthal, D. A. (1990). Absorptive capacity: A new perspective on learning and innovation. *Administrative Science Quarterly*, 35, 128–52.

accounting use of information technology

C. Janie Chang

Advances in information technology (IT) are pervasively affecting every aspect of the accounting profession. IT has made many companies more efficient and accurate in performing accounting, internal audit, and tax functions. The uses of IT in accounting are reflected mainly in accounting information systems (AIS) and in how accounting-related information is accessed.

ACCOUNTING INFORMATION SYSTEMS

An AIS collects, stores, processes, and reports information regarding the financial transactions of an organization. One major objective of an AIS is to provide internal control over the processing of transactions. This control is necessary to insure the organization's financial activities are recorded and reported accurately, fairly, and on a timely basis. The increasing importance of AIS is manifested by the scandals of Parma-latte in Italy and Enron and World Com in the US. There is an obvious worldwide trend of increased emphasis on internal controls over information systems. A particular important example is the US Sarbanes-Oxley Act. This Act, developed in 2002, currently is enforced by the US Securities and Exchange Commission (SEC) through rule making for publicly traded companies requiring them to maintain good internal controls of their AIS.

Accounting information systems are the most common information systems utilized in business. In general, they are a combination of manual (people-oriented) and automated (computer-based) components that work together to accomplish accounting system objectives. Due to the enterprise-wide role of many accounting applications, an organization's set of integrated accounting applications may be its largest information system. During the past decade, many firms have chosen to implement integrated systems to eliminate most manual parts of their accounting information systems.

Accounting information systems should perform business data processing with well-designed internal controls. In the input stage, the system collects and records data, such as sales/purchase orders, shipping/receiving data, and vendor/customer payments. If necessary, data from non-machine-readable documents (such as a handwritten price tag) are entered into machine-readable form for use in subsequent computerized processing.

In the processing stage, an AIS performs primary accounting operations, utilizing the data that were collected in the input stage. The most common data processing operation is the updating of organizational files and databases to reflect the completion of a transaction. IT has proved advantageous in processing accounting data in which rote calculations are involved and in linking financial records and tax records. For the past few decades, IT has been used to improve various accounting functions, such as the calculation of depreciation and amortization on assets and the printing of payroll checks and individual tax reports from electronic payroll data. Some accounting applications handle such functions as the flow of data from financial records to tax forms.

In the output stage, an accounting system produces documents that describe financial transactions that have been processed. These documents can describe single transactions or aggregated transactions. At the single transaction level, customer sales orders and bank deposit receipts are examples of outputs. Examples of outputs that depict aggregated transactions are corporate financial statements that summarize the financial transactions in which an organization has engaged during a specified period of time. The most important recent application of IT to improve financial reporting capabilities is the XBRL (Extended Business Reporting Language). Developed in 2000, XBRL is an XML-based specification for preparing, distributing, and analyzing financial information (*see* XML (EXTENSIBLE MARKUP LANGUAGE)). XBRL has been named as the next-generation digital language of business. It is expected to improve the integrity of electronic financial reports by standardizing financial reporting over the INTERNET. Companies will be able to use the web to report financial information in a timely, accurate, and understandable format.

ACCESSING INFORMATION

Given the advances in IT and web-based access, companies anywhere in the world can access financial information on companies that trade on the major stock exchanges and can access rules and regulations related to accounting standards and other documents. For example, the US Financial Accounting Standards Board (FASB) website has information on current activities related to drafting and reviewing new accounting standards and guidance. Copies of the various pronouncements can be ordered directly from the FASB website. Also, the SEC website has many types of items that previously could be obtained only by subscribing to a commercial service or by requesting them from the SEC. With the web, this information is available immediately at no cost. The SEC website provides links to statutes, press releases, special reports and studies, and regulatory actions. In addition, the well-known "EDGAR" service on the SEC website (www.sec.gov/) allows visitors to view or download copies of the financial reports (such as 10-Ks) filed by publicly traded companies.

Similar access is available from regulatory agencies in other countries.

ACM

The Association for Computing Machinery is the largest broad-based international computer and information system society (*see* ASSOCIATIONS AND SOCIETIES FOR INFORMATION SYSTEMS PROFESSIONALS).

ADA

ADA is a general-purpose programming language sponsored by the US Department of Defense. It is especially suited for the programming of large, long-lived systems with a need for ongoing maintenance. It supports modern programming structured techniques and concurrent processing.

Adobe Acrobat

see PORTABLE DATA FORMAT

agency theory applied to information systems

Soon Ang

Agency theory examines the contracts between a party (the principal) who delegates work to another (the agent). Agency relations become problematic when the principal and agent have conflicting goals and when it is difficult or costly for the principal to monitor the performance of the agent. When goals are incongruent, the agent is assumed to have a different set of incentive structures from the principal; the agent will consume perquisites out of the principal's resources and make suboptimal decisions. These activities produce efficiency losses to the principal. To counter these losses, the principal designs contracts to align the goals at the lowest possible costs. Costs can arise from providing incentives and from monitoring to insure that the agent is acting for the principal's interests.

Agency theory can offer insights for information systems. First, principals can design information systems to monitor the actions of agents. Electronic communication systems, electronic feedback systems, and electronic monitoring systems are examples of monitoring devices that can be implemented to insure that agent behaviors are aligned with principal interests.

Secondly, information systems professionals themselves often enter into agency relationships with other stakeholders in organizations and agency problems can arise. Important examples of such agency relationships include systems development, outsourcing (*see* IT OUTSOURCING), and end-user computing.

SYSTEMS DEVELOPMENT

As principals, users often engage information system (IS) professionals as agents to develop information systems on their behalf. Due to a lack of understanding and knowledge of each other's domain, goal conflict may arise between the two parties. To reduce agency costs, one or both parties must try to narrow goal differences. IS professionals can invite users to participate more actively throughout the development life cycle. This gives the users more opportunities to verify requirements and insure that the final system is aligned with user needs. Further, users may request that the information system produce information-rich documentation so that monitoring is made easier and more readily available to users.

OUTSOURCING

In any outsourcing arrangement, the client company (principal) is usually motivated to shift its IS operations to external vendors who can carry out the work at the lowest possible cost. The vendor, on the other hand, may be looking for high profit in the arrangement. There is thus an economic goal conflict. To protect its interests, the client will increase its monitoring of the vendor. This can be achieved by requesting regular operational performance measures from the vendor, frequent meetings with the vendor to review progress of outstanding projects, and independent auditors to review benchmarks and internal controls of the vendor.

END-USER COMPUTING

Agency theory can help explain the dynamics of end-user computing. End users develop information systems themselves with little IS involvement. End-user computing, interpreted in agency theoretic terms, is a mechanism for reducing agency problems by eliminating the agency relationship between the user and IS professional.

agile development

Manjari Mehta and Dennis A. Adams

Agile development (AD) combines accepted principles of programming and management into a new discipline for software development for rapidly changing environments. This development approach contains several different methodologies, one of which is the most popular "extreme programming." AD is a balance between highly structured and sometimes bureaucratic development processes and those processes that are very unstructured and ad hoc. For instance, although AD follows planning and modeling techniques such as data flow diagrams and UNIFIED MODELING LANGUAGE (UML), it avoids excessive reliance on them which can hinder the developer from meeting dynamic customer requirements. AD employs documentation only to the extent that it helps developers and customers understand the code. Instead, it relies heavily on face-to-face information sharing.

AD is based on the following tenets:

1   *Interaction among individuals* is preferred over strict adherence to formal plans, processes, and tools. The most efficient and effective way to share information is to use face-to-face communication. As a people-centric approach, the working environment must be conducive to the personality and working styles of those developing the system.
2   *Customer collaboration* is preferred over negotiating contracts. Because an organization's need can change frequently, it would

be better that managers communicate with the developers on a daily basis rather than employ a detailed requirements document. This insures that customer satisfaction is the highest priority and incremental changes of the working software quickly reflect customer's needs.
3   *Working software* is successful software. It is preferable to have working software with less documentation over non-working software with comprehensive documentation. The key is to keep it as simple as possible. Working software must be delivered frequently, ranging from two weeks to two months.
4   *Responding to change* is better than following a plan. Change is welcomed and even embraced late in the development process. Because software is developed and delivered in quick iterations, agile development enables the design team to quickly respond to new customer requests.

Some developers would say that AD flies in the face of the decades-old traditions of structured design and waterfall methodologies and that the frequent changes lead to scope creep, never-ending projects, budget overruns, and the like. Extreme programming is an example of an agile development methodology. The very name "extreme programming" would seem to indicate some sort of radical, perhaps careless method of systems development. Extreme programming, however, has a set of guiding principles that must be followed, lending structure to the methodology. These principles are interconnected and support one another.

1   *Paired programming*: A pair of programmers work together on a single workstation. One developer interacts with the workstation and the other explores, thinks one step ahead, and analyzes the current logic. Each reviews and supports the other and they only work together on the current task. After it is complete, they disband and circulate among the other teams. This is done at least once a day.
2   *Refactoring*: Refactoring (Fowler, 1999) is the process of rewriting existing code with the goal of making it easier to understand and more robust. Refactoring is done to a small piece of code, and tested immediately, in

order to insure that the external behavior of the code (features/functionality) remains unchanged.

3 *Collective ownership*: Anyone can write new code or refactor any existing part of the software at any time. Classes and methods are not owned by developers; this insures that complex or redundant code never lasts long.

4 *Short releases and deliveries*: A release happens only as often as the business decides to implement the software and put it to actual use. A delivery is simply submitting a modified software module for approval or feedback. Both of these happen with great frequency during the project.

5 *Planning*: In a series of short meetings, a dialogue occurs concerning what is possible (developer viewpoint) and what is desirable (customer viewpoint) where the customer determines the scope of the problem addressed in a particular software release, the priority of features in successive releases, and the dates of the releases. The developer estimates the time to implement a feature, the consequences of technical capabilities, and the development process. At the end of the planning process, a list of tasks is created and each developer volunteers for a particular task, refactors existing code to include the new feature, writes a test case, and then codes so that the test succeeds.

6 *Metaphors*: Extreme programming makes use of metaphors to communicate difficult concepts in order to provide contexts to discuss the difficult concepts. Metaphors can be used to articulate the central theme of the software and to develop a shared understanding among developers and customers.

7 *Continuous integration*: One of the key tenets of this type of agile development is to make sure that every module is tested and integrated with the rest of the software every few hours.

8 *40-hour week*: Developers using extreme programming methodologies are held to working a 40-hour week. None should work overtime, defined as 60 hours in a week, for two weeks in a row.

9 *On-site customer*: Customers must spend a significant amount of time with the development team. If possible, the customer should be a full-time member of the development team, and allowed to make decisions regarding the scope of the project and priority of deliverables. This is perhaps the toughest responsibility for the customer to bear.

10 *Coding standards*: As a result of paired programming and collective ownership, any programmer can write, refactor, and integrate code. Therefore, extreme programming cannot support a wide variety of programming styles and tools. Typical standards including name conventions for variables, placement of curly brackets for methods, and no duplicate code.

11 *User stories*: A customer writes user stories and tells the developer how he or she will use the system. A good user story is always testable with code, is focused, does not have optional plots, and is clearly understood by the title of the story. Once the customer writes a user story, he or she moves on to writing an acceptance test, which, if it succeeds, will be a measure of successful software.

12 *Test cases*: Once an acceptance test is written by the customer, the developer writes a code version of it. This test is written before the code is written. If the test runs, the team knows that it is "done" with the code. Tests also work as a type of documentation, recording the intentions of the actual software module.

Agile development is not recommended when the development project is large, or the customer is not willing to spend time with the development team and if the customer insists on having a complete set of software specifications before programming begins. It requires an environment that provides quick feedback to a coded module. As a development methodology, agile development is expected to gain more use as the need increases for organizations to react more quickly to their environments.

Bibliography

Adolph, S. (2004). Use cases. *Proceedings of SD West*.

Astels, D., Miller, G., and Novak, M. (2002). *A Practical Guide to Extreme Programming*. Upper Saddle River, NJ: Prentice-Hall.

Bain, S. (2004). Test cases. *Proceedings of SD West*.

Beck, K. (2000). *Extreme Programming Explained*. Boston: Addison-Wesley.

Fowler, M. (1999). *Refactoring: Improving the Design of Existing Code*. Boston: Addison-Wesley.

Fowler, M. and Highsmith, J. (2001). The agile manifesto. *SD Magazine*, August; www.sdmagazine.com/documents/s = 844/sdm0108a/0108a.htm?temp = 1ZL6j1GCzY, accessed June 28, 2004.

AIS

The Association for Information Systems is an international society for information system academics (*see* ASSOCIATIONS AND SOCIETIES FOR INFORMATION SYSTEMS PROFESSIONALS).

AITP

Formerly the Data Processing Management Association, the Association of Information Technology Professionals (AITP) is an international organization of information system professionals (*see* ASSOCIATIONS AND SOCIETIES FOR INFORMATION SYSTEMS PROFESSIONALS).

alignment of information systems to business

see STRATEGIC ALIGNMENT BETWEEN BUSINESS AND IT

allocating resources to IT/IS

Robert J. Benson

Allocating organization resources to information technology and information systems is often termed information economics. It is a management methodology for allocating resources among competing information technology (IT) and information systems (IS) alternatives. Originally created as a prioritization methodology for IT development projects, information economics has been widely extended for use in managing the complete organization expenditures on IT (the "IT spend"), including IT asset and portfolio management. The concepts defined as information economics are also applicable to prioritization and resource allocation in such business areas as marketing, research and development, and product development.

Information economics matches competing resource demands with a finite set of resources with which to satisfy the demands. For example, for IT development projects the management problem is to determine which of the many competing projects should be funded and scheduled. By analyzing each competing project for its financial impact, strategic fit (the degree to which the project supports management's strategies), operational fit (the degree to which the project supports improvement in the organization's performance), and risk (the degree to which risks of increased cost or project failure exist), management can identify which projects are the best for the organization to fund and schedule.

The underlying business issue addressed by information economics is how much to invest in information technology (as compared with marketing, new products, or new business acquisitions), and which IT investment will produce the greatest business impact. This is not a new problem. IT investments may include many possibilites such as cost-saving automation, management information systems, customer-focused systems, and electronic commerce (*see* E-COMMERCE). In every case, the central problem is to express in business terms how an enterprise can achieve maximum business impact from its investment in information technology, and then compare the investment with all the others to determine which investment mix is best for the organization.

BASIS FOR INFORMATION ECONOMICS ANALYSIS

Information economics assesses resource demands (e.g., IT projects) based on strategic effectiveness and operational effectiveness. These concepts are described by Michael Porter (1996) as an important basis for competitiveness, and are also used in shareholder value evaluations. The information economics methodology identifies the several strategic intentions management has for the organization, where the strategic intentions identify how management intends to improve the organization's strategic effectiveness (or, in the case of government, mission effectiveness) and operational effectiveness (e.g., cost, quality, etc.). The business case for each competing demand adds the financial measurements (e.g., ROI) and costs, schedules, and specialized resource requirements. Then, through cause-and-effect analysis, each competing demand for resources is evaluated as to the strength of support for those strategic intentions.

Information economics also identifies the risks for each competing demand for resources, where risk is defined as the risk of increased cost, or risk of failure of the initiative or project. The risk is included in the process of evaluating which of the many competing demands for resources is best.

The end result is a holistic, complete view of all competing resource demands, all assessed in a consistent fashion for financial impact, strategic fit, operational fit, and risk. The management team can then select those best for the organization.

INFORMATION ECONOMICS AS PORTFOLIO MANAGEMENT

The competing demands for resources (e.g., IT projects) are an example of a portfolio. By treating IT projects as a portfolio, information economics applies portfolio management objectives: squeeze out the low-value and invest in the high-value portfolio components.

EVOLUTION OF INFORMATION ECONOMICS TO THE COMPLETE IT SPEND

The initial information economics practice originally described in 1987–8 was focused on IT projects. Organizations rapidly evolved their use of information economics into portfolio methodologies for managing the complete IT spend. By evaluating the IT spend for applications, infrastructure, services, and management, management teams can understand their investments in IT and apply the information economics assessment tools against them.

The same issues apply to the IT spend as to IT projects, namely, that management is faced with competing demand for resources. In the case of the complete IT spend, this competing demand is not limited to new development projects. In many organizations, the proportion of IT spend devoted to keeping existing things going and maintained is the largest proportion of IT investment. This can be as much as 80 or 90 percent of the entire IT spend. These resources need to face competitive analysis and not receive a continuation of funding as an entitlement from prior period utilization. Information economics thus evolves into a methodology for assessing the effectiveness and desirability of the greatest proportion of IT spend, the existing set of applications and infrastructures.

In this information economics evolution, rather than being limited to "prioritization," information economics applies the same financial impact, strategic effectiveness, operational effectiveness, and risks analysis against the existing in-place application portfolio, the infrastructure portfolio, and the service and organizational portfolios. For each, the same issues apply as had originally been established for project prioritization: the degree of support for management's strategies, the degree of support for improving the organization's performance, and the degree of risk of increased cost or failure.

Similarly, information economics has evolved from merely an IT resource allocation process to one used by organization managers for all forms of resource allocation. In all cases, these resources are to be allocated and competed for, whether they are IT, research and development, new products, marketing programs, etc.

INFORMATION ECONOMICS METHODOLOGY

The information economics methodology engages management in assessing strategic fit, operational fit, and risk. Management looks at these issues from the organizational perspective rather than an organizational "silo" perspective. The holistic view of all competing demands subjects them to the same tests, irrespective of their organizational source.

Traditionally, IT investments and development projects have been assessed with return on investment (ROI) and cost-benefit analysis methods. These work well when the assessment applies to a single organization and the benefits are tangible and easily measured, as, for example, when benefits are primarily cost reductions in a single department. Many IT applications, especially distributed and infrastructure systems, affect multiple organizations, integrate activities across the enterprise, and significantly change how the enterprise does business. As a result, many of the benefits derived from IT projects are intangible relative to cost-benefit analysis.

Traditional cost-benefit analysis is especially difficult when an enterprise must make fundamental IT infrastructure investment decisions. The investments in infrastructure – for example, in networks and databases – are one step removed from the actual business activity that causes reduced cost, improved customer service, or new products and services. For example, a communications network needed to support an automated teller machine (ATM) network for a financial institution by itself cannot reduce operating cost or improve customer service. The network is simply one component of the overall business activity needed for an ATM service. How much should be invested in it? What alternatives should be considered? Should a network be built in-house or outsourced?

Information itself has similar attributes. For example, from a manager's perspective, it is important to have the full customer history available when making decisions in a financial institution. A loan officer can use the history to assess a proposed loan transaction. The IT investment issue is the value of this information and how much the financial institution should invest in providing it.

Information economics evaluates the impact information technology has on the enterprise in four domains:

- *Financial performance improvement*, such as increased profitability, productivity, and earnings.
- *Business performance improvement*, based on business measures such as customer satisfaction, product quality, time to market, time to process orders, inventory turns. Management expects that improvements in performance of this type will ultimately be reflected in improved financial performance.
- *Management's strategic intentions to improve business and financial performance*. These are management's goals, objectives, or agendas that must be accomplished for a business unit to meet its business and financial performance measures. Such items can often be stated as critical success factors. Managers expect that achieving their management agendas will ultimately produce improvements in financial performance.
- *Risk and uncertainty* include items that can affect the cost of the investment (e.g., uncertainty or disagreement about development project objectives, or risky new technology) or that can cause conditions leading to project or investment failure (e.g., unknown project requirements). When applied to installed IT systems, the items include factors leading to prospective failure or higher than necessary operating costs.

Information economics defines IT investment value in terms of IT contributions to business objectives in the four domains. Managers define specific management factors in each domain. These factors are applied consistently to each IT investment project for the enterprise. Each project – and each portfolio element in the complete IT spend – is compared to every other project or element in terms of impact on the business. A business value analysis and decision tool results.

By applying the factors from the four domains to all aspects of the IT spend, information economics connects each investment and proposed development project to the strategic intentions for the enterprise in a consistent way. Information economics asks what the effect of each project or investment will be on each strategic intention (e.g., on financial performance) if the investment is made.

BENEFITS

Organizations that employ information economics for resource allocation see these benefits:

- Overcome silo approaches to justification.
- Engage the management team with an organizational view.
- Provide a common documentation for all existing and prospective investments.
- Formalize the business case.
- Assess both benefits and risk.

Bibliography

Benson, R. J., Bugnitz, T. L., and Walton, W. (2004). *From Business Strategy to IT Action: Right Decisions for a Better Bottom Line*. New York: John Wiley.

McTaggert, J. M. et al. (1994). *The Value Imperative: Managing for Superior Shareholder Returns*. New York: Free Press.

Parker, M. M. and Benson, R. J. with Trainor, E. H. (1988). *Information Economics: Linking Business Performance with Information Technology*. Englewood Cliffs, NJ: Prentice-Hall.

Porter, M. E. (1996). What is strategy? *Harvard Business Review*, November/December, 113–18.

application service provision (ASP)

Wendy L. Currie

Application service provision (ASP) was an important proposed approach to delivering and enabling software applications over the INTERNET. The business reasons for the approach and its failure as originally marketed are useful in understanding business needs for software applications and the problems in the market meeting these needs. Application service provision emerged during the late 1990s as a "revolutionary" approach. The development of an ASP industry was fueled by the belief that *utility computing* offered a new business model to small and medium-size businesses, enabling them to purchase computer processing power using a subscription, pay-as-you go pricing model, similar to the way electricity, gas, and water are purchased. So instead of purchasing software as a product, customers would rent software as a service. Thus, the concept of *software-as-a-service* was created. This fueled the growth of numerous ASP startups in the late 1990s, some working with independent software vendors (ISVs) to offer hosted software applications and IT infrastructure, while others developed their own web-enabled applications. The ASP business model was also seen as a new form of applications outsourcing, different from traditional outsourcing in that it enabled suppliers to offer software on a one-to-many model, rather than forging a one-to-one customer relationship.

The ASP industry consortium (ASPic) was established in May 1999 by 25 technology sector firms. Its mission was to "promote the ASP industry by sponsoring research, fostering standards, and articulating the measurable benefits of this evolving delivery model." ASPic members defined ASPs as firms that "manage and deliver application capabilities to multiple entities from data centers across a wide area network. An ASP may be a commercial entity, providing a paid service to customers, or, conversely, a not-for-profit or government organization supporting end-users." Another definition claimed that "ASPs are service firms that provide a contractual service offering to deploy, host, manage and rent access to an application from a centrally managed facility. ASPs directly, or indirectly with business partners, provide all of the specific activities and expertise aimed at managing the software application or set of applications."

Other outlets to promote ASP emerged in the form of Internet reference or news sites. For example, WebHarbor.com described itself as "The ASP Industry Portal." Others were aspnews.com and aspindustrynews.com, with the mission to "cover the ASP marketplace." All these sites served to "educate" potential customers by providing market analysis on the latest software-as-a-service product offerings, market trends and surveys, mergers and acquisitions between industry players, ASP customer reference sites, gossip and industry/business analysis.

Technology market analysts predicted that the ASP market would grow to $18 billion (Gartner Group) or $24 billion (IDC Group) by 2005. Others also predicted similar growth rates (i.e., Forrester $23 billion; Dataquest $22.7 billion; Yankee Group $19 billion). These revenues would be derived mainly from the delivery of software-as-a-service in the business-to-business (B2B) and business-to-consumer (B2C) arenas.

By 2000, ASPs had emerged in various forms with diverse technology sector firms providing the services. Enterprise ASPs offered standard enterprise resource planning (ERP) (*see* ENTERPRISE SYSTEMS (ENTERPRISE RESOURCE PLANNING OR ERP)) software to small and medium-size firms; vertical ASPs targeted specific industry sectors (i.e., health, finance, manufacturing); horizontal ASPs offered business software applications (i.e., payroll, human resources, travel and expenses, etc.); pure-play ASPs dealt only in software applications designed to be web-enabled (these firms were largely Internet startups). In addition, ASP-enablers were primarily technology sector firms that provided the IT infrastructure (i.e., telecommunications firms, networking and data center providers, etc.) (Currie, Desai, and Khan, 2004).

While some commentators argued that *utility computing* was no different from the service bureaus of three decades before, the technology industry quickly became overcrowded with self-styled ASPs, each attempting to differentiate themselves from their competitors by offering either generic or specific hosted software applications.

Despite the hype surrounding the ASP business model, with promises to revolutionize business computing, 2001 saw a rapid decline in the fortunes of ASPs. This led to over 60 percent of ASPs going out of business. On closer examination, the first phase of the ASP market was characterized by flawed and failed ASP models (Hagel, 2002). So what were the reasons for the poor adoption and diffusion of the ASP model?

First, the large amounts ASPs spent on advertising and marketing failed to convince small and medium businesses about the value of using ASPs, especially as procuring commodity applications (email) on a price per seat/per month basis offered them few business benefits. Yet deploying ASPs for more complex software applications hosting exposed the customer to additional risks, such as data security infringement and theft. ASPs generally misunderstood the customer requirements of their targeted product/service and/or sector and unquestioningly believed that customers required 24/7 software application delivery and enablement over and above other key performance indicators. This was clearly misguided. Research shows that few customers were concerned about the *anytime, anyplace, anywhere* (the Martini) approach to software delivery and access (Currie et al., 2004). Rather, customers were more concerned about their data security and integrity than accessing their software applications continuously. Trusting their data to a third party was not something most potential customers were pre-

pared to do, particularly when startup ASPs did not have a brand identity, tangible assets, or customer reference sites.

Second, few ASPs offered mission-critical software applications on an affordable and secure basis. Most offered simple collaboration tools (i.e., email and office suites). Potential customers could not see any additional business value in paying for a hosted office suite, particularly in cases where the leading independent software vendors charged extra for this service even where the customer was already using the suppliers' products.

As ASPs found it difficult to generate revenues from commodity applications, and with ongoing concerns from potential customers to deploying ERP applications using a hosted model, they increasingly failed to turn a profit. This led to the refusal on the part of venture capital firms to award second-round investment funding, with the result that numerous ASPs went out of business.

Third, ASPs offering commodity applications found that scalability was critical to the survival of their business. ASPs had to scale the application to adequate numbers (i.e., thousands of paying customers) to generate revenues (Kern, Willcocks, and Lacity, 2002). Few managed to achieve this. Equally, ERP vendors found that potential customers did not wish to replace existing software applications with new ones. Rather, they wanted to maximize their legacy systems through integration. Most ASPs failed to take this on board. So by 2001, ASPs faced either a scale problem (i.e., commodity applications with too few customers to make a profit) or a scope problem (i.e., customers wishing to integrate hosted software applications across heterogeneous technology platforms and environments). These problems proved insurmountable to most ASPs.

Fourth, ASPs were faced with a serious technical problem in that the lack of broadband connectivity meant that hosted software applications did not meet customer demands for speed and availability. Traditional client server software applications were not well suited to be delivered using a hosted model. ASPs therefore needed to develop web-enabled products suited to a remote delivery environment. Quite simply, the technology was still too immature to enable the fast and efficient delivery of hosted software applications worldwide.

As ASPs continued to go out of business, those that survived the technology sector downturn increasingly associated the term ASP with dot.com failure. As a result, ASPs relabeled themselves using terms such as managed service providers, application infrastructure providers, and web service providers. While immature technology sector markets such as ASP show that an initial proliferation of firms eventually leads to market consolidation, the first phase of the ASP business model was flawed for the market, business, and technical reasons described above.

Recognizing that adding business value to the customer is critical to all technology sector firms, the second phase of the ASP market is evolving into a new business model called WEB SERVICES. Unlike ASP, which was populated by numerous dot.com startups, web services have the financial backing and commitment of large-scale technology industry leaders (i.e., Microsoft with its .NET™ and Sun Microsystems' J2EE™). Web services claim to offer a *new paradigm* for connecting business processes independent of their underlying implementation. Finally, web services are designed to extend the life of legacy systems and resolve many of the problems which ASPs failed to tackle.

Bibliography

Currie, W., Desai, B., and Khan, N. (2004). Customer evaluation of application services provisioning in five vertical sectors. *Journal of Information Technology*, **19**, 1 (March), 39–58.

Hagel, J. (2002). *Out of the Box: Strategies for Achieving Profits Today and Growth Tomorrow Through Web Services*. Boston: Harvard Business School Press.

Kern, T., Willcocks, L., and Lacity, M. C. (2002). Application service provision: Risk assessment and mitigation. *MIS Quarterly Executive*, **1**, 2 (June), 113–26.

artificial intelligence

Amit Das

The attempt to program computers to perform tasks that require intelligence when performed by humans is known as artificial intelligence (AI). Examples of such tasks are visual perception, understanding natural language, game playing, theorem proving, medical diagnosis, and engineering design.

Beginning in the late 1950s, AI researchers have modeled a variety of problems (such as playing checkers or proving theorems in mathematics) in terms of state space search. A *state* denotes a particular configuration of the components of a problem. The position of pieces on a chessboard and the structure of terms in a mathematical expression are examples of states (for the problems of chess playing and theorem proving, respectively). The application of a permissible operator (such as a legal move in the game of chess or an expansion of terms in a mathematical expression) alters the state of a problem. The set of all possible states, together with the operators that enable transitions among them, constitutes the *state space* representation of a problem.

The solution of an AI problem consists of a search through the state space, i.e., the successive application of operators until the final state of the problem matches the desired goal state (a checkmate in chess or the simplest expression of a theorem). Unless the problem is very limited in scope (e.g., playing tic-tac-toe), the state space is hopelessly large for an exhaustive search (the game of chess has more than 10^{120} states). Additional knowledge (beyond the rules of the game) is required to guide the state space search in promising directions. This search control knowledge is commonly called *heuristic knowledge*. The process of problem solving in AI described above is called *heuristic search* (Newell and Simon, 1976).

Chess playing and theorem proving are examples of tasks where the careful application of logic has to be supplemented by heuristic knowledge to produce an efficient solution. As AI research progressed, it was discovered that specialized tasks, such as diagnosis, design, and planning, require even more knowledge to formulate (in state space terms) and solve (through heuristic search). In order for knowledge to facilitate the solution of an otherwise intractable problem, the knowledge must be represented in a suitable form for use by a computer program. Methods of reasoning about the knowledge to apply it to a particular situation must also be specified. The representation of domain knowledge and efficient methods of reasoning with it have become central concerns of AI since the 1970s (Feigenbaum and McCorduck, 1983). Certain formalisms, including if–then rules, semantic networks, frames, and predicate logic, have been developed to represent and utilize knowledge efficiently in problem solving.

AI methods have been successfully applied to problems in computer vision, robotics, knowledge-based systems (*see* EXPERT SYSTEMS; KNOWLEDGE BASE), understanding natural language, and machine learning (the extraction of patterns from large volumes of data). AI-based computer systems have been successfully deployed in manufacturing to support the design and diagnosis of products and processes. In services, AI has been applied to a variety of tasks, including medical diagnosis, financial statement analysis, and logistics management. In addition to dedicated AI systems, AI techniques have also been used to improve the user interfaces of conventional information systems (*see* COGNITIVE SCIENCE AND INFORMATION SYSTEMS).

Artificial intelligence has complemented its focus on encoding explicit knowledge with methods to store knowledge implicitly, in a manner similar to the brain. Information for decision-making is encoded in connections among nodes in a network. This method automatically generates problem-solving knowledge from patterns in data, and such knowledge is automatically updated as more data become available.

See also *neural networks*

Bibliography

Feigenbaum, E. A. and McCorduck, P. (1983). *The Fifth Generation: Artificial Intelligence and Japan's Computer Challenge to the World.* Reading, MA: Addison-Wesley.
Newell, A. and Simon, H. A. (1976). Computer science as empirical inquiry: Symbols and search. *Communications of the ACM*, **19** (3), 113–26.

ASCII

A commonly used code for alphabetic, numeric, and special characters is the American Standard Code for Information Interchange (ASCII). The original ASCII standard code used seven bits. An extended ASCII code employs eight bits (*see* CODING OF DATA FOR INFORMATION PROCESSING).

assessment of management information system function

Gordon B. Davis

In order to evaluate the resources being spent on information management and whether or not it is meeting organizational needs, assessment of the management information system function can be performed periodically. The evaluation should be carried out within the context of the organization and its strategies and plans.

There are two persistent questions relative to the information systems of an organization:

1 How much should be spent on information systems? (Allocation of organizational resources to information systems.)
2 How good are the information systems and the function that supports them? (Evaluation of organization, management, and services of the information systems function.)

Within industries, spending levels on information systems differ substantially among successful companies. Within the constraints of resource availability, how much should be spent depends on two factors: (1) what the organization wants to achieve with information technology, and (2) how much it must spend to be competitive. Companies differ in culture, capabilities, and the way they use information technology, so what organizations wish to achieve will differ; industries differ in their use of information technology, so what organizations must spend to be competitive will differ by industry. This suggests that information systems can only be evaluated within their organizational and environmental context.

An in-context approach to information system assessment provides the framework for investigating these key management questions. The in-context assessment framework is presented as a complete assessment approach. A company may wish to perform a complete, comprehensive assessment, but it is more likely that the assessment will be targeted at a high-level evaluation or at a specific problem area. The value of the in-context assessment framework is in identifying factors to be included in assessment and in defining the overall context for targeted assessments.

THE CONTEXT FOR INFORMATION SYSTEMS

The information architecture of a company serves an organization which: (1) exists in an industry with a competitive environment; (2) has a specific organizational structure, management style, and culture; and (3) has specific information requirements. These define the overall context for assessment of the information management function and the portfolio of information system applications.

The existing *industry context and competitive environment* define what is expected of information systems at the current time. This can change as new applications and new information products (and other innovations) are used to change the industry structure and basis of competitive advantage. The relevant assessment questions should do more than merely determine whether information systems meet industry and environmental norms. Since information technology can help achieve competitive advantage by changing the way the organization or the industry operates, the management information systems (MIS) function and information systems should also be assessed on participation in competitive innovation and change.

Organizations differ in the way they approach problems and the way they respond to competitive pressures. These differences are reflected in the *organizational structure*, *culture*, and *management style* of the organization. This context is important in an assessment of how well the information systems fit the organization as it currently exists. The assessment can also identify changes in information systems that are necessary to support strategic changes in culture and organization.

OVERVIEW OF THE PROCESS

A complete, comprehensive assessment of information systems can be divided into four stages, each of which is subdivided into a series of assessment activities that focus on the major

areas of interest. The four stages represent a logical order of assessment in that there is a sequential dependency between the various stages. This suggests that assessment should proceed in a systematic fashion, since the activities within each stage build upon knowledge gained in prior stages. However, within each stage there is only a limited dependency between the individual activities, so the sequence of these may be determined by specific priorities or by convenience factors.

In general, it may be possible to postpone or even omit a particular activity within a given stage, although it is probably inadvisable to omit a stage altogether. When an assessment is targeted or limited in scope, the stages provide a framework for doing enough investigation to establish an appropriate context for the area of assessment interest. For example, a targeted assessment of end-user computing should first establish some context consisting of relevant organizational context and infrastructure context. For a limited assessment with a wide scope, the framework identifies the range of things to be considered, even though the depth of analysis may be limited. The framework of four stages and the areas of assessment are as follows.

Stage I: Analysis of the organizational context for information systems

1 Analysis of the industry and competitive environment of the organization.
2 Analysis of the historical development, culture, structure, and activities of the organization.
3 Analysis of the organization's requirements for information and technology support.

Stage II: Assessment of the information system infrastructure

4 Assessment of information systems architecture of applications and databases.
5 Assessment of the technical architecture for information systems.
6 Assessment of organization and management structure for information systems.
7 Assessment of the investment in information systems.

Stage III: Assessment of the organizational interface for information systems

8   Assessment of information system planning and control.
9   Assessment of information system use.
10   Assessment of end-user computing.

Stage IV: Assessment of information system activities

11   Assessment of application development and maintenance.
12   Assessment of information system operations.
13   Assessment of capacity planning and technology acquisition.
14   Assessment of information system support functions.
15   Assessment of information system safeguards.
16   Assessment of information system personnel management.

The steps in the assessment framework are organized in a top-down fashion. They proceed from the most general topic of competitive environment and company structure to the overall structure of information systems and the service level being provided to the management interface between information system and organization and then to the specific activities within the information system function. The evaluation of the information management function is an organizational evaluation; it deals with processes more than outcomes.

Stage I: Analysis of the organizational context for information systems. At the conclusion of this stage of analysis, there should be a clear definition of competitive forces, major competitors, and key success factors in the market. There should be an understanding of the way the organization has responded to the competitive environment through its organization, policies, culture, etc. There should be an appreciation at a general level of the organization's requirements for information and support services and how these relate to the context of the organization and its environment.

Stage II: Assessment of the information system infrastructure. After establishing the organizational context in stage I, stage II of the assessment analyzes the various components of the information system's infrastructure, i.e., the institutional structures and established processes that define the organization's information system's capability. The infrastructure is viewed in four dimensions: an *information dimension* (the application systems and databases that provide information support); a *technical dimension* (the architecture of computer equipment, system or non-application software, and telecommunications facilities); an *organizational dimension* (the organization and management structure of the information systems function); and an *economic dimension* (the organization's investment in information systems).

Stage III: Assessment of the organizational interface for information systems. Having assessed the institutional structures that represent the established information system's capability, the next stage is to evaluate the management processes that act as the essential interface between these structures and the rest of the organization. There is an assessment of information system planning and control to evaluate the existence of these processes and their quality. Assessment of information system use examines how effectively the organization uses its information system and meets the real needs of its users.

Stage IV: Assessment of information system activities. The last stage covers assessment of activities and management within the information system function. There are six activities that encompass the assessment of individual functions contained within the information system. Assessment of *application development and maintenance* is an evaluation of the methods and procedures for systems developed by professional programmers. The use of standard methods, methodologies, and development tools are included. Assessment of *information system operations* looks at the organization and management of operations. It includes an evaluation of facilities, use of operations software, and scheduling of work. Assessment of *capacity planning and technology acquisition* examines the processes by which the information management function tracks utilization, forecasts needs, employs performance measurement tools, and evaluates alternatives. The step also evaluates the processes by which new technologies are identified and considered for use. Assessment of *information system support functions* is an evaluation of the way that the function deals with its customers, the users of applications, and end users who need support. Assessment of *information system safeguards* is a study of the security measures and backup and recovery provisions. It may focus on how well the organization has done in studying security issues and in providing for backup and recovery. Assessment of *information system personnel management* considers the current personnel policies and procedures and evaluates how they are working in terms of recruitment, upgrading, and retention.

The assessment framework guides the assessment team in organizing its work, collecting data, and structuring its analysis and reporting. All activities performed by the MIS function are assessed within the organizational context of what is expected of MIS. These expectations are calibrated by the context of competitive environment and organizational strategy. Targeted evaluations, such as an assessment of MIS personnel management, are performed within the overall context.

associations and societies for information systems professionals

Ephraim R. McLean

Several associations and societies have been founded, or have evolved from other groups, since the invention of the electronic digital computer. Some of them are quite technical in nature, while others are strongly managerial in character. The latter group of associations is our primary focus here.

There is no one international body that captures the attention and loyalty of all those involved in information system activity, both professional and academic. Each country has one or more groups that cater to the specialized interests of its members. For example, in Australia, there is the Australian Computer Society (ACS), and in the United Kingdom, the British Computer Society (BCS). In the case of the US, there are several competing professional associations vying for members' attention.

The best-known broad international society is the International Federation for Information

Processing (IFIP), founded under the auspices of UNESCO in 1960 and currently headquartered in Laxenburg, Austria. It is governed by a general assembly, consisting of member representatives from 45 national computer societies. IFIP's mission is to be the leading, truly international, apolitical organization which encourages and assists in the development, exploitation, and application of information technology for the benefit of all people.

IFIP sponsors a general world congress every two years and has a regular newsletter. Most of its technical activities are conducted through special-interest technical committees (TC) and working groups (WG). Of special interest is IFIP Technical Committee 8 (TC8) on Information Systems. TC8 was founded in 1976 (growing out of WG2.6 on Databases) and at present contains seven working groups: WG8.1 on the Design and Evaluation of Information Systems (founded in 1976); WG8.2 on the Interaction of Information Systems and the Organization (1977); WG8.3 on Decision Support Systems (1981); WG8.4 on E-Business Information Systems: Multi-Disciplinary Research and Practice (1986); WG8.5 on Information Systems in Public Administration (1988); WG8.6 on the Transfer and Diffusion of Information Technology (1992); and WG8.8 on Smart Cards (1998). The titles of these working groups give a good indication of the scope of the interests of the members of TC8. Each of the working groups has an annual or biannual working conference, sometimes singly and sometimes in combination, with each conference having published proceedings. While TC8's scope of interest and international coverage is broad, it has a relatively small membership of a few hundred individuals, mostly academics.

The oldest computing association is the IEEE Computer Society, the largest of the 37 societies that make up the Institute of Electrical and Electronic Engineers (IEEE). It was founded in 1946 in the US and today has nearly 100,000 members worldwide. The Society is headquartered in Washington, DC. It has a number of conferences, technical committees, chapters, and publications, the most prominent of the latter being the monthly magazine *Computer*. As its name suggests, the Computer Society is primarily technical in its orientation.

The second oldest computing society (by one year) is the Association for Computing Machinery (ACM) founded in the US in 1947. Headquartered in New York City and covering all aspects of computing, computer engineering, and computer science, ACM now has 80,000 members worldwide. Its flagship publication is the monthly *Communications of the ACM*, first published in 1958. In addition, ACM publishes 33 other journals and numerous newsletters and proceedings from its 34 special interest groups (SIGs). All these publications are housed in electronic form in the ACM Digital Library. More than 60 technical conferences a year are sponsored by ACM and its SIGs, chapters, and regions. Among ACM's special interest groups, that on Management Information Systems (SIGMIS), formerly known as the Special Interest Group on Business Data Processing (SIGBDP), is the second oldest of all the SIGs, having been founded in Los Angeles, California, in 1961. Aimed at the organizational and managerial uses of information technology, this SIG has published *The DATA BASE for Advances in Information Systems* (or *DATA BASE* for short) since 1969. With an international readership of nearly 3,000, *DATA BASE* is the oldest scholarly publication devoted to the business aspects of computing. Another SIG of interest to information systems professionals is the Special Interest Group on Computer Personnel Research (SIGCPR). Founded in 1962 as an independent group and subsequently affiliated with ACM, SIGCPR has held annual conferences, with published proceedings, nearly every year since its founding. In 2003, it merged with SIGMIS and lost its separate identity, although it is continuing to hold its annual conference on computer personnel research.

While the primary focus of ACM and the IEEE Computer Society is on the computer, The Institute for Management Sciences (TIMS), headquartered in Linthicum, Maryland, is concerned with management processes and techniques, especially those using quantitative approaches. In 1995, TIMS merged with the Operations Research Society of America (ORSA) to form the Institute for Operations Research and the Management Sciences (INFORMS). The combined membership of INFORMS is approximately 13,000 worldwide. The main journal of INFORMS is *Management Science*, which began publication in 1953 and has been an important outlet for the publication of information systems research. In 1990, TIMS began publishing *Information Systems Research*, which has now emerged as INFORMS' primary publishing outlet for research in information systems. INFORMS also holds annual research conferences, both within the US and at international venues. A group within INFORMS, the INFORMS Information Systems Society, meets in conjunction with these conferences, as well as publishing a regular newsletter. The INFORM Information Systems Society currently has approximately 550 members, primarily academics.

The newest of the large academic information societies is the Association for Information Systems (AIS), founded in 1995 and headquartered in Atlanta, Georgia. With over 4,100 members worldwide, AIS is organized around three regions: Asia/Pacific, Europe/Middle East/Africa, and the Americas. Annual meetings are headed in each of the regions, with the International Conference on Information Systems (ICIS) being an international research-oriented conference for the entire association. ICIS was founded in 1980 and in 2001 became part of AIS. AIS publishes two journals, the *Communications of the AIS* and the *Journal of the AIS*, and supports the publication of the *Management Information Systems Quarterly* and the *Management Information Systems Quarterly Executive*, published by the University of Minnesota and Indiana University, respectively. These publications, as well as the proceedings of the various conferences that AIS supports, are housed electronically in the AIS e-Library.

In addition to academically oriented associations, there are a number of professionally oriented groups. The oldest and largest of these is the Association for Information Technology Professionals (AITP), founded in 1951 and renamed AITP in 1996. It was originally known as Data Processing Management Association (DPMA), and before that as the National Machine Accountants Association. There are currently 12,000 regular members and 5,000 student members organized into 260 chapters throughout North America. AITP has long had a strong emphasis on education for its members.

A noteworthy professional society is the Society for Information Management (SIM). Founded in 1969 as the Society for Management Information Systems, SIM consists of 2,500 members who are committed to advancing the management and use of information technology to achieve business objectives. SIM members are typically corporate and divisional heads of information systems (IS) organizations, their IS management staff, leading academics, consultants, and other leaders who shape or influence the management and use of information technology. SIM holds a national conference, SIMposium, each year and also supports the publication of the *Management Information Systems Quarterly Executive*, mentioned above.

asynchronous transmission mode

ATM is a high-speed switching protocol. It is an important data transmission method because it provides efficient use of band width in transmitting messages. An ATM cell or packet is a fixed length of 53 bytes. It accommodates well to transmissions requiring a constant bit rate, such as video and audio. It can operate at different speeds.

auctions

see INTERNET AUCTIONS

auditing of information systems

Rodger Jamieson, Paul L. Bowen, and Ron A. G. Weber

An audit of an information system (IS) is an examination, by qualified persons such as a CISA (*see* CERTIFIED INFORMATION SYSTEMS AUDITOR), of documentation, procedures, operations, programs, and data for the purposes of identifying and correcting weaknesses in an organization's information systems. Objectives of the IS audit function are to safeguard IS assets, maintain data integrity, and insure that IS functions are performed efficiently and effectively.

IS audits are undertaken by two types of auditors. *External auditors* are concerned primarily with financial information systems. They focus on evaluating IS controls that affect the reliability of financial data. *Internal auditors* recommend and design appropriate IS controls. They often serve on IS project teams or review the specifications produced by IS project teams.

RISKS ASSOCIATED WITH INFORMATION SYSTEMS

Information systems can significantly affect the success of many organizations. The development, implementation, operation, and maintenance of information systems, however, are subject to substantial risks.

1   *Information systems required for organizational continuity*. Many organizations cannot function without their information systems, e.g., airlines cannot schedule flights or book seats and banks cannot process checks. These organizations would cease to exist if their information systems remained inoperative for only short periods.
2   *High cost of information systems*. Many organizations have made substantial investments to develop and implement information systems. These investments sometimes account for more than 50 percent of their total capital investment. Moreover, information systems often are costly to operate and maintain. Significant losses can be incurred if they do not deliver expected benefits.
3   *Information systems affect employee behavior*. Information systems can be used to control and reward employee performance. Incorrect or inadequate information can result in dysfunctional behavior, e.g., employee morale may drop because employees believe that they have not been evaluated correctly.
4   *Intra- and inter-organizational information sharing*. Information systems enable information to be exchanged among individuals inside and outside organizations. An organization's ability to respond to change may depend on how well employees can exchange information among themselves. Its desirability as a trading partner may depend on how well it can exchange information with other organizations.

5   *High risk of failure.* Despite their high cost, many information systems fail, i.e., they are never placed in use, abandoned after a short service life, or not used for decision-making purposes. Even organizations known for their IS expertise sometimes have dramatic failures.

6   *High cost of software failures.* Software failures can cause both direct and indirect losses. Direct losses can occur from malfunctions that arise in physical processes or financial processes, e.g., environmental pollution by an out-of-control nuclear reactor or overpayments to creditors by a faulty electronic funds transfer system. Indirect losses arise through damage to reputation, e.g., loss of customer goodwill through errors in customer invoices.

7   *Data security violations.* Computer systems sometimes contain confidential information such as military secrets, financial data, and personal details. If IS controls fail to maintain the privacy of this information, national security can be jeopardized, competitive advantages can be lost, and individual lives can be ruined.

PERFORMING AN IS AUDIT

Auditors perform several phases of work during an IS audit.

Background investigation.   Audits are concerned with assessing and reducing risks. To assess the general risks associated with an organization and its information systems, auditors investigate and evaluate environmental factors, such as:

1   *Industry.* The reliance of organizations on information systems depends in part on the nature of the industry in which they compete. For example, information systems are likely to be more critical to financial services organizations than to mining companies.

2   *Organizational structure.* As control becomes more decentralized, the likelihood of variations in the quality of controls and personnel increases. Decentralized organizations also increase the demands on information systems to provide more diverse information about the performance of their subunits.

3   *Personnel.* The integrity and competence of senior management, internal auditors, and IS personnel affect how external auditors approach the audit. If senior management lacks integrity, external auditors may decline the entire engagement. If internal auditors lack competence, they may be unable to design appropriate controls or to properly evaluate IS functions and applications. If IS personnel lack competence, they may make inappropriate choices from hardware and software alternatives, develop error-prone systems, or fail to take advantage of strategic IS opportunities.

4   *Hardware.* When external auditors accept an engagement, they represent themselves as having the competence and knowledge required to conduct the engagement properly. For an IS audit, this includes having adequate knowledge of the hardware used by the client organization.

5   *Database management system (DBMS).* Many controls are implemented in an information system via the capabilities provided by a database management system. For example, IS personnel often use DBMSs to implement input, processing, and output controls. Auditors must have a thorough understanding of any DBMS used by an organization to be able to evaluate the quality of controls.

6   *Languages.* To evaluate application functions, auditors must understand the computer languages used by an organization. For example, at times auditors must read program source code to evaluate whether control weaknesses exist in a program.

Planning.   Once background information has been obtained, an audit must be planned. The following tasks must be undertaken:

1   *Setting priorities.* Auditors often cannot examine all an organization's information systems. Some systems (e.g., financial reporting systems) must be examined each year, others on a rotating schedule, and others not at all. Auditors select systems to evaluate based on the purpose of the audit and the importance of the system to the organization.

2   *Determining required procedures and evidence.*
Auditors consider the sensitivity, criticality,
pervasiveness, and implementation characteristics of each system when determining
procedures to perform and evidence to collect. Evidence is obtained from documentation, physical inspection, questionnaires,
interviews, and test data.

Evidence collection.   To evaluate the reliability of
controls in an information system, auditors use
various means of evidence collection including:

1   *Documentation.* Auditors usually begin their
procedures by inspecting documentation.
Documentation provides evidence about
how the system was developed, what controls are supposed to exist, and what functions the system is supposed to perform.
2   *Questionnaires and interviews.* Auditors use
questionnaires and interviews to gather information from IS personnel about how the
system operates, known weaknesses with the
system, and future plans. They may also use
questionnaires and interviews to gather information from users about the effectiveness
of the IS function and to identify problems
with specific information systems.
3   *Testing.* Auditors perform compliance
testing to verify that the system contains
the controls and performs the functions described in the documentation. They then use
test data to verify that the system responds
correctly to typical input, to unusual but
acceptable input, and to illegal input.
4   *Generalized audit software (GAS) and query
languages.* GAS and query languages allow
auditors to examine existing data. They use
these tools to identify potential problems or
inconsistent relationships among data, generate control totals that they can check
against other evidence, and produce samples
for further investigation, e.g., a list of customers to contact to confirm the unpaid balances of their accounts.
5   *Concurrent auditing techniques.* Concurrent
auditing techniques collect evidence about
the information system while it operates.
These techniques include software routines
embedded in a system that record random
or unusual transactions as they are being
processed.

Evidence evaluation.   Experienced IS auditors
evaluate and interpret the evidence gathered.
They use the piecemeal evidence collected
during an audit to arrive at overall decisions
about the quality of the information systems
they have examined.

Report.   The audit report should indicate both
strong and weak points in the systems examined
by the auditors. For each weak point, the report
should indicate its seriousness, suggest the priority for remedying the weakness, and where
possible indicate a way of correcting the weakness. Auditors address their report to the audit
committee of the board of directors or, if no
audit committee exists, to the chief executive
officer.

Follow-up.   Auditors follow up at appropriate
intervals to determine that IS strengths are
being maintained and that IS weaknesses are
being corrected.

INFORMATION SYSTEM CONTROLS

Information system controls consist of generalized IS procedures, generalized programmed
controls, application-specific programmed controls, and miscellaneous controls. Internal auditors help design and implement information
system controls. External auditors evaluate
whether the controls are working effectively
and make suggestions for improvements.

Generalized information system procedures.   IS procedures control the overall IS management environment in which information systems are
developed, implemented, operated, and maintained. They include IS planning, personnel,
disaster recovery, systems development, configuration control, and data administration
procedures.

1   In *IS planning,* management develops plans
to insure that information systems meet the
organization's strategic, managerial, operational, and regulatory information requirements. Management also establishes general
procedures and guidelines to control the development, implementation, operation, and
maintenance of information systems.
2   *Personnel procedures* include hiring, compensation, training, job assignments, and

supervision. They are important because IS personnel, especially highly skilled programmers, can often circumvent controls. Organizations attract and retain high-quality IS personnel by providing adequate compensation, ongoing training programs, and interesting job assignments.

3 *Disaster recovery procedures* protect data and insure that IS operations can be resumed in a timely manner if hardware, software, or facilities are lost, damaged, or destroyed. Disaster recovery techniques include making program and data backups, using fault-tolerant hardware and software, and establishing alternative processing sites.

4 *Systems development procedures* prescribe the steps to be used to build new systems. By following a defined methodology, systems can be developed that are more likely to meet cost and time constraints, to have high reliability, to integrate easily with other systems, and to be resilient to change.

5 *Configuration control procedures* define the approach to be used to modify existing systems. They insure that modifications are acceptable to all users, that these modifications do not introduce errors or inconsistencies, and that the system retains its resiliency.

6 *Data administration procedures* maintain and enhance the value of data stored in information systems. They embody the organization's strategy to insure data is authorized, accurate, complete, and timely.

Generalized programmed controls. Generalized programmed controls are software and hardware controls that apply to the operation of all information systems. They include boundary controls, communication controls, operating system controls, and database controls.

1 *Boundary controls* govern access to computer hardware, software, and data. They include physical access controls and passwords.

2 *Communication controls* maintain the integrity and privacy of data transmitted between the user and the system or between information systems. They include data transmission protocols, which determine that messages sent are the same as messages re-

ceived, and encryption, which scrambles messages so that they cannot be understood by unauthorized persons.

3 *Operating system controls* govern access to files and programs, regulate computer resource use (e.g., disk space and processor time), and manage and protect processes currently being executed.

4 *Database controls* provide more extensive access controls over data than operating system controls. Data in databases is often encrypted to insure that database controls are enforced, i.e., that users must access data through the database management system rather than accessing data directly. Database controls include concurrency controls to insure that changes made by one user are not corrupted by changes made simultaneously by another user and view controls to limit access to a subset of data in the database.

Application-specific programmed controls. Application-specific controls are software controls that apply to the operation of individual information systems, e.g., an inventory information system. They include input controls, processing controls, and output controls.

1 *Input controls* seek to minimize data errors entering the information system. They include menus, data entry screens, and interactive help to facilitate data entry; range and format checks to insure the accuracy of individual values; completeness and reasonableness checks to insure the accuracy of records; and batch checks (e.g., dollar amount totals) to insure the accuracy of groups of records.

2 *Processing controls* insure that correct files are accessed and that software executes correctly. Processing controls include file labels to insure that the correct data are accessed, file existence checks to insure that all the data needed for a process are accessible, and commit and rollback functions to insure that update processes produce consistent results.

3 *Output controls* determine the data that users can receive. They include physical restrictions that limit access to secure terminals, printers, and other output devices; and system backups to recover if the current

data or programs are lost or damaged. Because of the interactive nature of the exchange between the system and the users in online systems, the boundary and communication controls discussed above also function as output controls.

Miscellaneous controls. Miscellaneous controls are other measures organizations can take to maximize system availability and to protect against improper use of their information systems. They include fault tolerance, access logs, system logs, and security notices.

1 *Fault tolerance* involves using duplicate processing units, storage devices, and/or software to provide an immediate backup system. Fault tolerance becomes more desirable as hardware costs decline and the criticality of computerized information systems increases.

2 *Access logs* record who accessed or attempted to access an information system, when the access or attempted access occurred, and what applications or data were accessed. Proper control procedures include regular review and analysis of logs to detect security threats.

3 *System logs* record extraordinary events detected by the operating system. Internal events recorded on system logs include write failures, disk-capacity warnings, and device-access problems. External events recorded on system logs include repeated attempts by unauthorized users to access the system. Management must regularly review and analyze these logs.

4 *Security notices/patches.* When weaknesses in operating systems, database management systems, or similar software are discovered, known users are notified and provided with modifications (patches) to remedy the problem. Proper control procedures for organizations that use the software include reading the notices and applying the modifications correctly on a timely basis.

IMPACT OF CHANGING TECHNOLOGY

The incentives for organizations to implement successful information systems are increasing because of competitive pressures, gains in the expected net benefits from IS projects, and expanding access to information technology. Threats to information systems are increasing as access to and knowledge of computers increase. Public awareness of IS capabilities is increasing users' expectations and engendering less tolerance of weaknesses in organizations' information systems.

As the importance of IS increases, so does the significance of the IS audit function. Changes in information technology, integration of information technology with organizational functions, and threats to information systems are increasing the demands on IS auditors for technical knowledge, understanding of organizational functions, and integration of both areas with internal controls. The importance of the IS audit function and demands for greater expertise are causing many auditors to specialize in particular areas of technology.

For more information, consult the website of the Information Systems Audit and Control Assoication (ISACA), www.isaca.org/.

Bibliography

Standards issued by the Standards Board of the Information Systems Audit and Control Association: www.isaca.org/Template.cfm?Section = Standards& Template = /TaggedPage/TaggedPageDisplay.cfm& TPLID = 29&ContentID = 85, accessed August 9, 2004.

ISACA Standards and Guidlelines booklet: www.isaca.org/Template.cfm?Section = Standards& CONTENTID = 10114& ContentManagement/Content Display.cfm, accessed August 9, 2004.

authentication

William J. Caelli

Information systems employed by organizations for transactions such as purchases, sales, and payments must be able to authenticate the parties to the transactions. Authentication is simply the act of verification by a receiving party of the correctness of a claimed identity from a sender or the integrity of information transmitted or received. The term normally applies to the act of the entity, usually the receiver, who performs the appropriate checking operation and then relies upon the result of that checking operation to prove authenticity of a claimed identity or the integrity of a received message. Thus the integrity and veracity of the checking operations used are of extreme importance. In this way, authentication depends upon the trusted nature of three components as follows:

1 the system that enables the claimant to create and offer credentials that may be used to authenticate the claimed identity or to create and process a message for transmission in the same way;
2 the details of the path between the claimant and the verifier; and
3 the trusted nature of the schemes used by the verifier to perform the authentication function.

A simple example of this is the case of INTERNET-based home or small business banking operations. The bank's customer may use a commodity personal computer system at the "client" end of the banking or financial system and also have little to no detailed knowledge of computer or data network security technologies or procedures. The "server" end, at the bank or the appropriate data switch or the like, may, in reverse, be constructed from higher-trust mainframe or similar systems with advanced cryptographic subsystems incorporated and with management highly trained and skilled in related information security matters. The problem is that it is completely unreasonable to assume that the "client" is an information technology or systems expert. Authentication, in this case, takes on new dimensions and the trusted or trustworthy nature of the systems used has to come into overall consideration. It may be decided that, for example, the client system must be enhanced using some form of user-oriented high-trust subsystem, such as a "PINPad" of the type used in the retail industry for the entry of personal identification numbers (PINs) and the reading of appropriate account details and related information from an associated credit or debit card possessed by the user.

In this sense the processes used by the entity performing the check on the authenticity of information received must be themselves highly trusted and, if performed using computer software, for example, such software needs to have a very high level of assurance. Such software or even hardware/firmware-based systems should be evaluated against clearly stated and required security functionality using recognized international security evaluation standards, such as IS 15408, the "common criteria" for such evaluation. Normally, the act of authentication in the case of proof of identity is followed by some form of "authorization" whereby the user or end-use entity is granted various permissions to perform certain operations in an information system, e.g., access to pertinent data and/or programs, etc.

Attacks on authentication schemes can be performed in a number of ways, including techniques such as those that follow:

- breaking of any mathematical or cryptographic process that is used to enable authentication to be performed by the receiver, thus enabling fraudulent claims of identity or insertion of fraudulent messages in a transmission or undetectable modification of legitimate messages;
- exploitation of any problems or errors that may be found in the associated authentication protocols that are used in data network or database and computer systems; or
- insertion of illicit software or other subsystems into the authentication check generation and/or verification systems so as to produce a fraudulent result (*see* INFORMATION ASSURANCE).

Various standards, national and international, have been developed over the last 25 years covering the topic of authentication technologies and their implementation in real software or hardware-based products and services. Such standards often relate to specific industries such as the banking and finance sector, healthcare, and so on.

See also *biometrics; cryptography (crypto); identity theft; phishing*

automated teller machine

ATMs are used in consumer (retail) banking. Customers may withdraw cash or enter deposits from remote locations. ATMs are typically connected to a network that allows customers from different banks or holding different credit cards to use them (*see* ELECTRONIC FUNDS TRANSFER).

B

bar code

Gordon B. Davis

Bar codes such as the universal product code (UPC) are important to information processing because they provide a low-cost, well-defined method for identifying products, parts, equipment, etc. The bar code itself consists of sets of black and white bars of different widths. There is a human readable interpretation of the bar code at the bottom of the bar code space. The bar code can be read by a hand scanner or by a checkout counter scanner connected to a cash register. For sales purposes, a UPC is assigned to a product and placed on a small rectangular space on the product package. In the case of a retail store, the data scanned from the bar code are input to a computer that looks up the price and provides it to the cash register. The computer also collects data for inventory updating and sales analysis.

A bar code can be used internally without obtaining an assigned code. For commerce purposes, a company, Uniform Code Council (UCC), assigns a unique six-digit manufacturer identification number in return for an annual fee. The UPC used for a product consists of the manufacturer number plus a five-digit item number and a check digit (for error-checking purposes). There are rules for coding special situations such as coupons, items to be weighed on checkout, etc.

The advantage of the UPC bar code is its simplicity and the existence of inexpensive devices for creating tags for products. Separating the product identification from its selling price allows a retail store to change the price being charged without changing the price on each individual item. It reduces the need for a checkout clerk to enter a product identification number and a product price. A disadvantage is the possibility of a person making an unauthorized UPC for an item that shows a different (lower-priced) item code, applying it to the item, and going through checkout with a lower price being charged. An alternative to a bar code is a RADIO FREQUENCY IDENTIFICATION (RFID), which contains coded data that is transmitted to a reading device.

batch processing

A term applied to periodic processing of transactions that are assembled into batches. See PROCESSING METHODS FOR INFORMATION SYSTEMS.

biometrics

William J. Caelli

The term "biometrics" is defined in the US's NCSS Instruction 4009 (revised May 2003), an IT assurance glossary of terms, as encompassing "automated methods of authenticating or verifying an individual based upon a physical or behavioral characteristic."

The term relates to the original definition of three ways to verify a claim of identity that emerged in the 1970s. These are proof of identity claimed by:

- what you know, such as a password, personal identification number (PIN), etc.;
- what you possess, such as a smart card, mechanical/electronic token, etc.; and/or
- what you are, such as a fingerprint, eye retinal pattern, voiceprint, DNA pattern, etc.

The most common biometric, in a historical sense, is the usual fingerprint used in police and like investigations. For added security, two or all of these may be combined and products incorporating all three factors are now coming to the market. Examples include a smart card that can sense and read a fingerprint which holds it while the associated card reader requires a password to activate the card itself. Problems with the widespread introduction of biometric systems for increased overall system security and user identity AUTHENTICATION have included user acceptance and cost.

However, there are other problems that need to be considered in relation to the use of biometric systems. These include the following factors.

Should a biometric system be compromised in some way, e.g. a user's fingerprint be duplicated, it is more or less impossible to overcome the problem in a direct fashion. This is not the case with, say, the token or password situation where these can be changed and reissued.

In particular, it has to be observed that a biometric subsystem employed as a security scheme in an information system is only as good as the systems that protect the "string of bits" that represent the user's biometric measurement. So, for example, if a fingerprint scanner system is used and verification of the print pattern is performed by, say, a central server system, then the bit pattern that represents that fingerprint must be itself authenticated and kept confidential on an end-to-end basis. This usually means that some form of cryptographic algorithm and protocol set must be used to perform such a service, and this brings with it the necessity to manage that cryptographic subsystem and its associated keys with a very high degree of trust. It can also be argued that since such biometric systems may be used to produce data in the form of audit trails that provide evidence in a court of law, such systems should themselves be evaluated for their own security robustness using accepted national and international standards, e.g., IS 15408, FIPS 140 (for associated cryptographic services and related key management schemes), and so on.

The price of biometric units has collapsed since 2000 and such units as fingerprint scanners can now be observed in such items as laptop computers, cell phones, personal digital assistants (PDAs), access controls for doors, and other devices.

blog (weblog)

A blog is the web page that publishes the online journal of an individual. Many blogs are updated frequently, even daily, with entries describing events, emotions, or questions in the life of the individual. Some blogs become the basis for a discussion about issues such as health, handling personal problems, opinions, etc. The style is personal and informal.

See also *bulletin boards*

broadband

see ELECTRONIC COMMUNICATIONS

bulletin boards

Gordon B. Davis and J. Davis Naumann

Computer bulletin boards can be a valuable source of information for organizations. Three different types of information-sharing groups have evolved: (1) bulletin board systems; (2) commercial discussion groups; and (3) personal discussion groups. Bulletin board systems are independent systems created and operated by entrepreneurs or organizations. The largest bulletin board system is the Usenet. These news groups number in the tens of thousands and are globally distributed over the INTERNET. The Usenet evolved with no central organizational structure. It has been the source of controversy and even legislation because of the lack of control over its contents.

A second class of discussion groups and information services is provided by the major commercial online vendors. The services are marketed for a relatively low monthly fee and hourly charge. They are one of the primary sources of technical information provided by information industry vendors. Vendors assign staff to follow their bulletin boards, post replies, announce problem solutions, and post upgrades. A third source of bulletin board/discussion group information is a personal discussion group. Discussion groups may have a large number of users, but there are also specialized groups with small numbers of dedicated participants.

Search tools are available for discussion groups and bulletin boards. Many newsgroup discussions are archived. A user looking for information that might have been discussed in a particular newsgroup can search its archive and retrieve relevant comments. In some newsgroups, volunteers accumulate important information and periodically post it as FAQs (frequently asked questions).

Bulletin boards are commonly supported within organizations. Most electronic mail systems support bulletin boards. These may be used to access and disseminate useful information within the organization.

Blogs (weblogs) designed generally as an individual online journal are sometimes the basis for exchange of advice, opinions, and personal experiences (see BLOG (WEBLOG)).

byte

A byte consists of 8 bits. It is a basic unit for coding information for computer processing and for addressing units of computer storage. In processing, bytes may be combined for addressing or processing purposes.

See also *coding of data for information processing*

C

C and C++

C is a high-level programming language that takes into account machine-level considerations. There are a number of high-level instructions to simplify programming. It has been used in writing UNIX operating systems and for applications to be run on microcomputers and workstations. Programs in C for one computer tend to be easily transported to another computer.

C++ is a variation of the C language that incorporates principles of object-oriented programming. It has the advantage of being similar to the C language but the disadvantage of not meeting all of the conditions of an object-oriented programming language.

See also *programming languages*

Capability Maturity Model® (CMM®) and CMM Integration (CMMI®)

Mary Beth Chrissis, Linda Levine, and Sandy Shrum

Organizations that develop systems with software components have a vital dependence on processes that result in high-quality products and services. Capability Maturity Model Integration (CMMI) is important to these organizations because it provides a basis for evaluating their current process capabilities and tracking their progress in improving those capabilities. Capability Maturity Models (CMMs) are collections of best practices that organizations can use to guide their improvement. The success of the CMM for Software and development of other CMMs led to the development of the CMMI Product Suite, which consists of a set of models, an appraisal method, and training materials that support quality improvement related to product and service development.

HISTORY OF CMMs

First published in 1991 by the Software Engineering Institute (SEI), the Capability Maturity Model (CMM) was a model that contained the essential elements of effective software development processes and described an evolutionary improvement path from ad hoc, immature processes to disciplined, mature processes with improved quality and effectiveness. Although really the CMM for Software (SW-CMM), this model was often referred to as "the CMM" and was based on principles of product quality that have existed for over 60 years. In the 1930s, Walter Shewhart advanced the principles of statistical quality control. His principles were further developed and successfully demonstrated in the work of W. Edwards Deming, Joseph Juran, and Philip Crosby. These principles were adapted by the SEI into the creation of the first CMM.

The SW-CMM significantly influenced software process improvement worldwide. Consequently, other CMMs were developed and published for disciplines including systems engineering, software acquisition, human resource management, and integrated product and process development.

The development of multiple CMMs expanded process improvement to affect more disciplines and help organizations to better develop and maintain products and services. However, the expansion of CMMs to new disciplines also created challenges. Organizations found that differences among the discipline-specific models made improvement across the organization difficult and costly. Training, assessments, and improvement activities were repeated for each CMM used;

CMMs did not share a common vocabulary or structure; and best practices in one CMM would sometimes conflict with those in another CMM.

To respond to the challenges and opportunities created by the proliferation of single-discipline CMMs, the Office of the Under Secretary of Defense for Acquisition, Technology, and Logistics initiated the CMM Integration project at the SEI in 1997. Experts from a variety of backgrounds and organizations joined to establish a framework that could accommodate current and future models in a way that eliminated the need for redundant improvement, assessment, and training activities.

The project team initially developed a set of integrated models that covered three disciplines: (1) software engineering, (2) systems engineering, and (3) integrated product and process development. Today, the CMMI Product Suite covers these three disciplines as well as supplier sourcing and includes a module that provides guidance on acquisition. As did the original CMMs, CMMI identifies best practices that help organizations improve their businesses processes.

TECHNICAL DETAIL

The CMMI Product Suite consists of CMMI models, an appraisal method, and training materials. Each CMMI model covers one or more disciplines, including software engineering and systems engineering, and is designed to be tailored to the needs of the organization. Each model consists of required, expected, and informative elements that aid those improving processes in their organizations. Every model is available in two representations: staged and continuous.

An organization chooses the approach to process improvement that best suits its needs. This approach influences the organization's choice of model representation. The differences between the two CMMI model representations are mainly architectural (i.e., how the practices are organized and which are selected for emphasis); each representation has advantages, depending on the organization's approach to process improvement.

CONTINUOUS VS. STAGED REPRESENTATIONS

The continuous representation depicts process improvement using capability levels, while the staged representation depicts process improvement using maturity levels. The main difference

Table 1   Capability levels and maturity levels

Level	Continuous representation: capability levels	Staged representation: maturity levels
Level 0	Not performed	N/A
Level 1	Performed	Performed
Level 2	Managed	Managed
Level 3	Defined	Defined
Level 4	Quantitatively managed	Quantitatively managed
Level 5	Optimizing	Optimizing

between these two types of levels is how they are used to apply CMMI best practices:

- Capability levels, which appear in models with a continuous representation, apply to an organization's process-improvement achievement in individual process areas. There are six capability levels, numbered 0 through 5. Each capability level within a process area comprises a set of practices that, when implemented, improve processes within that process area.
- Maturity levels, which appear in models with a staged representation, apply to an organization's overall process-improvement achievement in a group of process areas. There are five maturity levels, numbered 1 through 5. Each maturity level comprises a set of goals that, when satisfied, improve processes across multiple process areas.

THE CMMI PRODUCT SUITE

A CMMI model consists of an overview section, the process areas, and the appendixes. Organizations using a model for process improvement primarily use the overview section to understand the model and repeatedly use contents of the process areas to guide their improvement efforts. Each process area is a group of related best practices organized into elements such as the purpose, introductory notes, goals, practices, and work products. Currently there are 25 process areas that cover topics such as requirements management, project planning, organizational process definition, and decision analysis and resolution.

CMMs typically have an accompanying appraisal method that allows users to have an evaluation of their progress conducted. The appraisal method currently available for use with CMMI models is the Standard CMMI Assessment Method for Process Improvement (SCAMPI^SM) Class A. To help insure that useful and credible results are obtained from SCAMPI appraisals, the SEI developed a certification and authorization process for SCAMPI Lead Appraisers^SM. To insure consistency, all appraisal methods must conform to the most current Appraisal Requirements for CMMI (ARC). Although SCAMPI Class A is the only appraisal method currently available from the SEI, the SEI also plans to support the development of additional appraisal methods that differ in cost, time to execute, and rigor.

PROCESS IMPROVEMENT

Process improvement objectives identify the processes and outcomes that an organization wishes to improve. Successful process improvement initiatives must be driven by the business objectives of the organization. Thus, process improvement objectives are derived from business objectives.

Process improvement is a significant undertaking that, to be successful, requires senior-level management sponsorship and a firm commitment of resources. Further, it is a long-term commitment for the organization that cannot be approached and accomplished quickly.

The costs vary depending on the organization and its goals. However, the support of process improvement typically requires additions to the organizational structure, such as an engineering process group (EPG).

ADOPTION RESULTS

CMMI is being adopted worldwide, including in North America, Europe, India, Australia, and the Pacific Rim. CMMI models and associated products are designed to fit the needs of small and large organizations from a variety of different industries. There are CMMI-adopting organizations in fields such as electronics, aerospace, health services, finance, defense, insurance, and transportation.

Many benefits are reported by CMMI users, including: lower development costs, more accurate schedules, increased quality, higher customer satisfaction, and substantial return on investment.

A recently published SEI report, *Demonstrating the Impact and Benefits of CMMI: An Update and Preliminary Results*, provides more information about the benefits of CMMI. It is available at www.sei.cmu.edu/publications/documents/03.reports/03sr009.html.

Bibliography

www.sei.cmu.edu/cmm/cmms/cmms.html
www.sei.cmu.edu/cmmi/

careers in information technology

Soon Ang and Sandra A. Slaughter

Information technology (IT) professionals are people who acquire, develop, manage, and maintain hardware, software, and telecommunication networks, and offer computing and information services to users. There is a wide spectrum of IT professionals who play various roles in the management and development of information systems. With the advent of client–server technologies, powerful personal computers, and software languages that are easy to use, end-users have been increasingly developing and managing their own computing applications, rather than relying on the organization's IT employees. This trend has contributed to the downsizing of the IT group within organizations. It also affects the nature of IT work. Rather than providing complete information system services to the organization, IT professionals may provide support for end-user-developed systems or may concentrate on developing and managing only major, company-wide applications.

Contemporary categories of IT careers include:

1 *Chief IT executives.* These IT professionals serve as the senior executives in the IT organization. Chief information officers (CIOs) are top corporate officers responsible for the overall IT function in organizations.

CIOs offer leadership in managing the information resources of the firm, and in directing the power of information technology toward the strategic objectives of the firm. Chief technology officers (CTOs) are responsible for technology planning, new technology evaluation and selection, and setting the vision for the firm's IT architecture. Given the increasing importance of information security, some firms have created another senior-level IT position, the chief security officer or chief information security officer (CSO). CSOs oversee and coordinate information technology security; establish, communicate, and implement IT security policies that support the firm's IT objectives; and act as the primary liaison with other security professionals inside and outside of the firm.

2 *Software development/engineering professionals.* These IT professionals comprise application programmers who develop software using programming languages and software tools; systems analysts who determine user requirements and design the systems specifications; and project managers who oversee and coordinate teams of programmers and systems analysts in developing specific application systems. Positions include: applications systems programmer, software applications specialist/engineers, software architect/engineer, data modeler, operating systems designer/programmer/engineer.

3 *Web development/administration professionals.* These IT professionals design, develop, and maintain web-based applications. They analyze, design screens, develop client–server applications, and provide quality assurance and testing. Positions include webmaster, web designer, web specialist/developer.

4 *Database/data warehouse professionals.* These IT professionals design and model databases, create objects, and monitor, test, and maintain the data integrity of the databases. Positions include: database administrator, data developer/modeler, and knowledge architect.

5 *IT operations, network design, and administration professionals.* These include computer operations and network specialists who are involved in computer capacity planning and

management; disaster recovery; security; hardware and systems software maintenance; and production or job scheduling. Contemporary network specialists are involved with INTERNET connectivity, intranets (*see* INTRANET), extranets (*see* EXTRANET), as well as local and wide area networks. They also analyze, install, monitor, and provide maintenance for hardware integration. Positions include network administrator, network engineer, network manager, and information systems administrator. Of increasing importance are security specialists who are responsible for protecting and recovering information resources.

6 *Technology support IT professionals.* These are responsible for the acquisition, installation, upgrade, maintenance, and help-desk support of IT use in the organization. Positions in this cluster of professionals include help-desk specialist, PC support specialist, call center support specialist, and maintenance or technical support engineer.

CAREER ORIENTATIONS OF IT PROFESSIONALS

Igbaria, Greenhaus, and Parasuraman (1991) found that IT professionals are diverse in their career orientations, i.e., in their interests, self-perceived talents, values, and motives that shape their career decisions (see also Ginzberg and Baroudi, 1988). Technical and managerial orientations are two dominant themes among IT professionals. People in technical jobs such as application programmers and systems engineers are more technically oriented, while those in managerial jobs such as systems analysts, project leaders, and managers are more managerially oriented. The study by Igbaria et al. (1991) found that the match between job type and career orientation of IT professionals is important because such a match leads to higher job satisfaction, stronger organizational commitment, and lower intentions to leave the organization. The implication of this study is that management should take into account differences in employee interests and orientations and provide job opportunities that match employee needs.

Joseph, Ang, and Slaughter (2004) tracked the career sequences of 347 IT professionals (i.e., individuals with at least one year of IT work experience) for a 21-year period using a US National Youth Longitudinal Survey sample and found that IT professionals are clustered into three types of career profiles: technical IT professionals ($N = 127$) who devote a majority of their careers to technical positions; managerial IT professionals ($N = 72$) who move to managerial positions after an average of three years of technical work experience; and ad hoc IT professionals ($N = 148$) who move in and out of the IT position during their career lifespan. Studies based on IT salary data (Ang, Slaughter, and Ng, 2002; Joseph et al. 2004) found that the returns to careers for managerial IT professionals were significantly higher than those of technical or ad hoc careers, suggesting that the IT labor market recognizes and pays a premium value for managerial competence in the IT profession. The average pay for each career profile (adjusted for inflation to base years 1982–4; Bureau of Labor Statistics 2004) is $26,589 for managerial, $22,185 for technical, and $16,854 for ad hoc.

OUTSOURCING AND IMPACT ON IT CAREERS

Traditionally, firms that require a specific skills set will employ a worker under a long-term employment contract where the worker works all year round at the employer's place of business, except for vacations and holidays. Unless they resign or have their services terminated, employees are assumed to remain with the employer until death or retirement. From the legal perspective, both parties have rights and responsibilities accorded to them by both common law and employment statutes governing the employer–employee relationship. Accordingly, it is not uncommon for IT professionals to remain attached to a single employer during their entire careers.

Careers built upon long-term employment relationships with single organizations work well in situations where the skills sets required by the firm are relatively stable over time. However, in information systems, firms are finding that alternative employment arrangements, such as contract work, are becoming more important and attractive because of the increasingly rapid evolution of technology (see Ang and Slaughter, 2001; Slaughter and Ang, 1995, 1996). Cutting-edge technologies typically enjoy lifespans of only two years. Skills of IT professionals therefore erode very rapidly. Operating in short windows of stable technological environments, IT organizations with a stable and static workforce anchored in traditional employment relationships continually face the problem of needing to upgrade the skills of the workforce. In many cases, organizations may feel that commitment to training the internal workforce is self-defeating. Because technologies move so rapidly, by the time an organization invests in and trains its IT staff in a certain technology, that technology may already have become obsolete.

Accordingly, the number of organizations using contract workers for IT work is growing dramatically, particularly with the rapid diffusion of IT OUTSOURCING and offshoring where organizations are contracting out the services of some or all of the IT organization to independent contractors or service providers (Ho, Ang, and Straub, 2003).

Consequently, IT careers no longer take place in single organizations. Rather, as contract workers, IT professionals are not attached to any single organization for a long period of time. Instead, they are independent and self-employed, hired on a fixed-term basis for a specific skill through an agreed-upon contract. The contract may provide a fixed duration of service or may operate on a job-by-job basis. From the worker's point of view, contract work provides an opportunity to establish a special expertise or professional status within an industry. In fact, it is often regarded as a way for workers to focus on the aspects of their profession they most enjoy (e.g., programming instead of managing software projects) without having to deal with corporate politics or pressures to move up the expected career ladder (see Ang and Slaughter, 2001).

The trends toward outsourcing and careers based on contract work arrangements imply an increasing inter-organizational division of IT labor in the future, as work formerly conducted within organizational boundaries and under the administrative control of a single enterprise is parceled out to more specialized individuals or organizational entities. The implication for IT professionals is that they can no longer solely rely on building careers by moving upwards in single organizations. Rather, IT professionals must consciously plan to upgrade and reskill themselves in light of competence-destroying technologies. They must also be cognizant of new career opportunities offered by outsourcing arrangements. For example, ideal IT professionals in outsourcing must possess a combination of not only technical and practical knowledge, skills, and abilities, but also negotiation and bargaining skills to sustain a flexible partnership that demands intense relationship building and continual recommitment from top to bottom of both client organizations and service providers.

Bibliography

Ang, S. and Slaughter, S. A. (2001). Work outcomes and job design for contract versus permanent information systems professionals on software development teams. *MIS Quarterly*, **25** (3), 321–50.

Ang, S., Slaughter, S. A., and Ng, K. Y. (2002). Determinants of pay for information technology professionals: Modeling cross-level interactions. *Management Science*, **48** (11), 1425–45.

Ginzberg, M. H. and Baroudi, J. J. (1988). MIS careers: A theoretical perspective. *Communications of the ACM*, **31** (5), 586–94.

Ho, V., Ang, S., and Straub, D. W. (2003). When subordinates become contractors: The persistence of managerial expectations of transplants in IT outsourcing. *Information Systems Research*, **14** (1), 66–86.

Igbaria, M., Greenhaus, J. H., and Parasuraman, S. (1991). Career orientations of MIS employees: An empirical analysis. *MIS Quarterly*, **15** (2), 151–70.

Joseph, D., Ang, S., and Slaughter, S. A. (2004). Economic returns on alternative IT careers: A sequence analysis. Information Management Research Center (IMARC) Working Paper, Nanyang Business School, Nanyang Technological University of Singapore (request papers from asang@ntu.edu.sg).

Slaughter, S. A. and Ang, S. (1995). Information systems employment structures in the USA and Singapore: A cross-cultural comparison. *Information Technology and People*, **8** (2), 17–36.

Slaughter, S. A. and Ang, S. (1996). Employment outsourcing in information systems. *Communications of the ACM*, **39** (7), 47–54.

CASE: computer-aided software/system engineering

Dzenan Ridjanovic

The term "computer-aided software/system engineering" (CASE) applies to tools that assist developers to analyze, design, and construct software applications or information systems. The objective of the tools is to automate software development. This requires an integrated set of features to support the development of models, requirements, design, and code generation. There are a large number of CASE tools, some with a very broad scope and some with limited capabilities.

CASE tools may be understood in terms of the process of developing an application using the tools. A software system is developed to provide a solution to a problem. This requires the problem domain to be analyzed before a solution is proposed and a solution to be designed before a software system is constructed. Once constructed, the system is maintained. After use, it may evolve and change. There are different approaches to the development (analysis, design, and construction) of software systems, as well as different formalisms and notations to represent requirements and design during the software life-cycle phase.

There are two broad categories of CASE tools: tools are used in both analysis and design and the construction of applications. Construction usually involves generating computer program instructions. All results of the development process using a CASE tool are stored in a repository. In this way, they can be used to maintain and evolve a software system from the analysis and design perspective, providing higher-quality software. In addition, they can be reused in other projects to increase software development productivity.

A CASE tool consists of a repository of analysis, design, and construction tools and results from using the tools in a graphical interface that presents the data in a specific notation (formalism or language). One of the important features of CASE tools is support for modeling of a problem domain and modeling information system components, such as external entities, business processes, data flows, and data stores. External entities provide specific entry and exit points to or from an organization unit being analyzed. Business processes transform, move, or store organizational data represented as data flows or data stores. A process relies on organizational resources to accomplish its tasks. If a process at hand is complex, it can be decomposed into lower-level processes that are graphically represented in another diagram.

In an information system application, business data, user applications (interfaces), business policies (rules), and business tasks (services) are represented and designed using an appropriate formalism. Business data, analyzed in the context of business processes, are described with the CASE tool. User applications are designed based on user data views using presentation layouts and use scenarios. A data view is derived from business data and is structured in such a way as to support user needs. View data may be presented to a user in different forms. The interaction between a user and various forms is documented by one or more use scenarios. Business policies are described in terms of their relationship to events, and conditions. Business tasks are specified.

case-based reasoning

see ARTIFICIAL INTELLIGENCE

CD-ROM and DVD

Nancy K. Herther

CD-ROM and DVD disks are used for computer storage. Both technologies are in current use, but DVDs are becoming more common. The newer DVD-ROM drives are designed to also read CD-ROM disks and most will also record to CD-R and CD-RW disks. These technologies are ideal for data sets that are relatively static or for which many copies of the same data are required. They are therefore important to information systems in organizations as well as for consumer products.

In a CD-ROM (compact disk read-only memory), information is permanently stored digitally and read by a CD-ROM drive system using low-intensity lasers. Each aluminum and plastic disk, measuring 120 mm in diameter and 1.2 mm thick, holds 700 megabytes (MB) of data. The technology began with audio CDs in 1982 (replacing vinyl long-playing records). CD-ROM was introduced in 1985. The standards

(called the "Yellow Book" in the industry) for CD-ROM are maintained by Koninklijke Philips Electronics NV (*www.licensing.philips.com/information/cd/video/*). Other versions of the CD include: CD-R (compact disk recordable) and CD-RW (compact disk rewritable), which can be written to one time and multiple times, respectively, and various interactive CDs (CD-I, CDTV, and other formats), which can store video, audio, and data. Photo CD is a format that holds digitized photographs and sound.

Although DVD (digital versatile disk or digital video disk) looks the same as a CD-ROM disk, the formats, physical specifications, and file specifications differ. A single DVD disk is able to store 13 times the data contained on a single, one-sided CD. Since DVDs are able to store data on both sides, the total storage capacity is 26 times that of a CD-ROM. DVDs allow for storage of video, audio, and data on a single disk. The DVD physical and file specifications were defined by the DVD Forum (*www.dvdforum.org/forum.shtml*).

Both CD-ROM and DVD systems store data in microscopic grooves that run in spirals around the disk surface. Both use laser beams to scan these grooves: tiny reflective bumps (called lands) and non-reflective holes (called pits) aligned along the grooves represent the zeros and ones of digital information. DVDs use smaller tracks (0.74 microns wide, compared to 1.6 microns on CD-ROMs) as well as different modulation and error correction methods.

There are several writable and rewritable DVD formats on the market (see specifications at *www3.toshiba.co.jp/dvd/e/whats/index.htm*). These DVD formats include:

- DVD-ROM: similar to DVD video, it is supplanting CD-ROMS.
- DVD-R: a write-once recordable format with a storage capacity of 4.7 gigabytes (GB), and compatibility with both standalone DVD players and DVD-ROM drives.
- DVD-RAM: a rewritable technology with read-write access. Current capacity is 4.7 GB per side with very high rewrite performance.
- DVD-RW: similar in capacity to DVD-RAM except that it features a sequential read-write access. DVD-RW media use rewritable disks that can be rewritten over

1,000 times under ideal situations. Most but not all standalone DVD players will play video recorded on DVD-RW disks.

Business acceptance of DVD has been insured owing to clear industry standards that feature a single interchange standard between computer and television applications, ability for DVD players to read and play CDs, compatibility across different DVD disks, a standard file system (UDF, ISO 9660), and very reliable error correction methods.

The use of DVD technology is likely to increase because of standard methods for increased storage. A single-sided disk can store 4.73 GB (enough for a 133-minute movie), a single-sided, dual-layer disk can store 8.5 GB, and a double-sided, dual-layer disk can store 17 GB. Future DVD development includes use of blu-ray lasers for reading information from the disks. Prototype systems using blue lasers have a capacity of 27 GB or more. Another future development is high-definition DVD systems.

In summary, the advantages of CD/DVD disks for storage include easily available and low-cost media and drive devices, standardization, large capacity, portability, a widespread installed base of drives, durability and stability of the medium, and the ability to store and retrieve multiple data types on a single disk. Disadvantages include the relatively slow access times (compared to hard drive systems) and the increasing availability of other high-density storage and distribution options (especially the INTERNET).

cellular technology in information systems

Gordon B. Davis

Cellular communication systems are used not only for telephone communications but also for information processing. A portable computer can download information from a central computer and upload customer or other information. Using this technology allows a salesperson or other customer representative to interact with a customer while communicating with applications and databases at a central location. For example, a sales representative at a customer's office can transmit an order via cellular technol-

ogy and receive immediately a confirmed delivery date for the order from the organization's main computer.

certified information systems auditor (CISA)

A CISA is a person certified by the Information Systems and Audit and Control Association to audit information systems (see AUDITING INFORMATION SYSTEMS).

chief information officer

Brian D. Janz

The chief information officer (CIO) is the highest-ranking manager responsible for the management of information resources and information technology within an organization. Although the job responsibilities of the CIO may vary somewhat from organization to organization, the CIO usually reports to the president and chief executive officer. The position typically has three broad responsibilities: (1) understanding the strategy of the overall organization and developing a technology strategy that is consistent with it; (2) the management of information technology (e.g., hardware, software, and networks); and (3) the management of the information resources (applications, databases, and personnel) used by the organization.

As the senior information technology (IT) officer, it is the CIO's responsibility to understand the organization's mission and objectives and the potential benefits of using information technology. The CIO's challenge is to seek out opportunities where existing as well as emerging information technology can be deployed to achieve organization objectives as well as to find ways in which information technology can be used to gain competitive advantage. This technology–strategy matching challenge is often termed "IT alignment" or "IT fit" within the organization.

The aggressive use of information technology and the growth in the creation, need, and use of information has forced the CIO to focus on corporate information and organizational knowledge as manageable resources. In this role, the CIO must understand how information is used by the organization in accomplishing its objectives and how to capture, store, and disseminate data, information, and knowledge to all parts of the organization whenever and wherever needed.

client/server architecture

Fred Niederman

The term "client/server" refers to a logical architecture that describes a way of subdividing tasks among processors in a network. Client/server applications and systems are distinguished from other logical architectures (such as hierarchical and peer-to-peer) by dividing tasks into two components: a client with which the user is generally in direct contact and a server that performs relatively standardized tasks for a set of clients. Multiple clients can be programmed to use the results of server activities; a single client can access one or more servers to perform a variety of tasks. Frequently, a personal computer or workstation is used for the client, while a workstation, minicomputer, mainframe, or supercomputer is used for the server. However, the logical client/server design can be implemented with other hardware patterns and may also be implemented on a single machine. One computer within a network can host both client and server programs. Middleware is generally required to provide communication routes for client requests to servers and server responses to clients. The simplest version of client/server architectures are organized in two tiers with clients interacting directly with servers; however, more robust designs use three or more tiers to provide queues, application processing, or other services (www.sei.cmu.edu/str/descriptions/clientserver_body.html).

The client/server architecture can be extended to computer resources in an enterprise network. In such a design, each client system has potential access to a variety of servers in the enterprise. The users have access to the entire range of enterprise computing (within their specified security-oriented limits). The client portion of the application typically provides a user interface, screens for data input or specification of data retrieval, text-editing capabilities, and error processing. Resources needed by the client, such as printers, database access, image processing, and security, are likely to be managed by a particular server. Sorting different tasks to appropriate hardware can provide advantages of efficient use of hardware while maintaining high performance levels.

Designers of client/server systems must decide where to conduct processing. The developer has the dual objectives of doing processing at client locations (which are presumably dedicated to a particular user), while not overloading network traffic by moving large volumes of raw data. In general, processing is more cost effective at the client site and input–output tasks more cost effective at the server site (Renaud, 1993).

The concept of client/server architecture is often linked to distribution of computing. Organizational computing is moved from the mainframe to smaller hardware. Using processing capabilities of both the client and server work sites, and replacing relatively expensive larger equipment with relatively less expensive smaller equipment, cost savings and more responsive computing are potentially attainable. By linking client/server architecture with reengineering or application redesign, additional streamlining can occur. In this scenario, redundant or unnecessary activities are eliminated and sequential processes can be replaced by concurrent or parallel processes.

By this definition, INTERNET computing is a kind of "client/server" computing with the browser typically serving as the "client" and the web server providing content of various levels of complexity. However, the term client/server computing is more often used to describe more tightly organized sets of operations that typically are designed to operate on the various products of a single vendor. The term "server" is also often used to reference hardware, such as a workstation, that comes with server software already installed and ready to use.

Bibliography

Client/server software architectures: An overview. Software Engineering Institute, Carnegie-Mellon University; www.sei.cmu.edu/str/descriptions/clientserver_body.html, accessed June 8, 2004.

Renaud, P. E. (1993). *Introduction to Client/Server Systems.* New York: John Wiley.

COBOL

Randy Snyder and Gordon B. Davis

COBOL is a procedural programming language designed to address problems in business data processing. The acronym COBOL stands for COmmon Business-Oriented Language. COBOL has been the most widely used programming language in business. Billions of lines of COBOL are in use throughout the world. COBOL is still an active, standard language but it is not suited to many current processing situations, such as INTERNET applications. Therefore, other programming languages are receiving greater use in new applications.

The effort to develop COBOL was started in the late 1950s by a group of private individuals from academia and industry. This group obtained assistance from the US Department of Defense to set up the Committee on Data Systems Languages (CODASYL). CODASYL was responsible for the first standard of COBOL, called COBOL 60. The US Department of Defense soon adopted COBOL 60 and propagated it as a standard. Other standards of the language have been defined by the American National Standards Institute (ANSI), beginning in 1974 with ANSI-74 COBOL.

The development of COBOL was motivated by business needs that were not well supported by other languages at that time. These needs included efficient retrieval and storage of large data files, manipulation of business financial data, formatting of business data onto reports, and English-like syntax that could be understood by non-programmers.

COBOL successfully addressed the need for retrieving and storing data files by supporting sequential, random, and indexed file access, as well as the ability to define hierarchical records of data. These features allowed COBOL programs to access data in any order from a file, process it, and store it in a new order. COBOL addressed the need to manipulate business data by supporting fixed-point arithmetic which prevented inaccurate computation of business data. COBOL addressed the need to format business data by providing data types tailored to the display of financial information. COBOL was unsuccessful in providing a syntax that could be understood by non-programmers. The language uses many English words in its syntax, but the meaning of a COBOL program cannot easily be understood by someone untrained in the language.

A COBOL program is composed of four divisions.

1 The *identification division* gives the name of the program, its author, the date the program was written, and other information that other users may find helpful in understanding or maintaining the program.

2 The *environment division* comprises two separate sections: the *configuration section*, which holds information about the way in which a specific machine implements COBOL, and the *input–output section*, which describes external devices that will be accessed during execution of the program.

3 The *data division* defines all of the program variables, data structures, and data types that the program uses. The data division contains the *file section* and the *working storage section*, among others. The file section describes data that come from external files and the working storage section describes data computed from program input. The data division defines three data types: numeric, alphanumeric, and alphabetic. Numeric data are represented by the number 9, alphanumeric data are represented by the letter X, and alphabetic data (which include the space character) are represented by the letter A (or the letter B for representing spaces). These types are combined to define the size of a program variable. For example, a numeric variable that is three digits long would be represented as 999.

4 The *procedure division* contains program logic to compute, manipulate data, and to iterate and branch through program execution. Most COBOL statements in the procedure division begin with a verb. Common data manipulation statements use the verbs *add*, *subtract*, *multiply*, *divide*, *compute*, and *move*. The *perform* verb is commonly used to iterate through program execution. The word *if* is used to begin statements that cause program branching.

A few lines illustrate COBOL program statements:

```
IF HOURS-WORKED OF PAYROLL-
RECORD IS GREATER THAN 40 PER-
FORM
PAY-CALCULATIONS-WITH-OVER-
TIME ELSE PERFORM PAY-CALCU-
LATIONS-NO-OVERTIME.
PAY-CALCULATIONS-NO-OVER-
TIME.
MULTIPLY HOURS-WORKED OF PAY-
ROLL-RECORD BY RATE-OF-PAY OF
PAYROLL-RECORD GIVING REGU-
LAR-PAY ROUNDED.
COMPUTE OVERTIME-PAY = 0.
```

coding of data for information processing

Gordon B. Davis and J. Davis Naumann

Coding is required for information processing because data in natural form (as data on documents, the documents themselves, voice, pictures, diagrams, etc.) are not suitable for computer storage or processing. The data in their various forms must be encoded in a representation using binary digits. For output, the process is reversed: digital codes are converted to representations such as printed characters, diagrams, pictures, voice, etc. Even though inputs and outputs take many forms, the concepts underlying coding data digitally are similar. Closely related to digital coding is data compression. Coding may be efficient for input but not efficient for storage or transmission. Most data coding methods result in significant redundancy. Compression methods reduce redundancy and thereby reduce the storage and transmission requirements.

ANALOG VS. DIGITAL REPRESENTATION

Information can be represented in either analog or digital form, corresponding to continuous or discrete representations. Although human processing of voice, sound, image, and motion is analog, computer information processing is based entirely on digital equivalents. This means that anything a computer is to process must be converted from analog inputs to digital coding. For output, it must be converted from internal digital coding back to analog for presentation to humans.

Analog methods are still in use in voice communication, entertainment media, and some telephone technology. In human speech communication, sounds are continuous waveforms that are produced by the speaker's vocal cords, sent through the air, and reconstructed by the ears of the recipient. When microphones and speakers are used, they also employ analog electromagnetic waveforms. Until fairly recently, methods for storing sound were based on storing analog waveforms on the magnetic surface of a disk or tape. Similarly, video programs are broadcast in analog signal form, flow over cable as analog signals, and are stored on VCR tape as analog signals.

In contrast, a digital signal is a voltage or current that represents two states. The digital codes represented by digital signals provide information for reconstructing an analog signal if there is need for an analog output. Newer data transport facilities, recordings, telephone communications, and other systems employ digital devices and digital coding. There are basically two reasons for the dominance of digital devices and digital coding. The first is the simplicity and low cost of electronic components based on the two states that represent binary digits; the second is the increase in quality by using digital coding error detection and error correction methods.

CODING OF ALPHANUMERIC CHARACTERS

If computers only processed numeric digits, the coding scheme could be quite simple. To encode the 10 numeric digits from 0 to 9 requires a code with a set of four binary digits (bits) with values of 0 or 1.

Numeric value	Digital code
0	0000
1	0001
2	0010
3	0011
4	0100
5	0101
6	0110
7	0111
8	1000
9	1001

Computers need to represent not only numeric characters but also alphabetic and special characters. The size of the code needs to increase. The basic coding and storage unit for personal computers consists of a set of 8 bits called a *byte*. An 8-bit code can encode 256 different input characters. A byte is sufficient for upper- and lower-case letters (which need different codes) as well as a large number of special characters. It is not sufficient when different non-Roman language characters such as Hebrew and Greek are included. The coding method must expand to use 2 bytes (which can encode 65,536 symbols). The fundamental principle is that the code size must increase as more characters are included. A commonly used code for alphabetic, numeric, and special characters is the American Standard Code for Information Interchange (ASCII). The original ASCII standard code used 7 bits. An extended ASCII code employs 8 bits.

Various coding schemes have implications for data processing and communication. The coding will affect the way data items are ordered. For example, if the capital letters are given a smaller numeric value than lower-case letters, the three words Alpha, Beta, Gamma will be sorted by the computer in that order; however, if the words are Alpha, beta, Gamma, they will be ordered as Alpha, Gamma, beta. There are ways to deal with this problem, but the underlying concept is that coding has implications for processing.

CODING OF PICTURES AND GRAPHICS

The screen used for computer output displays alphanumeric data, graphics, pictures, and video. If the screen needed to display only alphanumeric characters and simple line drawings, the display device could encode these as combinations of lines. However, in a full GRAPHICAL USER INTERFACE, the screen consists of thousands of tiny dots, each of which can have a picture value of white, black, gray, or color. These individual picture elements are called pixels (or pels). A digitized picture is composed of a large number of pixels. The number of pixels represented can vary with different implementations of the technology. The number of dots to be encoded per unit of area determines the size of each pixel and also the texture of the result. A fairly small number of pixels gives a rough picture in which the individual dots are clearly visible. A large number of picture elements makes the picture smooth and sharp, so that individual pixels cannot be identified by the viewer.

The size of the code for a pixel depends on the variations that must be encoded. If a pixel is either black or white, then the code for a pixel can be a single bit with 0 representing white and 1 representing black. If a pixel can be only a few basic colors, a half-byte of 4 bits can encode 16 different colors. If a pixel can represent 256 different colors, 1 byte is used for each pixel. This is currently sufficient for many high-resolution personal computer displays. If a pixel needs to represent more colors and shades of colors, a 3-byte (24-bit) coding is used to represent 256 levels for each of the primary colors. With 24 bits, over 16 million variations of color can be coded to represent the full range distinguishable by the human eye.

CODING OF VOICE AND SOUND

A sound is captured by a microphone or reproduced by a speaker as a continuous waveform. The analog method for coding voice and sound is to capture and store the waveform. With digital technology, however, analog waveforms are encoded with digital codes in such a way that they can eventually be reconverted to analog.

Analog to digital conversion is performed by measuring the analog signal at frequent intervals and encoding the measurement as a digital value. In telephony, for example, sampling is done at 8,000 times per second. Each measurement is encoded as one of 256 voltage levels using 8 bits. This means a voice or sound message requires 64,000 bits per second, or 480,000 bytes per minute. To produce the sound for humans, digital to analog conversion recreates the analog signal for a stereo speaker by generating the appropriate voltages from the digital codes. This same principle is used for other sound encoding such as music compact disk, but a much higher sampling rate is used to capture all of the music signal.

CODING OF VIDEO WITH MOTION

Motion video consists of separate pictures that change rapidly. Each new image is displayed often enough that the human vision system blends it into continuous motion. This occurs when a picture is completely redrawn about 15 times per second. For comparison, the US standard for broadcast TV, NTSC (National Television Systems Committee) video, has about 480 rows of 725 pixels repeated 30 times per second. If it were digitally encoded at 1 byte per pixel, it would require 10 million bytes per second of video (plus audio). High-definition television transmits a signal using a greater density of pixels, about double the standard signal (1,125 lines of signal versus 800).

COMPRESSION

The need for compression is based on costs of storage and communication, limits of storage technology, and convenience. Compression reduces the cost of storage by reducing the storage needed. For example, most software packages use compression to reduce the number of diskettes that must be distributed. The algorithm to decompress the data is included in the installation program. Information communication is often a significant cost. Compression reduces redundant information and speeds transmission. The costs of storage devices continue to decrease, but the architecture of most systems places limits on available storage capacity. When copying data files, compression makes the operation more convenient because it reduces the volume of media required.

There are many different procedures or algorithms for data compression. The simplest example of data compression is called "space suppression." Space suppression takes advantage of the presence of frequently occurring strings of the space character, something that was once very significant in computer-generated reports sent to remote printers. In space suppression, each string of spaces is replaced at the transmitter by a flag code and a count of the number of spaces. The receiver then replaces the flag code and count with the specified number of spaces. A similar scheme is used by facsimile transmission.

For data compression, variations on an algorithm by Lempel and Ziv are very common. Data files are compressed for storage and transmission, often to less than half of their original length. The LZ approach is related to space suppression, but is able to substitute short codes for virtually every string that repeats once or more in a file. Lempel–Ziv type algorithms are built into high-speed modems. They

are also the basis for many software products that effectively double the capacity of disk storage.

These approaches to compression are called "loss-less" since the exact bit-pattern of the original is always completely restored. Loss-less compression is often not necessary in communicating sound, graphics, and motion images. By carefully developing compression algorithms that leave out just the content of an image that is not noticeable (or least noticeable) to humans, high compression ratios have been defined. For example, the JPEG (Joint Photographic Experts Group) standard for images provides loss-less compression of about 3:1, but can approach ratios of 50:1 with some loss of the original signal.

Motion video compression can rely on all of the above techniques, and some additional characteristics of both the human vision system and motion pictures. Most of the time, only a small part of the video image changes from one frame to the next. By encoding only the changes over time, very high-quality compressed video can have compression ratios of more than 200:1. For example, the MPEG-2 (Moving Picture Experts Group) standard for high-definition TV will compress from an original picture of 1.2 billion bits per second to fewer than 6 million.

A popular coding for music is MP3. This is audio layer 3 for MPEG. It compresses the audio signals by removing redundant or unnecessary parts of the sound signal. The result is a substantial reduction by a factor of 12 without any perceived reduction in sound quality. This compression method provides a small, high-quality file for transfer over the INTERNET, use in MP3 players, etc.

cognitive science and information systems

Amit Das

Cognitive science is the interdisciplinary study of intelligent behavior. The disciplines contributing to cognitive science include ARTIFICIAL INTELLIGENCE, psychology, linguistics, anthropology, philosophy, and neuroscience (Gardner, 1985). The range of intelligent behaviors investigated by cognitive scientists extends

from commonplace tasks such as vision and loco-
motion to skilled problem solving in specialized
domains like medicine, engineering, and law.

A key area of focus within cognitive science
has been the development of computational
models of intelligent behavior. Computational
models identify the knowledge and reasoning
processes underlying an aspect of intelligent behavior and encode these representations and
processes in computer programs to reproduce
the behavior. Such computer programs have
been developed to model game playing, theorem
proving, natural language understanding, diagnosis of physical systems, and design of various
artifacts. The adequacy of a computational
model is assessed by examining the performance
of a computer program embodying the model.

The relevance of cognitive science to information systems is twofold. Frameworks drawn from
cognitive science improve our understanding of
work tasks that information systems are designed
to support. Understanding of work tasks enables
us to design more effective and usable information
systems. Cognitive science also contributes directly to the design of a class of information systems
called expert systems. These systems (which are
designed to mimic the problem-solving behavior
of human experts) are developed using principles
and methods of cognitive science.

Bibliography

Gardner, H. (1985). *The Mind's New Science: A History of the Cognitive Revolution*. New York: Basic Books.

collaborative filtering

see PERSONALIZATION TECHNOLOGIES

communications

see ELECTRONIC COMMUNICATIONS

competitive advantage with information systems

see STRATEGIC USE OF INFORMATION TECH-
NOLOGY

complexity and information systems

Eve Mitleton-Kelly and Frank F. Land

Systems theory usually underpins the thinking
in information systems (IS) management. However, the sciences of complexity have now provided a deeper and richer understanding of
systems. This entry outlines the contribution
made by complexity to IS, defines some key
principles, explains how they can enrich IS
thinking, and offers an example to illustrate
one of the principles.

COMPLEXITY THEORY

There is no single unified theory of complexity
but several theories, arising from various natural
sciences that study complex systems such as
biology, chemistry, computer simulation, evolution, mathematics, and physics. This includes
the work undertaken over the past four decades
by scientists associated with the Santa Fe Institute in New Mexico, and particularly that of
Stuart Kauffman (1993, 1995, 2000), John Holland (1995, 1998), Chris Langton (Waldrop,
1992), and Murray Gell-Mann (1994) on complex adaptive systems (CAS), as well as the work
of scientists based in Europe such as Peter Allen
(1997) and Brian Goodwin (1995; Webster and
Goodwin, 1996); Axelrod on cooperation (1990,
1997; Axelrod and Cohen, 2000); Casti (1997),
Bonabeau, Dorigo, and Theraulaz (1999),
Epstein and Axtel (1996) on modeling and computer simulation; work by Ilya Prigogine, Isa-
belle Stengers, and Grégoire Nicolis on
dissipative structures (Prigogine and Stengers,
1985; Nicolis and Prigogine, 1989; Prigogine,
1990; Nicolis, 1994); work by Humberto Maturana and Francisco Varela (Maturana and Varela,
1992) and Niklaus Luhman (1990) on autopoiesis (Mingers, 1995), as well as work on chaos
theory (Gleick, 1987), that on increasing returns
by Brian Arthur (1990, 1995, 2002), on economics by Hodgson (1993, 2001), and on management by Stacey (1995, 1996, 2000, 2001).

The above can be summarized as six main
areas of research on (1) complex adaptive
systems; (2) dissipative structures; (3) autopoiesis in biology and its application to social
systems; (4) chaos theory; (5) increasing returns
and path dependence in economics; and
(6) systems theory, cybernetics, social network

theory, and other work in social systems and management. These six areas of research form the background to the ten generic principles of complexity identified by Mitleton-Kelly (2003b) in developing a theory of complex social systems. Since these principles incorporate more than the work on complex adaptive systems, the term *complex evolving systems* (CES) will be used.

The principles are *generic*, in the sense that they are common to all natural complex systems. However, the nature of the entities (whether genes, molecules, numbers, computer agents, or humans) has to be taken into account and the application of the principles in each context has to be made both relevant and appropriate. Human systems, for example, do differ from all other complex evolving systems in one important respect, in that humans are able to reflect and to make intentional decisions.

CONNECTIVITY AND INTERDEPENDENCE

Complex behavior arises from the interrelationship, interaction, and interconnectivity of elements within a system and between a system and its environment. Murray Gell-Mann (1994) traces the meaning to the Latin root of the word. *Plexus* means braided or entwined, from which is derived *complexus*, meaning braided together, which gives the English word "complex." Complex behavior therefore arises from the *intricate intertwining or interconnectivity of elements within a system and between a system and its environment.*

In a human system, connectivity and interdependence mean that a decision or action by any individual (group, organization, institution, or human system) may affect related individuals and systems. That effect will not have equal or uniform impact, and will vary with the "state" of each related individual and system, at the time. The "state" of an individual or a system will include its history and its constitution, which in turn will include its organization and structure. Connectivity applies to the interrelatedness of individuals *within* a system, as well as to the relatedness *between* human social systems, which include systems of artifacts such as information technology (IT) systems and intellectual systems of ideas. In IS management the human–machine interface is part of that interconnectivity, as well as the integration of different IT systems following a merger or acquisition.

Complexity theory, however, does not argue for ever-increasing connectivity, for high connectivity implies a high degree of interdependence. This means that the greater the interdependence between related systems or entities, the wider the "ripples" of perturbation or disturbance of a move or action by any one entity on all the other related entities. Such a high degree of dependence may not always have beneficial effects throughout the ecosystem. When one entity tries to improve its position, this may result in a worsening condition for others. Each "improvement" in one entity therefore may impose associated "costs" on other entities, either within the same system or on other related systems.

Intense interconnectivity creates multiple and intricate dependencies throughout the system which cannot be pulled apart. Interdependence plays an important role in large IT systems, which becomes apparent when one part is changed and this results in unforeseen and often significant effects in other parts of the system.

Connectivity and interdependence is one aspect of how complex behavior arises. Another important and closely related aspect is that complex systems are *multidimensional*, and all the dimensions interact and influence one another. In a human context the social, cultural, technical, economic, political, and global dimensions may impinge upon and influence one another. But not all multidimensional systems are complex; machine-type systems, for example, are complicated. A sociotechnical system, however, may well be complex and demonstrate all the principles of CES.

The defining feature of a CES is that it is able to create *new order*, that is, the bringing about of new ways of working, or new structures, or new relationships, or even new entities such as a new organizational form. Technology tends to have a significant effect on an organization and does often help bring about significant change.

Complexity principles are *scale invariant* and apply at all scales from an individual to a team, organization, industry, economy, etc.

COEVOLUTION

Connectivity applies not only to elements within a system, but also to related systems within an ecosystem. As entities and organisms interact and adapt within an ecosystem, they alter "both the fitness and the fitness landscape of the other organisms" (Kauffman, 1993: 242).

The way each element influences and is in turn influenced by all other related elements in an ecosystem is part of the process of coevolution, which Kauffman describes as "a process of coupled, deforming landscapes where the adaptive moves of each entity alter the landscapes of its neighbors" (Kauffman and Macready, 1995).

Another way of describing coevolution is that *the evolution of one domain or entity is partially dependent on the evolution of other related domains or entities* (Ehrlich and Raven, 1964; Kauffman, 1993, 1995; Pianka, 1994; McKelvey, 1999a, b); or *that one domain or entity changes in the context of the other(s)*.

The main point to note, however, is that coevolution involves *reciprocal influence and change within a coevolving ecosystem*. If influence and change are entirely in one direction, then that would be more accurately described as "adaptation to" a changing environment. However, short-term adaptation may result in long-term coevolution if the entities in due course influence and change one another.

The notion of coevolution needs to be given serious consideration in IS management. The example given later will show that if the relationship between IT development and business strategy is seen in terms of facilitating their coevolution, many of the inherent problems in that relationship may be reduced.

DISSIPATIVE STRUCTURES, FAR-FROM-EQUILIBRIUM

Another key concept in complexity is dissipative structures, which are ways in which open systems exchange energy, matter, or information with their environment and which, when pushed "far-from-equilibrium," create new structures and order.

Ilya Prigogine was awarded the 1977 Nobel Prize for chemistry for his work on dissipative structures and his contributions to non-equilibrium thermodynamics. Prigogine has reinterpreted the second law of thermodynamics. Dissolution into entropy is not an absolute condition, but "under certain conditions, entropy itself becomes the progenitor of order." To be more specific, "under non-equilibrium conditions, at least, entropy may produce, rather than degrade, order (and) organization.... If this is so, then entropy, too, loses its either/or character. While certain systems run down, other systems simultaneously evolve and grow more coherent" (Prigogine and Stengers, 1985: xxi).

An external constraint may disturb the behavior of a system to such an extent that at a critical point it jumps to a new level and creates new order. In dissipative structures the tendency to split into alternative solutions is called *bifurcation*, but the term is misleading in that it means a separation into *two* paths, when there may be several possible solutions. Before the system settles into one solution, several alternatives were possible.

An observer could not predict which state will emerge; "only chance will decide, through the dynamics of fluctuations. The system will in effect scan the territory and will make a few attempts, perhaps unsuccessful at first, to stabilize. Then a particular fluctuation will take over. By stabilizing it the system becomes a *historical object* in the sense that its subsequent evolution depends on this critical choice" Nicolis and Prigogine, 1989: 72).

Innovation takes place at the critical point, when the existing order can no longer be sustained and new order comes into being. Once the decision is made, there is a historical dimension and subsequent evolution may depend on that critical choice; but *before* the decision is finalized, the alternatives are sources of *innovation* and *diversification*, since the opening up of possibilities endows the individual and the system with new solutions. When a social entity (individual, group, organization, industry, economy, country, etc.) is faced with a constraint, it finds new ways of operating, because away-from-equilibrium (established norms or patterns of work and behavior) systems are forced to experiment and explore their *space of possibilities*, and this exploration helps them discover and create new patterns of relationships and different structures.

EXPLORATION-OF-THE-SPACE-OF-POSSIBILITIES

Complexity suggests that to survive and thrive, an entity needs to explore its space of possibilities and to generate variety. Complexity also suggests that the search for a single "optimum" solution may be neither possible nor desirable. Any solution can only be optimum under certain conditions, and when those conditions change, the solution may no longer be optimal. If, however, a variety of possible solutions exists, then as the environment changes the system is able to draw on these alternatives, which may have become more appropriate in the new circumstances. The idea of an optimal solution is embedded in the IS community and often creates problems such as legacy systems, which were once appropriate but have become "stuck" in a narrow solution space. The move toward evolutionary development has helped, but the idea of allowing different alternatives to be tested in, for example, different sites may prove to be beneficial. Uniformity and homogeneity restrict future development and the drive toward tighter and narrower standardization is actively inhibiting exploration of possible alternatives, which may become significant when the environment changes.

SELF-ORGANIZATION, EMERGENCE, AND THE CREATION OF NEW ORDER

Kauffman (1993) brings the importance of self-organization in the evolutionary process to our attention. He calls Darwinian natural selection a "single singular force" and argues that "[i]t is this single-force view which I believe to be inadequate, for it fails to notice, fails to stress, fails to incorporate the possibility that simple and complex systems exhibit order spontaneously" (1993: xiii). That *spontaneous order* is *self-organization*. Kauffman argues that natural selection is not the sole source of order in organisms and suggests that both natural selection and self-organization are necessary for evolution; he then proceeds to expand evolutionary theory to incorporate both evolutionary forces.

Emergent properties, qualities, patterns, or structures arise from the interaction of individual elements. They are the structures or patterns that appear at the next macro level as a result of interaction at a lower micro level. The relationship between the micro events and macro structures is iterative – it is a *coevolutionary* process whereby the individual entities and the macro structures they create through their interaction

influence one another in an ongoing iterative process. Emergence is the *process* that creates new order together with self-organization.

In an organizational context, *self-organization* may be described as the spontaneous coming together of a group to perform a task (or for some other purpose); the group decides what to do, how and when to do it, and no one outside the group directs those activities.

Emergence in a human system tends to create irreversible structures or ideas, relationships and organizational forms, which become part of the history of individuals and institutions and in turn affect the evolution of those entities; e.g., the generation of knowledge and of innovative ideas when a team is working together could be described as an emergent property in the sense that it arises from the interaction of individuals and is not just the sum of existing ideas, but could well be something quite new and possibly unexpected. Once the ideas are articulated, they form part of the history of each individual and part of the shared history of the team – the process is not reversible – and these new ideas and new knowledge can be built upon to generate further new ideas and knowledge.

AN EXAMPLE: ENABLING COEVOLUTION BETWEEN IS DEVELOPMENT AND BUSINESS STRATEGY

The example (Mitleton-Kelly, 2004b) explores the idea that when coevolution between business strategy and IS development is enabled, the problems associated with legacy systems may be reduced.

The term *legacy systems* is taken to mean those IT systems which no longer fully support the business process and which constrain the development of new products and applications. Most systems described as legacy tend to be 20–30 years old, written in assembly, or an early version of a third-generation language (Chikofsky and Cross, 1990; Sneed, 1995; Adolph, 1996). Reengineering, reverse engineering, freeze and encapsulate (Bennett, 1995) have been suggested as viable solutions to the legacy systems' problem. They are associated with high maintenance costs (Warren, 1999) and they have become very difficult and expensive to change. Legacy can also be seen as a *gap* between the organization's business needs and technical capabilities.

However, legacy has also been recognized as a multifaceted sociotechnical situation (Gold, 1998).

Legacy is not merely a technical issue but arises from a multiplicity of intricately inter-related and interdependent sociotechnical factors. The degree of connectivity between the IS and business domains may improve the *fitness* of each domain, or it may result in *complexity catastrophe* owing to the increased constraints brought about through increasing dependencies. Increased fitness is here interpreted as the emergence of a *new organizational form*, which has helped to reduce the problem of legacy. Complexity catastrophe is interpreted as an extreme state of dependencies between the IT systems and the business applications that gives rise to an almost intractable problem of legacy. (The term information system is used to denote the entire sociotechnical system of information exchange using a variety of artifacts, while the term IT refers primarily to a computer-based system. The term IS domain, however, is used to refer to the professionals working in the IT depart-ment of an organization. They may be involved in the development of brand new systems, in the development of applications, or in maintaining the existing system.)

In the case under study, the organization (hereinafter the Bank) admitted to a significant legacy problem. It would prefer to jettison the old legacy systems, perceived as those systems that no longer support the current business objectives or are inhibiting future developments (e.g., the creation of new financial products). They are typically large, the cost of maintaining them is very high, and they constrain the business from responding fast enough to desired changes in the business domain. Legacy systems are not suffi-ciently flexible to allow significant modifica-tions, and cannot meet current and future architectural standards. However, the applica-tions supported by the legacy systems are typic-ally large, complex, and vital to the business.

The UK office acknowledged the complex nature of the problem and, by breaking the or-ganizational norms and actively encouraging a sustained dialogue over time between the IS and business strategy domains, created an enabling infrastructure, which in turn helped it overcome the technical constraints.

The dominant culture of the Bank supported one kind of *order*, i.e., a particular way of relating and working, which had inadvertently contrib-uted to a legacy problem. A different way needed to be found and the UK office *self-organized* and created a new order. Although certain individ-uals took particular actions, no one was deliber-ately *orchestrating* the process. Certain conditions were introduced that encouraged and supported a different type of interaction and enabled indi-viduals to coevolve in a reciprocal evolutionary context. In other words, certain individuals in the UK office initiated the conditions that helped to create a new enabling infrastructure, which in turn allowed a new organizational form to emerge through the interaction of a group from both the IS and the business domains. One of the outcomes of this initiative (which can also be seen as an *exploration of the space of possibilities*) was an amelioration of the legacy problem.

The legacy problem. The legacy system of the UK operation was based on IBM hardware, was at least 10 to 15 years old (with 30-year-old elements), was written in COBOL with assembler language components, and "needs resources that now are in their 50s or even 60s." With greater insight it was also described as "what is left behind by the previous organization – the system that was built for a different organization than the one we are today." This observation points to part of the problem. The systems were designed and built to support a different business environment. As the business environ-ment changed, the IT systems were modified, enhanced, partially replaced, and new elements added, in an effort to continue to support the business, but without full success. The con-stant modifications did not provide a system tailored to the changing business requirements but a "legacy system [that] becomes dysfunc-tional or it becomes disjoint [with] the current business." Furthermore, full replacement was not an economically and technically viable option.

A variety of business, organizational, and technical elements had combined to produce a complex sociotechnical system with a very high degree of interconnectivity and interdepend-ence. These multiple elements also explain why it was so difficult, if not impossible, to jettison the entire legacy system and to start afresh. The description may also be read as that of a socio-technical CES. If it is seen from that perspective, then certain generic characteristics common to complex evolving systems may be identified that are relevant and applicable to this example. The following interconnected elements contributed to the complexity of the system.

1 One element arose from increasing intercon-nectivity and interdependence among the *system components and the applications*. The Bank often customized or engineered solu-tions into its systems for individual custom-ers, and changed coded components. Over time a layered system infrastructure was created and the interconnectivity and inter-dependence became so intricately inter-twined that a point was reached when "to undo that complexity is almost insurmount-able." It became very difficult to fully tailor yet another application. Hence the Bank "cuts and pastes ... and you get to a situ-ation where you are suddenly generating subsets for different customers." With layering and new subsets, the systems became increasingly intertwined and gave rise to *emergent* properties, i.e., properties that were unexpected and unpredictable. If these properties also happen to be unnoticed, then changes in one part of the system could have significant consequences in other parts.

2 *Organizational restructuring* (a social aspect) *had changed the systems' architecture* (a tech-nical aspect). The main European system was on two hardware bases, using HP and IBM hardware. Originally the IBM system was implemented in six different countries and started in the late 1970s/early 1980s as a branch or country-centric system, referred to as "a bank in a box," which ran all the local bank's activities. Since then the Bank went through several phases of organizational re-structuring, which impacted the systems' architecture, until all the hardware for the six European countries with IBM systems became based in the UK.

3 A third component was that the Bank had made a conscious effort to try and isolate elements of the legacy "bank in a box" system and to *create stand-alone components*,

which still communicated with it. They were Windows NT-based front-end servers. But they had not succeeded in replacing the full set of legacy software. The part replacements used current technology.

4 *The identification of ownership of common com-ponents* and of the need for upgrading was much more difficult as multiple owners had to be identified and be persuaded of the benefits before they would sign off. There were so many interdependencies and link-ages that isolation of specific modules became extremely difficult. The technical problems impacted the organizational issue of ownership and the geographically dis-persed organizational structure added to the problem. The multi-ownership issue did not arise with systems that were managed and owned locally in a single country. This example shows how the intricate interrela-tionship between technological and organ-izational factors created the complex problem space of legacy: a technical problem impacted an organizational issue, while or-ganizational changes exacerbated the tech-nical concerns.

5 Another element contributing to the com-plexity of legacy was that the maintenance and further development of the IT systems had been centralized within the UK group, which controlled 16 systems on both HP and IBM platforms. Thus, as resources for the maintenance and support were held cen-trally, there was *no local knowledge* of the branch technology of the system. To over-come the loss of local knowledge, written formalized procedures were established to enable the day-to-day running of the system. However, when a relatively unusual request came, then "nobody knew how to use that part of the system anymore." Thus in for-malizing the procedures, the informal ways and means used to bypass certain problems, which were difficult to articulate, were not captured and that knowledge was lost.

Despite the above problems, the UK oper-ation did complete the project on time, by creat-ing an enabling environment that facilitated the interaction and the subsequent coevolution be-tween IS development and the business strategy.

The enabling conditions. The conditions in the UK operation that enabled closer working together between the business and information systems professionals can be summarized as follows:

- New procedures introducing regular monthly meetings, which enabled *good networking* and *trust* as well as a *common language* leading to mutual *understanding*.
- *Autonomy*: the project manager was left alone to introduce the new procedures.
- A *senior manager supported* the changes and allowed the necessary space for self-organization and autonomy.
- *Stability*: sufficient *continuity* to see the project through.
- An *interpreter* mediated the dialogue between the domains. This insured understanding on both sides but also protected the technologists from constant minor changes in requirements.

The process started when a new business product manager moved to the UK office and found a substantial disconnection between the business requirements and technical support in the *cash management business*. She then brought in a project manager to help bridge the gap. The procedures that the project manager introduced for the cash management business provided the necessary background and set the conditions, which in turn enabled the work to succeed. The outcome of these two projects was a significant improvement of the legacy issue.

When the project manager came in, he had to define his role and that of his group. A number of initiatives were taken. He created the conditions for the three environments of technology, business, and operations to talk together, but in doing so they went against accepted established ways of working. Initially, he acted as the *interpreter* between the business and the technology groups and used "control of the purse" to initiate the dialogue. But that was only to get the process started. The important initiative was instigating regular monthly meetings, supported by weekly information updates.

Senior managers from the business, the technology, and operations were invited to attend the monthly sessions. Every month they would go through each one of the projects reporting on the latest status, where the project was, what happened in the last month, what was planned for the future month, what the issues were. But something else was also taking place. The people involved in the different projects began to identify *cross-dependencies in terms of the business project relationships*, which led to new insights and new ways of working. "They're business-related dependencies. And . . . people suddenly open up and realize that maybe there's a better way of doing something. Maybe there is another view to take on this and in fact these sessions proved to be very useful." Once the conditions were provided, the individuals involved were able to make the necessary decisions and take the appropriate actions. This illustrates micro-agent interaction, which is neither managed nor controlled from the top. Once the inhibitors are removed and the enablers put in place, new behaviors and ways of working could emerge.

The monthly sessions improved communication between the different domains by improving understanding, but they also allowed for the *emergence of new ways of working*, and in the process helped the business become fitter and more competitive.

That monthly session was fairly well attended and as time went on, I think it proved itself out in terms of its value because we had good understanding between all of the project managers looking at the projects from a business perspective. We had ownership in that the business could see what we were doing so they were interacting with us. But also they were almost inadvertently interacting with technology because they were both in the same forum. And so I think what this did, it broke down any sort of barriers and we got *common understanding* and in fact we delivered projects that the business wanted to see and that the business has since found to be key. And since the Bank is the number one bank in cash management, we must have done some good.

The key was simplicity, regular communication, and a common language. The reporting was content based with the emphasis on "a simplicity of explanation on a regular basis of where a given project was." The technology person reporting and the operations person could both relate to the project. The business project manager, who owned the project, was also expected to present every month in a standard format to his or her colleagues who were all running the business projects for the cash management business. The business project managers were usually ex-bankers with 10–15 years' experience of the Bank. They therefore knew both how to network in the Bank and how to understand the rudiments of what the technologists were trying to articulate.

The meetings took half a day each month, with a continual rotation of presentations, which was a significant amount of time, yet people did attend regularly, and that regularity was a further key element of success. In a constantly changing environment, the meetings provided a necessary degree of stability and continuity: "the way the culture of the bank works, it changes so rapidly, people change so quickly from role to role."

Another important element was the articulation of business requirements as an iterative process, with regular face-to-face meetings between the technology specialists and the business project manager who owned the project and who "solicit(ed) well-articulated business requirements in writing from the business product people." These meetings were at a senior management level with (1) a vice president who would own the product and be responsible for the profit and loss. That individual would determine what he or she required. He or she would meet with (2) a senior and experienced business project manager who was a seasoned banker, with a good knowledge of the Bank, and (3) a senior technology project manager who would have to define the IS platform(s) and the technical development of the project. This constant dialogue created a willingness to communicate and a level of trust that were essential enablers of coevolution. "If you're willing to communicate and get down to a base level of discussion with technophobic individuals, then what you have is a willingness to participate and listen and over time you get a certain rapport and confidence level built up."

What was achieved at the UK Bank took a particular individual, supported by his senior manager, to create the conditions that enabled dialogue, understanding, and a good articulation of requirements. He created the initial conditions to improve the relationship between the domains, but he could not foresee how the process would work, or indeed whether it would work. As it happened it did work, and a substantial *network rapport* was established between the domains based on trust, a common language, and mutual understanding. They worked well together because the conditions were right and they were prepared to *self-organize* and work in a different way. The new relationships were not designed or even intended. They happened spontaneously in the sense that they were enabled but not stipulated.

The achievement, however, could be a one-off. Unless the new procedures and ways of working become *embedded* in the culture of the organization, they are likely to dissipate over time. Once the initiator is no longer in place, and there is no new energy to sustain the process, the danger of dissipation or reversion to the dominant mode of working will assert itself.

In this case there has been some embedding and some continuity, but the process is fragile. A new set of organizational changes could destroy it. Part of the embedding is the networking rapport that has been established. The business project managers know whom they have to talk to in the cash business, in operations, and in technology. That network is established. It is part of the social capital of the organization, but it is implicit and informal.

Because the network rapport is implicit and informal, it is under threat if there are too many and too frequent changes, and the Bank's culture is one of constant change in management positions. "Every two years someone else is in the post so that there is that lack of continuity." If the rate and degree of change are too great, then the network will become invalid.

There is a fine balance between stability and change. A degree of stability – a sense of continuity – is necessary. It strengthens the network of relationships, thus increasing the organization's social capital. A degree of change, on the other hand, insures a constant exploration of the space of possibilities. The two must be held in tension. If one predominates, then the fitness of the organization will decrease. In the example, a person who acted as *interpreter* and who helped to mediate the dialogue between the business and IT domains provided a necessary element of stability. This does not contradict what has been said above. The direct dialogue between the domains takes place face to face. The interpreter simply "protects" the technologists from constant minor changes in requirements. There is a distinction between (1) clarification and a good understanding of requirements and (2) the constant minor changes that the business people want to introduce. By providing a degree of needed stability, he gives the technologists space in which to work and to meet the agreed requirements.

CONCLUSION

In summary, encouraging coevolution (as opposed to the pursuit of separate evolutionary paths) between the domains requires an enabling infrastructure, which provides the conditions for self-organization, emergence, and exploration of the space of possibilities. In human systems, coevolution in the sense of the *evolution of interactions* places emphasis on the relationship between the coevolving entities. The example therefore focused on the relationship between the business and IS domains, and explored the assumption that the degree, intensity, and density of interaction between the two entities affect the rate of coevolution between the two domains. In this case, the enabling conditions were: (1) enhanced communication between the domains, based on trust and mutual understanding; (2) sufficient stability and continuity; (3) senior management support that allowed space for (4) autonomy and freedom to self-organize; and the realization that (5) "a cross-domain process was a successful way to run business-drive requirements."

One important outcome from this process was the emergence of a new organizational form, or a new way of working and relating, which helped to reduce the problem of legacy and thus increased the organization's fitness.

Bibliography

Adolph, W. S. (1996). Cash cow in the tar pit: Reengineering a legacy system. *IEEE Software*, May, 41.

Allen, P. M. (1997). *Cities and Regions as Self-Organizing Systems: Model of Complexity*. London: Gordon and Breach.

Arthur, B. W. (1990). Positive feedbacks in the economy. *Scientific American*, February.

Arthur, B. W. (1995). *Increasing Returns and Path Dependence in the Economy*. Ann Arbor: Michigan University Press.

Arthur, B. W. (2002). Is the information revolution over? If history is a guide, it is not. *Business 2.0*, March; www.business2.com/articles/mag/o,1640,37570,00.html.

Ashby, W. R. (1969). *Self-Regulation and Requisite Variety in Systems Thinking*, ed. F. E. Emery. Harmondsworth: Penguin.

Axelrod, R. (1990). *The Evolution of Cooperation*. Harmondsworth: Penguin.

Axelrod, R. (1997). *The Complexity of Cooperation*. Princeton, NJ: Princeton University Press.

Axelrod, R. and Cohen, M. D. (2000). *Harnessing Complexity: Organizational Implications of a Scientific Frontier*. New York: Free Press.

Bennett, K. (1995). Legacy systems: Coping with success. *IEEE Software*, **12**, 1 (January), 19–24.

Bonabeau, E., Dorigo, M., and Theraulaz, G. (1999). *Swarm Intelligence*. Oxford: Oxford University Press.

Casti, J. (1997). *Would-Be Worlds*. New York: John Wiley.

Chikofsky, E. J. and Cross, J. H. (1990). Reverse engineering and design recovery: A taxonomy. *IEEE Software*, January, 13–17.

Ehrlich, P. R. and Raven, P. H. (1964). Butterflies and plants: A study in co-evolution. *Evolution*, **18**, 586–608.

Epstein, J. M. and Axtel, R. (1996). *Growing Artificial Societies: Social Science from the Bottom Up*. Washington, DC: Brookings Institution Press.

Garcia-Lorenzo, L., Mitleton-Kelly, E., and Galliers, R. D. (2003). Organizational complexity: Organizing through the generation and sharing of knowledge. *International Journal of Knowledge, Culture and Change Management*, **3**, ed. M. Kalantzis and B. Cope, article MC03-0023-2003.

Gell-Mann, M. (1994). *The Quark and the Jaguar: Adventures in the Simple and the Complex*. New York: W. H. Freeman.

Gleick, J. (1987). *Chaos: Making a New Science*. New York: Cardinal, McDonald.

Gold, N. (1998). The meaning of "legacy systems." Technical Report 7/98, Department of Computer Science, University of Durham, UK; www.dur.ac.uk/CSM/SABA/meaning.html.

Goodwin, B. (1995). *How the Leopard Changed its Spots*. New York: Phoenix.

Hodgson, G. M. (1993). *Economics and Evolution: Bringing Life Back into Economics*. Cambridge: Polity Press.

Hodgson, G. M. (2001). Is social evolution Lamarckian or Darwinian? In John Laurent and John Nightingale (eds.), *Darwinism and Evolutionary Economics*. Cheltenham: Edward Elgar, pp. 87–118.

Holland, J. (1995). *Hidden Order: How Adaptation Builds Complexity*. New York: Addison-Wesley.

Holland, J. (1998). *Emergence: From Chaos to Order*. New York: Addison-Wesley.

Kauffman, S. (1993). *The Origins of Order: Self-Organization and Selection in Evolution*. Oxford: Oxford University Press.

Kauffman, S. (1995). *At Home in the Universe*. New York: Viking.

Kauffman, S. (2000). *Investigations*. Oxford: Oxford University Press.

Kauffman, S. and Macready, W. (1995). Technological evolution and adaptive organizations. *Complexity*, 1 (2), 26–43.

Lane, D. A. and Maxfield, R. (1997). Foresight, complexity and strategy. In *The Economy as an Evolving Complex System II: Proceedings*. Santa Fe Institute Studies in the Sciences of Complexity, 27, ed. B. W. Arthur, S. Durlauf, and D. A. Lane.

Lewin, R. (1993). *Complexity: Life at the Edge of Chaos*. London: J. M. Dent.

Luhman, N. (1990). *Essays on Self-Reference*. New York: Columbia University Press.

Maguire, S. and McKelvey, B. (eds.) (1999). Special issue on complexity and management: Where are we? *Emergence*, 1 (2).

Maturana, H. and Varela, F. (1992). *The Tree of Knowledge*. New York: Shambhala.

McKelvey, B. (1999a). Self-organization, complexity catastrophe, and microstate models at the edge of chaos. In J. A. C. Baum and B. McKelvey (eds.), *Variations in Organization Science: In Honor of Donald T. Campbell*. Thousand Oaks, CA: Sage, pp. 279–307.

McKelvey, B. (1999b). Visionary leadership vs. distributed intelligence: Strategy, microcoevolution, complexity. Proceedings of EIASM Workshop, Brussels, June.

Mingers, J. (1995). *Self-Producing Systems: Implications and Applications of Autopoiesis*. New York: Plenum Press.

Mitleton-Kelly, E. (1997). Organization as coevolving complex adaptive systems. British Academy of Management Conference, London, September 8–10.

Mitleton-Kelly, E. (2000). Complexity: Partial support for BPR. In P. Henderson (ed.), *Systems Engineering for Business Process Change*, vol. 1. New York: Springer-Verlag.

Mitleton-Kelly, E. (ed.) (2003a). *Complex Systems and Evolutionary Perspectives of Organizations: The Application of Complexity Theory to Organizations*. New York: Elsevier.

Mitleton-Kelly, E. (2003b). Ten principles of complexity and enabling infrastructures. In *Complex Systems and Evolutionary Perspectives of Organizations: The Application of Complexity Theory to Organizations*. New York: Elsevier.

Mitleton-Kelly, E. (2004a). An integrated methodology to facilitate the emergence of new ways of organizing.

Conference Proceedings of the 3rd European Conference on Research Methodology for Business and Management Studies (ECRM), April.

Mitleton-Kelly, E. (2004b). IT legacy systems. Enabling environments that reduce the legacy problem: A complexity perspective. In N. H. Madhavji, M. M. Lehman, J. F. Ramil, and D. Perry (eds.), *Software Evolution*. New York: John Wiley.

Mitleton-Kelly, E. (2004c). Coevolutionary integration: A complexity perspective on mergers and acquisitions. 20th EGOS Colloquium, Ljubljana University, Slovenia, July.

Mitleton-Kelly, E. and Papaefthimiou, M. C. (2000). Coevolution and an enabling infrastructure: A solution to legacy? In P. Henderson (ed.), *Systems Engineering for Business Process Change*, vol. 1. New York: Springer-Verlag.

Mitleton-Kelly, E. and Papaefthimiou, M. C. (2001). Coevolution of diverse elements interacting within a social ecosystem. In P. Henderson (ed.), *Systems Engineering for Business Process Change*, vol. 2. New York: Springer-Verlag.

Mitleton-Kelly, E. and Speh Birkenkrahe, M. (2004). Treasury operations in a multi-national oil company: Dialogue on the methodology of using natural experiments in complex evolving systems. In P. Andriani and G. Passiante (eds.), *Complexity Theory and Management of Networks*. London: Imperial College Press.

Nicolis, G. (1994). Physics of far-from-equilibrium systems and self-organization. In P. Davies (ed.), *The New Physics*. Cambridge: Cambridge University Press.

Nicolis, G. and Prigogine, I. (1989). *Exploring Complexity*. New York: W. H. Freeman.

Parker, D. and Stacey, R. D. (1994). *Chaos, Management and Economics*. Hobart Paper 125, Institute of Economic Affairs.

Pianka, E. R. (1994). *Evolutionary Ecology*. New York: HarperCollins.

Prigogine, I. (1990). Time and the problem of the two cultures. First International Dialogue on the Transition to Global Society, Landegg Academy, September 3–9.

Prigogine, I. and Stengers, I. (1985). *Order Out of Chaos*. New York: Flamingo.

Sneed, H. M. (1995). Planning the reengineering of legacy systems. *IEEE Software*, January, 24–34.

Stacey, R. D. (1995). The science of complexity: An alternative perspective for strategic change processes. *Strategic Management Journal*, 16, 6 (September), 477–95.

Stacey, R. D. (1996). *Complexity and Creativity in Organizations*. New York: Berrett-Koehler.

Stacey, R. D. (2000). *Complexity and Management*. London: Routledge.

Stacey, R. D. (2001). *Complex Responsive Processes in Organizations*. London: Routledge.

Waldrop, M. M. (1992). *Complexity: The Emerging Science at the Edge of Order and Chaos*. Harmondsworth: Penguin.

Warren, I. (1999). *The Renaissance of Legacy Systems: Method Support for Software-System Evolution*. New York: Springer-Verlag.

Webster, G. and Goodwin, B. (1996). *Form and Transformation: Generative and Relational Principles in Biology*. Cambridge: Cambridge University Press.

compression

Methods to reduce the storage requirements for program and data files (*see* CODING OF DATA FOR INFORMATION PROCESSING).

computer forensics

Rodger Jamieson

Computer forensics is a new field that deals with investigating computer-related crimes. Computer forensics, also referred to as electronic discovery, electronic evidence discovery, computer forensic analysis, digital discovery, computer examination, and computer analysis, is the process of methodically examining computer systems, computer networks, computer media, and peripherals for evidence (Rehman Technology Services, 2000). This includes the examination of any device that may contain evidence in a digital format. The method chosen to investigate a computer forensic crime may have consequences when the case is taken to court as any investigation has the potential to be contested on technical and evidentiary grounds; therefore, evidence needs to be gathered in a way that will be accepted in a court of law. Acceptance of evidence in a court of law is the key to the whole process so any action performed on the potential evidence must be forensically sound. Therefore, it is important to follow a methodology when investigating a computer system to insure that evidence is not destroyed, damaged, altered, or contaminated in any way, and so will be admissible in court (ACPR, 2003).

There is a significant difference between investigators and computer forensic analysts in that they play quite different roles in the investigation in terms of insuring the evidence will be admissible in court. The primary difference between an investigator and a computer forensic analyst (CFA) is that computer forensic analysis is one facet of an investigation. Often the two roles are held by two different people, where an investigator determines what evidence is required, consistent with the rules of evidence, and the CFA identifies, collects, and analyzes the digital evidence for the investigator. The CFA has no responsibility for putting an evidence brief together, so forensic analysis is a more objective approach. The admissibility of the evidence, defined by the rules of evidence and determined by the investigator, is independent of any computer forensic framework as there is no distinction between digital evidence (e.g., emails) and standard evidence (such as handwritten documents). The CFA must preserve the integrity of the evidence and maintain continuity of evidence. This entry focuses on the development of a framework for CFAs. The term investigation is used within the context of a computer forensic analysis investigation (the role of a CFA), and not that of a standard investigation (the role of an investigator).

A methodology is important to any computer forensic investigation as it insures that the investigation takes place in a structured and complete way that delivers evidence that is admissible in court. A computer forensics methodology will usually involve the following phases:

- *Preparation*: prepare the personnel, materials, tools, and equipment required for the computer forensic examination.
- *Identification*: secure the scene and identify the evidence from the data set.
- *Baseline*: test original evidence to provide a baseline or control result for future verifications to insure consistency and accuracy.
- *Preservation*: back up, protect, and preserve the evidence to prevent tampering and damage.
- *Verification*: test output/results to insure consistency and accuracy as failure at this stage may dictate a return to the identification and preservation phases.
- *Analysis*: extract, process, and interpret the digital data.
- *Presentation*: prepare the case and evidence for court.

Benefits of a standard computer forensics methodology include the following:

- beginners in the field can avoid the learning curve of having to develop a methodology;
- standardization can be achieved in the industry;
- provision of an agreed benchmark of parameters within which practitioners and judicial decision-making can be measured with more certainty of outcome;
- provides a framework for the development and application of techniques, tools, and practices;
- helps avoid questioning in court on methods used by providing a structure upon which to justify actions;
- uniformity across all jurisdictions with easy transference of evidence and data across jurisdictional boundaries;
- increased understanding by the legal system of computer forensics, thus removing some of the gray areas of practice;
- increased transparency in practices enabling members from other fields to more easily assist in investigations;
- provides a basis for the development of industry training and tertiary qualifications;
- justifies to the court that the case was approached in a structured, well-thought-out way that is generally aligned with fewer mistakes. Similarly, a set methodology helps to show to the court that investigators are aware of issues in the field.

While a standard computer forensics methodology provides many benefits, there are certain limitations, which include the following:

- the presumption that the desired outcome cannot be achieved by any other means and scrutiny of processes that fail to strictly comply with standardized/generic computer forensic methodology;
- the methodology may not be sufficiently generic and therefore restrict flexibility;
- it may not address enough detail for practitioners as it does not define specific procedures and practices;
- a methodology may be based on a small set of experiences and therefore may not encapsulate the broader approaches and issues;

- it may be difficult to develop a high-level methodology owing to the difficulty of achieving consensus among examiners;
- the methodology may not meet the needs of all jurisdictions;
- inexperienced people may adopt the methodology wrongly or simplistically, resulting in the risk that these people may lower the standard of the industry;
- the methodology may not be flexible enough to cope with the changing technology;
- a high-level methodology that can be used across jurisdictions may result in some jurisdictional freedoms being compromised by other restrictions.

Bibliography

ACPR (2003). *Seizing Computers and Other Electronic Evidence.* Australasian Center for Policing Research, Best Practice Guide, Adelaide.

Rehman Technology Services (2000). Computer forensics, electronic discovery, electronic evidence discovery, digital discovery, computer analysis, computer examination. *Computer Expert*, electronic-discovery.com; accessed October 26, 2000.

Tennyenhuis, A. and Jamieson, R. (2004). *An Investigation of Computer Forensics Methodologies and Competencies: A Research Report.* Sydney: SIRCA.

computer hardware architecture

Gordon B. Davis

Computer hardware is one of the elements in an operational computer system for information processing. The components of the hardware system form a computer hardware architecture. The basic building block for all computer hardware is the chip. Computer hardware systems differ in size, complexity, and power. However, every computer system for information processing includes hardware and software to perform processing functions and store data; most have communications capabilities.

COMPUTER HARDWARE CHIPS

A chip is a rectangular piece of silicon on which an integrated circuit has been etched. The process of producing computer chips starts with a crystal of silicon that is sliced into thin circular wafers. Circuits are etched on the wafer by a process of masking and diffusion. The process forms and connects transistors, resisters, diodes, etc. that make up circuits. The wafer is sliced into several chips. Each chip is mounted in a package with pins for plugging the chip into a board. Based on a projection termed Moore's law (after Gordon E. Moore of Intel), the complexity and storage capacity of computer chips doubles about every 18 months. This incredible growth in power and capacity and reduction in size have provided very large increases in capabilities and reduction in costs. Part of the effects have resulted in lower costs, but much of the processing power and storage capacity has been devoted to new applications and improved human–computer interfaces.

The circuits can be designed to be microprocessor chips, memory chips, or input–output interface chips. A microprocessor is a chip that contains the traditional functions of the central processing unit of a computer. It contains an arithmetic/logic unit, a control unit (to direct and synchronize operations), and registers to use during operations. The microprocessor is essentially a computer on a chip. It can be programmed to perform arithmetic functions, execute logic, select among alternatives, and direct functions. Memory chips are of two major types: read-only memory (ROM) and random access memory (RAM). The ROM chips are used for permanent programs written as part of the manufacturing process, and a user cannot alter them. The instructions are read from ROM as part of processing, but there is no writing to ROM chips. PROMs (programmable read-only memories) are like ROM memory but can be programmed after manufacture.

RAM chips are used for primary storage (main memory) containing user data and application programs being processed. Data may be read from this storage and data stored in it. It is volatile in the sense that data stored there are lost if power is interrupted. The storage capacity is expressed in thousands (using the symbol K for thousands of bytes of storage), millions (using the symbol MB for megabytes), and thousands of megabytes (using GB for gigabytes). A byte is the basic unit of storage. One byte can store, for example, one alphanumeric character. Sets of bytes are used for more complex elements.

The microprocessor uses an internal bus architecture. A bus is a common path for all signals. All functional units are connected to the bus. An electrical signal is sent down the bus and selects the connecting path that will take it to its destination. Different signals are kept from interfering by synchronizing signals and controls. Several internal buses may be used to increase speed. An important characteristic of chips and buses is the size of the internal data path on the chip and on the buses, i.e., how many signals are sent and used simultaneously. By analogy, it is the number of lanes on which traffic can move in parallel. At the PC level, high-performance computers have 32-bit or 64-bit architecture. Very large computers also use integrated circuits. However, the circuits are very dense and require special cooling and other design features.

Because of the basic power of the microprocessor, one approach to computer design has been to create microprocessors with a large number of complex instructions. This design is termed CISC (complex instruction set computer). The advantage is the ability to create complex instructions that handle complex situations. The disadvantages are the decoding delays and the need for more than one instruction cycle. An alternative approach is RISC (reduced instruction set computer) in which instructions are limited to simple ones that can be executed in one cycle. As a result, for some applications a RISC processor may require more instructions but may take less time to execute. For other applications, a CISC processor may be faster.

In the design of computers, both microprocessor code and software can be used to present the user with a machine that appears to have characteristics that are not in the physical hardware. The machine the programmer or user deals with is a conceptual or logical machine, often termed a virtual machine.

BASIC HARDWARE IN A COMPUTER SYSTEM

Basic hardware equipment in a computer system for information processing supports the following functions:

1   Entry or input of data and instructions to the computer.

2   Computation, control, and primary storage (central processing unit or CPU).
3   Secondary storage.
4   Output from the computer.
5   Data communications (not always present).

Equipment connected directly to the computer (through cables, communications lines, or wireless systems) during use is termed "online"; equipment used separately and not connected is "offline." In some cases the same device may be used online for some applications and offline for others.

Input of data for information processing comes from four hardware sources: direct online entry from a keyboard of a terminal, microcomputer, handheld device, or other input device; offline data preparation using terminals or microcomputers; reading of data from machine-readable documents or package coding; and data stored in files. "Entry" and "input" are often used interchangeably, although recording data at a keyboard is usually termed "entry," while reading of stored data is usually termed "input" (*see* INPUT DEVICES).

The CPU of a computer system contains the arithmetic logic unit, the control unit, registers, and primary storage or "memory." A clock establishes the timing for operations.

- The arithmetic logic unit contains circuitry that performs arithmetic operations (add, subtract, multiply, etc.) and logic operations.
- The control unit retrieves and interprets instructions, provides instructions to the other units, and sends timing signals.
- Registers are used to hold data during execution of arithmetic and logic operations. A computer will have a number of registers because of the need to hold several items at the same time.
- Primary storage is used for data and instructions to be processed. Access to primary or main storage is very fast compared to secondary storage access but still relatively slow compared to processing speeds. There are design methods to improve access; one of these is to use an additional, very fast access memory termed a *cache* memory to hold instructions and data that are actively being used.

The clock for the CPU provides signals that are used in synchronizing operations. A crystal delivers these signals at a predetermined rate. This rate, stated in terms of megahertz (MHz), is the clock speed for a computer.

Most computers use a sequential flow of instruction processing. Alternative processing architectures, found primarily in supercomputers, are pipelining or vector processing. In pipelining, operations are divided into a number of independent steps to be performed in parallel by different parts of the computer. In vector processing, the same operation is performed simultaneously on all the elements of a vector or pair of vectors.

Secondary storage is supplementary to the primary storage contained in the CPU. It has larger capacity and is less expensive but slower relative to primary storage. It is therefore used to hold data files plus programs not currently in use. Also, unlike most primary storage, it is not volatile; stored data are not affected by shutting off power (or a power outage). The most common secondary storage media are magnetic disk, magnetic diskettes, magnetic tape (reel and cassette), and memory stick (removable flash memory storage device). Storage technology is changing rapidly, with the storage capacity of each storage medium increasing and the cost per character stored decreasing.

Output employs devices such as the computer display screen, printer, or voice output unit (*see* OUTPUT DEVICES). One of the developments in hardware for output is multimedia output. A person using a computer may receive output from the display screen as text, graphics, or pictures. The picture can be still or moving. There can be sound in the form of music, tones, spoken words, and so forth (*see* MULTIMEDIA).

CLASSES OF COMPUTER SYSTEMS

There is a wide variety of computer systems in terms of size and power. Four classes are often identified: supercomputers, mainframe (large-scale) computers, minicomputers, and microcomputers. These labels are approximate because the increase in power and storage capacity means that the minicomputer today has the power of a mainframe a few years ago. Supercomputers are designed for applications requiring very high-speed computation and large primary storage. Large-scale or medium computers have very large secondary storage capacities, very powerful CPUs, and highly sophisticated operating systems. They can support multiple jobs executing concurrently and online processing from many remote locations at once. Minicomputers are smaller than the large mainframes and relatively less expensive. Each minicomputer may support online processing from multiple remote locations. In many organizations, multiple minicomputers with communications capabilities are used instead of a single large-scale computer. The term server is applied to a computer on a network that is dedicated in its function. A server may provide communications and INTERNET access for all the computers in an office. A server may handle all email functions.

Microcomputers are small and typically have a simple operating system, one keyboard input unit, one visual display unit, and one printer. Large-capacity microcomputers are often termed workstations.

Computers in an organization system are usually interconnected by networks. The processing work is distributed among the computers. The traditional architecture for interconnected computer systems was a hierarchy with the mainframe computer in control. An alternative architecture is for several computers, called clients, to make use of the facilities of a shared server (*see* CLIENT/ SERVER ARCHITECTURE). The clients are in control; the server makes available resources on demand such as programs and data.

OTHER COMPUTER HARDWARE DEVICES

Process control applications of information technology focus on managing the equipment in a production process. A computer, called a programmable logic controller, can be used to automatically control production equipment performing tasks, such as measuring and disbursing raw materials, executing the treatment steps, and feeding product (and labels) to packaging.

computer operating system

Jesper M. Johansson

The operating system (OS) provides the interface between the application programs and/or

the user and computer hardware. The operating system manages the resources provided by the computer hardware and allocates these services to application programs and users. There are several common features of an operating system: hardware input/output management; memory subsystem management; file system management; device management; user management; and user interfaces.

HARDWARE INPUT/OUTPUT MANAGEMENT

The hardware input/output feature of the operating system manages the execution and flow of data between the central processing unit (CPU) and the various subsystems such as temporary storage, permanent storage, input devices, and output devices. Most operating systems, particularly those running on commodity hardware, provide a driver model that allows the administrator to add or remove interface implementations (called drivers) that provide access to the particular hardware devices in the computer. The devices accessible through drivers may be physical, such as a printer, a video display card, or a network card; or they may be virtual, as in the case of a network socket. By abstracting a network socket, or even a higher-layer protocol, an application program may send and receive data from the socket simply by writing and reading to it as with an ordinary file.

Modern operating systems often have a *hardware abstraction layer* (HAL) that hides the implementation details of the actual hardware from the remainder of the operating system and user applications. This allows the same operating system to function on several different hardware implementations by replacing only the HAL. In addition, for security reasons, all access to the hardware must go through the operating system's hardware interface, including any drivers for particular hardware devices. Direct access to the hardware could allow circumvention of the security controls and is therefore not allowed. Only those portions of the OS that are part of the *trusted computing base* (TCB) have the right to access hardware. Any process that runs within the TCB can perform any requested action on the computer without being subject to security or abstraction restrictions.

With respect to processor utilization, the operating system may allow for seemingly simultaneous access to the computing resources. Such access is provided through *multitasking*, whereby several tasks can be executed at what to the user seems like the same time. This means that the operating system needs to somehow allocate the processing resources fairly to the different tasks. In order to insure that the system remains responsive, a multitasking OS needs a concept of task priority, such that user tasks cannot take precedence over critical operating system tasks, and to provide real-time response qualities to critical tasks.

MEMORY SUBSYSTEM MANAGEMENT

Tasks processed by the CPU need data. These data are held in the memory subsystem, consisting of several types of memory, such as random access memory (RAM), read-only memory (ROM), cache, and so on. The operating system is responsible for managing access to the memory in order to insure the integrity of the data stored there. The applications and the user thus do not need to specify where in memory something is to be stored. The OS assigns data to a storage location and maintains a record of it. Without this feature, a process might overwrite vital data used by another process. In addition, modern operating systems typically include a virtual memory manager, which abstracts physical memory for the applications using it. In this case, each application would typically be presented with a fixed, very large, memory address space (commonly 2 or 4 gigabytes in a 32-bit operating system) regardless of the physical memory in the system. This insures that applications can be hardware agnostic and function properly regardless of the amount of physical memory.

FILE SYSTEM MANAGEMENT

Data in the memory subsystem may need to be stored in secondary storage. This can be a hard disk, a floppy disk, a tape, or several other types of device. Regardless of the storage device, the OS manages the transfer and keeps track of storage so that data can later be retrieved.

DEVICE MANAGEMENT

Communication with users is accomplished through monitors, keyboards, mice, printers, hard drives, and so on. The management of these subsystems is also left to the operating system. In some operating systems this area coincides to a great extent with the file system management. The reason is that devices can be conceptually viewed as files; for example, to print something, the system copies it to the file associated with the printer. In other operating systems, each type of device is accessed through particular protocols unique to that type of device. Whatever the paradigm, devices need to be handled so that they can communicate with the rest of the computer, and this is also done by the operating system.

USER INTERFACE

Most operating systems today have some form of user interface. It may be very limited, as in the case of an embedded OS used to operate a gas pump, or it may be very complex, as in the case of a general purpose OS used for an ordinary user desktop computer. The user interface enables users to interact with the computing devices abstracted by the OS. Often, this is done through some sort of shell. The shell may provide a GRAPHICAL USER INTERFACE or a text-based one. The shell may be separate from the OS itself, or may be an integral part of the OS.

In some cases, many of the user-oriented features of operating systems are handed over to utilities running on top of the OS as any other application. For example, user management can be handled by a utility, and another shell can be substituted for the one that comes with the operating system. In some cases the operating system has become "kernelized," meaning that it only provides the most basic services and relies on other utilities to provide the higher-level services.

SECURITY FUNCTIONS OF AN OPERATING SYSTEM

It is often desirable to restrict the types of actions particular users, or applications acting on their behalf, can take on a computer. Not all operating systems are capable of doing so, but most modern operating systems provide at least some security functionality. For example, an operating system may provide all or some of these features:

- *Security principal*: the representation in the system of a user, computer, or application that acts on behalf of users or computers for security purposes within the system.
- *Identification*: the process of keeping the identities of security principals distinct from others on the system.
- *Authentication*: the binding of an entity, such as a physical user, computer, or an application acting on that user's behalf, to the security principal recognized by the operating system (*see* AUTHENTICATION).
- *Authorization*: the process of determining whether a security principal has the right to perform some requested action.
- *Auditing*: a feature that provides the ability to track actions performed by a particular security principal in such a way that a system administrator later can determine what the security principal did.

Not all operating systems support all these concepts. Nevertheless, they are fundamental to the design and operation of a secure operating system.

computer program

Gordon B. Davis

A computer program is a set of instructions that performs processing for a task. Examples of programs used in business processing are programs to update the payroll file, do depreciation analysis, apply customer payments to accounts receivable, and so forth. The instructions in a program perform input, output, and processing functions. A program written for an application does not contain all functions needed. Many standard functions are provided by the operating system of the computer (*see* COMPUTER OPERATING SYSTEM). For example, a program may specify data to be printed and the format; the management of the printing operation is handled by the computer operating system.

A computer program is typically subdivided into routines and modules. A program routine is a set of instructions within a program. It is a way of subdividing the program into parts for purposes of development and maintenance. A program module is a building block for a program or program routine. A subroutine is a reusable routine that is written to be used (called) by a program. A program object is a reusable routine that encapsulates both data and methods.

The instructions in a program are organized into program control structures to control execution within a module. The three basic control structures are sequence, alternation, and repetition. Sequence control means that instructions are executed in sequence, one after another. Alternation and repetition incorporate decisions. The program evaluates a condition described in a program statement as being true or false. Program execution follows different paths depending on the result. In alternation, a program selects from alternative program paths. The statement takes the general form of *if* (condition) *then* perform one set of instructions *else* perform another set of instructions. The repetition or looping control structure specifies repetition of a sequence of instructions. During each repetition, there may be changes in the data or execution. At each repetition, a condition is evaluated; when the condition is satisfied, the repetition ceases and the program continues with other instructions.

Two central concepts in program design are reusability and modular design. Reusability refers to the design of modules and program objects, so that they can be used over again in any program requiring the processing performed by the modules. Reusable code modules support standardization. Since they are carefully checked for errors, they reduce potential program errors. They are stored in a code module or program object library accessible by programmers.

Modular design (often called structured design) is based on decomposition of programs into modular structures. The concept is that a program should be divided into different functions and subfunctions. By subdividing in this way, modules can be designed to be relatively independent. Independence of a module means that there should be no instruction in some other module that affects it in unknown ways. In structured design, the modules are organized as a hierarchy. A high-level function is subdivided into several subfunctions, and so forth.

A program to be run by a computer is in the executable machine language of the computer.

This is termed an "object program." Programs are written in a computer programming language or using a program development system. The program in this language or notation is termed the "source program." The conversion from a source program to an object program is performed by a translation program termed an "assembler" or "compiler."

Computer programs of any size are complex artificial systems. Since there are many possible paths through a program, it is difficult and sometimes impossible to test a program for all possible conditions. To achieve correctness and other quality attributes, computer programs are developed by a process often referred to as SOFTWARE ENGINEERING. The process emphasizes a disciplined approach to requirement, decomposition into modules, coding and testing of modules, testing of the complete program, and documentation. The process of program repair and enhancement is termed maintenance (*see* SOFTWARE MAINTENANCE).

Traditional program design has emphasized a modular structure with reuse through subroutines. Data and processing using the data were separated, so that changes to processing statements or data would not require changing the programming statements or data definitions. An emerging program design paradigm is an OBJECT-ORIENTED PROGRAM in which reusable program objects are designed with processing methods and data encapsulated within the objects. An objective is to increase the reuse of program routines by providing tested program objects for common operations.

Macros are program routines that can be run (played) by other programs. They are often written in connection with microcomputer software to automate sequences of operations or add functionality to a spreadsheet or report program. Macro recorders are provided by application packages to assist users in developing macros. Macros can be developed by using a macro recorder. The user turns on the macro recorder, executes the instructions to be automated, and stores the result. This is programming by doing. It is effective for routines involving only sequences. To add alternation or repetition structures to a macro requires programming in the macro language. Macro programs can be employed to create applications that rely on the facilities of the package. A macro program written to be used with a spreadsheet processor will be a spreadsheet-based application. There are libraries of macros provided by software package vendors and independent suppliers.

computer-supported cooperative work

Gerardine DeSanctis and Douglas R. Vogel

Advances in technologies, such as networks, telecommunication, file-sharing systems, and MULTIMEDIA devices, have led to the development of computer-supported cooperative work or collaborative computing systems. Computer-supported cooperative work (CSCW) is the use of computer-based technology to facilitate work tasks involving multiple parties. CSCW refers to software applications and their use, and not to the more rudimentary technologies (such as networks, databases, videoconferencing, etc.) that make CSCW possible. In this sense, CSCW is not a type of technology but a technology application that diffuses and permeates an ever-widening variety of tasks and activities. CSCW designers take component technologies, integrate them, and develop functionality that will service the needs of a work group. Common examples of CSCW include electronic messaging, joint authoring, discussion databases, workflow management, and electronic meetings.

CSCW can be described in terms of collaboration concepts, computer systems design, application types, and impact on work groups.

COLLABORATION CONCEPTS

Because most, if not all, work involves some degree of interface between two or more parties, many organizational tasks can be conceived in terms of a cooperative work process. The unique focus of CSCW is on the interface between co-working parties, that is, on their collaboration. Those aspects of work which are done independently are of less concern in CSCW, except in so far as the inputs or outputs of one work process affect those of another work process. Tasks that are done entirely in a joint manner are of particular concern to CSCW designers. Business meetings and classroom learning represent extreme examples of CSCW, because all parties are present and actively working together in those contexts. Other collaborative work settings include systems development, business planning, project design, report development, forms passing, and joint decision-making. CSCW is concerned with the design of systems to support these kinds of collaborative work activities that increasingly occur in distributed contexts.

The parties involved in a cooperative work process are not restricted to people. They can be documents, machines, or transactions. Shared work among computer processors, for example, can fall within the domain of CSCW, as can the flow of paperwork through an office environment. Central to cooperative work processes is the concept of *coordination*. Coordination is the synchronous aspect of a cooperative work process, the juncture of dependency between two otherwise independent work tasks. Once the coordination required for a cooperative work task has been fully specified, a system can be designed to support coordination. Typically, a cooperative work task has many coordination processes within it, some of which are performed by people and some of which are computerized. CSCW is concerned with augmenting the computer-based coordination within cooperative work tasks.

COMPUTER SYSTEMS DESIGN

Whereas the development of user-friendly software for individual work has been driven by the principle of WYSIWYG, or "what you see is what you get," the development of collaborative systems has been driven by the principle of WYSIWIS, or "what you see is what I see." This can even embrace virtual reality with users sharing an artificially created environment with avatars. Collaborative design involves the creation of *shared workspaces* in which multiple parties access common computer files. Computer BULLETIN BOARDS exemplify this principle, as many people can post articles and share the bulletin board space. Similarly, collaborative word-processing applications allow multiple authors to develop a common document.

Major issues in CSCW design include data management, media selection, and multi-user interfaces. Data management involves specification of private versus shared information, determining which information will be exchanged and in what format, and specifying information se-curity and ownership procedures, such as which party involved in the collaboration is able to change common information and under what conditions. Issues of file updating and concurrency control are critical in CSCW design, since more than one party may have the capability to update a common data file at the same time. Maintaining accurate, current, and non-redundant data can be a complicated process in a CSCW system that is simultaneously utilized by many parties. Designers are increasingly interested in creating *group memories*, or a shared KNOWLEDGE BASE, whereby uses of CSCW applications result in historical repositories that can serve as resources for future coordination needs. Advances in group memory management may lead to further automation of coordination activities and the embedding of intelligence into CSCW applications.

Media for CSCW include text, sound, graphics, and/or video. Since so much of cooperative work involves interpersonal conversation, many CSCW designs include either a voice component or the ability to exchange text-based messages in real time (instantaneously). CSCW systems are increasingly multimedia, as in computer conferencing and electronic meeting systems. The CSCW designer must understand human communication processes and the relative impact of various communication media on the ability of people to work together effectively.

CSCW systems require multi-user interfaces, i.e., simultaneous access to system components by more than one party. The CSCW interface must accommodate different people, different input and display preferences, and different learning styles. As an example, consider a large electronic whiteboard used in a conference room setting. Some meeting participants may wish to draw freehand on the board, while others prefer to display documents typed within a word processor. More than one participant may want to use the board during the meeting; and everyone may want to leave the meeting with copies of material placed on the board so that they can work on it privately at a later time. The CSCW designer must assure flexibility for multiple forms of input, manipulation, and output of system data. Further, any one user may require the ability to track information as it stops or flows between various parties involved in the cooperative activity. The use of *threading* in electronic bulletin boards illustrates this latter capability; bulletin board postings are arranged to indicate the content, timing, and party involved in the posting:

```
The corporate plan is being
developed
(M. Jones), 6/9/04
Suggested item for the corpor-
ate plan
(K. Finch), 6/9/04
Comment on Finch's suggestion
(M. Blar), 6/10/04
Comment on Finch's suggestion
(E. Wharch), 6/12/04
Comment on Wharch's comment
(M. Jones), 6/16/04
Another suggested item for the
corporate plan
(G. Parch), 6/23/04
```

APPLICATION TYPES

CSCW applications are often referred to as *groupware*. The term "groupware" usually refers to a software system, whereas the broader CSCW term refers to the application of that software in a collaborative work task. Nevertheless, groupware and CSCW are sometimes used interchangeably.

CSCW applications can be distinguished along a number of dimensions, the most important being the *time* and *place* of the coordination involved. Four general types of CSCW settings are possible (see figure 1):

1 *Same time, same place.* All parties are co-located when the coordination takes place, such as in a group meeting.
2 *Same time, different place.* Parties coordinate at the same time but work in different physical locations, such as in a teleconference.
3 *Different time, same place.* Parties move through the same location but at different points in time, such as in shared office spaces or meeting rooms.
4 *Different time, different place.* Coordination is entirely asynchronous and physically dispersed, as in electronic bulletin board discussions. Coordination becomes more difficult, and the opportunities for computer support

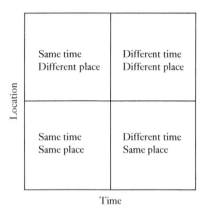

Figure 1 Computer-supported cooperative work

therefore greater, as coordination moves beyond the same time, same place setting to more dispersed, asynchronous work settings.

Some CSCW applications are commercially available as "off-the-shelf" software, whereas others are custom built to suit specialized coordination needs. Most commercial software vendors today offer some types of CSCW applications. In addition to the coordination settings that they support, CSCW applications can also be differentiated in terms of their various features, the numbers of parties they accommodate, and the type of work or task they support. Some of the more widely available CSCW applications today are as follows:

- electronic mail
- calendaring
- computer conferencing
- conversation management
- electronic bulletin boards
- electronic discussion groups
- electronic meeting systems
- group decision support
- project management systems
- group writing and editing
- document sharing
- joint authoring/editing
- workflow management
- knowledge management

Electronic meeting systems (EMS) are a special type of CSCW system designed specifically for group meetings. To the extent that an EMS contains facilities to support decision-making, it is a GROUP DECISION SUPPORT SYSTEM (GDSS). An EMS provides such facilities as electronic agendas, electronic whiteboards, shared notepads, and group writing programs. A GDSS may include these facilities as well but also includes group decision models, such as risk analysis, forecasting, and choice algorithms.

IMPACT ON WORK GROUPS

CSCW systems aim to smooth the linkages among the activities in a coordination task, resulting in tighter integration among otherwise independent or loosely coupled tasks. CSCW systems also aim to enhance the overall quality of the coordination endeavor.

Efficiency gains can be realized as CSCW systems automate systems that previously were done through manual means. For example, phone calls or typed memos can be replaced with electronic mail. Documents can be exchanged electronically instead of through traditional mail systems, and manual whiteboards in meeting rooms can be replaced with computerized boards. Automation can reduce costs, decrease the time required to complete a work task, and/or make the coordination process easier and less stressful for those involved.

CSCW systems also can create new possibilities for coordination, linking work processes that otherwise were not connected. For example, a CSCW system may allow participants in a project, who would otherwise work independently, to access each other's materials, even if project participants are not in the same location. Similarly, CSCW systems can enable strangers to discuss common problems and solutions via bulletin boards; popular Usenets on the INTERNET illustrate this CSCW application. CSCW systems that pool the knowledge of multiple parties to solve complex problems bring a level of sophistication to the work setting that inevitably will have a significant impact on the business or organizational setting in which that work is conducted.

CSCW systems are having a major impact on business process reengineering, on the support of mobile, dispersed workers, and on the creation of the "virtual organization." Business process reengineering requires that work be redesigned to yield a "leaner" organization, with a minimal number of business processes and rapid workflow. CSCW contributes to reengineering

as it supports specific, multiparty coordination tasks. Electronic communication systems, workflow systems, and project management software have been particularly helpful in reengineering efforts. Similarly, CSCW is facilitating the trend toward a more mobile, dispersed workforce. Work-at-home, virtual teams, the ability to communicate with coworkers while traveling, and the use of contract workers who electronically link to work facilities, are all made possible due to CSCW developments such as electronic mail, scheduling software, computer conferencing, and electronic meeting systems. Virtual communities beyond the workplace enable interaction on topics of mutual interest. Broad-based use of mobile devices such as wireless PDAs (personal digital assistants) and "smart-phones" blur the boundaries of time and space and activity focus as CSCW enters into the realm of ubiquitous computing.

The effectiveness of a CSCW system depends on the design of the technology, the task(s) for which it is used, and how it is used. Users may compare one CSCW system to another to see which is the most effective for a given work task. But equally significant in determining CSCW effectiveness is the way in which the CSCW system is managed. For example, researchers have found that the same electronic conferencing system brought many benefits to one group or organization but brought no advantages at all in other groups or settings. Solid understanding of how work is to change with a new system, adequate training of all parties involved, and a commitment to an efficient, participative management style are among the factors thought to be critical to successful CSCW adoption.

At the extreme, a geographically dispersed workforce makes possible an organization without physical facilities, i.e., a virtual organization. Collaboration occurs across time and space, with workers located in homes or office sites of their choice. Work occurs in shared computerized spaces connected via electronic networks; and there is little formal management structure, as workers operate with a high amount of professional independence. Research societies, consulting agencies, and brokerage firms illustrate the kinds of work suited to virtual forms of organizing. Many forecasters anticipate proliferation of virtual organizations in the future, with CSCW systems facilitating this trend.

The development of CSCW systems blends perspectives from the disciplines of economics, computer science, communication, social psychology, and management. Since CSCW is a comparatively new area of management information systems, techniques for systems design and methods for assessing CSCW impacts are still in their early stages.

Bibliography

Davis, G. (2002). Anytime/anyplace computing and the future of knowledge work. *Communications of the ACM*, **45** (12), 67–73.

Galegher, J., Kraut, R. E., and Egido, C. (eds.) (1990). *Intellectual Teamwork: The Social and Technological Bases of Cooperative Work*. Hillsdale, NJ: Lawrence Erlbaum.

Greenberg, S. (ed.) (1991). *Computer-Supported Cooperative Work and Groupware*. New York: Academic Press.

Olson, G. M., Malone, T., and Smith, J. (eds.) (2001). *Coordination Theory and Collaboration Technology*. Mahwah, NJ: Lawrence Erlbaum.

critical success factors

Critical success factors (CSF) is a method of eliciting information system requirements by asking informants to define factors critical to the success of their activity or system. Requirements are derived from these factors (*see* REQUIREMENTS DETERMINATION FOR INFORMATION SYSTEMS).

cross-cultural issues in MIS

Roberto Evaristo

In multinational and transnational organizations, there is a growing need to utilize information technology (IT) to achieve efficiencies, coordination, and communication. Clearly, however, cultural differences between countries may have an impact on the effectiveness and efficiency of IT deployment. Most of these differences are based on values and practices that people have. Despite their importance, their effect on information systems (IS) has until recently received limited attention from IS researchers (Straub, 1994; Evaristo and McCubbrey, 1995). In fact, the overall number of cross-cultural articles is still fairly low considering the number of practical and theoretical critical questions that remain unanswered. This incongruence can be partly explained by methodological and resource difficulties inherent in cross-cultural research (Karahanna, Evaristo, and Srite, 2002) as well as the long time horizon required to complete/conduct these types of studies.

Early research on cross-cultural influences in information systems use focused on group decision systems and decision-making. Current topics of interest include cross-cultural influences on trust as well as effects of culture on media choice. Decision-making continues to be a research topic.

A crucial change in the field was the introduction of journals with a charter on global information management; this made it easier to create a forum for cross-cultural research (Evaristo, 2003). Moreover, mainstream journals are publishing more cross-cultural work (e.g., Davison and Martinsons, 2003). As part of the field maturation, researcher attention is also moving from examination of specific issues in the context of multiple cultures to a more introspective consideration of what a cross-cultural theoretically based approach should be (Straub et al., 2002) or how different levels of culture (from individual to national) tend to affect specific IT behaviors (Karahanna, Evaristo, and Srite, 2004). A direct consequence of such is an expansion and redefinition of the meaning of culture. The key distinctions in cultural definitions and levels are presented in table 1.

Bibliography

Davison, R. and Martinsons, M. (2003). Guest editorial. Cultural issues and IT management: Past and present. *IEEE Transactions on Engineering Management*, **50**(1), 3–7.

Evaristo, J. R. (2003). Editorial preface: Cross-cultural research in IS. *Journal of Global Information Management*, **11** (4), i–ii.

Evaristo, J. R. and McCubbrey, D. (1995). Editorial: Special issue on cross-cultural management in information systems. *Information Technology and People*, **8** (2), 3–5.

Gouldner, A. W. (1957). Cosmopolitans and locals: Toward an analysis of latent social roles. *Administrative Science Quarterly*, **2**, 281–306.

Hofstede, G. (1984). *Culture's Consequences*. Newbury Park, CA: Sage.

Karahanna, E., Evaristo, J. R., and Srite, M. (2002). Methodological issues in MIS cross-cultural research. *Journal of Global Information Management*, **10** (1), 48–55.

Table 1   Levels of culture

Level	Definition
Supranational	Any cultural differences that cross national boundaries or can be seen to exist in more than one nation. Can consist of:
• Regional	• Regional: pertaining to a group of people living in the same geographic area
• Ethnic	• Ethnic: pertaining to a group of people sharing common and distinctive characteristics
• Religious • Linguistic	• Linguistic: pertaining to a group of people speaking the same tongue
National	Collective properties that are ascribed to citizens of countries (Hofstede, 1984; Trompenaars, 1993)
Professional	Focus on the distinction between loyalty to the employing organization and loyalty to the industry (Gouldner, 1957)
Organizational	The social and normative glue that holds organizations together (Siehl and Martin, 1990)
Group	Cultural differences that are contained within a single group, work group, or other collection of individuals at a level below that of the organization

Source: Karahanna et al., 2004

Karahanna, E., Evaristo, J. R., and Srite, M. (2004). Levels of culture and individual behavior: An integrative perspective. *Journal of Global Information Management*.

Siehl, C. and Martin, J. (1990). *Organizational Culture: A Key to a Financial Performance?* San Francisco: Jossey-Bass.

Straub, D. W. (1994). The effect of culture on IT diffusion: Email and fax in Japan and the US. *Information Systems Research*, **5** (1), 23–47.

Straub, D. W., Loch, K., Evaristo, J. R., Karahanna, E., and Srite, M. (2002). Toward a theory-based measurement of culture. *Journal of Global Information Management*, **10** (1), 13–23.

Trompenaars, F. (1993). *Riding the Waves of Culture*. London: The Economist Books.

cryptography (crypto)

William J. Caelli

The term cryptography simply refers to the art and science of "secret writing" whereby so-called plaintext, normal readable text, is transformed into ciphertext by the process of encryption, a scrambled form of the text that is unintelligible to anyone who does not possess the key to enable the ciphertext to be unscrambled or decrypted and converted back to the associated plaintext. It has an associated term, cryptanalysis, which refers to the action of attempting to recover plaintext from ciphertext without the aid of the secret key needed to perform the task in a ready fashion. Together, the terms cryptography and cryptanalysis are referred to as cryptology. These techniques have been known since antiquity and have been practiced by most civilizations in some form at some time.

The techniques used to perform the scrambling/unscrambling operation make use of a mathematical formula or procedure known as a cipher or cipher algorithm. Today, cryptography is a basic tool in most forms of information systems security including protection of databases, safeguarding of information flowing in telecommunications networks, provision of access control services for the protection of computer systems, and so on.

The US's CNSS Instruction 4009 glossary refers to cryptography as the "art or science concerning the principles, means, and methods for rendering plain information unintelligible and for restoring encrypted information to intelligible form."

Until the 1970s the form that cryptographic systems took was straightforward and known as "single-key" technology. In this scheme, a scrambling/unscrambling process is produced and controlled with one key. This key, in the form usually of some sequence of numbers and/or letters, needs to be known by both the scrambling and unscrambling processes, having been entered into a cryptographic device of some sort by a human user.

In the 1970s the US adopted a standard for a crypto algorithm that became known as the data encryption standard, or DES. This algorithm became widely accepted both in non-military government for unclassified usage and by the banking and finance industry, who incorporated it into systems for the then developing electronic funds transfer (EFT) schemes for enabling payments between banks, between banks and their customers, and even between merchants and banks and the merchants' customers. The DES enabled blocks of 64 bits of data to be encrypted/decrypted at a time through the use of a 56-bit-length key value. The standard was finally seen as being obsolete and was withdrawn in its usual form in 2004, to be replaced by other algorithms including a "triple" version of itself, i.e., encryption/decryption is performed on the 64-bit data using a sequence of three 56-bit keys.

Also in the 1970s a new cryptographic scheme was publicly proposed and finally adopted, i.e., so-called public key cryptography. The idea was simple but has proven to be mathematically complex to implement, with current implementations employing concepts from finite mathematics, including the problem of producing the factors of a number itself the product of two prime numbers. This technique is incorporated into the popular Rivest-Shamir-Adleman (RSA) algorithm. The idea was that separate keys be used to encrypt data and decrypt data and that it would be impractical to determine one key from the other. In this scheme, a user of an information system, for example, would create two keys.

One of these, the so-called public key, could be freely given to anyone who wished to send that person a secret message. The sender would use the associated encryption algorithm on the message text to be sent, usually a block of data in the form of binary bits, with the public key of the person to whom they wanted to send the message. This action would form the usual ciphertext for transmission.

Now, at the receiving end, the user would employ the other key, the so-called secret key known only to the user, to decrypt the message. Of course, it has to be noted here that there is no attempt at AUTHENTICATION of the message source or anything of that nature in this scheme. In principle, a user's public key could be widely published, e.g., it could be placed beside a telephone number in a conventional phone book, etc. Indeed, that idea, one of a public file, formed part of the first set of published ideas in this area. The problem was simple. The person wanting to send a message wants to be sure that she has the correct public key for the person to whom she wishes to send a confidential message and not that of an impostor. Later schemes developed to achieve this with some degree of trustworthiness and have become known as public key infrastructure (PKI) schemes, but they have had a mixed acceptance at the wider national and large-scale level.

However, public key cryptographic technology had another benefit that immediately became obvious. If it were possible for the user to invert the scheme and use his or her secret key to encrypt a message and send it out to anyone at all, then anyone who had possession of that user's open, public key could likewise decrypt the message and confirm that the message could only have been generated and come from the original user. Thus the concept of a digital signature (see DIGITAL SIGNATURES) was formed.

It should be noted here that the use of the term signature is unfortunate since, in legal terms, the word has a different connotation. A legal signature affixed to a document signifies the signer's acceptance of and agreement to the contents of the document by the act of attachment of his or her "mark" to the document in an indelible fashion. Moreover, in many cases, a witness or notary may be present or even required; a situation usually impractical in an electronic commerce (*see* E-COMMERCE) or system environment. In the case of a digital signature scheme, the user affixing that digital signature must be totally confident that "what you see is what you sign (WYSIWYS)." This implies, in turn, that the display on a computer screen, for instance, must be highly trusted and be an unaltered display of what is stored in the memory of the computer and used in the digital signature process. Current personal computer systems, for example, can give no such assurance as there is no "trusted path" between the memory and the display screen.

Of course, there would have to be something in the original message to indicate where it had come from, otherwise the receiver would not know which public key to use, i.e., an equivalent to the "from" address on the back of a normal written envelope. This address could then be confirmed by, say, its repetition in the body of the encrypted message received, similar to the sender's name and address on the envelope being repeated at the top of a letter contained inside the envelope.

Today, a digital signature is formed using public key cryptography by first forming a "hash" or compressed version of the data to be signed. This hash is then encrypted with the user's secret or, as it is sometimes called, "signing" key. This encrypted hash data block is now attached to the original message, which itself could be transmitted in plaintext if confidentiality is not required. The receiver can now perform the same hash operation on the received message to create a new summary block, then decrypt the encrypted hash block attached to the message received from the sender using that sender's public key to give another possible hash block, and then compare the two values. If they are equal, then the message must have come from the recognized sender and, incidentally, must not have been altered on the way since that would have caused the hash blocks to be different. Thus, a digital signature can serve two purposes:

- verification of the sender or at least the fact that the sender's secret key was used; and
- verification that the message has not been altered in transit.

Of course, all this absolutely depends upon the trusted nature of the computer systems used

since complex mathematical algorithms are employed and cryptographic key handling during these operations must be highly trustworthy. For this reason, it is becoming common for such operations to be performed by special add-in hardware subsystems in commodity computer systems or by specialized peripheral units attached to the computer.

As for biometrics, users will depend upon these cryptographic schemes to provide assurance of the security and integrity of information systems. Indeed, information from these operations will become important components of any evidence in legal proceedings, e.g., in the case of computer-based fraud. For this reason alone, the cryptographic mechanisms used must be beyond question in court proceedings. Software implementations of these processes in general purpose, commodity computer systems cannot be deemed to provide such trusted assurance.

Associated terms useful in searching for more information are:

- single-key cryptography
- public-key/dual-key cryptography
- public key infrastructure (PKI)
- Rivest-Shamir-Adleman (RSA) algorithm
- elliptic curve cryptography
- cryptographic protocols
- key storage and management
- key escrow
- digital signature
- data encryption standard (DES)
- advanced encryption standard (AES)
- DIGITAL RIGHTS MANAGEMENT

Additional INTERNET sources are www.rsa.com (RSA Inc., US) and www.certicom.com (Certicom Inc., Canada).

customer relationship management

Gediminas Adomavicius

From an information systems (IS) perspective, customer relationship management (CRM) typically refers to computer software systems designed to provide an enterprise with a comprehensive understanding about its customers, facilitate and improve customer service and support, and, more generally, support a wide range of customer-facing business processes. It is an important component of any modern business strategy, facilitating the organization to serve its customers more effectively. When adopting CRM technologies, the system integration issue plays an important role; CRM components have to be able to communicate with existing enterprise systems, such as enterprise resource planning (ERP) (*see* ENTERPRISE SYSTEMS (ENTERPRISE RESOURCE PLANNING OR ERP)) and supply chain management applications.

While CRM may be defined somewhat differently by different software vendors and companies using it, there is general agreement that the key functional areas where CRM capabilities are most important include the following:

- *Enterprise marketing automation*, where CRM technologies can significantly contribute to the activities of customer segmentation and analysis (e.g., new customer identification and acquisition, customer retention), telemarketing, and marketing campaign management.
- *Salesforce automation*, where the role of CRM tools is to help organize the sales process, including tracking current and potential customers (i.e., contact management), sales analysis and forecasting, sales content management (pricing, advertising, etc.), order management and tracking, and incentive management (e.g., sales commissions).
- *Partner relationship management*, where CRM can help enterprises to locate, recruit, train, and organize partners (e.g., wholesalers, distributors, dealers) for a variety of purposes, e.g., for coordinating the allocation of sales leads (matching sales leads to the most appropriate partners) or including partners in promotional programs or marketing campaigns.
- *Customer service management*, including the management of contact centers, field services, and self-service applications, where the goal of CRM technologies is to help enterprises manage the interactions with customers via phone, web, email, chat, or on customer's site. Most common customer service applications include inquiry handling (managing calls and interactions), technical support (including the knowledge base of

products and services), and the management of the customer service workforce.

Business analytics is a crucial component of CRM technologies that often overlaps with other functional areas of CRM mentioned above. Given a specific task (e.g., "provide a 360-degree view of a specific customer"), business analytics employs a variety of techniques to extract relevant and actionable knowledge from various internal and external data sources (e.g., files, databases, data warehouses, data marts; *see* DATA WAREHOUSING). The analytical techniques used by CRM technologies range from fairly simple reporting and online analytical processing (OLAP) tools to more sophisticated statistical analysis, DATA MINING, and personalization techniques (*see* PERSONALIZATION TECHNOLOGIES). Examples of typical tasks for business analytics in CRM applications include:

- sales analytics (e.g., monitoring key sales metrics, optimizing the sales process, interpreting sales trends);
- marketing campaign analytics (e.g., leads analysis, campaign effectiveness measurement, customer segmentation, customer profiling, cross-sell analysis);
- customer service analytics (e.g., optimizing the performance of call centers and field services);
- web and E-COMMERCE analytics (e.g., analysis of web content and advertising popularity, abandoned shopping cart analysis, optimization of business rules).

There are several CRM software vendors that provide extensive CRM enterprise suites. One of the latest trends in CRM is the development of vertical CRM solutions for specific industries, such as telecommunications, insurance, financial services, retail, pharmaceuticals, healthcare, manufacturing, automotive, and energy.

Bibliography

Greenberg, P. (2002). *CRM at the Speed of Light*, 2nd edn. New York: McGraw-Hill.

Technology Forecast: 2003–2005 (2003). London: PricewaterhouseCoopers.

D

data administration

Gordon C. Everest

Data management refers to the function of managing the data resources of an enterprise. This includes collecting, storing, and maintaining (updating) data, making it available for use, and protecting the integrity of data resources. Data management involves both a human component and a machine component. Human responsibility and accountability rest in the position of a data(base) administrator (DBA). Data management is enabled through the use of a DATABASE MANAGEMENT SYSTEM (DBMS) and related tools.

Data administration is the human and organizational locus of responsibility for data(base) management. It is responsible for creating and maintaining the information asset resources of an organization, particularly as embodied in computerized databases. Data administration includes the functions of:

- the design and formal definition of databases;
- evaluating, selecting, and installing database management tools;
- training and helping people use database management tools to access the databases;
- assisting in application systems development to insure that data requirements are satisfied;
- monitoring the operation of database systems to insure adequate levels of performance;
- protecting the existence, quality, integrity, security, and privacy of data.

Database administrators work with users, system developers, and managers. A data administration staff requires a complement of technical and administrative skills to carry out these functions. It may have a variety of computerized support tools to assist in its tasks.

data dictionary

Roger H. L. Chiang

The data dictionary is a reference of data about data, also called metadata. It defines each data element contained in an information system, specifies both its logical and physical characteristics, and provides information concerning how it is used. Historically, the data dictionary was created to provide information about data existing in the database systems. The database structures provide sufficient information for implementation by the DATABASE MANAGEMENT SYSTEM (DBMS). However, the database structures usually have insufficient information for those who use, manage, and maintain the databases.

The concept of a data dictionary has been extended to system development. When system analysts develop data flow diagrams during the analysis and design of an information system, they usually create a data dictionary. It is an information repository that defines the contents of data flows and data stores of data flow diagrams.

Many database management systems and CASE: COMPUTER-AIDED SOFTWARE/SYSTEM ENGINEERING tools have the data dictionary utility. This utility stores not only information about database structures and data flow diagrams, but also other information such as design decisions, usage standard, and user information. It facilitates the use as well as the maintenance of an information system. The terms system catalog and data repository are often used as synonyms.

data mart

see DATA WAREHOUSING

data mining

Gordon B. Davis

Data mining is an extension of information finding activities using one or more key words or phrases. In information finding, the search tools are designed to locate instances of the key words or phrases. Data mining extends the simple search to processes for discovery of complex relationships and facts that are not obvious. Data mining performs searches for these relationships and facts within data contained in one or more databases. The databases can be internal to the organization or external. An organization may prepare data warehouses that contain databases from internal and external data sources for data mining purposes (*see* DATA WARE-HOUSING).

Data mining implies the possibility of employing a variety of techniques to discover relationships and patterns in databases that are not obvious or not available from simple search using key words or phrases, for example, statistical analysis such as correlation, modeling to analyze relationships, pattern discovery, neural network analysis, personalization, and so forth. The objective is usually to discover rules and relationships that will allow prediction of future behavior, formulation of organization procedures, or development of marketing plans. For example, a fraud analysis may discover relationships that allow a predictive model to be developed to estimate the likelihood of fraud in a customer application for credit or services. Other examples are analysis of purchase relationships, evaluation of marketing efforts, segmentation of markets, and credit risk evaluation. Data mining is sometimes used in connection with discovery of knowledge that is employed in the organization but is not explicitly recognized in systems and procedures.

See also *customer relationship management; neural networks; personalization technologies*

data modeling, logical

Salvatore T. March

Logical data modeling is a process by which the data requirements of an organization or an application area are represented. A data modeling formalism defines a set of constructs and rules used in the representation. A logical data model represents (1) the things or events that are of interest (e.g., customers, employees, inventory items, orders); (2) their characteristics (e.g., customers are identified by customer number and are described by customer name, credit limit, etc.); and (3) their interrelationships (e.g., each order must be associated with a single customer). It can be validated by end users to insure accuracy of the data requirements.

Numerous data modeling formalisms have been proposed, such as the entity relationship model and the object relationship model. Such formalisms are termed *semantic* data models to differentiate them from *traditional* data models (hierarchic, network, and relational) used by commercial database management systems (DBMS) (*see* DATABASE MANAGEMENT SYSTEM) to represent a database schema. Object-oriented data models extend the semantic data modeling by explicitly representing processes (behavior) as well as data structure.

Four basic constructs are common among data models: entity, attribute, relationship, and identifier.

An *entity* is a category or grouping of objects (people, things, events) or roles (e.g., employee, customer), each sharing a common set of attributes and relationships. The objects are termed *entity-instances* (e.g., the employee with employee number 12314, the customer with customer number 5958). Some formalisms refer to the category as an *entity-type* and the instances as *entities*.

An *attribute* is a characteristic of an entity-instance. Attributes may be single- or multivalued, mandatory or optional. Each employee, for example, may be required to have exactly one value for the attribute social security number (single-valued and mandatory), and may be allowed to have zero or more values for the attribute dependent-first-name (multivalued and optional). A number of data modeling formalisms do not support multivalued attributes.

A *relationship* is an association among entities. Any number of entities may participate in a relationship and a relationship can associate zero or more instances of one entity with zero or more instances of other participating entities. The number of entities participating in a relationship is termed the *degree* of the relationship. A relationship between two entities is termed a *binary* relationship. A relationship among *n* entities is termed an *n-ary* relationship. Each entity in a relationship has a minimum and maximum *cardinality*, i.e., the minimum and maximum number of relationship instances in which one entity-instance must/may participate. Some data modeling formalisms only support binary relationships, while others support *n*-ary relationships. Some allow relationships to have attributes while others do not.

If the minimum cardinality of an entity in a relationship is one or greater, then that entity is said to be *dependent* upon the other entity or entities in the relationship. This type of dependency is termed a *referential integrity constraint*.

Data modeling formalisms vary in their definitions of attributes and relationships. A number of commonly used formalisms:

- limit attributes to a single value, i.e., disallow multivalue attributes;
- allow only binary relationships, i.e., disallow *n*-ary relationships;
- allow only one-to-one and one-to-many relationships, i.e., disallow many-to-many relationships; and
- allow only entities to have attributes, i.e., disallow attributes of relationships.

Proponents of such formalisms claim simplicity of formalism and consistency of definition. However, data models expressed in such formalisms must include additional entities to represent multivalued attributes, *n*-ary relationships, and many-to-many relationships.

Each entity has at least one set of attributes and relationships, termed an *identifier*, whose values uniquely distinguish its instances. Given the value of an identifier, there is at most one corresponding instance of that entity. Employee number 12314, for example, identifies one employee; customer number 5958 identifies one customer.

Figure 1 is a graphic representation of a data model in a variation of the entity relationship (ER) formalism. There are four entities: *Department*, *Employee*, *Project*, and *Assignment*. Each is represented by a rectangle with the name of the entity at the top. Attributes are listed inside the rectangle. Relationships are represented by arcs connecting the related entities. The relationship name is shown on the arc. Minimum and maximum cardinality are specified graphically on relationship arcs as discussed below. Identifiers are underlined.

Employee and *Assignment* are related through the relationship *Assigned to*. This is a one-to-many

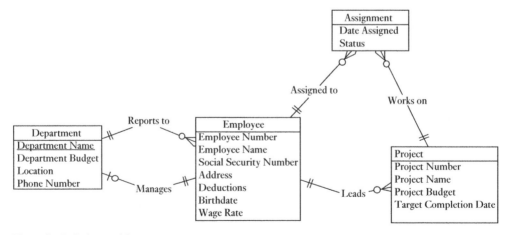

Figure 1 Basic data model

relationship (one employee can be related to many assignments but an assignment can be related to only one related employee), with *Assignment* being dependent upon *Employee* (an employee can have zero assignments but an assignment requires a minimum of one employee). That is, one employee can be *Assigned to* zero or more assignments but an assignment requires exactly one employee to be *Assigned to* it. *Project* and *Assignment* are similarly related through the relationship *Works on*. One project can have zero or more assignments *Work on* it but an assignment must *Work on* exactly one project.

There are two relationships between *Employee* and *Department*: *Reports to* and *Manages*. The first associates employees with the departments to which they administratively report. It specifies that each employee must *Report to* exactly one department and a department must have one or more employees *Reports to* it (maximum cardinality is one for *Employee* and many for *Department*; minimum cardinality is one for both *Employee* and *Department*). Thus, *Employee* and *Department* are mutually dependent along the *Reports to* relationship.

The second relationship associates each department with the one employee who *Manages* it. All departments must have a manager; however, not all employees manage a department. The fact that some employees participate in the *Manages* relationship suggests that the category *Employee* is heterogeneous. It contains at least two subsets of employees: those who manage departments and those who do not. The relationship *Leads* between *Employee* and *Project* is similarly defined, except that an employee can lead many projects. Thus there are possibly four subsets of *Employee*: department managers, project leaders, both, and neither.

Generalization was introduced to increase the fidelity of data models for such situations. Generalization allows the modeler to identify subsets of entities, termed *subtypes*, and to define how these subsets interrelate. This concept, central to the object-oriented paradigm, includes the notion of *inheritance*. A subtype inherits all attributes and relationships from the entity (its *supertype*). This type of relationship is also termed an *ISA* (is a) relationship – each instance of the subtype *is a[n]* instance of the supertype.

An entity may have many subtypes and it may be a subtype of many other entities. If all entities have at most one supertype, then the structure is termed a *generalization hierarchy*. If an entity is a subtype of more than one entity, then the structure is termed a *generalization lattice*. Two types of constraints characterize generalization structures: *exclusion* and *cover*. An exclusion constraint on a set of subtypes specifies that an instance of the supertype can be in at most one of the subtypes. A cover constraint specifies that each instance of the supertype is in at least one of the subtypes. Their combination, termed *partition*, specifies that each instance of the supertype is in one and only one subtype.

A more accurate representation of employees, department managers, and project leaders and their association with departments and projects uses generalization as shown in figure 2. *Manager* and *Leader* are subtypes of *Employee*. This is indicated by an arrow from the subtype to the supertype. Using generalization it is clear that the *Manages* and *Leads* relationships apply only to subsets of employees. An exclusion constraint specifies that employees who are department managers cannot also be project leaders (the *x* inside the triangle connecting the two subtypes of *Employee*).

Since each manager is an employee, *Manager* inherits all attributes and relationships from *Employee*. In addition, *Manager* has the attributes Parking Space Number and Credit Card Number that do not apply to employees who are not managers. Similarly, *Leader* has attributes Date Certified and Responsibility Level. If generalization were not used, these would need to be included as optional attributes of *Employee*.

Whenever a relationship has an entity whose minimum cardinality is zero or there are optional attributes of an entity, generalization can be used to decompose that entity into one or more subtypes. By using generalization in this way, the data model increases its fidelity to the domain; however, it also becomes more complex and may be more difficult to validate.

Data modeling is a part of an overall process of developing a system representation. Numerous techniques have been proposed; however, the process remains highly subjective. The key tasks are:

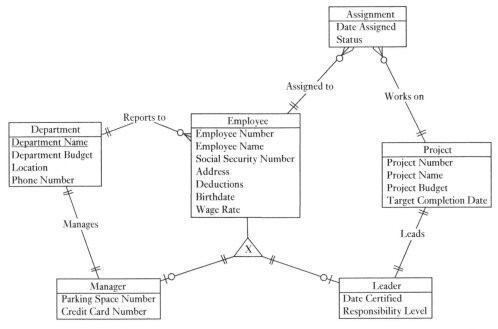

Figure 2   Data model with generation hierarchy

- identify the entities;
- establish relationships;
- determine and assign attributes to entities;
- represent constraints.

The developed data model must be cross-validated with other representations of the information system such as process and behavior representations.

Key approaches to data modeling are document analysis (transactions and reports) and analysis of sentences describing the operation of the organization. It is extremely common for an organization to create artificial identifiers for important entities. These identifiers invariably appear on reports or transaction documents as Number (or No. or num) or as some other obvious designator of an identifier. To analyze a document, examine each heading on the document and classify it as representing: (1) an entity (its identifier); (2) an attribute; or (3) calculated data. This determination is done by an analyst in conjunction with the end users.

Consider the invoice document illustrated in figure 3. A scan of that document reveals 21

headings: Invoice no.; Invoice date; Customer no.; Bill to address; Customer PO; Terms; FOB point; Line no.; Product no.; Product description; Unit of sale; Quantity ordered; Quantity shipped; Quantity backordered; Unit price; Discount; Extension; Order gross; Tax; Freight; and Order net. Recalling the definition of an entity as any "thing" about which information is maintained, we classify Invoice no., Line no., Customer no., and Product no. as entity identifiers. Tax, Order gross, and Order net are classified as calculated values. All others are classified as attributes. For each entity identifier, the entity is named: Invoice no. identifies *Invoice*, Line no. identifies a *Line item* on an invoice (hence its identifier is the combination of Line no. and its related *Invoice*), Customer no. identifies *Customer*, and Product no. identifies *Product* (see figure 4).

Secondly, we establish relationships. The following sentence describes the business operation. "Invoices are sent to customers." The nouns "invoices" and "customers" correspond to entities; the verb phrase "are sent" corresponds to a relationship. We choose to call the relationship *Responsible for* rather than *Are sent*

Sample Company, Inc.
111 Any Street
Anytown, USA

Invoice
Number Date
157289 10/02/04

Bill To:
  Customer No. 0361
  Local Grocery Store
  132 Local Street
  Localtown, USA

Customer PO : 3291
Terms   : Net 30
FOB Point   : Anytown

Line No.	Product Number	Product Description	Unit of Sale	Quantity			Unit Price	Discount	Extension
				Order	Ship	Backord			
1	2157	Cheerios	Carton	40	40	0	$50.00	5%	$1900.00
2	2283	Oat Rings	Each	300	200	100	$2.00	0%	$ 400.00
3	0579	Corn Flakes	Carton	30	30	0	$40.00	10%	$1080.00

Gross	$3380.00
Tax at 6%	$ 202.80
Freight	$ 50.00
Order Net	$3632.80

Figure 3 Sample invoice document

to better reflect the nature of the business concept. The relevant questions are: "How many customers are responsible for a single invoice?" (one); "Can an invoice exist without a customer who is responsible for it?" (no); "Can a single customer be responsible for more than one invoice?" (yes); and "Can a customer exist without having any invoices?" (yes). This specifies a one-to-many relationship between *Customer* and *Invoice* with minimum cardinality zero for *Customer* and one for *Invoice*.

Thirdly, we assign attributes. Attributes can be assigned using *functional dependencies* (or *multivalued dependencies* if multivalued attributes are supported). A functional dependency is a mathematical specification indicating that the value of an attribute is determined by the value of an identifier (xy, where x is an identifier and y is an attribute). Each attribute must be fully functionally dependent upon the identifier and on no other attributes or relationships. This process of assigning attributes is termed *normalizing* the data model.

Invoice is identified by Invoice no. and has attributes Invoice date, Customer PO, Terms, FOB point, Tax, and Freight. *Customer* is identified by Customer no. and has attributes Bill to

address and Terms. The attribute Terms has been assigned to both *Invoice* and *Customer*. That is, two functional dependencies were identified, Invoice no. $\rightarrow$ Terms and Customer no. $\rightarrow$ Terms. The attribute Terms is fully functionally dependent upon more than one identifier. There are three possibilities. First, there may be two different attributes referenced by the name Terms, the Invoice terms (for a specific invoice) and the normal Customer terms (which may be changed for a specific invoice). In this case, they should be given different names. Otherwise Terms must describe *either* Customer or *Invoice*. If Terms describes *Invoice*, then a customer could have invoices with different terms and the identified functional dependency Customer no. $\rightarrow$ Terms is in error. Terms should be removed from *Customer*. If Terms describes *Customer*, then all invoices for a customer must have the same terms and the functional dependency Invoice no. $\rightarrow$ Terms is a *transitive*. That is, Invoice no. $\rightarrow$ Customer no. $\rightarrow$ Terms. In this case, Terms should be removed from *Invoice*. Figure 4 illustrates the first case.

Continuing the analysis, the sentence "an invoice specified line items shipped" results in the one-to-many relationship *Specifies shipment* between *Invoice* and *Line item* with minimum cardinality zero for *Invoice* and one for *Line item*. That is, an invoice may have zero or more line items, each of which *Specifies [a product] shipment* on the invoice but a line item *Specifies [a product] shipment* for exactly one invoice. Note that Order price is the price of the product shipped, which may be different from the Unit price of the product. This differentiation is particularly important if the price of a product can change between the time a product is ordered and the time it is invoiced or if salespeople can negotiate prices for a specific order.

The data model specifies that *one product* can be *Sold on* many line items. This assumes that what is meant by *one product* is not one instance of the product, but one *type* of product. In contrast to Customer no., which identifies one instance of *Customer*, and Invoice no., which identifies one instance of *Invoice*, Product no. identifies one type of product, the instances of which are completely interchangeable. The customer is being invoiced for some quantity of this product. In figure 3, for example, "Cheerios" is Product no. 2157, sold in units of cartons. Local Grocery Store is being invoiced for 40 cartons of this product. Presumably 40 more cartons of this product could be shipped (and invoiced) to a different customer.

Finally, we review the model to insure that all attributes are assigned to an entity, that algorithms and base attributes are specified for all calculated attributes, and that all important generalizations are identified. The value of explicitly recognizing subtypes depends on the degree of heterogeneity within an entity. The purpose of the data model is to communicate the meaning of the data. If the introduction of subtypes confuses rather than clarifies, they should not be introduced.

Referring to figure 4, some customers may not have any outstanding invoices (*Customer* is not dependent upon *Invoice*). Thus there are two subtypes of customer: those with invoices and those without. If this is the only distinction, it is probably not worthwhile to explicitly recognize the subtypes. If, on the other hand, customers with invoices have additional attributes or are viewed differently from customers without invoices, then subtypes should be created.

data modeling, physical

Salvatore T. March

Given a description of the logical data content and activities for an application, physical data modeling is concerned with designing efficient

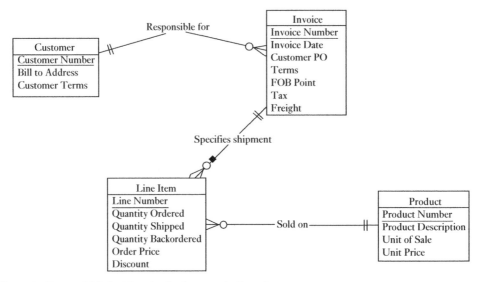

Figure 4   Data model derived from invoice document in figure 3

structures and algorithms for the storage and retrieval of those data. A physical data model describes the details of how data are stored and accessed. The efficiency of a physical data model is determined by such factors as: the volume and intrinsic structure of the data, the frequency and content of retrievals and updates, and the accessing characteristics of the data storage media.

There are two major aspects of a physical data model: *record structures* and *access paths*. Record structures define the representation, grouping, and interconnection of elementary data units (attributes and instances). Access paths define the algorithms and system data used to store and retrieve the data. Given the characteristics of common data storage media, a general rule for physical data modeling is to store data together that are used together.

A DATABASE MANAGEMENT SYSTEM (DBMS) can be characterized by the record structures that it supports. Relational database management systems typically restrict record structures to flat tables interconnected via data values (foreign keys). Object-oriented database management systems typically support complex record structures in which objects of different classes can be nested and interconnected via system pointers (object identifiers).

Record structures are defined from an application's logical data model. All information in the logical data model (i.e., attributes and relationships) must be represented in the record structures. Record structures may, however, *nest* or *fragment* logical entities, *replicate* attributes, and define *aggregate* data items in order to increase efficiency. Nesting entities implies storing attributes of related entities in the same file. Fragmenting an entity implies storing subsets of an entity's attributes or instances in separate files. Replicating attributes means copying specific attributes in related files. Aggregate data items hold values calculated from other attributes.

There are two types of access paths: primary and secondary. Both supply mechanisms for accessing records by their *key* attribute(s). Primary access paths use the *primary key* attributes to determine the physical positioning of records within the file. Secondary access paths use a secondary attribute in combination with supplementary system data (e.g., secondary indexes or hash tables) to locate records positioned by the primary access path.

There are three major types of primary access paths: sequential, indexed sequential, and algorithmic. Sequential access paths position records in physical sequence. Often they use chronological sequence as the key owing to the high cost of record insertion using an attribute-based key. Inserting a record anywhere but at the end of a sequential file requires all records in the file after the insertion point to be moved to make room for the inserted record.

Indexed sequential access paths also organize records in physical sequence, but only within disk *blocks* or *sectors*. Typically, a disk block can store a number of data records. An additional *index* file maintains the logical sequence of blocks. There is one record in the index for each block. It contains the primary key of the first record in the block and a pointer to the block (i.e., the block address). Records in the index are also stored in blocks and sequenced by primary key. An index may be indexed, forming a *tree-structured* or *hierarchical* index.

To insert a record into an indexed sequential file, the index is searched to find the appropriate block and all records in the block after the insertion point are moved to make room for the new record. If there is not sufficient room in the block, an *overflow* mechanism is invoked. A common overflow mechanism, termed block *splitting*, adds a new block to the file, moving half of the records (those with the larger primary keys) to the new block. A new record is added to the index. If there is insufficient room in the appropriate index block to accommodate a new record, the index block must be split.

Algorithmic or *hashed* access paths allocate a number of disk blocks for file storage and calculate the block in which to store records. For example, if 100 blocks were allocated for the storage of employee records, a possible hashing algorithm would be to take the last two digits of the employee number (primary key) as the block number for that employee (this results in a number between 00 and 99). If more records hash to the same block than fit on the block, an overflow mechanism is employed. *Dynamic hashing* and *extensible hashing* use index structures to enable file growth.

Consider the following simple record structure for an order processing application:

```
Salesperson [s-no, s-name, s-
address, s-commission]
Customer [c-no, c-name, c-ad-
dress, c-credit, c-terms, s-no]
Order [o-no, o-date, o-shipped,
o-terms, c-no, s-no]
Lineitem [o-no, l-no, p-no, li-
quantity, li-discount]
Product [p-no, p-description,
p-price, p-quantity-on-hand]
```

Consistent with relational database management systems, it has a file (table) for each entity having a field (data item) for each attribute and a field (foreign key) for each (many-to-one) relationship. Primary keys are underlined. Foreign keys are italicized. Consider producing a report of orders, including customer, salesperson, line item, and product information. All five files would need to be combined (joined). A number of different methods can be used to accomplish this, depending on the access paths implemented (e.g., merge join, index join).

Efficiency can be gained for this report by modifying the physical record structures. Joins with *Customer*, *Salesperson*, and *Product* can be eliminated if the needed *Salesperson* and *Customer* attributes (s-name, c-name, c-address) are *replicated* (copied) in the *Order* file and the needed *Product* attributes (p-description, p-price) are replicated in the *Lineitem* file. However, this increases the size of the *Order* file and of the *Lineitem* file and incurs additional update, storage, and data transfer costs. When an order is added, the replicated customer and salesperson data must be copied to it; when a line item is added, the replicated product information must be copied to it. Furthermore, it violates *third normal form* – if updates to salesperson or customer data must be reflected in the *Order* file, then additional update costs must also be incurred. A similar situation occurs for updates to the *Product* file. Efficiencies are gained if the reduction in retrieval cost exceeds the increase in storage and maintenance cost.

Alternatively, the *Lineitem* file could be nested within the *Order* file. That is, line items could be stored as a repeating group within the *Order* file.

In this way, order and related line item data are stored in the same block and accessed at the same time. While this has retrieval advantages for printing orders, it violates *first normal form* and may not be supported by the target database management system. Furthermore, it makes access to line items, e.g., for product sales analysis, more complicated.

For the record structure given above, producing a report of the gross sales for each order requires access to all line items for each order in the report. If an aggregate data item, say *order-gross*, holding the order's gross sale was added to the *Order* file, then only this file would need to be accessed and the cost to produce the report would be reduced. This data item would, of course, need to be maintained when line items for an order were added, deleted, or modified.

To select appropriate record structures and access paths for an application, trade-offs among retrieval and update activities sharing the database must be considered. Replicated and aggregate data can improve the efficiency of retrieval activities that use these data, but actually worsen it for retrieval activities that do not use them. Furthermore, it increases maintenance and storage costs. Similarly, secondary indexes can improve retrieval efficiency but increase maintenance and storage costs.

data processing

see PROCESSING METHODS FOR INFORMATION SYSTEMS

data structure(s)

Gordon C. Everest

Data structure refers to the method of organizing the data in a database. The database may be as a single file or a collection of files or tables. Multiple files and/or tables are generally explicitly interrelated, though formally defined interfile relationships are not necessary to constitute a database.

A database schema (or data model) is the *definition* of a data structure or a database, whereas the database contains the actual user data. For example:

```
[Employee: name(char), uni-
t(num,4),    jobcode(num,4),
title(char),    birth(date),
salary(money)]
```

would be a representation of the schema for the single file containing information about the entity type named *Employee*. The *Employee* entity is described by a set of defined *attributes* or data items, along with a definition of the type of values for each attribute. Data for an example *instance* of the *Employee* type entity could be:

```
[``Callagan, R. F.,'' 2100,
5210, Secretary, 1955/06/06,
$28,000]
```

These data could be stored in a *record* in the database. A collection of several such records constitutes a file or table in the database. In the relational model, a file is called a table with each record being a *row* and each attribute or data item being a *column* in the table.

A data structure can relate to three or four distinct levels, depending upon its perspective and purpose. The ANSI/SPARC Committee (1978) defined three levels of database schema: external, conceptual, and internal.

The *external schema* defines how a particular user, group of users, or an application (program) views a portion of the database of interest to them. This view (also called a subschema or view) can relate to a screen display, a report, or a query.

The *conceptual schema* defines the entire database from the global perspective of the database administrator (*see* DATA ADMINISTRATION), who takes an enterprise-wide view (which is still a chosen scope of interest). The conceptual schema is generally a high-level logical view, expressed without the constraints of implementation in a particular DATABASE MANAGEMENT SYSTEM. This has led some to speak of the global schema on two levels: the conceptual schema and the *logical schema* definition for implementation.

The *internal schema* defines the physical stored representation of a database.

A data structure contains information about entities, their attributes, and relationships in the domain of interest. Data structures are classed into those that form records and those that do

not. In a record-based data-structuring scheme, the attributes are represented by data items or columns in a table. The attribute values are stored together in records. Similar records (describing the same type of entity) are collected together in files or rows in tables. All the data in a database may be collected into a single file structure or multiple file structures. Each file may be "flat," i.e., where there is at most one value for each attribute, or *hierarchical*, where data items may be multivalued; a record may contain nested repeating groups of data items. For example, an *Employee* record may contain multiple *Skills* for each employee or may contain multiple addresses (consisting of the group of items: street number and name, city, state, zip/mail code).

Network and *relational* data structures are both multifile structures. The main difference is that in a relational data structure, each table must have a flat file structure, i.e., all attribute domains are single valued or "atomic." More general network data structures may permit many-to-many relationships, as well as ternary (and higher) relationships. Non-record-based data structures can be thought of as "no file" structures (*see* OBJECT ROLE MODELING).

Data structures can also be distinguished on the basis of their physical structure and accessing mechanisms. The main access alternatives are indexing and key transformation ("hashing").

Traditionally, databases contained formatted fields of numbers and symbolic strings of characters. More recently, databases are intended to store heterogeneous information to support more complex applications such as MULTIMEDIA, graphics, computer-aided design, and geographic information systems. Extended forms of information include text, graphics (bit-mapped and vector graphics), audio, and moving video. Some database management systems allow the definition of a general purpose data item, called a BLOB (binary large object). A BLOB can be used to represent a graphic image, a spreadsheet, a complex text document, an audio clip, or a moving video clip. Usually some other application must be designated which stores, retrieves, displays, prints, and edits a particular type of BLOB. For example, MS Excel may be invoked to process a spreadsheet BLOB.

A *multidimensional* data structure is intended to support complex queries and reporting for executive information systems and management decision-making. They are the basis for DATA WAREHOUSING applications. A multidimensional database is characterized by extensive classification and cross-referencing of the data, and a retrieval facility that allows much richer manipulation and analysis of the data, now called online analytic processing (OLAP). Think of a multidimensional data structure as a traditional spreadsheet (which is two dimensions) extended to multiple dimensions.

See also *data modeling, logical; data modeling, physical*

Bibliography

ANSI/SPARC Committee (1978). *Information Systems*, 3 (3).

data warehousing

Hugh J. Watson

A data warehouse is created to provide a dedicated source of data to support decision-making applications (Gray and Watson, 1998). Rather than having data scattered across a variety of systems, a data warehouse integrates the data into a single repository. It is for this reason that a data warehouse is said to provide "a single version of the truth." All users and applications access the same data. Because users have access to better data, their ability to analyze data and make decisions improves.

While a data warehouse is a repository of decision support data, data warehousing is a broader concept. It includes the processes for placing data in the warehouse and the use of warehouse data.

WAREHOUSE CHARACTERISTICS

A data warehouse has the following characteristics (Inmon, 1992):

● *Subject oriented*. Warehouse data are organized around specific subjects, such as sales, customers, or products. This is different

from transactional systems where data are organized by business process, such as order entry, inventory control, or accounts receivable.

● *Integrated*. Data are collected from multiple systems and are integrated around subjects. For example, customer data may be extracted from internal (and external) systems and integrated around a customer identifier so that a comprehensive view of the customer is created.

● *Time variant*. A warehouse maintains historical data (i.e., time variant). Unlike transactional systems where only recent data, such as for the last day, week, or month, are maintained, a warehouse may store years of data. Historical data are needed to detect deviations, trends, and long-term relationships.

● *Non-volatile*. A warehouse is non-volatile – users cannot change or update the data. This is done to make sure that all users are working with the same data. The warehouse is updated, but through IT-controlled load processes rather than by users.

THE ARCHITECTURE FOR DATA WAREHOUSING

A variety of warehouse architectures exist (e.g., hub and spoke, data marts with conformed dimensions, federated). A typical architecture is shown in figure 1. It is the "hub and spoke" architecture recommended by Bill Inmon, who is considered to be "the father of data warehousing." It features a central warehouse (the "hub") and dependent data marts (the "spokes") that obtain their data from the hub. This architecture is sometimes referred to as an "enterprise data warehouse" or the "corporate information factory."

The left-hand side of the figure shows the various data sources. Much of the data come from transactional (i.e., operational) systems – production, accounting, marketing, etc. Data may also come from an ERP system, such as SAP or PeopleSoft (*see* ENTERPRISE SYSTEMS (ENTERPRISE RESOURCE PLANNING OR ERP)). Web data in the form of weblogs may also be fed into the data warehouse. Finally, external data, such as census data, may be used. These data sources often use different hardware and software, and a mixture of hierarchical, net-

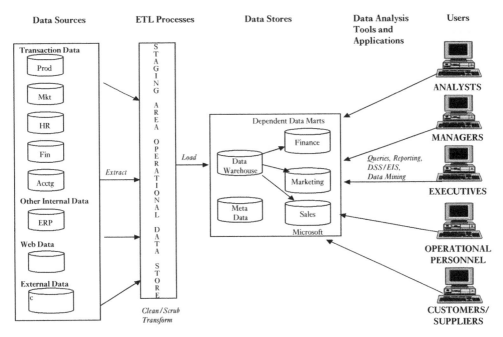

Figure 1   A comprehensive data warehousing architecture

work, and relational data models for storing the data. It is not unusual for a data warehouse to draw upon over 100 source systems.

The data are extracted from the source systems using custom-written software or extraction, transformation, and loading (ETL) software. The data are then fed into a staging area (i.e., a database) where they are cleaned, integrated, and transformed. Special purpose software may be used to facilitate data-cleansing processes. The processed data may then be placed in an operational data store, which is similar to a data warehouse but stores only recent rather than historical data. The data are then also ready for loading into the data warehouse.

The data warehouse provides the repository of data used for decision support. Subsets of the data may be used to create dependent data marts that support specific kinds of users, such as financial analysts or quality control specialists. The dependent data marts maintain "the single version of the truth" because they receive their data from the data warehouse. Typically, the dependent marts provide a multidimensional view of the data, such as by customer, by product, by location, and over time. A multidimen-

sional database that is designed to represent data multidimensionally and provide fast response times may be used. Metadata about the data in the warehouse (e.g., where and when the data are extracted, and the scheduled reports for users) are maintained so that they can be accessed by IT personnel and users.

A variety of users access the warehouse using data access tools and applications that are appropriate for their needs. Power users (e.g., analysts) who understand the underlying data model for the warehouse and how to write SQL queries (*see* SQL) may write their own queries. Many users (e.g., analysts, managers) employ a managed query environment to access data. These products provide a Windows-like interface for accessing reports and designing queries. Specially trained analysts may also perform DATA MINING using warehouse data. The data warehouse may also be used to support specific DECISION SUPPORT SYSTEMS (DSS) and EXECUTIVE INFORMATION SYSTEMS (EIS) applications, like electronic dashboards and scorecards. The warehouse is also used with specific application software, such as for CUSTOMER RELATIONSHIP MANAGEMENT

(CRM). A recent development is to give a wide variety of users including customers and suppliers (i.e., trading partners) access to warehouse data. A web browser is normally the client of choice for this purpose.

THE DEVELOPMENT METHODOLOGY

Building a data warehouse is a significant organizational undertaking because of the cost, technical complexity (e.g., the volume of data), and organizational factors (e.g., data ownership issues). Experts in data warehousing recommend a long-term development plan for the warehouse but that it be built incrementally (e.g., a subject area at a time). Each increment should provide business benefits, thus maintaining support for the warehouse. Data warehousing is often referred to as "a journey rather than a destination" to emphasize that it is always an ongoing process.

REAL-TIME DATA WAREHOUSING

Because of the needs of business and the emergence of new technologies, organizations are now introducing real-time data warehousing. With this approach, warehouse data are updated almost as soon as there are changes in source system data. This pushes decision support from the strategic (traditional data warehousing) to the tactical and operational (real-time warehousing). This capability allows the warehouse to affect current decisions and business processes, and is particularly useful with customer-facing applications where a comprehensive knowledge of the customer is important.

Bibliography

Gray, P. and Watson, H. J. (1998). *Decision Support in the Data Warehouse*. Upper Saddle River, NJ: Prentice-Hall.

Inmon, W. H. (1992). *Building the Data Warehouse*. New York: John Wiley.

database management system

Gordon C. Everest

A database management system (DBMS) is a computer-based system for creating and maintaining databases. A basic DBMS performs the following functions:

- defines a database;
- stores and accesses data;
- retrieves and displays or prints data in response to a request;
- maintains data in the database (insert, modify, delete);
- maintains the integrity of the stored data according to its defined structure and constraint rules.

The request to a DBMS for data may come directly and interactively from human users or from programs or stored procedures through some application programming interface (API). A DBMS may be designed to operate in a variety of environments: multi-user, client/server, host-based, etc., in which case additional functionality and interfaces are required.

DBMSs can be classified on various bases, e.g., underlying data structure (*see* DATA STRUCTURE(S)), purpose or role within an information system (client or development). A common classification is the underlying data structure: hierarchical, network, and relational. Note that this is not a complete structure taxonomy since it leaves out the single flat file and the object-role data model (*see* OBJECT ROLE MODELING). Another basis for classifying DBMSs is purpose or role within the platform of an information system, client or development. Client DBMSs are primarily intended for the ad hoc interactive end user. They usually have simplified data-structuring capabilities and rich, easy-to-use data access, query, reporting, and manipulation capabilities. They may or may not offer the ability for a user-written program to access the database, either from a standard programming language such as COBOL or C (*see* C AND C++), or using a built-in programming language (such as VBA in MS Access or PAL in Paradox).

Development DBMSs provide capabilities for system developers to build application systems. They provide an interface to one or more programming languages (which may include their own built-in language). They generally provide facilities to define menus, screens, queries, reports, and user views, which can all be combined to build an application system. DBMSs primarily intended for system developers may also include facilities for the interactive end user.

DBMSs differ in complexity and functionality, in part based on the type of computer system for which they are designed. Many DBMSs run mainly on a personal computer platform, and this limits functionality. The next tier of DBMS primarily runs on mini- or mainframe computers or in a network environment (though most also run on PCs) and generally offer higher levels of functionality. Most include facilities for both the interactive end user and the system developer. Compared to DBMSs designed for PCs, they are generally distinguished by offering a rich programming language interface, triggers and stored procedures, enhanced backup and recovery, greater access and quality control, concurrent update control, synchronization and replication management, etc. Another class of DBMS is the database server, intended primarily to run in a network and provide services to a set of clients. A database server does not normally interface directly with human users (although such facilities could be provided by the same vendor).

In the evolution of DBMSs, three generations are often identified. They are associated with the evolution of data languages. The first generation of DBMSs was identified with so-called third generations of programming languages, such as COBOL and PASCAL. The data management facilities of these third-generation languages were designed to read and write records one at a time from a single file. The next generation of data languages was termed fourth-generation languages (4GL). They were designed to process and retrieve sets of records, even from multiple files or tables, in a single statement. The dominant 4GL is SQL (pronounced "sequel"), for which there is now an ANSI and ISO standard. The second-generation DBMS incorporated a fourth-generation language. Most DBMSs today provide some flavor of SQL, whether directly to the end user, to the application programmer (perhaps as extensions to a conventional programming language), underneath an easy-to-use prompting interface, or at the interface between the client DBMS and the database server.

The next or third generation of DBMS is an object-oriented DBMS (*see* OBJECT-ORIENTED DATABASE MANAGEMENT SYSTEM). An OODBMS incorporates the principles of object orientation in its programming language and its user interface(s), while still providing all the functionality of a second-generation DBMS. The third generation of DBMS is marked by some of the following features:

- higher level of semantics in the definition of the database (or object base);
- handling heterogeneous, multimedia forms of information;
- explicitly representing the temporal and spatial dimensions of information;
- offering a natural language user interface;
- employing rules of inference (as in expert systems);
- operating in a distributed or client/server environment.

debugging of computer programs

Randy Snyder

Debugging is a programming technique or process used to find and correct computer program errors or mistakes, known as bugs. Debugging is performed to create robust programs, programs that compute reliable results for a broad range of input values, and reject illegal input. Different types of errors (bugs) in computers are identified and corrected using different debugging techniques. Bugs are commonly divided into three types: syntactic errors, logical errors, and algorithmic errors.

Syntactic errors occur when one or more program statements violate the construction rules (syntax) of the language being used. For example, the syntax of many languages requires that a period be placed at the end of a program statement. If a period is not present where required, a syntactic error will occur. Syntactic errors can exist in an otherwise logically correct program. The errors may occur because of statement entry mistakes or careless programming, or because the programmer had an incomplete or flawed understanding of language syntax. Syntactic errors are usually the easiest type of error to debug. The program compiler or interpreter that detects a syntactic error can produce diagnostic messages that identify the part of the program that contains the error and may also identify the kind of syntax error as well.

To debug syntactic errors, a programmer locates and displays the portion of the source code identified in the error message. The programmer determines how to modify the source code by comparing it to a correct definition of the programming language being used. This can be accomplished by examining a description of the language syntax or by looking at examples of correct code that use similar syntactical constructs. The programmer then modifies the source code and attempts to compile or interpret it again to see if the error has been corrected. All syntax errors must be corrected before a program can be executed.

Logical errors occur when a program instructs a computer to execute valid instructions that produce an unwanted behavior in the computer. Logical errors are sometimes called *semantic errors* because the meaning of the program instruction is inconsistent with desired behavior. Typical logical errors include causing programmed loops to run erratically, misassigning memory, or improperly formatting output data.

One debugging technique used by programmers to locate a logical error is to strategically embed temporary print or display statements in the program flow, allowing them to limit error search to small portions of the program. Programmers also limit their search for logical errors by using their knowledge of a program to focus on the parts responsible for program behaviors in error. After narrowing the search area, programmers examine the suspect logic and mentally rehearse the program's behavior to determine exactly how the logic is in error. To correct the bug, the programmer rewrites program statements, resolves any new syntactic errors that are introduced, and reexecutes the program to verify that its behavior is correct.

Algorithmic errors occur when a program works correctly for most, but not all, combinations of program input. Algorithmic errors can be difficult to detect and correct because it is often unfeasible or impossible to test every possible combination of program input. A common approach for detecting algorithmic errors is to test the program with widely varying input values and with large samples of data the program is written to process. Incorrect results identified for only a specific combination of input data alert a programmer to the existence of algorithmic errors. The peculiarities of the input data used in the test are used to locate and rewrite parts of the program.

decision support systems

Fred Niederman

Decision support systems (DSS) process, store, and present information to support managerial decision-making. The task of decision-making can vary greatly between functions within an organization, between individual decision-makers who have different styles of taking action, between different tasks or types of decisions, and between organizations. Therefore, decision support systems take many different forms. The DSS supports decision-makers in understanding the nature of the environment and in assessing probable consequences of various alternative actions, but generally does not "make the decision."

DSSs consist of applications built from tools with a user interface appropriate to decision-makers. The applications access data and employ models to support managerial decision-making. Data may be gathered from a single process from within an organization (such as customer transactions), from multiple processes (these often provide links between separate processes for receiving revenue and for disbursing funds), and/or from outside data sources such as online databases or customer help (or complaint) lines. Data-oriented DSS can be used, for example, where a hospital might be bidding on a contract with a health maintenance organization. Such an application would be built from data for clinical costs, patient or insurance billing, and physician profiles gathered from various departments based on historical data derived from various operational processes. Where such bidding on contracts might be a recurring task, the application would be built to be updated periodically with current data. Such an application would need to be tested to assure high levels of accuracy across scenarios (such as when receiving poor data from feeder systems), reliability, capacity, performance in a production environment, and security. If such a decision were not likely to recur, the DSS might be built using a prototyping approach with a series of iterations and refinements until a satisfactory level of performance were reached.

Models in a DSS are frequently financial or statistical in nature but may also include optimization and other mathematical tools. Financial models can be used for "what if" analysis in projecting the effect of changing policies or macroeconomic conditions on the probable effectiveness of various actions. Modern DSS will also incorporate DATA MINING tools to look for hidden relationships and "surprising" elements observable in past transactions. Results from this sort of DSS use may also be integrated with knowledge management systems that gather and organize facts and observations for purposes of supporting continual organizational learning.

The DSS user interface allows the user to directly manipulate data and/or models and to format the output as desired. For example, a DSS can draw data from organizational transaction processing systems and deposit it within a spreadsheet or database package on the user's desk for further manipulation. While providing extraordinary flexibility and timely use of data, organizations must be careful to avoid proliferation of out-of-date versions and must pay careful attention to data security and integrity issues.

DSS support one or more of Herbert Simon's phases of decision-making: intelligence, design, and choice. Intelligence is the gathering of information about the nature of the problem; design is formulating alternative action plans or solutions to the problem; and choice is selecting among the alternatives. In the hospital scenario, the DSS may support the intelligence activity by periodically drawing information from clinical and financial transactions, by integrating internal data with information drawn from external sources that provide baselines of activity or a basis for forecasting. The DSS can support alternative designs by comparing proposed contracts for profitability, given varying demand and cost scenarios. It can support choice by comparing alternative scenarios on various criteria selected by senior managers. It will present ranking of alternatives and the relative sensitivity to changes for particular criteria.

A DSS may be designed for top, middle, and lower management levels. In the hospital scenario, for example, a comprehensive DSS can provide information for high-level executives formulating major contracts; for middle managers insuring that medical resources are available for implementing the contract; and for operational managers selecting the most cost-effective techniques for arranging staffing on a holiday weekend.

The purpose of a DSS is to provide relevant data as a mechanism for managers to make decisions based on an understanding of the environment and an examination of relevant alternatives. As a by-product, managers tend to have more confidence in their decision, knowing that their investigation has been thorough. They have more effective means to communicate their decision to peers and to persuade others to implement the decision. A successful DSS will provide some combination of better decisions (where the link between decisions and outcomes can be demonstrated), more efficient use of time in decision-making, and more satisfaction or confidence with the decision-making process.

The term DSS has historically been used to describe both specific systems for supporting particular decisions and packages that facilitate a type of decision-making such as financial planning. Increasingly, DSS is interconnected with other organizational systems such as ERP (*see* ENTERPRISE SYSTEMS (ENTERPRISE RESOURCE PLANNING OR ERP)), CUSTOMER RELATIONSHIP MANAGEMENT (CRM), or more specialized data warehouses (*see* DATA WAREHOUSING). DSS can be used to automate "routine" decision-making, such as automatically rerouting airline passengers on a delayed flight as part of a CRM initiative. It can alternatively be used to support higher-level decision-making such as the selection of retail site locations where quantitative data must be blended with intangible factors based on managerial preferences and values to form a final decision.

Expanding on the original concept of DSS are EXECUTIVE INFORMATION SYSTEMS (EIS) and GROUP DECISION SUPPORT SYSTEMS (GDSS). The EIS supports senior managers in terms of specific decision-making and in monitoring key indicators of progress for their organization. The GDSS supports decision-making by groups or teams rather than by single individuals. In addition to tools for supporting data and modeling, the GDSS generally will have meeting support tools that automate brainstorming and voting functions.

Bibliography

Alter, S. L. (1980). *Decision Support Systems: Current Practice and Continuing Challenges.* Reading, MA: Addison-Wesley.

DeSanctis, G. and Gallupe, B. (1987). Group decision support systems: A new frontier. *Management Science,* 33(5), 43–59.

Gorry, G. M. and Scott-Morton, M. S. (1971). A framework for management information systems. *Sloan Management Review,* 13(1), 55–70.

Houdeshel, G. and Watson, H. J. (1987). The management information and decision support (MIDS) system at Lockheed-Georgia. *MIS Quarterly,* 11 (2), 127–40.

Silver, M. S. (1991). Decisional guidance for computer-based decision support. *MIS Quarterly,* 15(1), 105–22.

Simon, H. (1977). *The New Science of Management Decision.* Englewood Cliffs, NJ: Prentice-Hall.

Sprague, R. H., Jr. (1980). A framework for the development of decision support systems. *MIS Quarterly,* 4 (4), 1–26.

Sprague, R. H., Jr. and Carlson, E. D. (1982). *Building Effective Decision Support Systems.* Englewood Cliffs, NJ: Prentice-Hall.

Watson, H. J. et al. (eds.) (1992). *Executive Support Systems.* New York: John Wiley.

desktop publishing

Rosann Collins

Desktop publishing is the use of a computer-based hardware and software system to design and produce high-quality documents. The features of desktop publishing systems enable combinations and enhancement of text and graphic elements (photographs, line drawings, borders) in a design that is appropriate for a document's audience and purpose. Desktop publishing is commonly used to prepare short documents such as brochures, newsletters, announcements, and programs, as well as lengthy documents such as books, catalogs, and technical manuals.

Before desktop publishing became available in the 1980s, document design and production involved many manual processes, such as cutting and pasting text and graphics on a layout board and the services of specialists (graphic designers, typesetters). The process was slow, required much coordination between activities, and was expensive. At various stages in document preparation, decisions about text, graphics, and format were final. Changes made after those decision points were very expensive and time consuming.

Low-end desktop publishing programs are available for occasional, personal use. These programs are easy to use, have a reduced set of features, and include templates for common publications, such as newsletters and flyers. Full-featured, professional-level programs are used by desktop publishing specialists, who may work out of their homes as freelancers, in advertising and publications departments of large organizations, or in small businesses that specialize in professional document creation and production.

With desktop publishing, the entire document preparation process can be done by one person at a workstation, and changes to any aspect of the document can be quickly and easily done at any time. The typical desktop publishing workstation includes a microcomputer with a large, high-resolution graphics screen; a scanner; a mouse or digitizer board; a desktop publishing program; word and graphics processing programs; and a laser or inkjet printer. The text and graphics for a publication are entered and edited by using the keyboard, mouse, scanner, and the word and graphics processing programs. Layout, editing, and enhancement of the text and graphics are done in the desktop publishing program. Many desktop publishing programs include multiple templates for common document formats that enable individuals with few design skills to produce professional-looking publications.

Basic word processing program functions (column formats, text alignment, multiple type fonts and styles, graphics insertion, style sheets) offer limited document design capabilities. For example, text can be put into columns with a word processing program, but if graphics or more than one font size or type is used, it is difficult to align text at the top and bottom of columns. Desktop publishing programs enable such fine control of text through features such as kerning (minute adjustments in placement of letters on a line), leading (spacing additions between lines of text in very small increments), ligatures (letter combinations such as "fi" that typesetters usually place close together), and text wrap (specification of the space between text and graphics for each line of text). Photographs, drawings, and text can be cropped, sized, rotated, and stretched for design effect and for exact placement on the page. Many programs include extensive font and graphics libraries as well as functions that manage multiple projects and associated files. Printing of proofs and camera-ready copy of documents is typically done on a laser printer at the workstation, although some programs will also produce four- and six-color separations and Postscript or PDF files that directly drive very high-resolution commercial printers. Digital printers for multiple-copy production continue to increase in capability, especially in color consistency and exact matching, and, combined with desktop publishing software, have enabled publishing on demand.

diffusion of information technology

see INNOVATION AND INFORMATION TECHNOLOGY

digital cash

Gordon B. Davis

Business transactions depend upon payments being sent and received along with appropriate documentation. Although traditional methods of billing, payment, checks, and credit cards can be adapted to E-COMMERCE, there are transactions that can be made more efficient by the use of digital cash. Also known as e-money or e-cash, digital cash refers to various electronic systems for transferring payments. The digital cash systems differ in the methods used. Some digital cash methods result in an anonymous transaction in which a payment cannot be traced back to the sender. Other methods provide documentation of both senders and receivers. There are online systems using the INTERNET and offline systems

using cards. Digital cash has had some successes and some failures. Various methods are still in development and experimentation. Using the Internet to process very small amounts, referred to as micropayments, has not been very successful, although it may be implemented in the future. Examples of methods for digital cash are a stored-value card, Internet-based bank payment, and email cash transfer.

An example of an offline method of digital cash is a stored-value card, which is a credit card or smart card method for transferring funds. The card is issued by a machine that accepts funds and stores a digital record of the amount on the card. At each transaction, such as a train fare, the amount is transferred from the card and available funds are reduced. The card can be replenished by adding funds at a machine that issues the cards and adds value to them. A common use of a stored-value card is a bus or train card. The amount paid is stored in a digital record on a magnetic stripe on the card; at each use, the amount available is reduced when the passenger completes a journey. Another illustration is the American Express stored-value TravelFunds Card. It is a prepaid, reloadable card, sold as an alternative to carrying cash or debit cards. It is not linked to a bank account and, if stolen, it is refundable. It may be used for purchases and for obtaining cash from an ATM (*see* AUTOMATED TELLER MACHINE).

Internet-based bank transfers of funds are electronic transfers of funds from the bank account of the person making a payment to the bank account of the organization or person receiving the payment. The transfer is enabled by cryptographic methods (*see* CRYPTOGRAPHY (CRYPTO)) using public and private keys to provide a high level of security. In one system, for example, a digital cash certificate is purchased from a bank. The certificate, when transferred to a vendor as payment, is deposited in the vendor's bank. The receiver of a certificate can obtain assurance that the certificate is valid.

Email transfer of funds is an electronic method of payment using email. Email transfers are managed by a provider of a funds transfer service. An example of such a system is PayPal, an eBay company. It enables an individual or business with an email address to send and receive payments online.

digital convergence

Amit Das

Digital convergence refers to the coming together of functions that were traditionally provided by separate devices. Common examples of digital convergence include printers that also scan and fax, mobile phones that take pictures and play video games, and audio/video players that play back media formats associated with computers (MP3, Windows Media, DivX) in addition to conventional CDs/DVDs. This entry examines the factors driving the trend toward digital convergence, the technological developments that enable convergence, and the business consequences of convergence.

DRIVERS OF DIGITAL CONVERGENCE

An obvious attraction of convergence for consumers is the opportunity to replace multiple devices (such as a printer, a scanner, and a fax machine) with a single piece of equipment that combines multiple functions. Especially when a consumer uses a particular function only occasionally, he or she may be reluctant to acquire, operate, and maintain a dedicated device for this specific function. For example, a small office may print documents quite often, but scan and fax documents only occasionally. Though scanners and fax machines are fairly inexpensive to buy, they contribute to office clutter, consuming scarce desk space and adding to the already dense network of wires running through the office. For such an office, a printer that can also scan and fax represents a major saving, not just in purchase price but in the cost of operation and maintenance. The reduction in complexity arising from fewer devices is even more attractive to home users, who face tighter space constraints.

For equipment manufacturers, digital convergence exploits overlaps in components to deliver multiple functions for a cost lower than the sum of individual devices. For example, the paper-handling mechanism of a printer can also be adapted to move documents for scanning. Since the scanner creates (digital) images of a document, and the printer can print out such images, the combination of printer and scanner also acts as a copier (for light usage). With the addition of a modem, the digital image of a document created by the scanner can be transmitted over phone lines, yielding the functionality commonly associated with a facsimile (fax) machine. Inbound faxes received by the modem can be printed out by the printer for hard-copy output. The device resulting from the convergence of a scanner, a printer, and a modem usually costs less than the sum of the cost of three dedicated devices (scanner, printer, and fax) because the duplication of common components is avoided.

In the same fashion, the availability of an LCD screen, a keypad, and some amount of storage in a mobile phone makes it an attractive target for incorporating other functions – those of an organizer (personal digital assistant or PDA), a music player, a handheld video gaming console, and a camera. The organizer utilizes the memory, screen, and keypad of the phone, the music player the memory and sound-processing circuitry, the gaming console the screen, memory, and keypad, and the camera the memory and the screen. Thus the same screen, keypad, and memory are used for multiple functions. What makes this example interesting, however, is that the convergence of functions might, in this case, create new value for the consumer. Now that the same device stores contact information and makes phone calls, looking up a rolodex/PDA and dialing the selected number on a phone becomes a single seamless process. On an incoming call, the contact details of the caller (telephone number, as recorded by the Caller-ID function) can be saved directly into the phone book. Since the phone also provides connectivity to a GPRS/3G wireless digital network, the gaming console built into the phone can exploit this connectivity for multiplayer gaming. With the rise of multimedia messaging, pictures/video clips taken by the camera (and stored in memory) can be instantly shared over the GPRS/3G network.

In summary, therefore, we see that consumers like convergence because it enables them to replace many devices with one device. Manufacturers leverage convergence to sell functions to segments that might not invest in dedicated equipment for the function. It also helps them to differentiate gadgets in a crowded marketplace, though most instances of successful convergence are rapidly copied by all competitors.

Finally, convergence can also enable novel applications by combining the component functions in new ways – such as copying with a printer/scanner, automatic telephone dialing with the PDA/phone, and multiplayer gaming with the phone/game console.

ENABLERS OF DIGITAL CONVERGENCE

A key enabler of digital convergence is the progressive digitization of content. Now that vinyl records and audio cassettes have given way to digital compact disks (CDs) almost completely, many other types of traditionally analog content are also undergoing a shift to digital processing and distribution. Thus we have digital radio and television broadcasts, digital recorders on which media can be stored for later listening/viewing, digital still and video photography, digitized voice in mobile phone calls, and online delivery of news services. The main attraction for digitizing originally analog content is that the cost of electronic circuits that play, store, and distribute digitized content is falling at a rapid rate – approximately halving every 1–2 years (this improvement can be traced back to Moore's law – the density of transistors on an integrated circuit doubles every 18 months). Falling costs, reflected in lower prices, boost demand, and the resulting economies of scale drive costs down even further.

Until recently, the voice telephone network used to transmit analog voice and high-speed computer networks to carry digital data developed independently of each other, except perhaps for modems that transformed digital data into and out of analog format for transmission on phone lines. Cable TV networks, where available, were also analog networks laid for the express purpose of carrying television programming into the home. In the age of digital convergence, digitized content including voice and video can be transported over digital networks, bypassing the purpose-built analog networks. For instance, voice-over-IP telephony carries digitized voice over the INTERNET rather than existing phone lines. To survive, traditional analog networks have transformed themselves into conduits for digital data, phone lines and cable TV outlets turning into broadband connections (DSL and cable, respectively) to the ubiquitous Internet. The combination of increasing network bandwidth (mainly through the use of optical fiber instead of copper wires) and sophisticated data compression techniques has enabled the transmission of digital sound, images, and video in real time over these networks. Over time, the once sharp distinction between analog and digital networks has blurred to the point of irrelevance. Of course, the new generation of wireless telephone and data networks has been designed from the start to carry digital data.

Not only is digital information cheaper to process, store, and distribute, but it is also easier to manipulate through computer programs (software). When pictures, sounds, and moving video images are all similarly represented in the form of bits (1s and 0s), software can be used to transform and combine such information in innovative ways. A digital photograph can be imparted a blue tint through image-processing software, an operation that used to require expensive filter lenses in the past. Software can overlay a piece of digital music as a soundtrack on a digital video, with the original sound accompanying the moving images enhanced or muted. Software processing enables effects such as the transition between sounds or images that were difficult or even impossible to achieve with analog equipment. On the other hand, computer manipulation of pictures, sound, and video can transform them so subtly that the authenticity of media has become a contentious issue in modern journalism.

The three main enablers of digital convergence described above are the falling cost of digital circuitry, the rise of high-speed digital networks, and the availability of software to manipulate content more cheaply and flexibly than hardware-based approaches.

CONSEQUENCES OF DIGITAL CONVERGENCE

The marketplace today is abuzz with converged products: printers/scanners/copiers/fax, phone/PDA/camera, and so on. Once the functionality of these converged devices passes the minimum acceptable threshold, they start to threaten conventional single-purpose devices. The standalone PDA market is facing significant competition from phone/PDA hybrids, and digital cameras might be the next to be threatened by camera/phones. Aided by competition that forces prices down, the consumer obtains access to a broad array of functions through small (sometimes portable) multifunction devices. Of course, the ultimate convergent device is perhaps the desktop PC, which has acquired capabilities in a wide variety of functions – music and video playback, media editing and encoding, sound mixing and music composition, home automation, and video gaming (single-player as well as multiplayer). Conscious of the versatile position of the PC in the space of convergent devices, many PC makers are dropping the traditional beige and boxy appearance for more sleek and stylish looks, preparing the PC for a place in the living room next to conventional entertainment devices such as stereos and TVs.

The value of the digital content flowing through communication and distribution networks (such as telephone and cable TV networks) has tempted infrastructure providers to enter the business of providing content. To date, success in the content production business has eluded most of these infrastructure providers.

Many new services are being launched to capitalize on the opportunities presented by digital convergence. Multimedia messaging service (MMS) providers anticipate a world where consumers move up from text messaging to exchanging pictures and media clips captured with their camera/phones. Mobile online gaming, touted by many as a prominent application on 3G wireless networks, is predicated on the success of the convergence of the mobile phone with the handheld game console. Digital radio and TV broadcasts have plans to go "interactive" so that listeners and viewers can access additional customized content through options embedded in broadcast content.

The digitization of all content has been accompanied by problems in protecting the intellectual property rights of those who develop content. It is as simple to copy a piece of music or a movie as it is to copy any other computer file. Pervasive broadband networks make it easy to traffic in stolen intellectual property. In response, businesses that produce content have tried to place tight restrictions on the distribution and consumption of content owned by them. Whether such restrictions conflict with the rights of legitimate paying customers is often a matter of dispute. The amicable resolution of intellectual property disputes is likely

to be a key factor in the progress of digital convergence.

Bibliography

Yoffie, D. B. (ed.) (1997). *Competing in the Age of Digital Convergence*. Boston: Harvard Business School Press.

digital divide

Frederick J. Riggins

The digital divide is a phrase used to describe the separation that exists between those who have access to digital information and communications technology (ICT) and those who do not. The phrase typically is used to highlight the view that certain individuals are not able to obtain access to personal computers or the INTERNET owing to a variety of factors, including socioeconomic status, age, place of residence, level of education, adeptness with technology, and social associations. While some factors may be beyond the control of the individual, the phrase has also been applied to those who have an aversion to technology and so choose, for one reason or another, not to make use of ICT. There are significant differences in digital divide among countries. For example, the Scandinavian countries have the highest access, while poor countries have the lowest access and largest digital divide.

ISSUES AND CONTROVERSIES: THE US EXAMPLE

During the 1990s the digital divide took on political and public policy implications in the US as certain groups and policy-makers claimed that many individuals were being left behind in the digital revolution and would have trouble catching up in a technically advanced society. Not having access to digital information and communications technology would result in certain people having less access to information in general, and thereby cause disconnected individuals to lag behind educationally, economically, socially, and democratically. This led to calls for public subsidization of access to the Internet through schools or public libraries, or for financial incentives for certain households to invest in personal computers and Internet access. Just as the government adopted a universal telephone policy in the early twentieth century, there were appeals for a policy encouraging universal Internet service at the close of the century. At the same time, others argued that no such digital divide existed, or, if it did, that it would diminish over time without public assistance as the technology advanced and society became more saturated with ICT.

In July 1995, the US Department of Commerce issued a report entitled "Falling Through the Net: A Survey of the 'Have Nots' in Rural and Urban America." Not surprisingly, this study found that computer ownership rose dramatically with income. However, the study showed that within an income category, those located in rural areas were much less likely to own computers. Similarly, the study found that computer ownership lagged for minorities, seniors, and those with less education. Subsequent studies released over the next few years showed steady adoption rates for personal computers and the Internet, but with the same gaps occurring in certain demographic categories ("A nation online: Internet use in America," www.ntia.doc.gov/opadhome/digitalnation/).

In an unbiased effort to clarify the issue and further determine the extent of the divide, the Pew Internet and American Life Project was initiated in the late 1990s with the objective of creating and funding research that would examine the impact of the Internet on individuals and American society. The project began releasing periodic research reports on a variety of issues related to its mission in early 2000. In addition to studies that examine how people in different demographic profiles use the Internet, studies also address issues that include habits regarding downloading music, individuals' views of online trust and privacy, why people choose to not go online, and the impact of the Internet on political activities, the practice of religious faith, and personal relationships (these reports can be downloaded from www.pewinternet.org). A Pew report released in April 2003 ("The ever-shifting Internet populations: A new look at Internet access and the digital divide," www.pewinternet.org/reports/pdfs/PIP_Shifting_Net_Pop_Report.pdf.) found that

- those with higher incomes are far more likely to be online than lower-income individuals, causing the report to state "independent of all other factors, having an income above $50,000 annually predicts Internet use";
- the percentage of whites and Hispanics who have online access is about 6 to 12 percent higher than African Americans with similar education;
- 82 percent of college graduates use the Internet, but only 45 percent of those with a high school diploma are online; and
- of non-Internet users, half are over age 50, compared with just 14 percent being between 18 and 29.

From a managerial perspective, the concept of the digital divide encompasses much more than those who do and do not have access to the Internet. Whatis.com defines the digital divide as a term that "describes the fact that the world can be divided into people who do and people who don't have access to – and the capability to use – modern information technology, such as the telephone, television, or the Internet" (whatis.techtarget.com). Even for those individuals who have access to the Internet, a divide exists between those who make use of many of the more advanced features associated with online commerce, such as online auctions, configuration of personalized shopping sites, product comparison sites, and high bandwidth functionality, and those who do not make use of such services. For example, in a follow-up study to the one just cited ("America's online pursuits: The changing picture of who's online and what they do," December 2003, www.pewinternet.org), researchers for the Pew Internet and American Life project found that

- females were more likely to seek online health and religious information, while males were more likely to seek online financial, sports, and political information;
- African Americans often use the Internet to do school-related research and seek religious information, while Hispanics were more likely to use instant messaging and download music;
- young people are more likely to do instant messaging and download music, while

seniors are more likely to gather health and government-provided information; and

- those with higher incomes and college degrees were more likely to access government information, do online banking, and engage in online auctions than other people.

Indeed, the earlier Pew Internet report outlines a spectrum of Internet use. For example, in 2002 only about 13 percent of the US population were home broadband users, making for a fairly narrow population segment likely to make use of high-bandwidth services such as music or video downloads. In addition, over 40 percent of those considered to be not online had some experience with the Internet and were classified as either "net evaders," defined as those who avoid using the Internet but have someone close to them do their online tasks for them, or "net dropouts," who have tried but then discontinued use of the Internet for various reasons. Even of those who were considered to be online, nearly half may simply be "intermittent users."

THE INTERNATIONAL DIGITAL DIVIDE

In a 2003 report by two economists from the World Bank, Carsten Fink and Charles Kenny note that we should distinguish between an *international digital divide*, where there are measurable between-country differences in access, and a *domestic digital divide* measured as within-country differences ("W(h)ither the digital divide?" January 2003, www.itu.int/wsis/docs/background/themes/digital_divide/fink-kenny.pdf). Their report confirms that an international digital divide exists; however, the extent of the gap is a matter of interpretation. They point out that there is an obvious divide in terms of number of mobile and fixed telephone lines per capita, or teledensity, where high-income countries boast more phone lines than people, while there are three telephones per 100 people in developing countries. Further, about one in three people in high-income countries use the Internet, while penetration is about 0.4 percent in low-income countries. However, their study shows that the gap is closing for both teledensity and Internet use, as the adoption rates for both are higher in developing countries than the more saturated developed nations. In addition, they find that developing nations have actually surpassed use in developed countries when usage is measured using a per income measure of access to telephones and the Internet.

THE ORGANIZATIONAL DIGITAL DIVIDE

In addition to the between- and within-country distinction, it is also important to note that these differences in access, ability, usage, and resulting impact of ICT can occur between organizations, or what we might call an *organizational digital divide*. At the organizational level, some organizations use IT to gain advantage over their rivals and redefine the rules of engagement within their industry, while others lag behind as technological followers, putting themselves at a strategic disadvantage. Innovative organizations that make use of information and communications technology may do so for a variety of reasons, including visionary top management, a better-educated workforce, proprietary patents and copyrights, or threats from competitive pressures, just to name a few.

For those in the management and policy communities, the existence of the digital divide should have a profound impact on how firms compete globally, the creation of the information age organization, and the diffusion of online commerce, strategies for offering online services, and policies for promoting access to IT and the Internet. Further measurement of the phenomenon at the national level, the corporate level, and the individual level is needed to confirm changes in adoption and usage trends and the overall impact of the divide on society and competition.

digital products

see INFORMATION GOODS

digital rights management

William J. Caelli

Digital rights management (DRM) refers to any scheme that is used to protect copyright ownership in any digital product or system. It usually refers to products from the entertainment industry, such as audio digital recordings on compact disk (CD), movies on digital versatile disk (DVD), and others. However, this is not the only use of the term as the protection of copyright and other rights to intellectual property can be of note for any individual person or enterprise. Thus DRM is of importance, for example, in the protection of correspondence produced electronically, of user manuals and like documents produced to support some other product or service, governmental papers, and so on. In this more general usage the term encompasses many aspects of traditional security activity, such as the classification of documents into various levels such as "secret," as well as the use of related copyright protection mechanisms, such as password restrictions placed on electronic documents that control the ability to modify or even print a document, and so on.

The term implies that the owner of the rights in a digital product wishes to have those rights respected and enforced. It also implies that the owner will use some technological or other mechanism to enable such enforcement to be possible and that those mechanisms will be honored by the end user of the product and incorporated into any device used to "read" the copyright materials.

In some jurisdictions it has become illegal, for example, to tamper with or remove any system that enforces such copyright, e.g., the US's Digital Millennium Copyright Act (DMCA), let alone make illicit and unauthorized copies of the digital material itself.

digital signatures

Joel R. Helgeson

Information systems have changed the nature of many business documents. Documents are converted to digital codes before storage or processing. Paper documents can be inscribed with evidence of authenticity by signatures, initials, stamps, and other marking. Digital documents presented on video displays or printed from the digital representations require alternative methods of authentication. Digital signatures are a method of authenticating digital information.

When parties to a transaction agree to use electronic authentication, the electronic signature is as valid as one created with pen and paper. The validity of these signatures is supported by laws and court cases in most countries. For example, both the US and UK have laws for digital signatures: the Digital Signature and Electronic Authentication Law of 1998 (US) and the Electronic Communications Act 2000 (UK).

The terms electronic signature and digital signature are often used interchangeably; however, there is an important difference. Electronic signatures generally refer to signatures that can be delivered by fax, or a signature on paper that has been transmitted using electronic means. Digital signatures commonly refer to cryptographic AUTHENTICATION of an electronic transaction or document (*see* CRYPTOGRAPHY (CRYPTO)).

Most digital signatures rely on public key cryptography, which is built upon the public key infrastructure (PKI). This is a system by which users can be definitively identified by means of a trusted third party. These trusted third parties are referred to simply as certificate authorities (CA) and are analogous to notary publics for the digital domain. These CAs issue cryptographically unique digital certificates to individuals and companies once they have proved their identities and paid a nominal fee.

When a CA issues a certificate, it is actually issuing a pair of cryptographic keys. One key is a public key and the other is a private key. The purchaser of the keys retains the private key and uses it to decrypt messages that have been encrypted using the public key. A vital element of the process is that the public key can only be used to encrypt data and therefore it can be freely distributed to anyone who wishes to encrypt a message destined for the private key owner. The private key can only be used to decrypt data and therefore the private key must be kept private by the person or organization authorized to receive and decrypt (and thereby authenticate) messages. The key pairs can be authenticated at any time by checking with the CA.

As a practical example, if Bob and Alice wanted to exchange secret messages, Alice must obtain Bob's public key, from Bob or the CA, and use it to encrypt messages she sends to him. Conversely, if Alice wishes to receive encrypted messages, she must obtain her own set of keys, and send the public key to Bob. If Alice wishes to authenticate the messages she sends to the public, she can use her key to digitally sign the message. The message itself is sent in clear text combined with a digital signature. This signature provides proof of the source and can also prove that the message itself has not been altered. The validity of the signature itself can be verified by the CA as having come from Alice, and no one else, thereby preventing repudiation of the message.

But what if you don't need a notary, you just need a "witness"? You can create your own digital certificate. The drawback to this is the lack of the trusted third party, the CA. Anyone wanting to verify that you were in fact the original signer of the document in question must send the document back to you in order to see if the cryptographic signatures match.

disintermediation

see E-COMMERCE

distributed systems

Sangkyu Rho

A distributed system is a collection of computer systems that are interconnected within a communication network and that provide users and applications transparent access to data, computational power, and other computing resources. With the advances in communication networks such as the INTERNET, most computer systems including PCs are connected to some kind of network. Therefore, it is not unreasonable to state that most computer systems are distributed systems to some extent. However, we cannot call networked computers a distributed system.

WHAT IS A DISTRIBUTED SYSTEM?

The term distributed system has been applied to systems with widely different structures and characteristics (e.g., computer network, multiprocessor system). Rather than trying to pre-cisely define the term, we describe a distributed system by answering the following questions: (1) What is being distributed? (2) What are the characteristics of a distributed system? and (3) What are some examples of distributed systems?

What is being distributed? The definition of a distributed system assumes that multiple computers or *processing units* are connected via some communication network. A processing unit is an autonomous computer system including central processing unit (CPU), storage, and operating system. In addition to processing units, the following could be distributed.

1 *Process*: Processes of applications may be divided into subsets and distributed to a number of processing units. For example, in web-based order processing systems, processes are distributed over web servers, application servers, database servers, credit authorization servers of a credit card company, etc.
2 *Data*: Data used by applications may be distributed to a number of processing units. For example, on the worldwide web (WWW) data or information are distributed to a huge number of computers across the world.

Characteristics of a distributed system. Although difficult to define, a distributed system in general has the following characteristics:

1 multiple, possibly heterogeneous processing units;
2 electronically connected via a communication network (e.g., LAN, Internet, etc.);
3 single-system image providing transparent access to at least some of its resources (e.g., file, application); and
4 significant interaction among processing units.

As processes and data are distributed to multiple processing units, coordination is required to provide adequate services. If the services can be provided to users without much interaction between processing units (i.e., communication and coordination between units), it would be difficult to call such a system "distributed."

Such coordination should be transparent to users. Transparency is the key to a distributed system. Ideally, users should not see a distributed system at all. They should see a single system that provides a number of services and resources. They should not have to know where the resources are in order to accomplish their tasks. In reality, this ideal situation is not typically achieved and users are aware that they are using a distributed system.

Examples of distributed systems. Figure 1 shows a peer-to-peer system such as Napster. In this system, a huge number of PCs are interconnected via the Internet to share data such as music files. Is this a distributed system? This system has multiple processing units. It has a single-system view to a certain extent since users can get the data they want without knowing where they are stored. There are interactions among PCs to share data. Therefore, it is a distributed system.

Figure 2 shows a GRID system where a number of geographically distributed supercomputers, data archive systems, and sensors are connected via a high-speed network to solve complex problems such as weather forcasts and human genome projects. This system has multiple processing units. There are interactions among processing units to share processing power and storage. Does it have a single-system view? Ideally, it does. However, in most cases programs must be written to distribute the work among processing units. Therefore, a current GRID system may not be an ideal distributed system. We, however, consider a GRID system as a distributed system.

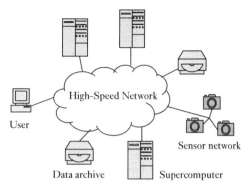

Figure 2 A GRID system

Figure 3 shows a distributed database system where the database is stored at several computers (i.e., database servers). In this system, users can write a query against the database as if it were stored at a single computer. If the data required by a retrieval request are located at the requesting node, then only local accessing and processing are needed. However, if some needed data are not located at the requesting server, then data must be accessed from, and possibly processed at, other servers. Is this a distributed system? There are multiple processing units and they are interconnected via a communication network. Users see only one database. If the user's query requires data that are stored at more than one server, the servers must cooperate to answer the query. This is clearly a distributed system.

COMPONENTS OF A DISTRIBUTED SYSTEM

A distributed system consists of several components. These include network, directory service, file system, security system, etc.

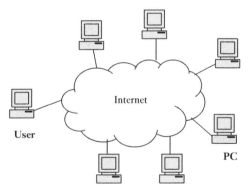

Figure 1 A peer-to-peer system

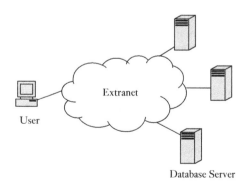

Figure 3 A distributed database system

Network. In order to provide transparency, processing units must be able to communicate with one another. A network provides such a mechanism. A computer network consists of a set of computer systems, termed *nodes*, interconnected via communication *links*. It allows multiple computers to exchange data and share resources (e.g., printer).

Given a set of nodes, the network topology defines how these nodes are connected. Examples of network topologies are meshed, star, bus, and ring topologies. The links in a network can utilize different technologies and have varying speeds and channel capacities.

Distributed directory service. In addition to being connected, a distributed system must know where resources are located. Finding resources (e.g., data and application) in a distributed system is the task of the directory service. It must map a large number of system objects (e.g., files, functions, printers, etc.) to user-oriented names. A distributed directory service makes distribution transparent to users. Users do not have to know the location of a remote file, application, or printer.

Distributed file system. A distributed file system provides transparent access to any files on the network. It utilizes a directory service to locate files. To enhance retrieval efficiency, files can be redundantly stored at multiple nodes. Such redundancy increases the complexity of a file system. If there are multiple copies of the same file, the file system first locates its copies using the directory service and must determine how and where read-only access will be performed. Furthermore, consistency among multiple copies of data must be maintained by the file system as the files are updated. Concurrency control/recovery mechanisms are responsible for maintaining consistency among multiple copies of the same file.

WHY DISTRIBUTE?

Distributed systems can yield significant cost and performance advantages over centralized systems for organizations. These advantages include improved system performance (i.e., response time), reduced system costs, improved reliability/availability, and scalability.

System performance can be improved by exploiting the parallelism inherent in distributed systems. Furthermore, massively distributed systems can achieve system performance that no single central computer can achieve.

Reliability/availability is improved since system crashes or link failures do not cause a total system failure. Even though some of the resources may be inaccessible, distributed systems can still provide limited service. If the same resources are provided by more than one node, reliability/availability is further improved, since only one of the nodes providing the resources needs to be available.

Scalability is improved. In a distributed environment, it is much easier to accommodate increases in system capacity. Major system overhauls are seldom necessary. Expansion can usually be handled by adding processing and storage power to the network.

However, there are several disadvantages. Distributed systems are much more complex than centralized systems. First of all, there are many more components in distributed systems. Therefore, distributed systems can be quite difficult to implement and manage.

Maintaining adequate security can be a serious problem. Since users as well as resources are distributed, maintaining security over the network is much more difficult than in a centralized environment.

A distributed system is a collection of autonomous, not necessarily homogeneous processing units that are interconnected via a communication network. It is more than a network. It must provide users with transparent access to its applications, files, and so on. Ideally, users should not see the difference between a centralized system and a distributed system.

Bibliography

Ozsu, M. and Valduriez, P. (1999). *Principles of Distributed Database Systems*, 2nd edn. Upper Saddle River, NJ: Prentice-Hall.

Tanenbaum, A. S. and van Steen, M. (2002). *Distributed Systems: Principles and Paradigms.* Upper Saddle River, NJ: Prentice-Hall.

document image processing systems

Andrew P. Jansma

An electronic document image processing system is a computer-based system that converts the contents of paper or microfilm documents to digitized images that can be viewed at a computer workstation. The digitized images can be held and manipulated in the memory of the computer, stored on magnetic or optical disk storage media, transmitted over networks and communications lines, and converted back to a paper image by a laser printer.

The electronic document image processing system, as illustrated in figure 1, includes a scanner to convert a paper image to a digitized image, a computer with sufficient memory and monitor graphics capability to hold and display digitized images, a magnetic or optical media drive to store images for processing and retrieval, and a laser printer. Additional hardware components may include network interfaces, erasable optical drives, optical jukeboxes, digital cameras, and other output devices.

ACQUISITION

Documents are entered into the system by a scanner. The scanner is operated much like a paper copier machine. The scanner converts the figures on paper or microfilm to a sequence of binary codes representing the presence or absence of dots or pixels of ink on the paper or microfilm. Currently, 300 pixels per inch is deemed sufficient to retain the information in the documents, but scanner technology is advancing in parallel with printer technology, so documents can be scanned at much higher resolutions, which significantly increases file sizes and storage requirements. The coded image is displayed on a computer workstation to allow the person scanning it to view the image and make adjustments, or rescan the image. When the document is scanned, the image is compressed to reduce storage requirements. All images are compressed for storage and decompressed for viewing.

The standard file format for acquisition of images is TIFF (Tagged Information File Format). This standard has been placed in the public domain. Tools to encode and manipulate the images are widely available in both proprietary and open-source forms.

Another very popular format for electronic document storage is the Adobe Acrobat format, widely recognized by its .pdf file extension.

Adobe Acrobat has two main functions. It extracts the textual and visual information from documents produced by widely used desktop software and displays it in a canonical form that can be widely distributed and viewed using an application that Adobe provides for free.

The Adobe Acrobat tool also allows the capture of a digital print stream of an application and allows it to be viewed with the same application. Generally, files acquired by a scanner are converted from TIFF documents by a one-to-one mapping of the pixels to the Adobe format. This conversion yields no size reduction; the primary benefit from the conversion is the availability of the free viewer. Adobe owns the encoding and viewing technology, and this presents a risk for archival storage since Adobe may choose to adopt a fee for viewing in the future. There is also a technical risk, because Adobe can abandon support for a feature used in the document archive in subsequent releases of both its creation and viewing products.

STORAGE

Other than magnetic media, the most commonly used and economical media for storing the digitized images are optical storage systems. There are currently two types of optical storage systems that are used for image archival:

- WORM or write-once-read-many optical technology is the most popular and is excellent for archiving document images. CD-ROM (compact-disk-read-only-memory) media is the most popular technology for publishing retrieval-only applications. The CD-ROM has large storage capacity and disk writers and readers are inexpensive. DVD (digital versatile disk) is a larger-capacity technology that has evolved through several technologies to sets of standards with relatively inexpensive writers and readers.
- Rewritable or erasable optical technology allows the user to reuse areas of the disk but requires additional protection procedures to protect valuable information. There are erasable technologies available for both CD-ROM and DVD solutions (*see* CD-ROM AND DVD).

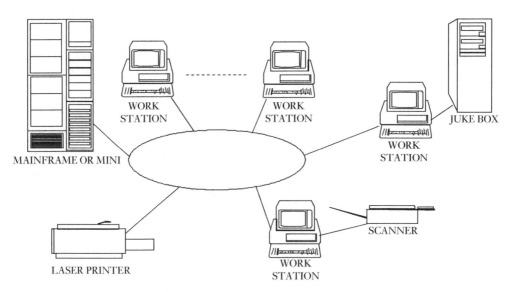

Figure 1   An example image processing management system

INDEXING

Computer indexes are prepared for easy and rapid retrieval of documents. The indexes are often stored in databases with links to the document images. It is common to have two or more different indexing schemes to facilitate retrieval using different methods. Some systems have optical character recognition (OCR) capability to convert the digitized representation of characters to text. This allows the system to create a full test image, to automatically index the document by keywords in the text, or by specific fields in a form document.

BENEFITS OF A DOCUMENT IMAGING SYSTEM

The technology offers an opportunity to reduce labor costs and improve service, but many of these savings come from the review and redesign of the way information is represented, processed, and disseminated through an organization. Analysis includes document management and workflow automation. The process can help redefine activities and make the entire organization more productive. To effectively implement a document image, the organization's processes should be studied to determine opportunities for more efficient and productive ways to distribute electronic information throughout the organization.

An effective document image processing system offers numerous benefits to users. Some of the benefits include:

- reduced storage space compared to storage of paper files;
- elimination of the need to refile microfilm and paper documents after use, which also eliminates misfiling or losing important documents;
- all users can have immediate access to the document;
- worker productivity is increased by allowing users to share a document image with others and allows them to work with the same document at the same time;
- documents can be easily faxed or mailed electronically to remote locations.

Document image processing technology historically has been limited to large corporations, government entities, and other large organizations because of the cost and proprietary nature of each system. The development of more powerful personal computers and local area network (LAN) systems has led to the design of inexpensive desktop-based document image systems. Today, an organization can purchase the image processing hardware for a few thousand dollars. Many organizations already have computer hardware that can be integrated in the system, further reducing the cost.

Industry experts (www.iaphc.org/news/tmn/archive/2002/feb1/) have reported that organizations spend from 10 to 15 percent of their annual revenue on production, distribution, and storage of documents. Through better management of their imaging and printing environment, businesses can reduce these costs significantly.

Document imaging systems support document retention and retrieval requirements of governments and regulatory authorities. For example, the systems are used to maintain archives of public corporation financial documents and internal control documentation.

dot.com

see E-COMMERCE

DVD

see CD-ROM AND DVD

E

e-commerce

Alina M. Chircu

When an enterprise engages in electronic commerce, the information systems function must provide the organization with specialized communications and information processing capabilities for this method of commerce. These capabilities are reflected in the information technology (IT) infrastructure, applications, operations, and support staff that are the responsibility of the information systems (IS) function.

DEFINITIONS

E-commerce, also called electronic commerce or EC, is the "use of electronic means and technologies to conduct commerce" (Choi, Stahl, and Whinston, 1997). E-commerce encompasses the delivery of information, products, and services, and payments over electronic networks, as well as the automation of the supporting business transactions and workflows (Kalakota and Whinston, 1997). Some authors differentiate e-commerce initiatives, focused on individual business transactions, from e-business initiatives, defined as any tactical or strategic initiative that transforms business relationships. E-commerce can therefore be thought of as one of the many ways firms can use electronic networks to generate and exploit new business opportunities and drive efficiencies, speed, and innovation in their quest for new value creation (Kalakota and Whinston, 1997).

E-commerce electronic networks consist of interconnected physical electronic networks such as wired and wireless telephone networks, local area networks (LAN), wide area networks (WAN), and the Internet. Electronic devices such as personal computers, web servers, personal digital assistants (PDAs), mobile phones, and vending machines enable consumers and businesses to connect with one another using these networks and a specialized software infrastructure consisting of communication protocols, applications, and standards.

TYPES OF E-COMMERCE

Central to the idea of electronic commerce is the business transaction, or exchange between a buyer and a seller. E-commerce transactions can be classified based on the identity of the buyer and the seller: individual consumers, businesses, or governments. Some of the most general types of e-commerce transactions are:

- *Business to consumer (B2C)*: These transactions describe situations where consumers acquire products, services, or information from firms online, either directly or through an intermediary such as an online retailer. Examples include purchasing books from Amazon.com (www.amazon.com) or apparel from Land's End (www.landsend.com), downloading digital music from Apple's iTunes service (www.apple.com/itunes/), ordering flowers through 1-800-flowers (www.1800flowers.com), buying computers and accessories from Dell, Inc. (www.dell.com), solving computer problems using online technical support tools (support.dell.com/), and renting movies from Netflix (www.netflix.com). In 2002, 73 million US consumers engaged in B2C transactions, generating $76 billion in sales, 3 percent of total US sales (Plunkett Research, 2004).
- *Business to business (B2B)*: These transactions involve exchanges of goods and services among firms through specialized

ELECTRONIC DATA INTERCHANGE

(EDI) links or online marketplaces such as Covisint (www.covisint.com) or Ariba Supplier Network (service.ariba.com/Supplier.aw). According to estimates by Gartner, worldwide B2B sales reached $1.9 trillion in 2002 and are expected to grow to $8.5 trillion by 2005 (Plunkett Research, 2004).

- *Business to government (B2G)*: This involves businesses selling information, goods, and services to government entities. E-commerce procurement of goods and services, an area receiving much attention lately from local and state governments, fits into this category.

- *Consumer to consumer (C2C)*: This refers to situations where consumers buy and sell goods, services, and information among themselves, usually with the help of an intermediary firm. Online auctions such as eBay (www.ebay.com) are the most popular form of C2C e-commerce. In 2002, 22 million US consumers participated in online auctions (Plunkett Research, 2004). In 2003, eBay, the leading auction provider in the US, listed 5.23 billion items and attracted 21 percent of all US INTERNET users (Plunkett Research, 2004). Another emerging C2C model is the online marketplace model. For example, Amazon.com allows individual sellers to list items for sale next to Amazon's own product listings. Other examples of C2C e-commerce include peer-to-peer (P2P) file-sharing networks such as KaZaA (www.kazaa.com) and online communities such as iVillage (www.ivillage.com).

- *Consumer to business (C2B)*: This refers to situations where firms acquire information, services, and even goods from consumers, or where consumers name their own price for a firm's products. Examples of the former include consumers participating in online market research activities or providing reviews of a firm's products and services, while examples of the latter include consumers bidding for travel services using Priceline's reservation system (www.priceline.com).

- *Government to consumer (G2C)*: This refers to situations where citizens obtain information and government services online. Currently, about 10 percent of Internet users in the US connect to government websites (Plunkett Research, 2004). Renewing a driver's license, paying parking tickets, viewing and paying utility bills are services now offered by many state governments in the US and similar services are starting to be offered online around the world. For example, Hong Kong's portal (www.esd.gov.hk/home/chi/default.asp) is one of the many G2C e-commerce developments to date.

- *Government to business (G2B)*: This refers to situations where businesses interact with government entities online for services such as paying sales taxes or obtaining various business permits and occupational licenses. As in the case of G2C e-commerce, such services are now offered by many governments around the world.

INTERMEDIATION AND E-COMMERCE

Another way of describing e-commerce transactions is by analyzing how the transaction is performed: directly between buyer and seller or through an intermediary that helps connect buyers and sellers and facilitate the transaction. For example, an online auction provider such as eBay acts as an intermediary for C2C e-commerce transactions, enabling the seller and buyer to list and respectively view product description, process payments, and manage the seller-rating mechanism that enables buyers to evaluate sellers based on performance of past transactions. A retailer connecting to its suppliers through specialized EDI links provides another example of direct B2B e-commerce transactions. In a similar vein, B2C book shopping over the Internet could be characterized as a direct e-commerce transaction if the unit of analysis is the interaction between a retailer such as Amazon.com and an individual consumer, or as intermediated if the unit of analysis is the interaction between a book publisher and an individual consumer, in which case the interaction is mediated by an intermediary such as the e-commerce retailer Amazon.com.

Intermediaries exist because buyers and sellers interested in trading among themselves have traditionally encountered a range of transactions costs associated with identifying suitable trading partners, negotiating the terms of the contract, and fulfilling the terms of the contract. Because emerging e-commerce technologies were hypothesized to reduce, sometimes significantly, these transactions costs, researchers have proposed that traditional intermediaries will be disintermediated, either by total elimination or replacement with e-commerce firms. Both e-commerce practitioners and researchers have come to recognize that intermediaries still have important transaction support roles in e-commerce, such as setting prices, coordinating, monitoring, and processing transactions, managing inventories, providing quality guarantees, lowering the probability of an unsuccessful transaction, and reducing the time required to find a suitable trading partner. In fact, e-commerce seems to create both disintermediation opportunities, where e-commerce entrants try to replace traditional intermediaries, and reintermediation opportunities, where traditional players adopt e-commerce capabilities and compete against their e-commerce opponents. For example, in B2B e-commerce transactions such as corporate travel reservations, e-commerce entrants such as Sabre BTS and GetThere.com, formerly ITN (www.getthere. com), have initially disintermediated traditional travel agencies such as American Express (home. americanexpress.com/home/corporations. shtml) and Carlson Wagonlit Travel (www. carlsonwagonlit.com/) by offering e-commerce travel reservations for reduced fees. However, the powerful travel agencies have successfully reintermediated by offering e-commerce travel reservations themselves along their traditional phone reservation services (Chircu and Kauffman, 2000a, b).

E-Commerce Transactions

In order to understand the technological and managerial issues associated with e-commerce, is it also useful to analyze e-commerce transactions from the perspective of individual transaction phases (Kalakota and Whinston, 1997):

- Pre-purchase intentions, which include product search, comparison shopping, and negotiation of transaction terms.
- Purchase consummation, which includes order placement, payment authorization, and product receipt.

- Post-purchase interaction, which includes customer service and support.

Each of these individual phases poses different technological and management challenges to buyers and sellers, as discussed in the following sections.

E-Commerce Applications

The success of e-commerce depends on the availability of appropriate communication, transaction facilitation, and e-commerce software applications that support each step of an e-commerce transaction, from the initial contact between a buyer and a seller until the final delivery of the product from the seller to the buyer and the provision of service and support.

For sellers, e-commerce technologies provide support in the following areas:

- Describe e-commerce offerings using protocols such as HTTP (hypertext transfer protocol) and XML (see XML (EXTENSIBLE MARKUP LANGUAGE)). HTTP provides a way of delivering information and application programs on web pages (see MARKUP LANGUAGES). XML combines the capabilities of HTTP with additional data-structuring abilities that allow the creation of web pages with embedded attributes – in fact, a page's own markup that could be used to automate data input, output, storage, and communication.
- Publish e-commerce content. Portal applications deliver personalized e-commerce content and applications to the end user, thus supporting the pre-purchase steps of the transaction. Content management tools enable firms to manage and publish on the web content gathered from various other business information systems in a consistent manner. Collaboration tools enable joint work on common projects and information sharing.
- Advertise e-commerce products and services. Sellers can advertise their e-commerce offerings either manually, by listing themselves with search engines or with aggregator sites, usually for a fee, or automatically, using WEB SERVICES. Web services are an emerging set of e-commerce communication

standards that include protocols for automated communication among e-commerce applications offered by a variety of providers. Using web services, sellers can automatically advertise their presence to potential buyers using the Universal Description, Discovery, and Integration (UDDI) protocol. UDDI "is one of the major building blocks required for successful web services. UDDI creates a standard interoperable platform that enables companies and applications to quickly, easily, and dynamically find and use web services over the Internet" (www.uddi.org).

- Sell. Relevant activities related to the selling process include inventory management, ordering, payment, fulfillment, and privacy and security guarantees. The following technologies provide support for these activities. Commerce servers are application systems that support e-commerce transaction steps such as display of information about products and services, online ordering, communication with online payment systems for payment processing, and inventory management. Settlement mechanisms insure the payment is correctly and securely processed. CUSTOMER RELATIONSHIP MANAGEMENT (CRM), enterprise resource planning (see ENTERPRISE SYSTEMS (ENTERPRISE RESOURCE PLANNING OR ERP)), and supply chain management (SCM) systems enable sellers to automate their customer-facing, internal, and supplier-facing processes.

- Service. E-commerce enables sellers to provide instant, online customer service and support through a variety of applications. The most widely used procedure of customer support is listing all known problems, solutions, or customer questions on the seller's website, where buyers can easily access them without interacting with the seller. More recently, sellers have begun to use automated intelligent agents and customer support agents that can accept a written question from the buyer and provide a written or voice-based response, while also guiding the buyer to web pages on the seller's site that can provide more support. Buyers can also interact with live customer

support agents through instant messaging (IM) technology and callback technology. IM enables buyers to type in messages on the seller's website and receive quick written responses from human customer service representatives. Callback applications enable buyers to request a call from a human customer service representative. All these customer service technologies eliminate the need for buyers to visit or call the seller and possibly have to wait until a customer service representative becomes available.

For buyers, the most relevant e-technologies in support of e-commerce transactions are:

- Search technologies. These include general search engines such as Google (www.google. com) or Yahoo! (www.yahoo.com), specialized shopping search engines such as Froogle (www.froogle.com) that enable Internet-wide product searches, and comparison shopping services such as MySimon (www.mysimon.com) and DealTime (www. dealtime.com), online auctions such as eBay (www.ebay.com), and online marketplaces such as Yahoo! Shopping (shopping.yahoo. com/) that allow users to search for specific products from registered sellers.

- Evaluation technologies. These e-commerce applications enable buyers to sample products before purchasing in order to facilitate the product evaluation. They include 2D and 3D virtual product tours, comparison matrixes that enable buyers to compare the characteristics of several products side by side, virtual models that enable buyers to try on clothes and other accessories on virtual models built based on the buyer's specifications – such as Land's End's virtual model (www.landsend.com), and sampling technologies that enable buyers to listen to digitized CD songs or browse digitized books.

- AUTHENTICATION and security technologies. Authentication and security mechanisms verify the identities of the parties involved in the transaction and keep the transaction information secure. Because buyers usually transmit sensitive personal and payment information over the Internet, the misuse of that information needs to be prevented both during transmission and upon receipt. Protocols such as Secure Sockets Layer (SSL) and Secure HTTP (S-HTTP) insure secure data transmission. Trust mechanisms such as Better Business Bureau (www.bbb.org/) or TRUSTe (www.truste.org/) seal of approval enable buyers to evaluate the risk of a potential transaction with unknown sellers.

E-Commerce Management Issues

From a buyer's perspective, e-commerce technologies reduce significantly the cost of e-commerce transactions and have the potential of offering lower prices than in traditional transactions as well. Using e-commerce technologies, buyers can potentially consider a greater number of suppliers, obtain more product information, and compare offerings from multiple sellers in a shorter amount of time than in a traditional commerce environment. As a result, e-commerce can decrease information asymmetries between buyers and sellers and increase competition among sellers, resulting in lower e-commerce prices in general and lower price dispersion online. Recent B2C studies have proved that these effects occur to some extent in certain situations, such as in markets for books, cars, and insurance, among others. However, other studies show that consumers prefer to pay price premiums in order to buy products such as books and used cars from trusted sellers with recognizable brand names. In addition, e-commerce sellers such as online travel agents can target their pricing to specific customer segments, thus avoiding direct price competition. As a result, price differences between online and offline channels and price dispersion in e-commerce still exist. In B2B or B2G settings, e-commerce buying (also called e-procurement or e-purchasing) automates the approval processes and eliminates much of the work, delays, and costs associated with order processing in traditional procurement. It can also encourage price competition among suppliers that participate in the same Internet marketplace (public or private, buyer-supported). It also enables buyers to centralize their procurement spending, effectively increasing their negotiating power with sellers for volume discounts.

Some of the salient e-commerce challenges facing buyers, be they individual consumers, businesses, or governments, are:

- Deciding whether to buy online or use more traditional transaction outlets, such as brick-and-mortar stores or catalogues. When the buyers are individual consumers, this decision usually represents a trade-off between the increased information search and evaluation capabilities offered in e-commerce and the related price savings, on the one hand, and trust, privacy, and security concerns and the inability to handle, try on, or immediately take possession of products once purchased, on the other hand. When the buyers are businesses or governments, this decision is justified by analyzing the potential price and time savings associated with procuring goods and services using e-commerce transactions rather than paper, phone, or fax orders.

- Deciding what type of e-commerce transaction structure to use. The choices here are between buying from a retailer or other type of intermediary and connecting with sellers directly (as discussed above), and between using a fixed-price or an auction-price model (see Internet auctions).

- Searching for, evaluating, and selecting among products that fit the buyer's preferences. Buyer search strategies can focus on identifying the lowest possible price, or on combining price with other desirable product characteristics such as brand based on specific buyer preferences. The quality of the search results, product evaluation, and the final product choice depends on the quality of the search technologies made available to buyers.

From a seller's perspective, e-commerce offers opportunities for businesses to enhance their physical value chain (inbound logistics, production processes, outbound logistics, marketing and sales) with a virtual value chain. Rayport and Sviokla (1995) recommend that in order to succeed at e-commerce, firms should identify physical value chain activities that can be performed faster, more cheaply and efficiently, and with more flexibility online. Apart from just mirroring the physical value chain, companies should also look for new value-added services in the virtual value chain that they can exploit to create competitive advantage. Gathering, organizing, analyzing, and distributing the information from each stage of the physical value chain creates visibility for physical processes and opportunity for value-added virtual processes. E-commerce also enables individual consumers to become sellers with minimal technology investments, through intermediaries such as online marketplaces and auctions that provide the technological trust and payment infrastructure necessary to complete transactions.

Some of the most relevant e-commerce management issues faced by sellers are:

- Deciding what products, services, and information to make available online. A seller may decide only some products are suitable for e-commerce, e.g., non-commodity products that buyers cannot get through traditional means such as brick-and-mortar stores, products with sufficiently high prices so that shipping charges do not appear excessive for buyers, or products that can be easily delivered electronically, such as airline tickets or downloadable music files (*see* INFORMATION GOODS). Through mass customization, e-commerce enables buyers to specify their product preferences and sellers to offer buyers products that fit those preferences, past purchases, or customer profiles obtained by aggregating information from other customers that fit a buyer's profile through technologies such as collaborative filtering.

- Deciding whether to sell only online (as a pure-play e-commerce seller) or to take advantage of possible synergies with an offline channel. For example, the seller may take advantage of its own brick-and-mortar stores or partner with a brick-and-mortar seller to allow buyers to inspect products in store and pick up products in store instead of having them delivered at home. Such synergies can minimize problems created by e-commerce evaluation tools, which cannot perfectly communicate physical product attributes such as color, smell, fit, touch, or feel. Integrating with an offline channel can also min-

imize delivery delays and eliminate operational problems related to individual item fulfillment by allowing buyers to pick up items in a store. However, sellers need to be aware that such integration will also create additional operational burdens on local brick-and-mortar stores due to increased demand from e-commerce orders and returns.

- Deciding whether to sell products directly or through an intermediary. A direct selling model is appealing because e-commerce makes it easy to reach buyers all over the world. However, such a model can create additional costs of managing individual transactions, especially if the seller is used to dealing only with volume purchases from distributors and does not have an operational and fulfillment infrastructure designed to handle individual purchases. Customer acquisition costs could also be prohibitively high if the seller does not have sufficient critical mass to attract buyers. In addition, the direct model may also alienate traditional intermediaries.

- Deciding how to price online products. E-commerce makes it very easy for sellers to change prices more frequently than in traditional settings. Such changes can be part of a seller's own retail strategy using dynamic supply and demand analysis of e-commerce data in real time. Moreover, sellers can monitor pricing changes enacted by competitors on their websites using automated software agents and respond to those changes by adjusting their prices in real time. E-commerce also makes it easy to price product bundles and even offer personalized prices for individual products or product bundles with the goal of revenue maximization. Pricing and selling surplus inventory or capacity without compromising the value of the brand is also enabled in e-commerce through transaction mechanisms that hide the identity of the seller until after the purchase is completed. For example, Priceline (www.priceline.com) and Hotwire (www.hotwire.com) sell heavily discounted hotel rooms and airline tickets without communicating the specific airline or hotel brand to the buyer until the final step of the transaction. E-commerce technologies also make it possible for sellers to use auction mechanisms for price discovery.

See also *e-commerce business-to-business systems; e-commerce clicks and mortar*

Bibliography

Chircu, A. M. and Kauffman, R. J. (2000a). The "eBay of blank": Digital intermediation in electronic commerce. In S. J. Barnes and B. Hunt (eds.), *E-Commerce and V-Business*. Oxford: Butterworth-Heinemann, pp. 45–66.

Chircu, A. M. and Kauffman, R. J. (2000b). Reintermediation strategies in business-to-business electronic commerce. *International Journal of Electronic Commerce*, 4, 4 (Summer), 7–42.

Choi, S.-Y., Stahl, D. O., and Whinston, A. B. (1997). *The Economics of Electronic Commerce*. Basingstoke: Macmillan; www.smartecon.com/products/catalog/eecflyer.asp.

Kalakota, R. and Whinston, A. B. (1997). *Electronic Commerce: A Manager's Guide*. Reading, MA: Addison-Wesley.

Plunkett Research (2004). E-commerce and Internet statistics. In *Plunkett's Companion to the Almanac of American Employers*, pp. 25–44.

Rayport, J. F. and Sviokla, J. J. (1995). Exploiting the virtual value chain. *Harvard Business Review*, 73, 6 (November/December), 75–85.

e-commerce business-to-business systems

Qizhi Dai

Business-to-business (B2B) E-COMMERCE employs computer and communications systems to conduct transactions and exchange information. B2B e-commerce requires specialized systems provided and maintained by the information systems function. In this entry, the term business refers to any organization, private or public, non-profit or for profit, that conducts transactions with other organizations.

B2B e-commerce systems allow businesses to electronically carry out some or all of the following functions involved in inter-business interactions and cooperative activities.

- *Catalogue management* provides a suite of tools to create and manage electronic product catalogues, including consistently organize and classify product data from various suppliers and in heterogeneous formats.
- *Requisition and ordering* applications serve businesses in automating their procurement processes from requisition, approval, and purchasing to receiving.
- *Order management* applications are deployed on the supplier side to enable customers to place orders, generate quotations, and check order status and inventory level.
- *Trading* services are often used for spot buying, and include auctions, reverse auctions, and requests for quote. These services are designed to match demand and supply through dynamic trading and negotiating processes.
- *Transaction settlement* includes electronic billing and payment applications and services for transportation arrangements.
- *Supply chain management* enables businesses to collaborate on setting goals and performance measurement, forecasting demand and sales, planning production, and managing inventory.
- *Project collaboration* provides a central platform and repository accessible to project participants including vendors and external partners. The major functions include project management, communication management, document management, team membership management, and project reporting.

Four major B2B e-commerce systems have evolved to support electronic transactions, information exchange, and cooperative activities between businesses: EDI systems, extranets (*see* EXTRANET), e-procurement systems, and B2B e-marketplaces.

EDI systems. Before the arrival of the INTERNET, businesses leased direct lines or hired value-added networks (VANs) to build up inter-business electronic communication networks. A VAN is a networking service provider that leases communication lines to subscribers and offers such extra services as security, guaranteed message delivery, message buffer, and error detection.

Through these systems, B2B transactions are conducted by exchanging business data computer to computer in a standardized format, referred to as ELECTRONIC DATA INTERCHANGE (EDI). EDI is used primarily to electronically transfer routine, well-specified business transactions, including purchase orders, invoices, confirmations, shipping notices, and so on. There are two major EDI standards. The EDIFACT is an international format developed by the United Nations and is popular in Europe and Asia. In the US and Canada, the standard is ANSI ASC X.12. Both standards provide standard coding of business transactions.

The Internet has become an alternative channel for EDI transactions using leased lines and VAN services. By Internet-based EDI, businesses allow their trading partners to enter information in web forms that are transferred over the public telecommunication network and converted by the receiver to EDI messages or other documents.

Extranets.   An extranet is a restricted-access network for a business and its customers and/or suppliers. It is a secure private network that uses Internet protocols and the public telecommunication system. With an extranet, a business shares information with its customers, suppliers, and business partners at various levels of accessibility. These external users need authorization to access the information shared through the extranet. An extranet uses firewalls, user AUTHENTICATION (e.g., digital certificate), encryption, and a virtual private network (VPN) to insure security and privacy in data transmission over the Internet.

E-procurement systems.   Electronic procurement or e-procurement systems are another type of B2B e-commerce application that uses Internet protocols and web technologies. E-procurement systems serve the needs of buyer companies and their primary functions are to automate and streamline purchasing activities, including requisition, approval, ordering, receiving, and supplier catalogue management. Using an e-procurement system, employees can access the supplier catalogues and fill out order forms via web browsers on their desktops. Requisition approvals are routed via the browser or through email systems, and orders, when approved, are placed with the suppliers or vendors electronically.

B2B e-marketplaces.   B2B e-marketplaces are also developed on the Internet and web technologies, and transfer data over the public telecommunication network. A B2B e-marketplace function is an intermediary in industry value chains. It may be owned by an industry giant, a neutral third party, or an industry consortium. It provides a common platform over the Internet on which authorized users from various businesses can access information, exchange documents, and conduct transactions using standard web browsers. The services of B2B e-marketplaces range from product and supplier aggregation, request for quote, and multibusiness collaboration to process integration. Based on the focus of their services, B2B e-marketplaces fall into four major types: information portals, market makers, collaborative platforms, and value chain integrators.

Information portals provide industry specific information and aggregate product and supplier information with functions for easy search and comparison. *Market makers* enable businesses to negotiate and settle deals as well as search for products. *Collaborative platforms* offer document management or project management services so that multiple businesses working on the same projects can share data over the Internet. *Value chain integrators* provide platforms and services to streamline the inter-business transaction processes and to cooperate for supply chain management.

In addition to the basic Internet and web technologies that are required for e-commerce in general, two other technologies are employed in B2B e-commerce. One is XML (*see* XML (EXTENSIBLE MARKUP LANGUAGE)). XML is used as a protocol for representing data semantically. It has become the standard for synchronizing and exchanging business information between computer applications. Many industries have developed industry-specific XML specifications.

A second technology is the middleware technology. Middleware is a connectivity software with a set of functions that facilitate direct communication between computer applications across a network. The following forms of middleware are used for B2B application integration: remote procedure calls (RPCs), message-oriented middleware (MOM), object request broker (ORB), transaction processing (TP) monitors, and database-oriented middleware. Another protocol for accessing data and services from remote computer systems on heterogeneous platforms is simple object access protocol (SOAP), which is based on XML and HTTP (hypertext transfer protocol).

Bibliography

Kambil, A. and van Heck, E. (2002). *Making Markets: How Firms Can Design and Profit from Online Auctions and Exchanges.* Boston: Harvard Business School Press.
Kaplan, S. and Sawhney, M. (2000). E-hubs: The new B2B marketplaces. *Harvard Business Review*, **78**, 3 (May/June), 97–103.
Senn, J. A. (2000). B2B e-commerce. *Information Systems Management*, **17**, 2 (Spring), 23–32.

e-commerce clicks and mortar

David Bahn

The information systems function must frequently provide support for business strategy and operations that includes both electronic commerce (*see* E-COMMERCE) and traditional physical facility (brick-and-mortar) channels. This use of both channels by some organizations has become among the most significant challenges for business in recent years. Clicks and mortar is one term used to signify the use of e-commerce ("clicks") alongside traditional ("brick-and-mortar") business operations. Also known as "bricks and clicks," it connotes an approach to deploy e-commerce alongside conventional business operations in a manner that best utilizes the strengths of each channel in a complementary and synergistic manner (Stuart, 2000).

At a strategic level, the clicks-and-mortar approach to e-commerce raises some significant questions for executives. In order to successfully manage conventional business operations along with business-to-consumer (B2C) e-commerce, it is desirable to achieve a synergy between them that optimizes the costs and benefits of each channel. How can business volume grow through e-commerce without cannibalizing and adversely affecting growth in established retail channels? What degree of investment should be made in each channel? Is it possible to establish

an interactive synergy in such a way that the e-commerce and the conventional brick-and-mortar business operations are mutually supportive?

At an operational level, there are some even more fundamental questions that are raised by the clicks-and-mortar approach to e-commerce. First, organizations must distinguish those business activities that can be performed online from those activities that require a "high-touch" interaction with the customer and must therefore continue to be performed through brick-and-mortar operations. If certain retail activities such as marketing and pre-sales operations can be performed through e-commerce, then will the same brick-and-mortar facilities still be required or will they be reduced or reshaped? If manufacturers adopt e-commerce to sell directly to consumers, will this enhance the disintermediation of retailers or will it enhance opportunities for potential cooperation between manufacturers and retailers?

Following the winnowing of "pure-play" B2C e-commerce, this hybrid approach to e-commerce began to attract more attention from business practitioners. Many press articles have called for firms to embrace e-commerce alongside their traditional brick-and-mortar operations, but offered little in the way of methodological guidance on how to accomplish this transformation.

The current research literature offers several perspectives on how firms can implement e-commerce in synergy with parallel brick and mortar. Gulati and Garino (2000) have stated that the central issue for this implementation is the degree of integration between the two channels. A firm's integration of its e-commerce with its traditional business operations can vary on several dimensions: the actual business processes used to execute the firm's transactions, the brand identity of the firm, and how each channel is owned and managed. A firm can own and manage brick-and-mortar operations in conjunction with e-commerce, yet still not integrate the brand identity or business processes of each one. Alternatively, a firm like Barnes and Noble might integrate the brand identity of its traditional retail operations within its e-commerce, yet still not integrate the business processes used to execute transactions within each channel.

Another perspective by de Figueiredo (2000) posits that the characteristics of a firm's products or service primarily determine how e-commerce can be integrated alongside traditional business operations. He views the key determinant characteristics as being the degree to which a product varies in quality, and the degree to which a potential customer can easily evaluate a product's quality. Commodity products are typically of fairly uniform quality and are easy for customers to assess, and hence would lend themselves readily to a clicks-and-mortar approach to e-commerce. However, "look and feel" products that are more difficult for customers to evaluate will yield more capability for executing transactions through e-commerce.

More recent studies have asserted that a far more complex synergy exists between e-commerce and traditional brick-and-mortar business operations. Wilcocks and Plant (2001) state that there are two distinct paths firms can take in arriving at a clicks-and-mortar approach to e-commerce. One path involves the creation or extension of a firm's traditional brand identity into e-commerce operations. An alternate, less risky path is for firms to utilize e-commerce as a means to create service and quality improvements in the traditional brick-and-mortar arena. Bahn and Fisher (2003) contend that there are several distinct strategies that firms employ in achieving a clicks-and-mortar approach to e-commerce. These strategies vary according to several dimensions of business constraints that include not only the characteristics of a firm's products, but also the relationships that a firm has with its supply chain partners and the capability of a firm to articulate a strategy that is distinct from its brick-and-mortar strategy. Bahn and Fisher also found that, owing to these constraints, many firms find it strategically appropriate to minimize their involvement in e-commerce and relegate it to an auxiliary channel that supports brick-and-mortar operations.

Bibliography

Bahn, D. and Fisher, P. (2003). Clicks and mortar: Balancing brick-and-mortar business strategy and operations with auxiliary electronic commerce. *Information Technology and Management*, 4, 2/3 (April), 319–35.

De Figueiredo, J. (2000). Finding sustainable profitability in electronic commerce. *Sloan Management Review*, Summer, 41–52.

Gulati, R. and Garino, J. (2000). Get the right mix of bricks and clicks. *Harvard Business Review*, May/June, 107–14.

Stuart, A. (2000). Clicks and bricks. *CIO*, March 15, 76–84.

Wilcocks, L. and Plant, R. (2001). Getting from bricks to clicks. *Sloan Management Review*, Spring, 50–9.

education and training in use of information technology

R. Ryan Nelson

Effective use of information technology (IT) is one of the prime determinants of success for organizations as well as individuals. The rapid advances in IT have created a gap between what most individuals know about the technology and what is required for its effective exploitation. Research suggests that most information system failures stem from a lack of user acceptance rather than poor technical quality. Education and training in IT may therefore have priority in human resource development.

LEARNING KNOWLEDGE AND SKILLS

Learning is a relatively permanent change in behavior occurring as a result of experience. The distinction between learning via *education* and learning via *training* is important. In general, education teaches problem-solving approaches, while focusing on the ability to reason abstractly. Training, on the other hand, provides the tools (i.e., skills) for implementing problem-solving approaches, while focusing on the ability to work concretely. Education helps the student choose his or her activity; training helps the participant improve his or her performance in it.

Six general areas of knowledge/skills are required by employees using IT.

1   *Organizational overview*: includes objectives, purpose, opportunities, constraints, and internal and external functioning.
2   *Organizational skills*: includes interpersonal behavior, group dynamics, and project management.

3   *Target organizational unit*: includes objectives, purpose, functions, resources, links with other internal and external units, and problems.
4   *General IT knowledge*: includes hardware and software concepts, IT potential, organizational IT policies and plans, and existing IT applications.
5   *Technical skills*: includes methods and techniques required to perform IT-related tasks.
6   *IT product*: includes purpose, design, required procedures, and documentation of a specific information system.

The Learning Process

The learning process consists of three main phases: pre-education/training, formal education/training, and post-education/training. Additionally, trainee, software, task/job, and organizational characteristics influence key decisions made at each phase of the process.

1   *Pre-education/training phase*. This phase concerns a broad range of factors, from needs assessment to the development of instructional materials.
2   *Formal education/training phase*. A key question in this phase relates to the method of training delivery (face-to-face, video, computer-based, or some combination). Methods that incorporate hands-on use, behavior modeling, good conceptual models, manuals that encourage exploratory learning, and training previews have been shown to be effective. A second question is who will facilitate the training: outside consultants, in-house trainers, or the learners themselves through some form of self-study?
3   *Post-education/training phase*. The primary focus of this phase tends to be on the evaluation of the education/training process (e.g., was the instructor effective?). However,

Table 1   The content–level framework for education/training needs assessment

Level	*Content*		
	Person	*Task*	*Organizational*
Individual	*Cell 1.1* What knowledge and skills do specific individuals need to learn for effective performance?	*Cell 1.2* What are the knowledge and skill requirements necessary for the accomplishment of specific tasks by an individual?	*Cell 1.3* How do the goals of an individual affect or constrain performance, motivation to learn, or training effectiveness?
Subunit	*Cell 2.1* What skill mix is needed for successful job performance within a given work group, e.g., interpersonal skills, teamwork skills?	*Cell 2.2* What activities, technologies, and behaviors should be trained for effective task performance within a given subunit?	*Cell 2.3* How do work group goals and culture affect or constrain performance or training effectiveness?
Organizational	*Cell 3.1* How does the organization tie human resource planning (i.e., HR analysis, skills inventories, forecasting of workforce demand and supply, and forecasting of skill mix) to strategic planning?	*Cell 3.2* What are the core work processes and technologies of the organization?	*Cell 3.3* How do organizational goals, objectives, and resources affect whether and where training is needed?

managers are interested in the longer-term effect of education/training.

ABILITY, ACCEPTANCE, AND PRODUCTIVITY

Essentially, through its impact on end-user ability, education and training serve to enhance acceptance by impacting the perceived ease of use and usefulness of information technology. Ability refers to the quality of having sufficient IT-related knowledge/skill to accomplish an objective. An organization's desire to improve white-collar productivity through more effective IT utilization is the primary motivation for the measurement of end-user abilities. Productivity benefits from IT result from both efficiently supplied and effectively utilized IT products and services. In addition, the decentralization of computer usage via end-user computing has prompted arguments that utilization is directly related to user knowledge and skills.

Careful needs assessment (see table 1) and systematic evaluation are needed to guide improvements in user education and training. Where needs assessment identifies the objectives of education/training, evaluation measures the accomplishment of objectives.

e-government

Claudio U. Ciborra

The use of electronic technology, especially the INTERNET, in the delivery of government services and interaction with citizens is termed electronic government or e-government. The underlying objective of e-government is to simplify, improve, and speed the processes by which citizens obtain information about government activities and services and processes by which government delivers the services. E-government initiatives include PORTALS and other mechanisms to provide a single point of access for a set of services, electronic access to forms and regulations, interactive applications to allow citizens to submit applications and pay fees using the Internet, interactive applications to enable citizens to participate in government rule-making, and online access to information about government services.

The use of information and communications technology (ICT) in government operations, services, and citizen interactions is important to the organization function of management information systems (MIS) in three ways: e-government activities by a government unit involve the MIS function in the governmental unit; e-government activities impact organizations that do business with the government; and the success or failure of e-government initiatives may have important lessons for non-government activities enabled by information and communications technologies.

E-government is here described in terms of models of the state and its interaction with citizens and in terms of governance and development. Some examples of e-government systems are given to illustrate the types of applications.

E-GOVERNMENT AND MODELS OF THE STATE

E-government promotes major innovations in the way in which information and communications technologies are used in government as well as in how government activities are organized. Three types of innovation can be identified: the relationship (transaction) between the administration and the citizen (customer); the related reengineering of the activities internal to the administration; and the changing of boundaries between the state and the market by the creation of a more transparent, agile, and accountable government.

The way in which the transaction relationship between state and citizens is supposed to change is a crucial aspect. In e-government, public administration is viewed as the interface between *customers* and *provider of services* rather than as that between *citizens* and *state*. However, it is important to note that transactions with government providers differ in some respects from market transactions. Technology may be applied to both market and non-market transactions to reduce costs and increase speed and efficiency, but in other respects the transactions are different. The internal workings of the public administration can be described as a bureaucracy, and information and communications technologies can be used to decrease its internal coordination costs. The scope of operation of public administration is within an environment populated by loosely coupled organizations and individuals whose transactions are not purely economic.

Besides *economic transactions*, what matter in this domain are also *political exchanges*. While objects of transactions can be money, goods, and services, the objects of political exchanges can also be intangibles such as laws, regulations, plans, provisions (targeted to communities, organizations, or individuals) and subtle goods such as recognition, legitimacy, support, security, and trust.

There are different models to regulate the political exchange. Three models are the minimal state that guarantees public and private order through general norms such as the enforcement of private property and otherwise depends on the order defined by the economy and the market; the pluralist state that provides functions in response to movements and pressure groups in the civil society; and the planning state that actively regulates economic exchanges and interferes with the functioning of the market. Each of these different models has a different objective and therefore creates a different context and objectives for e-government. In the minimal state, e-government is harnessed to extend the markets for services, externalizing the functions of the public administration. In the pluralist state, e-government provides new services and capabilities in response to the requests of pressure groups. In a planning model, e-government is used to enhance the planning capabilities of the state. The impact of e-government in the different contexts on the workings of political exchange between the community and the state can be hard to assess. For example, one can transform for reasons of efficiency a local authority into a call center. But what will be the impact of such innovation on the level of trust between the citizens and the state, especially if the call center arrangement creates unemployment in the local community, and/or does not work smoothly in addressing the requests of callers?

E-GOVERNMENT AND GOVERNANCE AND DEVELOPMENT

Governance is understood as a broad process affecting the way decisions are taken and responsibility allocated among social and economic agents within the realms of politics, state administration, and bureaucracy. Good governance, in relation to late developing countries (LDCs),

means ability to manage effectively their transition to development and is conditional on the implementation of good policies. These policies aim to: (1) promote democracy; (2) reduce corruption; (3) increase transparency; and (4) expand human capabilities. Recently, international agencies like the United Nations development agencies, the World Bank, and various banking institutions have supported regional development policies that include the creation of an information society, and in particular e-government applications. The belief is that this will lead to better (or good) governance. E-government is seen as a beneficial action to connect government agencies and institutions, promote the reorganization of governmental internal and external information flows, and organize activities and functions to shift the delivery of government services from physical offices to delivery over the Internet and other communications facilities.

Various policy blueprints for e-government argue that information and communication technologies are essential to increase transparency and accountability of government agencies, reduce transactions costs in service delivery, and enhance participation of citizens, businesses, and civil society in the workings of governments. Better accountability and improved transparency are among the paramount characteristics of good governance. They also are becoming a necessary condition imposed by the rich states and international agencies for furnishing aid to the LDCs.

There is conflicting evidence about the effect of e-government initiatives on transparency, accountability, cost reduction, and citizen participation. The main reason for uncertain outcomes is that the model of state that guides most e-government projects is of a neoliberal type. This model has historically had a dubious impact on good governance during the transition to development. Therefore, it is unclear how external aid interventions supporting information and communications technologies for e-government can reduce costs. Paradoxically, it also seems that successful implementation of e-government presupposes a strong, efficient state, and not necessarily the other way round.

There have been e-government initiatives in developed and developing countries.

Noteworthy examples are in the UK and other countries in Europe, and there has been significant e-government activity in many countries. In the US, a major initiative at the federal level was begun in 2002. Most states in the US and most of its major counties and municipalities have implemented applications of e-government.

A few examples illustrate e-government applications.

- A single point of access for citizens to determine eligibility for government benefits and services.
- A single point of web-based access for citizens to get information about government recreation sites.
- International trade site to assist small and medium enterprises in obtaining information on conducting business abroad.
- Site that provides businesses with relevant rules and regulations and enables submission of forms over the Internet.
- Electronic voting.
- Provision of telecenters in deprived areas to meet the needs of remote communities.

electronic commerce

see E-COMMERCE

electronic communication

Reagan M. Ramsower

The word "telecommunication" was formed by adding the word "tele" to "communication." "Tele" comes from the ancient Greek for "at a distance" and is used as a prefix to create a word that represents a new communication form made possible by using electricity. Telecommunication is, therefore, long-distance communication using electromagnetic methods. It encompasses other words that use the "tele" prefix, such as telephone (speaking at a distance), television (seeing at a distance), telegraph (writing at a distance), and teleconference (conferencing at a distance).

When human beings wish to communicate, they exchange information in the form of messages. The form of the message is affected by whether the communication will be face to face or occur at a distance. In face-to-face communication, visual cues, such as facial expressions, hand gestures, and other body-language messages, are included in communication. Face-to-face communication also provides the ability to share reports and drawings. In face-to-face meetings, participants regularly look at the body language of other participants and view common reports and drawings to support the communication. When communication occurs at a distance, the number and quality of the messages are reduced. Body language, for example, cannot be viewed over the telephone, and the tone of the voice cannot be heard using email. The goal of telecommunications is to provide communication systems that span long distances and deliver an optimal set of messages to support particular communication needs.

Telecommunications can be viewed either as a set of communication services or as an infrastructure to support telecommunication services. Some common telecommunication services include telephone, television, teleconferencing, electronic mail (*see* EMAIL), voice mail, and the INTERNET. The telecommunication infrastructure includes various public and private networks that deliver telecommunication services.

TELECOMMUNICATION SERVICES

A large and growing number of telecommunication services are offered to people around the world. Figure 1 classifies telecommunication services according to their level of interactivity and the type of messages supported. Interactivity is the ability of the receiver to reply to the sender in a particular time frame. Messages can be thought of as words, graphics, audio, and video sent electronically in various combinations.

At the low end of interactivity, the receiver cannot respond to the message and communication is one-way. Radio and television are examples of the low end of interactivity. An application such as the WORLDWIDE WEB (WWW) allows some navigational feedback, but it basically remains a one-way method of communication.

Interactivity that is two-way can either be immediate or delayed. In delayed two-way communication, the receiver chooses when to accept the message and the sender and receiver are not required to communicate at the same moment in time. Electronic mail and voice mail are examples of delayed two-way communication. Immediate two-way communication requires the receiver and the sender to be engaged in communication at the same moment in time. The telephone is an example of immediate two-way communication.

TELECOMMUNICATION INFRASTRUCTURE

Underlying telecommunication services is the technical infrastructure that permits messages to be sent and received. This infrastructure uses electromagnetic methods to encode the communication message. The most widely used electromagnetic method for representing a message involves creating a wave, as shown in figure 2. This waveform can be produced by an alternating current over wires or as energy propagated through the atmosphere as electromagnetic waves.

The waveform can be varied by frequency. The frequency is the number of cycles that occurs in a second and is called a hertz. To represent a large number of hertz (Hz), the words kilohertz (thousands of hertz), megahertz (millions of hertz), and gigahertz (thousands of millions of hertz) are used. The telephone system uses frequencies between 0 and 4,000 Hz to represent the human voice over telephone wires. Broadcast television uses frequencies between 30 megahertz and 3 gigahertz to send television signals through the air.

The receiver of a telecommunication message must know what frequencies the sender is using to represent the message. Thus, a basic agreement must be reached between a sender and receiver before any message can be communicated. Such an agreement is called a *protocol*. When a large number of people agree on a protocol it becomes a standard. Fundamental to the entire telecommunications infrastructure is the establishment of protocols and the eventual development of standards. Standards permit the largest number of people to utilize the telecommunication infrastructure to develop telecommunication applications.

PROTOCOLS AND STANDARDS

Many protocols must be established before telecommunication services are possible. A useful approach to understanding protocols is to view

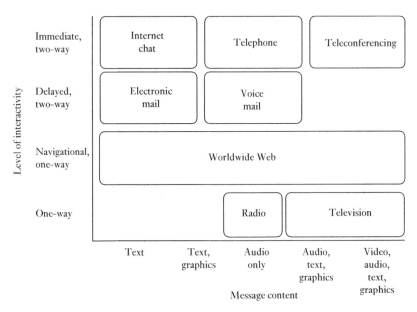

Figure 1   Telecommunication services

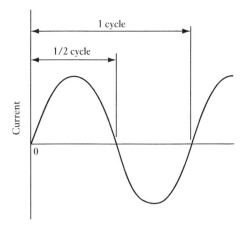

Figure 2   Electromagnetic wave

them as layers. Figure 3 shows a very simple four-layer model of telecommunication protocols.

Physical layer.   The lowest layer is labeled the physical layer because it concerns the physical characteristics of devices used to send and receive telecommunication messages. This layer includes protocols that address the physical specifications of wires, connectors, and devices that will send and receive electromagnetic frequencies. Sets of protocols which describe a particular type of wire receive names such as unshielded twisted pair (UTP), broadband coaxial cable, or single-mode fiber optic cable. Connectors that

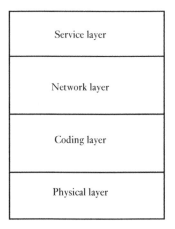

Figure 3   Four-layer model of telecommunication protocols

attach wires to devices are also specified with protocols and then labeled with names like RJ-11, RS-232, and phone jack. Protocols that govern the various devices used to send and receive microwaves, satellite waves, radio waves, television waves, and other electromagnetic waves are included in the physical layer. These devices and the frequencies of electromagnetic waves they use often involve significant government regulation so that interference with other users of electromagnetic waves is avoided.

Coding layer.   Above the physical layer are protocols that address how the frequencies on the physical wires or electromagnetic waves are coded to transmit messages. Messages can be encoded using either analog or digital coding techniques.

Human senses rely on analog signals such as sound and light waves. For example, ear drums vibrate to actual sound waves and then send the resulting signal to the brain, where it is heard. *Analog coding* protocols use the same technique to match electromagnetic frequencies with sound waves. The electromagnetic frequencies are transmitted over a distance and then used to reproduce the sound waves. Analog signaling thus uses electromagnetic waves that closely approximate the waves of sound and light.

To represent analog sound and light waves as digital signals, a protocol must be established to describe how a wave can be used to represent a binary switch symbolized by the digits 0 and 1. For example, a protocol may choose one frequency to represent a 0 and another frequency to represent a 1. Other methods include using different amplitudes (height of the electromagnetic wave), or using different pulses of voltage to represent the 0s or 1s. Regardless of the method chosen, the 0s and 1s must be grouped together to represent higher-order messages such as sound, video, or data. *Digital encoding* protocols are used to represent sound on CDs and video on video disks. Data consist of letters, numbers, and special characters. Data are usually represented by grouping binary digits (0s and 1s) together and establishing a protocol. The most common protocol to represent data is ASCII. ASCII, for example, represents the letter "j" with the binary pattern 1101010.

Network layer. The next layer is the network layer. This layer contains many protocols which address how private and public networks are developed and used to send coded signals. Networks can be grouped as either point-to-point networks or multipoint networks. In point-to-point networks, signals are transmitted between two points or nodes. Switching equipment creates a single circuit that allows for the transmission of signals between these two nodes. The telephone network is an example of a point-to-point network. Multipoint networks signal multiple nodes simultaneously. They are designed as either broadcast networks, in which the message is intended for every node, or as packet networks, in which the message is addressed to only certain nodes. The radio and television network is an example of a multipoint broadcast network. Multipoint packet networks are primarily used to transmit digital messages. The Internet is an example of a multipoint packet network.

Service layer. The service layer uses the underlying protocol layers to deliver telecommunication services. The form and type of the telecommunication service depend upon the firm selling the service. Some services are considered public services, such as radio, television, and telephone. Public telecommunication services are often operated by private companies, which, because of their public mission and monopolistic position, are highly regulated by national governments. Because of this regulation, public telecommunication services frequently differ among countries. This presents a significant challenge when trying to transmit messages across national boundaries.

Organizations create private telecommunication services, such as electronic mail or a system for taking customer orders. These private telecommunication services are established for the exclusive use of the organization. Private services are developed by building private networks. Portions of the private network may consist of purchased public telecommunication services. The security of the message must be protected by using encryption techniques when public telecommunication networks are used to deliver private services. Private telecommunication networks created by organizations generally transmit data and are critical to the survival of the firm. This branch of telecommunications is called data communication.

DATA COMMUNICATION

Data communication networks connect the computers of an organization and use digital coding to match the coding of the computers. The term data communication is used because data constitute the majority of the messages transmitted over digital networks; however, data communication services also transmit audio and video. Data communication networks are generally private networks established by companies to interconnect the computers of employees, customers, and suppliers. An exception is the Internet, which is a public data communication network. Data communication networks are constructed by building certain portions of the network and combining this internal network with purchased portions of the public network. The internal network covers a single geographic site, such as an office or building, and is referred to as a local area network (LAN). The interconnections of individual computers or of a LAN to other LANs or computers over larger distances are called wide area networks (WANs).

LOCAL AREA NETWORKS

Local area networks (LANs) interconnect personal computers. A card called a network interface card (NIC) is installed in each computer and connected using a wiring protocol such as Ethernet or Token Ring. A segment contains a group of computers that are on the same wire. Routers and bridges are used to connect segments. The data on LANs are coded in digital form and placed in packets that contain the address of the computer sending the message and the address of the computer to receive the message. NICs scan each message to see if the message contains its NIC address. Local area networks permit the sharing of common disk storage and access to common peripherals such as printers.

WIDE AREA NETWORKS

Wide area networks (WANs) interconnect computers over distances that can span the globe. Most WANs are constructed by purchasing the services of public telecommunication networks, but some companies own and operate their own

WAN network by using their own microwave or satellite transmission devices. The services purchased from public telecommunication companies to construct WANs are specified by protocols and receive labels such as ISDN and T1. Local area networks are connected to the WAN using routers. The Internet is a familiar public wide area network.

CONCLUSION

Telecommunication covers a very broad and rapidly expanding array of technologies. The telecommunications industry consists of some of the largest firms in the world. Electronic communication on a worldwide basis is critical to the success of companies, governments, and society. New telecommunication services are transforming the way people work, learn, and play, by supporting their communication over large distances. Understanding protocols and standards is fundamental to the construction of telecommunication services. One area of telecommunications, data communications, which involves the transmission of data among computers, is recognized as a crucial organizational asset. The telecommunication infrastructure, both public and private, and the services that are being delivered are transforming civilization.

electronic data interchange

Donald J. McCubbrey

Electronic data interchange (EDI) is the computer-to-computer exchange of standard business documents in a standard data format. Each of the three elements in the definition is important. "Computer-to-computer" means that paper business documents are not sent. The phrase "standard business documents" means that EDI is restricted to standard business documents such as purchase orders, order acknowledgments, shipping notices, invoices, and the like. "Standard data format" means that the trading partners have agreed that each standard business document (e.g., a purchase order) will always be transmitted using an agreed-upon standard data format, so that the computer systems on each end will be able to properly interpret the meaning of streams of data sent as

EDI transactions. Using EDI in place of paper-based transactions and the mail results in greater speed, increased accuracy, and lower costs. EDI is an essential feature of just-in-time (JIT) systems in the manufacturing sector and quick-response (QR) systems in the retailing sector.

EDI was a precursor to an emerging business paradigm called electronic commerce (*see* E-COMMERCE). EDI and e-commerce have been used to gain strategic advantage. EDI is also a special case of the larger business paradigm of INTER-ORGANIZATIONAL SYSTEMS (IOS). One of the ways that EDI in electronic commerce is used to gain competitive advantage is for two trading partners to use the techniques of EDI to reengineer the processes they share along a manufacturing, distribution, or retailing supply chain.

EDI has been in use for over 30 years. The dominant pattern of diffusion has been called "hub and spoke." In a hub-and-spoke pattern, a large customer (the hub) pressures its suppliers (spokes) to do business using EDI. From the perspective of a "spoke" company, they must use EDI when requested to do so by one of their important customers or they will not receive any more orders from them. In early systems, suppliers had to accept EDI transactions from their customers in a data format that was proprietary to the customer and not standard.

THE DEVELOPMENT OF STANDARDS

Initially, industry groups developed industry-wide standards for EDI transactions. In the US automobile industry, for example, it soon became apparent that if suppliers had to process incoming orders in a unique proprietary standard adopted by each of its major customers, the burden would be severe. Accordingly, the industry group MEMA (Motor and Equipment Manufacturers Association) facilitated the development of a standard that would be used by all of its members. Similar proprietary standards arose in other industries. When it became apparent that cross-industry standards would be beneficial, inasmuch as industry members did business with trading partners outside their own industry, or with government, the cross-industry standards ANSI X12 and, later, EDI-FACT were developed and put into widespread use. ANSI X12 is most popular with EDI users in the US, Canada, and Australia, while EDI-FACT is more widely used in Europe and in international trade generally.

The Role of Value-Added Networks

Value-added networks (VANs) have made it easier for trading partners to overcome the obstacles of connectivity and standards incompatibility, particularly when a company is dealing with hundreds of trading partners. Rather than establish an individual telecommunications link with each of its EDI trading partners, a supplier connects its computer with the VAN a few times each day and transmits all of its EDI transactions to any of its customers. The VAN receives them and places them in the electronic mailbox of each customer. When the customers' computers dial in to the VAN, they collect all EDI transactions waiting in their electronic mailbox. Before signing off, the supplier's computer will collect all EDI transactions in its electronic mailbox, placed there earlier by the VAN when it received them from the supplier's EDI trading partners.

In addition to the switching and store-and-forward messaging services offered by the VANs, they also offer translation services. For example, General Motors (GM) could transmit a purchase order to one of its suppliers in a format dictated by the design of GM's internal purchase order computer system. The VAN (for a fee) will translate the purchase orders into a predetermined standard format, such as ANSI X12. When the supplier picks up its orders from GM (and from other customers), they are all in the same standard ANSI X12 format. The supplier then has the VAN translate its customers' orders from ANSI X12 to the format required by its internal order entry computer system application. Should either trading party decide it would be cheaper to translate on their own premises, they would simply acquire one of the many commercially available software packages designed for that purpose. Some of the reasons for using a private network instead of a VAN are high performance, fixed costs, audit trails, and greater security.

VANs have played an important part in facilitating EDI. They will often offer to help hub companies engage their trading partners in an EDI relationship and offer consultation and training services, translation software, model trading partner agreements, and so on.

Organizational Placement of the EDI Function

Until recently, EDI did not have high visibility with top executives or with information systems (IS) executives. Sales professionals realized that EDI was an important business issue. The result has been that many EDI managers found themselves with a small EDI staff attached to the sales and marketing organization. As the strategic uses of EDI have become more generally known, many CEOs and CIOs have placed EDI much higher on their priority lists and the EDI function has assumed a more prominent role in many companies.

EDI's Status as a Legacy System

There are several initiatives underway to replace traditional EDI with schemes that reduce the complexity of standards-based EDI and make the computer-to-computer exchange of standard business documents available to more companies, particularly small to medium-sized businesses. Foremost among these are ebXML (*see* XML (EXTENSIBLE MARKUP LANGUAGE)) and WEB SERVICES. At this writing, however, traditional EDI is considered a legacy system by many hub companies and is expected to be in use for several years to come.

electronic funds transfer

Gordon B. Davis

Systems for electronic funds transfer (EFT) are used in both consumer banking and commercial banking. In consumer or retail banking, the most common application is the use of AUTOMATIC TELLER MACHINES (ATMs). ATMs are connected via networks so that a customer may access funds from remote locations. ATMs support both credit cards and debit cards. Credit cards result in charges to a credit card account. Debit cards provide immediate withdrawal of funds from a checking or savings account. In commercial banking, electronic funds transfer is used to transfer funds between banks or large corporations. These fund transfers are handled over specialized funds-transfer networks, both national and international. Banks that provide bill-paying services over the INTERNET will either pay the bills by electronic funds transfer or by writing and mailing checks. The preferred method is EFT because of its low cost.

electronic government

see E-GOVERNMENT

electronic meeting systems

see GROUP DECISION SUPPORT SYSTEMS

email

Gordon B. Davis

Email (electronic mail or e-mail) is important to information and communication system users, to the information systems function, and to management of organizations. It is important to users because it facilitates communications and may increase (or decrease) individual productivity. It is important to the information systems function because email requires significant resources to provide, monitor, and protect. It is important to management of organizations because it facilitates coordination and communication within an organization and with suppliers and customers. It is also important because it can increase or decrease organizational productivity.

Email has been available in various forms since the 1970s. It was developed in conjunction with ARPANET, the research network of the US Defense Department. In the mid-1980s, email became a significant application in conjunction with personal computers. It is now one of the principal uses for desktop personal computers and for various handheld computers and cell phones. Email can generally be accessed not only from a personal computer or handheld device, but also from any computer or device connected to the INTERNET. The number of individual email accounts (email mailboxes) is several hundred million and increasing rapidly.

The number of emails sent on an average day is in the thousands of millions.

Email is transferred with fairly small communications delay. The user can delay opening an email message. It remains available until it is opened and the user makes a decision about it. Computer users of email systems can have an audible signal indicating email is available. An alternate form of communications similar to email is INSTANT MESSAGING (IM). The email system establishes communication between two (or more) users. Written messages are exchanged instantly. It is essentially email with instant replies and responses to replies.

There are conflicting outcomes from the economics of email. The cost of preparing and sending email is very low. There is very little marginal cost associated with sending copies of an email. On the other hand, the low marginal cost encourages some organizations to send unsolicited email (*see* SPAM) to millions of email mailboxes. Unsolicited email may be one-third to one-half of the email traffic. Spam can reduce productivity if recipients have to spend time reading and deleting the messages or even deleting them without reading. Organizations devote resources to spam filters that block spam email. The computing industry is working on improved methods for reducing spam. One method is to force the sender to include a valid domain address; this would make it easier to track down senders. Other methods propose changing the economics of email to make it more costly to send spam emails. Some email is used for fraudulent purposes in a scheme termed PHISHING (fishing for personal information). The email is written with false indicators of identity such as logos in order to elicit a response from the recipient with personal information that may be used to access bank accounts, charge cards, etc.

Email messages can have files attached to them. The files can be text files or graphics, photographs, music, videos, and so forth. These attachments may also contain computer routines that can be useful to the recipients or may be destructive. These program attachments are activated by opening the files, so the advice of security experts is to not open unknown file attachments but delete the message and its file. One non-destructive but invasive file that a user may install without being aware of the consequences is SPYWARE. This program collects and sends data about computer use to the spyware owner. One problem is that the spyware may use computer resources and slow down the processing. Spyware may be removed by various programs that protect against viruses (*see* VIRUS). Viruses may come from files, email attachments, or from email with viruses. Virus protection programs are used to block and remove viruses.

To send and/or receive email, a person employs a personal computer, computer terminal, handheld device, or telephone with email capabilities plus an account with a supplier of email services. The supplier generally provides access to the Internet as well as email services. An organization may establish an internal email service, but the availability of public providers encourages the use of public service suppliers. An email is addressed to an email mailbox identified by a unique identification: username@domain.type-of-organization.country. The type of organization is a two- or three-character code. In the US, the code for an educational institution is EDU, a government body is GOV, and a commercial organization is COM, etc. Sponsored and unsponsored organization names have been approved. The domain is the organization that establishes the service and assigns the user names. Addresses for the US do not generally contain a country designation (but US may be used); other countries use a two-character code. For example, an email mailbox for an academic at the Nanyang Technological University (NTU) might read: aprofgb@ntu.edu.sg, where aprofgb is the username, ntu is the organization, edu indicates it is an educational institution, and sg indicates the organization is in Singapore. G.B.Davis@lse.ac.uk identifies the mailbox of G. B. Davis at an educational institution (lse for London School of Economics and ac for academic) in the UK. Different organizations establish naming conventions for the username.

The worldwide use of email and the Internet requires international cooperation. ICANN (International Corporation for Assigned Names and Numbers) is an internationally organized, public benefit non-profit responsible for coordinating the ICANN functions, which include Internet protocol (IP) address space allocation, protocol identifier assignment, generic (gTLD) and country code (ccTLD) top-level domain name system management, and root server system management functions. For more information, see their website (www.icann.org). Registration of domain names is required. This function is facilitated by organizations that perform the service and prompt users to renew registrations when they expire. Since domain names are used to access Internet sites, a domain name that corresponds with public perceptions of the name to use is a valuable resource. For example, NWA (for Northwest Airlines) is the domain name in the Internet address www.nwa.com.

There are two major approaches to email systems. In the simplest approach (called POP or post office protocol mail), the email system holds the messages for a user only until they are read. If the user wishes to process and save messages after reading them, they must be saved on the storage device associated with the computer being used to read mail. An alternative is IMAP (Internet message access protocol), which is a mail system protocol that allows the user to store and process messages on the mail server or download them for storage on a local computer. The POP method is simpler because it supports only reading the messages and doing all storage and processing locally; the IMAP method adds online processing and storage capabilities plus other capabilities. An extension of IMAP is MIME (multipurpose Internet mail extensions). MIME is a method for sending files as attachments and allowing the deferral of transferring selected parts of the message.

There are a number of operations and functions available in email. Some are optional and not provided by all vendors. Typical functions are reply, attach a file, indicate urgency, send copies, and send blind copies. Various editing facilities are usually available to set font, font size, color, etc. Also frequently available are other useful functions such as checking for spelling errors, obtaining a receipt that the message was read, etc. Some email systems allow instant messaging in which the messages are sent immediately and a conversation is carried on using the keyboard.

From the standpoint of the organization, there are three concerns: the first is the deployment of appropriate email technology, the second is security of the email systems, and the third is encouraging productive use of email. The appropriate technology includes spam filters to trap and discard spam or inappropriate email, virus checking software to trap and mark email with viruses, and backup and recovery software for use if there is a system failure. Security features are implemented to prevent unauthorized access and use of the email system. The technology issues are beyond the scope of this entry.

Productivity issues relate to use of email, timing of email use, copy feature use, and storage of emails. Email is efficient in sending messages for which a reply can be delayed. It is also efficient in providing documentation of communications. Emails are generally retained for long periods; in the case of some financial institutions, retention is for many years. The nature of email allows the recipient to schedule reading of emails at a time that does not interfere with concentration and attention on important tasks. However, there is a tendency for individuals to allow emails to interrupt work and break concentration. Indeed, in some organizations, a culture may emerge that demands immediate replies. In other words, the nature of email supports scheduling of work to allow concentrated attention to tasks, but personal and organizational norms may demand a break in current work to respond immediately. The copy feature allows communication with a number of interested parties; however, it can be misused and result in too many copies that must be read or at least noticed by people who do not need to know. The storage of email communication by individuals and the availability of search tools means it is much more efficient for an individual to find email communications than to search through paper documents and files. Folders can be used to organize emails, but even in the absence of folders, emails can be located easily using search tools.

See also *identity theft; malware*

encryption

Gordon B. Davis

Encryption is the coding of a data transmission or data in storage so that they cannot be under-

stood without decoding. The original data are processed using an encoding algorithm to create a complex data coding that is not meaningful without decoding. Encryption can be done using software or using processes built into encryption chips. Encryption systems typically employ a key used by the encoder to produce a ciphered output. The recipient of the message employs the same key in decoding. An alternative approach is a public enciphering key that is different from a private deciphering key. This allows the enciphering key to be distributed to multiple users without compromising the deciphering key.

See also *cryptography (crypto)*

end-user computing

R. Ryan Nelson

Prior to the 1980s, the information systems (IS) function maintained a virtual monopoly over the acquisition, deployment, and operation of information technology (IT) resources. Many of these responsibilities have been transferred to those who use the information. These are termed "end users." Three major forces explain the transformation process:

1 *Hardware and software improvements* have increased the availability, affordability, and usability of information technologies. Personal computers, productivity software, peripheral devices, networking, and the INTERNET support widespread individual use of information technology.
2 Enhanced *computer-related knowledge and skills* within the end-use community have motivated and enabled end users to use IS products and technologies.
3 An *organizational environment* conducive toward end-user computing (EUC) has fostered the employment of EUC products and technologies as productivity enhancement tools.

TYPES OF END USERS

End-user computing is a diverse phenomenon. End users can be categorized based on variables such as computer skill, method of use, application focus, education and training requirements, and need for ongoing support. Four categories represent end users:

1 *Non-programming end users.* These users access computer applications and data through a limited menu or GRAPHICAL USER INTERFACE (GUI)-based environment. They follow a well-defined set of procedures.
2 *Command-level users.* Users perform inquiries and simple calculations such as summation and generate unique reports for their own purposes. They understand the availability of database(s) and are able to specify, access, and manipulate information.
3 *End-user programmers.* These users utilize both command and procedural languages directly for their individual information needs. They develop their own applications, some of which are used by others. Use by others is a by-product of what is essentially analytic programming performed on a "personal basis" by quantitatively oriented managers and professionals.
4 *Functional support personnel.* They support other end users within their particular functional area. By virtue of their skill with information technology, they have become informal centers of systems design and development expertise. In spite of the time spent supporting other end users, these individuals do not view themselves as programmers or IS professionals. Rather, they are market researchers, financial analysts, and so forth, whose primary task within their function is to provide tools and processes to access and analyze data.

BENEFITS AND RISKS

There are a number of significant advantages to end-user development applications. First, EUC provides some relief from the shortage of development personnel. A common complaint by users is that they cannot get the IS solutions they need when they need them. There are not enough analysts and programmers to keep up with the demand.

Secondly, EUC eliminates the problem of requirements determination for information systems by IS personnel. One of the major problems in information systems is the eliciting of a complete and correct set of requirements. Various techniques and methodologies have been proposed, but it still remains a difficult process. The problem is made more difficult because the analyst is an outsider who must be able to communicate with users in eliciting the requirements that users may not fully understand themselves. While having users develop their own system may not eliminate the problem of obtaining requirements, it does place an "insider" in the role of requirements problem solver.

Thirdly, EUC transfers the IS implementation process to end users. This transfer effectively eliminates the potential conflict from technical system experts and non-technical users, one of the major reasons why systems are not utilized. Users may develop less sophisticated systems when they do the design and development themselves, but they will use them.

EUC also poses a number of serious risks to the organization. First, elimination of the role of systems analyst also results in the elimination of an external reviewer throughout the development process. The systems analyst provides an organizational mechanism for enforcing standards, supplying technical expertise, and providing an independent review of requirements.

Secondly, there are limits to a user's ability to identify correct and complete requirements for an application. For example, human cognitive limits stem from behavior based on anchoring and adjustment, concreteness, recency, intuitive statistical analysis, and the structure of the problem space. In addition, errors in decision-making relative to requirements result from over-analysis and inefficient search, solving the wrong problem, and applying a wrong analysis or model. Thirdly, there is often a lack of user knowledge and acceptance of application quality assurance procedures for development and operation. This quality assurance is evidenced by testing, documentation, validation procedures, audit trails, and operating controls. End users may not perform these quality assurance procedures because of either lack of knowledge or lack of motivation.

MANAGEMENT OF EUC

The challenge for organizations is to find ways to manage EUC to maximize the benefits of EUC while minimizing the risks. Though management may be perceived as encompassing many different attributes, the three most critical attributes relating to EUC are the following:

1 *Policy setting and planning*. Policy setting identifies appropriate EUC practices and clarifies the acceptable form of outcomes concerning EUC activities. Planning efforts are aimed at identifying goals/objectives and establishing the framework for coordination and allocation of resources to EUC activities.
2 *Support*. EUC support refers to activities such as provision of tools and training opportunities that enhance the development and growth of EUC in organizations.
3 *Control*. Control processes insure that planned activities are performed effectively/efficiently and in compliance with policies and plans.

End-user computing is expected to be a permanent phenomenon. It requires resources that must be managed carefully to insure proper diffusion and use within the organization. Technical and managerial infrastructures need to be created to support EUC at all levels of the organization (i.e., individual, departmental/work group, and organizational).

enterprise architecture and information technology

Robert J. Benson

Enterprise architecture (EA) is a family of methods, frameworks, and standards that model an organization and its application of information technology (IT). Enterprise architecture includes information architecture, organization and business process architecture, and information technology architecture. Each consists of architectural representations, definitions of architecture entities, their relationships, and specifications of function and purpose. EA is holistic and organiza-

tion-wide, and includes organization aspects such as vision, strategy, and business process, and technical aspects such as information, applications, and infrastructure.

For an organization, an enterprise architecture, through its models and frameworks, represents the organization at one point in time. It describes the structure of the organization in terms of means of production, customer service, strategy and objectives, and use of information and information technology. It portrays component parts of a company and how they work together to achieve its business mission and goals. It connects the company's business structure, use of information and information technology, and the technology architectures needed.

Enterprise architecture is extensively used by business and information technology managers to guide their organization's design, implementation, and use of information technology. Enterprise architectures are used to deal with intra-organizational processes, inter-organizational cooperation and coordination, and their shared use of information and information technologies. Business developments such as outsourcing, partnerships, alliances, and information sharing and interchange extend the use of enterprise architecture across organization boundaries.

NEED FOR EA

Organizations need enterprise architecture when the complexity of information technology increases risk of failure, adds costs to its implementation and use, and increases the time required to implement new functionality and applications. Managers apply enterprise architecture when IT becomes complex and multifaceted enough to demand an overall model or blueprint to guide its design and implementation throughout the organization.

These problems are caused by the widespread success organizations have had in implementing information technology and the challenges of new technologies to be added to the existing implementations. For example, client/server, network, and INTERNET applications enable distribution of information and computer applications throughout the organization and beyond to its customers and suppliers. As a result, this has created an environment that includes rapid information technology proliferation, incompatible and non-communicating application systems, multiple networks, inaccessible data in parts of the enterprise, piecemeal technical solutions to business problems, uncoordinated developments in common areas of the enterprise, unintegrated data, and inadequate integrity and security of results.

Enterprise architecture addresses the risks of failure, increased costs, and increased implementation time by establishing standards by which proposed infrastructures and applications are assessed, and specifying the desirable future states for the organization's information, infrastructure, and applications. EA methods are used to represent the current state of the organization and its IT, identify gaps to the desired to-be state, and establish a roadmap to make the transition. In the short run, enterprise architecture addresses risk, cost, and implementation concerns by enabling quicker, more flexible, and less costly implementations. In the long run, enterprise architecture creates a cohesive view of how all the many pieces of information technology and the organization fit together and evolve into an effective whole.

ROLE OF EA

In concept, enterprise architecture is a major part of business and IT strategic planning. The actual management practices followed in a given organization, however, differ widely. For some organizations, enterprise architecture is limited to a standards and "to-be" definition for IT infrastructure. For these, EA practitioners construct and review business projects for compliance to the to-be architecture, and propose primarily infrastructure development projects. For other organizations, EA practitioners are also involved in defining the "to-be" for business process and enterprise information. For these organizations, EA also contributes significantly to the business content of projects and, in many cases, the definition of the projects themselves.

EVOLUTION OF EA

In the early days of IT, individual applications were mostly independent with little interaction with other applications, and with little integra-

tion of the information stored. Early IT infrastructures were also simple and dictated by monolithic large mainframes. Typically, an organization had just one mainframe, or perhaps a few similar mainframes. This meant that all applications were similarly constructed, applied common technical approaches and designs, and were managed in a common environment.

With the advent of minicomputers, personal computers, and servers, along with networks and ultimately the Internet, the hegemony of the mainframe environment disappeared for practical purposes. Organizations lost the common environment of the mainframe, and along with it the de facto standards and common practices it imposed. Different parts of the organization became free to adopt their own approaches to infrastructure and applications. At the same time, the information processed and stored became more effective when integrated with information in other applications. While the implementation environment became fragmented and multifaceted, the value of integration and coordination increased. This led to complex application and infrastructure development projects to overcome the fragmentation, differing standards, and incompatibility inherent in the rapidly changing technical environment.

Other more pragmatic problems also emerged in the post-mainframe technology fragmentation. Simply maintaining multiple variations of servers, database managers, application development environments, and networks added considerable complexity and cost. Through great efforts, technical organizations typically managed to build interfaces across multiple technical environments, but with complexity and resulting reliability problems. The resulting complex patchwork of applications and infrastructures also has proved resistant to change. The cost of further adaptation and integration has consequently risen. Organizations have had increasing difficulties in successfully designing and implementing large-scale and integrated IT applications and infrastructure.

Enterprise architecture is an approach to treat these maladies. Just as tools of structured development brought order to complex application development projects, the concepts of enterprise architecture can bring the same kind of order across the organization. By having appropriate business models, information models, and technology models, management decisions can be made about how best to integrate, consolidate, and simplify. Sound enterprise-wide models for infrastructure and information and applications can lead to simplifying technical design and management. By having fewer standards, new implementations can converge on more easily integratible and more manageable results. By focusing on sound technical decisions such as standards and vendors, the organization can avoid ever-increasing complexity, costs, and inflexibilities.

While EA started as a blueprint for infrastructure and application development, it has evolved into a complex of management processes. EA concepts are used to model the business and its processes, which leads to business process reengineering. EA concepts are used to model and architect information, which leads to DATA WAREHOUSING and data marts for the collection and dispersion of information throughout the enterprise. EA concepts are used to review prospective hardware and software acquisition for suitability for the organization, including how such acquisitions fit into the organization's IT strategy. EA is used as the basis for IT governance, meaning the ways in which business and IT management work together to form the vision and direction for IT in the organization.

EA MODELS AND FRAMEWORKS

Enterprise architecture has developed into several distinct families and frameworks. Interest groups, consulting organizations, and governments have all developed distinct flavors and methodologies. Support for enterprise architecture comes from many governments and large businesses. For example, the US government requires its agencies to have an active EA program, to apply EA in project development, project review, and decision-making, and to use EA in overall assessment of ongoing IT activities. There is, however, no common agreement on exactly what the components, models, and frameworks should be. As EA has evolved, it has taken many forms in companies and government organizations. There are significant variations in the details of frameworks and models. However, every EA approach has commonalities.

An enterprise architecture consists of several related architectures. The set of related architectures describes different elements of the enterprise. Diagrams and schematics are commonly used to represent enterprise architecture. For example, an entity-relationship diagram may portray enterprise information architecture, and an organization chart may portray the enterprise management structure. Such diagrams and schematics come from other disciplines such as organizational design. They have been adapted to describe enterprise architecture.

Six common components make up an enterprise architecture: the enterprise environment, the enterprise organization and structure, business processes, information, application systems, and IT support infrastructures.

- The *enterprise environment* architecture describes the business and technical connections between the enterprise and its customers, suppliers, and competitors. ELECTRONIC DATA INTERCHANGE (EDI) is one common element of such connections, and the Internet is a critical addition to the enterprise environment.
- *Enterprise organization and structure* architectures are often represented as hierarchies or networks reflecting the organization of an enterprise. The models describe its components, its division or departments, the functions to be carried out by each part, and key business performance measures. Elements of the organization model include organizational roles, responsibilities, and relationships with other organizational units including customers, suppliers, and government.
- *Business process* architectures describe the business processes used in the enterprise to provide goods and services.
- *Information* architectures describe the information required to support the enterprise business activities.
- *Application systems* architectures specify the software portfolios that deliver business functionality to the departments and business processes.
- *IT infrastructure* architectures describe the organization's computers, ranging from mainframe through personal computers. It

also specifies the network architectures that define the communications and messaging technologies that connect the enterprise. Software development architectures define the environment in which the enterprise acquires or develops applications. This includes case tools, database and data management environments, and automated development tools. IT support architectures specify the configuration of IT organizations, whether centralized or decentralized throughout the enterprise. Such support architectures include help-desk and support services, as well as development and operational organization support.

The Importance of EA to Management

Enterprise architecture evolved in response to IT complexity and the increasing difficulty organizations have had in controlling costs and delivering new implementations. Any manager facing these issues can obtain benefits in dealing with complexity, cost, and successful implementation.

While the benefits depend on the extent to which an organization effectively embraces enterprise architecture and applies it in management processes, the general benefits can include:

- Alignment: assuring the consistency of IT implementations with business requirements.
- Organization-wide consistency and integration: a common set of information architecture principles applicable to business processes, information and information flow, applications, and infrastructures.
- Capability to implement and time-to-market: reduction of complexity and increased speed in the ability to add new features to organization processes and IT implementations.

More specific benefits are observable in organizations that employ enterprise architecture:

- Common documentation about business and IT practices in the organization.
- Better communication about business and IT practices.

- Better understanding of the complexity inherent in the organization.
- A roadmap to close the gaps between an "as-is" and a "to-be" EA model of the business.
- Better ability to support business innovation.
- Simpler designs and implementations, and reduced cost of development.

Bibliography

Boar, B. H. (1998). *Constructing Blueprints for Enterprise IT Architectures*. New York: John Wiley.

Cook, M. (1996). *Building Enterprise Information Architectures*. Englewood Cliffs, NJ: Prentice-Hall.

Fowler, M. (2003). *Patterns of Enterprise Application Architecture*. Reading, MA: Addison-Wesley.

Spewak, S. and Hills, S. C. (1993). *Enterprise Architecture Planning*. New York: John Wiley-QED.

Zachman, J. A. (1987). A framework for information systems architecture. *IBM Systems*, 26 (3).

enterprise systems (enterprise resource planning or ERP)

Gordon B. Davis

The core enterprise systems include the set of applications that are necessary for transaction processing, managerial reporting, and reporting to stakeholders including investors and government authorities. These applications keep records on customers, employees, and suppliers and activities associated with them. These applications tend to be fairly standard within an industry, produce databases that are interrelated, and produce necessary reports. Often termed enterprise systems or ERP (enterprise resource planning), the systems consist of an integrated set of software modules linked to a common database. They handle transaction and reporting for functions such as finance, accounting, human resources, marketing, materials management, and distribution. There are several vendors of enterprise systems, the leading firm being the German software company SAP. One of the drivers for enterprise systems is the need by many companies to replace their legacy systems. ERP systems provide a complete solution to fragmented legacy systems. There are significant potential benefits and significant risks in implementing ERP systems.

The potential benefits are a complete solution to the basic information processing systems of the organization and an integrated database. The implementation provides an opportunity to change business processes and redesign reporting structures and reports. The enterprise systems are said to incorporate best business practices in the software for the different parts of the system. The systems impose discipline on information processing and strict adherence to standard practices.

The risks are the high costs of ERP projects and a high failure rate. There is a significant learning curve to adjust to the new, complex software. The ERP package must be tailored to the company using options provided by the system. This involves a large project involving screens, forms, reports, processing option decisions, etc. It is generally accepted that tailoring of an ERP system should only use the tailoring options provided by the package; there should be no attempt to rewrite the system to achieve unique processing. This means the organization is limited in its innovations for basic processing; innovations can occur but should be in addition to and outside the basic ERP processes and ERP database. If the ERP system turns out to not meet organization needs, there is significant cost and difficulty in replacing it with custom software or another ERP package.

See also *software package solutions*

ER diagrams

Roger H. L. Chiang

An entity-relationship (ER) diagram is a conceptual data schema that depicts various categories of data and their associations within an organization or information system. It does not specify how the data are organized, implemented, used, or maintained physically within the organization or information system. An ER diagram is constructed according to the ER model invented by Peter Chen in 1976. The ER model is widely used in industry for conceptual data modeling, especially for database development. In 1988, the American National Standards Institute (ANSI) chose the ER model as the standard for

information resource dictionary systems. The basic modeling concepts provided by the ER model are entities, relationships, and attributes.

ENTITIES AND ENTITY TYPES

Entities represent instances of real-world objects. Any object about which someone chooses to collect data is an entity. Entities of the same class are collected into entity types, e.g., *employee* and *project*. Entity is the most fundamental modeling construct in the ER model. Each entity type is described by a name and a set of attributes to represent entities' properties. Entities from the same entity type have common attributes. Usually, the name of an entity type is a noun. In an ER diagram, entity types are depicted as rectangular boxes.

RELATIONSHIPS AND RELATIONSHIP TYPES

Relationships represent associations among entities. *Employees work on projects*, for example, represents associations between the entities *employees* and *projects*. There must be at least two entity occurrences participating in each occurrence of a relationship. Entities that take part in a relationship are called the participating entities of the relationship. Similar to entity types, relationships of the same kind are grouped into a relationship type, e.g., *work on*. In an ER diagram, relationship types are commonly depicted as diamond-shaped boxes, which are connected by straight lines to the rectangular boxes representing the participating entity types. Usually, the name of a relationship type is a verb, which is displayed in the diamond-shaped box.

Degree. The degree of a relationship type is the number of participating entity types. Although relationships can be of any degree, the ones that occur most commonly are binary. A binary relationship type has two participating entity types. For example, the relationship type *work on* between *employee* and *project* is a binary relationship type.

Cardinality ratios. The cardinality ratios specify the number of relationship instances in which an entity can participate. The cardinality can be represented by its lower and upper bounds, called *Min* and *Max*, respectively. Consider a binary relationship *work on*. The *Min/Max* values of the cardinality indicate the minimum and maximum occurrences of the entity type *employee* that can occur for each occurrence of the entity type *project*, and vice versa. If each occurrence of *employee* can have exactly one corresponding occurrence of *project*, then the *Min/Max* cardinalities for *employee* are (1,1). On the other hand, if each occurrence of *project* can have many occurrences of *employee*, then the *Min/Max* cardinalities for *project* are (1,*n*), where *n* denotes "many." There are three basic cardinality ratios for binary relationship types: 1 : 1 (one-to-one), 1 : *n* (one-to-many), and *n* : *n* (many-to-many).

ATTRIBUTES

Entities and relationships have properties, represented as attributes. Some attributes may be identifiers (keys). The identifiers form the set of candidate keys for an entity type from which one is designated as the primary key. Similar to entity types, relationship types can have attributes. Consider the binary relationship type *work on*. The start date that an employee works on a particular project can be a relationship attribute of *work on*. It is neither an attribute of *employee* nor an attribute of *project*, because its existence depends on the combination of participating entities in a relationship instance.

See also *data modeling, logical; data modeling, physical*

e-retailing (e-tailing)

see INTERNET-BASED SELLING AND INFORMATION SYSTEMS

ergonomics

Gordon B. Davis

As applied to information systems, ergonomics is the design of equipment and user interfaces that fit the capabilities of human users (*see* HUMAN–COMPUTER INTERACTION). In the design of the keyboard, for example, ergonomic principles will result in a keyboard that does not overstress the hands of the human operator. In the design of a GRAPHICAL USER INTERFACE, ergonomic and human–computer interaction principles result in a screen that fits human cognitive capabilities.

errors in information systems

Stefano Grazioli and Barbara Klein

Information system error is a failure of a system to achieve the outcome intended by its user or designer. As organizations rely more and more on information systems for conducting their operations, the consequences of information system error increase. Even small errors can be magnified through the repeated application of an automated process. Because of their interconnectedness, modern systems are vulnerable to errors made by other systems. Errors are generally considered unintentional and due to human inattention, complexity, or misunderstanding. The errors may originate in the system specifications, the software, or the input and output processes. The methods for dealing with errors may not be sufficient to deal with intentional threats to the integrity of the system. The presence of an adversarial agent intentionally causing a fault distinguishes errors from threats such as hacking and computer crimes.

Errors can be enabled either by faults in the user interface or by faults in system processing. Interface errors occur in input and output. Input interface errors are due to user failure (e.g., data entry errors) or poor quality of the input data (e.g., the use of obsolete data). Output interface errors are due to user failure (e.g., misreading a display of information) or poor quality of the output information (e.g., an incomplete report). Processing errors occur during the execution of computer programs that operate on acquired data. Processing errors can be categorized as knowledge errors, software errors, and execution errors. Knowledge errors occur when the system achieves its intended function but does not satisfy the requirements of the problem (e.g., the system uses the straight-line method of depreciation instead of the appropriate double-declining-balance method). Software errors occur when the system fails to achieve its intended function because of bugs in a computer program (e.g., the program creates a new record for a customer who has moved instead of updating the existing record). Finally, execution errors occur when the system fails to achieve the function specified by the software because of a hardware or operator failure (e.g., a computer operator executes an obsolete version of a program).

Both prevention and detection are employed to reduce system errors. Prevention of information system errors is based on increasing the reliability and accuracy of both the input and output interfaces and processing. Interface errors can be prevented by guiding or constraining user actions. This can be achieved through user-centered design or through user training. Processing errors can be prevented through SOFTWARE ENGINEERING practices such as systematic testing and reviews of requirements, designs, and code.

Complete prevention of errors is generally impractical and expensive, so error detection is also needed. Detection is based on exploiting redundancy and verifying consistency with standards. Redundancy checks are based on duplication of information. Examples at the interface level include redundant data entry and check digits. At the processing level, examples are various control totals used to verify completeness of processing. Redundancy checks are particularly effective in the presence of random disturbances. Consistency checks identify conflicts between information and a standard. Examples of consistency checks at the interface level include programmed integrity constraints and spell checkers. Consistency checks at the processing level insure that the relationships among processed data values are valid. Consistency checks can detect both random and systematic errors.

ethics of computer use

Richard O. Mason

Ethics is the study and evaluation of human conduct in light of moral principles. In an information society, human conduct is greatly influenced by the use of computers, communication devices, and other forms of information technology. Using information technology inevitably creates ethical issues: situations in which an agent's acts, which were undertaken in order to achieve his or her own goals, materially affect the ability of one or more stakeholders to achieve their goals. The affected parties may be either helped or harmed (ethics works for the good as well as for bad or evil).

A moral agent can be an individual, a profession, an organization, or an entire society. Agents must address several central questions when facing an ethical issue: "What action should I take?" "How should I live my life?" "What kind of person or organization do I want to be?" These questions are eternal; they deal with the good, the right, or the just. The context in which they must be answered, however, changes with every major change in technology and social organization. The transition from ancient Egyptian and Greek societies to the *polis* of fifth-century BC Athens required the reflections of a Socrates, a Plato, and an Aristotle to redefine the meaning of "the good" and of virtue in the newly emerged social system. Similarly, in the modern day, there has been a transition from an industrial society, rooted in machines that augment physical energy and the organizational values of Frederick W. Taylor and Henry Ford, to a knowledge- or information-based society. The new society is founded on computers and communication technologies and tends toward flatter, more highly networked organizational units with intensive external relationships. All of this change requires a fundamental reexamination of ethics and morality (*see* INTERORGANIZATIONAL SYSTEMS).

Ethics requires the examination of an issue from several crucial points of view. What is the agent's duty (deontology)? What are the results of the act (consequentialism)? What does it say about the agent's character (virtue)? Is the outcome fair (justice)? The questions are universal, but their application is shaped fundamentally by the nature of an information society. In the contemporary information society, at least seven crucial issues face moral agents at the individual, professional, organizational, and societal levels.

(1) Technologically induced social change. Technology is generally implemented in order to secure economic and social gains. In the process, however, the flow and the balance of benefits and burdens to the stakeholders in the social

system are changed. Some people win; others lose, physically, psychologically, economically, or socially. Resulting from this redistribution of social status is a set of ethical issues that managers and MIS professionals must resolve, such as worker displacement, under-employment or "dumbing down" of jobs, depersonalization, new health hazards, over-reliance on technology, spatial reallocation (e.g., telecommuting; *see* VIRTUAL WORK), technological illiteracy, and the need for education and training.

(2) Privacy.   Modern information technology makes feasible and economical both the acquisition and integration of information about people and their behavior, and its storage, processing, dissemination, and use. On the one hand, some of this information is wanted and needed by decision-makers in business, government, and other organizations; on the other hand, some of it is gathered at the ethical cost of invading individual privacy. Sensitive, sometimes quite intimate, information about people is revealed to those who do not have a legitimate need to know it or who are not authorized by the subject party to know it. Managers must balance their temptation to acquire these data against their obligation to respect the privacy and autonomy of others. This ethical issue has led to the adoption of principles of fair information practices based on the concept of informed consent: no personal information should be acquired on a secret basis; an individual should be able to discover personal information that is being kept about him or her; the individual should be able to correct the record; the individual who gives consent for the collection of information for one purpose should be able to prohibit its collection for use for any other purpose; and any party collecting and handling personal information must assure its accuracy and reliability (see also below) and take reasonable precautions to prevent its misuse. Relevant US legislation includes the Freedom of Information Act of 1966, the Fair Credit Reporting Act of 1970, the Privacy Act of 1974, and the Privacy Protection Act of 1980 (*see* PRIVACY IN INFORMATION SYSTEMS).

(3) Property.   Property is something that can be possessed, controlled, or owned while excluding others from these privileges. As John Locke argued in the seventeenth century, people earn the right to make something their property by virtue of their physical and intellectual labor. Because information is intangible and mental, however, and it is symbolic, readily reproducible, easily transmittable, easily shared, and highly "leakable," it is difficult to exercise this right effectively with intellectual property. One's intellectual property is a source of wealth and value; consequently, other people are motivated, tempted, and, frequently, able to take it without compensating its owner.

Managers must steward and safeguard their organization's intellectual property and insure that their organizations and employees respect the property of others. This leads to issues such as software piracy, fraud, and theft in electronic funds transfers (*see* ELECTRONIC FUNDS TRANSFER) and accounts, and copyright infringements of all types. A related class of issues is program damage such as is caused by software viruses (*see* VIRUS), worms, logic bombs, and Trojan horses. Relevant US legislation includes the Copyright Act of 1976, the Electronic Funds Transfer Act of 1980, the Semiconductor Chip Protection Act of 1984, the Computer Fraud and Abuse Act of 1986, and proposed computer virus legislation (*see* SECURITY OF INFORMATION SYSTEMS).

One's intellectual capability and know-how is also property. Initiatives in the name of ARTIFICIAL INTELLIGENCE and expert systems designed to delve into a worker's mind, to capture the principles of his or her reasoning, and to program them into computer systems may also violate or compromise the property rights of that individual (*see* KNOWLEDGE BASE).

(4) Accuracy and reliability.   In an information society most people rely on information to make decisions that materially affect their lives and the lives of others. They depend on computers, communication devices, and other technologies to provide this information. Errors in information can result in bad decisions, personal trauma, and significant harm to other, often innocent, parties. Users are entitled to receive information that is accurate, reliable, valid, and of high quality (at least, adequate for the purposes to which they intend to put it). But this also entails a significant opportunity cost. Error-free,

high-quality information can be approximated only if substantial resources are allocated to the processes by which it is produced. Consequently, managers must make an ethical trade-off between conserving the resources and competences under their control and allocating them to produce higher-quality information. In any case, a certain minimal, socially acceptable level of accuracy is required of all information and information systems.

(5) Burden. The cost of providing information at any level of accuracy or quality is borne, usually, by a limited class of people. For managers, this raises a question of fairness: are the providers unduly burdened and adequately compensated for their contributions? At the governmental level, the Federal Paperwork Reduction Act of 1980 represents an attempt to relieve US citizens of some of the burdens involved in filling out forms.

(6) Access. Information is the primary currency in an information society and in information-intensive organizations. Managers are responsible for its just and equitable allocation. In order to participate effectively in a democratic society, people must have access to information concerning things that affect their work and their lives; and, therefore, they must have access to a minimal level of technology for handling information and they must receive an adequate level of general and technological education.

(7) Power. Power is the ability to influence or control other individuals or organizations. Its acquisition and use engenders responsibility. Information, including the capability to produce and handle it, is a fundamental source of power and a generator of responsibility. The principal intent of the strategic and marketing use of information technology, for example, is to enhance this power base. Wielding this power, however, must result in considerable help or harm to others. In industry, for example, capturing vital information sources can result in monopolistic power, which, in a free-market economy, raises serious questions for managers and for government as to how this power is to be channeled, allocated, and used responsibly (*see* STRATEGIC USE OF INFORMATION TECHNOLOGY).

The combined forces of technological "push" and demand "pull" will only serve to exacerbate these ethical issues for managers in the future as the increased use of information technology results in more information being made generally available. The availability of information creates its own demand due to its perceived benefits; and, consequently, more parties hasten to use the information in order to secure its benefits for themselves.

Bibliography

Johnson, D. G. (1985). *Computer Ethics*. Englewood Cliffs, NJ: Prentice-Hall.

Johnson, D. G. and Snapper, J. W. (1985). *Ethical Issues in the Use of Computers*. Belmont, CA: Wadsworth.

Mason, R. O., Mason, F. M., and Culnan, M. J. (1995). *Ethics of Information Management*. Thousand Oaks, CA: Sage.

Oz, E. (1994). *Ethics for the Information Age*. Dubuque, IA: Wm. C. Brown Communications.

executive information systems

Hugh J. Watson

An executive information system (EIS) is a computer-based application system that provides executives with internal and external information relevant to their management responsibilities. Characteristics typical of an EIS include:

- custom-tailored to individual executives;
- extracts, filters, compresses, and tracks critical data;
- provides current status information, trend analysis, exception reports, and drill down;
- accesses and integrates a broad range of internal and external data;
- user friendly and requires minimal training;
- used directly by executives without intermediaries;
- presents graphical, tabular, and textual information;
- provides support for electronic communications;
- provides data analysis capabilities;
- provides organizing tools.

DEVELOPMENT OF AN EIS

An organization may develop an EIS for a variety of reasons. Typical reasons are to achieve more timely, relevant, concise, complete, or better information. Other reasons are to be more responsive to changing market conditions, to support a total quality management program, or to facilitate downsizing of the organization. Critical to the success of an EIS is a strong high-level executive sponsor (such as the CEO). The sponsor initiates the project, allocates the needed resources, participates in the system's design, uses the system, and handles political resistance. Usually an EIS is developed by executive mandate rather than a comprehensive cost-benefit analysis. Executive sponsors also appoint operating sponsors to oversee the day-to-day development of the system. The operating sponsor may be selected from information systems or a functional area. This sponsor selects the EIS staff, draws up plans for the system's development, and helps resolve routine issues and problems.

The EIS staff is responsible for building, operating, and enhancing the system. The group must combine solid technical, business, and interpersonal skills. This staff performs tasks such as determining information requirements, evaluating hardware and software, designing screens, installing local area networks (LANs), and accessing needed data. An EIS includes a variety of internal and external and hard and soft information. Organizational databases and analyst spreadsheets are major sources of internal data. External data may come from marketing intelligence and electronic news and stock price databases. Soft information in the form of explanations, assessments, and predictions is sometimes included as annotations to screens in order to enhance user understanding of the numeric information displayed. Electronic dashboards and balanced scorecards are similar to EISs and can be viewed as the same type of system.

EVOLUTION OF EISs

Most systems are currently developed using special purpose, web-based EIS software. EISs are developed using a prototype/evolutionary development methodology. There is seldom a final product; they evolve in response to new or changing information requirements, the need to add new applications and capabilities (e.g., DE-CISION SUPPORT SYSTEMS), and to satisfy the needs of additional users.

While the executives of a firm are the primary audience for an EIS, successful systems frequently spread to additional users. Powerful push/pull forces are at work. The executives want to "push" the systems down to lower-level organizational personnel so that they can benefit from the system, while lower-level personnel want to "pull" the system down in order to see the information that higher-level executives are using. This process tends to extend the EIS to a broader audience than the top executives.

expert systems

Amit Das

Computer programs designed to mimic the problem-solving activity of human experts in specialized domains are known as expert systems. Human expertise is characterized by extensive knowledge of the problem domain (Chi, Glaser, and Farr, 1988). For a computer program to attain a comparable level of performance, the domain knowledge of human experts must be captured and represented in the program. Because of the centrality of domain knowledge in problem solving, expert systems are also known as knowledge-based systems.

THE STRUCTURE OF EXPERT SYSTEMS

The development of an expert system begins with the acquisition of knowledge from a human expert. A systems professional (known as a knowledge engineer) works closely with a domain expert to accumulate and organize a body of explicit knowledge relevant to the problem being solved. Since expert knowledge is often tacit (difficult to articulate), a variety of methods are used in the knowledge acquisition process. These methods include interviewing, analysis of past records of expert decisions, and observation of experts engaged in their natural activity.

Once a body of domain knowledge has been acquired, the knowledge must be represented in a form suitable for use in a computer program. A number of knowledge representation formalisms have been developed over the years. The most common of these are if–then rules (also called condition–action rules or production rules), though other formalisms such as frames and predicate logic have also been implemented in some commercial systems.

If–then rules, as their name suggests, have two parts: a set of conditions necessary for the rule to "fire" (the *if* part), and a set of actions or consequences resulting from the application of the rule (the *then* part). Two hypothetical rules from the field of automobile repair may be:

Rule 1: if (car does not start) then (check battery), and

Rule 2: if (battery OK) then (check fuel subsystem)

A rule-based expert system contains a large number of such if–then rules. The set of rules in an expert system is collectively called the KNOWLEDGE BASE of the expert system.

Problems are solved by the expert system by composing the individual stored rules into sequences that connect the initial state to the goal state. The composition of individual rules into sequences is called *chaining*; both backward and forward chaining systems are possible. In *backward chaining*, reasoning proceeds from the goal state to identify the prior states leading to the observed outcome. Diagnostic expert systems often employ backward chaining to identify fault hypotheses that would account for the observed malfunction. In *forward chaining*, reasoning starts at the initial state and progresses through successive states until an acceptable goal state is found. A design expert system may use forward chaining to generate a configuration of components that satisfies certain constraints. Certain problems are better suited to backward chaining, while others are better solved by forward chaining. It is also possible to combine the use of both forms of reasoning in a single expert system. The part of the expert system program that performs reasoning on the knowledge base is called the INFERENCE ENGINE.

While each if–then rule has a simple structure, the programming of rule-based expert systems becomes complex as the number of rules in the system increases (commercial systems may have thousands of rules). Clever pattern-matching algorithms have been devised to identify all the rules whose *if* conditions are satisfied in each state of problem solving. Selecting one of the applicable rules as the most promising one to fire (called *conflict resolution*) is also a non-trivial programming task.

The knowledge in an expert system may not be completely deterministic, i.e., there may be uncertainty in the relation between the *if* and the *then* parts of a rule. For instance, finding a chemical pattern in a sample from a drilling site does not guarantee the presence of oil, it only provides probabilistic evidence. To represent such uncertainty in rules and propagate it through the reasoning process, a variety of methods (certainty factors, Bayesian networks, Dempster–Shafer theory, and fuzzy sets) have been developed. Because of their capacity to process uncertain information, expert systems are not restricted to choosing single alternatives; instead, they can rank a set of alternatives in order of their likelihood, given the information available.

Though the reasoning processes of expert systems are based on formal logic, human reasoning does not always closely follow the tenets of formal logic. One such characteristic of human reasoning is non-monotonicity – the possibility that conclusions, once accepted, may be revised in view of new information. Implementing non-monotonic reasoning enables an expert system to mimic the human expert's reasoning more closely, but implementing such a capability is a formidable programming task.

In addition to a knowledge base and an inference engine, some expert systems also have rudimentary capabilities for explaining the reasoning behind the system's conclusions or requests for information. In most cases, the explanation facility is little more than a trace of the rules fired to produce the conclusion, but even such a minimalist explanation is better than having none at all, and provides some insight into the operation of the system.

Some expert systems also attempt to automate the knowledge acquisition process by conducting a dialogue with the user. An analysis of the knowledge base identifies the items of knowledge that can be used to generate hypotheses or choose among them. The user is then requested to supply these items of information through a structured question-and-answer dialogue, and his/her responses are incorporated into the knowledge base. Automated knowledge acquisition opens up the possibility of improving system performance with usage.

COMMERCIAL APPLICATIONS OF EXPERT SYSTEMS

Significant commercial interest in expert systems was generated by the pioneering systems of the early 1980s: MYCIN (Buchanan and Shortliffe, 1984) in medical diagnosis; R1 (McDermott, 1982) in computer system configuration; and PROSPECTOR in mineral exploration. These programs amply demonstrated the power of knowledge-intensive approaches in solving otherwise intractable problems. The early programs were all hand-crafted in the LISP programming language, took multiple man-years of effort (from domain experts as well as software designers), and ran on special purpose hardware. Though some high-technology companies invested in similar hand-crafted expert systems for their own applications, the popularity of expert systems technology in the business world spread mainly after inexpensive expert system "shells" became available.

An *expert system shell* is a commercially available programming environment that allows the entry of domain knowledge in the form of rules. An inference engine (usually capable of forward as well as backward chaining) is included in the shell, and a GRAPHICAL USER INTERFACE facilitates the entry of rules and the observation of system performance. Many commercial shells also include interfaces to other software such as databases and programming languages. The availability of inexpensive shells running on desktop computers enabled individuals and organizations to create their own expert systems with minimal effort, and a large number of such systems appeared in organizations. With domain experts increasingly able to enter rules by themselves, the difficulties of knowledge acquisition were significantly reduced. In some ways, expert system shells became vehicles for END-USER

COMPUTING, by which means skilled professionals, such as engineers and scientists, could institutionalize their personal expertise.

Today, expert systems are widely used in businesses to perform tasks ranging from diagnosis of manufacturing processes to credit approval by credit card companies. By encapsulating human expertise in computer programs, expert systems make such expertise durable, portable, and affordable. Numerous organizational scholars have also written about the organizational impacts of formalizing knowledge into expert systems.

CURRENT DIRECTIONS IN EXPERT SYSTEMS RESEARCH

The first generation of expert systems, though commercially successful, had several shortcomings. They did not differentiate clearly between the knowledge used to construct the state space formulation of a problem and the knowledge used to guide heuristic search. This gave the knowledge acquisition process a somewhat haphazard character, making it prone to cost and time overruns. First-generation expert systems were made up entirely of an undifferentiated set of if–then associations. While this simplified the control structure of the programs, maintenance of the expert system in the face of rule additions became a problem (since the newly added rule could conflict with any of the existing rules). First-generation systems were also remarkably brittle, in the sense that any question even slightly outside the precisely defined scope of the system would evoke a "don't know" response.

Research into the second generation of expert systems (mid-1980s to the present) has sought to reframe the expert system development process as a modeling activity. Attempts are now made to create and use explicit models of the domain to which the expert system will be applied. The use of explicit models in expert systems overcomes many of the difficulties of the earlier-generation systems. Models provide a hierarchical organization for the knowledge in a system: the structure of the underlying model is clearly differentiated from associational if–then rules about the behavior of the model. The focus on a model also provides guidance to the knowledge acquisition process through the separation of domain knowledge from search control knowledge. Hopes have been expressed about the potential reusability of models across tasks and systems, thus simplifying maintenance. Finally, a model-based approach also has the potential to deal with novelty; hence it may produce less brittle expert systems.

Traditionally, knowledge acquisition has been a frequent bottleneck in the development of expert systems. An active area of current research is the attempt to bypass the knowledge acquisition bottleneck through machine learning. Machine learning programs take as input a set of past cases (containing observed symptoms as well as expert judgments) and attempt to detect regularities in the relation between the symptoms of a case and the judgment of the expert in that case. Given sufficient data, it is possible to approximate the heuristics used by the expert in making his/her judgments, alleviating the need for the first-hand acquisition of this knowledge. The machine-generated heuristic knowledge can be programmed easily into an expert system.

See also *artificial intelligence; cognitive science and information systems*

Bibliography

Buchanan, B. G. and Shortliffe, E. H. (1984). *Rule-Based Expert Programs: The MYCIN Experiments of the Stanford Heuristic Programming Project*. Reading, MA: Addison-Wesley.

Chi, M. T. H., Glaser, R., and Farr, M. (eds.) (1988). *The Nature of Expertise*. Hillsdale, NJ: Lawrence Erlbaum.

McDermott, J. (1982). R1: A rule-based configurer of computer systems. *Artificial Intelligence*, **19** (1), 39–88.

explanation systems

Explanation systems are incorporated into EXPERT SYSTEMS in order to explain to users the logic applied by the expert system in arriving at the recommended solution.

extranet

Gordon B. Davis

An extranet is an INTERNET that has restricted external access and use. Unlike the Internet, which is a public system, an extranet is a private network. It uses Internet protocols, so it appears to users the same as an Internet site, and access to files and other information is performed in the same way as at an Internet site. An organization implements an extranet by establishing a private website to share information with a group of external users, such as customers or suppliers. An external user uses a web browser to obtain information and services, but access requires a valid user name and password that the organization provides to appropriate users. Any type of information that can be shared over the Internet can also be shared over an extranet. This includes documents, video, audio, data, etc. The extranet is made secure by a firewall and passwords (*see* SECURITY OF INFORMATION SYSTEMS). The extranet may provide various levels of access, so that a given password may give permission to access part of the extranet resources but not other parts. An extranet is important in information systems because it allows an organization to share information with selected external parties in a controlled way.

See also *e-commerce business-to-business systems; Internet; intranet*

extreme programming

see AGILE DEVELOPMENT

failure of information system applications

Kathryn Ritgerod Nickles

There is a high failure rate in the design and implementation of information system applications. Failed information system applications result in high costs for organizations and potentially serious consequences for individuals whose lives or properties depend on them. Therefore, both management of organizations and those involved in information system projects should be aware of the factors that are associated with success; they should also understand how to diagnose and learn from failures.

Evaluation of information system applications does not usually result in binary judgment of success or failure. They are judged across a continuum that ranges from complete and obvious failure to high success. Applications found at the failure end of the spectrum are judged as failures because they do not meet or exceed some threshold of performance on one or more key dimensions. For example, an application may fail to meet user expectations for streamlining work or the implementation of an application may be plagued by delays. In either case, the application may be redesigned, under-utilized, or even abandoned. Although there are many reasons for abandoning an application, the clearest measure of failure occurs when the application is discarded with the *perception* that it was a failure.

Perceptions of system stakeholders (users and others who are interested in the success or failure of the application) are key to understanding or diagnosing information system failure. Stakeholder views vary, affecting their opinions and diagnoses of the system. An application that may be considered successful according to one view may be considered a failure by another. There-fore, in diagnosis and evaluation, it is important to identify the view being applied. Four major views are often applied: technological imperative view, organizational culture view, political view, and sociotechnical view.

An evaluator who holds a *technological imperative view* considers only the hardware, software, and data components of a system and thus sees information system failure as a hardware failure, software failure, data failure, or any combination of these. Remedial measures according to this view involve redoing (correctly) system analysis and design, accompanied by the willing participation of everyone involved in the development cycle procedures. Any failure according to this view is regarded as a failure of the developers or users and not a failure of the technology.

To those who hold an *organizational culture view*, the technology is seen as an artifact that must adapt to the needs of the people and the organization. A failed information system is one that does not serve well the individuals within the organization or fit organization activities or rituals. According to this view, redesigning an application to conform better to the organization may prevent system failure.

To the stakeholder who holds a *political view*, the development, implementation, and use of the information system application all provide a context within which power may be exercised by a person, group, or other organizational unit. The purposes of the information system are secondary to the exercise of power. Preventing application failure thus requires strong support from individuals or units within the organization whose primary interest is a political agenda.

Another view, the *sociotechnical view*, sees an information system as a social system that uses information technology. Because of the inter-action between technology and the social system, an application is likely to fail when the social and technical considerations are not well integrated. For example, if technical considerations dominate the development and implementation process and future users are ignored, user resistance may cause the application to fail. To prevent failure in this case, the sociotechnical view suggests that users become effective participants in the design process.

Bibliography

Davis, G. B., Lee, A., Nickles, K. R., Chatterjee, S., Hartung, R., and Wu, Y. (1992). Diagnosis of an information system failure. *Information and Management*, 23, 293–318.
Lucas, H. C. (1975). *Why Information Systems Fail*. New York: Columbia University Press.
Lyytinen, K. and Hirschheim, R. (1987). Information systems failures: A survey and classification of the empirical literature. *Oxford Surveys in IT*, 4, 257–309.

file transfer protocol

Gordon B. Davis and J. Davis Naumann

A provider of information may make it available in the form of a file to be copied by anyone who has access privileges and access software.

A protocol for file transfer is the file transfer protocol (FTP). Developed as part of the ARPANET project to aid transfer of research among universities and other research sites, it is now a standard INTERNET protocol. The FTP protocol is built in to many communication software tools. The user specifies file transfer using FTP by selecting an option.

FTP is employed to transfer data files, program files, software corrections, manuals, and a variety of other data. The transfer can be in either direction. For example, many software providers establish files that users can FTP in order to get software modifications. The software modifications obtained in this way are used in the same way as modifications on diskettes. In general, a user needs to know whether the data in the files are text data or are binary coded. This affects the options for file transfer.

The most frequent use of FTP for information retrieval is known as anonymous FTP. In this convention, the FTP server (the source of the information) establishes an account named "anonymous." Users (clients) connect to the account using "anonymous" as a user name with their email names as passwords. Many current versions of FTP client software hide technical and procedure details from their users and make anonymous FTP connections automatically. The user may use a graphical interface (*see* GRAPHICAL USER INTERFACE) to specify transfer to or from a remote computer directory.

firewall

see INFORMATION ASSURANCE; RISK ASSESSMENT AND RISK MANAGEMENT

flowchart

Flowcharts describe the flow of work in a system or the flow of processing and logic in a program. Both system flowcharts and program flowcharts employ the same set of symbols. Program flowcharts are typically used in informal design but are not usually included in formal documentation because of the difficulty of updating them when programs are altered.

FORTRAN

An algebraic programming language (FORmula TRANslator) (*see* PROGRAMMING LANGUAGES).

genetic algorithms

Sangkyu Rho

Many applications in information systems require a search for a solution where there is no well-defined algorithm to find the solution. Genetic algorithms (GA) are a class of robust and efficient search methods based on the concept of evolution in natural organisms. They have been successfully applied to complex problems in diverse fields, including optimization (e.g., traveling salesperson problem), machine learning (e.g., rule induction), and studying evolution (e.g., simulation of biological adaptation).

The basic ideas of GA are: (1) a representation of solutions, typically in the form of bit strings, likened to genes in a living organism; (2) a set of solutions likened to a population of living organisms, each having a genetic makeup; (3) a performance measurement of how good a solution is, likened to a Darwinian notion of "fitness," which represents how well a living organism has adapted to its environment; (4) genetic operators, which derive the genetic makeup of an offspring from that of its parents; and (5) a selection process where the fittest solutions survive into the next generation and the less fit solutions do not.

To illustrate these components, consider a simple optimization problem. Suppose we want to maximize the function $f(x) = -x^2 + 22x + 279$ on the integer interval [0, 31], as shown in figure 1. The optimal solution is $x = 11$. A solution, x, can be represented by five bits as a binary number. For example, 01001 represents $2^3 + 2^0 = 9$.

A genetic algorithm begins by randomly generating an initial set of solutions (i.e., the *population*). The population should be large enough to insure a reasonable sample of the actual solution space, but not so large as to make the algo-rithm approach exhaustive enumeration. Figure 1 and table 1 show an initial population of size 4 for the sample problem.

During each iteration, called a *generation*, the solutions in the population are evaluated using some measure of fitness or performance. In the example problem, the fitness of a solution can be defined as the value of the function (i.e., $f(x)$). Fitness should be defined such that it is non-negative and that the fitness of a better solution is greater than that of a worse solution. Therefore, in other problems such as minimization problems, the value of the function cannot be used as the fitness measure.

After evaluating the fitness of each solution in the population, some of the solutions are selected to be parents. Typically, parents are selected probabilistically with the selection probability for any solution being proportional to its fitness. Parents are paired and genetic operators applied to produce new solutions, called *offspring*. A new generation is formed by selecting solutions (parents and offspring) so as to keep the population size constant. Solutions to survive are typically selected based on their fitness.

The genetic operators commonly used to produce offspring are crossover and mutation. Crossover is the primary genetic operator. It operates on two solutions (parents) at a time and generates offspring by combining segments from both parents. A simple way to achieve crossover, as illustrated in figure 2, is to select a cut point at random and produce offspring by concatenating the segment of one parent to the left of the cut point with that of the other parent to the right of the cut point. A second offspring can be produced by combining the opposite segments. Selecting solutions based on their fitness yields the second generation shown in figure 2 and table 2.

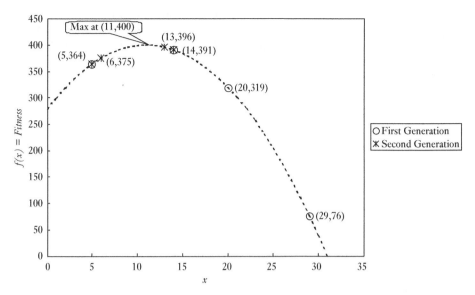

Figure 1   An example problem

Mutation generates a new solution by independently modifying one or more bit values of an existing solution, selected at random. It serves to guarantee that the probability of searching a particular subspace of the solution space is never zero.

Finally, a genetic algorithm terminates when a prespecified stopping condition is satisfied, typically some number of generations.

Table 1   Initial population

Solution	x	f(x)	Fitness
11101	29	76	76
00101	5	364	364
01110	14	391	391
10100	20	319	319

Table 2   Second-generation population

Solution	x	f(x)	Fitness
00101	5	364	364
01110	14	391	391
00110	6	375	375
01101	13	396	396

Although greatly simplified, the above example provides insight into why genetic algorithms are effective. As crossover combines solutions, a number of partial solutions, termed *schemas* (e.g., $0****$, $*1**1$, $01***$), having good performance, begin to emerge in multiple solutions.

Parents with above-average performance are expected to contain some number of good schemas (e.g., $01***$). With a probabilistic selection process, such parents are likely to produce more offspring than those with below-average performance (which are expected not to contain as many good schemas). Over successive generations, the number of good schemas represented in the population tends to increase, and the number of bad schemas tends to decrease. Therefore, the fitness of the population tends to improve and converges to that of an optimal solution(s).

Parent 1	0 0 1 0 1
Parent 2	0 1 1 1 0
	↑
	cut point
Offspring 1	0 0 1 1 0
Offspring 2	0 1 1 0 1

Figure 2   Crossover operation

Bibliography

Goldberg, D. E. (1989). *Genetic Algorithms in Search, Optimization, and Machine Learning.* Reading, MA: Addison-Wesley.

Holland, J. H. (1992). *Adaptation in Natural and Artificial Systems.* Cambridge, MA: MIT Press.

global positioning system (GPS)

Gordon B. Davis

GPS is a global positioning system. The system uses satellites to determine the exact geographic position of a receiver. The receiver can be a specialized global positioning receiver or it can be incorporated in another device such as a cell phone. GPS is important to information system applications in organizations because it allows instant identification of the location of a delivery truck, a person, an automobile, etc. It can be used in an application that involves identification of a location. For example, a small computer and communication device (such as a handheld computer) can identify its location by GPS and look up a map of the area, provide specification of the location, obtain instructions to go from that location to another specified address, or summon assistance with positive identification to guide assistance personnel to the location.

GPS technology enables a number of business applications that depend upon knowledge of the position of a customer, service facility, vendor, etc. For example, the exact location of service personnel may be determined, and service assignments made on the basis of this information. A disabled automobile may transmit its exact location in order for service to be dispatched. The location of a person wanting a hotel or restaurant can be used to identify the nearest hotel or restaurant meeting specified requirements and the driving instructions to reach the location.

graphical user interface

Gordon B. Davis

A graphical user interface (GUI) is used in almost all personal computer and workstation applications. The screen presents the user with an accur-ate representation of an input form, a document, a report, etc. Menus, icons, and buttons are represented graphically. This has been termed "what you see is what you get" (WYSIWYG). The graphical user interface extends to direct manipulation of objects of interest such as schematic diagrams, process control flows, simulations, and games. Graphical user interfaces are also used for menu selection, form fill-in, and icon selection to invoke operations. A mouse is usually used to move the cursor, but keyboard keys such as tab are also used.

graphics in information systems

Sirkka L. Jarvenpaa

Graphics are used for analyzing, presenting, and communicating data. Their increased use has occurred owing to a heightened need for better and more relevant information and the availability of low-cost computer graphics tools. Graphics can help identify key variables and trends, highlight important relationships among variables, and demonstrate subtle but important deviations or exceptions. However, confusing and misleading graphs can also be produced.

Graphics are abstract pictures conveying information about numbers and relationships among numbers using points, lines, a coordinate system, numbers, symbols, words, shading, and color. Statistical graphics, such as scatter plots, time-series charts, and multivariate displays, were invented during the period 1750–1800. Graphics capabilities became available to managers in the early 1980s with spreadsheet, database, and statistics software. The software allowed nearly automatic conversion of data already stored in computer-readable files to two-dimensional or three-dimensional graphics such as pie charts, bar or line graphs, scatter plots, and contour charts.

A common belief among professionals and managers is that graphs provide more appealing as well as more effective presentations of data. Graphical representations are inherently more appealing than text or tables. Graphs are free from clutter and can be richer, provide a "Gestalt" effect, have a higher level of abstraction, are more memorable, more fun, and so on. Graphics are, however, not necessarily more effective than text or tables. Different graphical formats are equivalent neither to each other nor to tables; each graphical format has its own particular uses and limitations. For example, horizontal bar graphs suffer from different human perceptual biases and limitations than vertical bar charts. The effectiveness of a particular graph is dependent upon other factors besides the particular graph format used, namely, the purpose of the task and the experience of the user (Jarvenpaa and Dickson, 1988).

In general, tasks where graphs perform well are those that require display of relational information. For example, in a bar graph the heights of the adjacent bars emphasize the relational perspective of the data, not the specific heights of each bar. By contrast, when the task involves presentation of specific data values, a tabular form is superior. The relational aspect of information typically becomes more emphasized with larger data sets. With small data sets, individual numbers are often as important as the relative dimensions of the data. Tufte (1983) recommends the use of tables for data sets of 20 numbers or less.

The leading theory explaining the effectiveness of presentation formats is "encoding specificity," which deals with how perceptual mechanisms and memory interact in human information processing. The theory argues that the recall of information is highest if the circumstances surrounding the acquisition of that information are recreated at the time of recall of the information. In the information systems literature, the theory has been extended to decision-making processes as "cognitive fit" (Vessey, 1991). Simply stated, this means that information should be presented in the form that creates a problem representation that best supports the decision and recall strategies (methods and processes) required to perform a particular task. In decision support, a graphic display form should directly support the structure of the problem. Besides the issue of task, there is a significant education and training component to the efficacy of presentation formats. Business people often prefer tables to graphics unless a large amount of data is summarized because they have more exposure to tables.

The two fundamental rules for the construction of graphics are that (1) physical measures on the surface of the graph should be proportional to the numerical values being portrayed, and (2) graphs are well labeled in terms of their scales, grids, and titles. These principles are violated, for example, when the starting baseline of a line graph is at a number other than zero or the time frame or scale varies from one graph to another without any notification. Used properly, graphs have an important role in analyzing, presenting, and communicating information for decision-making, but the use of graphics requires a manager to understand the relative advantages and disadvantages of graphs, as well as the ability to correctly perceive and interpret graphs.

Bibliography

Jarvenpaa, S. L. and Dickson, G. W. (1988). Graphics and managerial decision-making: Research-based guidelines. *Communications of the ACM*, 31 (6), 764–74.

Tufte, E. R. (1983). *The Visual Display of Quantitative Information*. Cheshire, CT: Graphics Press.

Vessey, I. (1991). Cognitive fit: A theory-based analysis of the graphs versus tables literature. *Decision Sciences*, 22, 219–40.

grid computing

Nellai Subramaniam and Dennis A. Adams

Grid computing seeks to provide an infrastructure to access computing resources such as central processing unit (CPU) processing power, storage, memory, and distributed applications in a consistent and pervasive manner. Typically, the infrastructure consists of the hardware required to network the resources, the software to manage and access the various resources, and the protocols and standards that are implemented to form the grid. A simple grid may consist of a dozen PCs with a homogeneous hardware architecture and operating system, and hooked together by means of a local area network (LAN), while a complex grid may include machines from different organizations with heterogeneous hardware architecture and operating system, hooked together by means of a wide area network (WAN). The grid within a single organization may be referred to as an intragrid, while a grid that spans organizations may be referred to as an intergrid.

One may consider grid computing as a logical extension of scalable and distributed computing concepts. As early as 1973, scientists working at the Xerox Palo Alto Research Center networked 100 computers together to perform shared computations (Buyya and Chetty, 2001). By replicating a worm program in the memory of each of the computers, the scientists were able to harness the idle computational processing power resident on the networked machines and generate realistic computer graphics. Advances in networking technology in the last decade have now resulted in computers being hooked through the INTRANET and INTERNET to form computational grids for high-performance computing. The computational grid may be considered as being analogous to the electrical power grid. Users within the electrical power grid have access to consistent and pervasive power. Though computational grids have not reached the same level of maturity of electrical power grids, nevertheless protocols and standards are being developed to allow users within and external to the grid to have consistent and reliable access to the computing resources provided by the grid.

The protocols and standards required to build a computational grid may be classified into four different layers (Foster, 2002): fabric, connectivity and resource, collective, and user application layer. The fabric is the lowest layer and includes the physical devices such as computers, storage media, and network systems. The next layer is the connectivity and resource layer, which contains protocols for communication, AUTHENTICATION, initiation, and monitoring of applications that facilitate resource sharing among users. The collective layer includes protocols to provide directory services for resource discovery, brokering services for resource allocation, data replication services, and services for monitoring user access. The user application layer, as the name suggests, consists of user applications that call on components in other layers to perform their tasks.

By creating computational grids, organizations can expect to cut costs and save time. Applications that are cost intensive and inconvenient for an organization to develop locally may be accessed on an on-demand basis from an external organization in a cost-effective way. Applications that consist of tasks and problems that take forever to complete in a single system

owing to lack of processing power can be completed by using the idle resources present in computers that reside in different departments, thereby reducing processing time. A recent research endeavor has shown that a supercomputer may be built with protocols similar to grid protocols, at a fraction of the cost of a traditional supercomputer. Scientists at the Virginia Tech University have built one of the fastest supercomputers in the world, which can compute at 7.41 trillion operations a second, by linking together 1,100 Apple Macintosh computers (Markoff, 2003). While typical supercomputers may cost between $100 and $250 million, the Virginia Tech supercomputer cost only about $5 million.

Major IT vendors are repositioning their computing strategies to include grid computing. More and more companies in fields such as biomedical, financial, oil exploration, motion picture, and aerospace are using grid computing for highly compute-intensive tasks (Taylor and Subramaniam, 2004). The worldwide grid spending is expected to increase from $250 million in 2003 to approximately $4.9 billion in 2008, with professional business services and financial applications accounting for the highest grid expenditures (Insight, 2003). Organizations need to be aware of what the grid can and cannot do and the associated risks. Nevertheless, grid computing is maturing into an attractive option for businesses and is gradually moving from academic and research institutes to commercially viable solutions.

Bibliography

Buyya, R. and Chetty, M. (2001). Weaving computational grids: How analogous are they with electrical grids? *IEEE Technical Reports*.

Foster, I. (2002). The grid: A new infrastructure for 21st-century science. *Physics Today*, February; www.aip.org/pt/vol-55/iss-2/p42.html.

Insight Research Corporation (2003). Grid computing: A vertical market perspective 2003–2008. *Insight Research Corporation Report*.

Markoff, J. (2003). Low-cost supercomputer put together from 1100 PCs. *New York Times*, October.

Taylor, R. and Subramaniam, N. (2004). Networking in the new millennium: Business applications for peer-to-peer and grid computing. *Proceedings of AMCIS 2004*, New York.

group decision support systems

Gerardine DeSanctis and Moez Limayem

Group decision support systems (GDSS) are a class of COMPUTER-SUPPORTED COOPERATIVE WORK (CSCW) system intended for use in group problem solving, planning, choice, and other decision tasks. A GDSS specifically targets group decision-making, whereas CSCW systems support a broader range of multiparty work activities. A simple GDSS may be created by applying a single-user decision support system (DSS) (*see* DECISION SUPPORT SYSTEMS) to a problem confronting a group. For example, a board of directors may use a forecasting model to project sales and expenses for a new business; a project team may apply risk analysis to compare possible courses of action; or an engineering group may use computerized optimization techniques to evaluate approaches to producing chemical compounds. These are very rudimentary forms of GDSS. More sophisticated GDSSs provide facilities designed for use by groups. In practice, most GDSS implementations involve facilities built specifically for group decision processes.

Implementations vary, but most GDSSs include two types of facilities to support group decision-making: (1) discussion management and (2) decision modeling. These are two general approaches to group problem solving that have been used in organizations for many years, and a GDSS adds computerization to each of these longstanding approaches.

The *discussion* approach to group problem solving involves bringing various experts and/or stakeholders together to identify issues and provide an environment for resolution. The strength of the discussion approach is that talking about a problem in a group setting can open divergent perspectives on the causes of a problem and creative thinking about how to solve it. Group discussion provides broad input on a problem, which can facilitate rapid idea generation and commitment to implementation of solutions. *Decision modeling* involves formulation of a mathematical representation of the problem and solution trade-offs. Once modeled, the problem is "solved" by using one or more algorithms deemed appropriate for the model. In some cases the models are spatial as well as mathematical, using graphical techniques to display variables and relationships to the group. The strengths of the group modeling approach are that it allows consideration of many variables and relationships simultaneously, and multiple parties can provide inputs to the model specification and analysis. Mathematical models facilitate rational analysis of complex problems and help to overcome the cognitive limitations of a decision-making group. Inputs to the model can be objective or opinion-based. A GDSS contains facilities to support group discussion and modeling.

GDSS FUNCTIONALITY

Discussion support.   To support group discussion, GDSSs include facilities for group note-taking, idea organization (clustering), voting and opinion polling, candid commenting, and storage and retrieval of meeting minutes. Additional facilities might include anonymous recording of individual inputs and step-by-step procedures for using the features within the system. Groups might create their own step-by-step procedures, piecing together features according to the particular needs of their meeting. Alternatively, they might use preestablished discussion procedures, such as Robert Rules of Order or a meeting protocol, to guide their discussion.

Decision modeling.   To support decision analysis, GDSSs take decision models developed for individual use, such as multicriteria modeling, forecasting, and risk analysis, and explode their components to accommodate input from multiple parties. For example, a multi-attribute utility model might be exploded to allow several $(2-n)$ people to (1) generate criteria; (2) weight criteria; (3) identify alternatives; (4) rate alternatives against criteria; and (5) calculate a relative score for each alternative. The model may generate various types of outputs for the group, such as lists of criteria, the average weight given by group members to each criterion, lists of alternatives, and average ratings given to each alternative on each criterion. More sophisticated GDSSs may provide extensive statistics on the model outputs, graphical display of group opinions, and the opportunity to change the parameters of the model and perform dynamic "what if" analyses. Expansion of individual decision models to accommodate multiparty input, processing, and output requires extensive computer programming and numerous design decisions regarding how data should be entered, processed, and displayed.

GDSS Operation

Typically, groups do not rely upon a GDSS for their entire problem-solving process but rather use a subset of available features at various points during their deliberations. Verbal discussion in a meeting, or electronic messaging in the case of dispersed groups, supplements use of the GDSS. The typical setting for GDSS use is the face-to-face meeting (rather than dispersed conferences) (see figure 1). In a GDSS-supported meeting, each participant has a workstation through which ideas, votes, comments, and so on can be entered. Usually, such information is entered anonymously. Simultaneous and anonymous entry of information speeds up the data gathering process and encourages group members to be creative and uninhibited in self-expression. Once entered, information then can be publicly shared on a common viewing screen or software window, which provides a focal point for the group discussion. In a face-to-face meeting the common screen is physically located in the front of the room. If group members are dispersed across a network, public information is viewed in a designated window or screen at the individual's private workstation. A network is needed to connect all of the workstations together into a common workstation, or server, where the heart of the GDSS software resides.

Design Rationale

GDSS design is based on a systems view of group decision-making in which the group's size, styles of interacting, and other characteristics are *inputs* along with the task at hand to the group decision *process*. The group's decision process occurs as members exchange information with one another and work to solve the problem that they confront. Depending on the nature of the group's decision and related processes, certain *outcomes* will result. Group decision outcomes can be described in terms of their quality, the time required for the group to reach the solution, the total number of ideas generated, the degree of consensus among members about the final solution, and members' willingness to implement the solution. *Feedback* in the system occurs as decision outcomes serve as inputs to future interactions that group members undertake. The entire group decision process takes place within

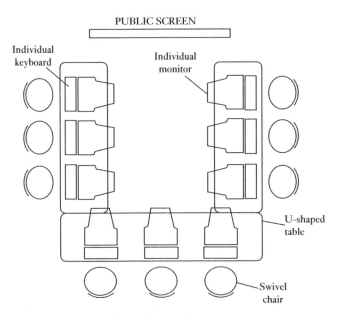

Figure 1   Typical GDSS configuration for a face-to-face meeting

a broader social context, such as a particular organization, institution, or society, which has a dynamic relationship with the group's decision system, affecting how inputs to interaction are defined and how the group decision process is conducted.

GDSS designers treat the inputs to the decision process as givens and proceed to consider how the group interaction process might be improved. That is, given a particular problem, a set of people responsible for resolving it, and a specific social context, how might technology be designed to facilitate analysis and resolution of the problem? GDSS designers have relied heavily on a large body of research that documents the difficulties that groups experience during decision-making and methods for overcoming these difficulties. The literature indicates that groups are more creative, engage in more thorough analysis, reach higher-quality decisions, and gain higher commitment to solution implementation when there is full and even participation in the decision process, rather than low participation or dominance by a few members. Unfortunately, groups often have difficulty achieving full and even participation in their deliberations owing to the *process losses* associated with interpersonal communication. In other words, when one person faces a decision, energy focuses solely on problem analysis and solution, but in a group setting, tremendous energy is expended in regulating interpersonal communication and dealing with socioemotional issues, such as conflict, influence, and the like.

Group researchers argue that process losses can be overcome and decision-making improved if groups are supplied with process interventions that promote more even participation, appreciation of multiple viewpoints, and systematic reasoning. Group discussion techniques and decision models provide these kinds of interventions, and GDSS designers often begin by automating techniques that originally were designed to be implemented manually or with minimal computer support. For example, computer files and view screens can be used instead of flipcharts or electronic blackboards; keyboards can be used instead of index cards or round-robin voice voting; and inputs to decision models can be made via electronic files or by members themselves, rather than by a special facilitator or modeling expert. A key aspect of the GDSS design is

separate but linked facilities for managing individual (private) versus group (public) work.

GDSS DESIGN ALTERNATIVES

GDSS design is centered around providing discussion and modeling support to a group's decision process. Table 1 shows how GDSS designers map system functionality to group process needs. Systems vary, of course, in their specific features and implementation, and there are several useful dimensions for distinguishing among GDSS designs.

Comprehensiveness. This is the degree to which the GDSS offers a full range of functionality. The more extensive the system's functionality, the more comprehensive it is. More comprehensive GDSSs can be applied to a variety of decisions, whereas less comprehensive systems target particular aspects of the group problem-solving process (e.g., idea generation, impact assessment) or particular types of decisions (e.g., transportation, agriculture). More comprehensive systems also may be more complex and may require training or other forms of guidance to facilitate their operation.

Restrictiveness. This is the degree to which the GDSS limits the decision-making process to a particular sequence of operation or problem-solving procedure. Whereas comprehensiveness concerns *what* functions are available, restrictiveness governs *how* the functional options are used. More restrictive GDSSs attempt to guide the group through a structured method of applying the available options. Less restrictive GDSSs offer no pre-specified decision path, so the group is free to choose among the options and use them in any order.

Decisional guidance. This is the degree to which the GDSS enlightens or persuades users as they choose among the system options. Decisional guidance is automatic (computer-based) facilitation. Decisional guidance provides users with *cognitive support* (explanations about how to develop and apply multicriteria decision-making models) and *group interaction support* (operators that trigger the timing of system explanations as the group's decision process unfolds). It may be *informative* (providing pertinent information that enlightens the selection or use of options

Table 1   Examples of GDSS functionality to support group processes

Group process	*Possible GDSS functionality*
Discussion	
Participation	Anonymous, simultaneous entry of ideas followed by display of idea lists on a common viewing screen
Influence	Weighting ideas (weights of all ideas sum to 1000 points); ranking, or ordering, ideas; rating, or scaling ideas (such as on a 1–7 scale); voting yes/no on each idea
Leadership	Combining weights either equally or according to a scheme that favors influence by certain members, such as the leader or experts
	Providing the leader with functions that are not accessible to other users
Emotional expression	Candid commenting, opinion polling
Conflict management	Issue identification and analysis, stakeholder analysis; statement of positions and graphics to illustrate shifts in positions over time
Memory	Group note-taking, storage and retrieval of meeting minutes, clustering ideas into common categories or themes
Decision analysis	
Problem structuring	Agenda management, outlining, problem formulation techniques, cognitive mapping
Idea generation	Electronic brainstorming, nominal group technique, creativity techniques
Alternatives evaluation	Multicriteria decision models, risk analysis, stakeholder analysis, contingency analysis
Impact assessment	Forecasting models, scenario analysis
Implementation planning	Planning techniques, budget models

but without suggesting how to proceed) or *suggestive* (providing judgmental recommendations on what procedures or data to apply and how to apply them). The guidance may be *predefined*, with a fixed set of guidelines that are available to all groups that use the system, or *dynamic*, applying intelligence so that the system can "learn" in response to the progress of the particular user group.

Interface. The GDSS software interface might be described along a number of dimensions, but a key dimension is the *representation* that members work with as they interact with the software. Representations may be *process oriented*, emphasizing actions that the group can undertake, such as defining the problem, evaluating alternative solutions, or formulating future strategies. The process-oriented interface presents the group with procedures for formulating or solving the problem, and data (usually in the form of member opinions or comments) are created as the procedures are applied. Alternatively, *data-oriented* representations emphasize information associated with the particular problem, such as health information, soil data, or public opinion surveys. The interface then allows the group to apply processes (such as decision models) to the available data. To date, most GDSSs favor the use of process representations as the dominant interface, with data representations being secondary.

Information exchange. Some GDSSs support creation and sharing of only *task-related* information (such as problems, alternatives, criteria, or strategies), whereas others support exchange of *socioemotional* information as well (such as expressions of frustration or praise, joking, or the overall mood of the group). The *pattern* of information exchange supported by the GDSS also can vary across system implementations. Information exchange patterns in GDSSs may include:

- *One-to-all communication*: all information entered into the system becomes public, or available to all members of the group.
- *One-to-one communication*: individual members can selectively communicate with other members as part of the group decision process.
- *Subgroup communication*: group members are divided into subgroups, and models or messages operate based on these subgroups.

Finally, the *storage* of information in the GDSS can affect information exchange in the group. Alternative storage designs include:

- *Complete histories*: comments, votes, model outputs, or other information created during the problem-solving process are stored as a continuing history with new information added as the group process unfolds.
- *Dynamic replacement*: only the most recently generated data are presented to the group; historical information is either deleted or stored outside of the group's active workspace.
- *Keyed storage*: data are organized according to some meaningful scheme, such as by date, by topic, or by group member.

The content, pattern, and storage of information exchange supported by the GDSS are critical design decisions that potentially can affect the decision process the group experiences as it attempts to understand and resolve the problem at hand.

Control over functionality. Who determines what functions are made available to the group, the sequencing of those functions, and when or how they are applied? Alternative designs include:

- *User controlled*: each group member has access to all system functions, and the members select and apply the functions as they see fit.
- *Leader controlled*: a group leader or facilitator, who has access to full system functionality, determines the subset of functionality that is presented to members.
- *Shared control*: system operation is divided among various parties, such as between the leader and members. The shared control mode can be implemented in a variety of ways. For example, to support negotiations, operations may be divided between members representing different sides of an issue. An alternative design is to share control among a leader, group members, and a technician, with the technician performing functions that are too complex for group members, such as file retrieval or complex data manipulations.

Private vs. public work. To support *private work*, the GDSS facilitates individual recording of ideas, comments, votes, and the like, and responds to whatever commands the individual enters at his or her workstation. *Public work* represents an aggregation of individual work and is located in the shared workspace. In some implementations, only a group leader or representative can control operation of the shared workspace. In other systems, each group member has direct access to the shared workspace and is free to control its operation. Usually, at least some of the public GDSS functions operate automatically. Determining the content and configuration of private and public workspaces is an important issue in GDSS design.

INTEGRATION OF GDSS WITH OTHER INFORMATION TECHNOLOGIES

Knowledge-based systems (KBS) technology. KBSs represent the knowledge and problem-solving expertise of human experts in narrow knowledge domains (*see* KNOWLEDGE BASE). A KBS provides two main types of support to its users: (1) analyses of the problem/case and (2) explanations that provide knowledge and reasoning about what the system knows and does, how it works, and why its actions are appropriate. The analyses and explanations provided by KBSs support the group decision-making process, resulting in greater efficiency and effectiveness.

Visual decision-making technology. Selection or the ranking of alternatives in a multicriteria evaluation is not an easy problem. It is difficult to represent a complicated situation by using text only. Text alone, in some situations, is not an efficient way to deliver rich enough information for decision-making. Graphic representation of the decision problem often allows a global view of conflicts among criteria and characteristics of actions. Visualization technology may help decision-makers to find hidden meaning in data. Studies have found that visualization of data, such as representing data in the forms of tree maps and metrics, helps GDSS users identify the best possible solutions faster and more accurately.

Agent-based technology. An agent is an encapsulated computer system that is situated in some environment and is capable of flexible, autonomous action in that environment in order to meet its design objectives. Negotiation agents have been incorporated into some GDSSs to help the decision-makers better understand one another's point of view. Negotiation agents are still in their infancy, and currently most negotiation agents are designed for simplified applications only.

Wireless technology. Wireless technology opens up the possibility of mobile GDSS. It allows mobile knowledge workers to cooperate and make group decisions seamlessly from remote locations. It is expected that, with breakthroughs in technologies, mobile GDSS will be used.

FUTURE USE OF GDSS

Existing GDSS technologies help to enhance support to group meetings and improve the effectiveness of group meetings at both the individual and organizational level. With the aid of new technologies, some innovative applications of GDSS are likely to be available. Examples are:

- new analytic methods based on diagrams and pictorial representations;
- intercultural meetings;
- integration with video and computer conferencing;
- interactive teaching;
- new forms of groups;
- issue-oriented GDSS;
- personnel decisions;
- new, temporary organizations;
- electronic mediated debates;
- hierarchical meetings that can communicate and also convene as a committee as a whole;
- eliciting system design requirements from users and from management;
- system design walkthroughs;
- eliciting expert knowledge from groups.

These future GDSS implementations involve the innovative use of the latest information technologies, such as knowledge-based systems technology, visual decision-making technology, agent-based technology, and wireless technology.

Bibliography

Bostrom, R. P., Watson, R. T., and Kinney, S. T. (1992). *Computer-Augmented Teamwork: A Guided Tour.* New York: Van Nostrand Reinhold.

Dennis, A. R., Wixom, B. H., and Vandenberg, R. J. (2001). Understanding fit and appropriation effects in group support systems via meta-analysis. *MIS Quarterly,* **25,** 2 (June), 167–93.

Gray, P. (1998). New directions for GDSS. ISWorld Net Virtual Meeting Center, ww2.cis.temple.edu/isworld/vmc/April98/gray/GRAY.htm.

Jessup, L. M. and Valacich, J. (eds.) (1993). *Group Support Systems: New Perspectives.* New York: Macmillan.

Nah, F. F.-H. and Benbasat, I. (2004). Knowledge-based support in a group decision-making context: An expert–novice comparison. *Journal of the Association of Information Systems,* **5,** 3 (March), article 5.

Nunamaker, Jr., J. F., Dennis, A. R., Valacich, J. S., Vogel, D. R., and George, J. F. (1991). Electronic meeting systems to support group work: Theory and practice at Arizona. *Communications of the ACM,* **34** (7), 30–9.

groupware

see COMPUTER–SUPPORTED COOPERATIVE WORK

history of organizational use of information technology to 1980

Eric S. Boyles

Individuals and organizations have come to depend on calculating and computing machinery for increasing amounts of accurate and timely information. Mathematicians and philosophers, among the first to use calculating devices, developed sophisticated techniques for representing, manipulating, and analyzing information. Entrepreneurs and inventors gradually adapted these tools and techniques to the problems faced by merchants, factory owners, and government agencies. By the twentieth century, engineers and scientists contributed fundamental insights into the design of calculating machinery, components, materials, and programming. At each stage in the development of computing machines, a constellation of economic, social, and technological factors combined to reduce cost while improving speed and reliability of computation. This history will recount the early aids to calculation and how mechanical and then electronic computational devices were developed. The early history ends in 1980, a critical year, with the introduction of a commercial-grade personal computer with an open architecture – the IBM PC. In other words, this history provides a background history.

EARLY AIDS TO CALCULATION

Efforts to mechanize calculation began in the early seventeenth century as mathematicians and philosophers like William Schickard (1591–1635), Blaise Pascal (1623–62), and Gottfried Wilhelm von Leibnitz (1646–1716) devised some of the first mechanical aids to calculation (Aspray, 1990). These devices represented numerical digits on gear wheels and performed

calculations as these components moved. By 1820 the first commercial adding machine, the "Arithmometer," was invented by Charles Xavier Thomas for the French insurance industry. Similar devices were developed by Frank S. Baldwin (1838–1925), Dorr E. Felt (1862–1930), and William S. Burroughs (1857–98), and improved the accuracy of accountants and office managers. Business professionals of the nineteenth century developed accounting techniques that relied heavily on mechanical calculating machinery and office equipment.

The English mathematician Charles Babbage (1792–1871) designed some of the most sophisticated mechanical calculating machines of the nineteenth century (Swade, 1991). Babbage's difference and analytical engines were never constructed during his lifetime, but they incorporated several of the key concepts found in later computer architectures and were designed to function automatically by following a sequence of instructions stored on punched cards.

PUNCHED-CARD TABULATING SYSTEMS

The growth of government bureaucracies and more complex business organizations heightened interest in the collecting, processing, and storing of information toward the end of the nineteenth century. Beginning in the 1890s, organizations like the US Bureau of the Census and the New York Central Railroad began to use punched-card-based tabulating systems developed by Herman Hollerith (1860–1929) to collate and analyze information (Norberg, 1990). Tabulating equipment used electrical sensors to read information encoded onto paper cards, and in turn perform a set of basic calculations. Hollerith incorporated the Tabulating Machine Company (TMC) in 1896 and produced a complete system of tabulating equipment. Hollerith's main competitor, James Powers, founded the Powers Accounting Machine Company in 1911. Between 1914 and 1930, these two firms introduced machines with increasingly faster sorting speeds, greater density of card data, and modest improvements in calculating ability. Eventually TMC was sold to the Computer Tabulating Recording Company (CTR) headed by Thomas J. Watson in 1911. In 1924 CTR changed its name to International Business Machines (IBM) and continued to manufacture and lease tabulating equipment until the emergence of electronic computers in the late 1950s. In general, tabulating systems prepared businesses and government agencies for many of the applications that would later be performed with digital computers.

Mechanical to Electromechanical Machines

While business organizations made heavy use of punched-card tabulating equipment, several mechanical and electromechanical calculating machines were developed during the 1930s and 1940s that foreshadowed the development of electronic digital computers. These machines used electromechanical devices to perform calculations, and functioned as special purpose machines for use by scientists and engineers (Ceruzzi, 1983). Konrad Zuse, an engineering student in Berlin, designed and constructed a series of electromechanical calculators beginning in 1938 with his Z1 machine. At Bell Telephone Laboratories, George Stibitz and Samuel Williams also developed special purpose, electromechanical computers beginning in 1939 that assisted engineers in the analysis of complex electrical networks. Howard Aiken, a Harvard University physics professor, joined with IBM to build an electromechanical machine, the Harvard Mark I or IBM ASCC, for scientific work in 1939. While Aiken's relationship with IBM was unstable, a series of machines was developed by Harvard that included the Harvard Mark II (1947), Harvard Mark III (1949), and the Harvard Mark IV (1952). A series of mechanically based analog computers, called differential analyzers, was developed under the direction of Vannever Bush at the Massachusetts Institute of Technology (MIT) from the 1920s to the 1940s that demonstrated the potential and limitations of analog computing devices. John Atanasoff at the University of Iowa, from 1938 to 1942, developed a computing device to solve systems of linear equations.

Early Electronic Digital Computers

During World War II the US military sponsored a number of R&D projects that resulted in some of the core technologies used in early computer designs. In June 1943 John W. Mauchley (1907–80) and J. Presper Eckert received a grant from the US Army to design and construct the ENIAC (Electronic Numerical Integrator and Computer) at the University of Pennsylvania (Stern, 1981). This machine was completed in December 1945. Weighing several tons and containing over 18,000 vacuum tubes, the ENIAC was programmed through plugboards and manual switches. Soon after the completion of the ENIAC, John von Neumann (1903–57) articulated the concept of the internally stored, automatically executed, programmable computer in his "First Draft Report on the EDVAC" of June 1945. This led to the construction of several stored program computers, such as the IAS machine. Started in 1946, this machine was constructed at Princeton under the guidance of von Neumann, and the design specifications for this machine quickly diffused to other projects, including the development of the IBM 701. British engineers, working at the University of Cambridge, Manchester University, and the National Physical Laboratory, made fundamental advances in computing technology during the 1950s. A significant accomplishment was the development of Williams's tube memory technology by F. C. Williams at Manchester University. Maurice V. Wilkes contributed to the development of true, stored program computers during this period.

MIT's Whirlwind computer project represents one of the last large machines constructed as a result of the war. It was designed to perform real-time simulation of aircraft performance (Redmond and Smith, 1980). Completed in 1951 under the direction of Jay W. Forrester, the Whirlwind computer made substantial advances in the design of high-speed circuits and pioneered the use of ferrite core memory. Many of these advances were later implemented in the

SAGE computer system to monitor aircraft that operated between 1963 and 1980.

EMERGENCE OF THE COMPUTER INDUSTRY

By the mid-1950s, electronic digital computers had migrated from scientific laboratories and military projects into the business sector (Cortada, 1993). While fewer than a dozen computers existed at this time, their numbers rapidly increased as firms started to view computers as a potentially profitable product. After purchasing the Eckert–Mauchley Computer Corporation in 1950, Remmington Rand developed the UNIVAC I with the first installation in 1951 at the Bureau of the Census. This machine's central processor contained some 5,000 vacuum tubes and used a mercury delay-line for main memory. The installation of one of these machines at General Electric, for use in payroll and general accounting applications, in 1954 marked the beginning of the commercial computer industry in America. The first business use of computers was in Great Britain in November of 1951 (Caminer et al., 1998). The Lyons Tea Company, in partnership with Cambridge University, developed the LEO computer (Lyons Electronic Office). It was innovative but survived only 12 years in the worldwide competitive environment. UNIVAC's customers used their machines for general accounting and transaction processing applications. Remmington Rand, renamed Sperry Rand in 1955, grew to be a major force in the early computer market and competed against IBM with its UNIVAC 80 and 90, UNIVAC II (1957), and UNIVAC 1108, 1110 computers.

In the 1940s IBM held a leadership position in the punched-card tabulator and office machine markets. Digital computers represented a potentially disruptive product to IBM's established line of punched-card tabulating equipment and IBM's senior management approached this technology with caution (Bashe et al., 1986). One of IBM's first efforts in digital computing involved the development of its Defense Calculator, later called the IBM 701, in 1952. IBM also developed a companion system, the IBM 702, for business customers.

By 1954 IBM had also developed a smaller system, initially intended to extend the capabilities of punched-card equipment, called the IBM 650. This machine used magnetic-drum technology for its main memory and was one of the most successful general purpose commercial computers. Organizations like Caterpillar Tractor and the Chrysler Corporation used the 650 for inventory control and manufacturing processing applications. Many universities also acquired their first digital computer through a discount leasing program for the IBM 650, and the availability of these machines encouraged the establishment of computer science departments in many American universities. While IBM came to dominate the computer industry by 1960, other computer manufacturers also developed so-called "first-generation computers." Some of the most prominent firms included the Datamatic Corporation, Burroughs, RCA, and the Philco Corporation, which introduced the first transistorized computer, the Philco Transac S-2000.

GROWING ACCEPTANCE

The computers developed in the late 1950s demonstrated the feasibility of manufacturing fast digital computers for a limited, largely scientific market; however, most of the calculations required in business activities continued to be done on punched-card equipment. In the first half of the 1960s, however, several new systems made their way into the market and increased the acceptance of digital computers. In general, these machines used individual transistors as logic circuit components and ferrite-core devices for memory. The lower cost and higher reliability of these systems convinced many business leaders to invest in computing technology. The development of higher-level languages like COBOL and FORTRAN (*see* PROGRAMMING LANGUAGES) also made these machines easier to program. As machines of greater power and flexibility emerged throughout the 1960s, business organizations began to explore the computer as a tool for management control and planning applications.

By the late 1950s, IBM's management had refocused its energies on the digital computing market and developed one of its strongest products of that period, the IBM 1401. Introduced in 1959, the IBM 1401 series used magnetic tape and punched cards for its input/output, ferrite core for its main memory, and a transistorized processor. Designed for commercial data processing tasks, the 1401 was available with a basic assembly language, SPS or Symbolic Assembly Language, and an assembler called "Autocoder." Various report program generators were also made available for both the 1401 and its subsequent series, the 1440, 1460, 1410, and 7010. Approximately 14,000 of the 1401 systems were installed, and the success of this system propelled IBM into a leadership position in the commercial digital computer market.

IBM competed against a number of other firms throughout the late 1950s and early 1960s for a share of the growing market for computers. US-based firms such as General Electric, Honeywell, Bendix, Philco, CDC, RCA, UNIVAC, and Burroughs developed competitive products for both the commercial and scientific markets. Computer companies were also formed in Europe. Only a few of the early entrants were able to gain a significant profitable market share.

TIMESHARING, NETWORKS, AND REAL-TIME APPLICATIONS

As large-scale computer installations became more prominent within business organizations, the task of managing these investments became a critical issue. One solution to the problem that received considerable attention involved the emergence of timesharing techniques in the 1950s and 1960s. Prior to this period, most computers operated in batch mode in which applications and data were processed serially, one "batch" at a time, at a centralized computer center. Such techniques were inconvenient for users and complicated the debugging of new applications. The initial concept of timesharing was articulated in 1959 by Christopher Strachey at the National Research Development Corporation in England and John McCarthy at MIT. Some of the earliest implementations of timesharing occurred in MIT's Compatible Time Sharing System and its Project MAC effort, the JOSS System developed at the Rand Corporation, and the development of timesharing systems at Dartmouth College.

A related development of the 1960s involved the creation of some of the first computer networks. In 1968, for instance, the Defense Advanced Research Projects Agency (DARPA) started development of the ARPANET. Based on packet-switching technology, the ARPANET eventually demonstrated that a heterogeneous network of different hardware, software, and data resources could operate successfully.

The early 1960s also witnessed the development of "real-time management systems" by some of America's leading corporate computer users. American Airlines began this movement with its collaborative effort with IBM to develop the SABRE airline reservation system. Similar systems were installed by other US-based airlines, and eventually became strategically important computer applications for these firms.

QUEST FOR COMPATIBILITY

While higher-level languages had eased the task of developing efficient programs, one of the persistent problems in early computing concerned the incompatibility of different processors even within the same product line. In 1964, IBM announced its S/360 family of upwardly compatible computers (Pugh, Johnson, and Palmer, 1991). The 14 models that eventually made up the 360 family featured a standardized input/output interface and subsequently spawned a separate peripheral devices industry. The IBM 360 series allowed users to run both character-based business applications and word-based scientific applications on the same machine. The IBM 360 was also part of a movement toward the use of integrated circuits, developed by Jack Kilby at Texas Instruments and Robert Noyce at Fairchild Semiconductor, in computer design (Braun and Mcdonald, 1982). This was followed by the IBM 370 in 1970. By all accounts the IBM 360 was a complete success, and by 1970 more than 18,000 installations of this machine were in operation. Some of IBM's competitors, like RCA with its Spectra Series, developed rival lines of 360-compatible computers, but the success of IBM's product series continued throughout the 1960s and 1970s.

MINICOMPUTERS

By the mid-1960s business organizations could lease an IBM mainframe or one of its competitors' products. While these systems were fast and expandable, they also were expensive, physically large, and required a team of specialists skilled in their operation and maintenance. Minicomputers rose to the fore in the late

1960s as a low-cost, small-sized alternative for many organizations. They resulted from continued technological development of circuit design, component packaging, and the shifting requirements of computing.

Digital Equipment Corporation (DEC) was founded in 1957 by Ken Olson and Harlan Anderson and emerged as one of the most successful developers of minicomputers (Rifkin and Harrer, 1988). Originally oriented toward large-scale mainframe, DEC's engineers turned to the problem of designing inexpensive, small computers. Beginning with the highly successful PDP-8 minicomputer (1965), DEC produced a series of minicomputers that included the PDP-11 (1968) and the VAX-11 in 1976. DEC's success spawned a series of other minicomputers, like Interdata's model-1, Prime's 200 mini (1972), and General Automation's SPC-8 and SPC-12 (1968). One of DEC's primary competitors in the minicomputer market was Data General. Data General developed its NOVA minicomputer in 1969, Eclipse in 1980 (Kidder, 1981). IBM also introduced its System 38 and AS/400 series of minicomputers.

THE PERSONAL COMPUTER REVOLUTION

Personal computers emerged in the 1970s as the cost of electronic components declined and people recognized a need for inexpensive, powerful, small systems. Initially, all of the established computer companies considered the potential market for personal computers to be too small to merit product development. Innovations in electronic component technology, particularly the development of the Intel 8080 microprocessor in 1974 by Marcian "Ted" Hoff, provided an opportunity for experimentation in small computer design. Electronics hobbyists were among the first to attempt to construct and operate small computers, building kits like EDP Company's System One (1973), Scelbi Computer's Scelbi-8h, and the MITS Altair 8800 computer (1975). These amateurs demonstrated that inexpensive, personalized computers were feasible. By the later 1970s, firms like Commodore and Radio Shack started to produce personal computers as either extensions of their handheld calculators or electronics businesses.

Working off a few thousand dollars of venture capital, Steve Wosniak and Steven Jobs developed their Apple II in 1977 (Butcher, 1987). Unlike many of the hobbyist machines, the Apple featured a full-sized keyboard and a separate floppy drive and monitor. The availability of software, particularly the program Visicalc written by Daniel Bricklin and Bob Frankston in 1979, made the Apple II an overnight success and accelerated the move to personal systems. After visiting Xerox's Palo Alto Research Center (PARC), Steve Jobs initiated a development project that ultimately resulted in the Macintosh computer in 1984. The Macintosh's user-friendly, graphically oriented system software created a paradigm for personal computing that has been widely emulated.

The growing popularity of personal computers prompted IBM to develop its own personal computer in 1980. Led by Philip Don Estridge, the IBM design team used outside contractors for many of the PC's components and system software. Bill Gates and Paul Allen, for instance, were contracted in 1980 to write the disk operating system or DOS for the PC. IBM's decision to create a PC with an open architecture that would allow outside firms to develop peripherals and other system components has had a lasting impact on the course of PC development.

Bibliography

Aspray, W. (ed.) (1990). *Computing Before Computers*, 1st edn. Ames: Iowa State University Press.

Bashe, C. J., Pugh, E. W., Johnson, L. R., and Palmer, J. H. (1986). *IBM's Early Computers*. Cambridge, MA: MIT Press.

Braun, E. and Macdonald, S. (1982). *Revolution in Miniature: The History and Impact of Semiconductor Electronics*, 2nd edn. New York: Cambridge University Press.

Butcher, L. (1987). *Accidental Millionaire: The Rise and Fall of Steve Jobs at Apple*. New York: Paragon.

Caminer, D., Aris, J., Hermon, P., and Land, F. (1998). *Leo: The Incredible Story of the World's First Business Computer*. New York: McGraw-Hill.

Ceruzzi, P. E. (1983). *Reckoners: The Prehistory of the Digital Computer, from Relays to the Stored Program Concept, 1935–1945. Contributions to the Study of Computer Science*, vol. 1. Westport, CT: Greenwood Press.

Cortada, J. (1993). *The Computer in the United States: From Laboratory to Market, 1930 to 1960*. New York: M. E. Sharpe.

Kidder, T. (1981). *The Soul of a New Machine*. Boston: Little, Brown.

Norberg, A. L. (1990). High-technology calculation in the early 20th century: Punched-card machinery in business and government. *Technology and Culture*, **31**, 753–79.

Pugh, E. W. (1984). *Memories that Shaped an Industry: Decisions Leading to IBM System/360*. Cambridge, MA: MIT Press.

Pugh, E. W., Johnson, L. R., and Palmer, J. H. (1991). *IBM's 360 and Early 370 Systems*. Cambridge, MA: MIT Press.

Redmond, K. C. and Smith, T. M. (1980). *Project Whirlwind: The History of a Pioneer Computer*. Bedford, MA: Digital Press.

Rifkin, G. and Harrer, G. (1988). *The Ultimate Entrepreneur: The Story of Ken Olsen and Digital Equipment Corporation*. Chicago: Contemporary Books.

Stern, N. B. (1981). *From ENIAC to UNIVAC: An Appraisal of the Eckert–Mauchley Computers*. Bedford, MA: Digital Press.

Swade, D. (1991). *Charles Babbage and his Calculating Engines*. London: Science Museum.

HTML (hypertext markup language)

see MARKUP LANGUAGES

HTTP (hypertext transfer protocol)

see INTERNET; PROTOCOLS

humans as information processors

David Bahn

The characteristics of humans as information processors are significant to the design of information systems. Well-designed applications support the unique capabilities of human users. Such applications can also potentially compensate for the limitations of human information processing in supporting critical decision-making activities.

Information processing is an innate human capacity. Several models of human information processing have been proposed. Newell and Simon's (1972) model of the human information processing system is patterned after the computer and it incorporates a central processing unit (CPU) along with three kinds of memory: short-term, long-term, and external. The speed and operation of the CPU are bounded not only by its incapacity to engage in parallel processing of data, but also by upper bounds on the speed of information retrieval from memory and the operating constraints of each kind of memory.

Short-term memory holds the rather small set of symbols that are immediately available to the CPU for information processing. The upper bound on the number of symbols available in short-term memory was identified by Miller (1956) as being about seven (plus or minus two). Although each symbol in memory might be equivalent to one piece of information or data, each symbol might also be a pointer to a larger (and topically grouped) set of data, known as a "chunk," that is resident in long-term memory. The speed of the retrieval of these symbols or chunks from short-term memory is much more rapid than from long-term or external memory. Further constraining the operation of short-term memory is the limitation that its contents begin to decay within a short time, particularly if the attention of the human information processor is being distracted by a new stimulus.

Long-term memory has a very large storage capacity but its data storage and retrieval operations are constrained. As humans acquire information through learning and experience, the information is organized associatively into patterns or chunks. Storage of information into long-term memory (i.e., memorizing) thus takes much longer to effect than retrieval from it.

External memory consists of the patterns or chunks of symbols that are stored by the human information processor in the external environment for later access and retrieval. Typically, this is written text, but it can also include objects, the configuration of objects, or even a network of people and things meaningful to the human information processor.

This model also postulates how human information processors solve problems confronting them. Human behavior occurs within a task environment of a problem. The task environment is mentally represented as a problem space. The structure of a problem space is what informs the human information processor as to how to achieve a solution to the problem.

Beyond the Newell and Simon model, the fields of psychology and decision science have found that human heuristics (judgmental rules of thumb) are quite limited in handling decision-oriented information for tasks of judgment and discrimination (and may even introduce biases). For example, when engaged in making a judgment of a situation, humans will typically establish an initial assessment of the situation and then subsequently make adjustments to that assessment in response to further data. The problem with this anchoring and adjustment heuristic (Tversky and Kahneman, 1974) is twofold: the final decision too closely resembles the initial assessment and that assessment may well have been flawed. Parallel to this is the representativeness heuristic that humans employ in order to assess the likelihood of an event. They assess how similar the properties of the event are to the most generally encountered and perceived properties of the type of event to which it belongs (Kahneman and Tversky, 1972). A third constraining heuristic is the concreteness bias, the preference of humans to evaluate only the most readily available information about the surface properties of alternatives presented to them. Humans also tend to mistake association or correlation between two events as implying a causal relationship, particularly when the events fit established patterns of expected sequences (Yates, 1990).

This tendency to fit experienced or perceived events into expected sequences of events is part of a larger feature of human information processing known as scripts. These are prototypical combinations of events, actions, and objects that people expect to encounter during the course of specific processes (such as an expected sequence of *ordering* some *food* listed on a *menu* from a *waiter* in a *restaurant*). Closely related to the notion of scripts as sources of organization for human information processing is that of narratives, which have been proposed (Bruner, 1990) as the basis for human experience and thought in that they both precede and underlie human language comprehension. Perceived causal relations between facts are embedded by humans into narratives.

Scripts and narratives are fundamental building blocks used by people to create mental models or representations of their experiences.

Narratives and scripts are quite advantageous because they provide cognitive economy by embodying a relatively small number of significant categories for understanding the world. Humans employ them in order to cope with an almost infinitely large number of potential relationships between objects in different categories. Scripts and narratives also underlie a key form of human information processing known as case-based analogical reasoning (Riesbeck and Schank, 1989). This type of problem-solving approach occurs when humans utilize scripts or narratives to recall from long-term memory past instances of a problem solution whose features are similar to the presenting problem at hand. The recalled solution is then adjusted according to those current problem features that are distinctive and the modified solution is applied to the problem at hand. Scripts and narratives can thus also counterbalance the intrinsic cognitive constraints of short-term memory (decay and limited space).

Also assisting to overcome cognitive constraints is the tendency for humans to perceive objects in the world as instances of types and supertypes arranged as hierarchies. This tendency is highly congruent with the storage of information as "chunks" in both short-term and long-term memory. However, it is so pronounced that if objects or entities in the world do not fit into some hierarchical grouping, they may be simply ignored by human information processors (Simon, 1988).

The use of theories and findings about human information processing has not been limited to the level of analysis of the individual problem solver or decision-maker. In fact, several theories of organizational decision-making and organizational function have extended information processing theory. Perhaps the most famous has been that of Simon (1976), who argued that human decision-making is based on "bounded rationality." Humans make decision choices that are rational but only within a limited set of alternatives and decision criteria. This occurs because humans, when functioning in real task environments, have a bounded cognitive capacity to fully determine the available alternatives and the appropriate decision criteria to employ. Cyert and March (1963) extended this idea and proposed that:

1 Organizations can only scan limited aspects of their external environment.

2 Organizations usually contain multiple and often conflicting goal sets based on the desires of competing subunits.

3 Organizations typically execute decision-making by engaging in serial attention to goals and problems, as well as following established operating procedures.

Situated cognition is a more recent perspective in cognitive science. It rejects the idea that human information capacity is a general purpose mechanism that can be invoked in disparate task domains (Lave, 1988). This perspective proposes that features of the external environment afford and constrain the possible set of actions by human problem solvers and are thus the primary determinants of human information processing.

Human capabilities and limitations as information processors are significant to the design of information system applications and the creation of user interfaces for those applications. For example, interfaces can be designed to minimize memorization and to assist recall, or even to present data in a way that diminishes the effects of innate human biases in decision-making. Superior applications of information technology can assist humans to identify hierarchies of objects or to recall scripts and narratives and thus enable efficient approaches to decision-making. Awareness of human information processing capabilities and limitations at the organizational level can be critical to teams of information systems designers as they implement new systems across a variety of distinctively structured organizations.

Bibliography

Bruner, J. (1990). *Acts of Meaning*. Cambridge, MA: Harvard University Press.

Cyert, R. and March, J. (1963). *A Behavioral Theory of the Firm*. Englewood Cliffs, NJ: Prentice-Hall.

Kahneman, D. and Tversky, A. (1972). Subjective probability: A judgment of representativeness. *Cognitive Psychology*, 3, 430–54.

Lave, J. (1988). *Cognition in Practice: Mind, Mathematics and Culture*. New York: Cambridge University Press.

Miller, G. A. (1956). The magical number seven, plus or minus two: Some limits on our capacity for processing information. *Psychological Review*, 63 (2), 81–97.

Newell, A. and Simon, H. (1972). *Human Problem Solving*. Englewood Cliffs, NJ: Prentice-Hall.

Riesbeck, C. and Schank, R. (1989). *Inside Case-Based Reasoning*. Hillsdale, NJ: Lawrence Erlbaum.

Simon, H. A. (1976). *Administrative Behavior: A Study of Decision-Making Processes in Administrative Organization*, 3rd edn. New York: Free Press.

Simon, H. A. (1988). *The Sciences of the Artificial*. Cambridge, MA: MIT Press.

Tversky, A. and Kahneman, D. (1974). Judgment under uncertainty: Heuristics and biases. *Science*, 185, 1124–31.

Yates, J. F. (1990). *Judgment and Decision-Making*. Englewood Cliffs, NJ: Prentice-Hall.

human–computer interaction

Michael J. Davern

To accomplish tasks using a computer, a dialogue usually occurs between the user and the computer. This dialogue is an iterative cycle of bidirectional communications with the user issuing instructions to the computer and the computer presenting the results (feedback) of carrying out those instructions. The field of human–computer interaction (HCI) is concerned with the study and design of this dialogue. An understanding of both the technological artifact and the user is needed in order to design the structure of the dialogue between the user and the computer. HCI draws on such diverse fields as computer science, psychology, ARTIFICIAL INTELLIGENCE, linguistics, anthropology, and sociology.

In early computer systems, the technology was relatively more expensive than the personnel who used the system. As a result, engineering considerations dominated designs and users were forced to adapt to the system. As technology has become relatively inexpensive and more powerful, there has been an increasing emphasis on fitting the system to the user. Although the emphasis is shifting, human–computer interaction is essentially a situation of mutual adaptation or accommodation (Norman and Draper, 1986).

To accommodate the user, the designer must employ (either explicitly or implicitly) some theory or model of user behavior. Much of the research in human–computer interaction is aimed at building such a theory or theories (Card, Moran, and Newell, 1983). System design involves constructing a conceptual model of how the system is to function. In adapting to the system, the user also develops a conceptual model of the system as a guide to his or her interaction and dialogue with the system.

Inconsistencies between the designer's model of the system and the user's model of the system create potential for error. Such inconsistencies arise because the primary means for communicating the designer's model to the user is through the physical system (and its accompanying documentation). Thus, inconsistencies can arise when the system fails to accurately reflect the designer's model (i.e., the system has bugs), or when the user's experience with the system results in a misinterpretation of the model embodied in the system. From this perspective a good system not only has few bugs but also has a conceptual model that is clearly evident in the technological artifact itself. The use of metaphors, such as the desktop metaphor popularized by Apple Macintosh, is a useful means of conveying a conceptual model of the system to users (Gerlach and Kuo, 1991).

In addition to having a conceptual or mental model of the system, the user also has a model of the task. It is the user's task knowledge that determines *what* functions or operations the user will require the computer to perform. The user's conceptual model of the system informs the user as to *how* to get the system to carry out the desired operations. From the standpoint of a human–computer interaction, a system should reflect a good understanding of the task domain. Without such an understanding, a system may still provide the functionality a user requires for a given task, but it may be inconsistent with the way the user thinks about accomplishing the task. In a well-designed system, the system model and the user's task model should be consistent, thereby enabling the user to work almost entirely in terms of the task domain. In such situations, the technology becomes virtually transparent.

There are several common design principles and guidelines that can aid HCI design. The use of a good metaphor as a basis for the system model is an important design principle. Consistency both within and across applications is an-

other important design goal. Consistency is desirable both in the manner in which an operation is initiated by the user, such as in the keystrokes required to carry out similar actions within or across applications, and in the presentation of information to the user.

Visibility is also an important design objective (Norman, 1988). A good design makes clearly visible the actions that are available to the user and the state of the machine. The on-screen buttons that pervade modern graphical user interfaces (*see* GRAPHICAL USER INTERFACE) are designed to make clear the actions available to the user. Similarly, disk drive access lights and flashing cursors are examples of visible cues to the current state of the computer.

While it is valuable to make the possible actions available to a user visibly obvious, it is also important to provide the user with feedback about the success or failure of an attempt to carry out some action. The beep that the computer makes when the user presses the wrong key is an example of such feedback. The beep is, however, not complete feedback; it merely signifies that an attempted action was erroneous. A better design not only signifies to the user that the action failed, but describes how or why it failed. It may provide guidelines on how to appropriately execute the desired action.

Human–computer interaction is also facilitated by placing appropriate constraints on both user and system behavior. Constraints can be physical, such as in the design of the 3.5 in floppy disk which cannot be inserted into a disk drive other than in the correct manner. User actions can also be constrained by software. Many software-imposed constraints are protection mechanisms intended to prevent user error. Examples include confirmation of critical actions such as file deletion and disk formatting. Nonetheless, errors can still occur, so it is also important to provide the ability to reverse or undo mistaken operations.

Providing a natural mapping between the logical action a user wishes the computer to perform and the physical action required by the user to get the computer to carry it out is also an important factor in system design. The popularity of the mouse as an input device owes much of its success to the fact that it exploits a natural mapping. To move the cursor in any direction, the user simply moves the mouse in that direction.

Within the bounds of these various design principles, the possible styles of interaction and interface devices vary. In terms of styles, the possibilities include simple command languages, question and answer dialogues, menu selection, on-screen forms (appropriately mapped to their paper equivalents), and "direct manipulation" (Shneiderman, 1992) or icon-based user interfaces. Common devices include keyboard, mouse, and monitor. Other emerging devices and methods are speech synthesis and recognition and virtual reality gloves and helmets. The appropriate design choice in all cases depends on the user and the task to be accomplished with the computer.

Bibliography

Card, S. K., Moran, T. P., and Newell, A. (1983). *The Psychology of Human–Computer Interaction.* Hillsdale, NJ: Lawrence Erlbaum.

Gerlach, J. H. and Kuo, F.-Y. (1991). Understanding human–computer interaction for information systems design. *MIS Quarterly*, 15, 527–49.

Norman, D. A. (1988). *The Psychology of Everyday Things.* New York: Basic Books.

Norman, D. A. and Draper, S. W. (1986). *User-Centered System Design: New Perspectives on Human–Computer Interaction.* Hillsdale, NJ: Lawrence Erlbaum.

Shneiderman, B. (1992). *Designing the User Interface: Strategies for Effective Human–Computer Interaction,* 2nd edn. Reading, MA: Addison-Wesley.

hypermedia/hypertext

Jesper M. Johansson

Hypertext is a method for linking documents (nodes) to each other through a network of semantic links. The term "hypertext" was coined by Ted Nelson in 1965 to refer to non-linear text. Nelson defined hypertext as "a body of written or pictorial material interconnected in a complex way that it could not be conveniently represented on paper." The power of hypertext lies in its ability to create a "virtual document" composed of several other documents. By adding MULTIMEDIA to hypertext, *hypermedia* can be constructed. Using hypermedia, the user

can be presented with a document which, while it appears to be a single entity, is actually composed of many different parts. The parts may be located separately on a single computer or on different computers (in some cases in different parts of the world).

Hypertext is extremely useful for combining information in a non-linear way. Humans think non-linearly, thus providing these linkages supports human cognition. As an example, hypertext is an excellent tool in manuals. By clicking on a link, the user is transferred to the document it represents. This makes it extremely easy to navigate between references, and related material can be linked to each other.

The basic concepts in hypertext are *nodes* (documents or concepts) and *links* (the relationship between the nodes). Hypermedia is created when nodes that contain media other than text are linked together. For example, a document can have pictures, video, and sound integrated so that it appears as though it were one document. By selecting a video, for instance, the user is able to see the video on the computer screen.

Hypertext is implemented through the use of a standardized language. The most common hypertext language today is the hypertext markup language (HTML) and its derivatives, such as dynamic HTML (DHTML), which is used in the WORLD WIDE WEB (WWW) of the INTERNET (*see* MARKUP LANGUAGES). HTML is a relatively simple derivative of another language, the standard generalized markup language (SGML). HTML works by enclosing text within tags in order to explain how that text should be treated by a browser (an application interpreting HTML). For example, the phrase "This text would be bold" is coded as bold by enclosing it within tags indicating beginning and ending of bold: This text would be bold. When the browser detects the (starting tag) and (ending tag), it converts the text in between to bold. Likewise, documents can be linked. An example is <a href = "http://www.w3.org">World Wide Web Consortium Homepage</a>. When the browser detects the text <a href = " ... "> it interprets this as a link. Anything after the first > sign is what the user sees when viewing the document in a browser, and the </a> marks the end of the link. Thus, from the previous excerpt, the user would see

"World Wide Web Consortium Homepage." These kinds of links, whether to other hypertext documents or other media, can be combined into a seamlessly integrated page. By implementing the simple set of semantics available in HTML, very complex documents can be produced.

In the last decade HTML has evolved significantly, to the point where the language now allows for production of very rich and complex documents. In fact, many personal productivity applications, such as *word processors*, *spreadsheets*, and even *presentation programs*, can now store their file types as HTML files, retaining the full richness of their original binary file format. In addition, using DHTML, a programmer can construct a dynamic document which responds to user input and reformats itself. For example, such a document can present a wizard that walks the user through completing a complex set of steps, where each step is dependent on the selections made in previous steps. Such documents can be self-contained and stored as a single entity.

Bibliography

Nelson, T. (1965). A file structure for the complex, the changing, and the indeterminate. *Proceedings of the ACM Twentieth National Conference.* New York: ACM Press.

I

ICIS

The International Conference on Information Systems is an annual international conference for information systems academics (*see* ASSOCIATIONS AND SOCIETIES FOR INFORMATION PROFESSIONALS). Begun in 1980, it is considered the leading international conference for academics in information systems.

identity theft

William J. Caelli

This term normally applies to the illicit act of one party in obtaining the identity parameters of another party and then, usually, making use of those identity parameters to fraudulently impersonate the original party from which they were stolen. This illegal act has been recognized as a major threat to the success of electronic commerce (*see* E-COMMERCE) over the INTERNET, for example, but the term applies more generally to any such activity such as usage of a stolen passport, credit card, or driver's license.

The use of untrusted commodity operating systems on home and small business computers linked, potentially on a permanently connected basis, to high-speed broadband data communications services, usually the Internet, presents major opportunities for such identity theft operations to be performed, particularly where the computer user's identity data may be permanently stored on the same computer system. The theft action is usually performed by the illicit insertion of unsolicited software systems, commonly called SPYWARE, into the computer system under attack.

See also *email; phishing*

IFIP

Begun in 1960, the International Federation for Information Processing (IFIP) comprises national information processing societies (*see* ASSOCIATIONS AND SOCIETIES FOR INFORMATION SYSTEMS PROFESSIONALS). Its technical activities are performed by technical committees. The most important technical committee for information systems is TC8 (Information Systems).

image processing

see DOCUMENT IMAGE PROCESSING SYSTEMS

implementation of information systems

Norman L. Chervany and Susan A. Brown

Implementation of information system (IS) projects focuses on the diagnosis and treatment – the resolution – of concerns that individuals and groups have about changes that an information system project will produce in their work life. This discussion of implementation processes is organized around three topics: (1) the change process; (2) the diagnosis of implementation problems; and (3) management actions for implementation. The relationship among these three components is illustrated in figure 1.

THE CHANGE PROCESS

To be successful, the implementation of an IS project must move an organizational work system from its current state to a desired new state. This movement involves passing through

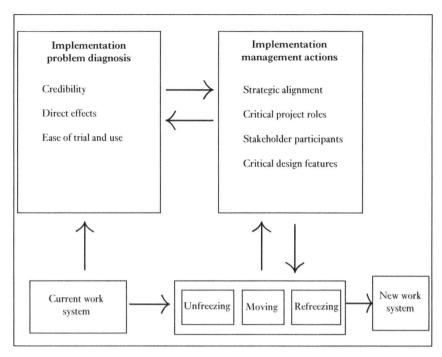

Figure 1   Implementation management process

three phases: (1) unfreezing; (2) moving; and (3) refreezing (for the original discussion see Lewin, 1952; for the use of this stage model, see Karahanna, Straub, and Chervany, 1999). The length of time for a phase depends upon the nature of the system being built, the nature of the organization for which the system is being built, and the management actions used to manage the transition. Mistakes that cause the implementation effort to failure can occur at each stage.

Management of IS implementation requires examination of the concerns of all the stakeholders to an information systems project – the diverse groups of people, inside and outside the organization, whose work life will be affected by the project. In addition, stakeholders also include groups of people whose actions can affect the success of the project. With respect to the successful implementation of a CUSTOMER RELATIONSHIP MANAGEMENT (CRM) system, for example, the stakeholder groups inside an organization include salespeople, sales management, logistics and customer service personnel, information systems personnel, plus upper man-

agement, and ultimately the owners of the business. Outside of the organization, the stakeholder groups include customers, competitors, and technology suppliers.

Unfreezing involves gaining recognition and acceptance from the stakeholders of the project that changes to the work system are needed. The data required for successful unfreezing differ according to the organizational position of the stakeholders. For upper management, owners, and other suppliers of capital to the organization, the required data focus on the projected improvements in organizational performance and increase in economic value added that the IS project will bring to the organization (e.g., increases in sales, gains in market share, reduction in costs, and improvements in quality). For others, such as mid-level managers, front-line workers, salespeople, IS personnel, as well as the organization's customers, the data focus on what benefits and costs the project will produce for them personally, not for the organization in general. Finally, for competitors and technology suppliers, the data focus on what their future actions may be. The primary cause of IS implementation failure during unfreezing involves overlooking significant concerns of one or more stakeholder groups.

Moving involves the definition and development of the functionality of the system. Obviously for IS projects, the functional requirements must be specified in terms of hardware and software. But the functional requirements must also be specified in terms of changes in operational and managerial work processes, management policies and procedures, and education and training specifications for the stakeholder groups. In fact, more often than not the primary cause of implementation failure during moving arises from the inappropriate specifications of the changes in work processes and not in the specifications of hardware and software.

The responsibility for developing the specifications falls within the domains of IS systems analysis and design, working in partnership with the various user and management stakeholder groups. It is through the successful completion of this partnership-based systems development process that the projected, as well as unforeseen, benefits and costs used as evidence in the unfreezing stage are achieved.

Refreezing involves activities that insure that the new operational and managerial work systems embedded in the IS project become institutionalized in the stakeholder groups. The focus is on demonstrating that the benefits and costs, projected in unfreezing and captured by the analysis and design efforts, are delivered to the various stakeholders. Assuming that the unfreezing and moving stages have been successfully completed, the primary cause of IS implementation failure during refreezing involves the failure to reinforce consistently how the proposed system addresses the concerns of stakeholder groups.

DIAGNOSIS OF IMPLEMENTATION PROBLEMS

Research on innovation in general (e.g., Rogers, 1983), and the implementation of IS projects specifically (e.g., Karahanna et al., 1999; Venkatesh et al., 2003), has identified three broad categories of criteria that stakeholders use to judge the value and acceptability of a proposed project: (1) the credibility of the people proposing the project, the credibility of the people developing the project, and the technology being employed; (2) the direct positive and negative effects of the proposed operational and managerial processes; and (3) the ease of trial and use of the proposed system. While each individual stakeholder evaluates a proposed system in terms of these three categories, IS implementation diagnosis focuses upon identifying the typical beliefs about the systems held by different groups of stakeholders. In the CRM example discussed previously, the evaluation of the system must be done in terms of the beliefs of salespeople, sales management personnel, customers, logistical and customer service personnel, etc.

The *credibility of proposers, developers, and technology* is important because it influences a priori perceptions of the proposed IS project. For example, if sales management is recommending the system, the credibility of the sales management in the eyes of the various stakeholder groups is critical. In IS projects, the reputation of the specific system developers involved in the project, as well as the credibility of information systems groups, is important. The reliability of the hardware and software employed in the project is important. Recent research (e.g., McKnight, Cummings, and Chervany, 1998; McKnight and Chervany, 2002) has examined the issue of credibility from the standpoint of the factors that produce trust – trust in the proposers, trust in the developers, and trust in the technology.

Direct effects of the proposed system consist of incremental benefits, incremental costs, and failure consequences. *Incremental benefits* may be monetary or non-monetary. As an example of monetary benefits to a stakeholder, a new sales support system may directly lead to an increase in sales and sales commissions. Most stakeholders, however, do not receive monetary payment; rather, they receive benefits such as the ability to complete a task faster with higher quality. *Incremental costs* for most stakeholders are not monetary. Rather, the costs may be the incremental effort to learn to use the proposed system and pressure to perform at higher levels of productivity with the new system. These incremental costs may be transitory or continuing. *Failure consequences* are encountered if a stakeholder adopts the new system and it temporarily or permanently fails. If, for example, a sales force moves to a CRM system and the system fails, it will affect sales effort.

Ease of trial and use of the proposed system focuses on five issues. The first two are *physical and intellectual ease of use* and *ease of conversation about the system.* If, for example, stakeholders can talk about and use a new system without learning complex technical procedures and terminology, they will be more likely to view the system favorably. The importance of these two issues explains the significance of graphical user interfaces (*see* GRAPHICAL USER INTERFACE) in personal computers and other mobile devices. The third issue is *compatibility* with other parts of the stakeholders' work processes. The more localized the effects of a proposed system, the more favorably it will be viewed. The fourth and fifth issues are ability to test a system *on a limited basis* before committing to full-scale use and ability to reverse the *usage decision.* The ability to try a proposed system on a limited, experimental basis and the ability to discontinue use if the actual system does not live up to expectations increase the likelihood that the system will be viewed favorably.

The three evaluative criteria categories and the specific dimensions within them define measures that the proposers and developers of a new system should monitor during the three phases of the change process. Positive responses across key stakeholder groups increase the likelihood that the project will succeed. Among all of the criteria mentioned above, however, *incremental benefits* are the most critical. Stakeholders will be willing to work to overcome a number of problems if they see a clear benefit in the system. Perception of no benefit or limited benefits by a stakeholder group is almost certain to cause implementation problems and may lead to the outright failure of an IS project.

MANAGEMENT ACTIONS
FOR IMPLEMENTATION

The diagnosis of implementation problems defines concerns that IS implementation management must resolve. IS implementation management can be defined in terms of four categories of action: (1) aligning the proposed system with the strategy of the organization; (2) filling critical roles within a specific IS project; (3) obtaining participation by representatives of key stakeholder groups; and (4) specifying the critical system design features.

Strategic alignment focuses on the relationship between the proposed system and the strategy of the organization. It explains why the system is important to the critical success factors of the organization. While the systems analysis process builds this linkage as it defines operational and managerial processes and the associated hardware and software requirements, this activity assures that all stakeholder groups understand the reasons for the proposed system. Although not all stakeholders will see personal *incremental benefits,* the strategic alignment explanation provides a legitimate reason for the system.

Critical project roles refer to positions and activities of sponsor, champion, and project leader. The sponsor is a senior-level manager in an organization who has the authority to spend the resources required by the proposed project. The sponsor is also the person who, by his or her support, communicates the alignment of the project with the organization's strategy. The project must also have a *champion,* usually an upper-level manager in the functional organization that will use the system. The champion is usually organizationally above the directly affected organizational stakeholders. From this position, he or she spends the time and energy to manage the negotiations and resolve the political issues that naturally arise from an IS project. Champions are usually at some political risk in the organization if the project fails. The *project manager* is the person responsible for managing the day-to-day activities of the project. For IS projects, the project manager usually comes from the systems development group in an organization. There should also be a co-project leader from the main user area. This dual project manager approach is necessary to insure that both the business issues and the technical issues are addressed during the development process.

Stakeholder participation refers to the active and appropriate involvement of the stakeholder groups in the systems analysis and development process. If there is a positive level of trust between the stakeholders and the project proposers and developers, stakeholder involvement can increase the quality of the functional specifications for the proposed system. The involvement of stakeholders helps to obtain their "buy-in" concerning the changes in operational and managerial work processes. In terms of the implementation problem diagnostic dimensions discussed in the previous section, involvement is a productive way of achieving favorable perceptions among the various stakeholder groups.

Critical design features refer to operational and managerial work processes, system functionality, and system user interfaces. These features are necessary to the success of the project, but they are not sufficient. The degree to which they will contribute to the success or failure of the project often depends on how well *strategic alignment*, *critical project roles*, and meaningful *participation* are executed.

Bibliography

Karahanna, E., Straub, D., and Chervany, N. (1999). Information technology adoption across time: A cross-sectional comparison of pre-adoption and post-adoption beliefs. *MIS Quarterly*, **23**, 83–213.

Lewin, K. (1952). Group decision and social change. In E. E. Maccoby, T. M. Newcombe, and E. L. Hartley (eds.), *Readings in Social Psychology*. New York: Holt, pp. 459–73.

McKnight, D. H. and Chervany, N. (2002). What trust means in e-commerce relationships: An interdisciplinary conceptual typology. *International Journal of Electronic Commerce*, **6**.

McKnight, D. H., Cummings, L., and Chervany, N. (1998). Trust formation in new organizational relationships. *Academy of Management Review*, **23**.

Rogers, E. M. (1983). *The Diffusion of Innovations*, 3rd edn. New York: Free Press.

Venkatesh, V., Morris, M., Davis, G., and Davis, F. (2003). User acceptance of information technology: Toward a unified view. *MIS Quarterly*, **27**, 425–78.

inference engine

Amit Das

An inference engine performs reasoning in a knowledge-based system (*see* KNOWLEDGE BASE). It applies formal logic to a set of facts to derive valid conclusions, which provide the basis for further reasoning. This continues until the goal is reached or all possibilities are exhausted. Inference engines perform forward reasoning, backward reasoning, or both.

See also *expert systems*

information assurance

William J. Caelli

The US Committee on National Security Systems (which replaces the earlier National Security Telecommunications and Information Systems Security Committee) defines the term information assurance (IA) as "information operations that protect and defend information and information systems by insuring their availability, integrity, authentication, confidentiality, and nonrepudiation. This includes providing for restoration of information systems by incorporating protection, detection, and reaction capabilities" (*National Information Assurance Glossary*, CNSS Instruction No. 4009, revised May 2003).

This definition, including the use of the term "information operations," owes a great deal to the circumstances of its creation, namely, the US military and federal government sectors. The publication referred to above is one of a series of such publications issued as relevant standards in the area. As such its usage by the commercial and non-government sectors has been somewhat limited until recently, where the more usual terms of privacy or information systems security have prevailed. However, the growth of concern for corporate governance, as evidenced in the US by the passing in July 2002 of the Public Company Accounting Reform and Investor Protection Act (Sarbanes-Oxley Act), often simply referred to as "SOX," coupled with the subsidiary concern of information technology (IT) governance, has meant that the IA term is growing in general usage. For example, in the UK, the relationship between IA and corporate governance, and thus the responsibilities of company directors, has been set out in a publication entitled *Corporate Governance and Information Assurance: What Every Director Must Know* from the Information Assurance Advisory Council (IAAC) in that country (www.iaac.org.uk, August 1, 2004). This publication clearly points out that the information assets of a company are vital to its survival and, as such, must be protected as much as any other asset of the company. It thus behoves company directors to be familiar with the overall information systems security employed in their operational information systems and to take oversight responsibility for this.

Now, from the definition it can be seen that the IA concept expands upon the usual "CIA" trilogy of concepts associated with the term "information security," namely, confidentiality, integrity, and availability. AUTHENTICATION and non-repudiation both come into the scene, as does the whole concept of restoration of services with the implied presence of appropriate audit and control facilities in information systems and data networks. In summary, relating to this IA term, and as outlined in the frequently asked questions (FAQ) website of the US's National Security Agency (NSA) (www.nsa.gov/isso/, August 1, 2004), the use of the IA term has increased in the relevant government arenas since the 1990s and has grown out of such terms as COMSEC (communications security), ITSEC (information technology security), and others to become a more inclusive term.

The IA paradigm can then be considered in two distinct ways:

• the associated responsibilities of the IT industry itself, including hardware, software, and service providers, to create and market products and systems that provide the necessary structures for users to implement information assurance policies in their organizations with a reasonable level of confidence that such policies will be capable of being represented in such systems and reliably and continuously enforced by the application systems they create; and
• the responsibilities of the users of these IT products and systems to define and maintain appropriate information assurance policies within their organizations and to allocate the resources needed, including human, computer, network, and other necessary resources, to insure that such policies are clearly understood and practiced.

Taking the second matter first, there are now accepted standards, nationally and internationally, for information systems security management practices and these form a major part of the information assurance regime in any enterprise, public or private. A prominent example is international standard IS 17799 Information Security Management from the International Standards Organization (ISO). This standard has been adopted in many countries as a benchmark of best practice in the area and presents a basic checklist of necessary concerns that need to be addressed. It is often referred to as a "baseline" for IT security. However, while this and other standards exist, they are ineffectual if an enterprise does not allocate people to the information assurance role and provide them with the necessary levels of education and training.

Given that these are new concerns, particularly in the private and commercial government sectors, it is highly likely that the IT professionals in any organization will not have the necessary education as part of their original tertiary/university education program. Indeed, it has been widely recognized that such education has simply not been widely available in the tertiary IT education sector in most countries and that this situation continues to the present day. It should be pointed out, however, that in the US, for example, attempts have been made since the mid-1990s to enhance such education programs through recognition of worthwhile programs by its NSA. Indeed, the NSA recognizes that education is the top "pillar" in five pillars of information assurance that it acknowledges:

• cyber security awareness and education;
• strong cryptography (*see* CRYPTOGRAPHY (CRYPTO));
• good security-enabled commercial information technology;
• an enabling global security management infrastructure; and
• a civil defense infrastructure equipped with an attack sensing and warning capability and coordinated response mechanisms.

Similarly, evidence is emerging that governments are starting to take a lead in defining the needs for information assurance in their own information systems. The US Federal Information Systems Management Act (FISMA) points in this direction, requiring relevant public sector management to take these matters seriously as part of their job function. In addition, there is evidence that governments are starting to place higher-level requirements on information assurance needs in public sector procurement activities for basic IT products, systems, and services as well as in the definition of "turnkey" information systems development and deployment contracts.

In relation to the IT industry itself, evidence of large-scale acceptance of the need to urgently upgrade products, systems, and services offered in line with these new requirements is rather hard to come by. While some efforts can be seen in such programs as Microsoft's "trustworthiness" direction, these efforts appear to be concentrated solely on such items as software quality activities and basic secure configuration of current products as default conditions.

In this sense, at government and military levels, the term information assurance is often associated with the evaluation of security in IT products and systems, usually by means of agreed criteria for such evaluation. The standard cited in this regard is IS 15408 Common Criteria for Information Systems Security Evaluation. Essentially, this standard sets out two parameters for the assessment of the security-enforcing properties of an IT system, i.e., the ability to cater for an enterprise's definition of security "functionality" required, and the level of "evaluation" of the reliability of the enforcement of that functionality by the system. This standard was developed in the 1990s, although its origins relate to the early 1980s with the publication in 1983 of its predecessor, the US's Trusted Computer System Evaluation Criteria (TCSEC), commonly known as the Orange Book by the color of its covers.

The problem, as defined in a paper some years later by members of the NSA, is that these standards were developed at the same time as a revolution was occurring in the IT industry itself, i.e., the move toward commoditization of the products and systems of that industry away from the mainframe- and even minicomputer-based data center approach of the period 1960–80. That NSA paper clearly argues that today's commodity-level computer operating systems, for example, were never designed with strong information security features or enforcement in mind. Moreover, the IT industry itself points to the fact that security was not specified by its customers as a major requirement until quite recently, and even then only by certain industries such as the banking and finance, healthcare and government services sectors. So, in the tradition of any industry, the IT industry did not respond with new levels of secure products.

From an information assurance viewpoint, then, incorporation of necessary security features and their enforcement in information and data communication products and services usually require the incorporation of add-in security products and subsystems from other vendors. Indeed, the last 20 years or so have seen the development of just such an IT security add-in industry, catering for the lack of such security features and structures in mainstream operating systems, middleware, database management, network control and management, and other systems. Examples include anti-virus software systems, firewall products, cryptographic products and subsystems, and many others (*see* SECURITY OF INFORMATION SYSTEMS).

In summary, the move toward responsibility for information assurance is emerging across the whole of society as a mandate for all IT and enterprise managers. However, these managers may not have the necessary education or training to fulfill this role, and such education has become a major concern in many countries. In particular, given the growing and massive complexity in current IT systems purchased off-the-shelf as commodity products, it is almost impossible for these managers to clearly state that those systems are indeed capable of enforcing the information assurance requirements of their enterprises, or even of catering for the definition of such requirements. As such, the future may lie in new forms of assignment of responsibility at both the purchaser and the manufacturer levels.

In particular, IT contracts may need new clauses related to this matter, since the IT vendor is usually in a position of total dominance and strength in relation to the purchaser; in other words, the end user does not and cannot be expected to have the levels of knowledge needed in order to be able to evaluate the security stance of products and systems offered. For example, an end user normally has no idea about the security-enforcing structures or reliability of a commodity operating system, nor does that user have any access to and/or have the capability to identify and assess security-pertinent sections of the relevant source code or like documentation in order to be able to make a reasonable assessment of the case.

Information assurance requirements, now being gradually invoked in legislative action in many countries, usually in an indirect way, at least for the present, will have an effect on both end-use information system developers and users and on the creators and vendors of IT products, systems, and services, i.e., the IT industry itself. It is likely that first steps in enabling information assurance through new levels of security technology in off-the-shelf products and systems will come from public sector-led procurement activities in the area as well as more specific legislative action. At the same time, growing formal education in the creation of trusted applications will help. For more information, consult the IEEE Task Force on Information Assurance website, ieee-tfia.org.

information concepts

Gordon B. Davis

Processing, delivering, and communicating information are essential objectives of the management information system of an organization. The system employs information and communications technology in achieving these objectives. The concept of information is therefore fundamental to the design of an information system.

In the context of information systems, information is data that have been processed into a form that is meaningful to the recipient and is of real or perceived value in current or prospective actions or decisions. Underlying the use of the term are several ideas: information adds to a representation, corrects or confirms previous information, or has "surprise" value in that it tells something the receiver did not know or could not predict. Information reduces uncertainty. It has value in the decision-making process in that it changes the probabilities attached to expected outcomes in a decision situation. It has value in motivation and building expertise about the organization and its processes and values.

The relation of data to information is that of raw material to finished product. An information processing system processes data into information. Information for one person may be raw data for another. For example, shipping orders are information for the shipping room staff, but they are raw data for the vice president in charge of inventory. Because of this relationship between data and information, the two words are often used interchangeably.

Information resources are reusable. When information is retrieved and used, it does not lose value; in fact, it may gain value through the credibility added by use. This characteristic of stored data makes it different from other resources. Since management information systems deal with information, it would be useful to be able to measure the information provided by the systems and how much comes from informal information channels. There is no adequate method for measuring the information provided by an information system. However, several concepts are useful in understanding the nature and value of information in organizations. These are (1) information theory; (2) message reduction concepts; (3) information quality; (4) the value of information in decision-making; and (5) the non-decision value of information.

INFORMATION THEORY

The term information theory refers to a mathematical theory of communication. The theory has direct application in electronic communication systems. It focuses primarily on the technical level of accuracy in information communication. It is limited in its practical application to management information systems, but it does provide useful insights into the nature of information.

Information theory was formulated by Norbert Weiner, a well-known mathematician, in connection with the development of a concept that any organism is held together by the possession of means for acquisition, use, retention, and transmission of information. Claude Shannon of Bell Laboratories developed and applied these concepts to explain telephone and other communications systems.

The purpose of a communication system is to reproduce at the destination a message selected at the source. A transmitter provides coded symbols to be sent through a channel to a receiver. The message that comes from a source to the transmitter is generally encoded there before it can be sent through the communications channel and must be decoded by a receiver before it can be understood by the destination. The channel is not usually a perfect conduit for the coded message because of noise and distortion. Distortion is caused by a known (even intentional) operation and can be corrected by an inverse operation. Noise is random or unpredictable interference.

As used in the mathematical theory of communication, information has a very precise meaning. It is the average number of binary digits that must be transmitted to identify a given message from the set of all possible messages to which it belongs. If there is a limited number of possible messages that may need to be transmitted, it is possible to devise a different code to identify each message. The message to be transmitted is encoded, the codes are sent over the channel, and the decoder identifies the message intended by the codes. Messages can be defined in a variety of ways. For example, each alphanumeric character may be a message, or complete sentences may be messages if there is a limited, predefined number of possible sentences to be transmitted. The size of the code is dependent on the coding scheme and the number of possible messages. The coding scheme for information theory is assumed to be binary (only 0 or 1 as values).

The information content (or code size in bits) may be generalized as:

$$I = \log_2 n$$

where n is the total number of possible messages, all equally likely. Some examples for a message selected from 8, 2, 1, or 27 possible messages illustrate the formula. If there are eight messages, a code with only 3 bits can be sent to distinguish among them, i.e., there are three combinations of 0s and 1s in three bits ($n = 8$, $I = \log_2 8 = 3$). If there are only two outcomes, a single bit (0 or 1) value can identify which of the two is intended ($n = 2$, $I = \log_2 2 = 1$). If there is only one message to select from, there is no need to transmit anything because the answer is already known by the receiver ($n = 1$, $I = \log_2 1 = 0$).

If the set of messages is the alphabet plus a space symbol, the number of bits required will average 4.75 per letter, assuming all letters to be equally probable ($n = 27$, $I = \log_2 27 = 4.75$). However, all letters are not equally probable.

The probability of an A is 0.0642 but for J is 0.0008. When probabilities are unequal, the average information content is computed by the following formula:

$$I = \sum_{i=1}^{n} p_i \log_2 \frac{1}{p_i}$$

A computationally equivalent form is

$$I = \frac{-\sum_{i=1}^{n} p_i \log_2 p_i}{}$$

A communication is rarely if ever completely composed of information. There are usually redundant elements. Redundancy reduces the efficiency of a particular transmission because more codes are transmitted than are strictly required to encode the message. However, some redundancy is very useful for error control purposes. A message may not be received as sent because of noise in the communication channel. The transmission of redundant data allows the receiver to check whether the received message is correct and may allow the original message to be reconstructed.

MESSAGE REDUCTION CONCEPTS

The mathematical theory of communication deals with the information content of messages that are assumed to be objective. However, the richness of language by which humans communicate, and the constraints on humans and organizations as information processors, means that humans typically receive too much information, and the interpretation of received messages is subject to misunderstanding. Information concepts for information systems therefore also include concepts of message reduction, either by sending or receiving efficiency or by selective distribution.

Two methods for reducing the quantity of information are summarization and message routing. Within organizations, message *summarization* is commonly utilized to reduce the amount of data provided without changing the essential meaning. Formal summarization is illustrated by accounting classifications. The president of an organization cannot normally review each sale to get information for decisions.

Instead, the accounting system summarizes all sales into a "sales for the period" total. The system may provide more meaningful information for decision purposes by summarizing sales by product group, geographic area, or other classification. The level of summarization is dependent on the organizational level of the decision-maker. For example, the president may need only the total sales by area, but the sales manager for the area may need sales by sales representative and sales by product.

In *message routing*, there is a reduction in communication volume by distributing messages only to those individuals or organizational units that require the information for some action or decision. This is illustrated by the transmission of copies of purchase orders to only those departments (production, distribution, billing) that take direct action based on the information on the order. The efficiency of message routing is often thwarted by individuals who have little or no use for information but require their own record of it "just in case."

In addition to message routing, individuals or organizational units exercise some discretion over the content and distribution of messages to control their workloads, to control distribution that may have perceived undesirable effects to the individual or unit handling the message, or as part of a presentation format. Messages may be delayed, modified, or filtered before being sent to a recipient. For example, customer complaints may be delayed, modified, or filtered as the information moves up the organization. Serious indicators of customer dissatisfaction may be blocked.

The way that data are presented will influence or bias the way they are used and the interpretation of their meaning. Three examples of presentation bias are (1) order and grouping in the presentation; (2) exception selection limits; and (3) selection of graphics layout. Order and grouping of data influence the perception of importance and affect the comparisons a user is likely to make. The selection of exceptions to be reported also causes presentation bias. In exception reporting, only those items that vary from an "acceptable level" by a fixed deviation are presented to the decision-maker. The choice of a limit automatically introduces presentation bias. A third example of potential presentation bias is the layout of graphics. Examples of ways in which bias is introduced are choice of scale, graphic, size, and color.

INFORMATION QUALITY

Even if information is presented in such a way as to be transmitted efficiently and interpreted correctly, it may not be used effectively. The quality of information is determined by how it motivates human action and contributes to effective decision-making. Andrus (1971) suggests that information may be evaluated in terms of utilities that, besides accuracy of the information, may facilitate or retard its use.

1 *Form utility*. As the form of information more closely matches the requirements of the decision-maker, its value increases.
2 *Time utility*. Information has greater value to the decision-maker if it is available when needed.
3 *Place utility* (physical accessibility). Information has greater value if it can be accessed or delivered easily.
4 *Possession utility* (organizational location). The possessor of information strongly affects its value by controlling its dissemination to others.

Given a choice, managers have a strong preference for improvement in quality of information over an increase in quantity. Information varies in quality because of bias or errors. If the bias of the presenter is known to the receiver of the information, he or she can make adjustments. The problem is to detect the bias; the adjustment is generally fairly simple.

Error is a more serious problem because there is no simple adjustment for it. Errors may be a result of incorrect data measurement and collection methods, failure to follow correct processing procedures, loss or non-processing of data, wrong recording or correcting of data, use of wrong stored data, mistakes in processing procedure (such as computer program errors), and deliberate falsification.

The difficulties due to bias may be handled in information processing by procedures to detect and measure bias and to adjust for it. The difficulties with errors may be overcome by controls to detect errors, internal and external auditing, adding of "confidence limits" to data, and user instruction in measurement and processing procedures, so they can evaluate possible errors in information.

VALUE OF INFORMATION IN DECISION-MAKING

In decision theory, the value of information is the value of the change in decision behavior caused by the information less the cost of obtaining the information. In other words, given a set of possible decisions, a decision-maker will select one on the basis of the information at hand. If new information causes a different decision to be made, the value of the new information is the difference in value between the outcome of the old decision and that of the new decision, less the cost of obtaining the new information. If new information does not cause a different decision to be made, the value of the new information is zero.

The value of perfect information is computed as the difference between the optimal policy without perfect information and the optimal policy with perfect information. Almost no decisions are made with perfect information because obtaining it would require being able to foresee or control future events. The concept of the value of perfect information is useful, however, because it demonstrates how information has value as it influences (i.e., changes) decisions. The value of information for more than one condition is the difference between the maximum value in the absence of additional information and the maximum expected value with additional information, minus the cost of obtaining it. The maximum expected value can change by a change either in the probabilities for the conditions or in the payoffs associated with them.

The quantitative approach suggests the value of searching for better information, but decisions are usually made without the "right" information. Some reasons are that the needed information is unavailable, acquiring the information is too great an effort or too costly, there is no knowledge of the availability of the information, and the information is not available in the form needed.

NON-DECISION VALUE OF INFORMATION

If the value of information were based only on identified decisions, much of the data that or-

ganizations and individuals prepare would not have value. Since the market for information suggests that it does have value, there are other values of information such as motivation, model building, and background building.

Some information is motivational; it provides the persons receiving the information with a report on how well they are doing. This feedback information may motivate decisions, but its connection is often indirect. The information may reinforce an existing understanding or model of the organization. It may provide comforting confirmation that results are within allowable limits. It also aids in learning as individuals receive feedback on the consequences of actions.

The management and operation of an enterprise both function with models of the enterprise within the minds of the managers and operations personnel. The models may be simple or complex, correct or incorrect. Information that is received by these individuals may result in change in or reinforcement of their mental models. This process is a form of organizational learning and expertise building. Since the models are used in problem finding, a change in the models will have an influence on identification of problems. The information also communicates organization values and culture, thereby providing a frame of reference for future decisions.

In decision theory, the value of information is the value of the change in decision behavior (less its cost), but the information has value only to those who have the background knowledge to use it in a decision. The most qualified person generally uses information most effectively but may need less information since experience has already reduced uncertainty when compared with the less experienced decision-maker. Thus, the more experienced decision-maker may make the same decision for less cost, or a better decision for the same cost, as the less experienced person. The value of the specific information utilized in a decision cannot be easily separated from the accumulated knowledge of the decision-maker. In other words, much of the knowledge that individuals accumulate and store (or internalize) is not earmarked for any particular decision or problem. A set of accumulated knowledge allows a person to make a better decision, or the same decision at less immediate cost, than one who lacks this expertise.

APPLICATION OF INFORMATION CONCEPTS TO INFORMATION SYSTEMS

Information theory, although limited in scope, provides useful insights about the surprise value and uncertainty reduction features of some information. It emphasizes the value of information in changing decisions. The idea that information has value only in that it alters a decision provides a useful guideline for parsimony of information. A common mistake in information system design is to produce volumes of data in the form of reports because they are easy to produce. In many cases, the actual value of the additional information is zero.

The theory explains that not all communications have information value, but there is value in redundancy for error control. In management information systems, there is substantial noise in the information being communicated owing to the unknown but differing backgrounds of humans, their differing frames of reference, varying prejudices, varying levels of attention, physical differences in ability to hear and see, and other random causes. Redundancy can be effectively used to overcome noise and improve the probability of messages being received and interpreted correctly.

Concepts of message reduction suggest ways to improve sending and receiving efficiency and reduce bias. Summarization and message routing reduce information being communicated. Filtering, inference by use of statistics, and presentation choices may improve efficiency but may also introduce bias. The quality of information received is not directly measurable. However, design can focus on achieving utilities associated with information and on processes to reduce bias and errors.

In decision theory, information is associated with uncertainty because there is a choice to be made and the correct choice is uncertain. The reason for obtaining information is to reduce uncertainty so the correct choice can be made. If there were no uncertainty, there would be no need for information to influence choice. Information received will modify the choice by altering the subjective estimate of the probability of success. The decision theory approach focuses the attention of the information system designer not only on the value of information in decision-making, but also on the fact that the cost of obtaining more information may not be worthwhile.

Many data are received and stored without reference to decisions being made. However, the data are meaningful to the recipient and are of real or perceived value in current or prospective decisions. They have value in building mental models and expertise that will be useful in future analysis and decision-making.

Bibliography

Andrus, R. R. (1971). Approaches to information evaluation. *MSU Business Topics*, Summer, 4046.

Cherry, C. (1957). *On Human Communication*. Cambridge, MA: MIT Press.

Gilbert, E. N. (1966). Information theory after eighteen years. *Science*, **152**, 320.

Shannon, C. E. and Weaver, W. (1962). *The Mathematical Theory of Communication*. Urbana: University of Illinois Press.

Weiner, N. (1948). *Cybernetics, or Control and Communication in the Animal and the Machine*. New York: John Wiley.

information economics

see ALLOCATING RESOURCES TO IT/IS

information goods

Gordon B. Davis

The information systems of an organization frequently provide support for the production, sales, and distribution of information goods. In providing this support, it is important for the management to understand the nature of information goods. Information goods consist of units that can be digitized. Examples are reports, books, movies, music, and news. They do not fit neatly into traditional economic or business profit analysis. The cost behavior and economics of information goods differ from traditional goods and services based on cost behavior (returns to scale), importance of experience in evaluating, and effect of use or consumption (appear to be like a public good).

A unit of a physical good traditionally has a cost based on an allocation of the fixed costs of producing the good plus the variable cost of producing each unit. The same applies to services with personnel and other service costs consisting of both allocation of fixed costs and variable costs that are identified with the services. Information goods differ in that virtually all costs are associated with the development of the first unit. These costs of the first unit are sunk costs; they can probably not be recovered if there are no sales. The marginal cost of duplication is close to zero. Unless the company can differentiate its information goods, competition will prevent it from recovering the sunk costs of the first unit.

Information goods are characterized by the need to experience them. Customers need to be provided with opportunities to preview or browse or at least obtain reviews that describe the goods.

The consumption of an information good does not reduce the amount available to others. For example, a family watching a television program does not reduce the availability of the same program to others. Various methods such as copyrights are used to limit access, so that there can be an economic return for the production of the good.

Another dynamic of the information economy is the low cost of storing information for access by the INTERNET and the close-to-zero cost of accessing it. This leads to an oversupply of information that is available but presents difficulty in locating relevant, worthwhile information. The time and cost dynamics of searching and evaluating information available on the web has led to search engines and recommender systems.

Bibliography

Shapiro, C. and Varian, H. R. (1998). *Information Rules: A Strategic Guide for the Network Economy*. Boston: Harvard Business School Press.

information overload

Roberto Evaristo

Information systems (IS) management faces frequent, recurring decisions relative to the introduction of new technology, new software systems, and new applications. One of the considerations in these decisions is the cognitive effort of users in learning and using the new systems. The cost-benefit evaluation considers the learning and using effort versus the perceived benefits in doing so. One of the yardsticks of effort is information load (Evaristo and Karahanna, 1998). The concept of information load was introduced in the IS literature in the early 1990s (Evaristo, 1993), and since then has been a relatively frequent subject of investigation (e.g., Schultze and Vandenbosch, 1998; Grise and Gallupe, 1999).

Information overload is one extreme of the construct of information *load*. Information load is a continuum in which both underload and overload are detrimental to human performance. When there are too few stimuli, *information underload* ensues and human attention is not maintained. Typical problems studied include those faced by night guards or submarine sonar operators. The other extreme is *information overload*. In these situations, information load is higher than the capacity to cope. Information overload has been researched in the management literature. The main focus of this literature has been decision-making behavior, such as purchasing in marketing and the relationship between amount of information available and satisfaction/performance in management. The implications of information overload for design, operation, and use of some specialized information systems, such as electronic mail, have also been researched.

Psychologists have investigated the construct of information load and not limited research to information overload. They have adopted the term "human mental workload" to include tasks that, besides processing information, pose other demands on the individual. Mental workload can be defined as the portion of one's available information processing resources demanded to accomplish a task. The concepts of underload and overload are important in the design of information system applications. To avoid underload, the task division between the computer and the human should give sufficient stimulus and activity to the human to maintain attention. To avoid overload, systems should be designed with human limits on amounts of information to be processed, and there should be structures, such as hierarchies, to facilitate human processing.

To research information load, the three main workload measurement methods are (1) secondary task method; (2) physiological measures; and (3) subjective ratings. The *secondary task method* requires the participant to perform a second task concurrently in order to assess process demands on the primary task. The most serious drawback of such a method is the intrusive aspect of the secondary task. Certain physiological functions usually show changes when an individual is under higher mental workload. Several functions have been investigated. These include sinus arrhythmia (heart beat rate changes), mean pulse rate, pulse rate variability, respiration rate, and pupil diameter. Although objective and hard to refute, physiological data are difficult to collect in the field or in large quantities in the laboratory. Moreover, special equipment is necessary. Subjective ratings provide generally valid and sensitive measurement. Two validated measurement scales are the subjective workload assessment technique (SWAT), sponsored by the US Air Force and developed by Eggemeier and associates (Eggemeier, 1981), and the NASA-TLX (Task Load Index), developed by Hart and associates (Hart and Staveland, 1988). A review and assessment of these methods can be found in Nygren (1991). A more recent discussion on subjective mental workload assessment sparking much controversy can be found in Annett (2002).

Bibliography

Annett, J. (2002). Subjective rating scales: Science or art? *Ergonomics*, 45 (14), 966–87.
Eggemeier, T. (1981). Current issues in subjective assessment of workload. *Proceedings of the Human Factors Society 25th Annual Meeting*, Santa Monica, CA, pp. 513–17.
Evaristo, J. R. (1993). An empirical investigation of the effect of information technology and information characteristics on individual information load. Unpublished PhD dissertation, Minnesota.
Evaristo, J. R. and Karahanna, E. (1998). The impact of mental workload in the evaluation of innovations. In T. Larsen and G. McGuire (eds.), *Information Systems and Technology Innovation and Diffusion*. Hershey, PA: Idea Group Publishing, pp. 48–70.
Grise, M.-L. and Gallupe, R. B. (1999). Information overload: Addressing the productivity paradox in face-to-face electronic meetings. *Journal of Management Information Systems*, 16 (3), 157–85.
Hart, S. G. and Staveland, L. E. (1988). Development of the NASA-TLX (Task Load Index): Results of empirical and theoretical research. In P. Hancock and N. Meshkati (eds.), *Advances in Psychology*, 52. Amsterdam: North Holland, pp. 139–84.
Nygren, T. (1991). Psychometric properties of subjective workload measurement techniques: Implications for their use in the assessment of perceived mental workload. *Human Factors*, 33, 17–33.
Schultze, U. and Vandenbosch, B. (1998). Information overload in a groupware environment: Now you see it, now you don't. *Journal of Organizational Computing and Electronic Commerce*, 8 (2), 127–48.

information retrieval

Nancy K. Herther

Critical to the research process are those activities in which existing, published information is gathered, analyzed, and used in some manner. The process of transferring information through various formal channels – from book or journal publication to speeches at conferences or preprint reports of research – is well understood today. Now, these various options or channels for collecting and reporting information are being challenged by the increasing use of informal methods of sharing information: self-publishing or use of INTERNET blogs and listserves, for example, which may result in a destabilizing impact on this system.

Traditional information transfer processes begin with the generation of research or data, from the government, private groups, or publicly funded sources such as higher education or government departments. As a critical part of traditional research, reports of work are shared with colleagues at various stages in the research process (as preprints, seminars, speeches at conferences, etc.) for critiques and input. Much of the information is accessible to subsequent researchers through indexes, databases, conference proceedings, etc. Primary publication in the form of journal articles, research reports, or other mechanisms follows. Secondary publication – summaries in books or research review sources – follows, usually at about a year after primary publication. At this point, indexes, bibliographies, library catalogues, and other organizational means are available to help identify and access these works or ideas.

Today, online databases, the Internet, and other channels have collapsed this process and have made the identification of research-in-progress much easier. Databases of stock data or corporate activities can help identify organizational shifts or anticipate product announcements when used by trained specialists. Full-text versions of major newspapers, industry newsletters, government reports, securities filings, journals, and even press releases have grown with the shift to an information-centered economy. This results in much more information being made easily available, but increases the need for sound judgment and careful study to avoid unnecessary work or to overlook critical information.

ANALYZING INFORMATION NEEDS

Given the glut of information available today, finding intelligent ways to navigate through all these data to gain the information needed is essential. The following questions may be asked.

- Do you need a particular document/resource/specialist or are you looking for a specific piece of information instead?
- Do you need background information or only a particular statistic?
- Are you looking to ultimately develop a perspective or make a decision concerning some issue, or are you hoping, more generally, to scan the environment for new developments in some particular area?
- Is this comprehensive, retrospective information that you need or a time-bound update (e.g., everything in the past two weeks)?

In order to get the information needed, an individual must clearly understand the dimensions of information need. Formulating a search strategy may be done by an individual, possibly aided by an information retrieval professional who assists in framing search questions.

WHAT INFORMATION SOURCES ARE AVAILABLE?

A second critical area is understanding what information may be available to help you answer a question. Does the information already exist? Is this something that some industry group or the government might track? Are the companies involved private or public? Would some of the information be mandated and kept by the government or other agencies? If trend data are needed, perhaps industry analysts or trade publications would be good sources. This is another area in which working closely with subject experts or information professionals can be helpful.

DATA GATHERING

Many data today are available in electronic format, making the process of gathering and organizing information much easier; however, many critical resources, including human experts, still require other methods of contact. Sophisticated database and information management programs can help to index information, to create spreadsheets, or to give free-text searching access to huge files. Many source databases are still very expensive to access and the use of subject experts or information professionals at this stage is often critical.

ANALYZING AND VALUING INFORMATION

Analyzing the information that is found will help in identifying gaps for further research, make initial conclusions about your subject, and may point out disparities or problems with available information. For example, estimates and projections from industry analysts may vary greatly, requiring an investigator to carefully reexamine what each expert evaluated, and how they evaluated their subjects. Often information is given by unnamed or unknown sources so that the validity of the data cannot be carefully checked.

CURRENT AWARENESS OR SELECTED DISSEMINATION OF INFORMATION

In the past 15 years a common service of database vendors and information centers has been the on-demand, ongoing provision of regular updates of information on specified topics. This allows researchers to get updated information from specified resources or databases on a regular basis. This is generally done once an initial, comprehensive search has been performed so that subsequent searches can target those points/issues/questions that are most critical and use only those databases or other resources deemed to be most relevant. Public libraries in major cities, research libraries, and private information brokers all provide information services today and should be contacted for information before starting any major research effort involving secondary or published information.

Bibliography

Brownstone, D. M. (1979). *Where to Find Business Information: A Worldwide Guide*. New York: John Wiley.

Daniells, L. M. (1993). *Business Information Sources*, 3rd edn. Berkeley: University of California Press.

Encyclopedia of Business Information Sources (1995–6). Detroit: Gale Press.

Kantor, P. B. (1994). Information retrieval techniques. *Annual Review of Information Science and Technology*, **29**, 53–90.

Lancaster, F. W. and Warner, A. J. (1993). *Information Retrieval Today*. Arlington, VA: Information Resources Press.

Salton, G. and McGill, M. J. (1983). *Introduction to Modern Information Retrieval*. New York: McGraw-Hill.

Stanfill, C. and Waltz, D. L. (1992). Statistical methods, artificial intelligence and information retrieval. In P. S. Jacobs (ed.), *Text-Based Intelligent Systems: Current Research and Practice in Information Extraction and Retrieval*. Hillsdale, NJ: Lawrence Erlbaum, pp. 215–25.

Strauss, D. W. (1988). *Handbook of Business Information: A Guide for Librarians, Students and Researchers*. Englewood, CO: Libraries Unlimited.

information system methodologies

T. William Olle

An information system development life cycle (SDLC) establishes a structured set of activities for developing and implementing information system applications. The set of methods to be applied is termed a "methodology."

INFORMATION SYSTEM LIFE CYCLE

In common with other complex artifacts, an information system goes through a life cycle (a term adopted from biological sciences). While the life-cycle view is widely accepted, there are varying opinions about the breakdown of this life cycle into stages (or phases). One example of the breakdown of an information system life cycle has been used by an international task group, IFIP Working Group 8.1 Design and Evaluation of Information Systems (Olle et al., 1991).

This life cycle identifies the following 12 stages.

1 strategic study;
2 information systems planning;
3 business analysis;
4 system design;
5 construction design;
6 construction and workbench test;
7 installation;
8 test of installed system;
9 operation;
10 evolution;
11 phase out;
12 post mortem.

In an attempt to be more specific, broad terms such as "development" and "implementation" are not used in this breakdown. Development covers roughly the stages from 3 to 6. Implementation covers either stages 5 and 6 or else 7 and 8, depending on the use of the term.

A *strategic study* is the preliminary stage in which it is determined whether new information systems are needed at this time and, if so, how to proceed. *Information systems planning* is a stage that covers a large business area (possibly the whole enterprise) and includes a broad analysis of information requirements. On the basis of this stage, it is possible to subdivide the business area for more detailed analysis.

The *business analysis* stage is the one in which the business is analyzed in detail to determine which business activities are performed and the detailed information requirements of each. Business analysis is more concerned with the business than with considerations of computer hardware and software. *System design* covers the specification of the external features of the system (the users' view). It is independent of any considerations attributable to the construction tools that are to be used to build the system.

Construction tools may not be selected until the system design is completed. *Construction design* is concerned with the system internals (which the users do not see). Furthermore, construction design depends heavily on the construction tools to be used. The term construction is used in preference to programming because, with recent advances in technology, programming is only one of a number of alternative ways of constructing the computerized part of an information system. It is already commercially viable for a system to be constructed automatically from the system design specifications.

The *evolution stage* is being recognized as of increasing importance and various distinct approaches exist for changing a system after it has been in the operational stage for some time. Typical distinct approaches are referred to as restructuring, reengineering, and reverse engineering.

INFORMATION SYSTEMS METHODOLOGY

Just as there are many different views of the information systems life cycle, so there are many different views on how one should progress through the life cycle toward an operational information system. Many approaches have been the subject of considerable formalization (usually not in the mathematical sense). The term *methodology* is used to refer to such an approach. It is noted that this term is etymologically incorrect since "methodology," strictly speaking, means "a study of methods." For this reason, some approaches carry the name "method," but the majority prefer "methodology."

Most methodologies cover only a few stages in the information systems life cycle. The stages in the above information systems life cycle that have received the most attention from methodology designers are business analysis, system design, and construction design. However, the information systems planning stage and the evolution stage are also supported in some methodologies.

Each information system methodology uses a number of techniques. Examples of techniques are data flow diagramming and data structure diagramming (*see* DATA STRUCTURE(S)). It should be noted that the term methodology is occasionally applied to a single technique. Many methodologies are referred to as system development methodologies. This usually indicates that the methodology covers the construction design stage and an activity preceding that which is often labeled "requirements definition" or "requirements specification." This view of the life cycle either combines or fails to differentiate between the business analysis stage and the system design stage.

Information systems methodologies have their origins in different aspects of data processing technology. Some methodologies spring from a programming language background (*see* PROGRAMMING LANGUAGES) and emphasize the processing that needs to be carried out by the computerized information system. Others have evolved from the use of DATABASE MANAGEMENT SYSTEMS. These methodologies focus more heavily on the data used in the business area and on a database that is central to the design of the system. Techniques based on preparing models of the data (*see* DATA MODELING, LOGICAL) are extensively used in this context. More recently, there have been claims that representations of events in the business and events that happen in the computerized system must be incorporated in a successful methodology. These various views are now converging and it is increasingly recognized that a good methodology should be able to support all of the three perspectives of data, process, and events.

Bibliography

Olle, T. W., Hagelstein, J., Macdonald, I. G., Rolland, C., Sol, H. G., van Assche, F. M. J., and Verrijn-Stuart, A. A. (1991). *Information Systems Methodologies: A Framework for Understanding*, 2nd edn. Reading, MA: Addison-Wesley.

information systems

Gordon B. Davis

In organizations, the term information systems, management information systems, or information management are equivalent and are applied to:

- the systems that deliver information and communication services for an organization;
- the organization function that plans, develops, and manages the information systems.

The name for the academic discipline more or less mirrors the organization use. Some of the names that are used for academic units illustrate the common theme:

- information systems
- management information systems
- information management
- management of information systems
- informatics (usually modified by organization, administration, or similar terms)

The term management information systems (MIS) reflected the strong theme that the function and the academic field were most concerned about the new powerful uses of computers to change the information presented to management and the analysis for management decision-making. Over time, there has been a trend to employ the simple term, information systems, in referring to the academic discipline and to the organization function, but there are still many variations of terminology in practice.

See also *management information systems*

information system stage hypothesis

Christina Soh

The stage model for information systems (IS) was first published in the early 1970s (Nolan, 1973; Gibson and Nolan, 1974). This model was presented as a description of information systems growth in organizations. Nolan initially hypothesized that an organization moves through four stages in the development of its computing resource. This hypothesis was based on Nolan's observation that the computing budget over time for three firms was approximately S-shaped. He stated that the points of inflection in the curve indicate the transition between stages. The four stages were named initiation, contagion, control, and integration.

Stage 1, *initiation*, is the introduction of computing into the organization, where the computing investment is treated like any other capital investment, and there is usually excess computing capacity vis-à-vis the initial computing applications. Stage 2, *contagion*, is a period of unplanned, rapid growth as users become aware of the potential benefits from computing.

As there are few formal controls over the computing resource at this point, the result is a steep rise in computing expenditures for hardware, software, and personnel. Senior management concern about burgeoning IS costs results in stage 3, where formal *controls* such as budgets, charge-out, and project management are implemented. Often an over-emphasis on control occurs and there is a failure to exploit information systems fully. Eventually, the organization reaches stage 4, *integration*, where it has settled many of the issues for managing the computing resource. Growth in the computing budget begins to level off.

In subsequent papers, Nolan modified the model in a number of ways. He noted that the growth in the computing budget did not level off at the integration stage, but that it continued to grow. He included two additional stages after integration: DATA ADMINISTRATION and maturity, to accommodate the then new database technology (Nolan, 1979). In this expanded model, stage 4, *integration*, marks the transition from management of computing resources to management of organizational data resources. At the beginning of stage 4, database and data communications have transformed key applications, and users experience significant increase in benefits from computing. User demand for information systems again escalates. Stage 5, *data administration*, therefore sees rapid growth in the computing budget, which eventually levels off in stage 6, *maturity*, when the applications portfolio is completed.

Benchmarks for characterizing each stage were also proposed. In addition to IT expenditure, there were benchmarks for technology, applications portfolio, data processing (DP) organization, DP planning and control, and user awareness (Nolan, 1979). The model also evolved from being primarily descriptive to being used for prescription as well. For example, Nolan proposed using the model to identify the organization's stage of computing development, and to apply the appropriate amount of management slack or control.

The model has, however, been the subject of several critiques (Benbasat et al., 1984; King and Kraemer, 1984). A major criticism has been the lack of empirical support. Empirical studies by other researchers have not supported the existence of an S-shaped budget curve, nor the benchmarks for each stage. It appears that the maturity criteria do not always move together; for example, "mature" IS organizations did not have more formalized data administration procedures, while increased user awareness did not correlate with reduced problems.

Nonetheless, the Nolan model was popular, particularly with practitioners, as it boldly and broadly framed the complex phenomenon of computing development within organizations. It is also noteworthy for proposing testable hypotheses, and for generating debate within the field.

Bibliography

Benbasat, I., Dexter, A. S., Drury, D. H., and Goldstein, R. C. (1984). A critique of the stage hypothesis: Theory and empirical evidence. *Communications of the ACM,* 27, 476–85.

Gibson, C. F. and Nolan, R. L. (1974). Managing the four stages of EDP growth. *Harvard Business Review,* 52, 76–88.

King, J. L. and Kraemer, K. L. (1984). Evolution and organizational information systems: An assessment of Nolan's stage model. *Communications of the ACM,* 27, 466–75.

Nolan, R. L. (1973). Managing the computer resource: A stage hypothesis. *Communications of the ACM,* 16, 399–405.

Nolan, R. L. (1979). Managing the crisis in data processing. *Harvard Business Review,* 57, 115–26.

infrastructure for information systems

see STRATEGIC ALIGNMENT

innovation and information technology

Norman L. Chervany and Susan A. Brown

An *innovation* is something new to the adopter. It may be new to the world and thus new to the adopter, or it may exist elsewhere in the world and thus be new only to the adopter. Organizations search for innovations because, for one reason or another, either an offensive or a defensive strategic move needs to be improved. When thinking about organizational innovation and information technology (IT), it is important to remember that information technology is a

means to an end (organizational performance improvement), and not an end in itself. More specifically, the target IT innovation is improved process performance and, within these processes, the improved design of work. These can be operational processes (e.g., manufacturing or consumer service call center processes) or managerial processes (e.g., budget planning or sales management processes).

All IT innovations, regardless of their specific focus, proceed through a common set of stages.

THE GENERAL STAGES OF IT INNOVATION

Based upon more than 3,000 studies, Rogers (1983) identified five general stages through which all innovations proceed: (1) knowledge; (2) persuasion; (3) decision; (4) implementation; and (5) confirmation. Rogers's definition was developed from the perspective of the individual adopter. It also provides a reasonable description of innovation at organizational level.

To understand Rogers's process, consider a potential wireless IT platform to improve the mobility of individuals using individual-centric products (e.g., cell phones, data and image transmission devices, medical implant devices, etc.) and how this potential innovation goes from an unknown entity to become a functioning part of organizational processes and individual product usage.

Taking the perspective of an organization that may ultimately decide to use wireless-based communication and data transmission systems for its sales force, at the outset (*knowledge*), this organization must become aware of the existence and operational characteristics of wireless technology. *Persuasion* occurs as the appropriate individuals in the organization form favorable or unfavorable attitudes toward the technology (e.g., believe that salesperson productivity could increase if they could access appropriate data without the "wired-to" constraint). *Decision* occurs when the organization engages in the evaluative activities required to make an adoption or rejection decision about the wireless-based applications. Assuming adoption has occurred, *implementation* starts when the technology is put into continuous use, in this example by the members of the sales force. Finally, in *confirmation*, the individual seeks reinforcement of the adoption decision from others in the organization. If the value of the technology is confirmed, continued usage follows; if not confirmed, the individual may reverse the adoption decision. What this last stage really means, in the sales support systems example, is that the individual salespeople and the individual sales managers will look to others to see if their decision is seen as a good one.

This overall innovation process description has stood the test of time. While refinements have been made, it is still consistent with the contemporary work on organizational innovation (see van de Ven and Poole, 2004.)

THE SPECIFIC STAGES OF IT INNOVATION

Starting with the work of Kwon and Zmud (1987), information systems researchers (e.g., Karahanna, Straub, and Chervany, 1999) have further articulated the IT innovation process. As defined in table 1, this stream of work modifies

Rogers's process in four ways. First, it explicitly recognizes that IT innovations involve both organizational and individual behavior. Second, it provides more details about each stage. Third, it recognizes that there is a process and a product associated with each stage. The process describes the activities that occur within a stage; the product, the outcome at the completion of each stage. Fourth, the modification redefines and extends the stages from five to six.

The revised stages are: (1) initiation; (2) adoption; (3) adaptation; (4) acceptance; (5) routinization; and (6) infusion. *Initiation* combines Rogers's stages of *knowledge* and *persuasion*. This recognizes that the acquisition and interpretation of basic facts about a potential IT innovation are integrated activities. Rogers's *decision* stage is equivalent to *adoption* and

Table 1 The information technology innovation process

Stage	Definition
Initiation	
Process	Scanning of organizational challenges and IT solutions occurs. Change arises from need-based pull or technology-based push
Product	A match between an IT solution and organizational need is found
Adoption	
Process	Rational and political negotiations are undertaken to obtain organizational backing for implementation of the IT application
Product	A decision is made to invest organizational resources in the IT application
Adaptation	
Process	The IT application is developed and installed; work and management processes are revised; training in the new processes and IT application is provided
Product	The IT application is available for use in the organization
Acceptance	
Process	Organizational members are encouraged to commit to the usage of the IT application
Product	The IT application is employed in the work of the organization
Use	
Process	Usage of the IT application within the new work and management processes is encouraged as a normal activity
Product	The IT application is no longer perceived as out of the ordinary
Incorporation	
Process	Increased organizational effectiveness is obtained by using the IT application in a more comprehensive and integrated manner to support work and management processes that are beyond the initial goals of the application
Product	The IT application is used to the fullest potential within the organization

adaptation. This change emphasizes that an IT innovation requires political support and resource allocation, as well as technical development and process reengineering. *Acceptance* and *routinization* equate with Rogers's *implementation* and *confirmation* stages. The logic is that the change process, including organizational confirmation, should be managed. Finally, *infusion* is added to recognize that IT innovations often have many applications beyond the initial *adoption* and *adaptation* target.

Bibliography

Karahanna, E., Straub, D., and Chervany, N. (1999). Information technology adoption across time: A cross-sectional comparison of pre-adoption and post-adoption beliefs. *MIS Quarterly*, **23**.

Kwon, T. and Zmud, R. W. (1987). Unifying the fragmented models of information systems implementation. In R. J. Boland and R. A. Hirschheim (eds.), *Critical Issues in Information Systems Research*. New York: John Wiley, pp. 251–67.

Rogers, E. M. (1983). *The Diffusion of Innovations*, 3rd edn. New York: Free Press.

Van de Ven, A. and Poole, S. (2004). *Handbook of Organizational Change and Innovation*. New York: Oxford University Press.

input devices

H. Kevin Fulk and Dennis A. Adams

Input devices accept data or information from outside the computer and convert it to a form the computer can manipulate. Input devices and their counterpart, OUTPUT DEVICES, typically do not include storage devices such as disks and tapes, which allow the storage of data that are external or secondary to the central processing unit (CPU) and its primary memory. Secondary storage devices must perform input and output (I/O) operations, but because their primary purpose is to store data, they are typically considered separately. Other devices that perform input and output functions are communications devices.

In the early days of data processing most input was done using a keypunch machine and 80-column computer cards (*see* PUNCHED CARDS). Data entry clerks transcribed the data from a source document into the cards by using a keyboard similar to that of a standard typewriter. The cards were then fed into a card reader, which converted the data into machine-readable form. While the cards have become obsolete, the keyboard remains a primary input mechanism. The basic keyboard layout is virtually unchanged from that of the first manual typewriters. This type of keyboard is also known as the QWERTY keyboard, based on the first six characters on the left of the top row of letters. A modern keyboard is generally divided into five different areas.

The first area, alphanumeric keys, includes all the letters of the alphabet, as well as the numerical digits from 0 through 9. It also includes punctuation mark keys and operational keys such as tab, backspace, shift, caps lock, enter (or return), and the spacebar. Many keyboards also have a variety of "shift" keys that change the operation of the standard keys. For example, pressing the "E" key along with the "ctrl" key creates a keystroke or character that is different from the upper-or lower-case "E." The "alt" key is a similar shift key.

The second area consists of the function keys, usually located across the top or to the left of the keyboard. These keys enable the user to perform a specific function by pressing the appropriate key. Most of the functions performed are controlled by the application software and vary from program to program. However, there are a few standard function keys that perform the same action independent of the application software (e.g. escape). For example, combining the shift key with the F7 key creates the shift-F7 keystroke, which in Microsoft Word invokes the thesaurus, while the same keystroke in WordPerfect prints the document.

The numeric keypad facilitates the entry of large amounts of numeric data. It is generally located on the right side of the keyboard, but may be a keypad separate from the rest of the keyboard. The layout of the telephone keypad and the 10-key are different, so that the integration of the telephone and the computer requires some compromises.

The fourth section of the keyboard contains the cursor-movement keys. These keys, as the name implies, permit the user to move the cursor up, down, left, or right around the screen. Depending on the key selected, the cursor can move as little as one character or as much as one page or more. Finally, indicator (or toggle-switch) lights show the status of certain features that can be set by specific keys. These include the num lock, caps lock, and scroll lock keys.

An increasing number of specialized keyboards are available for individuals who find it difficult to use the traditional keyboard. This includes those who incur repetitive stress injuries or carpal tunnel syndrome from long periods of time spent at the keyboard. Ergonomically designed keyboards that fold or split in the middle offer a more natural position for the hands, and those with wrist rests provide additional support. One-handed keyboards, keyguards, and keyboards equipped with sip-and-puff straws are other examples of available assistive technologies.

Two relatively new keyboard developments are increasing their usefulness. Increasingly common are wireless keyboards. First-generation wireless keyboards used radio signals to communicate between the keyboard and a receiver plugged into a computer's USB port (see the entry on output devices). This technique's usefulness was limited to only a few feet within line of sight between the two devices. Newer wireless keyboards utilize the Bluetooth wireless protocol to link keyboards and computers over larger distances and without the need to be within the line of sight. In addition, it is becoming more common for keyboards to employ keys that are highly customizable. Using customizable driver software, these features allow a user to activate useful functions, e.g., launching a web browser to surf the INTERNET.

While the keyboard gives the user an increasingly powerful and flexible tool for working with the computer, it can still be cumbersome, especially if the user is a slow or inaccurate typist. To increase the speed and effectiveness of user–computer interaction, a variety of pointing devices have been developed. These devices generally allow the user to execute commands by literally pointing at the screen and pressing a button. Common pointing devices include the mouse, trackballs, light pens, and joysticks.

Perhaps the most familiar pointing device is the mouse. It is standard equipment with almost every personal computer sold today. The mouse is a small, handheld device that is linked to the cursor on the screen. As the mouse is moved around, the cursor moves also. By manipulating the mouse, the user can position the cursor (or some other object) to the desired location. One or more buttons on the mouse increase the range of options available to the user. Depending on the application program, a mouse can be used to select and execute a large number of actions. Selecting an item on the screen can be done by moving the cursor to that location and clicking a mouse button.

Formerly, mice had to be used on a special surface. Optical mice eliminate this need and can be used on virtually any flat, non-reflective surface. Optical mice, as sealed devices, offer another benefit over mechanical mice. They do not need to be cleaned frequently. Similar in function to the mouse is a device called the trackball. The trackball is basically an upside-down mouse. It is a small ball, fixed in position on or near the keyboard. The cursor moves as the ball is rotated in place. Trackballs tend to be used with portable or laptop computers. Another pointing device is a light-sensitive tool shaped like a pen. Called light pens, these devices are placed directly on the screen at the desired location. By pressing a button on the pen, the user can select an item, highlight a menu choice, manipulate graphic objects, or even draw on the screen. Light pens are useful in graphic-intensive work or in situations where a keyboard would be impractical, such as dirty or dusty environments. Generally found with personal computers, joysticks are used like a mouse to position the cursor on the display screen and select items or commands. Initially developed for use with game applications, joysticks are also used more and more in industrial and medical applications.

The slowest link in data entry has historically been the human entering the data. One method used to speed up this process is source data automation, which uses a variety of input devices to capture the desired data related to an event in machine-readable form at the time and place the event occurs. Common methods of source data automation are magnetic ink character recognition, magnetic tape strips, and optical character recognition.

Magnetic ink character recognition (MICR) begins with documents being encoded with characters printed in a special magnetic ink. By processing these documents through MICR readers, the information can be captured and entered directly into the computer. MICR technology is used mainly for high-volume document processing, such as check processing by financial institutions. The checks are pre-printed with identifying information (the bank's routing and transit number, the customer's account number, and the check number). When the bank receives a check, the amount is then printed on the check in magnetic ink. As the check is processed, this information is used to update the customer's account and the bank's records. Magnetic tape strips are short lengths of magnetic tape encoded with data. The strips are passed through devices that read the data and forward them for processing. The most common examples of this technology are the magnetic strips on credit cards and ATM cards.

Optical character recognition (OCR) devices scan images and translate the data into machine-readable form. The three general types of OCR devices are scanners, bar code readers, and digitizer tablets. Scanners transform images, either printed characters or pictures, into digital form that the computer can process. This is done by converting areas of light and dark into digits. By literally mapping the digits (bitmapping), the computer can recreate, store, and manipulate or edit data from the source document being scanned. There are two main types of scanners: flatbed and handheld. Flatbed scanners are similar to office copiers, with the source document being fed into the scanner. Handheld scanners must be moved manually over the source document. Companies that handle large amounts of documents or correspondence, such as insurance companies or law firms, find scanners are particularly useful when used in conjunction with document imaging systems (see DOCUMENT IMAGE PROCESSING SYSTEMS). These systems create digitized images of documents, significantly reducing paper-shuffling by allowing firms to store, retrieve, and edit the document images through computer terminals or networks. This also allows multiple users access to the same document, eliminating time spent requesting, searching, and transferring a paper document.

Bar codes (see BAR CODE) are specially designed patterns of lines that are typically used to identify an item or product. By varying the width of the bars and the distance between them, a large amount of data can be represented. One example of bar codes is the universal product code (UPC), which is used on items in grocery and retail stores. By reading the bar codes with a special scanner, inventory, movement, and price data can be captured and processed. Other uses of bar codes include railroad cars, library books, inventory, and next-day delivery packages. As an extension to UPC bar code systems, RADIO FREQUENCY IDENTIFICATION (RFID) combines the usefulness of a bar code system with the ease of use of a wireless application by placing small transmitters in tags that are attached to products or other items. When those tags enter a radio field, the tags transmit their data contents to the reader nearby. That reader can store the data or transmit it as input to another system for further processing.

Digitizer tablets, or pen-and-tablet devices, transform handwritten data into machine-readable form. A special pen is used to write on a sensing surface which digitizes the input. These devices can be used to write, draw, or manipulate the screen cursor. They are useful in graphics applications and some inventory control and tracking situations. Substantial improvements have been made that allow the computer to convert the handwritten information into the appropriate corresponding computer character.

Tablet PCs have recently emerged and are gaining in popularity. These devices combine the keyboard found on traditional laptop computers with a flat surface for writing notes with a stylus. There are other devices used to input data into a computer system. With touch screens, a user touches a video monitor to enter commands or retrieve information. By touching the screen, the user's finger interferes with a fine mesh of light beams that crisscross the computer screen, thereby allowing the computer to determine where the user is touching the screen. Touch-screen systems are used often in retail stores and financial institutions in devices called kiosks where users make queries. Voice input devices change the spoken word into machine-readable form. These devices are still in their infancy, have limited though growing vocabularies, and often require the user to "train" the computer to recognize certain words. Still, voice input provides a quick, simple, and natural way to input data. It is also very useful for individuals who cannot use more traditional input devices.

Analog/digital sensors are becoming more commonly used as input devices. Used in a variety of scientific, industrial, and medical applications, sensors can monitor environmental or other conditions and feed the data directly to a computer for storage and analysis. The analog inputs, such as temperature or time, are converted to digital signals and processed by the computer.

With the advent of MULTIMEDIA computers, video and audio sources can be used as input. Using the appropriate software, laser disks, VCRs, audio cassettes, and CDs can be used as input sources. The VCR or audio player becomes the input device and transmits the data to the computer.

Virtual reality (VR) systems, while still in their infancy, are becoming more sophisticated. VR systems employ advanced technology to heighten HUMAN–COMPUTER INTERACTION by giving the user the feeling of immersion in a simulated environment. Input devices include data gloves, motion detectors, and pressure sensors which communicate user movement and actions to the computer. Areas using VR applications include airlines and the military (flight simulators and training), medicine (video fibers and microtools can be inserted into a body, allowing doctors to internally examine and treat patients without large incisions), and the entertainment industry.

As computer technology becomes part of consumer products and services, more natural and easy-to-use user interfaces will be needed. Input devices will become more sophisticated, with less entry from keyboard and mouse and more entry with microphones and touch screens. Interacting with a computer will become more natural for users.

instant messaging

Instant messaging (IM) is similar to EMAIL but a connection is established and maintained during a session, so that messages are sent and received immediately. It supports a conversation using keyboard entry of messages. More than one person may be part of the conversation. The advantage is the immediate sending and receiving of messages. This may be productive because it reduces delays and allows immediate clarification of ideas, instructions, comments, etc. The disadvantage is the lack of security for instant messages and the lack of checking that may be performed in a regular email message. A significant productivity disadvantage is the requirement that the participants must be online at the same time and therefore must interrupt other work to participate.

integrated services digital network

Gordon B. Davis

Integrated services digital network (ISDN) is a digital communications service over the telephone network. It provides higher transmission rates than an ordinary telephone service. An ISDN can, for example, support two voice connections or simultaneous transmission of voice and data. Narrowband ISDN operates over existing telephone systems; broadband ISDN requires higher-capacity fiber optic systems. ISDN is important in information systems because it provides higher transmission rates between computers and also allows online applications between users communicating by voice and working with displays of data being transmitted.

intelligent agent

see SOFTWARE AGENT

interface

An interface is the intersection between two systems or two subsystems. For example, in computer applications, the display screen is an interface between the application and the user.

Internet

Mark A. Fuller

Defined as a *network of networks*, the Internet is a large system of interconnected computer networks that spans the entire world, linking businesses, government agencies, educational institutions, as well as individual computer users. Thousands of networks and millions of individual computers are connected by this technology, with few limitations regarding the distance between networks or the number of computers on each linked network. From a hardware perspective, the Internet is much like a transportation system. It involves both wired and wireless communication pathways (equivalent to roads), carriers of messages in the form of information packets (similar to vehicles carrying goods), and finally PROTOCOLS that govern how this information can be sent through the network (roughly equivalent to the rules of the road as well as the language in which these rules are written). From a functional perspective, the user frequently thinks of the Internet in terms of what it can do, i.e., its ability to send and receive information via Internet applications such as EMAIL, FILE TRANSFER PROTOCOL (FTP), or web browsers, rather than its technology infrastructure.

In order to gain a full appreciation of the Internet, it is useful to understand its evolution. During the 1970s and 1980s many organizations (businesses, government agencies, etc.) began to adopt small-scale computer networks (called LANs or local area networks) to meet their data processing and data sharing needs. While LANs were useful in helping an organization distribute information more efficiently, it was clear that additional benefits could frequently be gained by connecting these distinct computer networks together. Unfortunately, many of these networks used different protocols for communication, and therefore sharing information between them was often challenging. Prior to this time, the US Department of Defense had also been interested in this problem for other reasons, most notably the desire for military installations to be able to share information reliably even in situations where part of the network would become inoperable – for example, in the event of a nuclear war. The Advanced Research Projects Agency (ARPA) was given the task of coming up with a network technology that would allow for the reliable and efficient communication and exchange of information across great distances under such conditions.

In the late 1960s and early 1970s, ARPA developed a technology called packet switching, which allowed information to be routed across a network in the form of small addressed packets that were then reassembled into a coherent message at the receiving end. This differed dramatically from the way information was transferred over networks prior to this point, i.e., by setting up a temporary circuit that was maintained for the duration of the communication. In contrast, with packet switching, not only could messages be broken up into smaller chunks, addressed, and then sent over multiple communication lines at the same time, but also an individual communication line could be shared by multiple messages. A key component of packet switching was a set of protocols termed TCP/IP, short for transmission control protocol/Internet protocol. Together, these protocols are responsible for insuring that each portion of the message is appropriately addressed for its intended destination, that any part of the message lost during transmission is resent, and that the individual packets comprising the message are reassembled in the correct order to insure that the message is coherent.

While the original set of Internet users were primarily scientists and researchers using simple tools like email and file exchange, the Internet has evolved to now include a variety of E-COMMERCE applications such as online journals and magazines, interactive catalogues, electronic banking, database retrieval, financial reporting, inventory tracking, career placement services, as well as online entertainment including games, music, and movies – and this list is far from exhaustive. When the National Science Foundation turned over the Internet technology backbone (major transmission links) to commercial interests in 1995, a new Internet infrastructure, termed Internet2, was created to once again serve scientists who needed the ability to share information over a high-speed worldwide network. In both cases, as bandwidth increases (i.e., as the roads for carrying the data become larger), the uses of the Internet and Internet2 will undoubtedly continue to grow. The Internet is currently (2004) estimated to provide services to around 600 million users.

Internet auctions

Charles A. Wood

Internet auctions are important uses of information technology in business transactions. They are used in both selling and purchasing goods and services. Online auction houses supply auction services for a wide variety of sellers. Generalized auction houses provide auction services for businesses purchasing goods and services. Internet auctions are important because they both support new business models for selling and purchasing and are used extensively.

The conventional auction is a seller's auction. The "host" of the auction is the *seller* who is auctioning *assets* to bidders, where the *highest* bid wins. An auction by purchasers of goods and services is termed a reverse auction. In *reverse auctions*, the host of the auction is the *buyer* who is auctioning *production contracts* to the bidders, where the *lowest* bid wins. Reverse auction exchanges have also flourished. Much B2B activity (*see* E-COMMERCE BUSINESS-TO-BUSINESS SYSTEMS) is done through reverse auction exchanges, where buyers place contracts online so that suppliers can bid for these contracts, the lowest bidder often winning the contract. As such, reverse auctions are also called *descending auctions* since the price decreases over time. Such exchanges have led to some extremely high initial savings. These reverse auctions are conducted by individual businesses and by exchanges for groups of businesses.

The Internet has transformed the way auctions typically occur and has led to some interesting changes in the auction phenomenon in terms of auction reach and auction timing as well as in available product and seller information. Traditional (non-online) auctions are typically conducted within minutes or less, where bidders gather in a specific location and an auctioneer accepts bids from bidders who compete against one another. The winning bid is the bid that is higher than every other bid. Traditional auctions are also *serial*, meaning that the auction

for the next item does not occur until the current auction is completed. Variants of this include sealed-bid auctions and reverse auctions, when dealing with supply contracts, government contracts, oil drilling, etc., but typically all traditional auctions are of a small scale, with a limited number of participants and a limited time frame. Also, many times in a traditional auction, the item can be viewed before purchase (in the case of artwork and rare coin auctions) or even sampled and tested (in the case of auctions selling oilfields for drilling).

Online auctions change much of these dynamics. Because technology has eliminated the need for an auctioneer, online auctions can be conducted over a period of many days or weeks rather than in minutes, as with traditional auctions. Online auctions are *translocational*, meaning that bidders do not need to be in the same location to enter a bid, unlike most traditional auctions. Thus, bidders from around the world can participate in the same auction. Online auction houses arrange auctions *concurrently*, so the bidder can see and bid upon every item up for sale rather than only a current item. Bidders can search through literally millions of items to find items they wish to bid upon. In figure 1, all 1888 Indian Head Pennies minted in the US that are for sale on eBay are listed. Bidders can compare prices and ending times for each auction and then click on an auction listing to bid.

Unlike traditional auctions, in online auctions bidders typically cannot view the product or investigate the seller to any great extent before purchasing. Thus, an unscrupulous seller could act anonymously by falsifying name, address, phone, and email address, leaving the consumer vulnerable to opportunistic behavior, such as lying about product quality or even selling products that do not exist. Even if the seller does not hide his or her identity, the consumer can still be victimized by a seller who typically is far away and, in online auctions, whose business does not depend on word-of-mouth and repeat business from satisfied customers. However, sellers who have much experience and history online have more to lose from negative reputation effects than sellers who are inexperienced. Auction houses typically implement a *reputation system* to reward good behavior and punish opportunistic behavior. Reputation systems track

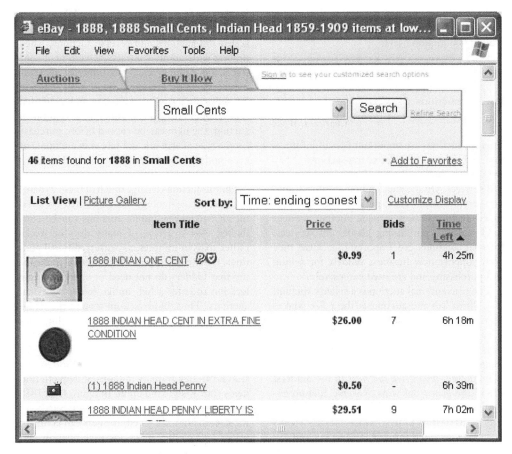

Figure 1   Items listed after a quick search

comments left by other bidders and sellers and report these comments. Figure 2 shows how eBay allows buyers and sellers to leave positive, neutral, or negative comments for their trading partner, and how those trading partners can reply to a comment.

There are a number of variations on the rules for an auction. These determine the winner and the amount that is paid by the winners. An *English auction* is an open, ascending auction where a single item (or multiple items sold as a single block) is sold to the highest bidder. Most online auctions and traditional offline auctions are English auctions.

A *multiple-unit English auction* is an auction where the seller offers multiple items for sale, and the bidder can bid for all or part of the lot. For example, if a bidder offers 100 rare coins in a multiple-unit auction, a bidder can enter a bid for only 10 of these coins. Thus, multiple-unit auctions can have multiple winners. Each winner pays the amount of his or her bid.

A *Vickery auction* (Vickery, 1961), also called a *second-price auction*, is an auction where the bidder with the winning bid still wins, as with English auctions, but pays the second-winning price. Vickery shows us that second-price auctions motivate the bidders to bid their true valuation, whereas English auctions motivate bidders to enter bids at less than their true valuation. Thus Vickery auctions often generate higher revenues.

A *multiple-unit Vickery auction* is similar to a multiple-unit English auction, except all winners pay the lowest winner's price. The term Dutch auction is sometimes used to describe a multiple-unit Vickery auction. Consider

Figure 2   An example of eBay's online reputation system

Table 1   English and Vickery multiple-unit auctions

Bidder	Quantity	Bid (each coin)	English auction amount paid	Vickery auction amount paid
A	50	$10	didn't win	didn't win
B	40	$12	20 @ $12	20 @ $12
C	30	$13	30 @ $13	30 @ $12
D	30	$14	30 @ $14	30 @ $12
E	20	$15	20 @ $15	20 @ $12

a hypothetical auction where 100 rare coins are auctioned off bids in table 1.

As shown in table 1, bidder A did not win because he bid too low. Bidder B only bid enough to win part of her auction, and thus only received 20 rare coins when she indicated that she would take 40 rare coins at this price. Bidders C, D, and E all received the items. In a multiple-unit Eng-lish auction, each bidder pays what was bid. In a multiple-unit Vickery auction, each bidder pays only what the lowest-price winning bidder, bidder B, has offered. Thus, in table 1, each bidder pays only $12 (the lowest bid entered by any winner), even though he or she offered more. Stock exchanges can be viewed as a type of mul-tiple-unit Vickery auction, since stocks do not sell for the bid price offered by investors, but rather the clearing price, which is the price point where all stocks for sale will sell.

A *reserve price* is a price set by the seller where bids below this price will not be honored. For example, if a seller feels an item is worth $100 dollars, she can set her reserve price at $100, and then any bid below $100 will be ignored. A reserve price can be of two varieties, a *public reserve price* or a *secret reserve price*. A public reserve price, also called *starting bid*, is the price the seller sets for the bidding to begin. Public reserve prices are known to all bidders, and thus no bidder will bid below this level. Secret reserve prices are not disclosed to the bidders usually until a bid passes the secret reserve price level. Auctions with secret reserve prices are also called *reserve price auctions*. Both online and traditional research has investigated the optimal reserve price setting and the motivation for setting a secret reserve price.

The previous definitions apply to all auctions. The changing nature of auctions to online auctions, however, has given rise to a language used when describing auctions, as shown by the following definitions:

- *Shilling* is the act of bidding upon your own item. In traditional auctions, shilling occurred when a seller hired another person, called an agent, to try to "run up the bid" if that agent felt that the high bidder is willing to bid more. In traditional auctions, however, shilling is difficult, since detection is more easily accomplished and it usually requires the assistance of another person. In online auctions new identities are easily created, and sellers can establish several identities to bid on their own items. Thus, in online auctions, shilling is more easily accomplished and more difficult to detect.
- *Bidding agents*, also known as using *proxy bidding*, are software tools that bid the lowest possible price and then bid the price up to an individual's valuation. There are some bidding agents that automate the timing of the bids as well, and some auction houses, such as eBay, provide simple bidding agents for free.
- *Sniping* is the act of waiting until the last possible moment to bid. In traditional auctions, which typically last only several min-

utes, there is no sniping since everyone bids at the same time. In online auctions, however, bid timing is more of an issue. The idea of sniping is that if you wait to bid, other bidders will not have time to bid against you. Sniping has become incredibly popular, to the point that companies have started up that allow sniping to be automated (such as www.auctionstealer.com). However, sniping seems to go against much economic theory, which holds that bidders should *not* be motivated to snipe but rather bid their true valuation when using a bidding agent. New research is delving into signaling and the possibility of receiving an item for below the second-bidder valuation as motivations for sniping.

The term *Dutch auction* is somewhat ambiguous. Traditionally, Dutch auctions derive their name from the old Dutch practice of auctioning tulip bulbs in a descending auction. The auction starts at a very high price, and at specific time intervals the price drops by a fixed amount. This continues until a bidder indicates a buy signal, at which time that bidder wins the entire lot. With *traditional multiple-unit Dutch auctions*, each bidder can take either some or all of the lot at the current price. If not all units are taken, the auctioneer continues dropping the price on the unpurchased portion of the lot. eBay has used the term Dutch auction to refer to a multiple-unit Vickery auction. The difference is that the bidder does not win the entire lot, but all winners pay the same ending price. *Buy it now* refers to an option placed on online auctions that allows the first bidder to purchase an item for a higher price rather than bid upon that item and a lower bid price. New research is being conducted to determine the optimal buy it now price.

Flash auctions are online auctions that mimic real-world auctions, with real-time bidding, auction times of minutes, not days, and a "going, going, gone" type of structure where the auction continues for up to several minutes until there are no more bids. The one difference between flash auctions and traditional auctions is that flash auctions are translocational, and thus bidders can participate from around the world.

Online auctions research is dedicated to examining how *sellers* and *bidders* interact through the online auction market structure.

As such, auction research can be characterized as typically conentrating on one of the following three auction characteristics: *seller behavior*, *bidder behavior*, and *auction design*.

Research on seller behavior includes setup strategies, seller opportunism (such as shilling; Kauffman and Wood, 2005), and seller comments left in an online reputation system. Other topics include shipping price, the effect of escrow, and insurance.

Research on bidder behavior includes the price a bidder pays, the bidding strategy employed by a bidder, buyer comments left in an online reputation system, buyer opportunism (such as colluding with each other when bidding), and factors that can cause a bidder to pay more or less for the same item (e.g., Kauffman and Wood, 2005). Note that in auctions, sellers do not set the price (although they do set the starting bid), so most research that examines the price paid in an auction is investigating a bidder behavior, not a seller behavior.

Research on online auction design typically involves the use of an analytical model that describes an optimal design of an entire online auction or some facet of an online auction, such as the optimal design of a reputation system or optimal auction house fee structure to encourage or discourage certain behavior (Kauffman and Wood, 2005).

Bibliography

Kauffman, R. J. and Wood, C. (2005). Doing their bidding: An empirical examination of factors that affect a buyer's utility in Internet auctions. *Information Technology and Management*, special issue on online auctions.

Vickery, W. (1961). Counter-speculation auctions and competitive sealed tenders. *Journal of Finance*, **41**, 1 (March), 8–37.

Wood, C. (2004). Current and future insights from online auctions. In M. Shaw, R. Blanning, T. Strader, and A. Whinston (eds.), *Handbook on Electronic Commerce*. New York: Springer-Verlag.

Internet-based selling and information systems

Jungpil Hahn

Internet-based selling, also known as e-retailing or e-tailing, is the selling of goods and services using information and communication technolo-gies of the Internet as the channel of choice. A classic example is Amazon.com – an online retailer that sells goods (e.g., books, music CDs, movie DVDs, electronics, etc.) directly to consumers via the WORLDWIDE WEB. In addition to such pure-play Internet retailers such as Amazon.com (i.e., those that do not have a physical store), traditional brick-and-mortar retailers can also adopt e-tailing strategies to augment their physical retail stores with an online presence. They implement a click-and-mortar (or brick-and-click) business model that combines both the offline and an online presence (*see* E-COMMERCE CLICKS AND MORTAR).

The online retail channel of Internet-based selling, like any other retail format (e.g., mail catalogues, TV shopping, etc.), must overcome the problem of adoption by consumers in order to succeed. Consumers will adopt online retailers (i.e., shop online) only if the utility provided by the online retailer to the consumer exceeds that provided by traditional retail formats. Hence, online retailers need to create value to consumers by creating online shopping environments that support consumer purchase needs. In essence, e-tailing success can only be achieved when e-tailers are able to offer quality products at good prices through excellent customer service. In this sense, the online and traditional channels are not very different. However, the digitization of the shopping experience has important impacts on how consumers shop for goods and how retailers provide the shopping environment.

A consumer's purchasing process is typically characterized as multistage information processing – need arousal, information search, product evaluation, purchase decision, and post-purchase evaluation. From the perspective of e-tailers, Internet-based selling websites can support the various stages of the consumer purchase decision-making process. In terms of need arousal, product recommendations offered at the e-tailer's website can trigger consumer purchase needs. Information search is facilitated by information technology since consumers can use search engines at e-tailer websites to find products sought without having to navigate extensively to arrive at the products, whereas in the physical store environment consumers have to find a way through the store's aisles to arrive at a specific product. E-tailing websites can bring to the consumer not only the product sought but also all other relevant products that the consumer may be considering.

Product evaluation, the stage at which the consumer uses perceptions about product attributes to form attitudes toward the products that are under consideration, can also be facilitated since the e-tailing website can offer not only detailed product information but also other useful information that may help the consumer evaluate the products. For example, Amazon. com, in addition to providing detailed product descriptions, offers product reviews (e.g., book reviews) written by other consumers to help consumers make purchase decisions.

Negotiation of transaction and payment can also be performed entirely online to streamline the purchase process. Currently most e-tailers take credit cards as the payment method of choice, but other technologies such as electronic cash or e-cash (e.g., PayPal), electronic checks or e-checks, or smart cards can be used to pay for online purchases. Finally, the post-purchase evaluation process can also be augmented via various technologies for customer support. Such technologies include FAQs (frequently asked questions), tracking capabilities for tracing the location of the product in the shipping process, and email messages with purchase confirmation, additional production information, and instructions to customers.

There are benefits to consumers who adopt online shopping. First, Internet-based selling provides a faster and more convenient shopping environment. Consumers no longer need to drive to physical shopping malls or retail stores, navigate through the store's aisles to find the products to purchase, and stand in line and wait at checkout counters. Rather, consumers can shop in the convenience of their homes using a computer with an Internet connection and a web browser. Second, consumers reap the benefits of better purchase decision-making and greater shopping satisfaction. Consumers who shop online have access to more information, and more importantly more relevant information, to make their purchase decisions. The availability of relevant product information typically results in better-informed purchases and

subsequently greater satisfaction with the purchasing process and outcome.

Just as the essentials of consumer purchase decision-making stay the same, the fundamentals of selling or retailing from the retailer's perspective are also largely the same. The same characteristics of Internet technologies that have provided consumers with a more convenient shopping environment can also be used to the advantage of e-tailers in conducting business. The retail business entails understanding consumer needs and providing a purchasing environment that can effectively deliver the product to the consumer.

The first major advantage of Internet technologies is the broad availability of access to the technology. The global network of the Internet eliminates distance barriers. Retailers are no longer constrained by the location of their physical stores. E-tailers do not need to have a physical presence in order to serve a local market; having one website can enable e-tailers to cost-effectively gain broader reach. Secondly, Internet technologies enable e-tailers to better understand consumer needs. Since all interactions with the e-tailing websites leave traces of consumer behavior as clickstream data in web server log files, e-tailers, by employing web usage mining (i.e., DATA MINING on clickstream data) techniques, can gain a better understanding of consumer purchase needs. Even though traditional physical retail stores can also gain insights into consumer purchase needs via data generated from POS (point-of-sale) systems, such data only identifies what products were actually purchased. Web clickstream data, on the other hand, by logging every click a consumer makes in the website, can also identify which products were in the consideration set in addition to which product within the consideration set was finally chosen to be purchased. Such additional information can be extremely useful to e-tailers in understanding the performance of their marketing mix.

An Internet-based selling strategy will not always be successful. Consumers will only adopt Internet-based selling channels if the utility provided by the online retailer exceeds that provided by traditional retail formats. From the e-tailer's perspective, there are several areas of concern that must be taken into consideration when planning an Internet-based selling strategy.

A negative impact of the digitization of the shopping experience is that despite the many benefits, online shopping also creates many risks to the consumer. The first is purchase transaction risk – will the online retailer effectively deliver the goods purchased? Consumers do not have the opportunity to inspect the merchandise prior to purchasing it. Such purchase transaction risks may inhibit consumers from adopting online shopping. However, the level of purchase transaction risk is not the same for all product types. For example, consumers may feel more comfortable purchasing pre-packaged commodity products (e.g., toothpaste) online than purchasing fresh produce items (e.g., fruit) or apparel without having a chance to touch and feel the freshness of the produce or the quality of the textile.

Internet-based selling also incurs delivery delays. There is a discontinuity between the time a purchase transaction occurs and the time when the physical product changes hands from the retailer to the consumer (i.e., when the product is shipped and delivered). Consumers may have a disutility toward waiting for a product to arrive. Hence, it is important for e-tailers to consider whether or not their products will overcome such purchase risks. As a side note, this is not to say that such risks are entirely unique to Internet-based selling – similar risks were present for other retail formats such as mail-order catalogues or television shopping.

A further negative impact comes from consumers' security and privacy concerns. Since, e-tailers can make use of customer information (e.g., demographic information, past purchase history, website navigation clickstream data etc.) in order to provide personalized shopping experiences, consumers are becoming increasingly aware that their personal information may be misused. Such security and privacy risks may also inhibit consumers from adopting Internet-based selling channels. E-tailers need to be careful about what kinds of information they collect, and how they employ private customer information. They need to assure customers that their privacy will not be violated.

Internet protocol

see PROTOCOLS

Internet telephony

see VOICE OVER INTERNET PROTOCOL

inter-organizational systems

Donald J. McCubbrey

Traditionally, information systems were constructed to serve the needs of a single organization. Opportunities soon emerged for companies with information systems to tie trading partners together in new and innovative ways (Kaufman, 1966). Such systems are called *inter-organizational systems* (IOS). The popularity of ELECTRONIC DATA INTERCHANGE (EDI) in most major industries and in many government operations is part of the reason for the interest in IOS, but EDI is just one form of IOS.

In 1989, Peter Drucker envisioned a future wherein "businesses will integrate themselves into the world economy through alliances." One of the reasons for this, Drucker argues, is that technology is moving so quickly that it is impossible for businesses to keep up with it without forming strategic alliances with other businesses, as well as with non-commercial entities such as universities and governments. Later, he notes that businesses in the future will follow two new rules: "One: to move work where the people are, rather than people to where the work is. Two: to farm out activities that do not offer advancement into fairly senior management and professional positions" (Drucker, 1989). He points out that neither of these two important trends would be reasonable options without the enabling and facilitating effects of computer and communication technologies.

STRATEGIC OUTSOURCING

The second of Drucker's new rules is termed "strategic outsourcing" by Quinn and Hilmer (1994: 43). They suggest that if firms

concentrate on their own unique "core competences" and strategically outsource those for
which the firm has neither a strategic need nor
special capabilities, managers can leverage their
firm's resources and skills for increased competitiveness. They cite examples such as Nike Inc.,
which outsources 100 percent of its shoe production. Nike prospers, they say, by focusing on research and development and marketing,
distribution, and sales, with all functions coordinated by a state-of-the-art marketing information
system. They note that while many companies look
at outsourcing only as a way of reducing short-term
direct costs, a strategic outsourcing (or partnership) approach can yield significant additional
benefits such as lower long-term capital investments and a leveraging of core competences.

Some of the new management approaches
necessary to obtain the benefits of strategic outsourcing arrangements include a much more
professional purchasing and contracting group
to deal with supplier selection, relations, and
management, and a greatly enhanced logistics
information system "to track and evaluate
vendors, coordinate transportation activities,
and manage transactions and materials movements from the vendors' hands to the customers" (Quinn and Hilmer, 1994: 54). Quinn
and Hilmer demonstrate that business partnerships and alliances can come into being as a
result of a "strategic outsourcing" decision
and be supported and facilitated by EDI and
other techniques of electronic commerce (*see*
E-COMMERCE).

McGee and Prusack (1993) label the approach
"pursuing cooperative advantage in a world of
electronic commerce." They note that one approach to cooperative systems is to attempt to
"lock in" customers by making it difficult or
expensive to switch from one technologically
supported business process to another. On the
other hand, they note that EDI systems are more
often pursued by trading partners in a cooperative mode, in an attempt to obtain mutual benefit
from streamlining the business processes that
their companies share.

Information Partnerships

Konsynski and McFarlan (1990: 114) identified
the potential for "information partnerships."
They describe several forms of information part-

nership beyond the typical customer–supplier
relationship, including joint marketing partnerships such as the airline coalitions of Amadeus
and Galileo, intra-industry partnerships such as
the ATM banking networks or MEMA's Trans-
net system, which connects manufacturers and
thousands of retailers. This research suggests
five key ingredients to successful information
partnerships:

1 *Shared vision at the top.* Top executives in the
   partnering companies must agree on the objectives of collaboration.
2 *Reciprocal skills in information technology.*
   Partnerships work better when both partners
   possess the necessary skills to manage the
   complex technologies that may be involved:
   databases, communications networks, and
   the like.
3 *Concrete plans for an early success.* Early successes give employees in the partnering companies confidence in the venture.
4 *Persistence in the development of usable information.* Attention must be given to packaging
   shared data in a way that is useful to both
   partners.
5 *Coordination of business policy.* Information
   partnerships go beyond merely sharing
   data. True information partnerships are supported by information systems that essentially ignore normal organizational
   boundaries between companies.

IOS Process Reengineering

Venkatraman (1994: 79, 83) notes that "Benefits
from business process redesign are limited in
scope if the processes are not extended outside
the local organizational boundary to identify
options for redesigning relationships with the
other organizations that participate in ultimately
delivering value to the customer. . . . I strongly
believe that the real power of IT for any firm lies
not in streamlining internal operations (efficiency enhancements) but in restructuring the
relationships in extended business networks to
leverage a broader array of competencies that
will deliver superior products and services."

The idea of partnership, and the potential
payoffs from partnership, should be foremost
in the benefits of IOS presented to general managers. Partnerships clearly seem to be an import-

ant strategic trend, and they can be facilitated by the electronic technologies of the world of electronic commerce: EDI, EMAIL, imaging, bar coding, etc.

IOS IN THE INTERNET AGE

Relationships are taking on new forms in the age of the INTERNET. Peter Keen and Mark McDonald note that e-commerce "more and more involves a complex network of relationships to operate between the enterprise, its customers, intermediaries, complementors and suppliers." Intermediaries are specialist companies that provide services better than its client companies can themselves. Examples include such categories as call centers and UPS deliveries. Complementors provide products and services that complement the offerings of the enterprise and thereby extend its value-adding capabilities to its customers. Yahoo!, for example, has 10,000 complementors providing services such as weather information, financial news, general news, and so forth that add value to the Yahoo! site. Keen and McDonald go on to emphasize the importance of trading partner relationships in forming a company's value network. A value network is all of the resources behind the click on a web page that the customer does not see, but that together create the customer relationship – service, order fulfillment, shipping, financing, information brokering, and access to other products and offers (Keen and McDonald, 2000: 5, 96, 99–100). Some of these resources are provided by software, some are outsourced to trusted trading partners, some are provided by electronic links to alliance partners, and others are handled by more efficient and effective business processes. Managers now have many more choices in how to deliver products and services to customers when, where, and how they want them. If a trusted trading partner can perform an essential function better, a company has the potential for a winning combination for itself, its trading partner, and its customers (Haag, Cummings, and McCubbrey, 2004: 260).

Bibliography

Drucker, P. (1989). The futures that have already happened. *The Economist*, October 21, 19–24.

Haag, S., Cummings, M., and McCubbrey, D. J. (2004). *Management Information Systems for the Information Age*. New York: McGraw-Hill Irwin.

Kaufman, K. (1966). Data systems that cross company boundaries. *Harvard Business Review*, 44.

Keen, P. and McDonald, M. (2000). *The eProcess Edge*. Berkeley, CA: Osborne/McGraw-Hill.

Konsynski, B. R. and McFarlan, F. W. (1990). Information partnerships: Shared data, shared scale. *Harvard Business Review*, 68, 114–20.

McGee, J. V. and Prusack, L. (1993). *Managing Information Strategically*. New York: John Wiley.

Quinn, J. B. and Hilmer, F. G. (1994). Strategic outsourcing. *Sloan Management Review*, 35 (2), 43–55.

Venkatraman, N. (1994). IT-enabled business transformation: From automation to business scope redefinition. *Sloan Management Review*, 35 (4), 73–87.

intranet

Gordon B. Davis

An intranet is an INTERNET that has restricted use inside an organization. Unlike the Internet, which is a public system, an intranet is a private network. It uses Internet protocols, so it appears to users the same as an Internet site. An organization establishes private, internal websites to share information with employees. An employee uses a web browser to obtain information and services. Access requires a valid user name and password that the organization provides to appropriate internal users. Any type of information that can be shared over the Internet can also be shared over an intranet. This includes documents, video, audio, data, etc. The intranet may provide various levels of access, so that a given password may give permission to access part of the intranet resources but not other parts. An intranet is important in information systems because it allows an organization to share information with employees in a controlled way. It can also be used to manage projects and support collaboration between individuals and groups in the organization. It can provide access (based on an appropriate password) from within the organization to human resource reports, personnel records, budgets and budget reports, procurement forms, and so forth.

See also *extranet*

IT outsourcing

Soon Ang and Christine Koh

IT outsourcing refers to the contracting out of some or all of an organization's IT functions, systems, or services to an external service provider. Though IT outsourcing has been around since the 1960s, interest grew in the early 1990s, when Eastman Kodak's landmark outsourcing decision triggered many firms to embrace the concept of total IT outsourcing. Total outsourcing refers to relinquishing the entire IT function to external service providers and legally transferring IT assets and human resources to the provider in the process. Total outsourcing is often motivated by cost reasons; senior executives who view IT as a non-core activity and a cost burden to be minimized often choose to outsource the entire IT function to external service providers, who can provide these services more efficiently owing to economies of scale and scope (Ang and Straub, 1998).

Increasingly, however, selective IT outsourcing has become the more dominant mode adopted, whereby firms outsource only selected IT activities while retaining ownership and control over other IT activities. Activities that are particularly suited for outsourcing are those for which the firm has neither a critical strategic need (e.g., IT infrastructure, such as data center operations, network management, and PC acquisitions and maintenance) nor special capabilities (e.g., knowledge in net-based applications development). IT outsourcing is thus viewed as a strategic decision that provides firms access to needed resources and capabilities to fill gaps in their current capabilities and supplement in-house competences. Outsourcing enables firms to leverage on provider capabilities to improve critical aspects of the business performance and deliver business impact through joint efforts that develop complementary skills and capabilities.

Managing the Outsourcing Efforts: Legal and Psychological Contracting

Proper management of the outsourcing effort is critical to success. Although much emphasis has been placed on the legal contract, it is equally important to manage the psychological contract to insure a close working relationship between the parties involved.

Since the outsourcing client and provider do not share the same profit motive, there will always be a potential built-in conflict between the two parties. A proper legal contract stating obligations and responsibilities of both parties is therefore essential to prevent opportunistic behavior of either party. Outsourcing firms must develop detailed performance standards and incorporate them into the legal contract. This must be coupled with careful measurement of the provider performance, and continual monitoring throughout the entire contract period to insure that all contractual terms are complied with.

Even though the legal contract provides the basis for effective monitoring and control, reliance on a legal contract alone is insufficient as a legal contract can never specify completely all contingencies that can arise. Rather, it must be balanced with efforts to build a strong relationship with the provider – a relationship characterized by trust, commitment, communication, cooperation, flexibility, and joint conflict resolution. Studies have shown that successful outsourcing arrangements are those with both tight contractual controls and a partnership-type relationship characterized by trust.

Essentially, what is important is the psychological contract between the two parties (Ang and Koh, 2000; Ho, Ang, and Straub, 2003). A psychological contract refers to people's mental beliefs and expectations about their mutual obligations in a contractual relation. It reflects the way the parties interpreted and understood their mutual obligations in the contract. IT outsourcing clients and providers hold certain beliefs of their mutual obligations in the outsourcing relationship. The concept of psychological contract highlights the mutual obligations between both the parties involved, emphasizing the importance of managing the dyadic relationship between the outsourcing clients and providers. In addition, it also highlights the fact that not all promises are incorporated into the legal contract, and the importance of going beyond the legal obligations to understand the psychological contract obligations. Since ambiguous promises are more likely to lead to misunderstanding and contract breach, outsourcing firms should work toward clarity of promises, making the obligations as explicit as possible.

According to Ang and Beath (1993) and Ang and Toh (1998), successful IT outsourcing requires parties to consider five critical contracting elements:

1   *Authority structures* where rights and responsibilities are assigned to either the client or provider to make discretionary decisions, issue orders, or demand performance. Examples of these decisions include identifying and changing key personnel; making price adjustments; and changing the scope of the contract as price–performance ratios of IT drop.
2   *Rule-based incentive systems* where rewards and punishments are tied to provider performance, and not to the market. Market incentives work well under conditions of certainty, where all performance contingencies are considered prior to contractual agreement. Rule-based incentive systems dissociate compensation from market-determined forces. They reflect locally determined inducements for desirable future performance. For example, if timely delivery is vital, penalties for delays beyond an agreed completion date and bonuses for early completion may be incorporated into the contract.
3   *Standard operating procedures* where routines are followed by parties in the contract to insure that the contract progresses as planned. Examples of routines include requiring the provider to produce formal progress reports; to conduct regular face-to-face meetings with clients; and to bring to the attention of the client potential IT operational problems and project delays.
4   *Non-market-based pricing systems* where pricing algorithms are designed to accommodate cost uncertainties in long-term IT contracts. Non-market-based systems are market-price established by competitive bidding but modified by cost-recovery procedures. A combination of market pricing and cost-recovery algorithms is designed to insure a reasonable balance between price risk for the client and compensation risk for the provider.
5   *Informal mechanisms for resolving disputes* where procedures are developed to settle conflicts without direct referral to court sanction. Unlike any typical arm's-length contractual arrangement, a series of private and informal appeals is embedded in the contract to insure that parties survive disputes. In the event of any disagreements, parties should agree to discuss and resolve the dispute informally and privately between top management of the client and provider organizations. In the event that such negotiation is not successful, parties should submit the dispute to mediation by a third party arbitrator – a mutually agreed-upon computer professional. Only if the arbitration fails does formal legal litigation commence.

EVIDENCE OF BENEFITS DERIVED FROM IT OUTSOURCING

Although IT outsourcing offers many potential benefits to firms, realizing these benefits is not always guaranteed. The benefits of outsourcing can be easily eroded by various hidden costs, such as provider search and contracting costs, initial and post-outsourcing transition cost, as well as the cost of managing the outsourcing effort (Ang and Straub, 1998). IT outsourcing is also laden with risks, including dependence on the provider, loss of critical business and technical skills, and loss of innovative capacity.

Overall, outsourcing success rates appear to have have improved over the years – from only 48 percent of outsourcing firms reporting that they had achieved expected results in the mid-1990s to 73 percent in 2000 (Lacity, 2002). Nonetheless, objective evidence of impact of IT outsourcing on actual firm performance remains relatively scarce. Although IT outsourcing is associated with positive stock market reactions (e.g., Hayes, Hunton, and Reck, 2000; Farag and Krishnan, 2003), Gilley and Rasheed (2000) found that outsourcing in general had no significant direct effect on overall firm performance.

IT OUTSOURCING TRENDS

The outlook for the IT outsourcing market remains robust. The worldwide outsourcing market is estimated to reach US$282 billion in 2006 (Gartner Group, November 2003). The US and UK remain the largest and most established markets, but other markets such as New

Zealand, Australia, and Asia are also growing rapidly.

The outsourcing landscape has changed over the years. The range and depth of services outsourced have increased, and outsourcing contracts are growing in size and scope, often involving multiple providers. This is propelled partially by the maturing marketplace, and partially by the increasing trend toward mergers, acquisitions, strategic alliances, and joint ventures among major service providers. This trend has enabled providers to consolidate their strength and position within the industry, and to provide larger, multidimensional outsourcing arrangements involving multiple providers (Currie, 2000).

Newer forms of outsourcing are also evolving.- While early outsourcing initiatives focused on IT management and development, business process outsourcing (BPO) is now becoming the fastest-growing segment, accounting for 42 percent of the total IT outsourcing market (Gartner Group, November 2003). BPO involves the outsourcing of the entire delivery of selected business processes to an external service provider. The most common processes outsourced are transaction-intensive processes such as payroll, credit card processing, and claims processing; outsourcing of process outsourcing is sometimes extended to enterprise processes such as human resources, finance, accounting, and procurement.

Outsourcing is also increasingly becoming global. Propelled by improvements in technology and the sophistication of offshore IT providers, companies are moving their outsourcing offshore, to countries such as India, China, and Russia. Spending on offshore software development and services reached US$10 billion in 2003, and is estimated to reach US$31 billion by 2008 (Global Insight, reported in *PC Magazine*, May 18, 2004). Offshore outsourcing is often motivated by cost differentials, as well as the availability of high skills in the face of a global IT skill shortage. The cost differentials are particularly significant when firms outsource to developing Asian countries; sending development work offshore to India, for example, can reduce costs by some 50 percent (Heeks et al.,

2001). However, managing offshore outsourcing projects involves greater challenges, because of the need to control the project remotely and to interact cross-culturally. This makes it more difficult for firms to maintain control over the outsourced activities and to monitor the provider, as well as to coordinate activities among the parties involved. This can be further exacerbated by differences in political and cultural environments.

Bibliography

Ang, S. and Beath, C. M. (1993). Hierarchical elements in software contracts. *Journal of Organizational Computing*, 3 (3), 329–61.

Ang, S. and Koh, C. (2000). Psychological contracting in IT contracts. In *Effective Management of IT Disputes*. Butterworth Asia, pp. 39–50.

Ang, S. and Straub, D. W. (1998). Production and transaction economies and IS outsourcing: A study of the US banking industry. *MIS Quarterly*, 22 (4), 535–52.

Ang, S. and Toh, S. K. (1998). Failure in software outsourcing: A case analysis. In L. Wilcocks and M. Lacity (eds.), *Strategic Sourcing of Information Systems*. New York: John Wiley, pp. 351–68.

Currie, W. (2000). The supply-side of IT outsourcing: The trend towards mergers, acquisitions and joint ventures. *International Journal of Physical Distribution and Logistics Management*, 30 (3/4), 238–47.

Farag, N. I. and Krishnan, M. S. (2003). The market value of IT outsourcing investment announcements: An event-study analysis. *Proceedings of the Ninth Americas Conference on Information Systems*.

Gilley, K. M. and Rasheed, A. (2000). Making more by doing less: An analysis of outsourcing and its effects on firm performance. *Journal of Management*, 26 (4), 763–90.

Hayes, D. C., Hunton, J. E., and Reck, J. L. (2000). Information systems outsourcing announcements: Investigating the impact on the market value of contract-granting firms. *Journal of Information Systems*, 14 (2), 109–25.

Heeks, R., Krishna, S., Nicholson, B., and Sahay, S. (2001). Synching or sinking: Global software outsourcing relationships. *IEEE Software*, 18 (2), 54–60.

Ho, V. T., Ang, S., and Straub, D. (2003). When subordinates become IT contractors: Persistent managerial expectations in IT outsourcing. *Information Systems Research*, 14 (1), 66–87.

Lacity, M. C. (2002). Lessons in global information technology sourcing. *IEE Computer*, 35 (8), 26–33.

knowledge base

Amit Das

Knowledge-based systems (also called EXPERT SYSTEMS) differ from traditional computer programs in that they maintain a clear separation between the domain knowledge and reasoning procedures used to solve a problem. The domain knowledge used by a knowledge-based system is stored in a knowledge base designed for efficient storage, retrieval, and updating.

Domain knowledge may be represented in several different ways in a knowledge base. The most common representation takes the form of *if–then* rules. Each rule has two parts – a set of conditions necessary for the rule to *fire* (the *if* part), and a set of actions or consequences resulting from the application of the rule (the *then* part). Other representations of domain knowledge, such as frames or semantic networks, are much less common than rules.

To perform complex tasks, such as medical diagnosis, a large amount of domain knowledge may be required. This translates to a large number of rules in the knowledge base and gives rise to several problems. During problem solving, many rules may have their *if* conditions satisfied at the same time, and selecting the most promising rule for further processing becomes difficult. Also, some rules in a large knowledge base may contradict one another and need to be reconciled. Checking for consistency becomes especially critical (and difficult) as new rules are added to an already large knowledge base to improve its problem-solving performance. Maintaining the integrity and performance of a large knowledge base can be an exceedingly difficult task.

knowledge management systems

Mani R. Subramani and Jungpil Hahn

The term knowledge management refers to organizational efforts to acquire, organize, and make knowledge available so that employees may make use of it to be more effective and productive. The organizational objective is straightforward; the solution requires a combination of organization efforts and information systems. Knowledge management systems (KMS) are tools to support the management of knowledge that employ information and communications technologies. Instances of knowledge management systems include information technology-based document repositories, expertise databases, discussion lists, and context-specific retrieval systems.

Knowledge can be either *tacit* or *explicit*. Tacit knowledge refers to knowledge that has a personal quality that makes it hard to articulate or communicate. It represents deeply rooted *know-how* that emerges from action in a particular context. In contrast, explicit knowledge refers to the codifiable component that can be disembodied and transmitted. It is also termed *know-what* – knowledge that can be extracted and shared with other individuals. Knowledge management systems can provide mechanisms to locate and use both tacit and explicit knowledge.

KNOWLEDGE PROBLEMS IN ORGANIZATIONS

In order to understand the role of knowledge management systems in organizations, it is useful to understand the knowledge management problems of organizations that are addressed by the systems. These problems fall into five broad classes: knowledge structure problems, knowledge distribution problems, knowledge coordination problems, knowledge transfer problems, and knowledge ownership problems. These problems arise from the complexities of recognizing the nature of knowledge needed to solve problems or make decisions, the difficulties in assembling the necessary knowledge, and difficulties due to the ambiguity of knowledge ownership.

Knowledge structure problems. Knowledge structure problems arise when it is difficult to clearly identify causes and effects because of the complex linkage between observed symptoms and one or more fundamental problems causing the symptoms. Knowledge structure problems underlie the descriptions of action in many contexts. Examples are clinical problem diagnosis in medical contexts and in online help desks. The major impediment created by knowledge structure problems is the inability to achieve repeatable problem solving and build up a clear set of decision rules or protocols for dealing with problems. In contexts characterized by knowledge structure problems, problem solving is consequently a non-structured activity with limited means to routinize problem solving.

Knowledge distribution problems. Knowledge distribution problems occur when knowledge to solve the problem exists (or is believed to exist), but the knowledge is not available at the location where the problem is encountered. Knowledge distribution problems are solved by accessing the knowledge, often located elsewhere (or available to another person), to solve the problem. The major impediment created by knowledge distribution problems is the physical and emotional distance between the source of the problem and the source of the expertise. This adversely impacts important factors such as the timeliness of problem solution, the level of priority accorded to addressing the problem, and the motivation for problem solving.

Knowledge coordination problems. Knowledge coordination problems are closely allied to knowledge distribution problems but are different in that knowledge coordination problems occur when the distribution of the knowledge is not known in advance. Unlike knowledge distribution problems where there is some prior understanding of the individual or group expected to have the knowledge required to solve problems, knowledge coordination problems occur where there is no broad, available map of "who knows what" and "who can be asked for help" for the problem to be solved. Often this knowledge resides in experienced individuals who, through their involvement in the organization, have personal networks that they can navigate to locate someone with the knowledge required. In contexts characterized by knowledge coordination problems, problem solving often involves a "search for expertise." The major hindrance created by knowledge coordination problems is that the ancillary activities related to problem solving can not only consume time and effort, but can also be difficult for individuals trying to solve the problem. Further, individuals possessing the knowledge to solve the problem often have their own personal and organizational priorities. Periodic requests for their assistance that rely on citizenship behavior and individual willingness to be helpful can often be disruptive and counterproductive to the particular tasks they are assigned. If overused, these sources may even become reluctant to be available for help.

Knowledge transfer problems. Once an appropriate source of knowledge is located (generally after solving the knowledge distribution and knowledge coordination problems), problem solution is often hindered by the knowledge transfer problem. Those experiencing the problem may have difficulty in recognizing the relevant factors characterizing a problem and describing them to another person who has the knowledge to solve the problem. Conversely, experts possessing knowledge also have difficulty transferring relevant knowledge to another person facing the problem to enable that person to solve it him/herself. In such instances, the knowledge is viewed as being "sticky."

Knowledge ownership problems. An overarching problem, cutting across all the previous knowledge problems, is the complex set of issues around ownership of knowledge. Knowledge can be conceived as existing at multiple levels – not only at the individual level but also at the group and organizational levels. Perceptions of knowledge ownership – whether it belongs to the organization or the individual – are influenced by factors such as the culture of the organization and the nature of knowledge. Knowledge ownership problems may be among the most complex issues surrounding knowledge management systems as the ability to productively create, deploy, and demonstrate knowledge is an extremely salient component of the identity of a knowledge worker.

Knowledge reuse problems. There are problems of motivation and reward related to the reuse of knowledge that is known to exist. Often, recognizing individuals for knowledge contributions (such as rewarding contributions to the organizational document repository or rewarding individuals for being helpful in sharing their expertise) appears paradoxically to create disincentives to reuse of the knowledge, particularly when reuse involves explicitly acknowledging the inputs or assistance received. Individuals in some instances indicate that they preferred to devise a unique solution to a problem through laborious knowledge coordination than reuse standard knowledge available in repositories. This often occurs when the individual believes that acknowledging a peer's input makes the solution seem like a rehash of a previously available solution and minimizes his or her own contribution to devising a solution. This is consistent with research suggesting that those who are helped are viewed as less competent than those who provide help.

Table 1   Knowledge problems in organizations

Knowledge problems	Description	Hurdle created by problem	Knowledge management systems addressing problems
Knowledge structure problem	Problems relating clusters of symptoms to specific problems	Problem identification Repeatable problem solving	Limited IT solutions
	Moving from P(Symptoms|Problem) to P(Problem|Symptoms)		
Knowledge distribution problem	Structural grouping of different levels of knowledge required to solve problem prevents ready problem solution	Accessing appropriate group for problem solving	Workflow systems Email lists Document repositories
Knowledge coordination problem	Knowledge dispersal – lack of understanding of who knows what	Need to locate appropriate knowledge and assemble knowledge components for problem solving	Document repository Knowledge maps Yellow pages Expertise profiles Collaborative filtering
Knowledge transfer problem	Ability to transfer knowledge limited by stickiness	Need to move problem to solution or solution to problem	Enable rich communication
Knowledge ownership problem	Unclear demarcation of ownership	Need to provide incentives for knowledge creation	Contribution tracking (both documents and email advice)
Knowledge reuse problem	Barriers to reusing knowledge, effort spent to resolve problems even though prior solutions are available	Lack of consistency in solutions	Reuse tracking systems

A FRAMEWORK FOR KNOWLEDGE MANAGEMENT SYSTEMS

Two important considerations determine the features of knowledge management systems to address knowledge problems in organizations. They are where the knowledge resides and the extent to which the knowledge is structured. The locus of the knowledge determines whether the KMS connects a user who has a problem or question to an artifact (e.g., a document) or to a person. The level of a priori structure determines the extent to which KMS use imposes the burden of a *translation* or *transformation* of the problem or question to a form that corresponds to implicit logic underlying the a priori structure. These dimensions categorize the different types of knowledge management systems currently used for knowledge management support. The framework is presented in figure 1 with a description of the assistance provided by knowledge management systems in each category.

The horizontal dimension of the framework focuses on the location of the organizational knowledge resources managed by the KMS – whether the knowledge is embodied within individuals or whether it exists as externalized knowledge artifacts. The vertical dimension describes the extent to which the KMS imposes or requires a structure, a priori.

Structured artifact access. Cell 1 comprises KMS managing knowledge artifacts that have an inherent structure (e.g., enterprise-wide data) or those where the KMS imposes a structure on the

contents (e.g., consulting reports tagged with keywords). Essentially, the domain of these systems is restricted to the organizational knowledge that is or can be effectively codified. Document repositories and DATA WAREHOUSING systems fall into this category. These systems typically use database management systems (*see* DATABASE MANAGEMENT SYSTEM) designed to capture and store documents with predefined keywords and metadata so that the contents can be accessed using the document categorization scheme. The systems may be repositories of documents, videos, and other artifacts.

Structured individual access. Cell 2 comprises systems where the knowledge resides in individuals, but the contents of who knows what is catalogued and structured employing a priori categorizing schemes. A database of experts is an instance of such a system. A "yellow pages" of experts is another. The contents of the KMS are created by employees filling out a questionnaire to describe their level of expertise in a predefined list of skill categories (e.g., Java programming, project management, vibration dampening, etc.). The "experts database" is intended for use in locating people with specific skills in domains where the user has a problem.

Unstructured artifact access. Cell 3 comprises systems where the knowledge is captured in artifacts but where the contents do not have a priori structure imposed on them. Instances include KMS systems incorporating document repositories that are fully indexed on the words

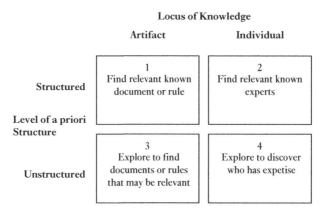

Locus of Knowledge

	Artifact	Individual
Structured	1 Find relevant known document or rule	2 Find relevant known experts
Unstructured	3 Explore to find documents or rules that may be relevant	4 Explore to discover who has expetise

Level of a priori Structure

Figure 1 Framework of knowledge management systems

they contain and KMS with document recommendation capabilities using *collaborative filtering* technology. The organization of the contents in such systems is dynamic and the systems provide employees with relevant documents on the fly. For example, many organizations currently deploy corporate intranets (*see* INTRANET) so that important documents can be posted and accessed by other users browsing or searching though the site. The documents do not follow a predefined structure. Search and retrieval are achieved via search engines that locate documents using full-text search. The use of collaborative filtering technology that *recommends* documents is an alternative approach to locating documents relevant to a user's question or problem without structuring contents a priori. The collaborative filtering system records user browse-and-search behaviors and recommends documents based on other users' past behaviors when they performed similar searches.

Unstructured individual access. Cell 4 comprises systems that provide means for users to access others who may be able to help and where the system imposes no a priori structure on the knowledge. In such systems, interpersonal contact enabled by the system is an important means for knowledge sharing and transfer. Instances of such systems include electronic discussion forums where employees may post questions to which other employees with answers or suggestions can post replies. Threaded discussions and email distribution lists (listservs) are typical technologies used in systems in this class.

The framework presents insights to the nature of assistance, the extent of assistance, and the limitations of different KMS. Implicit in this framework is the notion that different KMS implementations provide differing levels of support in locating knowledge and impose differing burdens on users of these systems. KMS that impose a priori structure are useful as they enable contents to be categorized in a manner that is consistent with the vocabulary of the community or constituency they serve. For instance, a Class 1 KMS would return a highly relevant set of documents as the results of a query on *compiler construction* as this specific keyword would exclude irrelevant documents that dealt with compilers but not with compiler construction. However, such a KMS imposes a burden on users as retrieval of relevant content is often difficult for someone without access to the local vocabulary. A Class 3 approach that supports a free-text search of documents would result in a much larger number of documents being retrieved in response to the same search, including a number of irrelevant documents that contain *compiler* and *construction* but don't address the specific issue of compiler construction. Such a system, while providing minimal barriers to use, burdens users with the task of handling irrelevant content to locate relevant content.

The framework also highlights the implicit assumptions regarding the nature of knowledge and sources of knowledge required for problem solving that underlie different KMS. A repository of information, say a Class 1 KMS, even if it contains all the information required to solve the user's problem, is unlikely to be useful if the information is not available in the form that the user can use. For instance, if the problem relates to a machine malfunction, having access to technical manuals is useful only if they address the malfunctions. If the malfunctions are known to repair technicians but are not documented, the person seeking knowledge needs to access a technician. If the knowledge is available both in documents and in people, locating knowledge is a resource allocation problem. For example, for a consulting firm that provides predefined systems solutions, a major source of knowledge is contained in knowledge artifacts such as project proposals and previous solutions to similar problems. A document repository is one knowledge management solution. An alternative for the reuse of such knowledge is an electronic discussion forum. The forum approach would probably lead to searchers posing questions such as, "Has anyone recently conducted a project with XXX product within the YYY industry? If so, can you send me your proposal?" Of these two methods, a document repository with an efficient indexing mechanism is probably more effective than a discussion forum for users to obtain the knowledge needed because it does not burden other employees with requests for help.

ISSUES AND CHALLENGES IN KNOWLEDGE
MANAGEMENT SYSTEMS

There are issues and challenges related to the utilization of information technology for knowledge management support in the setup phase, ongoing utilization and maintenance, and in evaluating the long-term effects of knowledge management support.

KMS setup: Balancing information overload and potentially useful content.   The reach of the knowledge management system is an important consideration, both in terms of size of the user group (those who are likely to request information and those who have the knowledge) and diversity of the group. This is an important issue because increases in the size and the diversity, while beneficial, involve an implicit trade-off between irrelevant content and potentially useful information. If usage of the system (e.g., a Class 4 email list) is restricted to a small group, users collectively lose valuable input that may potentially be obtained by an inclusive policy encouraging broader participation. However, if the reach of the system is too broad, then the system risks overloading users with irrelevant information. Deciding on an appropriate size and scope is important in order to leverage the strength of weak ties among people (relationships or recognition that exist but are not strong enough to obtain prompt responses).

When the knowledge sources are artifacts (Class 1 and 3), size may have a positive network effect – for example, the greater the number of documents in the document repository or the intranet, the higher the chances that a search will find documents of interest. However, size may have negative network effects when the knowledge sources are individuals (Class 2 and 4). Even though greater network size may increase the potential reach of an electronic discussion forum, which in turn increases the chances of generating an offer to help, greater network size tends to increase INFORMATION OVERLOAD in the form of multiple asynchronous yet concurrent threads of conversation. This increases the amount of effort required to follow and participate in the discussions, possibly reducing the overall incentive to participate. On the other hand, if the size of the network is too small,

it may offer insufficient resources to make participation worthwhile.

When knowledge sources are highly structured (Class 1 and 2), greater diversity of content poses minimal problems as long as the indexing scheme is appropriate. However, when the knowledge needed is loosely structured or unstructured (Class 3 and 4), diversity of content and domains can be issues. In case of low levels of diversity of those who are identified as having expertise, the names made available by the KMS would be limited, in some cases corresponding closely with known individuals. Hence, the knowledge management system is less valuable in finding new sources. On the other hand, diversity can also be overwhelming as it may become difficult to find the appropriate knowledge sources due to information overload and a lack of shared vocabulary. This situation is often apparent in the use of search engines on the Internet (Class 3). Recent research suggests innovative systems and techniques for dealing with the potential information overload associated with the use of KMS. For example, intelligent agent (*see* SOFTWARE AGENT) technology is used to filter out irrelevant content and locate potentially useful conversations on Internet relay chat (IRC). The agent builds a profile of the user through a keyword-based model and recommends current chat sessions by sampling IRC channels to find current conversations that match the user's profiles. Another line of research employs collaborative filtering methods to recommend potentially useful Usenet news posts to users. The system filters messages based on users' previous preferences and recommends useful Usenet news articles, those that other users with similar preferences have rated as being of high quality. Finally, several techniques have been developed to visualize and represent the conversational interface of synchronous and asynchronous discussion forums to express social patterns in online conversations.

KMS maintenance: Balancing additional workload and accurate content.   In a knowledge management system, maintaining a steady stream of contributions to content is important. Thus, motivating users to contribute is a critical problem. This may be more or less difficult depending on the level of structuring of the content in the

KMS. When the knowledge content is highly structured (Class 1 and 2), a great deal of effort is required up front to insure the appropriate structuring. Structuring requires employees to append appropriate keywords and metadata to their documents prior to uploading documents to a repository or filling out extensive skills and expertise questionnaires to be listed in an expertise database. While this may appear to be a simple, straightforward task, serious difficulties of knowledge representation and problems of motivation can exist. When employees are appending keywords and metadata tags to their documents or are evaluating themselves in terms of the skills or expertise they possess, they are in essence creating answers for questions that have not yet been posed and are implicitly addressing the issue, "to what queries should this document (or user profile) be a result?" Furthermore, motivation is also problematic since extra effort and time required for structuring contributions need to be allocated in addition to their regular job tasks and employees do not know a priori (and in some implementations, even ex post) if their document (or profiles) are later retrieved and used.

This is less of a problem when the knowledge sources are loosely structured on an ongoing basis (Class 3 and 4). Participants in an electronic discussion forum need only respond when questions are asked. Since response behavior is usually highly visible in such forums, participants may be greatly motivated to provide answers whenever possible since frequent responding can provide greater visibility and raise contributors' social standing as experts on a topic. Similarly, maintaining the knowledge resources is straightforward in the case of knowledge artifacts. Simply posting documents on the corporate intranet does not require extensive effort up front to insure the appropriate description of the document so long as the search algorithm is effective.

One potential consequence of increasing access to domain experts through KMS is that the small set of recognized experts may end up executing a significant portion of the work for users who seek their advice. If this shifting of the burden strains the experts' time and effort, it may result in reduced motivation to respond to inquiries and contribute in future periods.

There are a number of solutions that are employed. Some technological solutions have been proposed, but organizational solutions have been used most frequently. For example, one company adopts a management approach whereby domain experts in different engineering groups take turns operating the Usenet forum. This way, individual experts are able to concentrate on their own work when it is not their designated shift for monitoring requests for help. When designated employees receive a request for advice they cannot handle, they forward that request to an employee that has the expertise, who can later respond during his or her designated duty shift.

Another managerial practice for solving the knowledge repository maintenance problem without putting burden on knowledge workers is the creation of a new role within the organization – the knowledge librarian. The knowledge librarian is responsible for transferring content into the knowledge repository by tagging user submissions with appropriate keywords or metadata tags. While this solves the problem of increased burden on domain experts and users, this may also create coding errors.

Long-term effects of KMS: Balancing exploitation and exploration. The availability of existing knowledge for employees to retrieve and reuse can be very useful. However, there are possible undesirable long-term effects. Such systems may bias employees to adopt existing solutions rather than to search for or develop novel solutions that may be more effective. In the long run, reliance on existing solutions may result in competence traps that inhibit organizational learning and innovation. The literature on organizational learning suggests that experience plays a vital role in the learning process. In the case of knowledge management systems, experience will be tightly tied with the use of the system. Thus, in the long run, knowledge workers may gain extensive experience at *assembling* knowledge components to solve problems instead of actually *creating* the knowledge components themselves, an important consideration related to expertise development in knowledge-intensive firms that tend to promote heavy use of KMS. Further, the presence of KMS may encourage the use of easily available codified information rather than the harder-to-obtain tacit knowledge.

SUMMARY

As the basis of value creation increasingly depends on leveraging firms' intangible assets, knowledge management systems are emerging as powerful sources of competitive advantage. To be able to take advantage of KMS, managers need to consider the fundamental *knowledge problems* that they are likely to solve. A useful approach to selection of a knowledge management system is to use a framework for KMS based on the locus of the knowledge and the a priori structuring of contents. This framework provides a means to explore issues related to KMS and the unifying dimensions underlying different types of KMS.

Bibliography

Alavi, M. and Leidner, D. E. (1999). Knowledge management systems: Issues, challenges, and benefits. *Communications of the AIS*, 1 (7).

Argote, L. and Ingram, P. (2000). Knowledge transfer: A basis for competitive advantage in firms. *Organizational Behavior and Human Decision Processes*, 82 (1), 150–69.

Davenport, T. H. and Prusak, L. (1997). *Working Knowledge: How Organizations Manage What They Know*. Boston: Harvard Business School Press.

Orr, J. (1990). Sharing knowledge, celebrating identity: Community memory in a service culture. In D. Middleton and D. Edwards (eds.), *Collective Remembering*. London: Sage, pp. 168–89.

Szulanski, G. (1996). Impediments to the transfer of best practices within the firm. *Strategic Management Journal*, 17, 27–43.

Zack, M. H. (1999). Developing a knowledge strategy. *California Management Review*, 41 (3), 125–45.

knowledge work, use of information technology

Rosann Collins

Knowledge work involves the use of knowledge by those performing the work. It requires workers who have knowledge or can acquire it. Knowledge work involves the processing and production of symbols rather than physical materials. Knowledge workers are those whose activities are dominated by knowledge work, even though they may also perform some clerical and physical work. Today, knowledge is considered a primary resource for organizations and a source of wealth and competitive advantage for nations. Estimates, based on the US Bureau of Labor Statistics, suggest that knowledge workers may constitute nearly 70 percent of non-farm workers.

Knowledge work requires employees who can (1) use their own knowledge base; (2) acquire new information; (3) combine and process information to produce and communicate new information outputs; and (4) learn continuously from their experiences. Information technology provides support for these basic knowledge work functions and has had some unanticipated impacts on knowledge workers and their productivity.

USE OF PERSONAL KNOWLEDGE BASE

In order to perform knowledge work successfully, individuals must employ their own *intellectual capital*: a personal base of knowledge that includes both factual and procedural information. Knowledge workers build their intellectual capital through education and experience. Information technology can supplement the knowledge base stored in a knowledge worker's memory. For example, database management systems (*see* DATABASE MANAGEMENT SYSTEM) enable knowledge workers to store more information and retrieve and combine it in more ways than information stored in memory or in paper-based systems. Knowledge workers can build their own personal knowledge base by entering data directly or by importing data extracted from corporate databases and external sources. The personal database becomes a unique, external archive of the intellectual capital of the knowledge worker.

ACQUISITION OF NEW INFORMATION

Knowledge workers are expected to be lifelong learners, and their economic value is their existing knowledge and expertise combined with the expectation of continuous learning. The WORLDWIDE WEB of information accessed via the INTERNET has exponentially increased access to information. Acquisition of new information from traditional print resources is facilitated by bibliographic data storage and retrieval systems that provide references to (or in some cases, full text of) books, articles, and other printed materials. New information about one's own company can be retrieved from corporate databases, and information external to an organization pulled from a variety of commercial online services (e.g., Dow Jones). This new information can be stored in the personal database of the knowledge worker (as previously described) and/or manipulated (as described below). Advanced, high-speed communications have also expanded the ease and span of interpersonal communications, so that individual knowledge workers can acquire information from people anywhere, both synchronously and asynchronously, using an array of information technologies (EMAIL, discussion boards, groupware, teleconferencing, web meetings, KNOWLEDGE MANAGEMENT SYSTEMS).

COMBINE, PROCESS, PRODUCE, AND COMMUNICATE INFORMATION

Knowledge workers use a variety of information technologies to manipulate information. Systems like word processing and DESKTOP PUBLISHING support combinations of information from a variety of sources and of different types (text, numeric, graphic) to produce new documents. Processing of information may be accomplished by specialized applications (e.g., tax preparation software) in which decision and processing rules are already included and data can be entered or imported from other systems. Processing may also be accomplished via software that allows users to develop their own applications (e.g., spreadsheet programs). Technologies such as electronic mail, groupware, and information networks enable knowledge workers to share information with both individuals and groups, and knowledge management initiatives in organizations encourage such sharing of expertise. Mobile computing technologies allow knowledge workers to compute anytime, anywhere, and to keep in constant contact with their office and colleagues.

CONTINUOUS LEARNING FROM EXPERIENCES

A key advantage of using information technology for knowledge work is the ability of information systems to capture task data and processes. Once a knowledge worker bears the cost of learning how to use a technology and/or builds a system

to perform a task, a record of task inputs, processes, and outputs can be made. These computerized records can be recalled for subsequent task performance. When tasks are complex and repeated, but are not performed again for some time interval, the computer files can help knowledge workers remember what they learned from the last time they performed the task.

For example, suppose a manager uses a spreadsheet program to support budgeting. The manager will need to enter the data for that year in the appropriate categories, enter formulae that represent the relationships between the categories, and enter text that labels the categories and calculated data. The spreadsheet may be formatted so that a final document can be printed. Some benefits from using the spreadsheet program are realized immediately, since it enables the manager to consider many more budget alternatives than are feasible via hand calculations. Additional benefits are realized when the budget spreadsheet is retrieved at the next budget cycle, since the spreadsheet contains the content, rules, and format for the budgeting task. Only new or changed data or rules must be entered. The spreadsheet is a stored recipe for budgeting that the manager or others can recall and reuse. This helps prevent individual knowledge workers and the organization from "losing the recipe" for important tasks.

The organization can also benefit from using knowledge management and expert system (*see* EXPERT SYSTEMS) technology to capture the intellectual capital of knowledge workers. Knowledge management and expert systems can make an individual's expertise available even after that person has left the firm, and also can make it possible to extend that expertise to other, less knowledgeable employees in the firm.

IMPACTS ON KNOWLEDGE WORKERS AND THEIR PRODUCTIVITY

Information technology has many impacts on knowledge work, in particular in the areas of productivity and global competition. It seems logical that information technology support for the main functions of knowledge work, as described above, would lead to increased productivity. Computer systems equipped with a variety of software and communications capability are standard tools for knowledge workers, and as common as telephones in offices. The seemingly insatiable demand for more hardware with additional capabilities in increasingly smaller packages and for software to support new and existing tasks would appear to reflect the value of information technology for knowledge work.

However, in the late twentieth century economic data indicated that productivity in knowledge work-intense sectors had not improved with increased investment in information technology. Many top managers questioned whether they had realized performance benefits commensurate with the large and continuing costs of information technology acquisition and support. There are several possible reasons for this "missing technology payback" in knowledge work. One central reason may be that knowledge worker productivity is not accurately measured. While the benefits from information technology that replaced workers was easy to measure in reduced labor costs, information technology support for knowledge workers is intended to assist and enhance task performance. Higher-quality information products may not be captured by productivity measures. When technology speeds task performance, the knowledge worker may "use up" that efficiency gain in striving for non-measured improvements in task processes or outputs. Or, as described above, many of the benefits from technology use may accrue in the future, when a task is repeated.

Poor or no productivity gains may also be caused by changes in the labor-inputs part of the productivity equation. Most knowledge workers find that with the information technology-enabled anywhere-anytime workplace, work schedules have expanded, and many knowledge workers struggle to set boundaries between work and personal time. There are also changes in the division of labor, since knowledge workers may be assigned a larger task set because they have computer support. For example, some companies eliminate or drastically reduce the number of secretaries because the professional workers have tools such as word processing and electronic mail. Another reason for the missing technology payback is the cost of using information technology for the organization and individual knowledge workers. The organization experiences increased back-office costs to build and keep technology systems working. The individual knowledge worker bears time, attention, and cognitive costs to learn and use information technology. On an ongoing basis, knowledge workers have to find time and energy to learn and adapt completely new information technologies, but also new versions of their existing technology support systems. Periodically, knowledge workers even act as computer operators: recovering from problems like viruses and system outages, as well as preventing computer problems by backing up files and installing system upgrades.

Information technology support for knowledge work has also had an impact on global competition for these jobs. Given high-speed communications and anywhere-anytime computing technologies, the physical location of knowledge workers becomes increasing unimportant. For some knowledge workers this means telecommuting (see VIRTUAL WORK) is enabled, reducing their costs of commuting, the organization's costs of providing offices, and societal costs of transportation infrastructure and pollution. For other knowledge workers it means increased competition from workers in other countries who bring the same knowledge and expertise to the position at a lower wage. The trend in *offshoring* jobs in the early twenty-first century is a result of this competition.

LAN

see LOCAL AREA NETWORKS

legacy systems

The term legacy systems refers to old information system applications that are important, useful, and functioning. They were developed and implemented many years earlier. They were probably built using PROGRAMMING LANGUAGES and methods no longer in use. They have been improved and enhanced with so many modifications that documentation is not clear and complete. The applications are important but difficult to improve further and perhaps difficult to fix when there is a problem. Legacy systems present significant difficulties for organizations. Solutions include developing and implementing complete new systems, purchasing package solutions and adapting the organization processes to the package, and undertaking major revisions to update and reorganize the existing systems. A case study of the legacy problem in the context of complexity theory is contained in the entry for COMPLEXITY AND INFORMATION SYSTEMS.

linguistics and computers

Tarun Mital and Dennis A. Adams

The field of inquiry known as linguistics can be characterized as the systematic study of language, while computers are well known to be physical systems that convert data inputs into information output. Viewed together then, the study of natural language processing can have far-reaching implications for the design and use of computers.

Even as the human nervous system served as a model for computer hardware, human language has, to a large extent, driven the development of computer software. First- and second-generation computer languages performed elementary operations on data, while newer fourth- and fifth-generation languages seek to become more aligned with human natural language to facilitate software development and editing. Out of the five core areas of linguistics – phonology, morphology, syntax, semantics, and pragmatics – the latter three (syntax, semantics, and pragmatics) have a more direct influence on such computing technologies as the WORLDWIDE WEB.

Syntax examines how words in a sentence relate to one another, or word ordering more generally. The design of compilers, to cite one example, could greatly benefit from such analysis. Semantics looks at the meaning of words independent of context, while pragmatics studies the meaning of words within a particular context. A computer application of these disciplines is the semantic web, an endeavor that seeks to tag all of the content on the worldwide web in order to give it semantic meaning and thereby improve search capabilities.

Linguistics has numerous applications for information systems in the area of systems development. In particular, information requirements analysis can be benefited through improved conceptual schema development. Communication with users can be addressed by the area of sociolinguistics and such techniques as conversation analysis. Errors can be reduced, in many cases, by elimination of semantic ambiguity. Finally, naming conventions can be made less arbitrary through phonological analysis.

The design of natural language interfaces can also be aided by linguistics. Other applications requiring a better understanding of the interaction between language and the mind include fit of data and cognitive style, decision-making analysis, and organizational change, more generally. In addition, the allocation of computer memory can be improved by enhancing our understanding of the cognitive "lexicon" (i.e., dictionary).

Noam Chomsky's notion of generative grammar, which has given birth to the field of computational linguistics, can contribute to human–computer interface by basing it more upon natural language. A generative grammar is essentially a description of a native speaker's "competence," or intuitive knowledge about the construction of his or her language. This is generative in the sense that an infinite number of sentences can be produced based upon a limited set of rules or instructions. One might draw the computer analogy that an infinite number of applications can be developed from a single programming language in much the same fashion.

Computational linguistics can be defined as the research area having the goal of allowing computers to produce and interpret human language. Developments in this field could revolutionize robotics and ARTIFICIAL INTELLIGENCE. Thus, linguistics and computers seem to be most closely tied together with linguistics as the control mechanism whereby computers can be put to useful work.

Once relegated to the realm of science fiction, most researchers believe that human–computer speech interaction is a short time away. Questions remain as to how this will change work patterns and the way people interact with each other and with the devices.

Linux

see OPEN SOURCE; OPEN SYSTEMS

local area networks

Jonathan K. Trower

A local area network (LAN) consists of several different devices that have been connected to-

gether in relatively close proximity for the purpose of communicating and sharing files and other resources with one another. Generally, a LAN will serve the individuals in a department, building, or cluster of buildings in close proximity with one another. The early motivation to create LANs was to facilitate the sharing of files and expensive hardware resources, like laser printers, tape backup drives, and large hard drives. Today, those motivations still exist, but the uses of LANs have evolved to include the support of work group computing and connecting users on one LAN to other networks through a wide area network (WAN), or through the INTERNET. To fully understand the topic of local area networks, it is necessary to discuss several related topics: network topologies, PROTOCOLS, communications media, and network operating systems.

TOPOLOGIES

A network topology is the physical arrangement of the nodes (devices) along the cable that connects the nodes with one another. There are three dominant topologies for LANs in use today: star, ring, and bus. A *star network* (figure 1) consists of a centralized host computer which is linked individually to each of the other computers in the network. Data are sent from one computer to another through the host computer. Additional computers, or nodes, are added at the host computer, thus minimizing the impact on

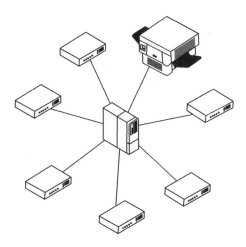

Figure 1   Star network topology

the network as a whole. Therefore, a star topology is easier to maintain than other topologies. The major disadvantage of a star network is that if the host goes down, the entire network is disabled.

In a *ring network* (figure 2) each node on the network is physically connected to the two adjacent nodes, forming a complete circle. Information is sent around the ring in one direction, from one computer to the next, until it reaches its destination. The final network topology is the *bus topology* (figure 3), which is also the most common. All devices are connected by a single circuit. Signals are broadcast in both directions along that circuit, and the network operating system determines which device will receive the signal. Because the circuit can only handle one message at a time, performance on this type of network can degrade if the volume of traffic is high.

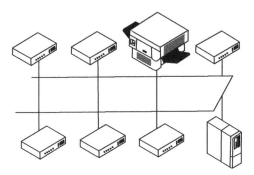

Figure 3   Bus network topology

PROTOCOLS

A protocol is a set of rules that govern how a device gains access to the cable in a LAN. There are two important protocols used extensively on LANs today: token passing and carrier sense multiple access with collision detection (CSMA/CD).

A network that uses a token-passing protocol requires a device to control the token before it can have access to the network. An empty token

passes from one device on the network to the next. If a device has some data to transmit, it must wait until an empty token passes. The device may take the empty token, attach its data to the token, then send it back out on the network. Once the token completes the circuit of the ring and returns to the original device, a new token is generated and passed, empty, back on the network. In that way, each device has equal access to the network, and there is no chance that more than one device will be using the network at a time. Token passing is typically utilized in a ring topology. This protocol supports transmission speeds of up to 16 million bits per second (Mbps).

When a network utilizes the CSMA/CD protocol, each device must contend for access to the network. If a node has data to transmit, it listens to the network. If no traffic is detected, it begins to transmit. Of course, it is possible that two or more devices may try to transmit at the same time, which would lead to collisions between the packets of data. If a collision is detected, both stations stop transmitting, and wait a random period of time before beginning the process again. Ethernet (developed by Xerox) is a protocol associated with the CSMA/CD protocol. As the number of users increases, the transmission speed degrades because the number of collisions increases. Depending on the physical media, speeds of 1 Gbps and more are possible.

COMMUNICATIONS MEDIA

Most local area networks today operate on one of three different media: twisted pair, coaxial, or fiber optic cable. Twisted pair is similar to the

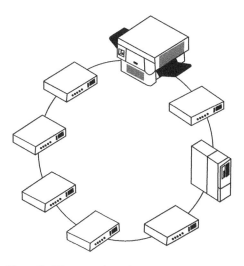

Figure 2   Ring network topology

wiring that is used in most telephone systems. It consists of two insulated copper wires that are twisted together to minimize electrical interference from other nearby wiring. The data transmission speeds vary widely for twisted pair, with speeds ranging from 14,400–56,000 bps over typical telephone lines to speeds of up to 100 Mbps possible on specially conditioned lines. These latter speeds make twisted pair useable in LANs. This feature, coupled with the low cost and ease of installation of twisted pair relative to coaxial or fiber optic cable, makes twisted pair the media of choice for many new networks.

Coaxial cable consists of a heavy copper wire at the center and a braided copper conductor separated by insulating material. This type of wiring is widely used in LANs, and in other applications like cable television. The advantage of coaxial cable over twisted pair is the greater transmission speeds possible, with speeds up to 200 Mbps.

Fiber optic cable consists of one or more strands of optical fiber, surrounded by insulation and reinforcing material. Instead of using electronic signals to transmit data, light is used. Relative to twisted pair or coaxial cable, fiber optic cable is capable of much greater transmission speeds, but costs more to purchase and install. Transmission speeds can range up to 6 Tbps.

Wireless LANs form a rapidly growing segment of LANs in operation today, where radio transmission replaces the physical media. The IEEE 802.11 standard has emerged as the dominant standard for wireless LANs. 802.11b is capable of 11 Mbps transmission speed, while 802.11a and 802.11g are capable of speeds up to 54 Mbps.

NETWORK OPERATING SYSTEMS

Just as every computer must have an operating system to control its operations, each network must also have an operating system to control access of individual nodes to the resources on the network. The services typically provided by network operating systems include file services to allow the sharing of data and application programs, print services to facilitate sharing of expensive printers and other OUTPUT DEVICES, security services to limit access to certain network resources to particular users, and communication services to support LAN-to-LAN, LAN-to-host, and remote-to-LAN communications. Leading network operating systems today include various versions of Microsoft Windows and Novell NetWare.

M

macro program

Gordon B. Davis and J. Davis Naumann

A macro is a program consisting of a few instructions that invoke underlying functions. Historically, a macro is a "superinstruction" because a single instruction results in a large program segment. The term "macro" is now widely used in computing to refer to a set of commands and menu selections stored in a file and executed (played) by a few keystrokes or a mouse stroke. A macro may be programmed by macro recording or by writing macro instructions provided by an application package.

Macro recording is a method of programming by doing. The user performs the sequence of activities that are to be automated, and the macro facilities create a program of instructions to perform the activities. For example, a user may perform a set of spreadsheet operations to create a heading, set fonts, define borders, establish row and column headings, etc. If these same operations are to be repeated frequently, they may be automated using a recording macro. The user specifies a name for the macro, turns on the macro recorder by an instruction, performs the activities to be automated, and turns off the recorder. The macro is stored. Subsequently, when the macro is "played," the activities are performed in exactly the same way. The advantage of macro recording is that the user need not understand the macro programming language; programming is by doing the activities. The main disadvantage is that only a sequence of actions may be programmed. No program logic to select from alternatives can be recorded. Because it is a fairly easy approach to automating a sequence of actions, macro recording is an important capability for improving productivity in using computer software.

The second approach to macro development is writing macro program instructions. Macro instruction languages resemble conventional procedural programming languages. Such languages are designed to write the procedures the computer is to execute and the logic to govern the execution of the computer actions. A generalized software package may have a macro language that is unique to it, or it may employ a macro language that is used across a suite of generalized packages.

Macros are programs. However, they tend to be short and limited in scope. They are developed and executed within a software package. The macro will not work without the software package. Although most macros tend to be short, many large, complex applications have been developed using a macro language. Spreadsheet macros have been used for complex applications based on spreadsheet processes. In the case of database packages, the macro language is designed as a development language for the development of applications that use the facilities of the database package for data storage and retrieval.

Many software packages include a set of pre-written macros for common functions. For example, a word processing package may include a macro that displays a common memo format or performs operations such as printing envelopes.

Pre-written macros are not limited to those included with the packages. Independent software vendors often offer macros for widely used packages. User groups share macros, and magazines for users of packages include them.

maintenance

see SOFTWARE MAINTENANCE

make or buy for software

William D. Nance

A key decision in an information system development project is how to acquire the software for the new system. The three options are to write the software code internally, hire external contract programmers to write the programs, or purchase a software package.

If the system development team chooses to develop the software internally, programmers employed by the company use the system specifications developed during the systems analysis and design phase to write, test, and debug the program code. The decision to produce software internally is typically based on a need for application programs that are unique or that must be tailored to specific company requirements and, as a result, cannot be found in the marketplace. In some instances, a company's search for a competitive advantage through sophisticated proprietary applications may lead to a decision to produce software internally. The primary advantage of producing software internally is that it can be designed to fit the specific, and perhaps unique, needs of the company. The major disadvantages are that it requires significant programming staff, takes notably longer than to purchase, and has a higher risk of cost overruns if problems arise during testing that require significant debugging and rework.

An alternative to internal software development that retains the advantage of tailoring the code to unique organizational needs is to hire, or "outsource," the programming activities to external contract programmers. These contractors may work independently on an individual basis, or they may work for an organization that specializes in providing system development staff. In either case, the contracting company provides the system specifications to the outsourcing programmers who write, test, and debug the code, and then provide the finished software product on a "turnkey" basis. In addition to enabling the code to be tailored to the company's particular needs, another major advantage of the contractor alternative is that the code is written by highly qualified programming staff, yet the company does not have to take on the responsibility of hiring, training, and supervising them. This lack of direct supervision over the programming staff can also be a disadvantage, however, since it transfers some control over the system development process to parties outside the organization. Although it depends on the nature of the contract, another potential disadvantage of this alternative is that the contractor may obtain the experience to develop and sell similar software to other companies (including competitors of the contracting company), and perhaps at even lower prices since the development costs have already been recovered under the original development project.

The third major option for acquiring software is to purchase a software package directly from a software vendor. This approach is applicable under three conditions. (1) The company can apply a standard set of software capabilities found in packages to its needs. (2) The company has little or no requirement for unique or system features that are difficult or impossible to obtain by tailoring a package system. (3) The company does not need a proprietary system designed with unique features to provide significant strategic advantage. If these three conditions are met and given the reduced time, cost, and risk from the use of packages, companies tend to use packages for applications that perform standard functions. The companies tend to prefer to modify their procedures to fit the software and employ the tailoring capabilities of the software package rather than building unique software internally. The internal "build" option is retained for applications that are unique or applications that contain proprietary features that give the organization a competitive advantage.

malware

Software such as viruses (*see* VIRUS) or SPYWARE that is installed on a user computer with the intention of obtaining personal information for fraudulent purposes or disrupting the functioning of the computer system.

management information system

Gordon B. Davis

The terms management information system (MIS), information system (IS), and information management (IM) are synonyms. They refer both to an organization system that employs information technology in providing information and communication services and the organization function that plans, develops, and manages the system (*see* INFORMATION SYSTEMS).

DEFINITION OF MIS AS A SYSTEM

The *management information system* is a system within an organization that supplies information and communication services and resources to meet organization needs. The system consists of information technology infrastructures to provide information processing and communication capabilities and application systems for delivery of specific information resources and services.

The infrastructures are core technology systems, core processing systems (often termed enterprise systems; *see* ENTERPRISE SYSTEMS (ENTERPRISE RESOURCE PLANNING OR ERP)), databases, and information management personnel. The infrastructures provide capabilities and services for applications. Application systems deliver information resources and services for specific organizational functions or purposes. Types of applications include systems embedded in products or services, transaction processing, communications, cooperative work support, reporting and analysis, decision support, and management support. The applications employ both automated and manual procedures. They may be associated with a single computer, an internal network, or an external network such as the INTERNET. They are human–technology systems because the results are obtained through an interaction of human users with the technology (*see* HUMAN–COMPUTER INTERACTION). The applications are model-based, i.e., the designs reflect models of decision-making, human–machine interfaces, social interaction, organization behavior, customer service, and so forth.

The objectives of the MIS infrastructures and applications are to meet an organization's information and communication needs, improve productivity in organizational activities, add value to organizational processes, and assist in achieving the organizational strategy. The systems apply information technology and information resources to add functionality and performance in products and services, quality and scope in analysis and decision-making, communication and sharing in cooperative work, and improved, faster operational and management processes at all levels. In a well-designed MIS, the different applications are not independent; they are interconnected subsystems that form a coherent, overall, integrated structure for information and communication services.

DEFINITION OF MIS AS AN ORGANIZATION FUNCTION

The management information system *organization function* plans, develops, implements, operates, and maintains the organization's information technology infrastructures and the organization's portfolio of applications. It also provides support and advisory services for systems developed and operated by individuals and departments.

The function employs, trains, and manages personnel with specialized knowledge and expertise for these purposes. The system development processes of the information management function include methods, techniques, and technologies for analyzing business processes, identifying system requirements, developing and implementing systems and related organization changes, and maintenance of systems. The management processes of the function include interaction with organizational strategic planning to identify ways information technology systems and capabilities may be used to achieve competitive advantage and other strategic goals, planning of infrastructures and applications, management of information system projects, operation of systems, consultation services to users, and evaluation of MIS performance.

The MIS function is needed by an organization because of organizational reliance on information technology, the risks of information system failure, the size of the investment, the need for organizational coordination and standards for the information system, and the need for expertise in processes for planning, development, and management of the information and communication infrastructures and applications for an organization. The reliance on information technology is pervasive in transactions and other business processes; few organizations could operate competitively without it. Risks include loss of systems, security breaches, incorrect processing, and improper use. The investment in information technology has, in recent years, been a significant part of the investment budget of organizations. The need for a function to coordinate information technology in the organization is increased as information technology innovation is diffused across all functions. Information technology use in business functions depends on an information technology infrastructure, organization-wide applications, and standards for systems that cross functional and organizational boundaries. The MIS function performs this important role. A fourth reason for the MIS function is the expertise required for planning, developing, operating, and managing the information technology infrastructure and organization applications.

BODY OF KNOWLEDGE ASSOCIATED
WITH MIS

The use of information technology is so pervasive that a certain level of expertise must be distributed broadly across the organization. Individuals and work groups within other organization functions may have significant responsibility for their own information management activities or local systems involving information technology. However, the management information system function has responsibility for maintaining expertise sufficient to assist individuals, groups, departments, and functions in their information management, to provide integration across the organization, and build and maintain the corporate information infrastructures and standards necessary for integrated information processes. The expertise associated with the MIS function consists of:

1   *Information strategies and structures.* Information system strategies and structures provide an organization with the capacity and capability for obtaining and using information, for applying information technology in its processes and systems, and for using infor-

mation and systems in its competitive strategy. The MIS function applies expertise in strategy and structures in the process of planning for information systems.

2   *Business process and information system development.* The information management function has special expertise in the design and implementation of business processes and systems. Information technology is a key element in most designs. Although all organization functions have some responsibility for their systems, the information management function has an ongoing expert role with primary technical responsibility for systems analysis and design, development, and integration.

3   *Organization and administration of the information management function.* This area includes organization of responsibilities for the functioning, hiring, and training of information systems personnel, budgeting and planning of activities, and assessment of management information system performance. Information system specialists are expected to have expertise to perform advisory and consulting services to users, build and maintain technical infrastructures, analyze requirements, and acquire or build solutions that employ information technology. The function may employ both internal employees and outsourcing.

4   *Information management operations.* The operations within the domain of MIS include the operation of organization-wide systems for information processing and communications. The activities include scheduling, operating, and controlling information and communications facilities, organization applications, and organization databases.

The body of knowledge for planning, implementing, and operating the MIS for an organization rests upon a number of underlying disciplines or bodies of knowledge. As examples, it relies on the SOFTWARE ENGINEERING principles and computational algorithms of computer science, the organization behavior and management principles of the field of management, the concepts and principles of human behavior in human–technology systems from cognitive psychology, principles of cooperation and communication from the field of communications, system concepts (*see* SYSTEM CON-CEPTS APPLIED TO INFORMATION SYSTEMS) and INFORMATION CONCEPTS from a variety of fields, and analysis of costs, benefits, and productivity from economics. From these reference disciplines, MIS has built a body of knowledge about the design, implementation, operation, and evaluation of information system infrastructures and applications in organizations.

EVOLUTION OF THE MIS CONCEPT

When computers were applied to business data processing in 1954, the first applications were document and report preparation based on batch input of transactions. Payroll checks, customer order documents, inventory analyses, and related reports are examples. In large part, computer technology was employed in early applications as a substitute for clerical labor and electromechanical devices. The systems were often referred to as electronic data processing (EDP) systems. Innovative organizations soon applied the computer to management reporting and analysis. The files that had been prepared for transaction document processing and transaction reporting provided the basis for more timely, analytical management reports. The computer made possible the use of quantitative modeling in support of business decisions. To reflect this change in emphasis from data processing to management support, the systems and function began to employ the term *management information systems*. The term included support for various levels of management and for decision-making.

The concept also included data as an organization resource. The data resource concept was implemented with database management systems (*see* DATABASE MANAGEMENT SYSTEM). Prior to computers, transaction data files were viewed as being "owned by" or the responsibility of a single business function. The marketing files were the responsibility of the marketing department, the accounts receivable records were the responsibility of the accounting department, and so forth. Database management systems and databases freed the organization from functional constraints on the use of data. Data from different organization activities were defined as an organization resource to be managed for broad organization use. Retrieval soft-ware was made available to selectively search and retrieve from the databases. Any authorized person could employ the software to access the databases.

Data could be organized, analyzed, and alternatives modeled in order to support decision-making. Since many models are applicable across the organization, a model base of analytical tools was developed to support decision-making and decision-making access to data. Software was provided as part of the MIS to support individual modeling of decisions and access to data for the model. Software was added to the system to support group decision-making and cooperative work (*see* COMPUTER-SUPPORTED COOPERATIVE WORK; DECISION SUPPORT SYSTEMS; EXECUTIVE INFORMATION SYSTEMS; GROUP DECISION SUPPORT SYSTEMS).

An early extension of the MIS concept was the strategic use of information technology to improve the competitive position of the organization and achieve competitive advantage. The MIS planning process became more closely tied to the strategy of the organization. The MIS function is expected not only to respond to requirements as defined by other business functions but interact in the planning process to suggest innovative uses of information technology to improve products, services, and business processes. New applications included inter-organizational applications that apply information technology to reduce cycle time and improve communications and transaction handling between the organization and its suppliers and customers.

THE STRUCTURE OF AN MIS

The structure of an information system may be visualized as infrastructures plus applications. The applications have a conceptual structure based on the purposes or needs being met and the functions of the organization that employ them. The four infrastructures that provide the general capacity and capabilities for information access and processing are technology, core enterprise systems, data, and personnel. The infrastructures enable specific applications and activities.

1   The *technology infrastructure* consists of computer and communication hardware, system software, and general purpose software

systems. The computer hardware consists of computers and related storage, input, and output devices (*see* INPUT DEVICES; OUTPUT DEVICES). Computers include large centralized computers, network servers, desktop computers, laptop computers, and handheld devices. The communications hardware contains devices to control the flow of voice and data communications within wired and wireless internal networks and with external network providers. Computer hardware is made operational through system software that provides generalized functions necessary for applications. Computer operating systems, communications software, and network software are examples. Generalized software is not specific to a single application but provides facilities for many different applications. An example is a database management system to manage databases and perform access and retrieval functions for a variety of applications and users.

2   The core enterprise systems include the set of applications that are necessary for transaction processing, managerial reporting, reporting to stakeholders including investors and government authorities. These applications keep records on customers, employees, and suppliers and activities associated with them. These applications tend to be fairly standard within an industry, produce databases that are interrelated, and produce necessary reports. Often termed enterprise systems or ERP (enterprise resource planning), the systems consist of an integrated set of software modules linked to a common database. They handle transaction and reporting for functions such as finance, accounting, human resources, marketing, materials management, and distribution.

3   The databases form a *data infrastructure*. They provide for storage of data needed by one or more organizational functions and one or more activities. There will be a number of databases based on organization activities. Planning of the database infrastructure involves determining what should be stored, what relationships should be maintained among stored data, and what restrictions should be placed on access. The result of database planning and implementation with database management systems is a capacity to provide data both for applications and ad hoc needs. Comprehensive databases designed for ad hoc use may be termed data warehouses (*see* DATA WAREHOUSING).

4   The information systems *personnel* can be viewed as a fourth infrastructure, which includes all personnel required to establish and maintain the technology and database infrastructures and the capacity to perform user support, development, implementation, operation, and maintenance activities. The personnel may be divided between an MIS function and functional areas. There may be, for example, general purpose user support personnel in the MIS function and functional information management support personnel in the functional areas of the organization.

The application portfolio provides the specific processing and problem-solving support for an organization. It consists of the application software and related model bases and knowledge bases. The application software consists of both applications that cross functional boundaries and applications identified with a single function. Although there is significant integration of applications because of the use of common databases and use of the same application by more than one function, the application portfolio reflects a federation of systems rather than a totally integrated system. A single, integrated system is too complex; the selective integration by interconnections among the federation of systems is more manageable and robust. A visualization of the MIS based on the application portfolio consists of applications in direct support of each business function (marketing, production, logistics, human resources, finance and accounting, information systems, and top management) plus general purpose applications and facilities. Although the database management system provides general purpose support, it also supports databases common to many functions and databases unique to a function. The applications can also be classed as being associated with transaction processing, products and services, and management. The management applications can be classified as related to operational control, management control, and strategic planning. This conceptual structure is illustrated in figure 1.

In terms of the use of technology and the frequency of use of the software, the applications in figure 1 differ in several respects. The transaction processing and goods and services applications tend to support lower-level management and operating personnel. The applications tend to incorporate programmed decision processes based on decision rules and algorithms. Applications supporting higher-level management processes are less structured and require human interaction to specify the decision process and data to be used. Because of these differences, the

application structure of a management information system is often described as a pyramid (figure 2).

INFORMATION SYSTEM SUPPORT FOR MANAGEMENT ACTIVITIES

In addition to its use in transaction processing, business processes, and within products and services, information systems support management processes such as planning, control, and decision-making. This use of information technology can provide significant value to the organization. The Anthony framework is used by both academic researchers and business practitioners to model and classify the

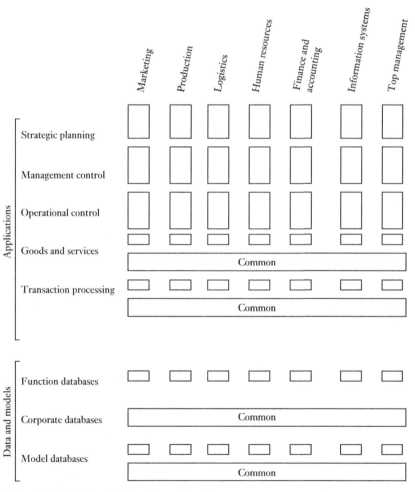

Figure 1   Organizational MIS applications, data, and models

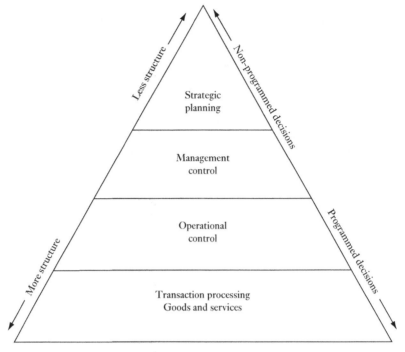

Figure 2   The MIS as a pyramid

information system support for management. The three levels of the Anthony hierarchy define the nature of the management support applications.

1 *Operational control* insures that operational activities are conducted efficiently and effectively according to plans and schedules. Examples of applications in support of operational management are scheduling, purchasing, and inquiry processing for operations. The decisions and actions cover short time periods such as a day or a week. An example of processing in support of operational control is the sequence of operations to authorize an inventory withdrawal. The balance on hand and on order is examined to determine the need for a replenishment order. The size of the replenishment order is based on reorder quantity algorithms to control inventory levels. An order document is prepared automatically for review and acceptance or modification by a purchasing analyst before it is released.

2 *Management control* focuses on a medium-term time period such as a month, quarter, or year. It includes acquisition and organization of resources, structuring of work, and acquisition and training of personnel. Budget reports, variance analysis, and staffing plans are typical of management control applications.

3 *Strategic management* applications were designed to assist management in doing long-range strategic planning. The requirements include both internal and external data. The emphasis is on customer trends and patterns and competitor behavior. Market share trends, customer perceptions of the organization and its products and services, along with similar perceptions for competitors, and forecasts of technology changes, are examples of information useful in strategic management.

A set of applications and retrieval/report facilities within an MIS designed especially for senior executives has been termed an executive information system (EIS) (*see* EXECUTIVE IN-FORMATION SYSTEMS). It focuses on the unique needs of senior management. These include an ability to formulate executive-level inquiries, construct special information requests, explore various alternative analyses, and so forth. The databases used for an EIS include portions of the corporate transactions databases, selected summary and comparative data, and relevant external data.

INFORMATION SYSTEM SUPPORT
FOR DECISION-MAKING

The decision-making support provided to an organization by its information system can be described in terms of Simon's three phases of the decision-making process: intelligence, design, and choice. The support for the intelligence phase of discovering problems and opportunities consists of database search and retrieval facilities. For example, an analyst investigating collections policy can use DATA MINING and retrieval software to obtain and interpret internal and external data on customers, sales, and collections for a representative period. The decision design phase in which decision alternatives are generated is supported by statistical, analytical, and modeling software. In the collections example, the decision design might involve correlation of collection times with customer characteristics and order characteristics. It might also compare company performance with competitors and others. The support for the choice phase includes decision models, sensitivity analysis, and choice procedures. A choice procedure for a collections policy might involve the use of models to compare collection policies on various dimensions and rank order the policies.

Management and decision-making support includes expert systems, decision support systems, and KNOWLEDGE MANAGEMENT SYSTEMS. Expert systems support decision-making by rule-based or knowledge-based systems. The most commonly used rule-based systems incorporate decision procedures and rules derived from the decision-making processes of domain experts. Data items presented to the rule-based system are analyzed by the expert system and a solution is suggested based on the rules derived from experts. The decision may be supported by an explanation facility that details the rules and logic employed in arriving at the decision. Unlike expert systems based on rules, NEURAL NETWORKS are a decision-support procedure based on the data available for a decision. The neural network is established (or recalibrated) by deriving the factors and weights that will achieve a specified outcome using an existing set of data. The factors and weights are applied to new data to suggest decisions. An example of neural network use is decision-making relative to creditworthiness for a loan or credit approval for a transaction.

The term decision support system (DSS) refers to a set of applications within an MIS devoted to decision support. Although some writers distinguish between MIS and DSS, the MIS concept is typically defined to include a DSS. The concept of a DSS incorporates the Anthony framework and the decision-making categories of Herbert Simon (1977). The classic description of the concept is by Gorry and Scott Morton (1971). Their framework for a DSS classifies decisions as structured, semi-structured, and unstructured within the three levels of management. Structured decisions can be incorporated in the programmed procedures of computer software, but unstructured (and many semi-structured) decisions are best supported by analytical and decision models and analytical and modeling tools. These facilities aid human decision-makers to deal with difficult problems that cannot be solved with algorithms. The concept of a DSS incorporates human–system interaction as the human decision-maker formulates scenarios, models alternatives, and applies analytical procedures in order to explore alternative solutions and evaluate consequences.

THE FUTURE OF THE MIS SYSTEM
AND FUNCTION

Systems based on information technology have become an integral part of organization processes, products, and services. The data available for analysis and decision-making have increased with the capabilities for computer-based storage and retrieval. The infrastructures have become more complex as more information and communications technology is distributed to individuals and departments. The planning, design, implementation, and management of information resources have become more complex and more vital to organizations. The need for a specialized MIS function has increased. Although some routine functions may be outsourced, the critical functions that affect competitive advantage are likely to remain part of an MIS function in the organization. When parts of the functions in information systems are outsourced, there is a crucial activity of managing the relationship with the oursourcing company.

Information technology is still changing rapidly, and new opportunities for organization use continue to emerge. The rate of innovation and change and the investment implications also underline the need for a vital, business-knowledgeable MIS function to support both routine and innovative organizational use of information technology for organization and management functions.

Bibliography

Anthony, R. N. (1965). *Planning and Control Systems: A Framework for Analysis.* Cambridge, MA: Harvard University Press.

Davis, G. B. and Olson, M. H. (1985). *Management Information Systems: Conceptual Foundations, Structure, and Development*, 2nd edn. New York: McGraw-Hill.

Gorry, G. A. and Scott Morton, M. S. (1971). A framework for management information systems. *Sloan Management Review*, 13 (1).

Simon, H. A. (1977). *The New Science of Management Decision*, rev. edn. Englewood Cliffs, NJ: Prentice-Hall.

manufacturing resource planning

see MANUFACTURING USE OF INFORMATION TECHNOLOGY

manufacturing use of information technology

Scott J. Hamilton

The backbone of information technology for planning and controlling a manufacturing company involves an enterprise resource planning (ERP) system (*see* ENTERPRISE SYSTEMS (ENTERPRISE RESOURCE PLANNING OR ERP)).

An ERP system provides the common database and communicates needed actions that coordinate operations across different functional areas, and with customers and vendors involved in the supply chain. The major information flows involved in an ERP system are explained below, followed by a summary of other IT applications that integrate with and build on the ERP system.

BUSINESS PLANNING

The business planning process results in annual budgets that establish the baseline for financial planning and measurement purposes. An ERP system defines budgets by general ledger account and tracks actual versus budgeted costs. Spreadsheet simulations can be used to develop budgets, drawing on information in the database and also updating the database with new budget data.

SALES PLANNING

Sales planning identifies independent demands for the company's products/services, such as sales orders and forecasts, and establishes an inventory plan as a buffer against demand variations. Forecasts and inventory plans are generally expressed for items at the highest possible stocking level, such as finished goods for standard products and intermediates for assemble-to-order products. They may also be defined for purchased materials with long lead times or supplier availability problems. Forecasts can be projected from historical sales, from existing quotes, and from other information such as leading indicators. Forecasts by product family provide aggregate planning, with planning bills to disaggregate the forecast based on product mix percentages.

SALES ORDER PROCESSING

Sales order processing starts with entry of the sales order and ends with shipment and invoicing. Many of the variations in sales order processing stem from differences between standard and custom products.

1   *Standard products.* Item availability can be checked against finished goods, or against scheduled receipts, for promising delivery dates/quantities. Pricing may be based on customer contracts or quotes, or on prede-

fined price books that reflect the customer and product types.

2 *Custom products.* The sales order defines a custom product configuration of what should be built. Delivery promises can be based on component availability and the lead time to produce the item. Pricing may be based on a cost-plus-markup or rolled-price approach.

A quotation may initially be developed and subsequently converted to a sales order. Credit policies are typically enforced during order entry. Order acknowledgments (and quotations) may be communicated to customers. Customer schedules can be used to indicate planned/firm sales orders, and ELECTRONIC DATA INTER-CHANGE (EDI) can be used to communicate customer schedules/orders electronically. A multisite operation may require sales order line items with shipment from several sites.

Sales order activities generate actions that need to be communicated to other functional areas. For example, an ERP system needs to communicate planner actions to produce make-to-order products, buyer actions to place drop-ship purchase orders or to procure non-stock items, credit management actions to review orders placed on hold, and stockroom actions to ship material. Shipping personnel can print picking lists, packing lists, box labels, and bills of lading. Shipment transactions update the general ledger for inventory and cost of sales, and pass information to accounts receivable for creating invoices. Shipments provide the basis for tracking warranty periods, reporting return goods authorizations, and analyzing historical sales.

Finishing Schedule and the Master Schedule

The finishing schedules and master schedules represent the company game plan for satisfying demands identified in the sales plan. A master schedule identifies production for stocked items, whereas a finishing schedule identifies production of make-to-order items. The planning calculations within an ERP system generate suggested supply orders which "chase" demands, and provide the starting point for finishing schedules/master schedules. A "level load" strategy can be employed by firming up these schedules over a time horizon such as an item's cumulative lead time. The planning calculations can use routing data to provide capacity planning to highlight overloaded periods, and to provide finite scheduling logic. Simulations can be used to analyze various alternatives.

Capacity Planning

Capacity planning compares work center load to available capacity to highlight overloaded periods. A work center's calendar and efficiency/utilization factors determine available capacity. A work center's load reflects routing operations for work orders, which have been scheduled based on infinite or finite scheduling logic. Drilling down to a period's load identifies the work orders and operations that can be rescheduled.

Material Planning

Material planning calculates supply/demand schedules for each item in the product structure and generates recommended actions to meet the finishing schedule and master schedule and final assembly schedule. Recommended actions identify the need to release, reschedule, cancel, and/or follow up orders. They are grouped by make items and purchased items. Recommended actions also apply to interplant transfers in a multisite operation when sites operate as feeder plants to other manufacturing or distribution sites.

Purchasing

Purchasing executes the materials plan through periodic negotiation of vendor agreements (buyer activities) and daily coordination of deliveries (vendor scheduling activities). In support of buyer activities, an ERP system identifies approved vendors, generates requests for quotes, defines price quotes and blanket purchase orders, specifies requisitions, tracks approvals, and measures vendor performance. In support of vendor scheduler activities, an ERP system generates vendor schedules, identifies recommended buyer actions, defines purchase orders, enforces receiving procedures, tracks material through inspection, and handles returns to vendor. Purchase orders can be defined for different types of items, such as normal material, expense items, and outside operations. Receipt information is passed to accounts payable for matching receipts to invoices and to general ledger for updating inventory and unvouchered payables.

PRODUCTION ACTIVITY CONTROL

Production executes the materials/capacity plan by coordinating production activity through work center dispatch lists and recommended planner actions. A work center dispatch list (or production schedule) lists work order operations in priority sequence, such as operation due date or order priority. Infinite or finite scheduling can be used to schedule work order operations. Additional coordination tools include a router/traveler of detailed work instructions (typically for custom product operations) and/or a visible scheduling system such as *kanban* tokens (typically for repetitive standard product operations).

A work order defines the quantity and start/complete dates for manufacturing the parent item and the version of the item's bill and routing to be used in manufacturing. The item's bill and routing, copied to the work order, can be modified to reflect material substitutions or alternative operations. This order-dependent bill forms the basis for picking components, although designated components can be automatically deducted (backflushed) upon reporting work order receipt or unit completions at paypoint operations. The order-dependent routing forms the basis for reporting labor by operation, although labor can also be backflushed. Labor and material transactions can be reported through a data collection system using technologies such as bar code readers. An ERP system tracks actual against planned costs, highlights variances, and generates corresponding financial transactions for updating the general ledger.

The ERP information flows utilize several key master files in the common database. These master files include information about product/process design, customers, vendors, locations, and employees.

PRODUCT/PROCESS DESIGN

The item master and bills of material define product design with engineering changes managed by date or serial number effectivity. The work center master and routings define process design. Standard operations minimize routing maintenance. The bills and routings can be used to calculate product costs.

CUSTOMERS

Customers can have different bill-to and multiple ship-to locations. Customer policies can be established for credit (such as credit limits and terms), applicable tax authorities (by ship-to location), and salesperson. Contracts and/or quotes can specify and summarize sales and receivables activities for each customer.

VENDORS

The system summarizes purchasing and payable activities by vendor. It specifies approved vendors for items and specifies vendor quoted prices with quantity breakpoints and effectivity dates.

INVENTORY LOCATIONS

An item's inventory can be stocked in multiple locations, typically identified by warehouse/bin within a plant. Inventory can also be uniquely differentiated by lot and serial number.

EMPLOYEES

The employee master is used for payroll and personnel application purposes. Employees are identified on labor transactions, so that pay rates can be used to track actual manufacturing costs.

Manufacturers have significant similarity in the need for information to manage their resources. They have the same information flows and key master files to perform aggregate planning – business, sales, and production planning – and coordinate detailed plans for execution in purchasing and production. Two other types of operations illustrate the similarity in information flows:

1 Distributors have similar information flows to manufacturers; the major difference is the lack of production activity. Production planning (for families of end items) and master scheduling (of purchased material) still apply, and capacity planning may focus on warehouse space/personnel.

2 Project manufacturers require additional functionality in an ERP system. Using a

project master file, business planning focuses on budgeting/estimating by project. Project budgets are frequently developed by using cost/schedule reporting capabilities to define the budgeted cost of work scheduled (with subsequent comparison to the budgeted and actual cost of work performed) by cost account and work package. Projects get identified in sales forecasts and sales orders, and the planning calculations translate these requirements by project through the product structure. Actual costs are tracked by project, along with performance against work packages (such as work order completions).

OTHER USES OF IT IN MANUFACTURING

Sales planning. Information technology has expanded the availability of external information useful in forecasting sales and identifying potential customers. Portable computers are used for doing proposals, presentations, and sales order entry. EXPERT SYSTEMS have been employed for automated product configuration to meet customer specifications. The shipping function can use a variety of information technologies (such as bar code readers) to record shipments and returns. Electronic communication of customer orders and shipments improves coordination with customers.

Product/process design. Information technology has been applied to schedule R&D efforts for product/process design, to directly design products via computer-aided design (CAD), and to simulate a product's performance.

Inventory and production control. Information technology has been employed for automated material handling systems and storage/retrieval systems. Data collection applications use a variety of devices (such as bar code readers) to minimize data entry efforts for reporting labor and material transactions. Expert systems are used for scheduling and assignment of workers/machines (e.g., based on skill attributes) to optimize utilization, throughput, or sequencing.

Quality. Quality management uses information technology to perform failure analysis, record and diagnose test results, and suggest corrective action. Lot and serial control are enforced and tracked through the ERP system.

markup languages

Roger Debreceny

Markup languages are used to define the content of files that are exchanged between different applications or different users. They are very important because they define the format and meaning of strings of characters or text within documents that are communicated within or between organizations. These documents can be as large as operations manuals for the maintenance of aircraft or as brief as shipping notes. In the absence of a markup language, each message or document would need to individually describe how the strings of characters being exchanged should be interpreted. The markup language is a standard way to describe the content of a range of documents. Without a markup language, for example, a document containing a financial report would need significant descriptive information to explain the elements of the report. The standard knowledge structures delineated in a markup language can be applied to a host of such reports.

There are many markup languages; the most significant are those accepted as standards. Some are limited in scope and use; others are broad and extensible. For example, HTML (hypertext markup language) is a standard markup language for INTERNET pages that interconnect with other pages. HTML has a static set of tags (tagset) that are primarily concerned with how to represent information on computer displays and how to link together a wide variety of Internet-based resources. XML (EXTENSIBLE MARKUP LANGUAGE) is one of the most important markup languages, because it is standard in its structure and yet can be extended to include new markup requirements and creation of new markup languages.

A markup language is coded in plaintext. Defined components of the file are interpreted as markup ("tags") instead of content. The text "<title>" and "</title>" in the string <title>This is the title of this document</title> are the opening and closing tags or markup that provide semantic value to, in this case, a fragment of text. Markup within a file may contain instructions for the application using and interpreting the plaintext file. The markup may alternatively provide semantic interpretation of the text contained within the markup. Semantic interpretation of the markup is defined by the markup language. SGML, XML, and the HTML are examples of markup languages.

m-commerce

see WIRELESS COMPUTING

methodologies for design, development, and implementation

see IS METHODOLOGIES

metrics for assessment of information systems

Sandra A. Slaughter

Information systems (IS) assessment is concerned with collecting accurate and meaningful indicators or metrics about software systems. Measures map a set of entities and attributes in the real world to a representation or model in the mathematical world, and this representation or model can be used to provide insight and increase understanding. Measurement helps to separate typical from unusual situations, or to define baselines and set goals. For example, consider three information systems written in the same programming language – system one is 100,000 lines of code and has had 1,000 defects discovered and corrected in the past year, system two is 50,000 lines of code with 50 defects discovered and corrected during the same time frame, and system three is 10,000 lines of code long with 10 defects. The numerical attributes about these systems can be analyzed in a mathematical model to reveal more about the systems. In this example, we learn that the average defect rate is about 7 defects per thousand lines of code, and that systems two and three have lower than

average defect rates while system one has a much higher than average defect rate. Such information could be used to focus attention on system one to determine why that system has had a higher than average defect rate and take corrective action, or it could be used to develop a predictive model of defect rates that associates system size with higher rates.

Measures capture information about the software product, process, or resources. It is important to measure information systems for several reasons. Information systems providers and users are under increasing pressure to improve productivity and quality. Measures can be used as a learning tool to monitor and evaluate the performance of information systems as well as their developers, maintainers, and users. They can also be employed to control the process of developing and maintaining information systems. Measurement information may reveal problems in the process. This information can be used to improve performance in software development and information system performance. Thus, measurement is an essential practice in software process improvement approaches such as the capability maturity model (Paulk et al., 1994). Metrics can also be used to predict the performance of systems over their life cycle. Finally, metrics can enhance communication among information system stakeholders including top management, software management and staff, users, and external stakeholders.

TYPES OF METRICS

Information systems metrics can be grouped into four major types: (1) internal performance; (2) growth and learning; (3) user/client perspective; and (4) business contribution (Grady, 1997; Jones, 1997). Many organizations first implement internal performance measures and gradually evolve to the use of more sophisticated business contribution measures.

An *internal performance* view focuses on the performance of the IS function relative to industry and organizational standards. Typical types of metrics include productivity, quality, and delivery rates. Productivity indicators measure the software delivery rate and the ability to support software. A key example is the function point metric that assesses the size of software functionality implemented (Albrecht and Gaffney,

1983). Quality metrics measure the technical quality of the software produced and maintained, and the quality of the SOFTWARE ENGINEERING process as practiced by the information systems function. A primary example is defects per line of software code. For systems developed using object-oriented methodologies (see OBJECT-ORIENTED PROGRAMS AND SYSTEMS), there are additional metrics that can be used to evaluate the quality of the design and code, such as measures of class coupling and cohesion as proposed by Chidamber and Kemerer (1994). Delivery metrics measure the information systems' organizational ability to meet time and cost commitments. An example is the number of elapsed days required to process a request for information services.

Growth and learning measures focus on assessing the capabilities of IS personnel and improving them. An important example is the maturity level of the information systems organization. This is measured using the CAPABILITY MATURITY MODEL developed by the Software Engineering Institute (SEI). Another example of a growth and learning metric is the number of training days per information systems employee.

User/client measures are concerned with assessing the relationship between the IS function and its customers. These measures indicate the extent to which business needs are met. An example is customer satisfaction metrics that measure whether users are satisfied with the system's functionality, ease of use and availability, and with the system development process.

Business contribution measures link the information systems function to the success measures used by the business to gauge business performance. Financial return, or business value of information technology, may be measured as the business benefit resulting from the use of the technology less the costs to develop or acquire the technology. Another example is strategic impact. This may be assessed by determining the amount of IS resources devoted to strategic business areas.

IMPLEMENTING METRICS

There is evidence of the value of the four types of metrics described above, but they tend to be difficult to implement. This is illustrated by

metrics for software development processes. Although software metrics provide insights that are essential to managing, controlling, and improving software development capabilities and processes, the successful implementation of software metrics programs is difficult. For example, an empirical study of software measurement and process improvement programs in 13 software firms in the UK (Hall, Baddoo, and Wilson, 2001) found enthusiasm in the firms for implementing measurement and a belief that software process improvement was substantially weakened without measurement. However, the firms actually implemented very few substantive metrics and found it difficult to implement measurement programs. The researchers concluded that, despite the importance of measurement to software process improvement, metrics are rarely implemented effectively. Even those organizations that have successfully implemented metrics programs "agonized" over the precise definitions of the metrics, and reported that the definitions, understanding, and use of these metrics continually evolved as the software development environment changed (Rifkin, 2001). Broad-based surveys of software organizations highlight the importance of management support in providing incentives for metrics use and in promoting a culture of measurement to facilitate the successful adoption of metrics programs (e.g., Ravichandran and Rai, 2000; Gopal et al., 2002).

Bibliography

Albrecht, A. and Gaffney, J. (1983). Software function, source lines of code, and development effort prediction: A software science validation. *IEEE Transactions on Software Engineering*, SE-9 (6), 639–48.

Chidamber, S. and Kemerer, C. (1994). A metrics suite for object-oriented design. *IEEE Transactions on Software Engineering*, 20 (6), 476–93.

Gopal, A., Krishnan, M., Mukhopadhyay, T., and Goldenson, D. (2002). Measurement programs in software development: Determinants of success. *IEEE Transactions on Software Engineering*, 28 (9), 863–75.

Grady, R. (1997). *Successful Software Process Improvement*. Upper Saddle River, NJ: Prentice-Hall.

Hall, T., Baddoo, N., and Wilson, D. (2001). Measurements in software process improvement programmes: An empirical study. In R. Dumke and A. Abran (eds.), *New Approaches in Software Measurement*. 10th International Workshop, IWSM 2000 Proceedings. Berlin: Springer-Verlag, pp. 73–82.

Jones, C. (1997). *Applied Software Measurement: Assuring Productivity and Quality*, 2nd edn. New York: McGraw-Hill.

Paulk, M., Weber, C., Curtis, B., and Chrissis, M. (1994). *The Capability Maturity Model: Guidelines for Improving the Software Process*. Reading, MA: Addison-Wesley.

Ravichandran, T. and Rai, A. (2000). Quality management in systems development: An organizational system perspective. *MIS Quarterly*, **24** (3), 381–415.

Rifkin, S. (2001). What makes measuring software so hard? *IEEE Software*, **18**, 3 (May/June), 41–5.

multimedia

Lester A. Wanninger, Jr.

Multimedia is the use of combinations of data, text, pictures, sound, animation, motion video, and graphics on a computer system. Multimedia uses both analog and digital representations of information along with the capabilities of the computing, telecommunication, consumer electronics, and media industries. It brings together very different technologies, approaches, and people. The blending of the underlying technologies and industries provides computing abilities to index, store, and randomly retrieve and interact with information, media abilities to create and deliver interactive content that affects many of our senses, wide availability and familiarity associated with consumer electronics devices, and capabilities of the telecommunications and television infrastructures to transmit content between locations.

DIGITAL IMAGES

Multimedia involves the processing, storage, retrieval, and transmission of large amounts of data. A typical typed page of text contains 1,000 characters. That document, when "digitized," by a fax or a scanner, is represented by about 1–10 million characters depending on whether it is stored as simple black and white or in full color. Recognizing that much of the document is contiguous white space, computer software "compresses" the digitized data by indicating the number of consecutive white or black dots rather than storing all of them. Compression reduces the amount of data to represent the digitized page of text to about 50,000 charac-

ters. Full-motion video typically shows 30 "frames" per second to represent the motion fluidly. Motion video requires about 30 million characters of data per second without compression. Compression to represent full-motion video reduces the data to 300,000 characters per second.

PHYSICAL COMPONENTS

The physical components of multimedia come from the consumer electronics, media, computer, and telecommunications fields. Consumer electronic devices include microphones and electronic amplifier/speaker systems, professional and home video cameras, television technology, home and professional still cameras, CD and DVD players, VCRs, audio tape players, and radios. Consumer electronics media include tape, disk, and film media that contain the creative content displayed by the devices. These devices and storage media have all traditionally been analog devices, but digital forms of most of the players have been introduced in the past few years.

Computer devices, storage, and communications media include magnetic and optical disks, magnetic tapes, digital monitors, room display devices such as LCD panels and digital TV-type displays, portable and desktop microcomputers, personal digital assistants (PDAs), scanners, fax, software, laser printers, modems for telecommunications, and LOCAL AREA NETWORKS (LANs). The computer devices are digital, although interfaces exist in terms of hardware cards and software drivers to integrate analog media devices into computer systems. Computer devices convert analog inputs such as full-motion video into digital form. Software capabilities include optical character recognition (OCR), which recognizes or converts a scanned page into text characters, and voice recognition technology, which converts speech into text and text to speech.

Telecommunication includes the transmission facilities of the communications companies, satellite transmission, television, microwave, LANs, devices including landline and wireless mobile phones, PDAs and pagers, and the software and PROTOCOLS that transmit the varieties of data between wide ranges of devices. Wireless telecommunications include various forms of wireless mobile phone and pager protocols and formats, infrared and wireless fidelity (802.11 WiFi or Bluetooth) for limited-range small networks to transmit voice and text (short message system or SMS) between mobile devices and computers in the telecommunications networks commonly called servers.

FUNCTIONAL CAPABILITIES AND BENEFITS

Functional capabilities of multimedia systems include the ability to generate, store, manipulate, retrieve, transmit, present, and interact with "images" from the physical devices. Scanned, faxed, written, voice, motion video, text, and still camera images can be used as input, processed, and presented as output, or communicated across geography via telecommunications and portable storage media such as optical and magnetic disk. Multimedia supports use of familiar forms and formats of information in a computer and communications system.

Multiple-party audio-video conferencing is a common multimedia system capability, having broad applicability. Conventional telephone communication, while simultaneous among the parties, is often viewed as not suitable for highly personal or social communications or group meeting situations, which require the parties to meet face to face for discussion or communication. Electronic mail (*see* EMAIL) and INSTANT MESSAGING (IM), even when simultaneous, have similar shortcomings. Video conferencing adds the important common capability of "looking the other person in the eye," and thus offers the potential to significantly change the way we work, become educated, and conduct transactions.

Indexing and electronic retrieval of multimedia audio and video clips and images is another basic capability that provides a foundation for many applications. In education, this supports remote access to multimedia libraries and videos of classes. In communication, it supports multimedia mail. In transactions, the purchaser can access a multimedia catalogue. In entertainment, it supports remote access to video libraries.

Multimedia can be employed in decision support systems to support groups in local and remote meetings. The addition of multimedia to games and simulations enables the situation to be represented in a manner that is very familiar to the users. Business games and simulations are used in class lectures, in labs, and at home to teach basic business processes and data uses. The use of multimedia in simulations allows the comparison of a variety of situations and operating modes, and can also be used as a tutor.

Mobile phones, pagers, and PDAs have unique functional capabilities of portability, "always on," always with you, and familiarity of operation. Their limitations are small screen, small keyboard size, limited power, and limited bandwidth.

Each of the individual media has unique functional characteristics which can result in some unique benefits. They also have limitations, particularly compared to other competing media. It is important to understand both the capabilities and the limitations in developing applications.

APPLICATIONS

The applications of multimedia can be grouped into four general categories: educate and inform; exchange and transact; entertain; and communicate. The functional capabilities of audio-video conferencing, indexing and retrieval of multimedia content, group decision support technology (*see* GROUP DECISION SUPPORT SYSTEMS), and multimedia games and simulations provide the basis for specific applications.

The following are examples of specific applications of multimedia to the education category, which also translate to the other application categories. Multi- and two-way interactive and real-time distance learning for remote students, faculty, and guests enables them to become an active part of the in-class delivery and is an important example of video conferencing. Implementation of distance learning, although difficult, offers significant opportunity to deliver courses differently and to a different mix of students. Video conferencing can also support remote individual or small group tutoring and grading.

Indexing and retrieval applications offer significant potential in education, in the classroom, in labs, and in remote access. Case discussions are widely used to relate conceptual material to actual situations. Cases are typically presented in written form. A multimedia case includes written case materials prepared by the faculty author, many of the materials used in developing the case, audio–video clips of case principals in a question/answer mode, and audio–video clips of pertinent products and facilities. Student preparation and the class discussion of the case can be enhanced by random access to motion video clips of principles of the case discussing certain points, and a "clip library" to illustrate or explain concepts, places, people, etc. Similarly, lectures can be enhanced by access in the classroom to multimedia content; for example, video clips of questions and answers, experts, specific situations, and instructor access to libraries of multimedia files, databases, etc.

Group meetings are typically limited to one person speaking at a time, by the listening and writing ability of the recorder, and by the ability of the meeting facilitator. Group decision support systems using multimedia allow simultaneous brainstorming input in the words and writing of each individual. This both speeds up the meeting and moves more easily to consensus. Video conferencing and retrieval applications also facilitate the group being separated in both time and place.

Simulations of very complicated or dangerous situations are typically mathematically based and as such difficult for most people to interpret. The use of multimedia allows presentations in color, three dimensions, in motion, etc. This allows people to examine the simulation results using more of their senses. Video conferencing and retrieval applications can also provide interpretive help for simulations.

Advertising has been a major application area for new media technologies throughout the twentieth century. Newspaper, radio, television, direct mail, 1–800 phone and fax each led to new ways to reach customers. However, until the INTERNET, essentially all of those media supported broadcast or one-way advertising communications. The WORLDWIDE WEB and Internet provided a revolutionary opportunity for interactive advertising communications, which is still in an adolescent phase as of 2004. Research has shown that websites can generate emotional responses, exhibit personality characteristics, and generate trust (all outcomes of broadcast advertising media and personal sales). SMS text messaging emerged in Europe and Asia in the late 1990s, growing to a volume of 400 billion text messages per year worldwide by 2004. Text messaging as an interactive advertising media capitalizes on the unique characteristics of the media combined with the proven psychological appeal of mobile phones and text messaging to youth and young adults. Research demonstrates that text messaging and mobile phones provide social acceptance, personalization, identity, social and group communication, fun and entertainment for youth and young adults.

With each new media, there is a significant period required for practitioners to learn how to capitalize on the unique capabilities and minimize the limitations of the media. As an example, one should consider the differences between three very familiar media – books, radio, and television. Television is a passive media that places words, sounds, and pictures in your mind. Radio requires you to make your own pictures. Books require you to make up your own sounds and pictures and to think.

networks

see ELECTRONIC COMMUNICATION; LOCAL AREA NETWORKS

neural networks

Loke Soo Hsu

Successful information systems require the ability to adapt to a changing environment. Often this entails the ability to learn, in real time, the latest trends/behavior from the current data inputs as well as past data. Once learned, these information systems will then modify their own behavior in accordance with the newly arrived data. Neural networks are important to information systems because the characteristics of this approach meet the needs of dynamic learning procedures. As an example, neural networks can be used in financial applications such as creditworthiness scoring where the importance of various variables in estimating creditworthiness may change rapidly with changes in the economy.

Briefly, a neural network is a software system that learns. Assume a data set with n pieces of input data, m pieces of output data, and k examples specifying input–output pairs. It is possible to analyze the data to come up with an algorithm specifying input and output relationships. A program can be written to execute the algorithm. Alternatively, the data can be used to train a neural network, a general purpose analytical program, to arrive at an algorithm. The factor weights, which are internal parameters of the general purpose programs, will be adjusted to suit the given problem. This produces a tailored neural network. With the input data from one of

the k examples, the system will reproduce the corresponding output data. With a new set of input data, it will produce a set of output data based on some relationship criteria. It is also a system that is massively parallel. The nodes in the network can perform simple computations independently. Since the computations are simple, it is assumed that they are completed at the same time. It is not necessary to check and make sure that other nodes have completed their job. This simplifies the algorithm and allows the system to arrive at a solution quickly.

The information stored in a neural network is distributed. If asked to remember ten pictures that the software should recognize, it does not store the bit patterns of these pictures. It learns the pictures to be recognized by using the picture bit patterns to calculate weights. These weights can be considered as a kind of weighted average of the bit patterns. When a noisy picture with some missing parts is presented as input, a degraded picture is output. The degradation is distributed throughout the picture instead of concentrating on the missing part. This is known as gradual degradation.

Internally, a neural network consists of a large number of interconnected processors called nodes. Each connection is represented by an arrow that points from a parent node to a child node. The nodes are classified into three types: input, output, and hidden. An input node has arrows radiating from it but no arrow pointing to it. The opposite is true of an output node. A hidden node is connected to both types of arrows.

The nodes are usually arranged in layers. Connections are allowed only between nodes in adjacent layers. For the purpose of computation, each node is characterized by a quantity called its *activation*, and each arrow is associated with a quantity called the *weight*. A parent node uses a transfer function to convert the activation into a message and sends it along the connections to its children nodes. The receiving node uses the message and the weights to perform simple computations to get its own activation. The process is repeated and the information is modified and passed along through the network. The network is essentially the algorithm for producing outputs from inputs.

There are two types of users of the neural network: the application programmer and the end user. The application programmer needs to know the structure of the neural network. Decisions are made about the number of layers, the number of nodes in each layer, the learning algorithm, and the transfer function to be used. K examples are used to train the network and test and make sure that the system produces the correct output when the k sets of input are presented. The end user sends new input to a tailor-made network and obtains output from the output nodes.

A neural network has its limitations. There is no proper theoretical basis for most of the models. The conditions for the learning process to converge are not known. When it converges, we do not know whether it reaches a global minimum or a local minimum. A few applications illustrate its use.

1 *Information retrieval.* Using a neural network, records can be retrieved from a database with over-specified condition or with conflicting information. In these cases, the system provides a prioritized list of answers.
2 *Logical inference.* Implementing EXPERT SYSTEMS by using a neural network as its INFERENCE ENGINE allows learning by examples. It is not necessary for the domain expert to provide rules. The neural network does not work by rules. The expert provides examples. This approach has been applied to systems based on classical, three-valued, probabilistic, and fuzzy logic.
3 *Financial forecasting.* A neural network can be used for time-series prediction. Examples are stock market, foreign currency market, and various other financial indices.

Bibliography

Aleksander, I. and Morton, H. (1995). *An Introduction to Neural Computing*. London: International Thomson.

Fausett, L. (1994). *Fundamentals of Neural Networks: Architectures, Algorithms, and Applications*. Upper Saddle River, NJ: Prentice-Hall.

Haykin, S. (1998). *Neural Networks: A Comprehensive Foundation*. Upper Saddle River, NJ: Prentice-Hall.

object-oriented database management systems

Gordon C. Everest

Object-oriented database management systems (OODBMSs) grew out of a marriage of object-oriented programming languages and conventional database management systems (DBMSs) (*see* DATABASE MANAGEMENT SYSTEM). They represent the next generation of DBMS.

OODBMSs are intended to handle more complex data in increasingly complex application systems. This includes heterogeneous MULTIMEDIA forms of data such as text, graphics (bitmapped and vector), three-dimensional graphics, moving video, audio, etc. They are also designed to handle complex object composition and complex inter-object processing. As such, they can produce substantially better performance compared to traditional relational DBMSs (*see* RELATIONAL DATABASE). Relational DBMSs are optimized to process one or a small number of large files, whereas OODBMSs are optimized for complex inter-entity processing. Typical applications include computer-aided design/computer-aided manufacturing (CAD/CAM), geographic information systems (GIS), document description, CASE repositories (*see* CASE: COMPUTER-AIDED SOFTWARE/ SYSTEM ENGINEERING), and others characterized by complex object descriptions and relationships.

The essential characteristic of an OODBMS is the encapsulation of objects or entities and the procedures used to access and process those objects. The system provides a formal mechanism that separates the referencing, accessing, and manipulation of objects from the methods that implement those actions. Thus the method of implementation is hidden from the outside world, i.e., the world of users and programmers who access and modify objects. The object-oriented approach provides for levels of abstraction in the design and implementation of systems (*see* OBJECT-ORIENTED PROGRAMS AND SYSTEMS).

OODBMSs differ from relational DBMSs in several significant ways. Object (entity) identifiers must be immutable, i.e., unchanging, whereas in a relational DBMS they are defined by users and can be changed by users. An OODBMS depends upon immutable object identifiers to maintain inter-object relationships. Good design in a relational environment requires records to be in third normal form. This means record decomposition. Then it is necessary for the user to perform JOIN operations to bring together the data pertaining to an object. Relational database design breaks down records and formally defines the result to the DBMS. However, relational systems provide no formal mechanism for defining record (re)compositions to get back to how end users actually think about objects. In contrast, OODBMSs provide formal mechanisms for defining inter-object relationships and complex object compositions.

OODBMSs are used primarily in environments where system developers write their own programs. Hence, the emphasis is on providing an application programming interface (API) to object-oriented programming languages such as C++ and SmallTalk. There has been less emphasis on providing a human interface for interactive processing and high-level query languages.

Initially, the main players in the marketplace for OODBMSs were new names. However, traditional DBMS vendors will eventually enter the marketplace as well with revised or new versions of their packages. Some OODBMSs are built as extensions of existing object-oriented programming languages, some are built from scratch, and some are hybrids of a relational system and an object-oriented system.

object-oriented programs and systems

Salvatore T. March and Charles A. Wood

Object orientation (OO) is a philosophy of software development based on the concept of autonomous *objects* requesting services from and providing services to other objects. Services are requested through *messages*. The metaphor for object-oriented programming is assembling a set of objects and coordinating their behavior with a script of messages that meet the application requirements. Object-oriented development is driven by two design principles, *encapsulation* and *inheritance*.

Objects are defined by a template-like structure called a *class*. Classes are defined and organized according to the services they provide. Following the *encapsulation* principle, objects are designed to be self-contained, i.e., they contain all *methods* (also known as *procedures* or *functions*) and *variables* required to provide their services. Other objects requesting a service do not know how the service is provided. They cannot directly access another object's variables. They only know the interface or *message signature* of the services provided. This insulates objects from changes in other objects. An object's implementation is said to be *hidden*

from other objects. Provided its message signatures remain constant, an object can be changed without affecting any other objects requesting its services.

Following the *inheritance* principle, classes are designed in a subtype-supertype structure where a subtype inherits the methods and variables of its supertype(s). This principle enables a designer to eliminate or at least minimize code redundancy.

Figure 1 illustrates an object-oriented computer program containing two classes. Four types of variables are defined in this program, global variables, local variables, class variables, and instance variables. *Global variables* can be accessed by all methods of all classes. That is, they are defined globally within the program. The encapsulation principle requires the ability to define variables that are *not* accessible globally. Hence *local variables* are defined within a method and can be accessed only within that method. Early non-object-oriented languages like COBOL and Assembler only supported global variables. Later non-object-oriented languages like C, PL/I, and Pascal introduced local variables that allowed them to support encapsulated procedures.

Object-oriented programming languages, like Smalltalk, C++, and Java, introduce *class* and *instance variables* to provide an additional level of encapsulation for variables required to implement a coherent set of methods. Object-oriented languages similarly differentiate between *class* and *instance methods*. Class variables and methods (also known as *static* variables and

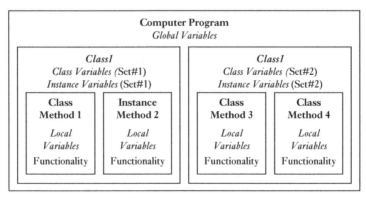

Figure 1　An object-oriented program

methods) apply to the class. Instance variables and methods apply to the objects of the class. A class method is executed when the corresponding message is sent to the class. An instance method is executed when the corresponding message is sent to an object of the class. Class methods have access to global variables, their class variables, and their local variables. Instance methods have access to global variables, their class variables, their instance variables, and their local variables.

In figure 1, for example, Class Variables (Set #1) is accessible by Class Method 1 and Instance Method 2, but neither is accessible by Class Method 3 or Instance Method 4. Instance Variables (Set #1) is accessible only by Instance Method 2.

By encapsulating variables within a class, modifications to its methods are unlikely to have any impact on methods outside the class. In this way, encapsulation can significantly reduce the effort and cost required to develop and maintain a complex system. The effect of encapsulation is so important that some object-oriented languages such as Smalltalk and Java do not allow global variables, requiring every variable to be encapsulated within a class. However, other object-oriented languages, such as C++, still allow global variables.

A class definition can be viewed as a *data type* similar to standard data types such as integer or character string. A class is *instantiated* when an object in that class is created. Each class must be instantiated at least once to set up the memory required for the variables and methods within the class.

A program can instantiate a class several times, i.e., create multiple objects of that class. Consider, for example, a program that retrieves employee information from a database, lists all employees within a specific department, and counts the number of employees. This program would define an *Employee* class and create one object (instance) of that class for each employee in the database. The *Employee* class would need instance variables for data values such as *salary*, *name*, and *department*. Each employee object would have its own value for each of these instance variables. The *Employee* class could also have class variables such as *maxFicaSalary* (maximum salary for FICA deductions) and *Fica_Rate* (the tax rate for FICA deductions). Each object of the

Employee class would share a single class variable, and all objects have access to *the same* class variables, so that changes made to a class variable by one object can be detected by every other object. Each *Employee* object can use its instance variables and all *Employee* class variables as needed, for example, in payroll processing.

Objects may be related to other objects in two ways. First, an object may *contain* other objects in its variables. For example, a *Department* object may include a variable that contains the *Employee* objects corresponding to employees who report to that department. Second, objects can be related to each other through a supertype-subtype structure. Subtypes (also called subclasses or child classes) *inherit* variables and methods from their supertypes (also called superclasses or parent classes). Inheritance occurs *without duplicating any of the supertype object's code*. Hence classes can be viewed as containers for variable and method definitions. Class variables and methods are inherited by subclasses. Instance variables and methods are inherited by objects in the subclasses.

Like encapsulation, inheritance can vastly reduce the time and effort required for new development and for maintenance. Continuing the above example, suppose *Employee* is responsible for producing the payroll via an instance method named *issuePaycheck*. This method must determine the employee's gross pay for the current pay period. Suppose further that there are two types of employees, salaried employees and hourly employees. Salaried employees are paid a fixed gross pay per pay period (i.e., based on their salary). Hourly employees are paid a gross pay equal to the number of hours worked multiplied by their hourly pay rate. Otherwise there is no difference in the way in which their paychecks are calculated.

Inheritance can be used to simplify the development of such functionality by creating two subclasses of *Employee*, *HourlyEmployee* and *SalariedEmployee*. The instance variable *salary* would be moved to the subclass *SalariedEmployee* since it describes only salaried employees, not all employees. Instance variables *hoursWorked* and *hourlyPayRate* would be included in *HourlyEmployee*. Both *HourlyEmployee* and *SalariedEmployee* inherit all *Employee* variables and methods, including the method *issuePaycheck*; however, each needs a different *calcGross* method to calculate the gross pay appropriately for that type of employee. Hence the code executed when a *calcGross* message is sent to an *HourlyEmployee* object is different from that executed when a *calcGross* message is sent to a *SalariedEmployee* object. Having different methods with the same name is termed *polymorphism*.

Since *HourlyEmployee* and *SalariedEmployee* are subclasses of *Employee*, changes made to the *Employee* class are *immediately* propagated to them. If, for example, a new payroll deduction is required or a change is made to the way in which a payroll deduction is calculated, changes can be made to the appropriate *Employee* methods without modifying any methods of *HourlyEmployee* or *SalariedEmployee* (assuming the changes are uniformly applied to both types of employees).

Inheritance is important to object-oriented development. In Java and Smalltalk, the class structure is a superclass/subclass hierarchy with the class *Object* as the root. All other classes are *subclasses* of it (i.e., children in the hierarchy). However, other object-oriented languages such as C++ allow classes to be defined that are not subclasses of another class.

Changes in software systems development allowed by object-oriented languages are beginning to have an impact on managerial structure. Generic objects that can serve as ancestors for specialized objects are developed and stored in an *object repository*. These can also serve as callable routines for a host of other objects. A *Reuse Engineer* or *Object Analyst* guides programmers during development to choose or create new objects that simplify software development and maintenance on an enterprise-wide scale. This differs from traditional information systems development where functional areas like production, finance, accounting, etc. each had their own programmers who, in turn, had little contact with programmers outside of their own functional area.

object role modeling

Gordon C. Everest

Object role (OR) modeling is a database design modeling technique based upon NIAM (Nijssen Information Analysis Method). The extensions and refinements to NIAM were primarily owing to Terry Halpin (1995). NIAM/OR modeling has also been called binary relationship modeling.

OR modeling builds a data model using two constructs: objects and relationships. This is in contrast to record-based data modeling techniques such as relational or entity relationship (ER) modeling (*see* ER DIAGRAMS). Record-based modeling uses three constructs: entities, attributes, and relationships. In OR modeling, entities and attributes are both treated as objects (this use of the term objects has no relationship to object orientation; *see* OBJECT-ORIENTED PROGRAMS AND SYSTEMS). In OR modeling, objects obtain attributes by virtue of being related to other objects.

OR modeling is more expressive than ER modeling, particularly in the expression of constraints on a data model. OR modeling does not cluster attributes into records. Building records should be the next step in the database design process. If done prematurely (and often incorrectly), building records can lead to a violation of normal forms. In record-based modeling, proper record design demands that records be in third normal form, i.e., not containing any multiple, partial, or transitive dependencies. A violation of third normal form is remedied by further decomposing the records in the design. OR modeling achieves the ultimate end of record decomposition, where each record has at most one non-key domain. Hence, normal form violations can never occur.

OR modeling views the world as objects playing roles in relationship with other objects. It begins with an expression of facts made up of nouns and verbs. The nouns are the objects and the verbs are the roles played by the objects in relationships. Facts are expressed in sentences. In an object role model, these are *elementary* (or irreducible) sentences. For example, an elementary unary fact might be "Jane smiles." This is an instance of the general fact type "the person named Jane smiles." An example of a binary fact might be "Bob likes Jane." At the type level, this is expressed "person named Bob likes person named Jane." It is possible to express higher-order facts. For example, employee with name–possesses skill–with proficiency rating of– is a ternary fact type.

These elementary sentences can be represented diagrammatically with circles for objects and arcs for relationships. The circle contains the name (noun) of the object. On the arc, a box is drawn with one or more parts. A line connects each part of the box to exactly one object. In each part of the box, a verb is used for the role the connected object plays in the relationship with the other object(s). For example:

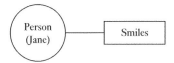

For the ternary fact type above, the diagram would appear as:

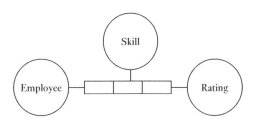

In a ternary relationship, if only two of the roles are needed for uniqueness, they can be separated out and made into a nested or objectified object, to which is attached the third object. In the above example, employee and skill could be together in one box, and then that could become another object by drawing a circle around the box with two parts and connecting that with another box to the rating object. Object types can be divided into subtypes relating to a supertype.

To any data model diagram, the following types of constraints are added:

- *Uniqueness* to specify the multiplicity (or cardinality) on the relationship, such as one to one, one to many, many to many.
- *Dependency* when it is mandatory that all instances of an object participate in the relationship (sometimes called the totality constraint).
- *Reference* scheme for naming or referencing objects.

- *Value set* for valid ranges or ennumerated sets of values.
- *Set constraints* such as IF (conditional), IFF (if and only if), subset, etc.

There are other types of constraints.

Bibliography

Nijssen, S. and Halpin, T. (1989). *Conceptual Schema and Relational Database Design*. Sydney: Prentice-Hall International; 2nd edition, Terry Halpin, 1995.

office automation

A term applied to a wide variety of equipment and software for automating or supporting clerical and professional activities in an office environment. The technology for office automation includes hardware and software for communications, data and text management, and image processing (*see* DOCUMENT IMAGE PROCESSING SYSTEMS). Communications support includes voice mail, electronic mail (*see* EMAIL), fascimile (fax), and teleconferencing. Examples of data and text management include optical character recognition, copier and printing systems, storage and retrieval systems, and access to external information sources. Image processing includes scanners and graphics packages.

OLE

Object linking and embedding (OLE) is a method for linking or embedding an object from one application into another application. For example, a spreadsheet or part of a spreadsheet can be embedded in a document and linked to the spreadsheet source. When the source object is changed, the embedded object is also changed automatically. The automatic change may, however, be disabled. Object linking and embedding is important for information processing because many applications use data or analyses from other files. OLE reduces the need to reenter changes when documents or spreadsheets are interconnected. OLE is a proprietary standard developed by Microsoft. A competing standard is Open Doc, developed by a consortium of other vendors.

on-demand computing

Gordon B. Davis

On-demand computing is an alternative to traditional purchase or leasing of information technology hardware and system software. Under traditional purchase or lease, an organization acquires the technology for its exclusive use. All of the resources are available for the acquiring organization's use; if the organization does not need all of the resources, the unused capacity remains idle. If more resources are required, they must be leased or purchased. A variation on purchase or lease is for the user organization to obtain the technology and operating personnel under an outsourcing arrangement. An external organization provides a given level of information technology infrastructure and service.

On-demand computing (*see* GRID COMPUTING) is a usage-based alternative. The company makes a contractual arrangement with an external computer technology vendor to buy information technology hardware and system software on a usage basis. If demand for information technology services increases, the provider of on-demand services delivers more resources to the using organization; if fewer resources are needed, fewer are provided. Payment is based on usage.

Why would an organization enter into a contract for on-demand computing? If usage fluctuates heavily but somewhat predictably, such as with organizations that have seasonal peaks, on-demand computing may result in reduced costs. The fixed costs of ownership are converted to variable costs based on usage. There is a predictable cost relationship related to volume, and the overall costs may be lower than with traditional purchase or leasing. An organization that is growing rapidly may be able to have necessary information processing resources to match its growth. The on-demand vendor, serving a variety of organizations, can achieve economies that may not be possible with a single organization and therefore costs of on-demand resources may be lower than in-house infrastructure.

Arguments against on-demand computing are that hardware is so inexpensive that companies can afford to have excess capacity for seasonal demand without going to an on-demand model. On-demand computing locks an organization into a single vendor and reduces interoperability with different vendors and platforms. Some organizations are concerned about security when the resources they use are shared with other organizations that are also served by the on-demand vendor.

online analytic processing

Christopher L. Carr

Online analytic processing (OLAP) is the acronym for a set of tools and a form of information processing that allows users to access, analyze, and represent organizational data in ways useful for management decision-making, control, and forecasting. OLAP tools allow end users to explore the historical databases of an organization, looking for patterns and anomalies that can lend insight into managerial decision-making and forecasting. OLAP addresses search and representation problems that highlight the difference between data and information. The problems are caused by the combination of the constraints inherent in the human cognitive processing system and the current functional architecture of relational database management systems or online transaction processing systems.

OLAP tools use a multidimensional representation of aggregated, summarized, and statistically manipulated data to make possible pattern recognition by end users. A typical example of this multidimensional representation might be a spreadsheet depicting the mean number of items sold by a distributor, by region of the country, by month of the year, with rankings within product groupings. This multidimensional representation (time, location, and product type are the dimensions) extracts patterns and trends in the data that are meaningful to the user instead of the row-by-column representation of raw data contained within the transaction data. These tools allow pattern extraction by the end user to operate in an intuitive and iterative fashion. Users create one form of summary or statistical analysis, the results of which naturally lead to "drill down" to a greater level of detail, or "roll up" to a higher level of aggregation, or view the data along another dimension. OLAP tools are found in many spreadsheet processors.

online systems

Online systems are applications with immediate data input and processing. Users interact with the computer to enter data and obtain results (*see* PROCESSING METHODS FOR INFORMATION SYSTEMS).

ontology

Jinsoo Park

The field of information systems involves significant bodies of new knowledge about technologies, systems, data, information, and domains in which systems are applied. It is important to have a well-controlled vocabulary for describing, representing, and sharing this knowledge. The term ontology is used for a knowledge representation in information systems; since there are several different applications for ontology, there are several "ontologies" in the field. The ontology concept is derived from metaphysics, but in the field of information systems it is used in the limited sense of a specification of concepts and relationships within a defined domain of information system knowledge. Note that it is common in information systems to use the term ontology to refer not only to the concepts of ontology, but also to the knowledge specifications.

In metaphysics, ontology is the study of being with regard to the aspect or essence of being or existence. More specifically, ontology deals with fundamental categories of things that exist or generic concepts that represent elements of the world. Different philosophers have different views on what the fundamental categories of being are. In the context of the information systems discipline, ontology consists of unambiguous specifications of a set of representational concepts for a shared domain of discourse or shared knowledge about information systems. An ontology is typically a hierarchical structure that contains definitions of classes, their relationships, properties, and rules within that domain. In other words, it is an explicit representation of the meaning of terms, their semantic interconnections, and some simple inference rules for that domain. In this sense, T. R. Gruber described ontology as "an explicit specification of a conceptualization."

Some argue that the concept of ontology may be applied very broadly to the entire field of information systems. According to the philosopher M. A. Bunge, the goals of scientific ontology are to analyze and to systematize the ontological categories and hypotheses pertinent to science. Wand and Weber have extended the concept of ontology delineated by Bunge as the Bunge–Wand–Weber (BWW) model. The BWW model is a conceptual framework that may be used as a foundation in the areas of information systems modeling, requirements engineering, and data quality dimensions.

In information systems, an ontology serves as a shared and common vocabulary (i.e., consensus knowledge of a community of people) that can be used to model a certain domain. In other words, an ontology is domain-specific metadata that describe the semantics of information sources. An ontology is a reusable building block; once an ontology is constructed, others can adopt and simply reuse it in many applications of similar domains. Accordingly, benefits of using ontologies lie in sharing and reuse. A computational ontology is a human artifact that can be processed by machines (e.g., computer programs and software agents), and is therefore useful in performing certain types of computation. Such ontologies can also be used as a means of achieving consistent communication between people and heterogeneous information systems.

Typically, ontologies are organized by concepts, not words, along with semantic relationships, such as subconcept–superconcept and part–whole. For example, *GraduateStudent* is a subconcept of *CollegeStudent*, and *BookChapter* is a part of *Book*. However, there is no consensus among scientists and practitioners on how the ontology should be structured or represented. The degree of formality in the construction of an ontology varies. Some ontology languages are very expressive and some are not. An ontology can be represented as a concept hierarchy, e.g., RDF (resource description framework) schema, a frame-based system, e.g., Ontolingua, a semantic net, e.g., WordNet, or a logical formalism, e.g., OWL (web ontology language) based on description logic language. Increased precision and formality can improve machine understanding. Ontologies have been developed independently for different pragmatic purposes in information systems. As a result, they often differ greatly from one another. Therefore, mapping and translation between heterogeneous ontologies are a very challenging problem.

APPLICATION AREAS IN INFORMATION SYSTEMS RESEARCH AND PRACTICE

Ontology is discussed in many areas of knowledge, such as philosophy and metaphysics. Within the field of information systems, ontology is applied in knowledge representation formalisms, knowledge sharing and reuse, knowledge management, commonsense reasoning, knowledge base, information systems development methodologies, business process modeling, information retrieval, INTERNET search, standardization, enterprise information integration, information systems evaluation, and SEMANTIC WEB. In order to illustrate the role of ontologies in information systems, the three main application areas of ontology technology are discussed.

Integration of heterogeneous information. Ontology can be used for semantic integration of information systems. Managing information in a heterogeneous environment has been one of the most challenging problems in information systems because much of a firm's valuable information lies in legacy systems stored in multiple, conflicting formats. For example, different business units employ different acronyms to refer to the same product, and each of them uses its own standard to represent units of measures and scales. As more businesses move to online marketplaces and confront new business opportunities and pressures such as mergers, acquisitions, deregulation, SUPPLY CHAIN MANAGEMENT, and new service offerings, firms face ever-expanding integration challenges. Information heterogeneity among distributed information systems limits how they communicate with one another. Therefore, the major challenge is to make diverse information systems interoperate at the semantic level while retaining their autonomy. The design of a semantically interoperable system environment that manages various semantic conflicts among different systems is a daunting task. It should provide

the capability to detect and resolve incompatibilities in data semantics and structures. At the same time, it should involve few or no changes to existing systems to preserve the local autonomy of the participating systems. The environment must be flexible enough to permit adding or removing individual systems from the integrated structure without major modifications. Since ontology can be used to describe contextual knowledge about data, it can also be used as a tool to resolve semantic conflicts. One viable approach to semantic heterogeneity resolution is to adopt a shared ontology as a basis for mutual understanding and semantic reconciliation. Such an ontology can facilitate communication and sharing of information between different systems.

Intelligent search. Organizations produce large amounts of information, such as departmental and technical memoranda, announcements of new products, summary of regular meetings, and so forth. Further, the unprecedented growth of information technology has made numerous resources on the web instantly accessible to various user communities. Therefore, it is increasingly difficult for knowledge seekers to choose useful keywords for representing their information needs and minimizing the amount of search results. Finding only truly relevant information among the overwhelming amount of information has become a critical issue. The primary issue is not how to efficiently process the data that are known to be relevant, but which data are relevant and where they are located. Ontologies can help improve user access to information on a large information space. For example, ontologies can support semantic-based intelligent search and filtering instead of keyword matching on the Internet. If search engines and users are guided by ontologies, users can avoid retrieving irrelevant information that uses a certain word in a different meaning. In addition, it can capture information where different words are used to describe the desired content. A good example is the semantic web. The semantic web is an extension of the current web with well-established infrastructure for expressing information in a precise, human-readable, and machine-interpretable form based on XML (EXTENSIBLE MARKUP LANGUAGE), RDF, and RDF schema.

The semantic web aims to use OWL as a standard language to build ontologies, making it easier for machines to automatically and efficiently perform sophisticated tasks for humans. Moreover, the ontology-based semantic web can facilitate the construction of the network of knowledgeable systems with various specialized reasoning services.

E-business. Ontologies can play an important role in e-business (*see* E-COMMERCE; E-COMMERCE BUSINESS-TO-BUSINESS SYSTEMS). An ontology can serve as a global infrastructure and be used as a de facto standard for e-business transactions. For example, different manufacturers can use a common ontology to build catalogues that describe their products. Afterward, the manufacturers could share the ontology for use in automated design systems. For the applications in WEB SERVICES, OWL-S (OWL for services) could be used to specify organization web service properties and capabilities in a machine-interpretable form. It can facilitate the automation of various web service tasks. Ontology can be used for automatic negotiation in the B2B environment. When software agents communicate with each other, it is important to provide participating agents with the standard communication primitives for negotiation and their semantics in terms of a negotiation protocol. Ontology can insure that the meaning of what one agent says is precisely conveyed to the other agent. Another important task to automate the negotiation process is to incorporate necessary knowledge into the agents that carry out the negotiation. Since ontologies can capture domain knowledge and problem-solving knowledge that might be in problem-solving methods specifying how to achieve goals, they can provide a means to incorporate human and enterprise negotiation knowledge. This enables negotiation agents to make automated negotiations effectively and intelligently. Another example of the use of ontology is business document exchange. Different organizations in the same industry or those in different industries can easily exchange business documents via ontology mapping and translation services.

AVAILABLE ONTOLOGIES AND ONTOLOGY LANGUAGES

There exist many ontologies and ontology languages that are used in a variety of application areas. WordNet and Cyc are well-known ontologies that are currently being adopted in many domains. KIF, Ontolingua, and OWL are widely used ontology languages to represent and construct ontologies.

WordNet. WordNet is an online lexical database for English. Its design was inspired by the assumption that words are stored differently in the human brain based on the current psycholinguistic theories of human lexical memory. Synset (synonym set) is used to categorize English words into noun, verb, adjective, and adverb. WordNet provides a short definition for each word and organizes the various semantic relations between these categories. WordNet is publicly available online (www.cogsci.princeton.edu/~wn/index.shtml). Since semantics of words are defined in natural language terms, its contents are not machine-processable. In this respect, WordNet shows a low level of formality. WordNet is used in many applications such as natural language processing, web navigation, automated word sense disambiguation, information retrieval, image retrieval, multilingual document analysis, and conceptual modeling.

Cyc. Cyc was developed in the Cyc project, which attempts to construct a comprehensive common-sense ontology. More than a million axioms that formalize common-sense knowledge are stored in the Cyc. The ontology of Cyc is organized around the concept of categories that are structured in a generalization/specialization hierarchy. CycL is a formal language based on first-order predicate calculus and used to express Cyc ontology. Cyc is a proprietary system of Cycorp (www.cyc.com/). However, a subset of the ontology is available as open source on the web (www.opencyc.org/).

KIF. Knowledge interchange format (KIF) is a formal language for exchanging knowledge between disparate computer programs such as software agents. KIF is a variant of first-order predicate calculus with extensions to support non-monotonic reasoning and definitions. Its design goal is to provide a standard interface that enables different programs to exchange knowledge by mapping into a standard, exchangeable format. Typically, each computer program has its own preferred format to represent knowledge serving its purpose. When communication with another program is required, each computer program maps its own syntax with that of KIF; exchanging knowledge between them can then be achieved. Since KIF provides a means for expressing the definitions of knowledge (i.e., knowledge about knowledge), it can be used as a language for representing and exchanging ontologies.

Ontolingua. Ontolingua is a frame-based language to support the design of ontologies. Ontolingua is based on KIF 3.0. It is an ontology-building language used by the Ontolingua server. Ontolingua provides an interface for ontology-to-ontology communication based on frame ontology, while KIF provides an interchange format for agent-to-agent communication based on predicate logic language. Without a shared and standard format for representing ontology, it is difficult to exchange knowledge between heterogeneous ontologies. In order for computer systems to communicate and cooperate effectively between heterogeneous ontologies, Ontolingua provides a language-neutral, knowledge-exchangeable environment between diverse ontologies by translating knowledge bases into a single canonical form.

OWL. Web ontology language (OWL) is a web-based ontology language designed to provide integration and interoperability of data in web documents. OWL can formally describe semantics of the classes/properties and how they are related. It is supported by XML, RDF, and RDF schema. XML provides a surface syntax for structured documents which has no semantic constraints on the meaning. RDF is a data model for objects and relations between them. It provides a simple semantics for this data model. RDF schema is a vocabulary for describing properties and classes of RDF, with a semantics for generalization hierarchies of such properties and classes. OWL adds more vocabulary for describing properties and classes, so it can be used to explicitly represent the meaning of terms in vocabularies and the relationships between those terms. OWL has three sublanguages: OWL Lite, OWL DL, and OWL Full. OWL can be used in a wide range of application areas, such as class definitions for conventional

software systems, automated negotiation, e-commerce, web services, web portal, content-based search, query answering, intelligent agents, and ubiquitous computing.

Bibliography

Bunge, M. A. (1977). *Treatise on Basic Philosophy.* Vol. 3, *Ontology I: The Future of the World.* Boston: D. Reidel.

Fensel, D. (2004). *Ontologies: A Silver Bullet for Knowledge Management and Electronic Commerce,* 2nd edn. Berlin: Springer.

Gruber, T. R. (1993). A translation approach to portable ontology specifications. *Knowledge Acquisition,* **5** (2), 199–220.

Wand, Y. and Weber, R. (1990). An ontological model of an information system. *IEEE Transactions on Software Engineering,* **16** (11), 1282–92.

Open Doc

A method for object linking and embedding (*see* OLE).

open source

Gordon B. Davis

Open source refers to software code that can be obtained without cost. The source code can be modified by the recipient without royalty or other fee. The basic rationale is that the open-source approach encourages the evolution and improvement of software. Users of the open-source software find defects and publicly suggest improvements and modifications. These modifications are made freely available to the user community. There is a non-profit corporation, Open Source Initiative (OSI), dedicated to managing and promoting open source. The operating system Linux is a well-known example of open-source software. The advantages of open-source software are an increase in modification and improvement of software and an increase in individual initiative to examine the software and make improvements. The disadvantages are the lack of control over development and the lack of economic incentives because of the absence of copyright or patent ownership. However, there is a business model for developers engaged in open-source development to obtain revenues to support their involvement. Although the open-source developers do not own the software, they can provide for-fee consulting, training, and integration services for the users of open-source software.

open systems

Gordon B. Davis

Open systems has a specific meaning in computing and information systems. As a system concept (*see* SYSTEM CONCEPTS APPLIED TO INFORMATION SYSTEMS), an open system, in contrast to a closed system, is one that accepts inputs and provides outputs. The term open systems, when used in reference to computing and information systems hardware and software, means that the application or software specifications are in the public domain and not proprietary to any one manufacturer or developer. Any developer can use the specifications, and any company can develop and sell products based on the open-system specifications. Open systems often have user groups that develop a shared understanding of the open-system specifications. The open-system concept has been applied to operating systems, such as Unix systems and Unix-based systems such as Linux, and to other hardware and software systems. The advantages of open systems are increased innovation without the dangers of copyright or other ownership restrictions and interoperability of systems that are built around the open-system specifications. The disadvantages are the lack of incentives for control over the specifications and orderly development and maintenance. Successful open systems generally have a user group that develops a shared understanding of the open-system specifications. This shared understanding can be very specific or can be a reference model that provides guidance but not detailed specifications. An example of an open reference model is the open systems interconnection, a reference model for electronic communication in a network. The purpose is to provide guidance to developers so that their products will work with other products.

optical character recognition

Gordon B. Davis

Optical character recognition (OCR) is a technology for reading and interpreting machine-printed or handwritten symbols. OCR can also include technology to read optical marks and magnetic ink characters. Examples of optical marks are the universal product code (*see* BAR CODE) and the US Postal Service bar code for zip codes. Magnetic ink characters are used on bank checks and similar bank documents.

OCR systems are used to read machine-printed fonts. Standard stylized fonts are available for optical character applications (OCR-A and OCR-B), but most machine-printed fonts are readable. In a typical business application, a customer returns a part of the billing form containing customer information, such as account number and amount due, printed on it. The turnaround document is read with an OCR reader.

Hand-printed characters can also be read. In order to achieve reasonable accuracy, the characters must be carefully printed. To aid users in entering data, forms typically provide a marked space for each character.

organization structure of the IS/IT function

Nicholas L. Ball

There is typically a separate organization function within an organization that has responsibility for planning, building, and maintaining an infrastructure of information and communications technology and a portfolio of applications that provide the capabilities and services needed by the organization. The function has responsibility for building or acquiring applications and providing services to support their use. It also has responsibility for personnel to perform development, operations, and support services. There are several alternative ways that the information technology/information systems (IS/IT) function may be structured in an organization. The choice of organization structure depends on factors that reflect the overall organization structure and its focus for information technology and information systems. Here,

"IT" will be used to refer to the "IT/IS" function and its organization structure.

The extent to which managers are able to appropriately design and structure the IS/IT function within the organization is an important determinant of how well the IS/IT function can service the rest of the organization. The literature related to the design and structure of the IS/IT function is quite well developed. Three perspectives from this literature can be used to understand the alternatives that are possible and the choices managers make with respect to the design and structure of the IT function: (1) the organizational focus or foci for the IT function; (2) the locus of control for IT-related decisions; and (3) contingencies.

ORGANIZATIONAL FOCI RATIONALE FOR IT ORGANIZATION STRUCTURE

Typical structural and design foci that may be used in deciding on IT organization structure include clients or customers, enterprise processes, portfolios of projects, or capability categories. Designing IT around clients or customers typically involves structuring IT to provide IT human and technical resources dedicated to meeting the needs of business and corporate units. Designing around enterprise processes involves structuring IT to provide IT human and technical resources dedicated to the creation and maintenance of integrated organizational processes. Designing and structuring around projects involves the creation of IT structures that provide human and technical resources dedicated to specific projects or portfolios of projects for the life of that project or set of projects. Where the other foci are more "permanent," the project orientation is more dynamic and might be laid on top of a capabilities focus. Organizing on the basis of competence or capability involves dedicating IT human and technical resources toward the creation or maintenance of specific IT capabilities or competences within the organization (such as systems development). Organizations may also adopt two (or more) foci as the logic for designing and structuring the IT function. Such organizations might apply a matrix structure, where resources are allocated on the basis of these multiple foci.

LOCUS OF CONTROL FOR IT DECISIONS

A second, more common perspective describes the locus of control of IT in terms of IT decisions that are made within the organization (Brown and Magill, 1998; Sambamurthy and Zmud, 1999). These decisions can be controlled either by the corporate IT function or by business units. There are three generic sets of IT decisions that are made within organizations: IT infrastructure, IT use, and IT project management. IT infrastructure decisions reflect choices made with respect to the hardware and software platforms as well as network and data architectures that support all organizational applications and systems. IS/IT use refers to decisions made with respect to long-and short-term plans for applications as well as planning, budgeting, and the day-to-day operations and services. Project management consists of decisions related to the acquisition, development, and deployment of IS/IT applications within the organization.

The organizational design and structure of the IT function can be described in terms of which organizational entities control these decisions. When managers within corporate IT control decisions related to infrastructure, use, and project management, then the IT structure is very centralized. At the other extreme, when all three types of decisions are controlled by managers in business units, the IT structure is decentralized. Finally, when some decisions are controlled by managers in corporate IT and some are controlled by managers of business units, IT employs a federal structure. Most organizations employ a form of the federal IT structure (Sambamurthy and Zmud, 1999). A common federal structure is reflected by corporate IT managers controlling infrastructure decisions and business unit managers controlling use of resources and project management. Another common federal structure highlights corporate IT control of infrastructure and shared control between corporate IT and business units of IT use and project management decisions.

CONTINGENCY APPROACH

The third perspective on the organizational design and structure of IT is based on organizational contingencies that impact the appropriateness of a given structure or design. This approach emphasizes the need to design the IT function such that the behaviors of IT employees and managers are consistent with desired organizational outcomes for IT. Much attention has been given to describe the contingency factors that influence the structural choices related to IT. Some of the factors that have been identified in this literature stem from industry and corporate characteristics. Examples are environmental volatility, complexity, and munificence, as well as firm size, absorptive capacity, structure, and strategy.

Sambamurthy and Zmud (1999) highlight the fact that these contingency factors often create a complex set of competing demands on the design of IT. Some factors may exert force on managers to employ one IT structure, while another equally compelling factor may exert force to employ another structure. The extent to which a given contingency factor is important to the design of IT is often dependent on the individual circumstances of an organization. Therefore, business and IT executives must design and organize the IT function in a way that best fits the set of contingency factors most relevant for their organization.

When one particular contingency factor is the dominant force in determining the IT structure, then the structure tends to be either centralized or decentralized. For example, if the structure of the enterprise is the most compelling force driving the structure of IT and that structure is decentralized, then the IT function will be decentralized to correspond with the structure of the organization. When multiple factors are influential in shaping the structure of IT, and those factors reinforce one another in their influence, then the IT structure also tends to be centralized or decentralized. For example, if the organizational structure is decentralized and the business units within the firm are unrelated (a factor that tends to lead to decentralization of IT), then both contingency factors will reinforce each other and the eventual IT structure is likely to be decentralized. Finally, when multiple factors are influential in shaping the structure of IT, and those factors conflict in their influence, then the IT structure tends to be federal. For example, if the business units within the organization are related, but the organization is quite large (a contingency that

tends to lead to decentralization of IT), then the eventual IT structure is likely to be federal in response to the conflicting pressure exerted by the contingency factors.

Bibliography

Brown, C. V. and Magill, S. L. (1998). Reconceptualizing the context-design issue for the information systems function. *Organization Science: A Journal of the Institute of Management Sciences*, **9** (2), 176.
Sambamurthy, V. and Zmud, R. W. (1999). Arrangements for information technology governance: A theory of multiple contingencies. *MIS Quarterly*, **23** (2), 261.

output devices

H. Kevin Fulk and Dennis A. Adams

Output devices take processed data or information from the computer and convert it to a form that the user (human user or another computer application) can understand and use. Logically, output is the inverse of input, and both are required to integrate information systems into human systems. There are devices that perform both input and output. These are called secondary or external storage devices and telecommunications devices and, although vital to the effective use of the information system, they are considered separately from the output devices discussed here.

Computers interact with the outside world using devices called *ports*. A port is an electronic gateway through which signals pass to and from the computer to the user and the world outside. Output devices typically use either parallel or serial ports. A *parallel port* sends multiple bits of data from the computer to the output device, while the *serial port* sends only one bit at a time. There are several different standards for ports and, with the increasing need for more data and more sophisticated output devices, more are being developed.

Two popular communications standards that enable device communications through ports are uniform serial bus (USB) and firewire. Both of these standards allow devices to be "hot-swapped," i.e., plugged into the computer quickly and used without turning it off. USB-compliant ports are currently a ubiquitous feature of desktop and laptop computers. The attractive feature of firewire that is causing it to appear more frequently with USB is that it enables much faster inter-device communication. This feature makes it especially good for MULTIMEDIA applications. An emerging standard is USB 2.0, which offers comparable speeds to those of firewire. Choosing between the two standards is made simpler by the fact that output devices typically support one standard but not the other.

Output can be divided into two very general classes: hard copy and soft copy. Hard copy, usually printed material (text or graphics), is more tangible and permanent than soft copy, which is usually displayed on the monitor screen or heard and is not considered a permanent record.

There are two basic types of printers: impact and non-impact. As the name implies, impact printers operate by impacting, or physically striking, the paper. Impact printers have two advantages over non-impact printers. They are generally less expensive, and they can print on multicopy forms such as invoices, shipping labels, and receipts. However, their print quality is usually not as good as non-impact printers; they are generally slower and noisier. The advantages of non-impact printers mean that they have largely replaced impact printers. Non-impact printers use a variety of methods to print characters. The three most common types are thermal, ink-jet, and laser. Thermal printers share the same basic design concept as dot-matrix printers. They have a rectangular matrix filled with heated rods. As the ends of the selected rods touch the paper, they literally burn, or brand, a character into the paper. Early thermal printers required special heat-sensitive paper, but modern ones can use regular paper. As with dot-matrix printers, the more rods in the matrix, the higher the print quality.

Ink-jet printers use a nozzle to shoot a stream of extremely small droplets of ink through electrically charged plates. These plates arrange the ink particles into the required characters. The quality of ink-jet printers is usually superior to that of dot-matrix, daisy wheel, or thermal printers. Certain ink-jet printers can also print

in color (red, green, blue, and black ink is combined to create the desired color). Care must be taken when selecting paper to be used in ink-jet printers, however. A soft grade of paper may absorb the ink, resulting in fuzzy-looking print.

Laser printers use a beam of light focused through a rotating disk containing a character set. The laser beam, now shaped like a character, is projected on a photosensitive drum. Powdered ink (toner) is then fixed to the paper with heat. Laser printers are capable of higher print quality and faster speeds than other printers, but with higher cost. Laser printers can print in color as well as black.

Print quality is generally defined as either letter quality or near-letter quality. Letter quality is comparable to typewriter or published print. Near-letter quality is less sharp. Impact and thermal print is usually considered near-letter quality, although some dot-matrix printers with a high number of pins can approach letter quality. Most ink-jet and laser printers are letter quality. Another measure of print quality is the number of dots per inch (dpi). This comes from the number of pins per inch in a dot-matrix printer. Once again, the higher the number, the better the print quality. Letter-quality print is considered to begin at around 300 dpi. Higher dpi is required for high-quality reproduction.

Printer speed can be clocked two different ways. Dot-matrix and ink-jet printers, which print one character at a time, are measured in characters per second (cps). These printer speeds can range from approximately 50 cps to over 400 cps. Because laser printers use a drum that prints line by line, their speed is measured in pages per minute (ppm). Using general approximations, laser printers operate between 4 and 25 ppm. Most laser printers used with personal computers are capable of around 6 ppm. By contrast, most ink-jet printers are rated in the neighborhood of 3 ppm, and dot-matrix printers are about half as slow as ink-jet printers. These speeds are for printers generally used with microcomputers. There are large-scale commercial printers which can generate over 20,000 lines per minute, or approximately 400 ppm.

Newer technology has made it practical for computer users to "burn" a wide variety of disk-based digital media to create durable output. These allow the recording of information on CD-RWs (compact disks read and write) and DVDs (digital versatile disks). DVDs differ from CD-RWs in terms of how much they can store, with DVDs being capable of holding far more information (4.7 GB per DVD vs. 650 MB per CD-RW). Burners for these media are frequently a part of the standard equipment of desktop and laptop computers today (*see* CD-ROM AND DVD).

Monitors, sometimes called video display terminals (VDT) or cathode ray tubes (CRT), are devices that display output on a video screen, similar to a television. Like a television, a monitor uses an electron gun to shoot a beam of electrons onto the inside, or backside, of a specially coated piece of glass. When the coating (phosphor) is struck by the electrons, it glows. The coating is organized into tiny dots, called picture elements, often called pixels. Since this glow quickly fades it must be refreshed, or restruck, by the electron stream. The refresh rate is measured in hertz (Hz) or cycles per second. If the refresh rate is too slow the screen will appear to flicker, which can lead to eyestrain and headaches. To avoid this, most monitors have a refresh rate of at least 60 Hz. Another technique used to reduce or eliminate flicker is by non-interlacing the screen. Televisions refresh every other row of pixels on each pass of the electron gun. Non-interlaced (NI) monitors refresh every row of pixels on every pass of the gun. This requires more processing capability, but has become the de facto standard for monitors.

Monitor resolution, or sharpness, is primarily determined by the distance between pixels (dot pitch, or dp). The lower the dp, the better the resolution. Dot pitch is expressed in millimeters and is usually around 0.28 mm. The number of pixels on the screen can also be an indicator of resolution. The more pixels, the better the resolution, all other things being equal. The number of pixels is usually shown by expressing the number of pixels per row, and the number of rows (e.g., 1024 × 768, or 1024 pixels per row, and 768 rows). Monitor size usually refers to its diagonal measurement with 14 inches being the generally accepted standard, although the number of readily available and comparably priced 15-inch and larger monitors is increasing.

Monitors come in black and white (monochrome) or color, although monochrome monitors are slowly disappearing. Monitors typically display 80 columns and 24 lines of text data.

One disadvantage of VDT or CRT monitors is their size and weight. This makes them impractical for portable or laptop computers. These PCs use flat-panel monitors. The most common type of flat-panel display is the liquid crystal display (LCD). This is the same technology used in some digital watches and calculators. There are three types of LCD monitors: passive matrix, dual-scan matrix, and active matrix. The basic difference between the three is the number of times the screen is refreshed and the size and shape of the matrix elements. Active matrix has the highest refresh rate and uses matrix elements that generate sharp, clear images that can be seen from almost any orientation of the screen. Passive and dual-scan matrix screens are more difficult to read.

Plotters are often used when a hard copy of a graphic image is required. Charts, blueprints, maps, and drawings are some of the items a plotter can produce. Plotters use multicolored pens, ink jets, or lasers to draw, rather than print, graphic images. They are slower than printers, but capable of much more detail. While laser and ink-jet printers have all but replaced smaller plotters, large plotters are still required to create large documents such as maps and schematic drawings.

There are several assistive output devices that enable handicapped users to use computers. Such a specialized printing device is a Brailler, which produces output in Braille format for the visually impaired. Voice synthesizers, or voice response units, convert digital output into versions of the spoken word. Output can be either mechanically synthesized or actual human speech that has been prerecorded and stored. Telephone information systems are one example of voice response units. Another is speech output devices for the voiceless or visually impaired.

Computer output microfilm (COM) is used to reduce images of hard copies to microfilm or microfiche. This reduces the amount of space needed to store documents, and is commonly used in the insurance and banking industries.

However, this is a mature technology and is gradually giving way to optical disk technology.

Output devices can also extend beyond the printer and monitor into the 3D world. Drilling, milling, and machining devices associated with computer-aided design and computer-aided manufacturing (CAD/CAM) can convert data into finished or semi-finished products. Virtual reality (VR) systems use output devices such as head-mounted displays, large projection screens, and headphones or speakers to enhance simulations.

As more and more emphasis is placed on using computers in our work and leisure activities, users will demand more natural means for interacting with these devices. Effective input and output devices are essential elements of information systems today and in the future.

Bibliography

Huber, J. (2003). Ask Mr. Technology. *Library Media Connection*, April/May, 51.

McEvoy, A. (2004). Walk on the wireless side. *PC World*, June, 140–2.

Metz, C. (2003). The great interface-off. *PC Magazine*, February 25, 100–5.

Reuters (2003). Tablet PCs finally taking off. *Wired News*, September 28; www.wired.com/news/print/0,1294, 60623,00.html, accessed June 25, 2004.

Thompson, R. B. and Thompson, B. F. (2002). *PC Hardware: In a Nutshell*. Sebastopol, CA: O'Reilly and Associates.

outsourcing

see INTER-ORGANIZATIONAL SYSTEMS; IT OUTSOURCING

P

personalization technologies

Gediminas Adomavicius

Users of computer applications differ in their requirements for services and responses. Personalization technologies are computer-based methods for personalizing user interactions with computer applications. Personalization is vital in E-COMMERCE applications, but it may be useful across a broad range of applications. The personalization process *tailors certain offerings* (e.g., content, services, product recommendations, communications, and e-commerce interactions) by *providers* (e.g., e-commerce websites) to the *consumers* of these offerings (e.g., customers, visitors, users, etc.) based on *knowledge about them* with certain *goal(s)* in mind.

Personalization takes place between one or several providers of personalized offerings and one or several consumers of these offerings, such as customers, users, and website visitors. Personalized offerings can be delivered from providers to consumers by computer programs called *personalization engines* in several different ways. These can be classified as provider-centric, consumer-centric, and market-centric approaches. The most common approach to personalization, as popularized by Amazon.com, is the provider-centric approach, where each provider has its own personalization engine that tailors the provider's content to its consumers.

Alternatively, the *consumer-centric* approach assumes that each consumer has its own personalization engine (or agent) that "understands" this particular consumer and provides personalization services from several providers based on this knowledge. This type of consumer-centric personalization delivered across a broad range of providers and offerings is sometimes called an *e-Butler* service (Adomavicius and Tuzhilin, 2002). Rudimentary e-Butler services are provided by such websites as Claria.com (formerly Gator.com) and MyGeek.com.

The *market-centric* approach provides personalization services for all participants of a specific marketplace in a certain industry or sector. In this case, the personalization engine performs the role of an *infomediary* (Grover and Teng, 2001) by knowing the needs of the consumers *and* the providers' offerings and trying to match the two parties in the best ways according to their internal goals. While this approach has not been extensively used before, it has a high potential, especially because of the proliferation of electronic marketplaces such as Covisint (www.covisint.com) for the automobile industry.

Although the above three approaches to personalization are general enough to be deployed in either online or offline personalization applications, in practice they are mainly applicable to the online computer applications. This is the case because personalization technologies in general are very information-intensive, i.e., they require rapid collection and processing of large volumes of data about the consumers, providers, and the market, as well as rapid responses to the results of the data analysis.

The result of personalization is the delivery of various *offerings* to consumers by the personalization engine(s) on behalf of the providers. Examples of the personalized offerings include:

- personalized content, such as personalized web pages and links;
- product and service recommendations, e.g., for books, CDs, and vacations;
- personalized EMAIL;

- personalized information searches;
- personalized (dynamic) prices;
- personalized products for individual consumers, such as custom-made CDs.

The objectives of personalization range from simply improving the consumer's browsing and shopping experience (e.g., by presenting only the content that is relevant to the consumer) to much more complex objectives, such as building long-term relationships with consumers, improving consumer loyalty, and generating a measurable value for the company. Successful personalization depends to a very large extent on the *knowledge* about personal preferences and behavior of the consumers that is usually distilled from the large volumes of granular information about the consumers and stored in *consumer profiles*.

An important aspect of personalization is that it constitutes an *iterative process* that can be defined by the *understand-deliver-measure* cycle:

- *Understand* consumers by collecting comprehensive information about them and converting it into actionable knowledge stored in consumer profiles. The data about consumers can be collected from multiple channels (e.g., over the web, phone, direct mail, etc.) in order to obtain the most comprehensive "picture" of a consumer. Such data can be solicited explicitly (e.g., via surveys) or tracked implicitly and may include histories of consumers' purchasing and online searching activities, as well as demographic and psychographic information. After the data are collected, they are usually processed, cleaned, and stored in a consumer-oriented data warehouse (*see* DATA WAREHOUSING), where various statistical, DATA MINING, and machine-learning techniques are used to analyze the data and build consumer profiles.
- *Deliver* personalized offering based on the knowledge about each consumer, as stored in the consumer profiles. The personalization engine must be able to find the most relevant offerings and deliver them to the consumer. Therefore, different delivery and presentation methods depend significantly on the quality of the underlying matchmaking technologies. Such technolo-

gies include rule-based matchmaking, statistics-based predictive approaches, and, most recently, recommender systems, which represent the most developed matchmaking technologies applicable to various types of personalized offerings (Balabanovic and Shoham, 1997; Pazzani, 1999; Schafer, Konstan, and Riedl, 2001). These technologies are based on a broad range of different approaches and feature a variety of methods from such disciplines as statistics, data mining, machine learning and information retrieval. After the most relevant offerings are found using matchmaking technologies, the personalized information can be delivered to consumers in several ways, including a narrative, a list ordered by relevance, an unordered list of alternatives, or various types of visualization. One classification of delivery methods is *pull*, *push*, and *passive* (Schafer et al., 2001). Push methods reach a consumer who is not currently interacting with the system, e.g., by sending an email message. Pull methods notify consumers that personalized information is available but display this information only when the consumer explicitly requests it. Passive delivery displays personalized information as a by-product of other activities of the consumer. For example, while looking at a product on a website, a consumer also sees recommendations for related products.

- *Measure* personalization impact by determining how much the consumer is satisfied with the delivered personalized offerings. It provides information that can enhance understanding of consumers or point out the deficiencies of the methods for personalized delivery. Therefore, this additional information serves as a *feedback* for possible improvements to each of the other components of the personalization process. This feedback information completes one cycle of the personalization process and sets the stage for the next cycle where improved personalization techniques can make better personalization decisions. Metrics for measuring personalization impact can range from *accuracy* metrics measuring how the consumer liked a specific personalized offering, e.g., how accurate the recommendation was, to more comprehensive metrics, such as consumer lifetime value, loyalty value, purchasing and consumption experience, and other ROI-based metrics that evaluate more general aspects of personalization effectiveness.

Bibliography

Adomavicius, G. and Tuzhilin, A. (2002). e-Butler: An architecture of a customer-centric personalization system. *International Journal of Computational Intelligence and Applications*, **2** (3), 313–27.

Balabanovic, M. and Shoham, Y. (1997). Fab: Content-based, collaborative recommendation. *Communications of the ACM*, **40** (3), 66–72.

Grover, V. and Teng, J. (2001). E-commerce and the information market. *Communications of the ACM*, **44** (4).

Pazzani, M. (1999). A framework for collaborative, content-based and demographic filtering. *Artificial Intelligence Review*, **13** (5/6), 393–408.

Schafer, J. B., Konstan, J. A., and Riedl, J. (2001). E-commerce recommendation applications. *Data Mining and Knowledge Discovery*, **5** (1–2), 115–53.

phishing

A message sent by EMAIL that is fishing for confidential information. The message appears to be from a bank, financial institution, or other trusted institution. However, it is from a sender intent on obtaining private information useful in conducting fraudulent transactions. For example, the email may have the logo of the recipient's bank and ask the person to access a website and provide confidential information in order to verify that the person's account is safe. The confidential information such as account number and PIN are then used by the senders of the phishing message. A recipient should never respond to phishing messages but should contact the institution that supposedly sent the message.

planning for information systems

William R. King

Information systems (IS) planning is an organizational administrative process that involves the consideration of alternative methods for employing information, computing, and communications resources in furtherance of the organization's objectives and its overall "business" strategy. IS planning takes place at a number of different levels in the organization. At the highest level of strategic IS planning, the relationship between the organization's objectives and strategy and its IS resources is articulated. At a much lower level, IS project planning involves the specification of the activities, resources, and relationships that will be required to develop a new computer system, install and implement new hardware and software, or perform any other complex task involving computer resources.

STRATEGIC IS PLANNING

Strategic IS planning is the core of IS planning since it directly involves the translation of organizational objectives and strategy into data, applications, technology, and communications architectures that can best support the implementation of that strategy and the achievement of the organization's overall objectives. It also involves the assessment of the "product market" opportunities that may be supported by existing and planned information resources (i.e., identifying whether the organization's information resources and competences may suggest opportunities for it to carry on its activities in ways that may make it more competitive in the market).

Figure 1 shows these two major elements of strategic IS planning in terms of two arrows that connect an "organizational strategy set" and an "information resources strategy set." The former represents the organizational mission, objectives, and strategies that have been developed through a strategic "business" planning process. The right-facing arrow shows that the information resources strategy set (composed of the information resources strategy and information infrastructure) is derived from the organizational strategy set. The left-facing arrow describes the assessment of information resources that may be conducted to identify important changes in the organizational strategy set.

EVOLUTION OF IS PLANNING

Tracing the development of IS planning can serve to describe its various levels, since the

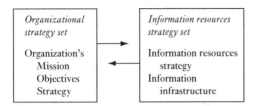

Figure 1 Strategic IS planning

forms of IS planning that represented its highest and most sophisticated level in past eras are still conducted today. Higher (more strategic) levels of planning have been added to the previously existing planning activities in each era as the IS planning field has evolved. This approach also offers the opportunity of identifying the underlying concepts and techniques associated with each planning paradigm.

The pre-strategic planning era.   In the early computer era, the most sophisticated level of IS planning involved assessing the future computing needs of the enterprise and insuring that adequate and appropriate computing capacity was available to fulfill those needs. An associated planning task was that of evaluating and selecting the applications and systems development projects that would be funded and implemented by the enterprise. At the project level, project plans were developed to insure that appropriate milestones were identified and that specific activities and tasks were assigned to appropriate IS professionals.

The systems development life cycle (SDLC) was the primary conceptual basis for planning in this era. The SDLC for information systems evolved from the basic SDLC for complex systems. The SDLC postulated that the development of all complex systems naturally evolved through a sequential series of phases that were most appropriately managed in different ways, and which demanded different mixes of resources to complete effectively and efficiently. An extremely simplified version of the SDLC is shown at the center of figure 2 where it is labeled "traditional SDLC."

In this era, the multiproject levels of planning (capacity planning and project selection and evaluation) were based on the concepts of forecasting and project selection, respectively. Capacity planning involved the forecasting of computing requirements and planning for the acquisition, installation, and testing of new generations of hardware and software. Project evaluation and selection were conceptually based on the project selection methodologies that had largely been previously developed and used in the research and development (R&D) context.

Because "cost avoidance" was the major criterion for project evaluation in this pre-strategic era, this project selection procedure was relatively straightforward, primarily involving the estimation of the costs that could be avoided if manual systems were to be automated. This criterion usually resulted in the approval of projects that were at the operational or operational control levels. Those projects that substituted computer systems for human operatives or those that measured and controlled the performance levels of operations were accepted as being cost effective. Projects whose rationale depended on the sometimes intangible benefits that they might produce were difficult to justify because of the emphasis on the cost-avoidance criterion and the relatively greater ease of forecasting costs versus benefits.

The highest-level plan that came into being in some organizations during the latter part of this pre-strategic era was the "IS master plan." This plan demonstrated the intended relationships among the various systems and subsystems that the organization operated or planned to develop. The need for a master plan was recognized by organizations that had developed independent and incompatible systems. While such systems may well have been individually effective to operate, they could not be readily integrated to provide information that might be of use to higher-level management. Illustrative of this situation were the many banks that had developed expensive and operationally effective product-oriented computer systems. Their checking account systems, loan systems, and trust systems, for example, had databases that were not readily cross-referenced to enable a marketing manager to readily determine which of the bank's many products and services were utilized by a given customer. The master plan was intended to insure systems integration. The adoption of this notion was the precursor to the IS strategic planning era.

The early strategic IS planning era. The simple idea of deriving the IS strategy directly from the overall organizational strategy, and thereby of developing the IS resources that best supported the organization's strategy, had profound effect on IS planning and on IS development activities (King and Cleland, 1975; King, 1978). When IBM incorporated the notion into this widely known business systems planning (BSP) methodology, strategic IS planning came into widespread use (IBM, 1981).

This expanded domain for IS necessitated a change from the simple, cost-avoidance IS project selection criterion that had been in common use to more sophisticated criteria that gave greater consideration of the potential benefits that might result from an IS project. Because cost remained a necessary consideration and benefits were often intangible and difficult to quantify, the net result was a multidimensional criterion that was conceptually similar to those that had been in use in R&D project selection for some time.

For the first time in the history of many firms, IS applications whose benefits were intangible, and/or more difficult to forecast than was cost avoidance, came to be given higher priority. The result was that top managers developed a greater appreciation of the IS function as a potential contributor to business value rather than viewing IS merely as a service function.

The expanded planning horizons of IS and the emphasis on assessing and evaluating systems in more sophisticated ways have been conceptualized in terms of the expanded life cycle shown in figure 2 (King and Srinivasan, 1983). Figure 2 shows a simplified version of the "traditional SDLC" embedded in a broader life cycle that also includes strategic planning, systems integration planning, evaluation, and divestment phases. These phases serve to extend the traditional SDLC, which applies to a single system, to a broader organizational context. The systems integration planning phase primarily involves the sort of systems integration functions that are implicit in the earlier notion of a "master plan." The strategic planning phase involves the development of an IS strategy that is derived from, and which directly supports, the business strategy.

In figure 2, the two phases that are shown to begin after the traditional SDLC – evaluation and divestment – reflect the growing attention that has come to be paid to the formal evaluation of systems and the need to phase out systems. In the evaluation phase, other measures, such as user satisfaction and business value assessments, are commonly used to complement traditional cost, time, and technical performance measures. These two phases further recognize that an IS, like any complex system, has a finite useful life. These phases reflect the need not only to evaluate systems, but *to plan for the shutdown, replacement, and phasing out of systems*. In the earlier eras of IS planning, little attention was given to divestment, leading many firms to make the implicit assumption that systems would function forever. This assumption inevitably leads to decisions concerning systems maintenance, updating, and modification that might be significantly different from what they would be under the assumption of a finite useful lifespan for a system.

The era of strategic planning for information resources. In the 1980s and 1990s, the initial notion of strategic IS planning was expanded to include the idea described by the left-facing arrow in figure 1. This involved the recognition that information resources could become a basis

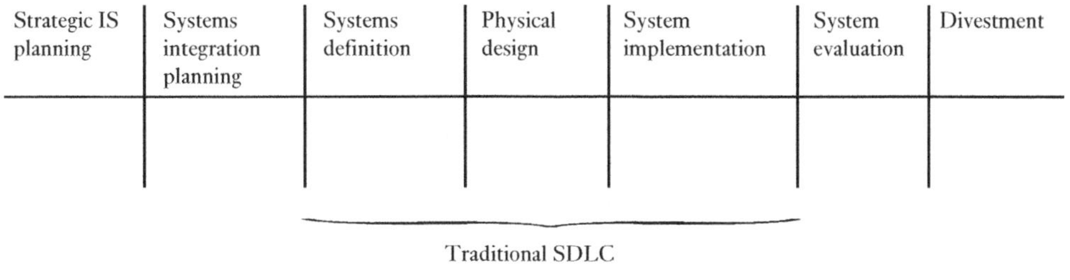

Strategic IS planning	Systems integration planning	Systems definition	Physical design	System implementation	System evaluation	Divestment

Traditional SDLC

Figure 2   Expanded systems development life cycle

for new organizational strategy as well as being supportive of existing organizational strategy. This idea, enunciated by King and Zmud (1981), has come to be a basic concept of the IS field.

The systems that have been developed as a result of the planning process described by the left-facing arrow in figure 1 are variously described as "strategic systems" and "competitive weapons" (i.e., systems that impact the "product market" strategies of organizations). Among such systems are Merrill Lynch's Cash Management Account (CMA), a "product" whose core technology is information processing, and American and United Airlines' reservation systems, which have been employed to achieve competitive advantages in the market rather than serving merely for transaction processing.

This new view of "information resources," as contrasted with "information systems," reflects both the greater organizational importance of computer-related entities and the rapid development of a wide variety of useful communications and information technologies that greatly transcend the traditional computer hardware and software dimensions of IS. LOCAL AREA NETWORKS (LANs), wide area networks (WANs), database management systems (see DATABASE MANAGEMENT SYSTEM), word and document processing, EXPERT SYSTEMS, and many other technology-based entities are now physically and/or conceptually integrated into an overall set of information resources that must be jointly planned for and managed. Moreover, in the modern information era, the important role of data *per se*, without regard to the technology that is used to collect, process, and disseminate data, has also increasingly been recognized. An organization can utilize these entities much as it has traditionally employed its human, financial, and physical resources to create business value.

The evolution of the criteria used to evaluate and select systems has moved toward a focus on "sustainable competitive advantage" in the era of strategic systems. Systems that have the potential to produce an identifiable advantage over competition, sustainable over time, are those that will be given highest priority (e.g., Sethi and King, 1994). Systems that promise cost avoidance or temporary competitive advantage will generally be less highly valued (unless, of course, in the former case, cost leadership is a strategy that is intended to produce an advantage in the market).

CURRENT TRENDS IN IS PLANNING

The modern era. The current era of IS planning involves the continuing evolution of two key trends as well as some important new foci of interest. The two key trends are: (1) the integration of IS planning into overall organizational planning, and (2) the integration of planning for various communications and information technologies.

New areas of opportunity for IS have also come into play that place substantial requirements on IS planning: ERP systems (*see* ENTERPRISE SYSTEMS (ENTERPRISE RESOURCE PLANNING OR ERP)), KNOWLEDGE MANAGEMENT SYSTEMS (KMSs), business processes reengineering (BPR) applications and support, and E-COMMERCE systems (*see* E-COMMERCE BUSINESS-TO-BUSINESS SYSTEMS). Each of these systems is sufficiently complex, costly, and important to warrant major attention in the IS planning of the firm.

Integration of IS planning and organizational planning. The recognition of strategic planning for information resources as a "free-standing" administrative activity may be beginning to reach the limits of its value. With the emerging view of information resources as one of the important kinds of resources that a general manager can employ to achieve organizational objectives, many organizations have embarked on the integration of IS planning with overall strategic "business" planning processes. Although this trend is not universal, it is clearly identifiable and, if successful, will undoubtedly become a major theme of future developments in the area.

When strategic planning for information resources becomes a process conducted under the aegis of the organization's general manager with the heavy involvement of non-IS personnel, it will have emulated the evolution of IS from a backroom technical service function to one that is critical to the organization.

Integration of communications and information technology planning. At the same time as IS planning is being integrated into overall organizational planning, its scope is being expanded because of the physical and conceptual integration of technologies. As ELECTRONIC DATA INTERCHANGE (EDI), telecommunications systems, the INTERNET, and a wide variety of other technologies become more integrated, and as the requirements for organizations to employ these various technologies in an integrated manner become clear, information resources planning has expanded to address a broad range of communications and information systems and technologies.

Planning for ERP systems. ERP systems have the capability of integrating all or most functions of an enterprise – e.g., accounting, human resources, marketing, input logistics, project management. The focus of such systems is usually on cross-functional business processes such as order fulfillment or product development.

ERP systems are widely deployed in business, but they are often "a work-in-progress." The magnitude of the effort required to choose a vendor-supplied system and then customize it (which is the way that nearly all such systems are implemented) is so great that it requires "selling" the concept to top management, feasibility studies, data standardization, software selection, process reengineering, and implementation planning.

The nature of an ERP project is so large and risky that it requires sophisticated project planning. However, since it involves all aspects of the enterprise, it also requires strategic planning.

Planning for KMSs. Knowledge management systems are those which seek to collect, store, and disseminate an organization's knowledge very much as information systems operate vis-à-vis information. Such systems are difficult and often time consuming to develop. They are so popular that a number of vendors offer systems that are labeled KMS; however, unlike vendor-supplied ERP systems, they are often not sufficient to allow an organization to begin with a vendor-supplied system and then customize it. Thus, many KMSs are developed in-house.

KMSs are of such great potential and fundamental importance that they require sophisticated project planning. In organizations that are making a serious attempt to become "knowledge based," strategic planning is also required.

Planning for BPR. The redesign of business processes has become a major organizational activity that usually has a high information systems and technology content. Information systems often are incorporated into newly designed business processes that are employed to enable process redesign. As such, BPR projects must be designed, selected, and implemented just as any other IS project. Since BPR is potentially of great strategic importance to the enterprise, in some organizations BPR planning is treated as an element of strategic IS planning.

Planning for e-commerce systems. Electronic commerce is an important innovation of the late twentieth century. Virtually all organizations engage in some form of e-commerce, even if it is only displaying products on a webpage. Some businesses are strictly e-commerce-based in that they offer products, receive orders and payment, and direct others, who maintain inventories, to make shipments and handle post-sales contacts such as warranty fulfillment. Most firms are "in between" these two extremes, but many firms see e-commerce as a necessary, ever-increasing, and ever more important aspect of their business.

E-commerce is not restricted to operations and marketing. It can also include "inbound" activities such as the purchase of raw materials or other inputs on electronic auctions (*see* INTERNET AUCTIONS) or the sharing of information with suppliers so that deliveries can be scheduled and coordinated.

E-commerce systems are closely related to ERP systems since they complement the internal focus of ERP with the external focus on supplies, sales, and post-sale relationships. CUSTOMER RELATIONSHIP MANAGEMENT (CRM) systems are traditionally offered in both "free-standing" modes and in forms that are integral parts of e-commerce and/or ERP systems. As such, these systems are of strategic significance and require both project-level and strategic planning.

CONCLUSION

Planning for information resources has become a complex and sophisticated administrative process. Its increasing integration into overall organizational strategic planning processes parallels the increasing regard of information resources as one of the most important varieties of resources that are at the disposal of managers in the pursuit of their organizational objectives. This development vividly contrasts with earlier eras when computer systems were backroom service functions of relatively limited importance to business and when information systems planning was a straightforward capacity- and requirements-driven process.

The increasingly important and visible role of the IS function and of communications and information resources represents both opportunity and challenge for the field. In earlier eras, failures of computer systems to perform in the manner that was expected were often not of enormous significance to overall organizational performance. Therefore, IS planning was not usually instrumental in determining long-run overall organizational success. Now, in many organizations, success is primarily based on the ability to develop and exploit information resources. In the future, such situations are likely to proliferate, as are situations in which the decline and fall of organizations can be explained by their failure to do so. In such an environment, IS planning is of fundamental importance.

Bibliography

IBM (1981). *Business Systems Planning: Information Systems Planning Guide*. IBM.

King, W. R. (1978). Strategic planning for management information systems. *MIS Quarterly*, **2** (1), 27–37.

King, W. R. and Cleland, D. I. (1975). A new method for strategic systems planning. *Business Horizons*, **18** (4), 55–64.

King, W. R. and Srinivasan, A. (1983). Decision support systems: Planning, development and evaluation. In R. Schultz (ed.), *Applications of Management Science*, vol. 3. Greenwich, CT: JAI Press.

King, W. R. and Zmud, R. (1981). Managing information systems: Policy planning, strategic planning and operational planning. *Proceedings of the Second International Conference on Information Systems*. Boston, December.

Sethi, V. and King, W. R. (1994). Development of measures to assess the extent to which an information technology application provides competitive advantage. *Management Science*, **40** (12), 1601–27.

portable data format (PDF)

A format for transmitting documents that preserves the format and layout as prepared by the author. The document can be sent to different computer systems and looks and feels the same with color and graphics intact. A suite of programs available from Adobe Systems, Inc. is used for creating and distributing the PDF documents. The software to read a PDF format is available over the INTERNET without cost from Adobe Systems, Inc.

portal

Gordon B. Davis

A term applied to a website that offers access to an array of services. The portal can provide access to a set of general services covering a broad range of topics and resources, provide a set of services for a given topic or subject, or provide services relative to an organization. Portals may be organized around the capabilities of a search engine, or a search engine may be included within a portal to search within the domain of the portal itself. An example of a general purpose portal is an online service such as Yahoo! and AOL that provides access to news, entertainment, stock quotes, forums, chat groups, a search engine, and so forth. An example of a specialized portal is a site that provides access to sites associated with a topic such as books. An example of an organization portal is a website that provides access to the individual departments and services of an organization both by a directory and by an internal search engine for finding individuals, services, and documents in that organization. A portal may be open to any user of the INTERNET or it may be restricted to internal personnel, customers, clients, subscribers, etc.

The information systems function in an organization may provide an INTRANET portal for internal access to the organization or an Internet portal for customers, vendors, suppliers, potential employees, etc.

privacy in information systems

Gordon C. Everest

Privacy is the freedom from unwarranted intrusion upon oneself, into one's private affairs, home, family, and relationships. Parts of the description of privacy in information systems are adapted from Everest (1986). Privacy as a separate right was first enunciated eloquently and profoundly in a paper by Warren and Brandeis (1890) as "the right to be let alone." (Note: it was not based on a legal court decision.) The common law right of privacy extends to the person (physically and psychically) and the space (territory and property) around the person. The fourth amendment to the US constitution speaks about the "right of the people to be secure in their persons, houses, papers, and effects." It is interesting that the legal community has defined a tort for each of three of these (assault, trespass, and theft), but none for "papers." We can only speculate why the authors differentiated papers from effects (possessions). Perhaps they really intended to mean the information on the papers, rather than the physical papers themselves!

Data privacy (sometimes called information privacy) extends the right of privacy from individuals to *data about* individuals. It derives from the assumption that all information about a person *belongs*, in a fundamental way, to that person, *regardless of who possesses that information*. Personal data become the surrogate for the individual. It is increasingly common for organizations to make decisions affecting individuals by looking only at data about the individual, having no interview or personal contact with that person. When was the last time you were offered a credit card that required a personal interview? Note that the notion of privacy does not encompass data about organizations, businesses, or governments. In the case of organizations, the equivalent notion considers the information to be confidential, classified, or secret.

Misuse or abuse of personal data can violate the privacy rights of individuals. In the latter third of the twentieth century, public concern grew as individuals found themselves unable to control the dissemination and use of information about themselves. Problems encountered include:

- denial of access to data pertaining to oneself;
- inability to discover the sources of adverse data;
- intrusive data collection practices;

- inability to have data corrected;
- continued dissemination of incomplete, old, or erroneous data;
- use of data for secondary purposes without one's knowledge or consent;
- inability to exercise control over disclosure of personal data to third parties.

These problems were further exacerbated and magnified through the use of computer technology and information systems.

Growing public concern led to the emergence of laws to protect individual rights and to circumscribe the behavior of organizations and government agencies that collect personal data. The Data Protection Act (1970) in the state of Hesse, West Germany, was the world's first law to specifically regulate governmental automated data systems. The next few years saw legal activity and laws passed in the US, UK, Canada, Sweden, France, Austria, Norway, Switzerland, and Australia, as well as multinational organizations such as the United Nations, OECD (1980), and the European Union (EU). Minnesota was the first state in the US to pass a comprehensive, omnibus (covered all types of personal data), public sector (only pertained to government-held personal data), data privacy law (1974).

The main purpose and rationale behind data privacy laws was to establish the basis for an open, honest, and fair relationship between organizations and individuals on whom data are collected, maintained, and used. These laws attempt to articulate three basic rights:

- *Personal privacy*: the right to determine what information about oneself to share with other persons and for what purposes, i.e., control over secondary disclosures.
- *Personal access and due process*: the right of an individual:
  - to know that his/her personal data have been or will be collected;
  - to know (and have interpreted) the contents of his/her data record;
  - to dispute those data and have them amended if they are inaccurate or incomplete; and
  - to know the sources and disclosures of one's personal data.

Due process affords protection against arbitrary and unfair procedures in judicial or administrative proceedings which could affect the personal and property rights of an individual. Due process begins with notice, i.e., being told the rules of the game in advance, or that something exists or has happened.

- *Public access*: the right of individuals to know what their government is doing. A strong democratic society depends upon the free flow of truthful information. This right is generally embodied in freedom of the press and freedom of information laws (FOIA in the US).

With this broader scope, such laws were more correctly referred to as "codes of fair data (or information) practices."

Before data privacy laws, or fair data practices acts, things were black or white in the legal community – disclosure was all or nothing (wholly public or wholly private). If private information was revealed to *anyone*, then it automatically became public – there was no middle ground. Limiting data collection is one solution. However, there may be legitimate needs for personal data to be collected. These new laws introduce the notion of *limited or selective disclosure* – to authorized persons, for authorized purposes. When an individual shares information with an organization, there is an implicit contract for how those data will be used and what benefits will flow back to the individual. Uses beyond that contract are *secondary uses* and require the permission of the individual; at the very least, the individual should have advance notice that such secondary uses are about to take place. For example, when you obtain a license to use a boat on the public waterways, you don't expect to receive spam mail offering to sell you marine insurance, because the government licensing agency sold its address list of licensed boats. At the very least, you need to have notice of such a secondary disclosure and have the opportunity to opt out.

None of these rights is absolute. There is an inherent conflict between privacy and access. For example, the writers of a letter of recommendation for a job applicant often expect their anonymity (privacy) to be maintained. However, the applicants also have a right to know what is being written about them, in case it is untrue. At the least, they have a right to know what is said about them and an opportunity to dispute it if they feel it is inaccurate or incomplete. Similarly with caller ID on telephones. One can argue that the caller has a right to remain anonymous and that the recipient has a right to know who is calling. It generally takes some time to develop appropriate protocols in such situations and to reach a balance of competing rights. When organizational information systems are involved, these same principles must be considered.

Fair Information Practices

Starting with the recommendations in a 1973 report from the US Department of Health, Education, and Welfare (Ware et al., 1973), followed by the reports of various commissions and research studies, a code of fair data practices has evolved to guide the development of laws and the data practices of organizations and governments.

- There shall be no personal data record-keeping systems whose very existence is secret.
- Limit personal data collection.
- Individuals have the right to know whether or not data on them have been collected, what that information is and what it means, how it is used and for what purpose, and by whom it is used.
- An individual should have notice and control over secondary disclosures.
- There must be a way for persons to correct or amend a record of identifiable information about themselves.
- Any organization creating, maintaining, using, or disseminating records of identifiable personal data must assure the reliability of the data for their intended use and must take precautions to prevent misuse of the data.

The fair code approach to developing legislation attempts to embody these principles in the law. It spells out the rights of data subjects, the responsibilities of organizations that handle personal data, and the mechanisms for carrying out the law.

An examination of various approaches reveals some important distinctions in terms of the scope of fair information legislation:

- Cover only computerized data vs. all forms of personal data.
- Cover organizations (legal "persons") as well as individuals (natural persons).
- Cover both public sector and private sector organizations.

ORGANIZATIONAL RESPONSE TO DATA PRIVACY CONCERNS AND LAWS

Data privacy and fair information practices are a significant and growing issue for information systems managers. As corporations find their data management activities receiving more scrutiny, they need to assess the risks: of legal liability, adverse reactions from the public, and the impact on their customers, employees, and shareholders. Information systems managers must be accountable to their organizations, and take steps to be responsive to provisions in the laws under which they operate and to embrace the principles of fair information practices.

Responsibilities of organizations handling personal data include:

- Limit data collection to specific needs or requirements, and avoid intrusive, deceptive, or unrestrained data collection practices.
- Give notice of intended uses or disclosures (what and to whom) when data are initially collected from the individual, and explain the consequences of refusal to provide the information.
- Maintain data quality.
- Control disclosure of private data to authorized individuals for authorized purposes. This requires appropriate access control mechanisms (identification, AUTHENTICATION, and authorization), ENCRYPTION mechanisms, and monitoring.
- Keep an audit trail of sources and disclosures.
- Retire data when no longer pertinent or timely to the purpose(s) for which they were collected and stored.

LEGISLATIVE APPROACHES TO FAIR INFORMATION PRACTICES AND REGULATION

Many different models of privacy regulation exist around the world. While overall legislative activity regarding information privacy is flourishing internationally, no single, standard policy regarding privacy issues has emerged. As described in Milberg et al. (1995), the predominant models appear to be those represented in figure 1. The models vary significantly in terms of governmental involvement in day-to-day corporate operations. At the low government involvement side (left end) of the continuum, the government assumes a "hands-off" role and allows corporations to monitor themselves, with reliance on injured individuals to pursue their own remedies in the court system. At the high government involvement side (right end) of the continuum, the government assumes authority to license and regulate all corporate uses of personal data, including the right to conduct inspections inside corporations and to examine all proposed applications of personal data before they are implemented.

The models can be described as follows:

1 *The self-help model* depends on data subjects challenging inappropriate record-keeping practices. Rights of access and correction are provided for the subjects, but data subjects are responsible for identifying problems and bringing them to the courts for resolution.

2 *The voluntary control model* relies on self-regulation on the part of corporate players. The law defines specific rules and requires that a "responsible person" in each organization insures compliance.

3 *The data commissioner model* utilizes neither licensing nor registration, but relies on the ombudsman concept through a commissioner's office. The commissioner has no powers of regulation but relies on complaints from citizens, which are investigated. The commissioner also is viewed as an expert who should offer advice on data handling; monitor technology and make proposals; and perform some inspections of data processing operations. This model relies to a great degree on the commissioner's credibility with legislature, press, and the public.

4 *The registration model* acts much like the licensing model with one exception: the governmental institution has no right to block the creation of a particular information system. Only in a case where complaints are

Figure 1 Regulation models: lower, medium, and higher refer to the level of government regulation in corporate privacy management (Milberg et al., 1995)

received and an investigation reveals a failure to adhere to data protection principles would a system be "deregistered." Thus, this model provides more remedial than anticipatory enforcement of principles.

5   *The licensing model* creates a requirement that each databank containing personal data be licensed (usually upon payment of a fee) by a separate government institution. This institution would stipulate specific conditions for the collection, storage, and use of personal data. This model anticipates potential problems and heads them off, by requiring a *prior* approval for any use of data.

The US is usually described as intermingling the self-help and voluntary control models. Germany is often viewed as a good example of the data commissioner model, the UK as the registration model, and Sweden as the licensing model. Some countries have no data protection laws at all (see Bennett, 1992; Madsen, 1992).

Bibliography

Bennett, C. J. (1992). *Regulating Privacy: Data Protection and Public Policy in Europe and the United States*. Ithaca, NY: Cornell University Press.

Everest, G. C. (1980). Non-uniform privacy laws: Implications and attempts at uniformity. In Lance J. Hoffman (ed.), *Computers and Privacy in the Next Decade*. New York: Academic Press, pp. 141–50.

Everest, G. C. (1986). Data privacy and fair information practices. In *Database Management: Objectives, System Functions, and Administration*. New York: McGraw-Hill, ch. 16.

Laudon, K. C. (1986). *Dossier Society: Value Choices in the Design of National Information Systems*. New York: Columbia University Press.

Madsen, W. (1992). *Handbook of Personal Data Protection*. New York: Macmillan.

Milberg, S. J., Burke, S. J., Smith, H. J., and Kallman, E. A. (1995). A cross-cultural study of relationships between values, personal information privacy concerns, and regulatory approaches. *Communications of the ACM*, **38** (12), 65–74.

Miller, A. R. (1971). *The Assault on Privacy: Computers, Databanks, and Dossiers*. Ann Arbor: University of Michigan Press.

Organization for Economic Cooperation and Development (OECD) (1980). *Recommendations of the Council Concerning Guidelines Governing the Protection of Privacy and Transborder Data Flows of Personal Data*. Paris: OECD, October.

Privacy Protection Study Commission (1977). David Linowes (chairman), *Personal Privacy in an Information Society*, final report. US Government Printing Office (Y3.P93/5), July.

Prosser, W. L. (1960). Privacy. *California Law Review*, **48**.

Smith, H. J. (1994). *Managing Privacy: Information Technology and Corporate America*. Chapel Hill: University of North Carolina Press.

Straub, D. W. and Collins, R. W. (1990). Key information liability issues facing managers: Software piracy, proprietary databases, and individual rights to privacy. *MIS Quarterly*, **14** (2), 43–6.

Ware, W. H. et al. (1973). *Records, Computers, and the Rights of Citizens*. Report of the Secretary's Advisory Committee on Automated Personal Data Systems, US Department of Health, Education, and Welfare, DHEW Publication No. (OS) 73–94, 1973 July.

Warren, S. C. and Brandeis, L. D. (1890). The right to privacy. *Harvard Law Review*, **4** (5), December 15.

Westin, A. F. (1967). *Privacy and Freedom*. New York: Athenaeum.

processing methods for information systems

Gordon B. Davis

Processing methods are generally associated with transaction processing. Transaction processing is a basic organization activity. Without transaction processing, business transactions would not be completed. Without it, bills would not be paid, sales orders would not be filled, manufacturing parts would not be ordered, and so on. Without it, data for management activities would not be available.

TRANSACTION PROCESSING CYCLE

The transaction processing cycle begins with a transaction that is recorded in some way. Although handwritten forms are still very common, transactions are often recorded directly to a computer by the use of an online terminal, desktop computer, or handheld device with communications capabilities. Recording of the transaction is generally the trigger to produce a transaction document or instructions that are displayed on a terminal, desktop computer, or handheld device. Data from the transaction are frequently required for the updating of master files; this updating may be performed concurrently with the processing of transaction documents or by a subsequent computer run.

The capturing of data on documents or by direct entry is a necessary first step preceding other activities in processing the transaction. For example, a sales order is manually prepared on a sales order form by a salesperson, a telephoned order is entered in a computer by a telephone salesperson, a cash withdrawal is entered in an automatic teller machine by the customer, and a reservation is entered by a travel agent using an online reservation terminal.

When a transaction is recorded manually, a copy of the document is usually used for data preparation. The transaction is keyed into a file using a terminal or data entry computer. The records of the transactions are used for processing. Many times, the documents involved are partially or completely coded. A bank check is precoded with the customer number and bank number; the amount of the check must be added. A turnaround document may be coded with much of the transaction data. An example is the part of the invoice returned with the payment; the turnaround portion may often be read with optical scanning.

Data validation is the testing of input data records to determine if they are correct and complete. This cannot be accomplished with complete assurance, but reasonable validation is usually possible. Validation tests applied against each data item or set of items may include tests for missing data, valid field size for each data item, numerical data class test, range or reasonableness test, valid or invalid values test, and comparison with stored data. Identification numbers and processing codes are very sensitive to errors. They can be validated for size, range, and composition of characters. An additional, very effective, validation technique for codes is a check digit. It is a redundant digit derived by computations on the identification number and then made a permanent part of the number. During data preparation and input validation, the check-digit derivation procedure is repeated. If the procedure performed during input results in a different check digit, there has been an error in recording or entering the identification number.

When input data items have been validated, the transactions are processed. Subsequently, two major activities occur during transaction processing: updating of machine-readable stored data (master file) related to or affected by the transaction, and preparation of outputs such as transaction instructions, documents, and reports. In these activities, control information is also produced.

Transaction data output can be classified as to its purpose. There are three major reasons for producing transaction documents or other transaction outputs: (1) informational to report, confirm, or explain proposed or completed action; (2) action to direct a transaction to take place or be completed; and (3) investigational for background information or reference by the recipient. Action documents include shipping orders, purchase orders, manufacturing orders, checks, and customer statements. These documents instruct someone to do something. For example, a purchase order instructs a vendor to ship, a check instructs a bank to pay, etc. When action is taken, the completed action (or lack of completion) is reported back to the organizational unit initiating the action. A sales order confirmation verifies receipt of an order. Lists of checks not paid by banks represent a confirmation of completed action (if not on list, checks have been paid) and lack of completed action (by being listed as unpaid). A single document or different copies of it may serve both action and informational purposes. For example, one copy of the sales order confirmation may be sent to the customer to confirm the order; a second copy may be used as an action document to initiate filling of the order.

Some transaction records are distributed to other departments in the organization to provide background information for recipients in the event that they need to respond to inquiries or need them for other reference. With online systems, a reference copy of the transaction can be stored in a computer file and may be retrieved via a terminal by anyone who is authorized and has need of the information. Transaction documents may also be used for managerial information or control scanning, as when a purchasing manager scans all purchase orders to spot unusual occurrences. In general, however, managerial information purposes are better met by reports or analyses that summarize transactions.

When transactions are processed, a transaction report is usually prepared for a period of time such as a day, a device such as terminal, or other basis for reference. The listing includes control totals for the number of transactions processed, total dollar amount of transactions, etc. The listing represents a batch of transactions received or input during a period of time. It provides a means of processing reference and error control.

METHODS FOR PROCESSING TRANSACTIONS

There are three different methods commonly used for processing transactions and updating master files: (1) periodic data preparation and periodic batch processing (usually termed batch processing); (2) online entry with subsequent batch processing; and (3) online entry with immediate processing (termed online processing). The choice of methods should reflect the underlying process being supported. If the underlying process is transaction oriented with immediate completion of the transaction desirable (as with order entry), online processing is indicated. If the process is periodic (as with payroll), batch processing is adequate.

Batch processing involves the accumulation of transactions until a sufficient number has been assembled to make processing efficient or until other considerations, such as a report cycle, initiate processing. The processing of batches can be daily, weekly, or monthly, depending on the volume of transactions and other considerations.

Batch processing of transactions can be very efficient in terms of data preparation and pro-

cessing of transactions. One major disadvantage of periodic batch processing is the delay in detecting and correcting errors. This is an especially serious problem for errors that can be found only when the transaction is compared against the master file. For example, if a transaction is coded with an apparently valid customer number for a nonexistent customer, the error will not be detected until processing is attempted against the customer file. The delay makes it difficult to trace the transaction back to the origination point and identify the correct customer.

With a batch system, the user prepares data input as a batch of transactions recorded over a period of time such as a day or week. A user responsible for processing data in a batch system must prepare input data in the exact format and with the exact codes required by the processing program, prepare control information used to insure that no records are lost or remain unprocessed, and check output received for errors (including checking against the control information prepared with input data). The user is also responsible for reviewing error reports, preparing corrections, and submitting corrections for processing.

When transactions are entered at an online terminal, the transaction is entered directly into the computer and validated immediately. The processing itself may be performed immediately or at a subsequent time as with periodic batch processing. One important advantage of online entry over periodic data preparation and input is that most of the validation may be performed while the transaction is being recorded. Many errors can therefore be corrected immediately while the person entering the transaction is available for correction. Often the user or customer originating the transaction is still available to make appropriate changes. In addition, the master files can be accessed for the detection of errors such as nonexistent master file records. In online entry with subsequent batch processing, the computer is used for direct data entry and validation, but valid transactions are stored for later periodic batch processing.

In *online entry with immediate processing*, the transaction is validated online and then processed immediately if valid. A response with the result of processing or a confirmation of completion of processing is generally provided to the user at the input terminal. The advantages of this approach are the same as direct entry with subsequent processing (i.e., immediate validation with opportunity for immediate corrections by the person doing the input) plus the additional advantage of immediate processing with immediate results. The master files are always up to date. For instance, after an item is sold, the inventory master file reflects the actual state of the inventory for that item. The disadvantages of immediate processing are the somewhat higher cost of online processing versus periodic batch processing (requires greater computer power and often data communications) and the extra procedures required to produce adequate control information and to safeguard the files against accidental or deliberate destruction during online updating.

In online processing, the user has a terminal, microcomputer, or handheld device for the input of transactions and output of results. The input devices are connected by wired or wireless communication lines to a remote computer where processing actually takes place. Transactions are entered and processed one at a time as they occur (in real time). The user generally has to be identified to the system as an authorized user before transactions are accepted. System sign on and authorization usually uses a password protection scheme. Users may have different authorization levels which determine what types of transactions they may perform. For instance, a user may be authorized (via his or her password) to process certain update transactions (e.g., a sale) but not others (e.g., alteration of payroll data). The mode of operation is a dialogue. The dialogue may be extensive and provide tutorial and help information for entry of data, or it may be very limited and require the user to understand what data to enter and how they should be entered. A user responsible for processing data in an online system must enter transactions in the proper format based on a dialogue, a visual form, or instructions in a manual; respond to error messages (since the system should reject any invalid data) with corrected input; and review control information. At the end of a period of processing transactions, the user signs off, so that an unauthorized user may not subsequently enter data.

RETRIEVAL IN TRANSACTION PROCESSING

Many online systems use data retrieval software to support transaction processing. Even in applications where batch updating is appropriate, the capability to access related records during transaction preparation is often desired. For instance, a bank may install online terminals so that customers may inquire about the status of their accounts. A customer complaint department in a retail catalogue company may check the status of an order when a customer calls. In these examples, online inquiry into master files is required.

Inquiries associated with a transaction processing system tend to be fairly structured, so that they may be programmed to use a standard set of commands that can be mastered fairly easily. In some systems, commands can be assigned to special function keys on the keyboard so that the operator needs only to press a single key rather than type in a command. Terminals that are only to be used for inquiries, such as terminals for customer use on a bank floor, may be specially designed with only function keys.

INFORMATION PROCESSING CONTROLS

Control of transaction processing begins with the design of the document or screen for initially recording the transaction. If the document is manually prepared, it should be designed to minimize errors in completing it. This requires adequate space, unambiguous directions and labels, and a sequence of recording that is natural to the preparer. Boxes, lines, colors, labels, and menus of alternatives are some of the methods used to aid the preparer. One serious problem is how to make sure every transaction is recorded and entered into processing. Interruptions or carelessness may cause a transaction to not be recorded or the source document to be misplaced. To prevent or detect such errors and omissions, the transaction processing system may have one or more controls such as the following: (1) computer-defined transaction number or prenumbered source document; (2) record anticipating a transaction (such as payment due); (3) document produced as a by-product; or (4) comparison with related transaction controls.

The use of a terminal, desktop computer, or handheld device to enter the original transaction has the advantage that a machine-readable record is produced at the same time as source documents needed for the transaction are prepared. If a source document is misplaced or lost, the computer record permits the tracking or reconstructing of the missing record. Accuracy and completeness considerations for source document design also apply to input screen design for the visual display terminal. Since online entry may also be performed without a source document (as with order entry by telephone), the machine record may be the only "document."

In the flow of control in batch processing, it is best to establish a control total of documents before the batch processing begins. The control total can be a record count, a financial total, or a "hash total" of numbers such as account numbers, which are not normally summed (hence the total is meaningless except for control purposes).

During the data preparation process, the control totals are checked to verify that no transactions are missing and that items used in control totals have been entered correctly. The control total is input with the data and checked by computer as part of data validation, processing, and output. The control totals appear on batch reports and on other control reports. The output (after adjusting for rejected transactions) should match the control total for the input batch. Computer programs and control personnel make control total comparisons during processing; users check controls on output against control totals for data they submitted for processing. This checking provides a simple but powerful control procedure to insure that all transactions in the document batch are processed.

In the case of online input from documents, there is no control total of transactions prior to entry. However, if there are reasonable control procedures to enforce entry of all transactions, control totals can be developed for logical batches of input (transactions that are logically grouped by some common feature). The logical batches provide a basis for listings for reference, follow-up, comparison with physical evidence, and so on. For example, the log of all transactions entered is sorted, and logical batches of

transactions are prepared by terminal, by operator, by type of transactions, etc.

There are special control considerations with online processing. The files change continuously, and therefore any error can disrupt a file and create additional errors as subsequent transactions are processed. The straightforward preprocessing batch control totals cannot be used to check batches before updating. Some examples of controls illustrate how control in online processing is handled. Restart procedures tell input personnel which transactions were lost if a system goes down. A separate backup file copy and transaction log are used for making file correction.

PROCESSING REFERENCE CONTROL

The audit trail (or a processing reference trail) is the trail of references (document numbers, batch numbers, transaction references, etc.) which allows tracing of a transaction from the time it is recorded through to the reports in which it is aggregated with other transactions, or the reverse, tracing a total back to amounts on individual source documents. The processing trail is required for internal clerical, analytical, and management use because of the frequent need to examine the details behind a total or to trace what happened to a transaction. It is also needed by external auditors and is required by certain tax regulations for tax-related records.

An audit trail should always be present. Its form may change in response to computer technology, but three requirements should be met:

1 Any transaction can be traced from the source document through processing to outputs and to totals in which it is aggregated. For example, each purchase of goods for inventory can be traced to inclusion in the inventory totals.
2 Any output or summary data can be traced back to the transactions or computations used to arrive at the output or summary figures. For example, the total amount owed by a customer can be traced to the sales and payments that were used to arrive at the balance due.
3 Any triggered transaction (a transaction automatically triggered by an event or condition) can be traced to the event or condi-

tion. An example is a purchase order triggered by a sale that reduced inventory below an order point.

programming languages

Gordon B. Davis

A computer program is a set of instructions that direct the computer to execute operations. Writing a set of instructions is termed "coding." The computer executes machine language instructions, but programs are not written in this form because they are expressed in some binary form that is difficult for human use. A symbolic assembly language was used in the early development of computers to allow programmers to code machine-level instructions using mnemonic names for instructions and symbolic names for storage locations. The difficulty with symbolic assembly languages is that they require one symbolic instruction for each machine instruction. Most programming is now done in a higher-level language. There are different types of high-level languages, but a common characteristic is that the program is written in instructions that describe the procedures or problem-solving steps to be performed. The high-level instructions are converted to a machine-level program by a computer program called a "compiler."

High-level languages used in information processing can be categorized by their orientation. The classification below is useful in thinking about the orientation of languages, but often programming languages do not fit exactly into any one category.

1 Algebraic, formula processing languages.
2 Business data processing languages.
3 Specialized languages.
4 General purpose languages.
5 Fourth-generation languages (4GL).
6 Screen-oriented languages.
7 Object-oriented languages.

Algebraic languages are oriented toward computational procedures for solving mathematical and statistical problems or problems that can be expressed in terms of formulas or numerical solution procedures. Algebraic languages have good facilities for expressing formulas, for describing computational procedures, and for specifying common mathematical functions. Typically, they are less useful for complex input and output and manipulation of non-numeric data. There are a large number of such languages, each one suited to a specialized environment. The most commonly used algebraic languages are FORTRAN (FORmula TRANslator) and BASIC (Beginners All-purpose Symbolic Instruction Code). FORTRAN has developed through a number of versions and is supported by standards efforts. BASIC was developed as a language for student use but is now widely used as a simplified language. Since most languages have facilities for expressing formulas and mathematical functions, many newer object-oriented languages with facilities for INTERNET applications are used for mathematical and statistical problems (*see* OBJECT-ORIENTED PROGRAMS AND SYSTEMS).

Business data processing languages emphasize information processing procedures involving manipulation of non-numeric data, large files, and high volume of input and output. They also have extensive formatting capabilities for reports. The processing procedures do not usually require extensive mathematical manipulation. COBOL (COmmon Business Oriented Language) has historically been the most widely used of these languages. As a historical note, a language often used with smaller business computers was RPG (Report Program Generator). In the development of business-oriented data processing, existing languages have been expanded to include user screen design and screen object operations. Newer object-oriented languages suited to applications involving microcomputers and Internet applications are often used for business data processing applications. Database packages include programming facilities for retrieval of data and formatting of reports. A standard language, SQL, is the most common query language. Many database packages have graphical user interfaces (*see* GRAPHICAL USER INTERFACE) for formulating queries, but the underlying instructions are generated in an SQL-like language.

Specialized languages are used for situations requiring functions that are not common to algebraic or business processing. An example is simulation languages, which are used to simulate operations involving queues. These can be quite complex and difficult without a specialized language. For example, a simulation of the operation of a job shop will involve many processing stations, many waiting lines of jobs to be processed, etc. Other specialized languages are used to write programs to control machine tools, do computations unique to engineering, etc.

General purpose languages are designed to support both algebraic and business data processing plus some common specialized functions. An example is ADA, a general purpose programming language. It is especially suited for the programming of large, long-lived systems with a need for ongoing maintenance. It supports modern programming structured techniques and concurrent processing.

Fourth-generation languages (4GL) are languages that produce programs based on high-level specifications rather than detailed procedural code. Fourth-generation languages are used by both professional programmers and experienced users to access data and build reports. Complete applications can be built using fourth-generation languages. This is frequently the case in applications that depend upon database use.

Screen-oriented languages are designed to assist in programming applications that are run by a user employing a graphical user interface to select operations from a menu, by a mouse operation to activate a screen object, or by keyboard entry.

Object-oriented languages are designed to assist in programming with reusable objects rather than writing extensive procedures. Each element of an object-oriented program is an object. Each object consists of data structures plus the operations, called methods, that can be performed on its data. Objects are activated by messages that come from other objects or are triggered by external events. Objects interact only by exchanging messages (which can include data). This characteristic of data and methods contained within an object is called "encapsulation," one of the main principles of the object-oriented approach. The effect of encapsulation is that data can only be affected through the methods of the object containing them. Another important characteristic of objects is inheritance. Once an object has been defined, a descendant object may be created that automatically inherits the data structures and methods of the original object. The two most widely used object-oriented languages are C++ and Java, but there are many others. Each of these language systems provides complete development environments tailored to the needs of object-oriented implementation.

The type of language or its orientation is useful in selecting the programming language that best fits the characteristics of an application. However, because most information processing functions can be programmed in almost any language, a programmer will often select a language that is known rather than the language that has the best functionality for the problem.

protocols

Gordon B. Davis

When two devices are communicating, there must be agreement as to the meaning of control information being sent with the data, and agreement as to how the control information and data will be packaged. This agreement is the protocol. There are a number of standard communication protocols. The most widely known communications protocol is the OSI (open systems interconnect) reference model developed by the ITU (International Transport Union). It has been standardized as the X.25 seven-layer model. In this model, separate sets of rules (protocols) are defined for different communication conditions and needs.

There are other models or collections of protocols. These models are often called communications architectures. Examples include IBM's SNA (systems network architecture) and TCP/IP (transmission control protocol and Internet protocol, two key elements of the protocol architecture). Communication on networks using a single protocol architecture is simpler and more efficient than communication involving multiple architectures.

prototyping

Julie E. Kendall and Kenneth E. Kendall

There are two schools of thought concerning the use of prototyping during systems analysis and design. The first view maintains that prototyping is a rapid development approach that replaces the traditional systems development life cycle (SDLC). AGILE DEVELOPMENT and extreme programming (XP) are development methodologies that rely heavily on prototyping. The second view suggests that prototyping is useful chiefly as a requirements determination technique within the conventional design methodologies.

Sometimes managers and systems analysts refer to prototyping as an alternative methodology that has supplanted the SDLC. This approach, however, may be rife with problems if the skills of the analyst and programmer have not evolved to handle this process. It may be true that through prototyping a system can be built more rapidly than when traditional SDLC methodologies are used, but good modular design may be sacrificed. A patched-up prototype might work, but it may be inefficient.

Prototypes can be developed and tested in a limited way. A prototype might be tested in one corporate branch or division and, if successful, might be implemented for use in the entire corporation. This kind of prototype is often used in manufacturing when an innovative product, such as a new model of an automobile, is developed.

When analysts use prototyping as a data-gathering technique, they interview, observe, and listen to feedback from users who make suggestions for improving the final system. Just as an architect builds a scale model before the actual building is constructed, a systems analyst may present a non-operational prototype that reveals the new designs for input, output, and user interfaces.

A systems analyst may choose to develop a prototype that only presents key features of the system. Users may suggest that additional features, such as help screens, might be incorporated into the revised prototype. Using feedback in this way permits users to become deeply involved with the information system they will soon be using. Prototyping goes through successive iterations until the user is satisfied.

Most CASE: COMPUTER-AIDED SOFTWARE/SYSTEM ENGINEERING tools used for systems analysis and design possess functions supporting the development of input and output design. These programs use information stored in the DATA DICTIONARY (e.g., the field lengths of all data elements) to aid a systems analyst in creating balanced and uncluttered input and output screens. User-interface design is typically left to the imagination of the systems analyst, with little automated support presently available.

There are three main advantages of using prototyping within traditional systems analysis and design approaches. By gathering data about use of the prototype, the analyst increases the potential for improving the system early in its development. Furthermore, the analyst gains valuable information that may become useful in the event that development must be halted. Thirdly, the final system is more likely to meet the needs of the users who desire valid input, meaningful output, and an appropriate user interface.

Bibliography

Alavi, M. (1984). An assessment of the prototyping approach to information systems. *Communications of the ACM*, 27, 556–63.

Kendall, K. E. and Kendall, J. E. (2005). *Systems Analysis and Design*, 6th edn. Upper Saddle River, NJ: Prentice-Hall.

Naumann, J. D. and Jenkins, A. M. (1982). Prototyping: The new paradigm for systems development. *MIS Quarterly*, 6, 29–44.

punched cards

Gordon B. Davis

Punched cards are of historical interest to information systems, because they were the basis for the development of mechanized data processing. Punched cards were originally developed by Herman Hollerith for the 1890 US census. Each card had 80 columns with each column encoding one character by means of punched holes. Machines were developed to punch data, sort and collate the cards, make computations based on data on the cards, and produce reports based on card inputs. Although there were several punched-card formats, the most common measured $7\frac{3}{8} \times 3\frac{1}{4}$ inches with 80 columns and 12 rows. This format was often referred to as the Hollerith or IBM card. The 80-column design of the punched card influenced the design of forms and early computer screens. Punched cards dom-

inated large-scale mechanized data processing until the advent of computers in the 1950s. Punched cards continued to be used for data entry with computers until the early 1980s when other data entry methods supplanted them.

quality in information systems

see ASSESSMENT OF MANAGEMENT INFOR-
MATION SYSTEM FUNCTION

radio frequency identification

Vlad Krotov and Dennis A. Adams

Radio frequency identification (RFID) is a recently developed, contactless auto-identification technology that involves use of electronic labels (tags or transponders) with the capability to transmit and receive data wirelessly. Objects, animals, or humans with an attached transponder can be detected and identified by a specialized device (reader or transceiver) over the air without direct physical contact or even without the transponder being within the line of sight of the reader. RFID technology can be used for inventory and animal control, security access, contactless transactions, and other applications. An RFID system is a member of a class of systems known as location-based systems. These systems interact with users and other systems based upon their location. Location-based systems assume that the system and/or user can be mobile and will need to interact with the system differently depending upon where it is being used. An RFID chip can provide input to a system or can be written upon as an output device, or both.

RFID technology relies on a body of knowledge developed over the centuries. In the 1600s the first observational knowledge on electricity and magnetism began to merge. During the nineteenth century such scientists as Michael Faraday, James Maxwell, Heinrich Hertz, Alexandr Popov, and Guglielmo Marconi advanced the body of knowledge on electromagnetism and radio waves. In the early twentieth century Ernst Alexanderson marked the beginning of modern radio communication and the first radar was developed. Probably the earliest paper on RFID technology was published by Harry Stockman in 1948. In the 1960s the first EAS (electronic article surveillance) solutions became available. The 1970s was a period of intensive research in the domain of RFID by government, academic, and commercial institutions. The 1990s marked the explosion of RFID applications, primarily in electronic tolling. In June 2003 Wal-Mart announced its plans to implement RFID in its supply chain. The announcement received wide attention from the mass media and made both the business world and general public aware of the technology.

RFID technology provides a number of advantages over traditional auto-identification technologies, such as bar code systems (*see* BAR CODE), OPTICAL CHARACTER RECOGNITION, biometric procedures (*see* BIOMETRICS), and SMART CARDS (Finkenzeller, 2003). First of all, RFID obviates the need for contact, line-of-sight, or static position for identification. Secondly, some RFID systems can scan an area for items automatically, being able to detect several hundreds of transponders in a second. Finally, tags can be very durable and hard to counterfeit. All these advantages may translate into substantial savings for businesses that decide to implement RFID.

RFID system architecture consists of three conceptual elements: transponder, reader, and host computer (see figure 1).

A transponder is an electronic identification tag that usually consists of a coil and an electronic chip being embedded into a plastic or glass housing. Transponders can be active, passive, semi-passive, read-only, or with both read and write capabilities. Active transponders contain an internal energy source that allows for autonomous transmission of data. Normally, active transponders can transmit data over a larger distance than passive transponders. Passive transponders do not contain an internal

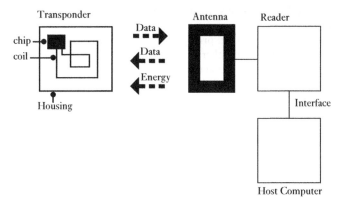

Figure 1   RFID system architecture

energy source – their chips are powered by the electricity generated in the transponder's coil when it is placed within the electromagnetic field of the reader (Faraday's law). Passive transponders are more reliable and cheaper. Semipassive transponders contain an internal energy source, but remain idle until they receive a signal from a reader. This allows for more efficient use of energy. Read-only transponders are capable only of broadcasting data, which is usually a unique identification number. Read–write transponders can store data in memory that can be rewritten. Some of the most common memory types used in transponders are EEPROM (electrically erasable programmable read-only memory), FRAM (ferromagnetic random access memory), or SRAM (static random access memory). Depending on the specific application, transponders also vary in shape, size, and housing materials. Transponders also vary in their memory size, starting with 1-bit transponders used in EAS and ending with transponders holding up to 128 K of data.

A reader uses an antenna to transmit and receive data from the transponder and supply it with energy (in the case of passive tags). Readers are also equipped with an interface that is used to transmit data to a host computer. The host computer uses software for storing and analyzing data received from the transponder. Such software vendors as Oracle and SAP are stepping into the market by offering software that can work with RFID.

RFID systems can be classified based on frequency used for communication, range over which data can be transmitted between transponders and a reader, and fundamental operating principles. Table 1 provides a summary of

Table 1   Frequency bands and applications

Frequency band	Characteristics	Typical applications
Low: 100–500 kHz	Short to medium read range, inexpensive, low reading speed	Access control, animal identification, inventory control
Intermediate 10–15 MHz	Short to medium read range, potentially inexpensive, medium reading speed	Access control, smart cards
High 850–959 MHz 2.4–5.8 GHz	Long read range, high reading speed, line of sight required, expensive	Railroad car monitoring, toll collection systems

Source: AIM (1999)

frequency bands used by RFID systems, their characteristics, and applications.

According to fundamental operating principles, RFID systems can be classified either as inductively (capacitively) coupled or as microwave (backscatter) systems (Finkenzeller, 2003). Inductively coupled systems typically have a shorter operating range in comparison with backscatter systems. Some other points of difference among RFID systems are memory capacity, detection/writing speed, requirement of line of sight, cost, penetration, collision avoidance, security, interoperability, etc.

RFID technology can replace traditional auto-identification systems in such areas as SUPPLY CHAIN MANAGEMENT, asset management, tollway payment systems, and security access control. Moreover, RFID technology can make it possible to use identification in areas where traditional technologies were ineffective or could not be used at all. For example, because of the durability of RFID tags, RFID can be used to identify items that undergo rough handling, such as gas cylinders and tools. Moreover, RFID can be used to manage hazardous materials without direct human involvement. Finally, RFID can be used to strengthen access and transaction security. A glass transponder can be implanted in a person's hand to grant the person the right to open a lock or fire a gun. Credit cards and access cards can be manufactured with an embedded transponder, providing an additional layer of security.

Most commercial applications of RFID (except EAS and tollway payments) are still in the emergent stage. Wal-Mart, one of the RFID pioneers, is still in the testing stage of implementing RFID in its supply chain. Delta plans to use RFID tags on passengers' luggage. Ford intends to use RFID tags to track parts. Taco Bell and KFC are experimenting with RFID to introduce wireless payment solutions for its customers similar to technologies already in use at service stations. The US Department of Defense is also employing RFID tags on some of its assets.

Despite enthusiasm present in the industry, RFID technology has several drawbacks that have not been fully addressed. First of all, the cost of RFID transponders is still too high to use them to identify inexpensive items. Secondly, radio waves cannot pass through metal or even water at certain frequencies and are sensitive to radio noise generated by other devices. Frequencies and protocols are not yet standardized, creating a chaotic abundance of proprietary RFID solutions. Privacy and security concerns are also serious problems that RFID vendors have to address in part by considering use of "kill switches" to deactivate RFID at point of sale and in part by developing effective AUTHENTICATION and ENCRYPTION algorithms.

In spite of numerous drawbacks associated with the technology, the market for RFIDs continues to evolve, with hundreds of vendors already offering RFID solutions for every possible application. The market for RFIDs is estimated to grow to $2 billion by 2007 (Shim, 2003). It is expected that as the size decreases and transmission distances increase, RFID systems will proliferate.

Bibliography

AIM (1999). RFID basics. www.aimglobal.org.
AIM (2001). Shrouds of time: The history of RFID. www.aimglobal.org.
Finkenzeller, K. (2003). *RFID Handbook*, 2nd edn, trans. Rachel Waddington. Chichester: John Wiley.
HiPoint Technology (2002). Benefits of RFID. www.hi-point.com/resources.html.
Mital, T. (2003). The emergence of RFID technology. University of Houston Information Systems Research Center, www.uhisrc.com.
Shim, R. (2003). Smart label consortium identifies itself. *New York Times*, March 17.

reengineering and information technology

Boon-Siong Neo

Process reengineering is an analysis and design approach for achieving significant break-throughs in important organizational performance indicators such as cycle time, quality, service, and cost. The scope for change may be limited to one function within an organization, may include processes across several functions, or may extend to external processes linking separate organizations. Reengineering focuses the change on business processes, and often results in concomitant changes to job requirements, organizational structure, management systems, culture, and values.

An organization implements its strategy, creates customer value, and achieves desired business results through its products, processes, and people. In advanced manufacturing firms, non-production processes may account for up to 75 percent of total product value. In service firms, such as banks and hotels, business processes describe virtually every step to meeting customer needs. Business process examples are the *order–delivery–payment cycle* in distribution, *customer account management* in financial services, and the *systems development life cycle* (SDLC) in software firms. A strategic view of process management requires organizations to invest to develop capabilities in mapping key processes, measuring process performance, redesigning processes, and executing new processes to realize business strategies.

The structure of a business process refers to the way that tasks are differentiated and performed according to knowledge and skill requirements, and how the tasks are coordinated to achieve integrated outcomes that are of value to customers. Traditionally, tasks are divided into narrow specialized duties and then coordinated in an assembly-line manner by supervisors and staff units organized in a hierarchy of authority relationships.

Reengineering is not about speeding up or automating existing process steps. Process reengineering in essence is:

1 Rethinking of what is required to accomplish business goals and strategies.
2 Designing new processes to integrate and implement these requirements.
3 Using information technology (IT) to enable such processes.
4 Institutionalizing dynamic new ways of doing business based on these processes.

Reengineering seeks to change process designs by empowering motivated front-line workers to make decisions that have outcomes that are aligned to organizational mission, and by providing access to relevant information that enables workers to make the best possible decision in a timely manner. It links worker motivation to performance by aligning each process to explicit goals, and by informing and rewarding workers according to desired results.

Many reengineering solutions employ case management techniques such as case worker, empowered customer representative, and self-managing teams.

Successful reengineering efforts require a change in mindset affecting five critical dimensions of organizational culture. Organizational change along these five dimensions distinguishes successful applications of process reengineering. Altered information flows accompany each shift:

1 *Convention to innovation.* Reengineering improves performance by challenging traditional practices, as in the invoiceless accounts receivable system developed by the Ford Motor Company. The efficacy of rules and assumptions underlying existing business practices was questioned and reevaluated to determine their validity. New rules that better reflect current business reality were used as the bases of new process designs.
2 *Independent to interdependent processes.* The logic of integrated logistics, rapid replenishment in distribution, and value-added partnerships among independent firms substitute information for expensive resources such as capital, space, inventory, people, and time. A centralized database may be used to coordinate and communicate information among organizational units without undermining autonomy to decide and act.
3 *Sequential to integrated processing.* Reengineering shifts the organization from dependence on a fragmented series of process steps to an integrated set of processes performed by a case worker or by a cross-functional team. The integrated case team processes all the tasks required for a major category of business transactions with access to the information necessary to do the job without the need for time-consuming hand-offs or approvals.
4 *Equal misery to differentiated service.* Reengineering shifts process design from one-size-fits-all to custom-tailored processes that serve more finely defined groups of customers. A triage is usually designed to filter customers into differentiated processes designed to better meet their needs.
5 *Bureaucratic control to entrepreneurial initiative.* New process designs are used to

transform rigid bureaucracies based on central command and control into dynamic organizations of informed workers guided by performance measures that are aligned with goals.

IT plays a crucial role in enabling the reengineering of business processes by overcoming basic limitations to performance, such as time differences, geographic dispersion, social distances, and organizational boundaries. Fundamentally, IT capabilities enable time compression and non-hierarchical communications across social barriers and geographic distances to add value in the performance of business processes. IT facilitates process innovation by changing the manner in which business processes traditionally capture, manipulate, store, present, communicate, and use information as a complement to the performance of physical activity. Data may be automatically captured at source via bar coding (*see* BAR CODE), validated by programs in handheld computers, and transmitted to a shared database. Unlike paper documents, a shared database simultaneously distributes information to many uses simultaneously. Unlike human experts, an expert system (*see* EXPERT SYSTEMS) provides a co-worker with consistent advice round the clock. Unlike catalogues, a video disk helps customers or trainees to interact with content. And unlike a typical trip log, automatic identification and tracking means mobile assets, such as vehicles or containers, and tells dispatchers where they are now, instead of forcing the dispatcher to find the location. Developments and applications in work group computing, enterprise-wide integrated systems, and e-business (*see* E-COMMERCE) enable organizations to take greater advantage of IT in reengineering the way that work is structured to deliver value to customers and other stakeholders.

When firms should consider initiating reengineering depends on the driving force for reengineering and whether the target is to resolve performance issues or to exploit new opportunities. Many reengineering efforts are triggered by *major performance shortfalls*. Other projects start because of major efforts to *develop new IT systems* to support new business strategies. *Business startups* present natural opportunities to design the new business with a clean slate. *Tech-nological breakthroughs* present yet another opportunity since they give organizations new capabilities for overcoming the limitations of human cognitive abilities, physical constraints of geography, and differences arising from separate time zones.

Although reengineering may be carried out without the use of IT, it is highly unlikely that new process designs can be implemented efficiently without enabling information systems. At the same time, reengineering is not merely process automation, as speeding up broken processes cannot result in major performance improvements. Reengineering seems to have the best results when it applies out-of-the-box thinking to traditional business practices, together with creative uses of IT capabilities in developing new process designs that enable more competitive performance.

relational database

Roger H. L. Chiang

This is the most commonly used database system across all types of computers, ranging from mainframes to personal computers. In relational databases, data are organized according to the relational model introduced by E. F. Codd (1923–2003) in 1970. The relational model employs the concept of a mathematical relation, which looks somewhat like a table of values and has its theoretical basis in set theory and first-order predicate logic. It allows database designers to focus on the logical representation of the data and their relationships, rather than on the physical storage and implementation. The relational model is widely recognized as one of the great technical innovations of the twentieth century.

A relational database is a collection of relations. A relation can be thought of as a two-dimensional table consisting of rows and columns of data. Each row of the relation is called a *tuple*, representing a collection of related values. These tuples are facts describing a real-world object or relationship. Each relation's column has a name and represents an attribute. The values of an attribute are drawn from a data domain, which specifies the valid set of values for one or more attributes. Attributes should contain atomic values. The relation names and attribute names are used to help in interpreting the meaning of data in a relation.

A relational database can be created and maintained by the DATABASE MANAGEMENT SYSTEM (DBMS). The relational DBMS is a general purpose software system that facilitates the creation, modification, and update of the database, the retrieval of data, and the generation of reports. The structured query language (*see* SQL) is composed of a set of commands. SQL is the internationally accepted standard for creating, manipulating, and querying the relational databases. All relational DBMS software supports SQL, and many software vendors have developed extensions to the basic SQL command set.

Consider the following simple example with two relations: *Department* and *Employee*. There are four attributes for *Department*. Each row (tuple) of the *Department* relation represents one individual department (e.g., *Marketing*). Each column represents a unique property (e.g., *Birthday*). The *Manager* attribute represents the relationship employees manage departments. Likewise, the *Dept#* of *Employee* relation represents the relationship employee works for departments.

Department

Dept#	Name	Office	Manager
D12	Human Resource	0501	02357
D13	Marketing	0409	02348
D14	Information Systems	0510	10023

Employee

Emp#	Name	Birthday	Salary	Dept#
02357	William Bowser	12/05/78	94,500	D12
02348	Anne Smithson	05/23/72	101,750	D13
10023	Walter Brewer	06/09/83	100,500	D14
10046	Gerald Robertson	07/11/89	51,000	D14

report generators

Facilities for producing reports by specifying data to be included and the format of the report. Report generators are included in some PROGRAMMING LANGUAGES; they are an integral part of database management systems (*see* DATABASE MANAGEMENT SYSTEM). Report generators allow a user to specify headings, groupings of data, subtotals, totals, etc; they simplify report preparation.

requirements determination for information systems

James C. Wetherbe and Glenn J. Browne

Information requirements determination is the process in which a systems analyst develops an understanding of the problem to be solved and a definition of users' needs for a proposed information system. Behavioral and technical information is gathered concerning goals, processes, tasks, and data requirements for the system (Browne and Rogich, 2001). Requirements determination is generally thought to be the most critical phase of information systems development, and poor requirements determination is one of the leading causes of information systems failures (Davis, 1982; Wetherbe, 1991; Ewusi-Mensah, 1997). The requirements determination process can be divided into three stages: information gathering, representation, and verification (Browne and Ramesh, 2002; Larsen and Naumann, 1992). Here we focus on the information gathering stage.

There are three levels at which information requirements need to be established in order to design and implement computer-based information systems:

1 *Organization-level information requirements.* These requirements are used to define an overall information system architecture and to specify a portfolio of applications and databases. Often termed "enterprise analysis," the process of organization-level information requirements determination obtains, organizes, and documents a complete set of high-level requirements. The requirements are factored

into databases and a portfolio of applications that can be scheduled for development.

2 *Organization database requirements.* These arise both from applications and ad hoc queries. User ad hoc query requirements and application requirements are referred to as conceptual or logical requirements because the user views of data are separated from the organization of data in physical storage. Requirements for physical database design are derived from user requirements and hardware and software environments.

3 *Application-level information requirements.* An application provides information processing for an organizational unit or organizational activity. There are essentially two types of information system application requirements: behavioral and technical. The behavioral or social requirements, based on job design, specify objectives and assumptions such as work organization and work design objectives, individual role and responsibility assumptions, and organizational policies. The technical requirements are based on the information needed for the job or task to be performed. They specify outputs, inputs, stored data, and information processes.

There are different strategies for determining information requirements, which we now describe in detail.

Strategies for Determining Information Requirements

There are three broad strategies for determining information requirements:

1 *Asking directly.* In this strategy, the analyst obtains information requirements from people who perform the business processes by asking them to describe their requirements. From a conceptual standpoint, this strategy assumes that users have a mental model (or can build one) to explain their information requirements. These conditions may hold in very stable systems for which a well-defined structure exists or in systems established by law, regulation, or other outside authority.

2 *Deriving from an existing information system.* Existing information systems that have an operational history can be used to derive requirements for a proposed information system for the same type of organization or application. The types of existing information systems that are useful in deriving requirements for future systems are the system to be replaced, a system in a similar organization, and a proprietary system or application package. In this strategy, users and analysts start with (anchor on) an existing system and adjust from it. If the information system is performing fairly standard operations and providing fairly standard information for business processes that are stable, the use of an existing system as an anchor may be appropriate.

3 *Asking indirectly by eliciting characteristics of business processes.* Requirements for information stem from the activities that occur within the business processes. In eliciting requirements, questions focus on the activities and responsibilities that lead to the need for information. This approach is therefore especially appropriate when the business processes are changing or the proposed information system is different from existing patterns (in its content, form, complexity, etc.), so that anchoring on an existing information system or observations of information needs will not yield a complete and correct set of requirements.

When an initial set of requirements has been elicited by one of the methods, the requirements may be extended, modified, and refined by using a prototype of the application to allow users to adjust initial requirements through experimentation with an evolving information system.

The strategy of asking indirectly is used when requirements cannot be obtained by asking directly or by studying an existing system. Because of its importance and value in information requirements determination, the asking indirectly strategy will be our focus in this discussion.

Improving the Process of Eliciting Requirements Indirectly

Four recommendations for improving the process of eliciting information requirements indirectly are to (1) consider cross-functional requirements and sharing of information; (2) use group interviews for stakeholders;

(3) use sets of questions that elicit different patterns of thinking about requirements; and (4) use a prototype of the system to elicit user refinements and extensions to requirements.

Elicit cross-functional requirements.   Many users and analysts view systems as functional as opposed to cross-functional (Wetherbe and Vitalari, 1994). This perspective is too narrow. For example, when developing a new budgeting system, a focus on the information needed by the budget managers or budgeting staff members is not sufficient. People other than budgeting staff make use of budgeting information.

Order processing illustrates the need to develop systems cross-functionally. To process orders, salespeople have to decide which customers to call, what to sell them, and what is available to sell. The credit analysts must decide which customers should be extended credit and how much credit to extend, which customers need past-due notices, and which customers' credit should be discontinued. The warehouse

must decide what and how much inventory to stock, when to reorder, when to unload slow-moving inventory, and which customers should be allocated limited inventory. Shipping must decide such things as what merchandise to send to which customers, what orders can be shipped together to save delivery costs, and when trucks should depart. These decisions are summarized in table 1.

A system should provide information so that all decisions can be improved. In eliciting requirements to improve the quality of the decision, cross-functional factors that should be considered include customer importance to the business, customer need for prompt delivery of the order, the profitability of each order, credit status of customer, shipping schedule for delivery to each customer, and customer reaction if a previous order was late.

For example, consider the last decision listed for the warehouse department in table 1 (allocating available inventory to customers). If the

Table 1   Decision centers involved in order processing

Decision center	Activity	Examples of major decisions
Sales staff	Selling merchandise	Which major customers to call What to sell customers What is available to sell
Credit department	Accounts receivable management	Which customers to allow credit How much credit to allow Which customers need past-due notices Which customers' credit should be discounted
Warehouse	Inventory management	What inventory to stock How much inventory to stock When to reorder stock When to unload slow-moving stock Which customers to allocate available inventory
Shipping department	Packing and shipping orders	What merchandise to sell to what customers What orders can be shipped together to save delivery cost When trucks should depart

warehouse has five orders but only enough inventory to fill three, it must make a resource allocation decision. Typically, this decision is made on a first-in-first-out (FIFO) basis. That seems equitable and fair, given the information the warehouse people have available to them. However, this rule can result in a bad decision. What if we have a customer who does a lot of business with the company and needs this shipment promptly, who recently received an order late and was furious about it, who is paying a high profit margin on the order, and who always pays his bills promptly, and it so happens that a truck is routed to deliver a shipment to another customer nearby the same afternoon? A FIFO decision may cause the inventory to be allocated instead to someone who hardly ever does business with the company, to whom the order is not urgent, who yields a low profit margin, who does not pay bills on time, and who is at a location to which a truck is not going for the next three weeks (during which time inventory could have been restocked). Note that the information needed to improve the decision-making in the warehouse comes from outside the warehouse. For example, customer need, importance, and profitability come from sales, creditworthiness comes from credit, and shipping schedule comes from shipping.

Use group interviews. In the determination of information requirements, the system design team usually interviews managers individually instead of using a group process (also known as joint application design). Performing each interview separately often places cognitive stress on a manager and hinders his or her ability to respond adequately to questions.

A second reason for a joint application design is that different functional areas of an organization have different agendas in developing a new information system. For example, in the order processing system portrayed in table 1, each decision center is likely to emphasize different design criteria. Sales may view the primary importance of order processing as insuring prompt and correct delivery of orders to customers. Credit, on the other hand, may be primarily concerned with insuring that the company receives full payment for all orders. Those responsible for inventory management are, of course, interested in facilitating good inventory management, reducing inventory costs, etc., while those responsible for shipping are interested in insuring good routing of trucks to minimize delivery costs. It is difficult to achieve this overall perspective if each manager is interviewed individually.

Use questions that elicit different patterns of thinking. Research has shown that common questioning methods used by analysts are frequently ineffective in eliciting requirements from users (e.g., Browne and Rogich, 2001). For example, system developers often ask direct questions such as: "What information do you need from the new system?" Such a direct question is not helpful to managers desiring better information for problem solving, decision-making, and understanding business processes. The reason the direct question may not work well is that managers think in terms of the need for information and not the list of information needed.

Instead of direct questions, methods that encourage users to think in creative ways are most likely to lead to improved sets of requirements (Browne and Ramesh, 2002). The best way to elicit requirements is therefore through the use of *indirect* questions. For example, in determining what lawnmower someone needs, questions such as "How big is your yard? How steep is it? Do you have fences or trees?" are indirect questions that determine appropriate blade width, horsepower, and the need for a rear or side bagger. Those designing information systems should follow the same approach to understand users' requirements.

A straightforward, useful indirect question approach to interviewing users (instead of simply saying "What information do you need?") to determine information requirements is based upon three different but overlapping sets of requirement determination questions as shown in table 2. By combining questions from these three different approaches, a comprehensive, reliable determination of conceptual information requirements can be achieved. This method is explained in more detail in the next major section.

Use a prototype to elicit user refinements. After providing an initial set of requirements, users should be allowed to extend and refine their

Table 2 Comprehensive interview approaches, implementations and developers

Comprehensive approach	Information system implementation	Developers
Specify problems and decisions	The executive interview portion of business systems planning (BSP)	IBM
Specify critical factors	Critical success factors (CSF)	Rockart
Specify effectiveness criteria for outputs and efficiency criteria for processes used to generate outputs	Ends/means analysis (E/M analysis)	Wetherbe and Davis

conceptual requirements and provide detailed information requirements through trial and error. Trial and error, or experiential learning, is an important part of problem solving. It is also a part of determining detailed information requirements. It can be incorporated into the system design process through the use of a prototype or mock-up of the system. Using state-of-the-art technology, a prototype of a new system can usually be constructed quickly. As in manufacturing, much can be learned about final requirements through a prototype before "building the new factory."

Ideally, users should be able to observe and experience a prototype within a few days of being interviewed. This prototype can then be shaped into a final design. Once the prototype is accepted, a revised schedule and budget can be established for building the system. Although systems must evolve over time and should be built with evolution in mind, a system that is initially "right" will not need substantial immediate modifications. Evolutionary change of such a system is therefore much more manageable.

THE ELICITATION PROCESS IN THE ASKING INDIRECTLY STRATEGY

Before conducting the interview, an agreement on the overall goals of the business activity should be established in a joint application design session. For example, for the order processing system discussed above, the objectives of the system could be to insure prompt, correct delivery of orders to customers, maintain credit integrity, facilitate inventory management, and insure good shipment routing and scheduling. Once this has been established, questions can be asked that determine information needed to insure that those objectives are accomplished.

As explained earlier, a robust approach employs questions that overlap in their coverage (table 2). The three sets of questions trigger different patterns of thinking, and therefore should result in a more complete set of requirements.

Elicit problems and decisions. These questions define information requirements by asking indirect questions about problems and decisions. Example questions are:

1   What are the major problems encountered in accomplishing the purposes of the organizational unit you manage? For example, in an order processing system, problems include being out of stock too often, allocating limited inventory to the wrong customers, and allowing a truck to leave on a route unaware that another order going to the same destination will be arriving at the shipping dock within an hour.

2   What are good solutions to those problems? For example, to solve the problem of being out of stock too often requires better inventory management. To solve the problem of incorrectly allocating orders requires letting the warehouse know the importance of customers and the importance of orders to specific customers. It would also be helpful to know customer credit status. To solve the scheduling of truck departure problems requires letting shipping know the destination of orders that are being processed but have not yet arrived at the shipping dock.

3   How can information play a role in any of those solutions? For example, to improve inventory management, out-of-stock and below-minimum reporting could be provided electronically. Also, an automatic re-ordering system could be implemented.

Electronic access to customer importance, importance of order, and credit status could allow the warehouse to make appropriate allocation decisions when inventory is limited. If the shipping department has access to orders received and in process, it can make better decisions about routing and scheduling trucks.

4   What are the major decisions associated with your management responsibilities? Major decisions for order processing include which customers to call and what to sell them, credit, inventory, reordering, allocation of limited inventory, and scheduling and routing deliveries.

5   What improvements in information could result in better decisions? Table 3 illustrates the way decisions relate to information requirements.

Elicit critical success factors (CSF).   A second line of questions is based on critical success factors. Table 4 provides an illustration of critical success factor/information results. Questions to ask include the following.

1   What are the critical success factors of the organizational unit you manage? (Most managers have four to eight of these.) For example, critical success factors for order processing include adequate inventory to

Table 3   Decisions elicited for order-processing system

Decision	Information
Which customers to call on and what to sell them?	Customer-order history; inventory available
Credit for whom? How much? When to discontinue?	Credit rating; current status of account, payment history
What and how much inventory to stock? When to reorder?	Inventory on hand; sales trends on inventory items; market forecasts
How to allocate limited inventory?	Priority of order; importance of customer; credit status of customer; shipping schedule
When to unload slow-moving inventory?	Sales trends
Destination of ordered inventory?	Customers' addresses
What orders can be shipped together to save delivery costs?	Shipping schedule and customers' destination for orders awaiting shipment

Table 4   Critical success factors and information requirements

Critical success factor	Information
Adequate inventory to fill customer orders	Percentage of orders filled on time – overall and also categorized by customer and product
Prompt shipment of orders	Deliver time – overall and also categorized by customer
High percentage of customer payments	Delinquency report on nonpaying customers
Vendors (suppliers) promptly fill reorders	Exception report on vendor reorders not filled on time

fill customer orders, prompt shipment of orders, high percentage of customer payments made, and vendors (suppliers) promptly filling reorders.

2 What information is needed to monitor critical success factors? For example, to determine whether adequate inventory is available, management needs summary and exception reports on percentage of orders filled on time. In addition to overall reports, orders should also be categorized by customer and product. To determine whether orders are being shipped promptly, management needs to have summary and exception reports on delivery time, including reports categorized by customers.

Elicit effectiveness and efficiency (ends/means). Effectiveness measures relate to the outputs or ends from a process, whereas efficiency measures relate to the resources (means) employed. Ends/means questions elicit requirements by causing managers to think about both effectiveness and efficiency and information needed to monitor both (Wetherbe, 1991). Questions to elicit this thinking are:

1 What is the end or good or service provided by the business process?
2 What makes these goods or services effective (useful) to recipients or customers?

3 What information is needed to evaluate that effectiveness?
4 What are the key means or processes used to generate or provide goods or services? For example, means for order processing include processing orders, processing credit requests, and making shipments.
5 What constitutes efficiency in the providing of these goods or services? For example, efficiency for order processing is achieving low transaction costs for orders and credit checks. It is also minimizing shipment costs.
6 What information is needed to evaluate that efficiency? Examples of information needed to assess efficiency include cost per transaction with historical trends, and shipment cost categorized by order, customer, region, and revenue generated.

Tables 5 and 6 illustrate the use of effectiveness and efficiency questions in an ends/means analysis for order processing.

Using these three sets of indirect questions as the basis for obtaining a correct and complete set of information requirements is both simple and powerful. It is simple because it consists of components that can be learned by an analyst and a manager in a relatively short time. It is powerful because it overcomes human limitations in thinking about information requirements.

Table 5 Eliciting effectiveness information for order-processing system

Ends	*Effectiveness*	*Information*
Fill customer orders	Customer orders delivered as ordered, when expected, and as soon or sooner than competition	Summary and exception reports on customer deliveries; number of order corrections made; comparative statistics on delivery service *v.* competition
Provide customer service	Promptly provide credit to qualified customers	Customer credit status and payment history
	Quick response to and reduction of customer complaints	Report of number and type of complaints by customers and average time to resolve complaint
	Customers are satisfied	Customer attitudes toward service perhaps determined by customer surveys

Table 6   Eliciting efficiency information for order-processing system

Means	Efficiency	Information
Process orders	Low transaction cost	Cost per transaction with historical trends
Process credit request	Low transaction cost	Cost per transaction with historical trends
Make shipments	Minimize shipment costs	Ship cost categorized by order, customer, region, and revenue generated

The redundancy in the questions increases the reliability of the structured interview results. For example, the set of questions concerning *problems* may identify poor allocation of limited inventory to customers. The need to allocate limited inventory may also be identified as a *decision* that must be made. In other words, if the concept of allocating limited inventory is not recalled as a problem, it can still be identified as a decision, and so forth.

Requirements determination is critical to information systems development since all subsequent stages of the development process, including design and implementation, depend on the requirements elicited. Thus, utilizing appropriate and useful techniques, such as those described, is crucial to the successful development of information systems.

Bibliography

Browne, G. J. and Ramesh, V. (2002). Improving information requirements determination: A cognitive perspective. *Information and Management*, 39, 625–45.

Browne, G. J. and Rogich, M. B. (2001). An empirical investigation of user requirements elicitation: Comparing the effectiveness of prompting techniques. *Journal of Management Information Systems*, 17, 223–49.

Davis, G. B. (1982). Strategies for information requirements determination. *IBM Systems Journal*, 21, 4–30.

Ewusi-Mensah, K. (1997). Critical issues in abandoned information systems projects. *Communications of the ACM*, 40, 74–80.

Larsen, T. J. and Naumann, J. D. (1992). An experimental comparison of abstract and concrete representations in systems analysis. *Information and Management*, 22, 29–40.

Wetherbe, J. C. (1991). Executive information requirements: Getting it right. *MIS Quarterly*, 15, 51–65.

Wetherbe, J. C. and Vitalari, N. P. (1994). *Systems Analysis and Design*. St. Paul, MN: West.

risk assessment and risk management

William J. Caelli

The development of a plan for a statement of the "trustworthiness" of any information system (IS), and thus any concept of INFORMATION ASSURANCE in a working system, depends upon a thorough risk assessment and associated risk management program for the target information systems. This leads, then, to the acceptance of relevant information security baselines for the system and for a total program of information security management (ISM). Over many years, national and international standards relevant to this area have been developed and used with mixed results and with varying acceptance. Indeed, in the public sector it is now common for regulations to specify that risk assessment and management programs be undertaken on a regular basis and that appropriate reporting is done to relevant government agencies or even to the relevant government itself, e.g., the US Congress.

Growing concern for national information infrastructure protection (NIIP) means that such activities are starting to receive enhanced attention and the roles of the private and public sectors in this regard are being widely discussed. The problem that emerges is essentially one related to cost of performance of such assessments and the education and training of the people necessary to perform such functions and to provide such assessments.

NCSS Glossary No. 4009 gives each of these terms the following definitions:

- *Risk assessment*: "Process of analyzing threats to and vulnerabilities of an IS, and the potential impact resulting from the loss of information or capabilities of a system. This analysis is used as a basis for identifying appropriate and cost-effective security countermeasures."

- *Risk management*: "Process of identifying and applying countermeasures commensurate with the value of the assets protected based on a risk assessment."

The major themes here relate to the identification of threats to the information system itself and the determination of cost-effective countermeasures to overcome those threats. A major problem in this regard is that related to the availability of necessary information regarding the vulnerabilities of the systems used, particularly in the software area. This includes such vital areas as operating systems, middleware, network and file subsystems, database management systems (*see* DATABASE MANAGEMENT SYSTEM), generic applications, and so on.

It is likely that any end-user organization will not have access to the underlying technology on which their applications have been built and, indeed, may not even have access to large-scale application systems that may be adapted to their enterprise needs. This is particularly so for small to medium enterprises (SMEs) who make use of commodity, "off-the-shelf" systems in nearly all stages of the development and deployment of their enterprise critical information systems. Examples include use of small business accounting systems, inventory control and management systems, banking and finance packages, etc. with, in many cases, "always-on" broadband connection to the global INTERNET.

At the US federal government level, for example, risk assessment and management takes on new imperatives under Public Law 107–347 (Title III), the Federal Information Security Management Act (FISMA) of 2002. In relation to this, Katzke of the National Institute of Standards and Technology (NIST) has presented a checklist that expands the risk management function into a number of subheadings, as follows:

- Risk assessment
- Security planning
- Security policies and procedures
- Contingency planning
- Incident response planning
- Physical security

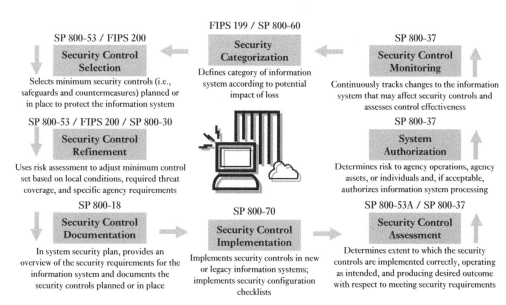

Figure 1   Risk management framework

- Personnel security
- Security assessments
- Security accreditation

This work ("Protecting the Nation's Critical Information Infrastructure: An Overview," presentation available from the FISMA project website of NIST) pays particular attention to the problem of classification and categorization of information resources in a general sense that is equally applicable to any enterprise, public or private. Such an activity forms the first part of any real risk assessment applied to an enterprise's information system. This role of classification and categorization is expanded in figure 1 from Katzke.

However, such risk-related activity does fully depend upon the existence of a complete and accurate inventory of all information systems in use in the enterprise, including the difficult problem of clearly identifying all client, server, and infrastructure systems that exist in the data network that comprises that information system. In current schemes, this may also include an assessment of other systems attached to the actual enterprise information system but outside the direct control of the enterprise, such as systems owned and operated by business partners, customer organizations or the like.

Risk assessment and management must also be considered in an IT-outsourced environment, particularly where information systems relevant to the critical operations of the enterprise may exist and be controlled offshore (*see* IT OUTSOURCING). It may be necessary to enter into appropriate contracts to cover the security of information systems in these cases but this does not mean that a thorough risk assessment can be avoided. Essentially, legally binding contracts act only as a form of "insurance after the fact," in case problems occur.

Associated terms useful in searching for more information are business continuity, security planning, information security management (IS 17799), and COBIT (Control Objectives for Information and Related Technologies).

risk management of information systems

Rodger Jamieson

Risk management is part of information systems security and auditing information systems and involves the identification, analysis, treatment, communication, and monitoring of risks within information systems. Information security risk management methods and techniques may be applied to complete information systems and facilities, or to individual system components or services, such as networking or E-COMMERCE interfaces.

See also *auditing of information systems; information assurance; risk assessment and risk management*

Bibliography

Standards Australia (2000). *HB231: 2000 Information Security Risk Management Guidelines*. Sydney: Standards Australia/Standards New Zealand.

S

SCM

see SUPPLY CHAIN MANAGEMENT

search engine

Gordon B. Davis

A search engine is a program that searches a database and, based on criteria for the search, presents the results. The information systems function may need to employ a search engine as part of an internal PORTAL for employees or an INTERNET portal to the organization for customers, vendors, prospective employees, etc. Employees of an organization will use a variety of search engines to obtain information from the Internet.

Search engines employ bots (program robots) to search the web for data. The bots examine the websites and index the contents. This information may be found in websites and databases. When a user specifies search terms, the indexes are searched and the results are presented, often in order by expected relevance.

There are a number of search engines that search the WORLDWIDE WEB. They differ in their approach to indexing and evaluating relevance. One approach, illustrated by Yahoo!, is to organize the available information using a hierarchical index. Relevance is associated with "fit" of the query to the hierarchical index. Another approach, illustrated by Google, is to use the content of the websites or databases to create large indexes of search terms. Relevance is identified using an algorithm based on frequency of access. Because of the different approaches by search engines to indexing content and computing relevance, some users prefer to employ more than one search engine. There are metasearch engines that search using a variety of search engines and present the results. Some metasearch engines combine and integrate the results; others present the results but do not integrate them.

The search engines for the worldwide web perform the searches without cost to the user. The business model for search engine providers is to obtain revenue from the companies that want to be "found" in a search. This is done by selling space on the pages that display results and by selling "results spaces" that are defined as paid. Popup ads may also be sold.

security of information systems

see INFORMATION ASSURANCE; RISK ASSESSMENT AND RISK MANAGEMENT

semantic web

Jinsoo Park

The semantic web is the evolution of the current WORLDWIDE WEB, which provides a global-scale infrastructure for explicitly expressing web data in a well-defined, human-readable, and machine-interpretable semantics. The semantic web is the vision originally of Tim Berners-Lee, known as the inventor of the worldwide web (WWW). In his book *Weaving the Web*, Berners-Lee said, "The first step is putting data on the Web in a form that machines can naturally understand, or converting it to that form. This creates what I call a *Semantic Web* – a web of data that can be processed directly or indirectly by machines." Note that "machines" refer to computer programs (e.g., software agents) that perform some tasks on the web.

The current web is originally designed for human consumption. The web information is typically based on HTML (*see* MARKUP LANGUAGES), and thus is machine-readable but not machine-interpretable. As a result, it is difficult for machines to automatically understand, process, and communicate. The intent of the semantic web is to serve as an information intermediary in support of humans, allowing information to be shared and reused across various applications, enterprises, and communities. It is the abstract representation of data on the web based on a set of standards and technologies, which can facilitate global semantic interoperation between machines. It is a collaborative effort led by the WWW Consortium (W3C) with participation from various research communities and industrial partners (www.w3c.org/2001/sw/).

Fundamental to the semantic web infrastructure is the implementation of layers of web technologies and standards as shown in figure 1. The basic layer of data representation is RDF (resource description framework) and RDF schema, which are built on the top of existing standards such as XML (EXTENSIBLE MARKUP LANGUAGE), URI (uniform resource identifier), and Unicode. RDF is used to support metadata for web resource description, while RDF schema extends RDF to provide semantics about RDF. The ONTOLOGY layer features

OWL (web ontology language), which is a family of ontology languages. The logic layer consists of rules that allow agents to make logical inferences to perform daily tasks. The proof layer supports the validation of those rule executions. The trust layer is the topmost layer, which serves as a mechanism to evaluate whether to trust the given proof or not. The DIGITAL SIGNATURE layer supports the notion of trust by checking integrity of the source documents. The logic, proof, and trust layers are not standardized yet.

The success of the semantic web will be largely determined by the availability of established ontologies and various contents that could be easily accessible by computer programs. Furthermore, as witnessed by the success of HTML-based web, various tools should allow non-experts to create ontologies and contents for the semantic web without any difficulty. The semantic web can be used in a wide range of application areas, which include, but are not limited to, WEB SERVICES, knowledge management (*see* KNOWLEDGE MANAGEMENT SYSTEMS), intelligent search, e-marketplace, E-COMMERCE, ubiquitous computing, natural language processing, virtual community, and intelligent integration of information. Semanticweb.org is the semantic web community PORTAL, which is dedicated to be a forum for people interested in the semantic web. This site provides available technologies and approaches related to the semantic web. Another interesting website for the information systems community is www.sigsemis.org/, which is maintained by

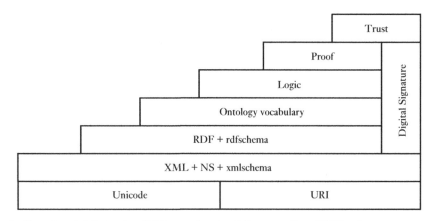

Figure 1   Semantic web infrastructure (W3C semantic web activity, www.w3.org/2001/sw/)

the Semantic Web and Information System Special Interest Group (SIG SEMIS).

SIM

The Society for Information Management is an international organization of information system executives (*see* ASSOCIATIONS AND SOCIETIES FOR INFORMATION SYSTEMS PROFESSIONALS).

smart cards

Gordon B. Davis

Smart cards are used for personal identification and access to services. Smart cards contain significant data to identify the smart card holder and hold information about transactions. The transaction information can be updated at each transaction. Examples of smart card use for access control are entry to buildings, access to bank accounts, access to medical services, and so forth. Smart cards are about the size and shape of a plastic credit card. In contrast to a credit card, which has a magnetic stripe with information about the card and its holder, a smart card contains a computer chip. This allows the card to communicate more data and to interact with the application for which the card is required. Smart cards are used more in Europe than in the US, where most access cards use magnetic stripes. The advantages of a smart card are increased interactive storage. It is more secure than a magnetic stripe. Some applications are banking, charging for purchases, identification, and security. For example, a smart card is used in Germany for health insurance and a smart card reader can be attached to a personal computer for use in secure INTERNET transactions.

sociotechnical concepts applied to information systems

Jim Coakes and Elayne Coakes

Sociotechnical thinking is important to the design, development, implementation, and use of information technology systems in organizations. It addresses vital issues in combining the use of powerful information and communication technologies with effective and humanistic use of people. Sociotechnical concepts are recognized by many academics and practitioners as vital to the design and use of work systems in organizations; the difficulty has been in incorporating them into the methods and methodologies that are employed by system designers and developers.

SOCIOTECHNICAL THEORY AND CONCEPTS

Sociotechnical thinking is a part of social theory and of philosophy. Its original emphasis was on organizational design and change management. In Coakes, Willis, and Lloyd-Jones (2000), the foundations and modern applications of sociotechnical theory are explored and the classic concepts extended. While much of the early work of the sociotechnical pioneers related to the shop floor and factory automation, later work looked at the impact of computer developments on office work. The concepts of sociotechnical design were found to be effective in redesigning work for computer-supported white-collar work, just as they had been beneficial in factory automation.

Two sources of the fundamental concepts of sociotechnical approaches are Follet and Cherns. Enid Mumford, the pioneer in using sociotechnical approaches for the design of information systems (IS), was influenced by the work of Mary Parker Follett, who wrote in the early 1900s. According to Mumford (1996a), there are a number of general principles that can be derived from the work of Follett, including:

- participation: in work and process design;
- representation: all users should be represented in the design group;
- joint problem solving: all are equal in decision-making and all should agree on the route to change and problem solving;
- freedom of speech: there should be face-to-face communication and honest exchanges of views; solutions will be obtained through integration and not compromise;
- gaining power: groups should recognize that joint work increases their power in relation to other organizational groups;

- integration of all factors: all relevant factors must be considered in the situation; and
- staying together: groups should maintain their cohesiveness over long periods.

Cherns's seminal papers (1976, 1987) provide well-accepted definitions of sociotechnical principles that cover all the main areas of participation. Of particular importance to IS development are: the involvement of staff in setting work boundaries; keeping power and information flows at lower levels of the organization; keeping the specification of work to a minimum (in order to minimize interference); making systems work compatibly with the rest of the organization; and keeping variances in views close to the holders of those views. Cherns's principles recognize that the design of work, organizations, and systems is forever reiterating, and that at the same time organization values are continually evolving. Cherns also outlines philosophies of stakeholder involvement, together with regulations and policies; he emphasizes (1987) that mechanisms are needed to resolve conflict, but he does not develop such mechanisms.

As applied to information systems, the term "sociotechnical" means a design approach that is intended to optimize both the application and development of technology and the application and development of human knowledge and skill. The underlying philosophy of sociotechnical approaches is based essentially on two ideas focusing on the individual and the organization. The first is the humanistic welfare paradigm, involving the redesign of work for autonomy, self-actualization, the use of self-regulating teams, individual empowerment, and thus stress reduction. In this view, the design of work systems is performed to improve the welfare of employees. The second (and perhaps contradictory philosophy) is the managerial paradigm, focusing on improving the performance of the organization (Land, 2000). Here change is intended to improve the organizational performance, which is measured by:

- added shareholder value;
- improved competitiveness;
- bottom-line improvements; and
- responsiveness to change.

If applied within the constraints of this paradigm, sociotechnical change methods will lead to a more "contented" workforce and thus improved performance that can be measured against these targets. Many would argue (see Land and Mumford's work) that there is an evident link between implementation of these principles and organizational effectiveness.

SOCIOTECHNICAL APPROACHES

Two sociotechnical approaches to IS development illustrate its use: the "ETHICS" (Effective Technical and Human Implementation of Computer-based Systems) methodology devised by Enid Mumford and the "Multiview" development approach.

ETHICS AND ENID MUMFORD

Enid Mumford's sociotechnical goal is to obtain joint optimization of the technical and social systems in an organization. Her work builds on the sociotechnical writings of the Tavistock Institute, London.

Mumford describes ETHICS as a set of sequential steps that enable the needs of businesses and people to be incorporated into the design effort. It is a subjective approach to IS development (ISD); it emphasizes order and does not prioritize the investigation of conflict. Potential users of systems are helped to diagnose their requirements and problems and set their own objectives for efficiency and effectiveness and even job satisfaction. Users can assess alternative technical and organizational strategies in order to select the ones that fit their highest-priority objectives most closely.

Mumford (1996b: 11) describes the specific details of ETHICS as follows:

> The ETHICS method includes the following systematic steps:

- Diagnosing user needs and problems, focusing on both short- and long-term efficiency and job satisfaction.
- Setting efficiency and job satisfaction objectives.
- Developing a number of alternative design strategies and matching them against these objectives.

- Choosing the strategy which best achieves both sets of objectives.
- Choosing hardware and software and designing the system in detail.
- Implementing the new system.
- Evaluating the new system once it is operational.

ETHICS incorporates the following diagnostic and design tools.

1 A framework to assist the identification of mission, key tasks, important constraints and factors critical to effective operation.
2 A variance analysis tool to assist the identification of significant problems and problem areas.
3 A questionnaire to measure job satisfaction.
4 A framework to identify likely changes in the internal and external environments.
5 A set of guidelines for individual and group work design.

These objectives, steps, and tools are used as a general problem-solving approach to assess the non-technical aspects of systems design, including organizational design and the quality of life.

Mumford emphasizes that the ETHICS approach may enable the system stakeholders to increase their ability to manage their own organizational change, thus reducing the role of external experts and indicating a shift of power both from the technological imperialists (the IT department and IT vendors) and a limited number of managers to more broadly based staff.

The key challenges in sociotechnical implementation, it has been argued (Langefors, 1973), include the development of user participation and interpretation of findings when establishing requirements. Also, there is a challenge in retaining stakeholder involvement in design and development when scaling up the sociotechnical approach to large organizational systems or large multinational establishments (Mumford, 1996b).

STRENGTHS AND INSUFFICIENCIES OF ETHICS

Sociotechnical approaches, while they clearly contribute to IS development, also have insufficiencies. Sociotechnical thinking contains an agenda that is not necessarily achieved in the ETHICS method. The concepts describe consensus building in groups, but there are difficulties in implementing the concepts. Sociotechnical thinking has, in general, also emphasized emancipation as an objective, but sociotechnical methods in information systems do not deal comprehensively with the issue.

Sociotechnical agendas. Sociotechnical change models have an agenda behind their methods and processes. This agenda is related to the moral and ethical imperative which underpins the way in which they examine the workplace and workforce. This moral imperative is highlighted by sociotechnical approaches to information system development where it is intended to "use system development approaches as a vehicle to rethink the social work environment in which the new system would be implemented," with the aim of achieving: "job satisfaction, learning, opportunities for advancement . . . and the use of new skills" (Hirschheim, Klein, and Lyytinen, 1995: 36). Pasmore (1988) also interprets the sociotechnical systems change model as being initially agenda driven; he enumerates nine preordained stages of work, arguing that investigations are constrained by the narrow methodological scope and that for sociotechnical approaches, semi-autonomous teams have become an answer for every change situation. The sociotechnical agenda is also seen by some as management manipulation to reduce worker resistance to systems (Bjerknes and Bratteteig, 1995).

The most well-known sociotechnical system development and change methodology is that of Enid Mumford (see above), who draws up schematics of the stages of the ETHICS methodology in which the work starts by identifying the problem before identifying boundaries. At this stage, the analyst does not have much information from stakeholders about their perceptions, culture, or daily work. The sociotechnical analyst starts as an expert in that agenda and framework of analysis, primarily addressing issues established by the client. Mitroff and Linstone (1993) state that this leads to the filtering out of images that are inconsistent with (the analyst's) past experience.

Later in the sociotechnical development process the analyst facilitates the user, rather than the more broadly defined stakeholders, to resolve his or her issues. The analyst's role (Avison and Wood Harper, 1995) becomes that of an "agent for social progress" putting change into place, or as a "change agent" encouraging users to develop such changes themselves.

As always, the theory and principles are not the same as the practice of an approach. This is highlighted in Mumford's work, where, having spelt out the ETHICS approach, she emphasizes that designing and implementing sociotechnical systems is unlikely to be easy, since implementation requires the enthusiasm and involvement of management, staff, and other stakeholders. The approach also requires leadership and conviction, elements that are very difficult to encapsulate in the descriptions and principles of a methodology. Furthermore, Mumford expects practitioners to have a belief in the right of employees to work in humanistic work systems and to believe that a sociotechnical approach can benefit all participants, help the creativity and development of individuals and groups, as well as contribute to the commercial success of the organization.

Thus, the agendas of sociotechnical work, in terms of the client's commission and methodological framework for implementing change, support the IS development, but at the same time color the findings with the predetermined agendas of the researchers, however positive these may be toward stakeholders. Research has shown that, in some circumstances, the effects of predetermined agendas can be mitigated through application of ethnographic approaches (Coakes, 2004).

Linking representations with the working world. Sociotechnical approaches such as ETHICS originate from social science and ethical disciplines that readily accept divergent views and qualitative inputs. ETHICS analyzes and develops models of the work system in order to enhance that system and the participation of its users, and to meet management goals. ETHICS models represent, for example, roles and responsibilities; missions, key tasks, and critical success factors; social systems and relationships; and value-adding activities. ETHICS also identifies and prioritizes information needs in order to create a core IS. However, discursive and word-based sociotechnical models are not formal representations; their links with formal data and process models that inform computerized IS (CIS) design, and with the working world, are limited.

Mumford (1983) says that users can and do design properly. Pava (1990) additionally recommends that sociotechnical design should be used to see different perspectives on situations, which enable stakeholders to develop their own processes, matching these to organizational needs within a changing environment. However, stakeholders are then likely to design information systems for their own use, rather than aiming to meet the needs of a wide range of users. Therefore, for instance, when integration of database-driven CISs is required, systems analysts still have to provide the expertise required to develop, for example, integrated data-related object models that can support a range of functions within one set of broadly based CISs.

We can see from the discussion above that sociotechnical approaches such as ETHICS offer more richness than hard approaches, and complement soft approaches (Checkland, 1981, 1984). By starting from different objectives, they aim to insure deeper investigation and representation of stakeholder-oriented issues.

COMBINING APPROACHES: MULTIVIEW

Sociotechnical approaches such as ETHICS do not cover all stages of IS development. For example, the discursive sociotechnical models show us how people interact with one another and their organizations, but do not give us the formal data and process models that are needed to inform CIS design. Multiview (Wood-Harper, Antill, and Avison, 1985), updated as Multiview2 (Avison et al., 1998; Avison and Wood-Harper, 2003) combines the ideas of sociotechnical and soft approaches with those of "hard" methodologies such as information engineering, and reconciles task-based and issue-based concerns.

The Multiview framework. Multiview links organizational analysis, information modeling, sociotechnical analysis and design, and the technical aspects of system design. It recognizes the importance of context by offering "a contingency approach . . . that . . . will be adapted according to the particular situation in the organization and the application" (Avison and Fitzgerald, 1995: 375).

Avison and Fitzgerald argue that, to be complete in human as well as in technical terms, the methodology must provide help in answering questions about the IS that:

- furthers the aims of the organization concerned;
- fits into the working lives of users and considers their relationship to its use and output;
- insures that individuals best relate to the machine in terms of operating it and using the output from it;
- identifies information system functions; and
- identifies the technical specification that will come close enough to achieving the above.

Multiview addresses these issues in five stages, which are to be emphasized according to context:

1 analysis of the human aspects, applying soft approaches;
2 analysis of the information, data, and functions required;
3 analysis and design of the sociotechnical aspects;
4 design of the human–computer interface;
5 design of the technical aspects.

Multiview2 moves away from the more traditional waterfall-oriented approach of ISD to an iterative and less sequential operation. In Multiview2, the first (soft analysis) stage is expanded to cover organizational issues such as strategy, organizational change (e.g., business process redesign), and analysis of possible future developments. Also, the fourth and fifth stages detailed above are combined, and all stages are coordinated by a mediation process, which promotes responsible participation, taking into account the organizational structure and stakeholders' attitudes.

Thus Multiview combines hard, soft, and sociotechnical approaches. It combines the strengths of people-oriented soft analysis and sociotechnical approaches with the hard analysis

demanded by the database-based CIS. This still leaves some insufficiencies in that predetermined agendas still color findings, group psychological factors (Coakes, 2004) can hide some stakeholders' contributions, and there is room to enhance the development and linking of the representations that inform CIS design.

CONCLUSION

Sociotechnical approaches facilitate the involvement of stakeholders in the design of IS and jobs. The concepts do not provide a complete development methodology. In order to execute all stages of the CIS development process, sociotechnical work needs to be complemented by analytical approaches, such as the "hard" analytical methods. Soft approaches are also relevant in assessing issues of people and politics; and ethnographic approaches produce findings that are less influenced by developer agendas. The challenge is to find practical ways of combining several approaches. One such combined effort to bring sociotechnical work into IS development is Multiview.

Bibliography

Avison, D. E. and Fitzgerald, G. (1995). *Information System Development: Methodologies, Techniques, and Tools*. Maidenhead: McGraw-Hill.

Avison, D. E. and Wood-Harper, A. T. (1995). Experience of Multiview: Some reflections. In F. Stowell (ed.), *Information System Provision*. Maidenhead: McGraw-Hill, pp. 102–17.

Avison, D. E. and Wood-Harper, A. T. (2003). Bringing social and organizational issues into information systems development: The story of Multiview. In S. Clarke, E. Coakes, M. G. Hunter, and A. Wenn (eds.), *Socio-Technical and Human Cognition Elements of Information Systems*. Hershey, PA: Information Science, pp. 5–21.

Avison, D. E., Wood-Harper, A. T., Vidgen, R. T., and Wood, J. R. G. (1998). Multiview2: A further exploration into information systems development. *Information, Technology, and People*, 11, 124–39.

Bjerknes, G. and Bratteteig, T. (1995). User participation and democracy: A discussion of Scandinavian research on system development. *Scandinavian Journal of Information Systems*, 7 (1), 73–98.

Checkland, P. B. (1981). *System Thinking, Systems Practice*. Chichester: John Wiley.

Checkland, P. B. (1984). Systems theory and information systems. In T. M. A. Bemelmans (ed.), *Beyond Prod-*

uctivity: Information Systems Development for Organizational Effectiveness. Amsterdam: Elsevier North-Holland, pp. 9–21.

Cherns, A. (1976). The principles of sociotechnical design. *Human Relations*, 9 (8), 783–92.

Cherns, A. (1987). The principles of sociotechnical design revisited. *Human Relations*, 40 (3), 153–62.

Coakes, E., Willis, D., and Lloyd-Jones, R. (2000). *The New SocioTech: Graffiti on the LongWall*. London: Springer-Verlag.

Coakes, J. (2004). Discovering and representing stakeholders' requirements for management information systems, in context. PhD thesis, Royal Holloway College, University of London.

Hirschheim, R., Klein, H. K., and Lyytinen, K. (1995). *Information Systems Development and Data Modelling*. Cambridge: Cambridge University Press.

Land, F. F. (1976). Evaluation of systems goals in determining a design strategy for a computer-based information system. *Computer Journal*, 19 (4), 290–4.

Land, F. F. (2000). Evaluation in a socio-technical context. LSE working papers, London.

Land, F. F. and Hirschheim, R. A. (1983). Participative systems design: Rationale, tools, and techniques. *Applied Systems Analysis*, 10, 91–107.

Langefors, R. (1973). *Theoretical Analysis of Information Systems*. Philadelphia, PA: Auerbach.

Mitroff, I. I. and Linstone, H. A. (1993). *The Unbounded Mind: Breaking the Chains of Traditional Business Thinking*. Oxford: Oxford University Press.

Mumford, E. (1983). *Designing Secretaries*. Manchester: Manchester Business School.

Mumford, E. (1996a). Designing for freedom in a technical world. In W. Orlowkowski, G. Walsham, M. R. Jones, and J. I. DeGross (eds.), *IT and Changes in Organizational Work*. London: Chapman and Hall, pp. 425–41.

Mumford, E. (1996b). *Systems Design: Ethical Tools for Ethical Change*. Basingstoke: Macmillan.

Pasmore, W. A. (1988). *Designing Effective Organizations: The Socio-Technical Systems Perspective*. New York: John Wiley.

Pava, C. (1990). Redesigning socio-technical systems: Concepts and methods for the 1990s. *Applied Behavioral Science*, 22 (3), 201–21.

Wood-Harper, A. T., Antill, L., and Avison, D. (1985). *Information Systems Definition: The Multiview Approach*. Oxford: Blackwell.

soft systems methodologies

Frank F. Land

Soft systems methodologies were developed in reaction to the lack of success in applying mathematical (hard) methodologies to certain types of problems. A short review shows the historical context for soft systems. A new discipline labeled operational (or operations) research emerged from World War II. It applied mathematical techniques to solving a variety of operational problems. Problems ranging from the best deployment of checkout counters in a supermarket to metaproblems relating to the world's use of non-sustainable resources appeared to be susceptible to the new mathematical treatments offered by the disciplines of operational research, mathematical programming, industrial dynamics, and systems analysis. The availability of computers enabled larger and more complex problems to be tackled.

These so called "hard" techniques were useful only if it were possible to define the problem to be solved in clear and unambiguous terms. In wartime, it was often possible to define the objective of a system clearly and in terms that could be quantified. Moreover, there was an expectation that all stakeholders shared the goals. In situations where there were conflicts in the desirability of outcomes, the techniques took second place to what were often political judgments. Hard approaches worked well when the problem situation was well understood and clearly defined, there was broad agreement on desirable outcomes, and outcomes lent themselves to quantification and measurement.

For many business problems, instead of a definable problem, there is a feeling of unease, perhaps triggered by some unexpected changes in performance. Human behavior is frequently unpredictable and responses to situations contradict expectations. The outcomes looked for from an action, say the introduction of a new system to monitor the performance of a group of employees, turns out to reduce rather than increase productivity. A system introduced into different branches of an enterprise, all apparently identical, nevertheless results in a wide range of outcomes, some meeting all targets, others having to be abandoned as failures. Many of the desirable outcomes from an action may be classed as intangible. They do not lend themselves to measurement, or the outcomes are the consequence of so great a range of external and internal factors that it becomes impossible to relate the outcome to any single cause. Cultural and political factors may influence the actions of stakeholders. The problem situation may be unstructured.

The failure of "hard" methods to cope with this kind of situation led to the development of so-called "soft" approaches. Peter Checkland, of the University of Lancaster in England, has developed the best-known method. He was schooled in the hard systems methodology that had so successfully helped to solve some problems, but he was dissatisfied with the limitations noted above. He observed that "human activity systems," systems in which humans participated as planners, decision-makers, and operators, did not behave as the "hard" school anticipated. He sought to develop techniques that would enable systems analysts to work on human activity systems. His methodology, now widely used in many parts of the world, is called *soft systems methodology* (SSM) (Checkland, 1999; Checkland and Howell, 1997).

SSM provides a way of developing insights to illuminate unclear problem situations. It guides an analyst to view an organization as a "human activity system." In SSM, the first task of the analyst is to determine the system under investigation. In information system studies, it is the part of the organization where the problematic situation lies. The analyst's study should, at its conclusion, lead to a plan of action that will improve the system's function. The analyst needs to insure that a proposed plan of action is acceptable to the relevant stakeholders and can be implemented by the organization and by the people who work there. In other words, a plan must be formulated that is not just desirable in terms of the goals of the organization, but that can be feasibly implemented in the organization in question.

Figure 1 illustrates the SSM approach (the description of how SSM is used is taken from Avgerou and Cornford, 1993). It represents SSM as a process with seven stages. In the first two stages, the analyst finds out what makes the situation problematic. To do that, it is useful to build up the richest possible picture of the situation studied by observing the processes taking place, by interviewing different stakeholders, and by examining reports and other organizational documents. It is important that the analyst gains an understanding of the functioning (and

personalities) of the informal system that exists in all organizations, as well as the formal, designed system. A rich picture may be expressed in terms of structures, such as the power hierarchy and the communication patterns and processes, decision-making, and operations. It should also capture the various viewpoints from which the problem situation can be perceived. Conflicting views about a problem are likely to stem from different ways of viewing the world: the stakeholders' *Weltanschauung*. Displaying the situation in a way that reveals the different points of view helps in deciding the range of possible actions to follow.

In stage 3 of SSM, the analyst uses what has been discovered about the problem situation to define notional human activity systems that seem relevant to the problem. Checkland calls these *root definitions*. Several root definitions can be developed, according to the various *Weltanschauungen* revealed in the rich picture of the situation. Each root definition must give a clear statement of the system under study. The differences in the root definitions indicate the extent to which issues such as goals and objectives are shared, as well as understanding what some of the organization processes are intended to support.

In stage 4 of SSM, the analyst forms a model of activities for each root definition. An activity model is a description of the activities that need to be carried out for the system to perform the transformation process of the relevant root definition.

In stage 5, the analyst compares the conceptual activity with what actually happens in the part of the organization under study. The objective of this stage is to tease out the complexities, contradictions, and perceived and actual inadequacies of the existing situation.

At stages 6 and 7, the analyst opens the debate about possible changes that can be made to improve the perceived problem situation. The task is to find which of the suggested changes can be implemented. The actions for change must be compatible with the culture of the organization and acceptable to its stakeholders. The analyst should seek a consensus solution: there must be agreement on the validity and utility of the proposed changes.

The wavy line in figure 1 indicates the split between two different classes of activities. Those

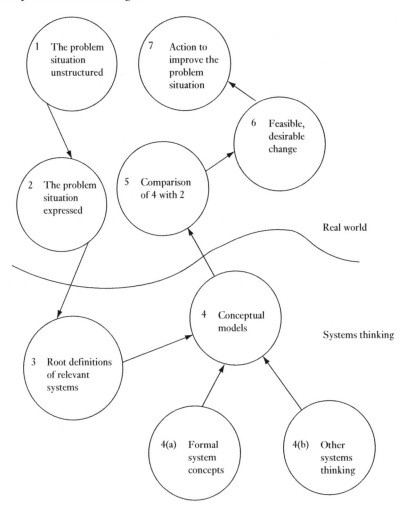

Figure 1   Outline of soft systems methodology (Checkland, 1999; reprinted by permission of John Wiley & Sons, Ltd)

stages lying above the line involve interactions of the analyst with the stakeholders of the organization concerned. Those lying under the line are desk work, where the analyst applies and uses systems concepts in order to formulate and structure his or her perceptions of the problem situation and to model its functioning.

The main value of SSM lies in its making the analyst aware that organizational problems are embedded in human activity systems where alternative points of view govern behavior and where successful change requires acceptance and commitment from the relevant stakeholders. It provides an approach that enables the analyst

to get a better understanding of the organizational realities that determine the effectiveness of the enterprise.

SSM is just one approach to dealing with the uncertainties, informality, and unstructuredness found within most organizations (Rosenhead, 1989). Other methods tackle different aspects of the problem. Fuzzy logic provides a method for dealing with the problem of partially indeterminate relationships between the entities of a system. Multiple objective, multiple criteria evaluation methods enable the analyst to select solutions where different stakeholders have varying objectives and, even if they agree on objectives, may attach very different values to them. The analytic hierarchical process (AHP) developed by Saaty provides a way of selecting from a range of options where the characteristics of some options can be defined in quantitative forms, but those of others only in words of the form "I prefer A to B." "Soft" methods are now regarded as an important weapon in avoiding failure in systems design and development and in helping to design effective systems.

Bibliography

Avgerou, C. and Cornford, T. (1993). *Developing Information Systems: Concepts, Issues and Practice*. London: Macmillan.

Checkland, P. (1999). *Systems Thinking, Systems Practice: Includes a 30-Year Retrospective*. Chichester: John Wiley.

Checkland, P. and Howell, S. (1997). *Information, Systems and Information Systems: Making Sense in the Field*. Chichester: John Wiley.

Rosenhead, J. V. (1989). *Rational Analysis for a Problematic World*. Chichester: John Wiley.

software

Gordon B. Davis

The term *software* is contrasted with *hardware*. In computer hardware, elementary operations and functions are fixed by the equipment design and circuitry; software creates operations and functions based on a set of instructions termed a program. The software instructions make use of the hardware operations and functions to create a variety of more complex functions and sequences of operations. Software allows a single hardware design to be used for a large number of different purposes. The program of instructions is not permanently stored in the computer; it is input when needed. A program that is to be executed is brought into the main memory of the computer; when not in use, it is stored on disk or other accessible storage.

The set of instructions that comprise a computer program can be written so that it modifies itself as the instructions are executed. A program can, in essence, build the execution path as the program is run. There are usually numerous program paths that may be selected; the actual path of instructions executed depends on the data being processed, instructions provided by the user at execution, and the way the solution process was programmed. The potential number of unique combinations of instructions that can be executed by a program can easily number in the millions. This is why software is so useful in processing complex procedures required for human systems. It is also a reason why it is difficult to make sure software is correct.

All business systems that use computers are designed as *human–machine systems* (*see* HUMAN–MACHINE INTERACTION). Software is used in connection with human input, human review, and human decision-making. The advantages of computers are that they are very fast and consistent. The consistency of processing is very valuable in performing procedures required by organizations. However, humans are still needed in most business processes. Even though software can be flexible with program paths to deal with different situations, it cannot innovate and respond to unanticipated inputs in the same way as humans.

Software in the information system is of two general types: *application software* and *system software*. The application software performs the information processing required by the organization; system software provides services needed by applications and supports the development of application software.

SYSTEM SOFTWARE

System software consists of software that provides facilities and functions to allow applications to be developed and to operate. General types of system software are the operating system, communications software, database software, and development software. System software is purchased or leased from software vendors and not developed by user organizations.

The operating system is the most fundamental system software. It is loaded in the computer prior to application programs, because it provides facilities for hardware utilization by the application program and monitors program execution for various types of errors related to hardware use. The basic operating system functions include job execution control, allocation and management of system resources, and standard methods for the use of input and output devices (*see* INPUT DEVICES; OUTPUT DEVICES). For example, the application program may specify reading data from a record stored on a disk; the operating system provides the instructions to manage the physical reading of the record from disk storage. It also provides facilities for common activities such as sorting, although these are often referred to as utilities. Other system software extends the operating system concept to provide general facilities to manage user interfaces, provide database management facilities, and manage electronic communications (*see* EMAIL).

Graphical user interfaces (*see* GRAPHICAL USER INTERFACE) are generally provided to improve ease of use. The user interface software provides facilities that improve the user interaction with the operating system and allows switching among programs, transferring data between them, copying files, and other user-support facilities.

Communications software provides facilities for applications that rely on data communications. A single data communications package is installed to manage all transfer of data, deal with transmission errors, handle protocols, and so forth. In a local area network (*see* LOCAL AREA NETWORKS), the network is managed by a local area network operating system. In a wide area network, the communications software manages the communications over telephone lines or other network facilities. Database management software extends the data and file management facilities of the operating system. The DATABASE MANAGEMENT SYSTEM (DBMS) may be used by application software to manage access and storage of data.

The general category of system software includes support for application development. The development of applications requires software development tools, such as high-level software to generate programs from specifications, computer language software for writing processing procedures, and software to assist in various parts of the program development process. The database management software package that supports application programs also contains program development facilities.

APPLICATION SOFTWARE

Application software is designed for specific business activities such as transaction processing, data analysis, business processes, report preparation, and so forth. Applications software can be purchased as complete packages, developed using high-level program generators, or developed using programming language facilities. The way they were acquired or developed affects how they use the operating system and facilities for user interface, communications, and database management. Application software packages are typically written to be used with a certain operating system. For example, an application package for a microcomputer may require a specific operating system and version number; a large mainframe package may require a specific mainframe operating system.

PROGRAMMING LANGUAGES

Computer hardware is instructed by a program of machine-language instructions in primary storage. For all practical purposes, programmers never write computer instructions in machine language. The programmer writes instructions in a language more suited to human use and the instructions are translated to machine language. The programmer may also employ development tools that generate programs from specifications. The translation process from the source program written in a programming language to an object program in machine-level instructions uses software called an assembler for low-level languages or a compiler for higher-level languages. There are also a number of facilities in the development software to assist in linking programs, editing programs, testing programs, and maintaining programs in libraries.

A programming language (*see* PROGRAMMING LANGUAGES) consists of a syntax, command words, naming rules, and rules for constructing instructions and specifications. There are hundreds of different computer languages. Languages may be designed to support the writing of programs as a sequence of procedures (a procedural language) or as separate program objects that encapsulate the instructions and data associated with business functions (object-oriented languages). There are different levels of programming languages. The lowest level is a symbolic assembly language close to the machine level, the middle level is a language oriented to the procedures and steps in processing or problem solving (such as COBOL), and the third level consists of problem-oriented programming facilities and very high-level language (often called fourth-generation languages or 4GLs) designed to focus on describing the output to be achieved or the problem to be solved (rather than detailed processing or solution procedures). Object-oriented programming centers program design around program objects, each of which encapsulates all the data and procedures associated with it (*see* OBJECT-ORIENTED PROGRAMS AND SYSTEMS). The most common high-level languages in business use are business data processing languages, algorithmic languages, and database languages. As part of these languages, there may be facilities for designing and building graphical user interfaces with which humans interact with computer programs.

Data processing languages are designed for handling business transactions and preparing business documents and reports. The dominant language for many years was COBOL (COmmon Business-Oriented Language), a procedural language. More than two-thirds of all business applications were written in COBOL and many COBOL programs are still in use. Most new applications use other languages more suited to the environment of microcomputers and INTERNET applications. A language that has had use with microcomputers is C, a language with some low- and some high-level features. C++ is an object-oriented language based on the C language. Java is an object-oriented language similar to C++. Java programs are compiled into a format that can be executed by a Java interpreter available on most computers. Java has features that make it useful in programming applications for use on the Internet.

Algorithmic languages facilitate writing formulas and computational procedures. There are many different languages to match special conditions; one of the most common is FORTRAN. It has been used extensively in scientific and engineering work, but newer languages suited to interactive applications and Internet applications are frequently used. A simplified algorithmic language for user programmers is Basic.

There are several database query languages. The standard approach to a query language is termed SQL (structured query language) designed for programming access to a RELATIONAL DATABASE. It is important because of the extent of use, the fact that it can be used across a large number of computer types and sizes, and that it has been standardized. Data can be selected with SQL, using various criteria, and combined in a number of ways. The language also provides facilities for data entry, report formatting, and other procedures. Many query languages provide simplified interfaces for users and others writing queries, but they tend to be based on the standard SQL language.

ACQUISITION OF APPLICATION SOFTWARE

There are several options to be considered in the acquisition or development of application software. Three major choices are application package, application generator, and custom development using a programming language.

Commercial application packages are written to be used by a large number of organizations for a common business processing application. They are identical in general purpose to application software written by an individual company. They are, however, written and maintained by a software company that sells or leases the software. The software vendor takes responsibility for all aspects of development and maintenance, including documentation, user instruction manuals, error corrections, and enhancements. The vendor usually provides training for users and maintains helplines to answer questions about the software. There is a growing trend toward acquisition of application packages as the preferred approach to software acquisition.

Application packages may be used without change, customized with input/output changes, and customized by adding unique features. The one chosen will depend on a number of factors. In the no-change approach, the company changes its processes and procedures to adapt to the package. This is often a useful approach to process redesign, especially if the package is based on leading-edge practices. The inputs, outputs, reports, and procedures are all defined by the package. The configuration options provide a limited number of alternatives for modeling company operations; these permit users to select the alternative that provides the best fit with company procedures. Many commercial packages have a number of options for making input/output or similar changes to the package. Examples of input/output changes include the design of inputs, reports, external documents (such as purchase orders and invoices), and the meaning of user-definable codes. The input/output changes do not change the basic logic and functions of the package.

In the customizing approach, the application software package defines the basic requirements and forms the starting point for adding unique features. The changes can be done in-house or by the package vendor. The advantage is that the basic features are well tested and meet general requirements, while the additions or changes provide unique capabilities for the company. The disadvantages are that the company may be constrained by the package's basic functionality and must take responsibility for updating the application when the basic package is altered.

In general purpose application generator packages, much of the application is generated from simple user-defined specifications. Such packages have facilities for common tasks such as spreadsheet computation, statistical analysis, and data management. When a person uses a software package for a task, such as preparing a spreadsheet, the package does the processing based on the specification that the user has given. It is a very cost-effective way to program. It fits the concept of END-USER COMPUTING, although such application generator packages are also used by professional developers. The packages may be used to develop applications. Simple commands create an application complete with input/output screens, editing of input data, storage and retrieval of data, computations, and other processes. Examples of application development facilities in software packages are a macro-language, user-defined menus, and user-defined error handling.

THE SOFTWARE DEVELOPMENT PROCESS

SOFTWARE ENGINEERING is a systematic approach to the development of quality software. The hierarchy of systems and relationships of subsystems in applications are the basis for a design approach termed *structured design*. The software engineering approach follows a basic engineering principle for dealing with complexity by dividing programs into modules, routines, and subroutines based on tasks, functions, and actions to be performed.

software agents

Gove Allen

An agent is an individual who is authorized to act on behalf of another person. Software agents are computer programs that either act on behalf of a person, or take the place of a person in a system designed for human interaction. As the INTERNET and WORLDWIDE WEB (WWW) gained broad acceptance, software agents have proliferated. The WWW is designed to allow humans to retrieve documents from a server and quickly reference documents located on other servers. Because web documents were originally designed strictly for human access, any software program that systematically requests web documents may be termed a software agent.

Among the first software agents widely used on the Internet were search engines (*see* SEARCH ENGINE) such as AltaVista, InfoSeek, Excite, Lycos, and Google. The interfaces of search engines that Internet users see (e.g., www.google.com) are not software agents. The interface simply allows a user to query the search engine's index of Internet content. The program that generates the search engine's index is the software agent. These agents request a document from a server on the web. When the page is retrieved, the contents are parsed for at least two different kinds of data. First, the text of the document that would be visible to a user is stored in an index so it can be searched quickly. Second, each hypertext reference (or hyperlink) to other documents contained on the page is extracted. The documents these hyperlinks reference are requested in turn and parsed in a similar manner. The software agents that request and parse these documents are often called "crawlers" because they arbitrarily "crawl" the entire web by following hyperlinks from one document to another. These crawlers are sometimes also called "spiders." Major search engines use thousands of computers to simultaneously run such software agents to keep their indices up to date.

Some software agents fit the more general definition of agent not only by interacting with a system designed for use by humans, but also by acting on behalf of a human. Several online auction agents (e.g., sniperight.com) allow an individual to configure a program to interact with online auctions (e.g., ebay.com) that are designed for human interaction. These agents will place bids on behalf of their principals and "decide" which auctions to pursue and which auctions to disengage based on the behavior of other bidders and the outcomes of other auctions. In such a situation, the software agent truly "acts for" the principal – even entering into contracts that may be legally binding.

Software agents are also used in other Internet contexts. The web has allowed companies to get information to potential customers on an unprecedented scale; however, such information (often including pricing) is also readily available to competitors. Software agents can easily be configured to allow a company to monitor the online offerings of competitors. Academic researchers are also using software agents to collect information about how individuals and companies (and other software agents) behave in electronic environments.

The term "software agent" and "intelligent agent" are often used synonymously. However, for an agent to be termed "intelligent" it must exhibit behavior that is normally associated with intelligent individuals. Although the term does not enjoy a universally accepted definition, some software does exhibit "intelligent" behavior. One such example is the class of programs termed "recommendation systems."

Recommendation systems (e.g., netperceptions.com) do not interact with systems intended for use by humans; however, they do perform a service normally reserved for intelligent beings. By supplying information about likes/dislikes and interests (either directly or indirectly), recommendation systems are able to suggest other products or services that an individual may also enjoy. Whether such systems expressly collect preferences about movies or songs an individual has seen or heard to recommend others, or determines which product to advertise along with a particular online news article, they perform a task that until very recently was reserved for intelligent beings. As such they are also categorized as intelligent agents or software agents.

software engineering

Sandra A. Slaughter

Software engineering is the application of formal engineering principles, concepts, and methodologies to construct software systems. It involves the use of a systematic, disciplined, quantifiable approach for the development, testing, implementation, operation, and maintenance of software systems. The focus of software engineering tends to be large systems that have substantial performance, capacity, reliability, security, quality, and safety requirements. The software engineering discipline addresses how such systems are built and maintained in ways that are economically viable for the producers and users.

Software Engineering Institute

Mary Beth Chrissis, Linda Levine, and Sandy Shrum

The Software Engineering Institute (SEI) is known internationally for its work on improvement of SOFTWARE ENGINEERING practice. The mission of the SEI, a federally funded research and development center (FFRDC) located at Carnegie Mellon University, is to advance the practice of software engineering. The primary beneficiaries of the SEI are the US Department of Defense (DoD) and the SEI's principal sponsor, the Office of the Under Secretary of Defense for Acquisition, Technology, and Logistics (OUSD (AT&L)); US military services; government agencies; the contracting organizations that serve the government; commercial organizations that develop, support, or maintain software-intensive products; and academic and commercial providers of education and training.

The SEI mission includes four objectives:

● to accelerate the introduction and widespread use of high-payoff software engineering practices and technology by identifying, evaluating, and maturing promising or underused technology and practices;

- to maintain a long-term competence in software engineering and technology transition;
- to enable industry and government organizations to make measured improvements in their software engineering practices by working with them directly;
- to foster the adoption and sustained use of standards of excellence for software engineering practice.

The SEI's strategic approach to achieving its mission can be summarized in three words: create, apply, and amplify:

- The SEI works with the research community to help *create* and identify new and improved practices.
- The SEI works with leading-edge software developers and acquirers to *apply* and validate the new and improved practices.
- The SEI works through the global community of software engineers to *amplify* the impact of the new and improved practices by encouraging and supporting their widespread adoption.

For more information, consult the SEI website: www.sei.cmu.edu.

software maintenance

Sandra A. Slaughter

Software maintenance refers to the process of modifying an existing software system following its general release to users (IEEE, 1998). It applies to both system software and applications. There are several different kinds of maintenance activities including adaptive, corrective, and perfective maintenance (Swanson, 1976). Adaptive maintenance is performed to change software when its technical environment changes, such as when a new operating system or hardware platform is implemented. Corrective maintenance is performed to correct software defects. Enhancement is a type of maintenance often called perfective maintenance that is performed to add new capabilities to a software system.

Reengineering is maintenance that improves the design of some or all of a software system, often using refactoring, so that the system can be more easily maintained in the future. Repairs tend to dominate the maintenance activity for the first few months of operation of a new software system. Later in the system life cycle, most of the maintenance is enhancement. Software maintenance can be performed by the system developers, a separate maintenance group, or by an external firm if it is outsourced.

PRODUCTIVITY IN SOFTWARE MAINTENANCE

Software systems are long-lived and expensive to maintain. It is estimated, for example, that the average age of enterprise general ledger systems in Fortune 1000 companies is 15 years (Kalakota and Whinston, 1996). To satisfy changing information requirements, software systems are often modified and enhanced over their life cycles. In fact, the activities occurring post-launch (i.e., after initial implementation) can account for as much as 90 percent of the total product life cycle for software (Bennett, 1996).

It is thought that many problems in software maintenance are caused by inadequacies in the initial software design (Schneidewind, 1987). Poor choices in software development may result in low-quality software that is difficult to modify. A particularly problematic aspect of the software that ensues from bad design is software complexity. Software complexity refers to the characteristics of the data structures and procedures in the code that make the software hard to understand. Numerous studies have suggested the importance of software complexity for performance in software maintenance (Kemerer, 1995). Software complexity is believed to interfere with the critical maintenance activity of software comprehension. Software that is large in size or that has complicated data interactions or logic paths is difficult to understand. There are several measures of software complexity. For procedural PROGRAMMING LANGUAGES, the most noted are Halstead's (1977) software science metrics, which measure software volume, and McCabe's (1976) cyclomatic complexity metric, which counts the number of decision paths in the software. For object-oriented approaches, complexity can be assessed by determining class cohesion or the degree of coupling between classes (Chidamber and Kemerer, 1994). These measures, as well as others, can be used to assess the quality of software design. Such assessment is important to insure that maintainability is built in to the software when it is initially constructed.

The productivity benefits of design for maintainability have been demonstrated in several empirical studies (e.g., Gibson and Senn, 1989; Banker and Slaughter, 2000). In a study of business-oriented information systems at two firms, Banker and Slaughter (2000) show that structured design is most advantageous for the more volatile software systems in terms of reduced maintenance costs and errors. The results of this study imply that high investment in practices such as structured design may not be economically efficient in all situations. In resource-constrained environments, software managers should therefore focus their efforts on promoting efficient design choices.

Maintenance Management Concerns

There are several managerial issues related to software maintenance. A critical task is to effectively manage the system portfolio, or set of systems. As software systems age, they tend to become more complicated, with frequent modifications and enhancements. In addition, there may be few information systems personnel and users familiar with these systems. Thus, a key decision concerns whether to continue to repair a system or replace it entirely. Software managers are often faced with budget constraints in fulfilling maintenance requests from users, and hence focus on incremental maintenance to the system. However, in order to reduce long-term maintenance costs, it may be economically beneficial to rework the entire software system through major improvements in designs or use of efficient technology. Although a major rework or replacement of the system may require significant investment, it will also improve consistency in the system and increase familiarity of the code to the developers. Some researchers have developed decision models that can be used to help managers understand when it is economically efficient to perform major software rework or system replacement (Chan, Chung, and Ho, 1996).

Another maintenance management concern is how to organize the software maintenance func-

tion. Software maintenance can be organized together with software development, so that personnel work on both development and maintenance tasks. Another alternative is a life-cycle arrangement where there are separate development and maintenance staffs. While this arrangement has potential advantages for quality assurance and user service, it may have disadvantages of coordination and political costs (Swanson and Beath, 1990). Motivation of maintenance personnel is a final important managerial concern. Studies by Couger and Zawacki (1980) and Swanson and Beath (1989) indicate that information systems personnel may not consider maintenance work to be sufficiently interesting or challenging. Especially when technological obsolescence is prevalent, information system workers may fear that unless they are continuously involved in development work, their skills will deteriorate, and this will affect not only their future earning power but also their ability to do work they enjoy.

Future of Software Maintenance

Several software development innovations, such as object-oriented design, structured design, design patterns, component-based development, computer-aided software engineering tools, and software reuse, promise to reduce the software maintenance burden. In addition, there have been tools and techniques developed to improve software maintenance performance. Some of the most prominent maintenance aids include software complexity analyzers, code structuring tools, debugging tools, and reverse engineering tools. These software development and maintenance practices may lower the need for maintenance and increase the maintainability of systems.

Bibliography

Banker, R. and Slaughter, S. (2000). The moderating effects of software structure on volatility and complexity in software enhancement. *Information Systems Research*, **11** (3), 219–40.

Bennett, K. (1996). Software evolution: Past, present and future. *Information and Software Technology*, **39** (11), 673–80.

Chan, T., Chung, S., and Ho, T. (1996). An economic model to estimate software rewriting and replacement times. *IEEE Transactions on Software Engineering*, **22** (8), 580–98.

Chidamber, S. and Kemerer, C. (1994). A metrics suite for object-oriented design. *IEEE Transactions on Software Engineering*, **20** (6), 476–93.

Couger, J. D. and Zawacki, R. A. (1980). *Motivating and Managing Computer Personnel*. New York: John Wiley.

Gibson, V. R. and Senn, J. A. (1989). System structure and software maintenance performance. *Communications of the ACM*, **32** (3), 347–58.

Halstead, M. (1977). *Elements of Software Science*. New York: Elsevier North-Holland.

IEEE. (1998). Standard for Software Maintenance #1219–1998.

Kalakota, R. and Whinston, A. (1996). *Electronic Commerce: A Manager's Guide*. Reading, MA: Addison-Wesley.

Kemerer, C. (1995). Software complexity and software maintenance: A survey of empirical research. *Annals of Software Engineering*, **1**, 1–22.

McCabe, T. J. (1976). A complexity measure. *IEEE Transactions on Software Engineering*, **SE-2** (4), 308–20.

Schneidewind, N. (1987). The state of software maintenance. *IEEE Transactions on Software Engineering*, **SE-13** (3), 303–10.

Swanson, E. B. (1976). The dimensions of maintenance. *Proceedings of the Second International Conference on Software Engineering*. New York: IEEE, pp. 492–7.

Swanson, E. B. and Beath, C. M. (1989). *Maintaining Information Systems in Organizations*. New York: John Wiley.

Swanson, E. and Beath, C. M. (1990). Departmentalization in software development and maintenance. *Communications of the ACM*, **33** (6), 658–67.

software package solutions

Scott J. Hamilton

The availability of software packages for major business processes and problem domains has introduced alternative approaches to developing software and reengineering business processes. Software packages are the preferred approach to software for knowledge workers. Business solution packages may have significant advantages, depending on the industry in which they are used and the need for customized solutions. Information systems that have organization-wide, mission-critical, and/or competitive advantage implications typically require serious consideration of the make/buy decision. Package solutions for some applications (such as accounting) have been widely accepted and implemented; other applications are more dependent on package evaluation.

KNOWLEDGE WORKER SOFTWARE PACKAGES

Most computer users work with one or more software packages such as word processor, spreadsheet, statistical software, presentation graphics, electronic mail, numerical database management, text database, and personal computer management software (such as the computer operating system). Other useful knowledge worker packages include cooperative work software, finance modeling software, scheduling and project management software, forecasting software, and possibly expert system shells (*see* EXPERT SYSTEMS). Knowledge workers in specific functional areas may have domain-specific packages such as a computer-aided design (CAD) package for engineers, a statistical process control (SPC) package for quality personnel, or an executive information system (EIS) (*see* EXECUTIVE INFORMATION SYSTEMS). The key issue usually is not make or buy because packages typically are the only viable option; the issue is selection among packages.

BUSINESS SOLUTION PACKAGES

A generalized business package often applies to firms within an given industry, since these firms have common information processing requirements. Example industries include manufacturing, distribution, retail, professional services, hospitals, and clinics. An application software package that fits a large percentage of a firm's system requirements has several advantages over custom-developed applications. The package has typically been written by specialists who have considered industry standards, best practices, key requirements, and integration issues. The package is typically documented and tested. Almost all of the costs are known in advance. The software is available for immediate use; there is no development delay. The vendor has economic incentives to keep the package up to date and running on industry standard hardware/software. The vendor (or an affiliated consultant organization) usually provides training and professional assistance to insure successful implementation. These advantages reduce the risks associated with a firm's ability to complete software on schedule and within budget, to maintain software and the associated documentation/training, and to retain system-knowledgeable personnel.

One disadvantage of an information system package solution is generality, so that the package cannot meet unique requirements in comparison with software developed in-house. A related issue involves the constraints that a generalized package may place on innovative applications. These disadvantages can be addressed by customizations and extensions to a package, but extensive customizations can lead to problems with future upgrades to new releases from the software vendor. In addition, customizations can be very time consuming, expensive, and error prone because of the complexity and/or underlying technology (such as the database management system and software development tools) of the software package. Customizations for an integrated system can have an unintended ripple effect that creates errors in other parts of the application.

Multiple software packages may be employed to achieve a comprehensive information system. Manufacturing information systems, for example, may require use of ERP (*see* ENTERPRISE SYSTEMS (ENTERPRISE RESOURCE PLANNING OR ERP)), computer-aided design (CAD), and quality management application packages, in addition to the database management system and software development tools.

APPROACHES TO USING A SOFTWARE PACKAGE

There are three major approaches to using application packages: (1) use without change; (2) customizing with input/output changes; and (3) customizing by adding unique features.

1 *Using package without change.* The package vendor typically offers configuration options to tailor the software to operations. The company in this situation selects options and changes its business processes and procedures to adapt to the package. This approach makes sense for a company that lacks good business practices. The software package provides a way of introducing innovative organizational changes, typically with a faster implementation cycle.
2 *Customizing inputs/outputs.* Cosmetic changes to reports, queries, user-definable codes, external documents (such as invoices), and input screens can be made without changing the basic logic and functions of the software package. Supplementary applications can also be developed that interface with the software package without affecting source code. These changes help fit the package to the way personnel view the application, with minimal impact on the ability to upgrade to new releases from the software vendor.
3 *Customizing package with unique features.* The software package can provide an integrative framework and a starting point for adding unique features. While the additions/changes can provide unique and innovative capabilities, the changes may constrain the ability to upgrade to new package releases, especially when appropriate development tools and configuration controls have not been utilized. The company must take responsibility for ongoing maintenance of software, documentation, and training, and the responsibility for retaining knowledgeable systems personnel.

spam

William J. Caelli

The term "spam" refers to unwanted and unsolicited electronic mail (*see* EMAIL) or like messages. The word is taken from a brand of canned meat product and was originally used in a Monty Python humorous sketch and song wherein the word was repeated over and over again. This concept of constant, unwanted repetition led to the adoption of the word "spam" to cover the flood of unwanted email messages received by INTERNET users worldwide. By 2004 some governments had enacted legislation to attempt to limit this "epidemic" of unwanted messages that, at times, could cause denial of service problems with some large enterprise users of the Internet.

Often, such "spam" messages may present further security challenges in that they may contain "Trojan Horse" or virus programs, unknown to the receiver. They may also resemble a message from a source known to the user, such as his or her bank, with a request to perform some compromising action such as entering bank account details, passwords, etc. In this case the use of such spam messages has become known as PHISHING.

speech recognition and synthesis

Gordon B. Davis

Speech synthesis is the generation of voice output by a computer system. Applications in information systems include systems for providing information to customers about account balances, transactions processed, status of projects, etc. For example, a bank customer connecting to an automated system may issue a request via a touch-tone telephone for account balance, recent deposits, etc. The computer system synthesizes a voice reply over the telephone.

Speech recognition by a computer program is based on an analysis of the user speech. Speech recognition has been very successful for small vocabularies of words, especially in applications where the user's hands are not available for entering data. With a small number of commands, recognition accuracy is very high.

Full-text speech recognition is difficult because of the large number of variations in speech, differences in clarity of diction, lack of pauses between words, and the large number of words that sound alike or somewhat similar. Homonyms (words that sound the same but have different spelling and different meanings) present a problem (examples are "two," "to," and "too"). Human recognition of speech is based on a complex process of recognizing words in context, so lack of pauses between words or differences in diction or accent do not prevent understanding. For example, a person may say "yabetchyalife" with no pauses between words. The listener knows the colloquial expression and interprets the meaning as "you bet your life."

Personal computer speech recognition systems are available for dictation of words, text, and numbers into cells in a spreadsheet. The software requires a period of training to adjust the software to the diction of the individual user. The user must employ discrete speech with distinct pauses between words. Background noise must be minimal. When the software has difficulty in recognition, alternative words are displayed for the user to select. Over time, the software can refine the recognition algorithms to select words the user is likely to use. For ordinary dictation with a variety of words in different contexts, the error rate for current speech recognition software may be fairly small but the time required for correcting the errors means keyboard entry is more productive. However, with a limited vocabulary and mainly present tense, such as professional notes or memoranda, the rate of correct recognition may rise to a very satisfactory level. Successful applications include simple memoranda or notes in business and dictation of notes by users such as lawyers, pathologists, and physicians.

Full-text entry by voice requires significant processing power to achieve a low error or non-recognition rate. The error or non-recognition rate is reduced by extensive processing to match a user's vocabulary, common words employed, strings of words usually used together, and grammatical usage. Speech recognition is important in some information processing applications and, with the availability of substantial processing power, routine text input for reports is becoming more feasible.

spyware

Term applied to software installed on a personal computer for the purpose of obtaining personal information or displaying advertising during sessions on the INTERNET. The spyware may be installed without user knowledge during downloading of Internet files. The software may be intrusive and obtain confidential information. It may also slow down the operation of regular applications. The spyware software may be removed by anti-virus software or spyware removal software.

See also *email; identity theft*

SQL

Salvatore T. March

Structured query language (SQL) is a comprehensive database language implemented in numerous commercial database management systems (*see* DATABASE MANAGEMENT SYSTEM). Originally called SEQUEL (Structured English QUEry Language), SQL was designed and implemented at IBM Research in the mid-1970s as the interface for an experimental RELATIONAL DATABASE system called SYSTEM R.

SQL has two components: (1) a data definition language (DDL) in which the structure of the database is defined; and (2) a data manipulation language (DML) in which queries on the data are specified.

DATABASE DEFINITION

A database is defined as a set of *tables* (relations), each having *columns* (attributes) and *rows* (tuples). Columns define the data elements in a table. Rows correspond to instances. Each row contains one data value for each column. The database illustrated in figure 1 has two tables: *Department* and *Employee*. *Department* has columns for *Department Number* (DNO), *Name* (DName), *Budget*, and *Manager*. Each department has a corresponding row in the *Department* table containing the data values describing that department.

Each table has a column or set of columns designated as its *primary key*. Each row must have a unique value for its primary key. DNO is the primary key of *Department*; ENO is the primary key of *Employee* (underlined in figure 1).

Relationships between tables are specified using corresponding columns. The column in one table must be a primary key; the column in the related table is termed a *foreign key*. In the database illustrated, there are two relationships between *Department* and *Employee*: (1) *Dept* is a foreign key in *Employee*, containing the department number of the department to which the employee reports; and (2) *Manager* is a foreign key in *Department* containing the employee number of the employee who manages that department. For example, David Jones, employee number 15342, reports to the *Operations* department, department number 002. This department is managed by John Young, employee number 57211.

DATA MANIPULATION

Query specifications in SQL are based on relational calculus. The result of a query is a table which can be saved or used in other queries. A basic query can have four clauses:

```
Select     <attribute list>
From       <table list>
Where      <condition list>
Order by   <sorting list>
```

<attribute list> is a list of columns and column calculations; <table list> is the list of tables in which these columns are defined;

Department table

DNO	DName	Budget	Manager
001	Marketing	$220,000	50124
002	Operations	$400,000	57211
003	Accounting	$100,000	22054

Employee table

ENO	EName	Salary	Dept
10231	Smith, Joseph	$40,000	003
15342	Jones, David	$55,000	002
22054	Swanson, Jane	$75,000	003
24519	Neff, Arnold	$22,000	001
28332	Homes, Denise	$38,000	002
50124	Naumi, Susan	$83,000	001
57211	Young, John	$71,000	002

Figure 1   Example of an SQL database

`<condition list>` defines rows to be included in the result table; `<sorting list>` defines the order of the result. `Select` and `From` clauses are required. `Where` and `Order by` clauses are optional.

The following query produces the *Employee Number*, *Name*, and *Salary* of all employees with salary greater than $50,000, sorted by employee name.

```
Select      ENO, EName, Salary
From        Employee
Where       Salary > 50000
Order by    EName
```

More complex queries can access data from multiple tables (e.g., *join* and *union* queries), perform data aggregations such as sums, counts, and averages (*group by* queries), and use queries within the Where clause to define conditions for row inclusion (*nested* queries).

The following join query includes departments whose budgets exceed $200,000 and employees in those departments whose salaries exceed $30,000, sorted by employee name within department name.

```
Select      DNO, DName, ENO, E-
            Name, Salary
From        Employee
            JOIN Department
            ON Employee.
            Dept=Department.
            DNO
Where       Budget > 200000
            and
            Salary > 30000
Order by    DName, EName
```

The *join condition*, `Employee.Dept = Department.DNO` is written in the fully qualified form, `<table name>.<column name>`. Earlier versions of SQL have join conditions in the `Where` clause rather than in the `From` clause. Variations of this type exist in different commercial implementations of SQL. Both American National Standards Institute (ANSI) and International Standards Organization (ISO) are developing standards to provide consistency across different implementations.

standards for information technology

T. William Olle

Standards can be de jure or de facto. A de jure standard is formally accepted as a standard because it has been authorized by a recognized standards-making body such as the International Standards Organization (ISO). A de facto standard is informally recognized as a standard because it is widely recognized and accepted even though it has not been through the standardization process of a formally recognized standards-making body.

It is also useful to recognize "installation standards." Organizations making use of information technology often find it convenient to adopt standards for the way information technology is used in the installation. Some of these standards may be either de jure or de facto standards. However, there are many situations for which no such standards are available and an installation using information technology may find it convenient to develop their own installation standards.

The process by which de jure standards are developed is lengthy and complex. The process of standardization that preceded the advent of information technology has been largely adopted and applied to information technology. Most countries in the world have a standards body, which is responsible for developing standards in that country. Some larger countries, such as the US, may have more than one such body. The US has an umbrella organization for information technology standards, the American National Standards Institute (ANSI). The most significant US technical group under ANSI for information technology standards is the InterNational Committee for Information Technology Standards (INCITS).

In other countries, each national standards body is a member of the ISO, which currently has over a hundred members. However, only a few of these bodies participate in the development of information technology standards.

Most countries involved in information technology standards tend to focus their work on the work of the ISO. After a standard has been agreed by the ISO, a country's member body may choose to issue its own standard, which is usually an exact copy of the corresponding ISO standard.

Since the progression of standards in the international arena has been shown to be slower than within a single country, a country's member body may choose to develop its own standard for a specific area and then submit it to ISO for progression through one of the available sets of standards procedures.

In 1986, as a result of a perceived overlap between the information technology work of the ISO and the International Electrotechnical Commission (IEC), a merging of efforts took place. One result was that the distinction between information technology standardization and other kinds of standardization was more clearly visible. This distinction was manifested by the formation of ISO/IEC Joint Technical Committee 1 (JTC1), a special committee with the name Information Technology. The scope of this committee is quite simply "standardization in the field of information technology." One of the original ISO Technical Committees and one or two IEC Technical Committees became part of JTC1. Those not joining were considered to be concerned with standardization outside the scope of information technology.

A list of the 17 subcommittees currently active in JTC1 provides insight into the scope of ISO/IEC. These are as follows:

JTC 1/SC 2	Coded character sets
JTC 1/SC 6	Telecommunications and information exchange between systems
JTC 1/SC 7	Software and system engineering
JTC 1/SC 17	Cards and personal identification
JTC 1/SC 22	Programming languages, their environments and system software interfaces
JTC 1/SC 23	Optical disk cartridges for information interchange
JTC 1/SC 24	Computer graphics and image processing
JTC 1/SC 25	Interconnection of information technology equipment
JTC 1/SC 27	IT security techniques
JTC 1/SC 28	Office equipment
JTC 1/SC 29	Coding of audio, picture, multimedia and hypermedia information
JTC 1/SC 31	Automatic identification and data capture techniques
JTC 1/SC 32	Data management and interchange
JTC 1/SC 34	Document description and processing languages
JTC 1/SC 35	User interfaces
JTC 1/SC 36	Information technology for learning, education, and training
JTC 1/SC 37	Biometrics

Each subcommittee has a secretariat, which is typically one of the member bodies active in the work of that subcommittee. Each subcommittee also has two or more working groups, which are responsible for carrying out the detailed technical work. Each member body involved in the work is expected to send a delegation to the plenary meeting of the subcommittee at which formal decisions are taken on the progression of the work.

Not all the countries represented in the ISO participate in the work of JTC1. In fact, only 23 countries participate actively. This means that each country participates in one or more of the 17 subcommittees. A further 44 countries have observer status in JTC1. The number of countries having a vote in the work of any one subcommittee may be fewer than 23, while the number actually participating in the work may be even less. Countries such as the US (ANSI), UK (BSI), Japan (JISC), and Canada (SCC) play an active role in most JTC1 subcommittees.

In addition, JTC1 maintains internal liaisons with other subcommittees within ISO and external liaisons with organizations outside ISO.

ISO has extensive procedures that are to be used in the carrying out of the technical work. International standards are developed using a five-step process:

1 proposal stage;
2 preparatory stage;
3 committee stage;
4 approval stage; and
5 publication stage.

The success of a de jure standard can be assessed by two criteria:

1   Are products being implemented based on these standards?
2   Are products conforming to these standards being used?

One of the major issues related to information technology standardization is whether an information technology standard should be preemptive, prepared prior to the availability of products indicating the need for the standard, or post facto, prepared after products have become available. In some cases one approach is better, and in other cases it is the other. The issue is complicated by the rate at which new developments in information technology are emerging.

Up-to-date information on ISO standards can be obtained from the ISO webite: www.iso.ch.

storage of digital data

Thomas M. Ruwart

Digital storage technologies originated in the mid-1940s with the advent of the digital computer. Special data storage devices were used to store data that would not fit into the computer's memory space and data that needed to be retained even when the power to the computer system was removed. These are referred to as "permanent" data storage "peripherals" – "permanent" because of their ability to retain their data indefinitely, and "peripheral" because they existed at the periphery of the computer system whose center was the central processing unit (CPU).

There have been many different types of permanent data storage technologies employed over the past 60 years, but the most enduring are magnetic, optical, and, more recently, flash memory devices. At the time of this writing, these storage devices are almost ubiquitous in western society and will most likely be more widespread in the coming years.

Permanent magnetic storage first appeared in the 1940s as magnetic tape. This tape was a flexible, thin plastic tape about 1 inch wide with a thin coating of a ferrous magnetic material applied to one side. Data were recorded by passing the tape under a magnetic recording "head" that would set the magnetic orientation of the ferrous magnetic material in one of two directions on a very small piece of the tape, usually about 1/500th of an inch long. This would constitute a single digital "bit" of information and could easily be decoded as either a 1 (oriented in on direction) or a 0 (oriented in the other direction). This process of recording bits on a magnetic material is also known as "writing" data. In order to make the process of writing bits to the tape more efficient, several bits (either 7 or 9 bits) were written simultaneously across the width of the tape. These 7 or 9 bits would constitute what is referred to as a "byte" of data. In the early days of computing a byte was 6 bits, whereas now it is universally accepted as 8 bits. The 7th or 9th bit is referred to as the "parity" bit that is used to detect potential data errors.

Tape devices, however, are inherently slow because they are essentially linear. Data must be accessed by starting at the beginning of the tape and positioning to the point on the tape where the required data reside. This positioning process can take a very long time if the data are at the end of a 2,400-ft spool of tape. Furthermore, as the speeds of the computers increased, it because necessary to find alternative data storage technologies. This led to the development of more randomly accessible data storage devices such as the disk drive.

A disk drive is similar to a tape drive in that the data are stored as magnetic bits in a ferrous material. However, that is where the similarities end. The disk is actually a round, rigid platter that is coated with the ferrous recording medium on both sides. This platter spins about its central axis at a constant angular velocity. The recording head moves perpendicular to the axis of rotation and "floats" over the surface of the platter at a very small distance. (The head never touches the medium on hard disks because the relative speed of the disk medium to the head would cause significant or permanent damage to the head and/or the medium.) The recording tracks on a magnetic disk platter are concentric circles, each track being about the same width as a similar track on a piece of tape medium.

The advantage of a disk drive over a tape drive is that the head can more easily and more quickly move from one track to any other track, thereby accessing the requested data much faster. Furthermore, since each disk platter has its own head, the time to access any piece of data is simply the time to move to a specific track and then wait for the rotation of the platter to bring the data under the head. Rotational speeds are typically in the tens to hundreds of revolutions per second on hard disks. Floppy disks are much slower but still faster than tape.

Ultimately, tape and disk drive became the dominant data storage technologies in the computing industry. As of 2004, tape is still used as a backup medium in some applications but more generally it is used as an archival medium. Archival media are generally used for data that need to be kept for long periods of time and are seldom accessed. Furthermore, archival media require minimal power and maintenance to store the data.

Disk drive technologies, on the other hand, are used primarily for storing frequently accessed and/or modifiable data. At the time of writing however, there is a significant overlap between the use of tape and disk technologies. This overlap is in the form of disks being used in applications previously ascribed to tapes. The end result may be the extinction of tape as a data storage technology, but only time will tell.

An interesting cross between magnetic tape and magnetic disk technologies is that of optical data storage. Optical data storage technologies surfaced in the early 1980s and soon the compact disk (CD) became the recording medium of choice for the consumer music industry, replacing the incumbent vinyl records. Shortly thereafter, in the early 1990s, CDs were adopted by the personal and commercial computing industries for storing digital data. CDs have the unique characteristic of being relatively fast, random access, permanent data storage devices. Instead of recording bits magnetically on a ferrous medium, however, bits are stored as "holes" in a thin Mylar film sandwiched between two pieces of transparent plastic. The advantage of this is that CDs are far less susceptible to various sorts of damage and can therefore store the data for potentially longer periods of time. DVD technologies are essentially the same as CDs with the difference being in the overall capacity: a single piece of

DVD medium is many times that of a traditional CD. The problem, though, is that CDs and DVDs can be recorded once and do not work well for more spontaneous uses. (*see* CD-ROM AND DVD). There has been and always will be a need to move small amounts of data between two physically/logically separate computers.

To meet the transportable data need in the 1970s and 1980s, it was necessary to have a "transportable" data storage medium that could be used to quickly move these data between computers. Hence, the "floppy" disk was developed. The floppy was given this name because it is a flexible medium similar to the medium used in a tape, but it was in the shape of a disk: round with concentric tracks written into the ferrous magnetic coating by a head similar to that of a disk drive. The disks started out at about 8 inches in diameter and eventually decreased to about 3.5 inches before becoming all but extinct by 2004. The floppy was effectively replaced by the flash drive.

Flash memory is a solid-state memory device similar in some respects to the memory used inside of a computer. It has the advantage of having no moving parts, requires no power to retain the data indefinitely, is small and lightweight, and is very durable. By the early 2000s the "density" of flash memory had increased to the point where it became feasible to use it to replace the floppy disk drive. Furthermore, the growth of the consumer electronics market that uses flash memory pushed the prices of flash memory down to the point that it became technologically and economically feasible to replace the floppy.

To summarize, the 1940s provided data storage devices that could store thousands of bits of information at enormous cost and very long latencies. As of 2004, a single flash memory stick could store all the digital data that existed on the planet in 1950 for about $20. The magnetic, optical, and solid-state data storage technologies continue to evolve and will provide the ability to store and retrieve data at any given time and place. The coming years will allow most anyone to have their own personal copy of the Library of Congress as well as their entire video and audio library in the palm of their hand.

strategic alignment between business and IT

Nicholas L. Ball

The alignment of IT to the business is one of the most cited managerial issues facing top IT executives. (IT is used here to refer to both the information technology infrastructure and systems and the information systems function.) One reason for this is that many practitioners believe the performance of the IT function within an organization is highly correlated with the level of business/IT alignment. The persistence of alignment as a key issue may also be evidence that a large percentage of senior IT executives are not satisfied with the level of alignment achieved within their organizations. The difficulty managers face in creating and sustaining alignment can been traced to two fundamental alignment challenges: (1) the ability to measure or assess alignment between IT and the organization and (2) the ability to design appropriate organizational mechanisms for creating and sustaining alignment.

At a high level, the alignment of IT to the business can be defined as the fit between an organization and the IT strategy, structure, processes, and resources within that organization. Henderson and Venkatraman (1993) provide a comprehensive and operational definition of alignment. They argue that alignment consists of both strategic fit and functional integration.

Strategic fit occurs between IT strategy and IT operations. The IT strategy position of an organization describes the role of IT within that organization, the IT capabilities necessary for filling that role, and the governing policies and principles that guide the delivery of those capabilities. The IT operating position consists of the design and structure of IT, as well as the configurations of IT processes and resources that are utilized in the delivery of IT capabilities. Strategic fit occurs when the IT operating position supports and enables the execution of the IT strategy.

Functional integration consists of the degree to which IT supports the business domain of the organization. Integration exists at both the strategic and operational levels. Strategic integration occurs when the IT strategy (IT roles, capabilities, and governance) supports and enables the execution of the business strategy. Operational integration occurs when IT operations (IT design and structure, processes, and resources) match with business operations (organizational structure, processes, and resources).

Business/IT alignment is therefore a broad topic that encompasses both the fit between IT strategy and IT operations as well as integration between business and IT. Alignment may also be described in terms of three subalignments, namely, fit between IT strategy and IT operations (internal IT alignment), integration between IT strategy and business strategy (business/IT strategy alignment), and integration between IT operations and business operations (business/IT operational alignment).

Two types of research have been conducted on alignment: content research and process research. Das, Zahra, and Warkentin (1991) describe the distinction between content and process research as it relates to IS/IT strategy planning. The same distinction can be used to describe alignment content and process research. Alignment content research is concerned with describing what alignment is. Alignment process research is conducted to describe how alignment is achieved. Both types of research are necessary for aiding practitioners in creating and sustaining alignment within their organizations.

Alignment content research can be used as a basis for dealing with the measurement of alignment. The work of Sabherwal and Chan (2001) is an example of alignment content research that could be used as a starting point for organizations to measure alignment within their organizations. Because alignment is a broad concept that touches on many elements of the organization, it is difficult to quantify. Even with these difficulties, it is important to develop and use alignment measures. Without the ability to assess the degree of business/IT alignment within an organization, it is difficult to ascertain the extent of an alignment problem if it exists and to identify elements of the IT strategy or operating positions that need to be modified to improve alignment.

Alignment process research can be the basis for designing organizational arrangements and mechanisms that create and sustain alignment. Such mechanisms may include: senior business executive support for IT, IT management involvement in organization strategy development, IT management understanding of the business, IT leadership within the organization, a strong partnership between business and IT, and well-prioritized IT projects (Luftman and Brier, 1999). Other mechanisms might include a more elaborate alignment process that is utilized periodically to assess the current level of alignment within an organization and identify areas of misalignment to be corrected.

Bibliography

Das, S. R., Zahra, S. A, and Warkentin, M. E. (1991). Integrating the content and process of strategic misplanning with competitive strategy. *Decision Sciences*, **22**, 1.

Henderson, J. C. and Venkatraman, N. (1993). Strategic alignment: Leveraging information technology for transforming organizations. *IBM Systems Journal*, **32**, 4–16.

Luftman, J. and Brier, T. (1999). Achieving and sustaining business–IT alignment. *California Management Review*, **42** (1), 109–22.

Sabherwal, R. and Chan, Y. (2001). Alignment between business and IT strategies: A study of prospectors, analyzers, and defenders. *Information Systems Research*, **12** (1), 11–33.

strategic use of information technology

Blake Ives

Early business information systems were usually intended for automation of back-office functions, routine information processing, or support of decision-making. Starting in the mid-1980s, however, management began to envision how information systems might be used in the pursuit of strategic objectives. At first these systems were typically designed to align information technology investments with the strategic objectives of the firm. These systems were increasingly justified based on increased sales and market share rather than just cost savings. In other cases, a competitor's strategic application of technology might motivate investment in similar systems to help recover from a strategic disadvantage. Today, we increasingly see information technology driving strategy. These strategic systems often provide new marketing or distribution channels or entirely new products or services. Unlike early strategic applications, they increasingly rely on non-proprietary communications networks, particularly the INTERNET, to reach directly to consumers, corporate customers, suppliers, or distribution partners. These new applications and businesses have begun to dramatically reshape commerce and industry as well as many other economic and social institutions.

Business managers at all levels of the organization need to understand the strategic value of systems and services that depend on information technology. Even routine data processing can have a strategic impact if it provides unique services and excellence in services.

TYPES OF STRATEGIC USE

Information technology is now commonly deployed in IT-based products and services. Charles Schwab, for instance, rewrote the rules for the big stock brokerages by offering online trading services at far lower costs than its major competitors. The electronic gaming industry, with far greater revenues today than the movie industry, is another illustration of an IT-based product.

Sometimes the nature of the product can be significantly enhanced by IT. For instance, Pacific Pride, a retailer of fuel for commercial vehicles, differentiated its service offering by providing commercial customers with a card-lock fueling system that enhances control over the fuel charges incurred by commercial drivers.

Another opportunity to use information for strategic advantage is to control a distribution channel. Early examples included the computer reservation systems developed by United and American Airlines. Until forced to stop by antitrust legal action, the owners of the reservation systems were able to bias travel agents and passengers toward their own flights. Today firms such as Amazon and Apple have pioneered new distribution channels on the information superhighway. Amazon has migrated a large investment in online shopping technology for book sales to a dozen other product categories. Similarly, Apple's iPod music player and iTunes music store threaten to dramatically reshape music distribution.

Another type of strategic information system is information intermediaries. While initially strategic applications of information technology were predicted to disintermediate distribution channels, say by allowing manufacturers to sell directly to consumers, in many instances we have instead witnessed the emergence of powerful new "infomediaries," whose primary power comes through the information they possess. eBay is a classic example in the consumer space. Its online site and associated services provide a trustworthy market for consumers to buy and sell a remarkably wide range of products. Priceline.com is a similar example of an infomediary, but one focused on the travel industry.

Inter-organizational systems are another way to use IT strategically. Wal-Mart, for instance, is using its market clout to require its largest suppliers to employ RADIO FREQUENCY IDENTIFICATION (RFID) systems on pallets of merchandise shipped to Wal-Mart's distribution outlets. These smart pallets, combined with data transfers between suppliers and Wal-Mart, provide powerful tools for inventory management.

Strategic advantage can also be achieved by personalizing the service or product to meet the unique needs of a specific customer. The June 2004 issue of *Reason* magazine, for instance, was individually tailored for each of *Reason*'s 40,00 subscribers. Each magazine cover included a unique aerial photograph of the subscriber's neighborhood. Inside the magazine subscribers found customized statistics and personalized advertising. Customization is also now becoming popular in the world of fashion. Land's End's custom-tailored apparel program, for instance, provides its customers with trousers and shirts that have been manufactured based on customers' own sizes and tastes.

Often, significant cost advantages can be achieved by leveraging scarce expertise. Large consulting firms, for instance, have extensive databases that permit them to reuse, from anywhere in the world, expertise emerging from previous projects. Softer information, such as the firm's experiences with particular client managers, can also be retained and made available throughout the firm. Sharing expertise with customers or channel partners can enhance revenues. A large chemical company, for instance, leverages the scope of its product offerings by providing customer designers with detailed tools for identifying and selecting appropriate materials. Dupont Chemical's plastics

division also makes online collaboration rooms available for use by customer designers who can be joined in their virtual rooms by Dupont engineers.

Firms are also reducing costs by electronically relocating knowledge work to sources of low-cost labor. The Internet provides a relatively low-cost means to partition knowledge work across country boundaries. Software developers, for instance, can significantly reduce their labor costs by using programmers in India rather than California. This opportunity, which was initially popular for software development and staffing help desks, is increasingly expanding to other business processes such as drafting and medical diagnosis.

SUSTAINING COMPETITIVE ADVANTAGE

Some contend that information technology is a commodity that cannot be leveraged for sustainable advantage. They argue that hardware innovations and software packages can be easily acquired and implemented. Even custom-tailored systems can, according to this argument, be easily, quickly, and inexpensively reverse engineered.

Others believe that information technology can provide a sustainable advantage if is carefully planned and integrated into the firm's unique business processes and capabilities. Proponents of this position contend that sustainable advantage can be created and defended by attention to the following four barriers to competitive erosion.

The development and implementation barrier. The time required by a competitor to duplicate an IT initiative actually varies considerably. Among the factors impacting this barrier are the visibility or uniqueness of the technologies used, the complexity of either the technologies or the process required to implement them, and the amount of process change required. For instance, duplicating all of the functionality currently available on the Amazon website would inhibit all but the largest potential competitors.

IT assets barrier. Another barrier to erosion derives from leveraging unique IT assets. IT assets include past investments in IT infrastructure or information repositories, as well as both technical and management skills. Amazon, for instance, has an extensive database of past customer purchase behavior. In addition to using this to suggest future purchases, the firm provides Amazon customers with a running total of the current resale value of past merchandise purchased on the site, thus promoting the firm's resale marketplace.

Complementary resources barrier. This barrier is made up from the non-IT resources, business processes, and capabilities as well as external resources. Amazon, for instance, has successfully defended its patent on a unique business process, its one-click® ordering system. Amazon also was able to best its early and traditional rivals in the bookselling business by leveraging its merchandising software into other product categories – thus also creating rich cross-selling opportunities.

First-mover advantage barrier. Getting there first can sometimes produce a significant real or psychological barrier. For instance, customers of online banking services are inhibited from switching to another bank because they would have to reenter all their payee information when they switch.

Bibliography

Ives, B. and Learmonth, G. (1984). The information system as a competitive weapon. *Communications of the ACM*, **27** (12), 1193–1201.

McFarlan, F. W. (1984). Information technology changes the way you compete. *Harvard Business Review*, **62** (3), 98–104.

Mata, F. J., Fuerst, W. L., and Barney, J. B. (1995). Information technology and sustained competitive advantage: A resource-based analysis. *MIS Quarterly*, **19** (4), 487–505.

Piccoli, G., Bass, B., and Ives, B. (2003). Custom-made apparel at Land's End. *MISQ Executive*, **2**, 2 (September).

Porter, M. E. and Millar, V. E. (1985). How information gives you a competitive advantage. *Harvard Business Review*, **63** (4), 149–60.

structured programming

Gordon B. Davis and J. Davis Naumann

This is an approach to coding computer instructions in any procedural programming language (*see* PROGRAMMING LANGUAGES). The fundamental idea is that programs can be constructed from a very limited set of control or decision structures. The major benefit of structured programming is to make programs understandable to humans so that they can be correctly written, modified, and maintained.

Structured programming employs three basic control structures: sequence, alternation, and repetition. The *sequence control structure* is one instruction after the other, executed from beginning to end with no possibility of change. The instructions in a sequence are processing instructions such as arithmetic calculations, operations on strings of characters, retrieval of data, displaying outputs, etc.

The *alternation structure* is the way choices are controlled. The basic implementation of alternation is *if–then–else–end if*. There are a number of additional implementations of alternation. The additions are conveniences and each can be translated to the basic *if–then–else–end if* control structure. The basic alternation structure is shown below.

```
if conditional expression then
    Sequence of statements if condition is true
else
    Sequence of statements if condition is false
end if
```

There is a frequently occurring special case where no action is to be taken when the condition is evaluated to be false. In this special case no *else* statements are specified.

```
if conditional expression then
    Sequence of statements if condition is true
end if
```

Case is an extension of alternation that may be used to select among more than two possible actions. One and only one action is selected based on the value of a condition. A case statement has the following structure:

```
select case conditional expression
case value-1
    Sequence of statements to be executed if the
    expression evaluates to case value-1
case value-2
```

Sequence of statements to be executed if the expression evaluates to *case* value-2
case value-*n*
Sequence of statements to be executed if the expression evaluates to *case* value-*n*
case else
Sequence of statements to be executed if none of the above apply
end select

do while employee records exist
Input employee name, status, dependents
if status = retired *then*
Compute health benefit cost for retired
else
Compute health benefit cost for not retired
end if
Display employee name, status, dependents, health benefit
end while

The *repetition structure*, often termed a loop, is a way of conditionally repeating a sequence of instructions. The repetition structure evaluates a conditional expression every iteration of its loop. The statements within the loop effectively control the number of repetitions since they alter the values being tested by the conditional expression. The basic repetition structure is shown below.

do while conditional expression is true
Sequence of statements to be executed
end while

In the *do while* control structure, the value of the conditional expression is evaluated before any action is taken. If it initially evaluates to false, the entire sequence of statements is bypassed. If it is true, the sequence of statements is executed and control returns to the beginning, where the conditional expression is evaluated again. There are useful variants of the basic repetition structure. One repetition variant is used when a sequence of statements is to be executed a predetermined number of times. The *for* loop is often called indexed repetition because repetition is controlled by an index variable that is automatically incremented at each execution.

for index initial value *to* index ending value
Sequence of statements to be executed
end for

An important control structure related to repetition is recursion, in which modules in effect repeat themselves.

Control structures may be "nested." One control structure may be wholly contained within another. Alternation nested within repetition is shown below.

In addition to the use of a limited set of control structures, structured programming conventions also involve the use of embedded comments, readable coding, indentations, and paragraphs to clearly indicate structure. Structured programs are inherently readable and therefore easier to maintain and modify than programs lacking a regular structure.

success of information systems: measuring the effectiveness of information systems

William H. DeLone, Ephraim R. McLean, and Stacie Petter

US businesses are currently spending 50 percent of their capital investments on information technology (IT). Thus they are naturally interested in knowing the return on these investments and, by extension, the overall success of their information systems departments. Since the impacts of IT are often indirect and influenced by human, organizational, and environmental factors, the measurement of information systems success is both complex and elusive.

The success of information systems (IS) is dependent on several sequential and interdependent activities and is therefore multidimensional. IT components are organized into information systems that produce management reports or customer information that are then used by managers and customers to make decisions and take actions that impact the ability of an organization to achieve its objectives. Organizations seek to measure the value of information systems and technology beyond tangible or financial approaches, such as return on investment (Rubin 2004), using methods such as balanced scorecards and benchmarking (Seddon, Graeser, and Willcocks, 2002).

There have been multiple models that strive to explain why people use certain technologies or what makes information systems successful. Davis's (1989) TECHNOLOGY ACCEPTANCE MODEL (TAM) used the theory of reasoned action and theory of planned behavior to explain why some information systems are more readily accepted by users than others. Acceptance, however, is not equivalent to information system success, although acceptance of a system is a precursor to success.

Early attempts to define information system success were ineffective owing to the complex, interdependent, and multidimensional nature of IS success. To address this problem, William DeLone and Ephraim McLean of American University and Georgia State University, respectively, performed a review of previous research and created a taxonomy of IS success (DeLone and McLean, 1992). They identified six dependent variables of IS success: system quality, information quality, use, user satisfaction, individual impact, and organizational impact. However, these six variables are not *independent* success measures but are *interdependent* variables. Figure 1 shows this original IS success model as developed by DeLone and McLean (D&M).

The D&M model of IS success was intended to be "both complete and parsimonious" and, as such, has proved to be widely used and cited by other researchers, with over 300 citations to date. To use this model to predict IS success, all six constructs within the IS success model must be measured and/or controlled. This enables a richer understanding of success and reduces possible confounding results related to measuring IS success.

Shortly after the publication of this success model, IS researchers began proposing modifications to the original model. Accepting DeLone and McLean's call for "further development and validation," Seddon and Kiew (1996) evaluated a portion of the IS success model (i.e., system quality, information quality, use, and user satisfaction). In their evaluation, they modified the construct of *use* because they "conjectured that the underlying success construct that researchers have been trying to tap is *Usefulness*, not *Use*." Seddon and Kiew's concept of *usefulness* is equivalent to the idea of *perceived usefulness* in Davis's (1989) TAM. The researchers argued that for voluntary systems, *use* is an appropriate measure; however, if system use is mandatory, *usefulness* is a better measure of IS success than *use*. DeLone and McLean responded that, even in mandatory systems, there is still some variability of use and therefore the variable *use* should not be omitted.

Researchers have also suggested that service quality be added to the D&M model. An instrument from the marketing literature, SERVQUAL, has become salient within the IS success literature. SERVQUAL measures service quality of information technology departments, as opposed to individual applications, by measuring and comparing user expectations and their perceptions of the information technology department. Pitt, Watson, and Kavan (1995) evaluated the instrument and suggested that the construct of service quality should be added to the D&M model. Some researchers resisted this change (Seddon, 1997), while others seemed to embrace the addition (Jiang, Klein, and Carr, 2002).

Some of the most well-known proposed modifications to the D&M model are those offered by Seddon (1997). He argued that the D&M model in its original form was confusing, partly because both process and variance models were combined within the same framework. While he claimed that this was a shortcoming of the model, DeLone and McLean responded that they believed that this was one of its strengths. Seddon furthered suggested that the concept of *use* is highly ambiguous and suggested that

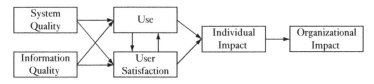

Figure 1   DeLone and McLean's IS success model (1992)

further clarification was needed to this construct. He derived three different potential meanings for the *use* construct, as well as parsing out the process and variances portions of the model.

In addition to Seddon's proposed modifications, there have been many other calls to revise or extend the model. Some researchers have modified it to evaluate success of specific applications such as knowledge management (Jennex and Olfman, 2002) and E-COMMERCE (Molla and Licker, 2001; DeLone and McLean, 2004). Other researchers have made more general recommendations concerning the model (Ballantine et al., 1996).

In their follow-up work, DeLone and McLean acknowledged these modifications and revised the original model accordingly (DeLone and McLean, 2003). Based on a literature review of the empirical studies that had been performed during the years since 1992 and the proposed changes to the model, DeLone and McLean developed an updated IS success model, shown in figure 2.

This updated IS success model accepted Pitt et al.'s (1995) recommendation to include service quality as a construct. Another update to the model addressed the criticism that an information system can affect levels other than individual and organizational levels. Because IS success affects work groups, industries, and societies (Myers, Kappelman, and Prybutok, 1997; Seddon et al., 1999), DeLone and McLean chose to replace the variables *individual impacts* and *organizational impacts* with *net benefits*, thereby accounting for benefits at multiple levels of analysis. This revision allowed the model to be applied to whatever level of analysis the researcher considers most relevant. The final enhancement made to the updated D&M model

was the further clarification of the *use* construct. The authors explained the construct as follows: "Use must precede 'user satisfaction' in a *process* sense, but positive experience with 'use' will lead to greater 'user satisfaction' in a *causal* sense" (DeLone and McLean, 2003). They went on to state that increased *user satisfaction* will lead to a higher *intention to use*, which will subsequently affect *use*.

The D&M model has also been found to be a useful framework for organizing IS success measurements. The model has been widely used by IS researchers for understanding and measuring information systems success. The six major success dimensions of the updated model include:

- *System quality*: the desirable characteristics of an information system. For example: ease of use, system flexibility, system reliability, and ease of learning, as well as system features of accuracy, sophistication, flexibility, and response times.
- *Information quality*: the desirable characteristics of the system outputs, i.e., management reports and web pages. For example: relevance, understandability, conciseness, completeness, understandability, currency, timeliness, and usability.
- *Service quality*: the quality of the support that system users receive from the information systems department and support personnel. For example: responsiveness, accuracy, reliability, technical competence, and empathy of the personnel staff. SERVQUAL, adapted from the field of marketing, is a popular instrument for measuring IS service quality (Pitt et al., 1995).
- *System use*: the degree and manner in which staff and customers utilize the capabilities of

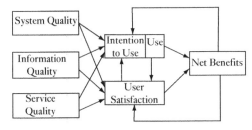

Figure 2   DeLone and McLean's updated IS success model (2003)

an information system. For example: amount of use, frequency of use, nature of use, appropriateness of use, extent of use, and purpose of use.

- *User satisfaction*: users' level of satisfaction with reports, websites, and support services. For example, the most widely used multi-attribute instrument for measuring user information satisfaction can be found in Ives, Olson, and Baroudi (1983).

- *Net benefits*: the extent to which information systems are contributing to the success of individuals, groups, organizations, industries, and nations. For example: improved decision-making, improved productivity, increased sales, cost reductions, improved profits, market efficiency, consumer welfare, creation of jobs, and economic development. Brynjolfsson, Hitt, and Yang (2000) have used production economics to measure the positive impact of IT investments on firm-level productivity.

The practical application of the D&M IS success model is naturally dependent on the organizational context. The selection of success dimensions and specific metrics depend on the nature and purpose of the system(s) being evaluated. For example, an e-commerce application would have some similar success measures and some different success measures in contrast to an enterprise system application (*see* ENTERPRISE SYSTEMS (ENTERPRISE RESOURCE PLAN-NING OR ERP)). Both systems would measure information accuracy, while only the e-commerce system would measure personalization of information. Figure 3 includes specific success dimensions and metrics for an e-commerce system evaluation. Seddon et al. (1999) developed a context matrix that is a valuable reference for the selection of success measures based on stakeholder and level of analysis (individual application or IS function).

As information technology and information systems become more critical to organizational performance, the need to measure information system impact and success will only become more important. The DeLone and McLean IS success model has proved that it provides a useful framework for developing success evaluation metrics and for increasing the understanding of this complex phenomenon.

Bibliography

Ballantine, J., Bonner, M., Levy, M., Martin, A. I. M., and Powell, P. L. (1996). The 3D model of information systems success: The search for the dependent variable continues. *Information Resources Management Journal*, 9, 4 (Fall), 5–14.

Brynjolffson, E., Hitt, L. M., and Yang, S. (2000). Beyond computation: Information technology, organizational transformation and business performance. *Journal of Economic Perspectives*, 14 (4), 23–48.

Davis, F. D. (1989). Perceived usefulness, perceived ease of use, and user acceptance of information technology. *MIS Quarterly*, 13, 3 (September), 318–46.

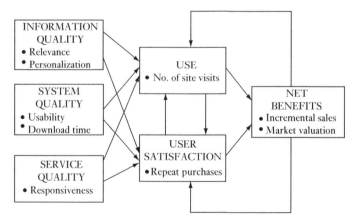

Figure 3 IS success model for e-commerce

DeLone, W. H. and McLean, E. R. (1992). Information systems success: The quest for the dependent variable. *Information Systems Research*, 3, 1 (March), 60–95.

DeLone, W. H. and McLean, E. R. (2003). The DeLone and McLean model of information systems success: A ten-year update. *Journal of Management Information Systems*, 19, 4 (Spring), 9–30.

DeLone, W. H. and McLean, E. R. (2004). Measuring e-commerce success: Applying the DeLone and McLean information systems success model. *International Journal of Electronic Commerce*, 9, 1 (Fall), 31–47.

Ives, B., Olson, M., and Baroudi, J. (1983). The measurement of user information satisfaction. *Communications of the ACM*, 26, 10 (October), 785–93.

Jennex, M. E. and Olfman, L. (2002). Organizational memory/knowledge effects on productivity: A longitudinal study. *Proceedings of the 35th Hawaii International Conference on System Sciences*. Big Island, Hawaii, US.

Jiang, J. J., Klein, G., and Carr, C. L. (2002). Measuring information system service quality: SERVQUAL from the other side. *MIS Quarterly*, 26 (2), June, 145–66.

Molla, A. and Licker, P. S. (2001). E-commerce systems success: An attempt to extend and respecify the DeLone and MacLean model of IS success. *Journal of Electronic Commerce Research*, 2 (4).

Myers, B. L., Kappelman, L. A., and Prybutok, V. R. (1997). A comprehensive model for assessing the quality and productivity of the information systems function: Toward a contingency theory for information systems assessment. *Information Resources Management Journal*, 10, 1 (Winter), 6–25.

Pitt, L. F., Watson, R. T., and Kavan, C. B. (1995). Service quality: A measure of information systems effectiveness. *MIS Quarterly*, 19, 2 (June), 173–87.

Rubin, H. (2004). Into the light. *CIO*.

Seddon, P. B. (1997). A respecification and extension of the DeLone and McLean model of IS success. *Information Systems Research*, 8, 3 (September), 240–53.

Seddon, P. B., Graeser, V., and Willcocks, L.P. (2002). Measuring organizational IS effectiveness: An overview and update of senior management perspectives. *DATA BASE for Advances in Information Systems*, 33, 2 (Spring), 11–28.

Seddon, P. B. and Kiew, M.-Y. (1996). A partial test and development of Delone and McLean's model of IS success. *Australian Journal of Information Systems*, 4 (1), 90–109.

Seddon, P. B., Staples, S., Patnayakuni, R., and Bowtell, M. (1999). Dimensions of information systems success. *Communications of the Association for Information Systems*, 2 (November), 2–39.

supply chain management

Gordon B. Davis

Supply chain management (SCM) is one of the important applications of information technology in organizations. The supply chain is the set of activities that begin with the acquisition of goods and services, continue with activities that the organization performs, and end with the delivery of goods and services to customers. Typical activities include forecasting of demand, estimating delivery times, purchasing, inventory management, production planning and scheduling activities, scheduling delivery of goods and services, and customer service. Supply chain management may involve online collaboration with suppliers and customers. Private exchanges may be established to allow suppliers to bid on procurement needs. The requirements for obtaining information related to the supply chain and the complexity of scheduling and coordinating the supply chain activities make information system applications for supply chain management an important and valuable application in organizations.

See also *manufacturing use of information technology*

system concepts applied to information systems

Gordon B. Davis

System concepts provide a useful way to describe many organizational phenomena, including the information system, features of applications, and development processes.

DEFINITION AND GENERAL MODEL OF A SYSTEM

Systems can be abstract or physical. An abstract system is an orderly arrangement of interdependent ideas or constructs. For example, a system of theology is an orderly arrangement of ideas about God and the relationship of humans to God. A physical system is a set of elements that operate together to accomplish an objective. Examples of physical systems are the circulatory system of a body, a school system (with building, teachers, administrators, and textbooks), and a computer system (the hardware and software that function together to accomplish computer processing). The examples illustrate that a system is not a randomly assembled set of elements; it consists of elements that can be identified as belonging together because of a common purpose, goal, or objective. Physical systems are more than conceptual constructs; they display activity or behavior. The parts interact to achieve an objective.

A general model of a physical system comprises inputs, process, and outputs. The features that define and delineate a system form its boundary. The system is inside the boundary; the environment is outside the boundary. In some cases it is fairly simple to define what is part of the system and what is not; in other cases the person studying the system may arbitrarily define the boundaries.

Each system is composed of subsystems made up of other subsystems, each subsystem being delineated by its boundaries. The interconnections and interactions between the subsystems are termed *interfaces*. Interfaces occur at the boundary and take the form of inputs and outputs. A subsystem at the lowest level (input, process, output) is often not defined as to the process. This system is termed a *black box*, since the inputs and outputs are known but not the actual transformation from one to the other.

TYPES OF SYSTEM

Although many phenomena as different as a human and a computer program can be described in systems terms, they are still quite different. Two classifications of systems emphasize key differences. Systems are deterministic versus probabilistic and closed versus open. These concepts can be applied to the concept of the human–machine system employed in management information systems.

A *deterministic system* operates in a predictable manner. The interaction among the parts is known with certainty. If one has a description of the state of the system at a given point in time plus a description of its operation, the next state of the system may be given exactly, without error. An example is a correct computer program that performs exactly according to a set of instructions. The *probabilistic system* can be described in terms of probable behavior, but a certain degree of error is always attached to the prediction of what the system will do. An example is a set of instructions given to a human who, for a variety of reasons, may not follow the instructions exactly as given.

A *closed system* is defined in physics as a system that is self-contained. It does not exchange material, information, or energy with its environment. In organizations and in information processing, there are systems that are relatively isolated from the environment but not completely closed in the physics sense. These will be termed closed systems, meaning *relatively* closed. A computer program is a relatively closed system because it accepts only previously defined inputs, processes them, and provides previously defined outputs.

Open systems exchange information, material, or energy with the environment, including random and undefined inputs. Examples of open systems are biological systems (such as humans) and organizational systems. Open systems have form and structure to allow them to adapt to changes in their environment in such a way as to continue their existence. They are "self-organizing" in the sense that they change their organization in response to changing conditions. Living systems (cells, plants, humans, etc.) are open systems. They attempt to maintain equilibrium by homeostasis, the process of adjusting to keep the system operating within prescribed limits. Organizations are open systems; a critical feature of their existence is their capability to adapt in the face of changing competition, changing markets, etc. Organizations illustrate the system concept of *equifinality*: more than one system structure and process may achieve the same result (but not necessarily at the same cost).

Artificial systems are systems that are created rather than occurring in nature. Organizations, information systems, and computer programs are all examples of artificial systems. Artificial systems are designed to support the objectives of the designers and users. They exhibit, therefore, characteristics of the system that they support. Principles that apply to *living systems* are also applicable to artificial systems that support human or other living systems.

Information systems are generally human–machine systems; both human and machine perform activities in the accomplishment of a goal (e.g., processing a transaction or making a decision). The machine elements (computer hardware and software) are relatively closed and deterministic, whereas the human elements of the system are open and probabilistic. Various combinations of human and machine are possible. For instance, the computer can be emphasized and the human simply monitors the machine operation. At the other extreme, the machine performs a supporting role by doing computation or searching for data while the user performs creative work. An appropriate balance in the division of functions is critical to the successful performance of each component in accomplishing its objective; the division between human and machine will thus vary from application to application.

SUBSYSTEMS

A complex system is difficult to comprehend when considered as a whole. Therefore, the system is decomposed or factored into subsystems. The boundaries and interfaces are defined, so that the sum of the subsystems constitutes the entire system. This process of decomposition is continued with subsystems divided into smaller subsystems until the smallest subsystems are of manageable size. The subsystems resulting from this process generally form hierarchical structures. In the hierarchy, a subsystem is one element of a suprasystem (the system above it).

Decomposition into subsystems is used both to analyze an existing system and to design and implement a new system. In both cases, the investigator or designer must decide how to factor, i.e., where to draw the boundaries. The decisions will depend on the objectives of the decomposition and also on individual differences among designers. A general principle in decomposition is functional cohesion. Components are

considered to be part of the same subsystem if they perform or are related to the same function. As an example, a payroll application program to be divided into modules (subsystems) will divide along major program functions such as accumulating hours worked, calculating deductions, printing a check, etc.

The process of decomposition could lead to a large number of subsystem interfaces to define. For example, four subsystems which all interact with each other will have six interconnections; a system with 20 subsystems all interacting will have 190 interconnections. The number can rise quite quickly as the number of subsystems increases. *Simplification* is the process of organizing subsystems so as to reduce the number of interconnections. One method of simplification is clustering of systems, with a single interface connection from the cluster to other subsystems or decoupling. If two different subsystems are connected very tightly, very close coordination between them is required. The solution to excessive coordination is to decouple or loosen the connection so that the two systems can operate in the short run with some measure of independence. Some means of decoupling are inventories, buffers, or waiting lines. Slack or flexible resources allow some independence. Standards of various types also reduce the need for close coordination.

SYSTEM ENTROPY

Systems can run down and decay or can become disordered or disorganized. Stated in system terminology, an increase in *entropy* takes place. Preventing or offsetting the increase in entropy requires inputs of matter and energy to repair, replenish, and maintain the system. This maintenance input is termed *negative entropy*. Open systems require more negative entropy than relatively closed systems to keep at a steady state of organization and operation.

SYSTEM CONCEPTS APPLIED TO MANAGEMENT INFORMATION SYSTEMS

System concepts are applicable to many aspects of management information systems. A few examples illustrate the application of these concepts. The information system of an organization is a system. It receives inputs of data and instructions, processes the data according to instructions, and outputs the results. The basic system model of inputs, process, and outputs is suitable in the simplest case of an information processing system. However, the information processing function frequently needs data collected and processed in a prior period. Data storage is therefore added to the information system model, so that the processing activity has available both current data and data collected and stored previously. The information processing infrastructure system has subsystems, such as the hardware system, operating system, communication system, and database system. It also has application subsystems, such as order entry and billing, payroll, and personnel. The application subsystems make use of the infrastructure subsystems.

Information systems and other artificial systems are human artifacts; the systems exist only because humans design and build them. The fact that information systems are human artifacts means that they reflect characteristics and objectives of human systems. The design and operation of living systems allow them to adapt and survive. Likewise, there is an objective of survivability in artificial systems. In order to achieve this survivability objective, information systems are designed with characteristics that simplify the system structure, reduce tight coupling, and allow system repair and change.

System concepts can be applied in the development of information system projects. The information system is defined and overall responsibility assigned, major information processing subsystems are delineated, each subsystem is assigned to a project, the project leader factors the job into subsystem projects and assigns responsibility for each. The structured design approach encourages definition of subsystems from the top down; at each level of the hierarchy, the interfaces between the lower-level subsystems are clearly defined. This allows development personnel to clearly define the objectives of each subsystem and provide checkpoints for its accomplishments.

The concept of *black box* is also useful when subsystems, boundaries, and interfaces are being defined: lower-level subsystems can be defined as black boxes, while the higher-level subsystems are being designed. Later in the development process a systems analyst is provided with the defined inputs and required outputs and assigned to define the rules inside the black box.

System concepts assist in understanding various features and practices of information systems. The principle of equifinality explains why many designs may work but are not equal in effort to develop and use. The principle of entropy explains why systems decay, and why maintenance to repair and update systems is vital. The human–machine nature of information systems is the basis for sociotechnical design that emphasizes the consideration of both human/social and technical factors (*see* SOCIOTECHNICAL CONCEPTS APPLIED TO INFORMATION SYSTEMS).

Some researchers have begun to examine systems and system behavior using the perspective of complexity. This research suggests that many complex systems evolve in ways that are not predicted by simplification and decomposition analysis (*see* COMPLEXITY AND INFORMATION SYSTEMS).

Bibliography

Checkland, P. (1999). *Systems Thinking, Systems Practice: Includes a 30-Year Retrospective*. Chichester: John Wiley.

Churchman, C. W. (1968). *The Systems Approach*. New York: Dell.

Davis, G. B. and Olson, M. H. (1985). *Management Information Systems: Conceptual Foundations, Structure, and Development*, 2nd edn. New York: McGraw-Hill, ch. 9.

Emery, F. E. (1969). *Systems Thinking*. Baltimore: Penguin.

Katz, D. and Kahn, R. L. (1978). *The Social Psychology of Organizations*, 2nd edn. New York: John Wiley.

Miller, J. G. (1978). *Living Systems*. New York: John Wiley.

Simon, H. A. (1981). *The Science of the Artificial*, 2nd edn. Cambridge, MA: MIT Press.

system software

Gordon B. Davis

Software is often divided into system software and application software. System software enables application software to be developed and executed. Application software performs the specific processing needed by the computer users. System software, as a broad term, therefore encompasses any software with functions used by applications or by personnel who operate the computer and manage its resources. The dominant system software is the operating system. The operating system includes many functions that are also available as separate software packages. Examples of other system software include utilities to perform common processing functions, performance software to monitor system performance and assist operations in managing resources, and security software. The GRAPHICAL USER INTERFACE for microcomputer users is system software that may be separate from the operating system or packaged with it. System software is usually obtained from software vendors; this is contrasted with application software, which is often developed by the organization or person using it.

See also *computer operating system; software*

systems analysis and design

Kenneth E. Kendall and Julie E.Kendall

This is a systematic and complex endeavor that has as its goal the improvement of a business through the skillful use of computer-based information systems in an organization. Systems analysts are typically educated in universities or technical schools. Systems analysis and design demands an entire spectrum of skills, ranging from computer programming to effective interpersonal skills. Numerous categories of information systems, serving each functional area of business, as well as all different levels of management, are developed. These extend from transaction processing systems (TPS) on the operations level all the way up the organizational hierarchy to EXECUTIVE INFORMATION SYSTEMS (EIS) on the strategic management level. Complicated projects involving large amounts of financial and human resources are often directed by systems analysts.

ISSUES

A systems analyst approaching a new project deliberates about several issues that are important to the project's overall plan and eventual implementation. Most of these decisions are not taken unilaterally, but rather are made in consultation with management, users, and other analysts who are involved in the systems project. These issues include, but are not necessarily limited to, the scope and boundaries of the systems project; how many people are involved in the project directly; how many people ultimately will be affected by the proposed changes; assessing the level of motivation and resource commitment for the project; how to involve key decision-makers and users in the systems project; choosing a systems development methodology from both structured and other approaches; and whether it is necessary to create unique software applications for the client or whether customizing off-the-shelf software is appropriate. Many additional issues are subsumed under these broad concerns.

The issue of choosing an alternative methodology not only revolves around the systems analyst's skills and preparation, but also must reflect the way in which management and users envision their future. For instance, the enterprise might consider that it is a complex machine, working precisely toward its goals in a structured, orderly, and predictable way. Other organizations believe they are on a long journey, one beset by disorder and chaos, although a clear goal is stated. Still another company might hold that it is a family. Choosing an appropriate systems development methodology can help enrich and extend this organizational perspective.

A fairly recent development in systems development is extreme programming (often abbreviated as XP). Extreme programming is an approach that takes what we typically designate as good software development practices and extends them to extreme lengths. For instance, XP uses more intense, ever-shorter feedback cycles during software development, providing ever more feedback. An important part of XP is its values: communication, simplicity, feedback, and courage. XP practices include pair programming, a 40-hour work week, short release cycles, and the inclusion of on-site customers. A similar method of development is called agile modeling (*see* AGILE DEVELOPMENT).

Another approach to systems development is the use of object-oriented systems analysis and design (*see* OBJECT-ORIENTED PROGRAMS AND SYSTEMS). Each object is a computer representation of some actual thing or event. Objects are part of a general concept called classes. Many advocates felt that the main benefit of the object-oriented approach would be the "reusability" of the objects. However, another benefit is that maintaining systems can be more cost effective by creating objects that contain both data and program code, because a change in one object will have minimal impact on other objects. The industry standard for object-oriented systems analysis is the UNIFIED MODELING LANGUAGE (UML).

No matter what approach is used, the systems analysis has to describe the opportunities and problems, gather data, analyze something about the current system and processes, design a new system, and create or help programmers create a working version of the new system that is tested, evaluated, and eventually marinated. Whether analysts recommend that organizations purchase commercial off-the-shelf (COTS) software or instruct programmers how to code and customize systems, they need to possess many diverse skills to carry out all of these demanding tasks.

For the most part, this entry covers the most widely taught and used approach to systems analysis and design, which is embodied in structured analysis and design methodologies (some with proprietary names such as STRADIS and SSADM) and which is supported by popular CASE: COMPUTER-AIDED SOFTWARE/SYSTEM ENGINEERING tools.

Machine-like organizations, as well as those involved in a game mentality, are well served by structured methodologies, but if the organization houses individuals who are autonomous, and make different evaluations leading to a variety of actions, use of SOFT SYSTEMS METHODOLOGIES may be more appropriate. ETHICS, a sociotechnical design method (*see* SOCIOTECHNICAL CONCEPTS APPLIED TO INFORMATION SYSTEMS), may be useful in family-like organizations. Organizations on journeys may feel PROTOTYPING is the methodology of choice.

SYSTEMS ANALYSIS AND DESIGN PROCESSES

There are many processes in which the systems analyst must engage, regardless of which development methodology is used. Completing these processes helps insure that the organization will meet its goals and objectives. The processes often referred to as the systems development life cycle (SDLC) fall into five broad phases: information requirements determination; analysis of the existing and proposed system; design, development, and documentation of the new system; implementation; and evaluation of new system performance.

INFORMATION REQUIREMENTS DETERMINATION

Major processes include collecting data about existing information systems, and analyzing and documenting the data, systems, and user needs. Many methods are used to accomplish these processes. Analysts use interviewing, observation, archival data collection, and questionnaires to investigate user information requirements as well as system needs. They may also use prototyping, which permits the interaction with working or non-working models of the input, processing, or output stages of information systems. In order to document what they have found, analysts use field notes to document structured interviews with information-system users; interview forms; diagrams of offices; examples of existing forms and screens; and system specifications for the existing system (*see* REQUIREMENTS DETERMINATION FOR INFORMATION SYSTEMS).

ENTITY-RELATIONSHIP DIAGRAMS

One tool a systems analyst can use to define system boundaries is an entity-relationship model (*see* ER DIAGRAMS). It is critical that the systems analyst understand early on the entities and relationships in the organizational system. An entity may be a person, a place, or a thing, such as a customer, the New Jersey warehouse, or a CD-ROM product. Alternatively, an entity may be an event, such as the end of the month, or a machine malfunction. A relationship is the association that describes the interaction between the entities.

Two symbols (a rectangle and a diamond) are used to draw an entity-relationship diagram, as shown in figure 1. The rectangle depicts the entity, while the diamond shows the relationship between that entity and another entity. In the

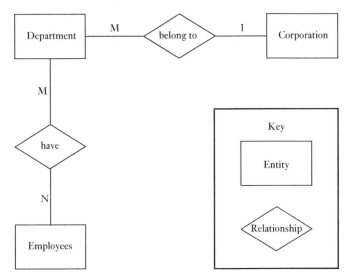

Figure 1   An entity-relationship diagram

example one can see that many (M) departments belong to 1 corporation and many (M) departments have many (N) employees.

A systems analyst may identify many entities and relationships and then decide where the boundary will be. For example, a physician may have relationships with the patient, the healthcare provider, a hospital, and pharmaceutical representatives. If the systems analyst decides that the system will include only scheduling office visits with patients, then the physician and patient would be the only relevant entities. Entity-relationship diagrams are useful in data modeling (*see* DATA MODELING, LOGICAL).

DATA FLOW DIAGRAMS

Data flow diagrams (DFD) are a structured analysis technique the systems analyst can use to put together a graphical representation of how data proceed through an organization. The data flow approach includes describing the existing system, and then describing the logical data flow as it would occur in the improved system. After the logical flow is described, a physical data flow diagram can be developed that includes not only data movement but also hardware and manual procedures. Finally, the physical data flow diagram can be partitioned, enabling the programmers to program the system using sensible, meaningful modules.

Figure 2 is a data flow diagram using symbols developed by Gane and Sarson (1979). Four symbols describe external entities, data flows, processes, and data stores. The external entity (e.g., a company, department, customer, or manager) is a main source or main destination of data, and is drawn as a double rectangle. Data flows are represented by arrows showing the movement of data from one point to another, with the head of the arrow pointing toward the data's destination. Data flows depict data in motion in the organization. Processes (the transformation of data into a different form of information) are drawn as rectangles with rounded corners. Processes always denote a change in or transformation of data; hence, the data flow leaving a process is always labeled differently from the one entering it. Data stores are drawn as open-ended rectangles. In logical data flow diagrams, the type of physical storage, whether it is tape, diskette, or other, is not specified. Therefore, the data store symbol simply shows that data are stored for use at this point or elsewhere in the system. Data stores depict data at rest in the organization.

Data flow diagrams are usually drawn from the most general to the most specific, typically top down. The first diagram the systems analyst draws is called a context diagram, which shows only the entities and one process, the system itself. This context diagram is then "exploded" to show more detail. At this point, data stores are identified and drawn. The diagram can be exploded further into child diagrams. Detailed logic, however, is not revealed in a data flow diagram. This is done in process specifications.

DATA DICTIONARY AND DATA REPOSITORY

Using data flow diagrams, the systems analyst begins compiling a DATA DICTIONARY, which contains data about data (metadata) on all data processes, stores, flows, structures, and elements within the system being studied. The data repository is a larger collection of project information. An important reason for compiling a data dictionary is to sort out the proliferation of uncoordinated names or aliases for data items that may exist if a variety of computer programs and systems are developed over time by different systems analysts. The data dictionary also serves as a consistent, organization-wide standard for data elements.

While a data dictionary should be as inclusive as possible, it is never complete. In fact, it should be updated as changes are implemented, just as other documentation is. In order to be useful, data dictionary entries should contain specific categories of information including: the name and aliases of the data item (e.g., customer or client); a description of the data item in words; data elements related to the entry (e.g., name, address, telephone, and credit card information); the allowable range of the data item (September cannot have more than 30 days); its maximum length in characters (e.g., a US social security number may never exceed nine numbers); proper encoding (e.g., Tuesday is coded as "Tue" not "Tues"); and any other pertinent editing information.

The data repository is structured to contain much more than the data dictionary, including: information maintained by the system such as data flows, data stores, record structures, and elements; logic specifications; screen and report

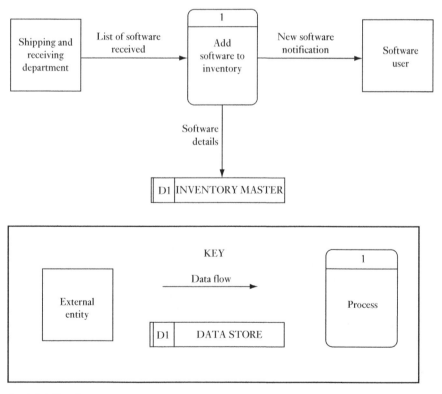

Figure 2   A data flow diagram

design; data relationships; project requirements and final system deliverables; and project management information, including delivery schedules, achievements, and issues that need resolving. Many CASE tools now feature active data dictionaries and extensive data repositories that include reusable program code as well as data elements. They are valuable for their capacity to cross-reference data items, since necessary program changes can be made to all programs sharing a common element. Additionally, data repositories can help to reduce the amount of new computer program code that must be written. New CASE tools prompt and assist the systems analyst in creating the data dictionary and the data repository concurrently with the analysis of the information system. This reduces the time necessary for documentation once the system is complete.

Process Specifications and Logic

After data flow diagrams are drawn and data dictionaries are well underway, the systems analyst will need to describe the logic of decision-making in a more detailed manner. A large part of a systems analyst's work involves identifying and diagramming structured decisions; i.e., decisions that can be automated if identified circumstances occur. A structured decision is repetitive, routine, and has standard procedures to follow for its solution. An example of a structured decision is approval of a credit card purchase by a credit card company. Three commonly used methods for describing structured decision processes are structured English, decision tables, and decision trees.

Structured English uses accepted keywords such as IF, THEN, ELSE, DO, DO WHILE, and DO UNTIL to describe the logic used and, when written, phrases are indented to indicate the hierarchical structure of the decision process (*see* STRUCTURED PROGRAMMING). CASE tools tend to favor structured English to express logic in terms of sequential, decision, and case structures, as well as iterations. Structured English is easy to understand, and therefore is a good way to communicate simple decision processes.

Decision tables provide another familiar way to examine, describe, and document decisions. Four quadrants (viewed clockwise from the upper left-hand corner) are used to: (1) describe the conditions; (2) identify possible decision alternatives such as Yes or No; (3) indicate which actions should be performed; and (4) describe the actions. The use of decision tables promotes completeness and accuracy in analyzing structured decisions.

A third method for decision analysis is the *decision tree*, consisting of nodes (a square depicts actions and a circle depicts conditions) and branches. Decision trees do not have to be symmetrical, so trees may be more readable than decision tables and are essential when actions must be accomplished in a certain sequence.

Modularity and Structure Charts

By using these tools, the analyst is eventually able to break apart the system into logical, manageable portions called modules. This kind of programming fits well with top-down design because it emphasizes the interfaces or relationships between modules rather than neglecting them until later in systems development. Ideally, each module should be functionally cohesive so that it is charged with accomplishing only one function in the program.

There are many advantages to modular program design. Modules are easier to write and debug (correct errors) because they are virtually self-contained. Tracing an error in a module is less complicated, since a problem in one module should not cause problems in others. Modules are easier to maintain because modifications usually will be limited to a few modules, rather than spreading over an entire program. Logic within modules is easier to understand since they are self-contained subsystems.

In order to represent the modules, the systems analyst may use a structure chart, which is a diagram consisting simply of rectangular boxes and connecting lines as shown in figure 3. Additional information noted on a structure chart includes "data couples," which show which data must pass from one module to another, and "control flags," which show which instructions must pass between modules. Ideally, the analyst should keep this coupling to a minimum. The fewer data couples and control flags one has in the system, the easier it is to alter the system in the future.

Structure charts are used to communicate the logic of data flow diagrams to the computer programmers while child diagrams are used to communicate process specifications. Process specifications describe the order and conditions under which the child diagram will execute. Process specifications may be used to analyze the data flow diagram and data dictionary through a method called horizontal balancing, which dictates that all data flow output elements must be obtained from input elements and process logic. When unresolved areas appear, they can be posed to users as follow-up questions in interviews.

DESIGNING OUTPUT, INPUT, AND USER INTERFACE

There are six main objectives in designing output of information systems:

- to serve the intended purpose;
- to fit the user;
- to deliver the right quantity of output;
- to deliver it to the right place;
- to provide output on time;
- to choose the right output method.

Once limited in scope to paper reports, output now can take virtually any form, including print, screen, audio, microforms, CD-ROM, and electronic output such as EMAIL and faxes. Output technologies differ in their speed, cost, portability, flexibility, storage, and retrieval possibilities, and users often prefer some technologies over others (*see* OUTPUT DEVICES). The systems analyst needs to consider all of these factors as output is designed. Data that are not already stored in a database, or data that are unavailable via scanning or electronic transfer, must be captured with more traditional methods. These include paper forms and computer screens. In either case the design of the form is critical, especially with regard to the logical way in which the data are to be entered. Systems analysts can take advantage of a variety of fonts, icons, and colors to help make forms more readable and easier to fill out. Proper input design encourages more accurate and valid data.

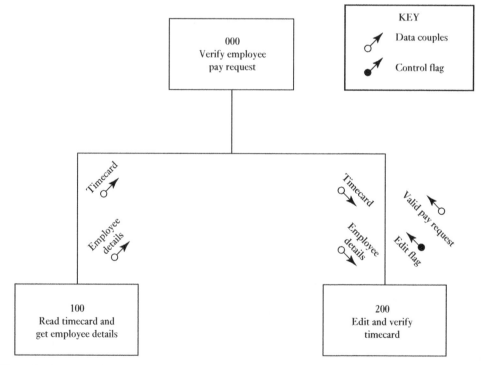

Figure 3   A structure chart

Systems analysts must often design interfaces as well. Interfaces are the means by which the system user interacts with the machine. Some interfaces include: natural language, command language, question-and-answer, menus, form-fill, and graphical user interfaces (GUI), which is pronounced "gooey" (*see* GRAPHICAL USER INTERFACE). Systems analysts also design powerful queries, which are developed to help users extract meaningful data from a database. Finally, analysts need to design *feedback* for users. System feedback is necessary to let users know:

- if their input is being accepted;
- if input is or is not in the correct form;
- if processing is going on;
- if requests can or cannot be processed;
- if more detailed information is available, and how to get it.

DELIVERABLES

The term *deliverables* refers to an installed and working information system, including all of the tangible items and training needed to support and maintain the new or upgraded system, which the systems analyst agrees to deliver to management and other involved parties throughout the project and at its end.

A written systems proposal typically presents three alternatives (only one of which the analyst will recommend), given to management after some feasibility and data analysis has been performed. At this juncture, management and the systems analyst examine each alternative for costs and benefits, as well as whether they are technically, operationally, and economically feasible. Once management and the analyst have agreed on an option, they agree to go forward with the project during a specified time frame.

The systems analyst (particularly one who has chosen a structured methodology that is supported by a CASE tool) delivers logical diagrams depicting new data flows, physical data flows, a data dictionary, a data repository, and process specifications. These deliverables were described earlier. No matter what systems analysis approach is adopted, the output, input, and user interface design are critical components for which the systems analyst is responsible. No matter how completely the data flow and logic are described, if there is meaningless or unintelligible output, invalid input, and/or an ineffective user interface design, the resulting project may be unsuccessful.

It is incumbent on the analyst to provide as much assistance as possible to the programmers who will code the software for the system. Structure charts are used to promote modular program design, and process specifications (also called minispecs) help transfer logic to programmers.

When purchases of hardware and coding of software are complete, the system is installed and tested with the analyst's help. System hardware and software are among the most easily identifiable and visible deliverables provided to management. An overall plan to test the system for accuracy, reliability, and usefulness is implemented at this time.

Clearly written and thoroughly tested documentation, such as manuals and online help systems written to accompany the hardware or software, its installation, operation, and maintenance, are also deliverables for which the systems analyst is responsible. Manuals range from highly technical documents for use by maintenance programmers to online, context-sensitive help directed at end users who must use the system as part of their daily jobs, but who are not computer experts.

Finally, as the analyst assists in getting the system into production, an evaluation plan, already written as part of the systems proposal, is implemented. This can include interviews and questionnaires designed both to assess user satisfaction with the system and to measure the actual system performance based on the benchmarks established earlier (*see* ASSESSMENT OF MANAGEMENT INFORMATION SYSTEM FUNCTION). Systems analysts may be involved up to a year or more after the system is installed in order to complete necessary refinements based on this feedback. The project is then officially ended.

Bibliography

Alavi, M. (1984). An assessment of the prototyping approach to information systems. *Communications of the ACM*, 27, 556–63.

Avison, D. E. and Wood-Harper, A. T. (1990). *Multiview: An Exploration in Information Systems Development*. Oxford: Blackwell.

Checkland, P. B. (1989). Soft systems methodology. *Human Systems Management*, 8, 271–89.

Davis, G. B. and Olson, M. H. (1985). *Management Information Systems: Conceptual Foundations, Structure, and Development*, 2nd edn. New York: McGraw-Hill.

Downs, E., Clare, P., and Coe, I. (1988). *Structured Systems Analysis and Design Method: Application and Context*. Hemel Hempstead: Prentice-Hall.

Gane, C. and Sarson, T. (1979). *Structured Systems Analysis and Design Tools and Techniques*. Englewood Cliffs, NJ: Prentice-Hall.

Jackson, M. (1983). *Systems Development*. Englewood Cliffs, NJ: Prentice-Hall.

Kendall, J. E. and Kendall, K. E. (1993). Metaphors and methodologies: Living beyond the systems machine. *MIS Quarterly*, 17, 149–71.

Kendall, K. E. and Kendall, J. E. (2005). *Systems Analysis and Design*, 6th edn. Upper Saddle River, NJ: Prentice-Hall.

Mumford, E. (1983). *Designing Participatively: A Participative Approach to Computer Systems Design*. Manchester: Manchester Business School.

Mumford, E. and Weir, M. (1979). *Computer Systems in Work Design: The ETHICS Method*. London: Associated Business Press.

Naumann, J. D. and Jenkins, A. M. (1982). Prototyping: The new paradigm for systems development. *MIS Quarterly*, 6, 29–44.

Yourdon, E. (1989). *Modern Structured Analysis*. Englewood Cliffs, NJ: Prentice-Hall.

task/system fit

William D. Nance

The concept of task/system fit focuses on the "fit" or "match" between the capabilities or functionalities provided by a given information system and the information processing requirements of the task in which the system may be used. Task/system fit models contain two key components: information processing requirements of a given task and information processing functionalities in an information system. The degree to which the information system capabilities "fit" or are "aligned with" the needs of the task determines system usefulness for that task. This degree of fit, or system usefulness, in turn, influences user task performance when the system is used to complete the task.

The concept of technology fit or alignment originated among contingency theorists at an organizational level of analysis to explain organizational effectiveness as a function of the extent to which organizational variables fit the context in which the organization operates. Subsequent extensions of research on contingency fit have utilized less aggregate levels of analysis such as organizational work units, groups, jobs, and individuals. Researchers have also examined several different dimensions of fit itself. Some have assessed fit from an objective, "engineering" perspective that excludes any individual component. Other researchers have included a strong individual dimension in their evaluation of task/system fit. They focus on dimensions such as individual perceptions of an application fit for tasks and on the cognitive fit between three components: the task information processing requirements, the capabilities of the information system, and the cognitive information processing style of the individual completing the task.

Regardless of the level of analysis or dimension of task/system fit, a key idea is that task performance improves when the information system application used in the task provides the appropriate functionalities for the task that needs to be completed. When other factors are the same, the task performance of a user who takes advantage of the appropriate system capabilities is generally better than the performance of one who uses a system with less useful capabilities relative to the task needs.

The task/technology fit concept has implications for the development of information systems. To develop systems that are likely to improve user performance, the systems development team must understand the key information processing needs of the task(s) the users will perform. They design into the new application the functionalities that support these information processing requirements.

TCP/IP

Transmission control protocol/Internet protocol is a widely used routing protocol. The Internet protocol routes data packets across networks and the transmission control protocol enables flow control and reliable transmission.

See also *Internet; protocols*

teams in system development

Brian D. Janz

Central to developing information system applications is determining business requirements that such systems must address. Given the interdependent and systemic nature of the functions and processes within business organizations, the knowledge and skills needed to completely understand business requirements and the complex interrelationships among them require a number of participants. In practice, teams made up of participants from various affected business functions come together to provide necessary expertise. Cross-functional system development teams represent knowledge work experts from both business functions and information technology areas.

Once the business requirements have been identified, development methodologies and tools are employed in order to articulate the requirements into technical specifications. An understanding of the potential hardware, software, and networking technologies is required. Development skills are necessary to build and maintain application systems. Today's teams come together for numerous kinds of application development activities. Rapid application development (RAD), PROTOTYPING, and joint application design (JAD) all require a team-based approach, and the knowledge and skills required for development suggest that teams of knowledge workers will be an ongoing need in systems development activities.

technology acceptance model

Viswanath Venkatesh

A persistent issue in information systems is acceptance of new technologies and new applications. The technology acceptance model, widely known by its acronym TAM, is the most dominant theoretical model explaining individual acceptance and use of technology. The parsimonious and intuitive model, developed by Fred Davis in the 1980s, has been applied to a wide variety of technologies and settings. TAM suggests that perceptions of usefulness and ease of use will together determine an individual's decision to use a new technological system.

See also *technology acceptance: unified model*

technology acceptance: unified model

Viswanath Venkatesh

For technologies to improve productivity, they must be accepted and used by employees in organizations. Explaining user acceptance of new technology is often described as one of the most mature research areas in the contemporary information systems (IS) literature. Research in this area has resulted in several theoretical models, with roots in information systems, psychology, and sociology. These models explain well over 40 percent of the variance in individual intention to use technology (e.g., Davis, Bagozzi, and Warshaw, 1989; Taylor and Todd, 1995; Venkatesh and Davis, 2000). Researchers are confronted with a choice among models. This entry summarizes the findings from an extensive review of the models and development of a unified model of technology acceptance (Venkatesh et al., 2003).

REVIEW OF USER ACCEPTANCE MODELS

IS research has studied *how* and *why* individuals adopt new information technologies. Within this broad area of inquiry, there have been several streams of research. One stream of research focuses on individual acceptance of technology by using intention or usage as a dependent variable (e.g., Davis et al., 1989). Other streams have focused on implementation success at the organizational level (Leonard-Barton and Deschamps, 1988) and task/technology fit (e.g., Goodhue and Thompson, 1995), among others (*see* TASK/ SYSTEM FIT). While each of these streams makes important and unique contributions to the literature on user acceptance of information technology, the theoretical models in this review, comparison, and synthesis employed intention and/or usage as the key dependent variable. Although the goal here is to understand usage as the dependent variable, the role of intention as a predictor of behavior is critical and has been well established in IS and the reference disciplines (see Sheppard, Hartwick, and Warshaw, 1988; Ajzen, 1991; Taylor and Todd, 1995). Figure 1 presents the basic conceptual framework underlying the class of models explaining individual acceptance of information technology that forms the basis of this research.

Venkatesh et al.'s (2003) review resulted in the identification of eight key competing theoretical models: theory of reasoned action, TECHNOL-OGY ACCEPTANCE MODEL (TAM), motiv-ational model, theory of planned behavior (TPB), combined TAM and TPB, model of PC utilization, innovation diffusion theory, and social cognitive theory. The models hypothesize between two and seven determinants of accept-ance, for a total of 32 different constructs across the eight models (see Venkatesh et al., 2003). These determinants fall into the left-most box of figure 1. In addition, four constructs were identified as key moderating variables: experi-ence, voluntariness, gender, and age.

Longitudinal field studies were conducted at four organizations to test and compare the eight models (Venkatesh et al., 2003). All eight models explained individual acceptance, with variance in intention explained ranging from 17 percent to 42 percent. Also, a key difference across stud-ies stemmed from the voluntary versus manda-tory settings – in mandatory settings, constructs related to social influence were significant, whereas in the voluntary settings they were not significant. Finally, the determinants of inten-tion varied over time, with some determinants going from significant to non-significant with increasing experience. Following the test of the baseline/original specifications of the eight models, Venkatesh et al. (2003) examined the

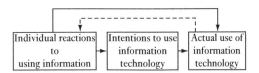

Figure 1 Basic concept underlying user acceptance models

moderating influences suggested in the litera-ture, either explicitly or implicitly – i.e., experi-ence, voluntariness, gender, and age. Overall, as expected, the moderators added to the predictive validity of the models with intention as the de-pendent variable. Intention was the strongest predictor of actual behavior at all times.

FORMULATION OF THE UNIFIED THEORY OF ACCEPTANCE AND USE OF TECHNOLOGY

A unified theory of acceptance and use of tech-nology (UTAUT) was formulated (Venkatesh et al., 2003). UTAUT theorizes that four con-structs, created from the overlap across con-structs in different models, will play a significant role as direct determinants of user acceptance and usage behavior: *performance ex-pectancy, effort expectancy, social influence,* and *facilitating conditions.* Figure 2 presents the propositions of UTAUT.

Performance expectancy is defined as the degree to which an individual believes that using the system will help him or her better

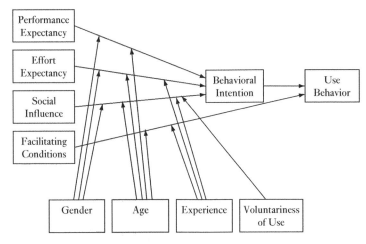

Note: All interactions shown are higher-order terms.

Figure 2 Unified theory of acceptance and use of technology (UTAUT)

attain significant rewards. Also, the influence of performance expectancy on behavioral intention will be moderated by *gender* and *age*, such that the effect will be stronger for men and particularly for younger men.

Effort expectancy is defined as the degree of ease associated with the use of the system. Also, the influence of effort expectancy on behavioral intention will be moderated by *gender*, *age*, and *experience*, such that the effect will be stronger for women, particularly older women, and particularly at early stages of experience.

Social influence is defined as the degree to which an individual perceives that important others believe he or she should use the new system. Also, the effect of social influence on behavioral intention will be moderated by *gender*, *age*, *voluntariness*, and *experience*, such that the effect will be stronger for women, particularly older women, particularly in mandatory settings in the early stages of experience.

Facilitating conditions are defined as the degree to which an individual believes that an organizational and technical infrastructure exists to support use of the system. Facilitating conditions are *not* expected to have a significant influence on behavioral intention. However, the influence of facilitating conditions on usage will be moderated by *age* and *experience*, such that the effect will be stronger for older workers, particularly with increasing experience. Finally, as noted earlier, *behavioral intention* will have a significant positive influence on usage.

UTAUT was strongly supported via empirical tests in six different organizations among employees being exposed to new technology. UTAUT was consistently more predictive than the previous models. This, of course, is to be expected given that UTAUT builds on and integrates the different models and also includes a superset of moderating variables. UTAUT explained over 75 percent of the variance in intention in a preliminary test and a cross-validation, thus providing perhaps a very comprehensive explanation of the phenomenon of employee acceptance of technologies over the short and medium term.

UTAUT is a definitive model that synthesizes what is known and provides a foundation to guide future research in this area. By encompassing the combined explanatory power of the individual models and key moderating influences, UTAUT advances cumulative theory while retaining a parsimonious structure. UTAUT highlights the importance of contextual analysis in developing strategies for technology implementation within organizations. While each of the existing models of technology acceptance is quite successful in predicting technology usage behavior, it is only when one considers the complex range of potential moderating influences that a more complete picture of the dynamic nature of individual perceptions about technology begins to emerge. Despite the ability of the existing models to predict intention and usage, current theoretical perspectives on individual acceptance are notably weak in providing prescriptive guidance to designers.

Future research is expected to focus on integrating UTAUT with research that has identified causal antecedents of the constructs used within the model (e.g., Karahanna and Straub, 1999; Venkatesh, 2000; Venkatesh and Davis, 2000) in order to provide a greater understanding of how the cognitive phenomena that were the focus of this research are formed. Examples of previously examined determinants of the core predictors include system characteristics (Davis et al., 1989) and self-efficacy (Venkatesh, 2000). Additional determinants that have not been explicitly tied into this stream but merit consideration in future work include task/technology fit (Goodhue and Thompson, 1995) and individual ability constructs such as "g" – general cognitive ability/intelligence (Colquitt, LePine, and Noe, 2000).

While the variance explained by UTAUT is quite high for behavioral research, further work should attempt to identify and test additional boundary conditions of the model in an attempt to provide an even richer understanding of technology adoption and usage behavior. This might take the form of additional theoretically motivated moderating influences, different technologies (e.g., collaborative systems, E-COMMERCE applications), different user groups (e.g., individuals in different functional areas), and other organizational contexts (e.g., public/government institutions). Results from such studies will have the important benefit of enhancing the overall generalizability of UTAUT and/or extending the existing work to account for additional variance in behavior.

Future research should investigate other potential constructs such as behavioral expectation (Warshaw and Davis, 1985) or habit (Venkatesh, Morris, and Ackerman, 2000) in the nomological network. Employing behavioral expectation will help account for anticipated changes in intention (Warshaw and Davis, 1985) and thus shed light even in the early stages of the behavior about the *actual likelihood* of behavioral performance, since intention captures only internal motivations to perform the behavior. Recent evidence suggests that sustained usage behavior may not be the result of deliberated cognitions and is simply routinized or automatic responses to stimuli (see Venkatesh et al., 2000).

One of the most important directions for future research is to tie this mature stream of research into other established streams of work. For example, little to no research has addressed the link between user acceptance and individual/organizational usage outcomes. Thus, while it is often assumed that usage will result in "positive" outcomes, this remains to be tested. The unified model presented here might inform further inquiry into the short- and long-term effects of information technology implementation on job-related outcomes such as productivity, job satisfaction, organizational commitment, and other performance-oriented constructs. Future research should study the degree to which systems perceived as "successful" from an IT adoption perspective (i.e., those that are liked and highly used by users) are considered a "success" from an organizational perspective.

Bibliography

Ajzen, I. (1991). The theory of planned behavior. *Organizational Behavior and Human Decision Processes*, **50**, 179–211.

Colquitt, J. A., LePine, J. A., and Noe, R. A. (2000). Toward an integrative theory of training motivation: A meta-analytic path analysis of 20 years of training research. *Journal of Applied Psychology*, **85**, 678–707.

Davis, F. D., Bagozzi, R. P., and Warshaw, P. R. (1989). User acceptance of computer technology: A comparison of two theoretical models. *Management Science*, **35**, 982–1002.

Goodhue, D. L. and Thompson, R. L. (1995). Task-technology fit and individual performance. *MIS Quarterly*, **19**, 213–36.

Karahanna, E. and Straub, D. W. (1999). The psychological origins of perceived usefulness and ease of use. *Information and Management*, **35**, 237–50.

Leonard-Barton, D. and Deschamps, I. (1988). Managerial influence in the implementation of new technology. *Management Science*, **34**, 1252–65.

Sheppard, B. H., Hartwick, J., and Warshaw, P. R. (1988). The theory of reasoned action: A meta-analysis of past research with recommendations for modifications and future research. *Journal of Consumer Research*, **15**, 325–43.

Taylor, S. and Todd, P. A. (1995). Understanding information technology usage: A test of competing models. *Information Systems Research*, **6**, 144–76.

Venkatesh, V. (2000). Determinants of perceived ease of use: Integrating perceived behavioral control, computer anxiety and enjoyment into the technology acceptance model. *Information Systems Research*, **11**, 342–65.

Venkatesh, V. and Davis, F. D. (2000). A theoretical extension of the technology acceptance model: Four longitudinal field studies. *Management Science*, **46**, 186–204.

Venkatesh, V., Morris, M. G., and Ackerman, P. L. (2000). A longitudinal field investigation of gender differences in individual technology adoption decision-making processes. *Organizational Behavior and Human Decision Processes*, **83**, 33–60.

Venkatesh, V., Morris, M. G., Davis, G. B., and Davis, F. D. (2003). User acceptance of information technology: Toward a unified view. *MIS Quarterly*, **27**, 425–78.

Warshaw, P. R. and Davis, F. D. (1985). Disentangling behavioral intention and behavioral expectation. *Journal of Experimental Social Psychology*, **21**, 213–28.

telecommunication

see ELECTRONIC COMMUNICATION

telecommuting

The substitution of travel to a workplace through the use of telecommunication technology. See VIRTUAL WORK.

telework

Accomplishment of work outside a central office through the use of computer and telecommunications technology. See VIRTUAL WORK.

transaction processing

Transaction processing refers to applications that process business transactions such as order entry and billing. See PROCESSING METHODS FOR INFORMATION SYSTEMS.

trust in information technology

D. Harrison McKnight

On its voyage to the moon, the Apollo 13 spacecraft's primary means of propulsion was damaged, so NASA had to devise another plan. The technology to do this existed, but, since it was built for other purposes, it had never been tested for in-space propulsion. If you were the Apollo 13 captain, with your crew's lives at stake, to what extent would you trust the alternate technology to propel you home?

The import of trust is only noticed when trust becomes scarce. Usually, we trust human-made technical marvels, such as spacecraft, planes, autos, bridges, and buildings. As long as they work, we seldom think of trust. When they don't (e.g., the Apollo spacecraft or the Columbia space shuttle), the trust question arises.

The basic nature of trust is found as one feels the tension between depending upon another and instituting controls to make sure that other performs. The more situational the risk, the higher the stakes. Whether the object of trust is another person or an information technology, one trusts the other to the extent that one chooses to depend on the other and reconciles away fears by being willing to become vulnerable to the other without controlling the other (Mayer, Davis, and Schoorman, 1995).

Trust in information technology (IT) is an important concept because people today rely on IT more than ever before. For example, at the airport, you rely on IT (a reservation system) to remember that you are booked on a particular flight in an acceptable seat. When you send an important package by express mail, you rely on IT to tell you, hour by hour, whether the package has arrived. When you deal with cash transactions at a bank ATM, you rely on the system both to track your transactions accurately and to prevent others from accessing either your money or your account information. When you buy items on sale, you expect the point-of-sale system to ring up the correctly discounted price. The INTERNET has increased reliance on IT by encouraging millions to download music or software, upload digital pictures, buy goods, or seek new information or new services. Because of the Internet's open, non-secured structure, trust in the web itself is an issue. Trust in IT has to do with relying or depending on infrastructure systems like the web or relying on specific information systems like Microsoft Excel.

Formally, the overall trust concept means secure willingness to depend on a trustee because of that trustee's perceived characteristics (Rousseau et al., 1998). Three main types of applicable trust concepts are used: (1) trusting beliefs, (2) trusting intentions, and (3) trusting behaviors. These concepts are connected.

1   Trusting beliefs means a secure conviction that the other party has favorable attributes (such as benevolence, integrity, and competence), strong enough to create trusting intentions.
2   Trusting intentions means a secure, committed willingness to depend upon, or to become vulnerable to, the other party in specific ways, strong enough to create trusting behaviors.
3   Trusting behaviors means assured actions that demonstrate that one does in fact depend or rely upon the other party instead of on oneself or on controls. Trusting behavior is the action manifestation of willingness to depend.

Each of these generic trust types can be applied to trust in IT. Trusting behavior-IT means that one securely depends or relies on the technology instead of trying to control the technology. For example, one who hits a website's "Download now" button demonstrates a willingness to be vulnerable to the software sent to one's computer – software that may contain viruses. Trusting intention-IT means one is securely willing to depend on or be vulnerable to the information technology. This is the psychological state one possesses before hitting the "Download now" button. Trusting beliefs-IT means a secure conviction that the technology has desirable attributes. For example, one may believe the system sending the software is reliable, safe, and timely in completing its task.

Most of these trust in IT definitions are very similar to their trust in people counterparts. The difference is the object of trust (McKnight and Chervany, 2001–2) – a specific technology or technologies versus a specific person or set of persons. For example, just as you can behaviorally depend on a person (as in trusting behaviors) to do a task for you (such as calculating numbers), so you can behaviorally depend on a piece of software (e.g., a statistical system) to do a task for you (such as making a statistical computation). With trusting intentions, just as you are willing to depend on the person, you can be willing to depend on an IT. Similarly, you can as easily believe an IT has favorable attributes as you can a person.

The major difference between trust in people and trust in IT lies in the applicability of specific trusting beliefs. People and technologies have both similar and different attributes, and those similarities and differences define which trusting beliefs apply.

In terms of similarities, both an information technology and a person have the quality of competence in terms of what they can do. Trusting belief in a person's competence means the person is perceived to have the capability to do a task or fulfill a responsibility. Trusting belief in an IT's competence means the IT is perceived to have the functionality or functional capability to do some task the trustor wants done. Another example: people can be said to act in predictable or consistent ways. Similarly, a technology can be said to perform in predictable or consistent ways. With people, we say the person's behavior is predictable, reliable, or easily forecast. With IT, we say the predictable system operates reliably, by which we mean it does what it is designed to do without frequent "crashing," delays, or unexpected results.

In terms of differences, whereas people can be described as having benevolence and integrity, these are harder to ascribe to IT without reverting to unwarranted anthropomorphisms. With trust in people, one trusts a morally capable and volitional human; with trust in IT, one trusts a human-created artifact with a limited range of behaviors that lacks both will and moral agency. Thus, one cannot ascribe moral or volitional attributes to information systems – only capabilities or predictabilities. One can't say an IT cares (related to trusting belief-benevolence) or tells the truth (related to trusting belief-integrity). Further, when commercial airline pilots decide to turn the plane over to a co-pilot or to autopilot, their decision reflects comparisons of the co-pilot's *willingness and capability* to fly the plane and the auto-pilot's *capability* to fly the plane. Because technology lacks moral agency, trust in technology necessarily reflects beliefs about a technology's capability rather than its will or its motives. Because auto-pilot technology has limited capabilities to deal with dangerous or unusual conditions, trust in the auto-pilot IT cannot be extended as far as can trust in a fully trained and experienced co-pilot.

Trust in information technology has several interesting implications. First, trust in IT should influence use or adoption of a technology. Unless one trusts a software product to reliably fill one's needs, why would one adopt it? Second, trust in IT is a general assessment of the technology that probably affects other IT perceptions, such as relative advantage or usefulness of the technology. Thus, it may influence beliefs and attitudes that affect intentions to use a technology.

Trust in technology is built the same way as trust in people. When users first experience technology, signals of well-done user interfaces and good vendor reputations will build trust. Reliable, dependable, quality IT performance is the key over time. Effective help functions also improve trust in IT. The entire system infrastructure should demonstrate quality, for deficient software at one level may hurt perceptions at several levels. For example, system security issues must be addressed before an application is trusted.

In addition to trusting beliefs, trusting intentions, and trusting behaviors, two other types of trust deserve mention – dispositional and institution-based trust (McKnight, Cummings, and Chervany, 1998). Disposition to trust is an individual differences concept originating from personality psychology that means a tendency to trust general others. Its IT equivalent is disposition to trust IT, the general tendency to be willing to depend on technologies across a broad spectrum of situations and specific ITs.

Institution-based trust is a concept from sociology that relates to structures and situational favorableness that support trust. In terms of IT, institution-based trust in IT means a belief that success with the specific technology is likely because, regardless of the characteristics of the specific technology, one believes either that the technical situation is favorable or that structural conditions like guarantees, contracts, or other safeguards exist. Both disposition to trust technology and institution-based trust in technology foster trusting beliefs, trusting intentions, and trusting behaviors regarding a specific technology.

Bibliography

McKnight, D. H. and Chervany, N. L. (2001–2). What trust means in e-commerce customer relationships: An interdisciplinary conceptual typology. *International Journal of Electronic Commerce*, **6** (2), 35–59.

McKnight, D. H., Cummings, L. L., and Chervany, N. L. (1998). Initial trust formation in new organizational relationships. *Academy of Management Review*, **23** (3), 473–90.

Mayer, R. C., Davis, J. H., and Schoorman, F. D. (1995). An integrative model of organizational trust. *Academy of Management Review*, **20**, 3 (July), 709–34.

Rousseau, D. M., Sitkin, S. B., Burt, R. S., and Camerer, C. (1998). Not so different after all: A cross-discipline view of trust. *Academy of Management Review*, **23** (3), 393–404.

ubiquitous computing

Fred Niederman

Ubiquitous computing is an important direction for information systems in organizations. The basic concept is to provide computing and communications services at the time and place where the employee or customer or other user needs the services. This is in contrast to traditional information systems that provide computing and communications services in offices or other fixed locations. The persons who need these services (clients) receive them in factories, offices, corridors of building, hotels, and so forth. Ubiquitous computing applications also provide services to clients while they are in motion between locations. Examples are a knowledge worker participating in a virtual meeting while on a subway or train between metropolitan areas, or a manager walking through a warehouse and receiving messages from the inventory pallets about the amount of inventory and its age. Consumer examples are services provided to individuals visiting a shopping center or recreational area such as a botanical garden.

In all the examples, clients could be accessing services using devices such as intelligent phones, personal digital assistants (PDAs), laptop computers with wireless access, and other similar devices. The computing and communications capabilities required by the clients are included in the locations and may be embedded in local objects. For example, a client passing through a botanic garden might receive identification messages from various flora or artistic pieces such as statues. At a basic level, these identification messages may indicate what the tree or sculpture is named. At a more detailed level, the identification may trigger a set of additional functions such as displaying information about the origins,

natural location, design, or history of the object. Ultimately, the identification could trigger transactions or invitations for transactions such as purchasing a simulation or artist's rendition of the piece; or forwarding related information to friends or family. While these scenarios describe the central tendency of ubiquitous computing, the term has also been used in describing other applications such as wearable computers and virtual organizations/teams.

The broad definition of ubiquitous computing reflects the fact that most ubiquitous computing applications are in conceptual, prototype, or developmental phases and few, if any, have been broadly implemented. Therefore it is difficult to define a clear and agreed-upon boundary. Some applications, such as virtual organizations/teams, are in relatively early stages in their evolution and will continue to develop additional services so that full implementation may eventually fully utilize both mobile and pervasive aspects, even if, at present, versions of these applications do not require the full range of features that would clearly mark them as ubiquitous computing.

Some of the major areas in which ubiquitous computing can be expected to provide services include:

1. business production and supply chain, for example, linking process machines or robots on the shop floor with business information such as arrival of raw materials, updating of inventory, and shipping orders;
2. public spaces and accommodations, for example, broadcasting identification messages from public buildings in a downtown area such that a visitor could quickly access historical, locational, and consumer information – perhaps even connect to a "virtual

city" that links local residents with visitors through various institutions;

3 recreation and public activities, such as in the botanical garden example;

4 in the home, for example by linking home appliances such as refrigerators and ovens, washers and driers, music and entertainment systems for intelligent home systems, automatic inventory updates, and personal security systems; and

5 for knowledge workers, for example by providing seamless connections with project teams, transactional data, evolving customer relations, and individual knowledge base.

From a technical perspective, there are difficulties that limit the diffusion of ubiquitous computing. These difficulties appear in the areas of

1 developing "client" standards such that differences in client hardware, formats, and configuration are transparent to the "server";

2 developing application logic for the wide range of different user needs and services;

3 developing database tactics for anticipating needed data, storing them in efficient formats, and retrieving them within usable time allotments;

4 networking and scaling applications to the handling of large bodies of data over available bandwidth;

5 sorting through large amounts of data, which may include much redundancy and irrelevant messages; and

6 identifying the functionality that will justify the expenditure of investment dollars.

From a social perspective, ubiquitous computing offers significant potential benefits in terms of streamlining existing tasks and creating new products, services, and experiences for workers, consumers, citizens, and students. On the other hand, as with most new technologies, there can be unintended consequences. Ubiquitous computing, if not monitored, could create a society where even minimal levels of privacy are difficult or impossible to realize. By providing constant access to communication technologies, the line between work and non-work time can become increasingly blurred, producing negative social consequences. It potentially can

render many existing jobs obsolete while creating new ones, with all the related issues that such change creates. Modern society is already very dependent on computer technology for providing basic and complex social interactions. Ubiquitous computing increases that dependence and therefore increases the potential for failures and disruptive consequences.

Bibliography

Davis, G. B. (2002). Anytime/anyplace computing and the future of knowledge work. *Communications of the ACM*, 45, 12 (December), 67–73.

Lyytinen, K. and Yoo, Y. (2002). Issues and challenges in ubiquitous computing. *Communications of the ACM*, 45, 12 (December), 63–5.

Siewiorek, D. P. (2002). New frontiers of application design. *Communications of the ACM*, 45, 12 (December), 79–82.

Weiser, M. (1991). The computer for the 21st century. *Scientific American*, 263, 3 (September), 94–104.

unified modeling language (UML)

Theresa M. Quatrani

In defining, designing, building, and implementing an information system application, it is important to be able to document ideas and designs and to communicate with those who are building the application and those who will use it. Visual modeling is a way of thinking about problems and systems using models organized around real-world ideas. Models are useful for understanding problems, communicating with everyone involved with the project (customers, domain experts, analysts, designers, etc.), modeling enterprises, preparing documentation, and designing programs and databases. Modeling promotes better understanding of requirements, cleaner designs, and more maintainable systems.

Notation plays an important part in any model – it is the glue that holds the process together. Notation has three roles:

- It serves as the language for communicating decisions that are not obvious or cannot be inferred from the code itself.
- It provides semantics that are rich enough to capture all important strategic and tactical decisions.

- It offers a form concrete enough for humans to reason and for tools to manipulate.

The unified modeling language (UML) is an important, well-supported modeling language. It provides a very robust notation, which grows from analysis into design. Certain elements of the notation (e.g., classes, associations, aggregations, inheritance) are introduced during analysis. Other elements of the notation (e.g., containment implementation indicators and properties) are introduced during design.

During the 1990s many different methodologies, along with their own sets of notations, were introduced to the market. Three of the most popular methods were OMT (Rumbaugh), Booch, and OOSE (Jacobson). Each method had its own value and emphasis. OMT was strong in analysis and weaker in the design area. Booch 1991 was strong in design and weaker in analysis. Jacobson was strong in behavior analysis and weaker in the other areas.

As time moved on, Booch wrote his second book, which adopted a lot of the good analysis techniques advocated by Rumbaugh and Jacobson, among others. Rumbaugh published a series of articles that have become known as OMT-2, which adopted several of the good design techniques of Booch. The methods were beginning to converge but they still had their own unique notations. The use of different notations brought confusion to the market since one symbol meant different things to different people. For example, a filled circle was a multiplicity indica-tor in OMT and an aggregation symbol in Booch. The term "method wars" was used to describe this period of time – is a class a cloud or a rectangle? Which one is better?

The end of the method wars as far as notation is concerned comes with the adoption of UML. UML is a language used to specify, visualize, and document the artifacts of an object-oriented system under development (*see* OBJECT-ORIENTED PROGRAMS AND SYSTEMS). It represents the unification of the Booch, OMT, and objectory notations, as well as the best ideas from a number of other methodologists.

The first public draft (version 0.8) was intro-duced in October 1995. Feedback from the public and Ivar Jacobson's input were included in the next two versions (0.9 in July 1996 and 0.91 in October 1996). Version 1.0 was presented to the Object Management Group (OMG) for standardization in July 1997. Additional en-hancements were incorporated into the 1.1 ver-sion of UML, which was presented to the OMG in September 1997. In November 1997, the UML was adopted as the standard modeling language by the OMG. Over the next few years, minor modifications were made to the UML. The current version is UML 1.5. UML 2.0 is the first major revision to the notation. This version is expected to be approved in late 2004 or early 2005.

A model is made up of many different dia-grams showing a static view as well as a dynamic view of the system (see figure 1). The major UML diagrams are shown below.

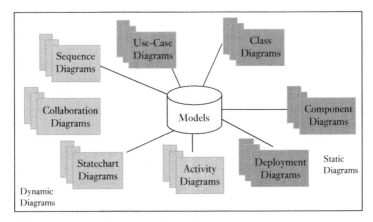

Figure 1   A model shows static as well as dynamic views of the system

ACTIVITY DIAGRAMS

Activity diagrams represent the dynamics of the system. They show the flow of control from activity to activity in the system, what activities can be done in parallel, and any alternate paths through the flow. Early in the life cycle, activity diagrams may be created to represent the flow across use cases or they may be created to represent the flow within a particular use case. Later in the life cycle, activity diagrams may be created to show the workflow for an operation.

Activity diagrams contain activities, transitions between the activities, decision points, and synchronization bars. In the UML, activities are represented as rectangles with rounded edges, transitions are drawn as directed arrows, decision points are shown as diamonds, and synchronization bars are drawn as thick horizontal or vertical bars.

USE-CASE DIAGRAMS

The behavior of a system under development (i.e., what functionality must be provided by the system) is documented in a use-case diagram, which illustrates the system's intended functions (use cases), its surroundings (actors), and relationships between the use cases and actors. The most important role of a use-case diagram is one of communication. It provides a vehicle used by the customers or end users and the developers to discuss the system's functionality and behavior. In the UML, use cases are represented as ovals and actors are represented as stickmen.

Each system typically has a Main Use-Case diagram, which is a picture of the system boundary (actors) and the major functionality provided by the system (use cases). Other use-case diagrams may be created as needed. Some examples follow:

- A diagram showing all the use cases for a selected actor.
- A diagram showing all the use cases being implemented in an iteration.
- A diagram showing a use case and all its relationships.

SEQUENCE DIAGRAMS

A sequence diagram shows object interactions arranged in time sequence. It depicts the objects

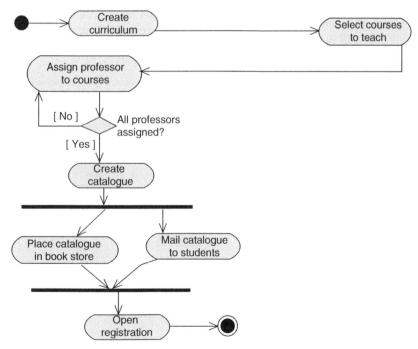

Figure 2   Activity diagram

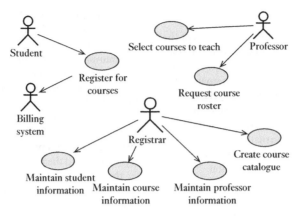

Figure 3   Use-case diagram

and classes involved in the scenario and the sequence of messages exchanged between the objects needed to carry out the functionality of the scenario. In the UML, an object in a sequence diagram is drawn as a rectangle containing the name of the object, underlined. An object can be named in one of three ways: the object name, the object name and its class, or just the class name (anonymous object). Object names can be specific (e.g., Algebra 101, Section 1) or they can be general (e.g., a course offering). Often, an anonymous object (class name only) may be used to represent any object in the class. Each object also has its timeline represented by a dashed line below the object. Messages between objects are represented by arrows that point from the client (sender of the message) to the supplier (receiver of the message).

COLLABORATION DIAGRAMS

A collaboration diagram is an alternate way to show object interactions. This type of diagram shows object interactions organized around the objects and their links to one another. In UML, a collaboration diagram contains:

- objects drawn as rectangles;
- links between objects shown as lines connecting the linked objects;
- messages shown as text and an arrow that points from the client to the supplier.

CLASS DIAGRAMS

Class diagrams are created to provide a picture or view of some or all of the classes in the model – they show the static structure of the system. A class is a collection of objects with the same structure

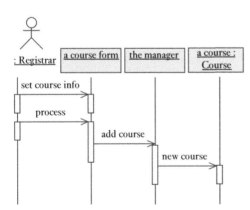

Figure 4   Sequence diagram

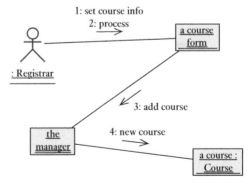

Figure 5   Collaboration diagram

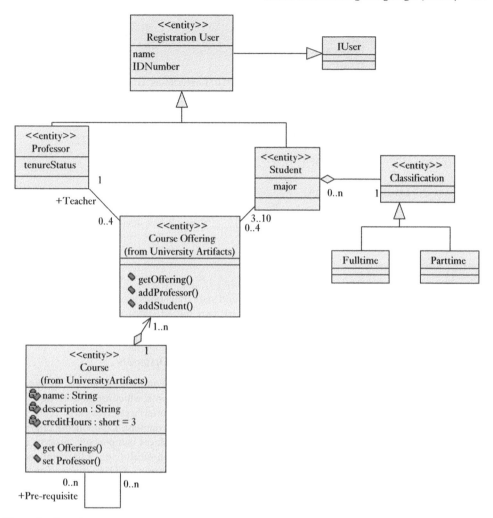

Figure 6 Class diagram

(attributes) and behavior (operations). In the UML, a class is shown as a rectangle with three compartments. The first compartment contains the class name, the second compartment contains attributes, and the last compartment contains operations. There are different types of relationships between classes. They are: association, aggregation, composition, dependency, realization, and inheritance. An association is a bidirectional relationship between two classes and it is drawn in UML as a line connecting the classes. An aggregation is a stronger form of association that shows a whole–part relationship between the classes. In UML an aggregation is shown as a line with a diamond closest to the class representing the whole. A composition relationship is a stronger form of aggregation that depicts lifetime dependencies between the whole and the part. A composition is drawn as an association with a solid diamond closest to the class representing the whole. A dependency is a weaker form of an association that shows a client–supplier relationship between the classes. In UML, a dependency is drawn as a dashed arrow pointing from the client to the supplier. A realization relationship shows the relationship between a specification and its implementation (i.e., the realization of an interface) and is shown as a dashed line with a triangle

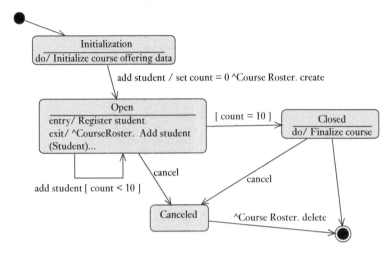

Figure 7   Statechart diagram

pointing to the class representing the specification. Finally, inheritance is a relationship between a superclass and its subclasses. UML inheritance relationships are shown as a solid line with a triangle pointing to the superclass.

STATECHART DIAGRAMS

A statechart diagram shows the states of a single object, the events or messages that cause a transition from one state to another, and the actions that result from a state change. A statechart diagram will not be created for every class in the system, only for classes with "significant" dynamic behavior. Sequence diagrams can be studied to determine the dynamic objects in the system – ones receiving and sending many messages. Statechart diagrams are also useful to investigate the behavior of an aggregate "whole" class and of control classes. In UML, states are represented as rectangles with rounded corners

and state transitions are shown as arrows. There are two special states – the start state, represented as a filled-in circle, and the stop state, which is shown as a bull's eye.

COMPONENT DIAGRAMS

Component diagrams show the relationships between components, which are modular units with well-defined interfaces that are replaceable within its environment. Components can be logical (e.g., business components, process components) or physical (e.g., EJB components, .NET components, COM components). In UML, components are drawn as rectangles with two small rectangles protruding from the side.

DEPLOYMENT DIAGRAMS

A deployment diagram is a hardware diagram – it shows processing nodes and their connections. In UML, a node is shown as a cube.

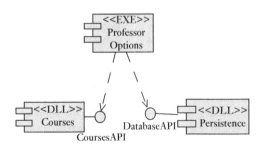

Figure 8   Component diagram

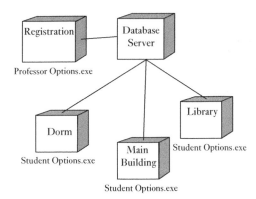

Professor Options.exe

Student Options.exe

Student Options.exe

Student Options.exe

Figure 9   Deployment diagram

More detailed information on the UML can be found in the Rational domain on IBM developerWorks (www-136.ibm.com/developer works/rational/).

URL (uniform resource locator)

see INTERNET; WORLDWIDE WEB

user acceptance of information technology

see TECHNOLOGY ACCEPTANCE MODEL; TECHNOLOGY ACCEPTANCE: UNIFIED MODEL

user evaluation of information systems

Gordon B. Davis

User evaluations are employed to assess the success of applications and services provided. Equating system success with usage is not satisfactory because some systems are required in order for a task to be completed, while others are elective. Some evaluation instruments have been based on job satisfaction; others have examined attitudes toward systems and resulting behaviors. An alternative performance approach may be more useful in evaluation. When the functionality and characteristics of the technology have a good fit with the task needs and abilities of individuals using the systems (*see* TASK/SYSTEM FIT), better performance will be achieved and the users will be satisfied. Research has shown that users are able to evaluate the fit of the technology with the tasks being performed.

virtual organization

A collection of geographically and functionally distributed organizational entities that are linked by computer and telecommunication technologies. *See* VIRTUAL WORK.

virtual reality

Virtual reality provides a user with computer-generated, full-color, three-dimensional imagery with possible attributes of touch, sound, and motion. The virtual reality application allows a user to experience the essence of reality for a physical space, operational environment, etc. Virtual reality displays can be supplemented by virtual reality gloves so that a user can manipulate screen objects and feel weight and texture. Applications of virtual reality for information systems include walkthroughs of physical space being planned (such as a new office design), simulation of new product use, and training in new procedures.

virtual team

A collection of individuals using computer and telecommunication technology to work across time and space in order to accomplish an organizational task. *See* VIRTUAL WORK.

virtual work

Priscilla Arling

Virtual work refers to the accomplishment of work, spanning time and space boundaries, through the utilization of computers and telecommunication technologies. Various terms relating to virtual work are often used interchangeably but have slightly different definitions. These terms include telecommuting, remote work, telework, virtual teams, and virtual organizations.

Nilles (1975) is credited with first using the term "telecommuting" to describe the substitution of travel to a workplace through the use of telecommunication technology. Telecommuting's focus on travel reduction was due in part to the oil crisis experienced in the US in the 1970s that spurred calls for reduced gasoline consumption. Today the idea of substituting travel to the office through technology use is still the defining feature of telecommuting.

In the early 1980s businesses began concentrating less on energy conservation and more on leveraging the ever-increasing capabilities of personal computing and communication technologies. The term "remote work" appeared during that time, referring to work performed outside of a central office and outside of normal working hours. While technology was seen as a facilitator for the accomplishment of remote work, the emphasis was on retaining workers by allowing flexibility in the location or scheduling of work. This could be accomplished through satellite centers, neighborhood centers, flexible work arrangements, or work-at-home (Olson, 1983). Satellite centers are geographically dispersed mini-offices where complete functional units of an organization are located so as to be close to where employees live. In a similar manner, neighborhood centers bring technology and office space to a location close to employees' homes, but these centers can be used by multiple organizations. Flexible work arrangements reflect a more part-time remote work environment where employees stay home occasionally to work on reports or other non-collaborative tasks, or arrive early or stay late at the office in order to accommodate childcare or other personal needs. Finally, work-at-home in the 1980s was at its nascent stages for most businesses, with only a small percentage of employees being allowed to spend an entire day or several days a week working from home. Even fewer employees were permitted to work full-time away from the central office. The work-at-home option was often viewed primarily as an accommodation for new mothers and it was expected to be a temporary arrangement.

By the 1990s, however, rapid improvements in technology and a rising need for skilled knowledge work combined to increase the use of virtual work. Advances in telecommunications technology not only expanded the type of work that could be performed away from a central office, but it also greatly improved the quality of virtual personal communication. Cellular phones, personal digital assistants (PDAs), and computer laptops increased the mobility of many workers. As video conferencing costs declined and the quality improved, this technology became commonplace in most large firms by the mid-1990s. While technology was changing rapidly, so were human resource requirements. Organizations found that they needed more highly skilled workers and that local labor markets often could not supply essential human capital. Those same skilled workers, realizing their value in the marketplace, demanded more flexibility in terms of work location and schedules. It was during this period that "telework" programs were spawned in companies across the globe. The term reflected a shift in emphasis away from specific remote work locations to leveraging technology to allow individuals to work anytime, anyplace. Flextime arrangements expanded to allow a broader variety of employees to work at home several days a week. Full-time teleworkers also grew in number, due in part to increased use of contractual employees who were geographically dispersed. Initially created as a job benefit for individual workers, companies soon realized that teleworking had the potential to reduce physical capital costs as well. By the end of the century, several firms had implemented mandatory telework programs, with entire regional divisions of employees working from home. Central office space was drastically

reduced and employees shared desks, phones, and other facilities in an arrangement called "hoteling." For some firms this resulted in substantial cost savings.

Today, the same need for flexibility and access to diversely skilled workers that initiated telework programs is now spawning virtual teams and even virtual organizations. Virtual teams are groups of individuals who use technology to work together across time and space to accomplish an organizational task (Jarvenpaa, Knoll, and Leidner, 1998). Since the individuals are brought together for the purpose of accomplishing a specific task, the team typically only exists for the life of the project or task. This is in contrast to organizational telework programs, where individuals generally work virtually across project lifetimes. Also, whereas telework connotes working away from a central office, virtual team members may all work in separate offices, with each office being the "central location" in its business unit or geographic area. Similarly, a virtual organization is a collection of geographically and functionally distributed entities that are linked by electronic forms of communication (DeSanctis, and Monge, 1999). Each of these entities is usually a self-sustaining organization in its own right. They form dynamic relationships with one another to facilitate production, coordination, and control of a shared product. As with other forms of virtual work, the emphasis is on dispersion of the organizations across time and space and the accomplishment of work that is achieved through use of information and communications technology.

Even while virtual work implementations continue to grow globally, the advantages and disadvantages of the practice continue to be debated. Virtual workers who work outside a central office tend to experience increased productivity owing to fewer distractions, increased autonomy, and improved flexibility in their work schedules. Members of virtual teams and organizations also benefit from access to expertise and other resources that were previously unavailable locally. Such groups are able to take advantage of time zone and cultural differences to truly work 24 hours a day to produce products suitable for a global marketplace. On the negative side, individuals working at home or in small offices can often feel isolated and can be left out of both formal and informal group communication. Managers may find it difficult to supervise virtual workers and performance evaluations and opportunities for promotion can suffer. For virtual teams and organizations, differences in time zones and culture can also hinder productivity and make communication both technically and socially challenging. For all virtual workers, the use of technology-mediated communication has both benefits and drawbacks. Technology-mediated communication has been found to be more efficient than face-to-face communication and it also increases the range of people with whom an individual interacts. However, using technology to communicate tends to diminish the ability to convey the intended meaning and context of messages, and in doing so negatively affects individual and group effectiveness.

Despite the above debates on advantages and disadvantages, virtual work is a mode of work that will only increase in use in the coming decade. Environmental and energy-conservation concerns, worker demands for flexible work location and schedules, the need for access to a global workforce, and opportunities for physical plant cost reductions will all continue to promote virtual work implementations. As virtual work grows, new terms and meanings are likely to evolve that will reflect the ever-changing environment in which technology is used to accomplish work across time and space.

Bibliography

DeSanctis, G. and Monge, P. (1999). Introduction to the special issue: Communication processes for virtual organizations. *Organization Science*, **10** (6), 693–703.

Jarvenpaa, S., Knoll, K., and Leidner, D. (1998). Is anybody out there? Antecedents of trust in global virtual teams. *Journal of Management Information Systems*, **14** (4), 29–64.

Nilles, J. (1975). Telecommunications and organizational decentralization. *IEEE Transactions on Communications*, **23**, 1142–7.

Olson, M. (1983). Remote office work: Changing work patterns in space and time. *Communications of the ACM*, **26** (3), 182–7.

virus

William J. Caelli

The concept of a computer "virus" has been seen as being inherent in the very structure of a computer system, whereby a "program" may see itself or any other program as "data." The US's CNSS 4009 glossary of terms, however, narrows this definition somewhat. It defines a computer virus as a "self-replicating malicious code that attaches itself to an application program or other executable system component and leaves no obvious signs of its presence."

In this sense, a computer virus can be seen as the manifestation of a failure in system integrity policy. In simple terms, an application program, for example, should not have the authority to read, modify, delete, or otherwise tamper with another application program unless this is specifically and explicitly granted. For example, a final, executable, binary form of a program should only be readable by the computer operating system's "loader" program, which copies that program file from secondary storage to main memory for execution. If it has to be "patched," in binary form, then that patching program needs to have full system management authority at the highest level to perform such a function. At another level, an application program, of which a virus is an example, must not have permission to alter overall operating system settings or tables needed for the operation of all applications and the service of all users in the system. It could be argued that with such higher security systems as those implementing a "mandatory" access control or security regime, the actions of application-level virus programs would be severely curtailed, and even potentially stopped.

Computer viruses, first described in the early 1980s by F. Cohen, have become a major threat to globally interconnected computer systems on the INTERNET. The problem in this case is not the Internet itself, a data communications service, but rather the level of security provided by the computer and basic operating systems that form the end-elements in such a network. The topic is explained in detail in Cohen (1990).

The modern computer virus takes many forms and can be coded in many ways, including the use of "macro languages," provided as services in other applications such as word processor programs, high-level scripting languages that provide for usually small, dedicated programs to be created and used for specific purposes in a dynamic way, and others. These latter virus programs are considered to be "cross-platform" viruses in that they are independent of the particular computer type being used. The problem in modern computer networks based around the Internet, particularly as so-called "web-based" applications emerge, is that a client user, for example, will find it almost impossible to completely trust all programs that arrive at the client computer system for execution and operation. This concern points to the need for a "next generation" of operating system structures to cater for such a new environment, e.g., an operating system that permits only applications approved by the system's owner to execute through use of cryptographic checksum operations controlled by the owner, etc.

See also *cryptography (crypto); information assurance; malware; risk assessment and risk management; spyware*

Bibliography

Cohen, F. B. (1990). *A Short Course on Computer Viruses.* Pittsburgh, PA: ASP Press.

voice over Internet protocol

Joel R. Helgeson

Internet voice, IP telephony, voice over IP and VoIP are all terms used to describe what is known as voice over Internet protocol (VoIP). VoIP is the technology that has enabled the full convergence of the legacy telephone (voice) networks and digital data networks. This convergence started taking place first within corporate networks (intranets; *see* INTRANET), and then spread across the INTERNET, where it is often referred to as simply Internet voice.

Prior to VoIP, companies had to deploy two disparate networks, one for voice and one for data. Each network essentially required separate administration teams. The telephony administrators responsible for the voice network generally reported to the facilities department, whereas the data administrators reported to the information technology department.

By combining the voice and data networks, companies received a rapid return on investment (ROI) with VoIP as they were able to utilize data connections to carry voice traffic between their offices and obtain significant savings by eliminating inter-office long-distance charges and costly PBX tie-lines. These companies saw further returns when they merged telephony and network administration responsibilities into a single department.

Traditional telephone system vendors (e.g., Lucent/Avaya, Nortel) began integrating VoIP technologies into their existing product line. By 2001, two years after it gained initial use, every major telephone system manufacturer had VoIP telephone systems on its roadmap, or had abandoned its legacy voice network designs entirely. Major issues in the adoption of VoIP are its economics, reliability, and time delays.

Major telephone carriers have begun to replace existing telephone network infrastructures with VoIP. Handling voice calls as data is very efficient, enabling the carriers to better utilize and manage their network infrastructure. This efficiency is gained primarily in two ways. The first is efficiency from placing multiple data calls into the space that previously could handle only one traditional voice call. The second efficiency is because VoIP faces fewer governmental regulatory requirements. In the US, these efficiencies have enabled carriers to offer long distance at rates that fall below $0.05 per minute.

Reliability has always been central to adoption of VoIP. Telephone systems are generally built using what is commonly referred to as a five-nines architecture, which means 99.999 percent uptime guarantee. That equates to just 5 minutes of unplanned downtime per year. When a customer picks up a phone, he or she expects to hear a dial tone. Therefore, the entire voice infrastructure has been built with resiliency and redundancy in mind, not to mention a high degree of efficiency in providing services and billing for them.

VoIP is now generally as stable as the traditional telephony networks. The problems that early adopters experienced with reliability were primarily due to improper design and limitations within the VoIP protocols themselves. As the technology has matured, design considerations have been made and communication protocols have been updated to better handle the need for redundancy and self-healing networks. Major IP telephony vendors, such as Cisco and 3Com, claim 99.999 percent reliability.

Voice traffic is very sensitive to time delays, more sensitive than many Internet services, such as EMAIL. Any transmission delay over 250 ms is generally unacceptable and makes holding a conversation very difficult. As a result, VoIP systems must limit delay to less than 150 ms in one direction. It is for this reason that voice calls are not generally routed over the public Internet, where 500 ms delays are quite common.

The exceptions to this are free, publicly available phone services over the Internet. These free services use the public Internet and therefore have lower voice quality and reliability compared to commercial carriers.

The future of VoIP is promising. Currently, the major issue with VoIP is vendor interoperability, since vendors tend to have slightly different standards. These problems are expected to be resolved by national and international standards.

voice recognition

see SPEECH RECOGNITION AND SYNTHESIS

weblog

see BLOG (WEBLOG)

web portal

see PORTAL

web services

Wendy L. Currie

Web services are emerging as a systematic and extensible framework for application-to-application integration. Built upon existing web protocols and open XML (EXTENSIBLE MARKUP LANGUAGE) standards, information can be seamlessly passed between remote applications running in different environments. This architecture heralds the way for web services, promising to provide real business delivery mechanisms, system integration, and strategic opportunities for firms. This new distributed computing model is described as the next generation of service-oriented INTERNET applications.

In the past, consistent implementation was necessary to enable distributed application integration. But with web services, the playing field may be leveled, enabling the construction of new composite applications using business functions from other internal or external applications without being dependent on an implementation. This services-oriented approach aims to integrate applications within and across firms. The key difference between a traditional web application and a web service is that the data and information returned can be easily integrated into INTRANET, server, or desktop applications

(Currie, 2004). Definitions of web services vary, with some pundits focusing on the business features and others on the technical aspects. Thus,

> Web services are loosely coupled software components delivered over Internet standard technologies. A web service represents a business function or business service and can be accessed by another application ... over public networks using generally available protocols. (Gartner Group, 2001)

> A web service is a software application that is identified by a URL whose interfaces and bindings are capable of being defined, described, and discovered by XML artefacts, and supports direct interactions with other software application using XML-based messages via Internet-based protocols. (W3C Web Services Architecture Group, www.w3.org/TR/wsa-reqs)

The drive toward web services is built upon the premise that significant benefits will arise from integrating software applications across heterogeneous organizations, sites, and departments. One of the failings of the application service provider (*see* APPLICATION SERVICE PROVISION (ASP)) business model of the late 1990s was the implication that *legacy* software applications and infrastructure needed to be replaced, or at least reinforced with *web-enabled* technology. For banks, insurance firms, and many others who have invested heavily in information technology, the prospect of web-enabled "add-ons" is insignificant in the context of their overall IT infrastructure and human capabilities. Investing further sums of money with no discernible business benefits is both impractical and undesirable. The key issue for these industries is not to replace IT but to explore ways to better integrate legacy systems. Yet the cost of integrating numerous disparate systems (e.g., compliance, order management, reconciliation, data attribution, performance analysis, treasury, etc.) requires a large commitment in terms of money, time, and skill. So what is the impetus behind the perceived growth in web services?

According to the Gartner Group (2001),

The need for e-commerce, collaborative commerce (c-commerce) and involvement with other divisions or departments is pushing vendors to honour enterprises' requests for easy integration, if not out-of-the-box then certainly without having to rely on extraordinary resources.... Through 2006, service-orientated development will change the way software is built, packaged and sold by more than 80 percent of ISVs (Independent Software Vendors). By 2005, new licences for software that use Web Services standards will represent 21 billion in sales.

The business requirement for integration is expected to become a multibillion dollar market.

The Aberdeen Group estimated that new enterprise information integration technology would become a $7.5 billion market in 2003. Like its ASP forerunner, web services is an e-business model which is spearheaded by the technology sector. It is based on the service-oriented architecture (SOA) framework to provide a technical foundation for making business processes accessible within enterprises and across enterprises to allow customers to communicate with their suppliers at all levels.

Some believe that web services will create new, and transform existing, business and customer-facing software applications. Unlike stand-alone and self-contained software applications deployed in fixed locations like thick-client desktop machines or centralized application servers, web services are not tied to specific technology platforms and operating systems. Applications based on delivery via web services will benefit the customer through their simplicity of use within a single IT structure.

Table 1   Phases of web service (WS) adoption

Integration	Collaboration	Innovation	Domination
• Experimentation with WS with small, internal integration projects • SOAP-enablement of legacy applications and ERP, CRM systems • Fast cycles of learning reach the limits of early WS, unprepared IT architectures • Increase in shared information across the business	• Experimentation with WS outside firewalls • Increasing interaction with trading partners and customers • Close trading partners implement WS to drive shared value • External trading partners begin sharing information to drive industry value chain benefits	• Lessons from integration and collaboration applied to new processes and business models • New distributed WS processes and applications drive business change • Dramatic business results are achieved as WS are applied in many ways, driving new value propositions	• First movers begin to assert their dominance over respective markets and industries • Industry dominance achieved by innovating new business models as well as out-executing competitors • WS leaders win through rapid innovation and cycles of learning • WS mastery creates new company and industry structures as boundaries are redefined

Source: Marks and Werrell (2003: 19)

The maturity of web services is expected to move through four distinct phases: integration, collaboration, innovation, and domination (Marks and Werrell, 2003: 19). In the first phase of web services adoption, firms will engage in internal system integration projects. This requirement is driven by the myriad of information silos created by proprietary enterprise applications implemented to support various activities (i.e., general ledger, accounts payable, accounts receivable for financial management; and costing systems, order management, procurement, and production scheduling more generally). These enterprise applications are likely to be large, client/server implementations built with an internal organization-facing view of the world, and oriented toward internal efficiency and controls. Integration will employ specialized features of XML that are being standardized under the acronym SOAP.

The second phase of web services is expected to drive process and operational improvements in many business areas, provided that the integration hurdles can be overcome and that the tools and technologies are mature enough to enable collaboration. The third phase is innovation. This will see firms devising new ways of doing business using web services. These firms will leverage what they have learned in previous (integration and collaboration) phases with outside customers, partners, and suppliers. The fourth phase, domination, is the culmination of the three previous stages. Market leaders will emerge, which drive superior business value through the use of web services in distributed business process execution (DBPE). The four phases are presented in table 1.

Like other emerging technologies, it is important to distinguish between the reality and the hype surrounding web services. Currently, web services offers the potential to resolve the perennial problem of poor software applications integrations, yet much remains to be seen.

Bibliography

Currie, W. (ed.) (2004). *Value Creation from E-Business Models*. Oxford: Butterworth-Heinemann.
Gartner Group (2001). Web services 2002 and beyond. Author David Smith. December 14, 1–3.
Marks, E. and Werrell, M. J. (2003). *Executives' Guide to Web Services*. Chichester: John Wiley.

wifi

This abbreviation of wireless fidelity refers to wireless networking. It may be used to refer to any wireless networking for communication among computers, computing devices, and peripheral devices such as printers. It may refer specifically to wireless networking using the IEEE 802.11 standard. See WIRELESS COMPUTING.

wireless computing

Joel R. Helgeson

Wireless computing is used synonymously with the term mobile computing. These terms are used to describe the application of portable, wireless computing and communication devices. Examples of devices employed in wireless computing are laptop computers with wireless local area network (LAN) technology (*see* LOCAL AREA NETWORKS), mobile phones, and personal digital assistants (PDAs) with Bluetooth or infrared wireless interfaces. Wireless networks are also referred to as WIFI or wireless fidelity, a reference to the rapid adoption of wireless technology by home hobbyists, similar to that of high-fidelity (hifi) stereos.

The terms wireless LAN and wifi both refer generically to any wireless network that conforms to the 802.11 specifications for wireless networking. Some of these specifications are as follows:

- 802.11 – the base standard defines transmission rates between 1 and 2 Mbps.
- 802.11b and 802.11g specifications use the 2.4 GHz spectrums. They can transmit data at speeds up to 11 and 54 Mbps, respectively.
- 802.11a uses the 5 GHz spectrum and can transmit data at speeds up to 54 Mbps.

The 802.11b standard was the first specification that came to market and is therefore the most widely adopted. 802.11b was followed by 802.11a, then 802.11g. Devices that support 802.11g are also backwards compatible with 802.11b as they both use the 2.4 GHz (gigahertz) spectrum.

Wireless devices that support any of the wireless LAN specifications are able to communicate with a wireless base station, referred to as an access point, from distances as far as 300 ft (100 m). Alternatively, wireless devices can communicate directly with one another in what is referred to as a peer-to-peer network. One major drawback of using wireless technologies on mobile devices is the additional power consumption of the wireless network adapter.

Bluetooth is a wireless communications protocol that also uses the 2.4 GHz spectrum and was designed for use primarily by mobile devices to create a personal area network (PAN). PANs were designed simply to eliminate the need for interface cables and are designed to connect mobile devices to peripherals such as printers, keyboards, and mice that are located within 30 ft (10 m) of the mobile device. Bluetooth's smaller area of coverage, combined with the lower throughput (723.1 kbps), creates less drain on batteries and is therefore an attractive option used primarily by cell phones and PDAs.

Bluetooth is often used on cellular phone handsets to communicate wirelessly with headsets and automotive hands-free kits. Alternate uses of Bluetooth-enabled cell phones are beginning to include using a cell phone to pay for purchases. Current trials enable users to use their cell phones to pay for incidental purchases such as soft drinks from a vending machine. Future uses anticipate using a cell phone to pay for gasoline at the pump or groceries at the store.

There are multiple versions of the Bluetooth technology. They are versions 1.1, 1.2, and the soon to be 2.0. Each version offers various feature enhancements over the others that essentially provide enhanced device interoperability and security. Versions prior to 1.1 were primarily used for testing and development of the technology and did not have commercial deployment.

Infrared data association (IRDA) defines the specifications for the use of infrared light to transmit data over short distances. IRDA is commonly used to transfer data between mobile devices, such as business cards between PDAs, or for a mobile device to send data to a printer or synchronize a PDA with a laptop or desktop computer. IRDA uses very little battery power; however, its biggest drawback is that it operates only in line of sight and is only useful at distances of less than 10 ft (3 m).

Security is often cited as the number one concern for wireless computing. There are reasons for this concern. It is very difficult to dynamically balance the need for security with the desire for flexibility. Therefore, users have been forced to make a difficult choice, to have either a flexible wireless network or a secure one. Companies and users often deployed flexible yet insecure wireless networks. This has resulted in criticism of wireless systems on the basis of security. Recent standards have provided more security features.

The original 802.11 specification was designed for use in targeted industries, such as retailers and warehouses for the purposes of inventory management. Because of the targeted application, security was almost an afterthought and was not designed with scalability in mind. The default security used in 802.11 networks is called wired equivalent protocol (WEP) and was designed to encrypt data between wireless devices and access points, to provide a level of security that was roughly equivalent to that of a wired device. When mobile devices increased in use and started the widespread adoption of wireless LANs, the shortfalls of 802.11 security became readily apparent. 802.11 security was simply never designed for these uses.

As a result, there have been several amendments to the 802.11 specification, specifically 802.11i, n, and 802.11x. These advances in security were designed to increase the flexibility and security that are missing from the original specification. Users that implement these are faced with the challenge of integrating legacy devices that do not support the newer specifications. As a result, companies are turning to wireless gateways to provide a segmentation of their networks.

The term wireless gateway refers generically to a device that behaves similarly to an INTERNET firewall. Where a firewall typically segments the internal corporate network from the public Internet, the wireless gateway segments the wired network from the wireless network. Users of wireless devices must first authenticate with the wireless gateway before they are allowed to access resources located on the wired network. Additionally, by using wireless gateways, companies offer guest users access to the Internet, whereas employees have full access to internal resources once they are authenticated. This helps to balance the flexibility versus security issue.

There have been numerous concerns regarding the security of devices supporting Bluetooth. In a technical sense, someone may be able to download the contents of your PDA or your cell phone address book just by simply walking past you and making a wireless connection. In the case of infrared connections, the limits of range and need for line of sight makes security less of a concern. However, there is a new proposed use of IRDA called IRFM (infrared financial messaging), also known as "Point and Pay," which integrates unique security features to pay for transactions using a personal device.

wireless communications

see WIRELESS COMPUTING

worldwide web

Mark A. Fuller

In 1993, a new INTERNET function was introduced by the CERN physics laboratory in Switzerland termed the worldwide web. The worldwide web is a service that provides an Internet-accessible network of hyperlinked documents. The documents are standardized in their underlying structure, facilitating the exchange of complex types of information. Until this time, most people had not found the Internet to be particularly useful. While some businesses and many universities used the basic functions of the Internet, i.e., message and file exchange, the ability to gather useful information from remote locations was still a reasonably complex task, beyond the skill and interest of many. The worldwide web (also known as the web or WWW) changed usage by making it possible to exchange information more easily and in richer forms.

Information on the worldwide web is organized into pages and accessed through software called a web browser. Each page may contain information in the form of text, images, sound files, or full-motion video. The worldwide web has evolved into an interactive media as well. Programs running in the background of some web pages allow the user to respond to questions online, fill out forms, access remote databases, or interact with other types of programs. These interactive capabilities have the potential to change the way users run both their personal life (through applications involving activities such as online banking, shopping, or entertainment) and their work (through online systems that assist in business activities such as inventory control, product ordering, and communication).

Web pages typically contain hypertext links to other pages and resources. When links are activated, the user may be retrieving data from the same computer where the original page resides, or from a computer in a remote location thousands of miles away. Each page and computer combination has a unique address called a uniform resource locator (URL). This addressing system enables users to store the location of a resource for access in the future. Web documents are created in a particular language which browsers recognize and translate. The language, termed hypertext markup language (or HTML), is reasonably simple to learn, allowing even relative computer novices to create basic web pages in a short amount of time (*see* MARKUP LANGUAGES).

The earliest web browser, called Mosaic, was designed at the University of Illinois and incorporated the ability to interpret graphical images on the screen. Since that time, a variety of other browsers have been developed, including Netscape's Navigator and Microsoft's Internet Explorer. The web became a rapid success, changing Internet usage from primarily the governmental and educational sector to nearly 10 million users by 1994, just one year after its inception. As of 2003, the estimated number of users was nearly 600 million. In that year, these users accessed over 6 billion web pages and spent nearly $100 billion dollars purchasing goods and services on the Internet's worldwide web.

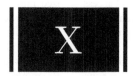

XML (extensible markup language)

Roger Debreceny

MARKUP LANGUAGES are used to define the content of files that are exchanged between different applications or different users. They are very important because they define the format and meaning of strings of characters or text within letters, documents, forms, and other business documents that are sent within an organization or between organizations. In the absence of a markup language, each message or document would need to describe how the strings of characters being exchanged should be interpreted. The markup language is a standard way to describe the content. Without a markup language, for example, a document containing a financial report would need significant descriptive information to explain the elements of the report and how the recipient should format the elements in the report.

There are many markup languages; the most significant are those accepted as standards. Some are limited in scope and use; others are broad and extensible. For example, HTML (hypertext markup language) is a standard markup language for INTERNET pages that interconnect with other pages. XML (extensible markup language) is one of the most important markup languages, because it is standard in its structure and yet can be extended to include new markup requirements and creation of new markup languages.

XML was developed in response to the need for a general purpose markup language that could be widely deployed on the Internet. The World Wide Web Consortium (W3C) created the extensible markup language version 1.0 (XML 1.0) as a foundation for the development of new Internet-based standards and applications in electronic commerce (*see* E-COM-MERCE), metadata management, and other application areas. XML is a metalanguage, designed to support the creation of new languages. XML is a subset of the standard generalized markup language (SGML), which is expressly designed for the Internet and the WORLDWIDE WEB.

A markup language is coded in plaintext. Defined components of the file are interpreted as markup ("tags") instead of content. The text "`<title>`" and "`</title>`" in the string `<title>` This is the title of this document `</title>` are the opening and closing tags or markup that provide semantic value to, in this case, a fragment of text.

Markup within a file may contain instructions for the application using and interpreting the plaintext file. The markup may alternatively provide semantic interpretation of the text contained within the markup. Semantic interpretation of the markup is defined by the markup language. SGML, XML, and HTML are examples of markup languages. In contrast with the predefined set of tags (tagset) defined in the HTML specification, XML has an extensible tagset. XML makes no semantic restriction on the tags that may be incorporated within a particular application. Indeed, HTML 4.0 is reproduced in XML as XHTML.

XML semantic content can be incorporated within both tags and/or attributes of tags. The XML code fragment shown below illustrates the use of both tags that are designed to impart semantic content to the text they encompass (e.g., "`<paragraph>`") and tag attributes that add semantic meaning to the encompassed content (e.g., "`<display = ``Yes''>`").

```
<?xml version = ``1.0''?>
<helloworldtext>
```

```
<title>
My First XML Document
</title>
<paragraph display = ''Yes''>
Hello World.
</paragraph>
</helloworldtext>
```

XML 1.0 has, by design, a highly limited set of features. XML provides no direct support for presentation of content on interactive displays or in print. It has no mechanism for transporting XML content on the Internet or any other network architecture. It provides no direct support for externally defining the semantic meaning of the extensible tagset within XML documents. For example, the semantic meaning of the markup such as "`<title>`" and "`<paragraph>`" shown in the code fragment above will be completely dependent on the application under development. In this case, the markup has semantic value within the English language. The tags (elements) could equally as well have been represented by the terms "`<ax74t>`" or "`<xi3f5>`." Support for the prerequisites for any complete application such as presentation, transport, and semantic definitions are found either elsewhere in the suite of standards defined by the W3C and that make up the XML family, or in the wider body of Internet standards defined by organizations such as the Internet Engineering Task Force (IETF).

The suite of companion XML standards developed by the W3C is both broad and deep, covering presentation, namespaces, semantic structuring, information querying, and hyperlinking. Support for transformation and presentation of XML documents is covered by the extensible stylesheet language family (XSL). XSL transformations (XSLT) provides a means for transforming XML documents from one form ("source tree") to another ("result tree"). The content and structure of the transformed document will depend on the way in which the consuming application has utilized a template that is associated with an XML document. XSL 1.0 (previously XSL Formatting Objects (XSL-FO)) provides a means for formatting a result tree in a particular display format, typically a print-based layout.

The core XML specification makes no restriction on the naming of elements or attributes and there is, consequently, no central registry of elements or attributes. It is highly likely, then, that application designers will each identically name elements or attributes. In designing an inventory application, for example, it will be common to have elements such as "`<part _id>`" or "`<bin_location>`." The XML Namespaces specification provides a mechanism, based on standard Internet universal resource identifiers (URIs), to uniquely identify the authority for a given element or attribute. This will allow the consuming application to differentiate "`<my:part_id>`" from "`<your:part_id>`."

The foundation of SGML, of which XML is a subset, was in the processing of textual documents for publication purposes. Whilst these documents typically have complex structures, they are of quite a different character to the semantic structures required for processing business or e-commerce information. SGML provides a method for externally imposing a data structure upon one or more instance documents through the document type definition (DTD) mechanism. Whilst this mechanism is also supported in XML, it has been effectively replaced by the relatively recent XML Schema specification. XML Schema was created in response to a clear need for a more efficient and effective method for enforcing data structures over instance documents in a wide variety of application domains, notably in all aspects of e-commerce. XML Schema provides a more data-centric approach to specifying knowledge structures in instance documents. The specification provides a systematic approach to defining both simple and complex data structures that can be consistently enforced on a set of instance documents by an application. XML Schema defines a host of simple data types that are commonly found in database schema languages, including `string`, `decimal`, `integer`, `negativeInteger`, and `positiveInteger`. The specification provides a mechanism for deriving further specializations of the predefined simple types. For example, `negativeInteger` and `positiveInteger` are both specializations of the integer simple type.

XML Schema also supports the creation of complex types, such as a "`purchaseOrder`" or "`customerAddress`." These complex types incorporate sets of simple data types or complex types. The complex type can impose both ordering or sequence and cardinality on sets of simple and complex types. Data structures can be reused by associating different names with predefined simple or complex types. Specialization is also supported by allowing new types to be created that are extensions of existing types. Types may be associated with rich sets of attributes that may, in turn, be associated with enumerated lists.

XLink and XPath are components of the companion suite of XML standards that collectively provide a significantly enhanced set of hyperlinking functionality, as compared with HTML. XLink supports both simple and complex ("extended") hyperlink structures. The HTML hyperlink based on the anchor construct is functionally equivalent to the simple link in XLink. Extended links, however, allow designers to incorporate highly complex link structures in their applications ("linkbases"). Links in XLink at their simplest level join two resources such as content in XML instance documents together over an arc. The manner by which those links are established can be derived in complex ways. An extended link associates an arbitrary number of resources. XLink provides mechanisms for the developer to bind resources together by networks of links, associate human-readable titles to a given hyperlink, set rules for traversal between resources, and define the resources that may be accessed by a given hyperlink.

XML instance documents will frequently have highly complex internal structures. Information that is of value to applications may be stored within some subsection of the instance document. XPath provides syntax for applications based on other standards such as XPointer and XSLT to address given components of an instance document. The choice of components may depend on some processing logic and selection criteria by the application using (consuming) the data. XPath provides a mechanism for applications to locate parts of XML documents. XPath sees documents as a tree of nodes that include text, attribute, and namespace nodes and then provides a mechanism for retrieving sets of nodes. A revised version of the XPath specification is also an important component of the architecture to query sets of XML instance documents, along with the nascent XQuery. XQuery is designed to allow consuming applications to query documents that are of a primarily textual nature (semi-structured) as well as sets of documents that correspond to a database in nature (structured). Both the revised XPath and XQuery are designed to interoperate with XML Schema.

A knowledge store defined in XML Schema is functionally equivalent to the semantic structure of an object-oriented database (see OBJECT-ORIENTED DATABASE MANAGEMENT SYSTEMS). In a RELATIONAL DATABASE, database structures are typically homogeneous, regular, and flat; the order of rows in tables is immaterial and missing information is typically represented by null values. In a database of XML instance documents, metadata are typically heterogeneous, with semantic structure being drawn from multiple XML schemas; ordering is intrinsically semantically significant; and missing information is represented by the absence of an element. XQuery is a strongly typed object query language that provides a wide array of functions, including math, sequences, Boolean, string manipulation, and regular expressions. Developers may also derive their own functions.

The World Wide Web Consortium has also developed several knowledge management (see KNOWLEDGE MANAGEMENT SYSTEMS) and ONTOLOGY specifications that are either based on XML or include XML documents within the resources described in the ontology. An early and important specification was the resource description framework (RDF). This framework provides a mechanism to describe any resource that can be encapsulated within a URI, including information that may be accessed on the Internet (such as websites, HTML documents, or a gateway to a Z39.59 library database), or animate or inanimate objects that are not reachable on the Internet. RDF ontological data describe both the location and properties of information resources. RDF/XML allows the exchange of structured information about these resources. OWL (web ontology language) is a new specification that provides a formal means for developers to provide a rich set of descriptives on web resources, including XML instance documents. OWL is in three versions, each of increasing functionality ("Lite," "DL," and "Full"). OWL can describe resources in terms of XML Schema datatypes, equivalence, cardinality, versioning, and characteristics of the resource.

XML and the suite of companion specifications have provided a common language for the development of a wide range of knowledge interchange standards. XML is used as a common means to specify them. Some of the most important XML-based standards have been in the broad sweep of e-commerce. One of the most significant uses of XML in this segment is by RosettaNet, a consortium of more than 500 corporations primarily in the electronics sector. RosettaNet defines partner interface processes (PIPs) that provide the requisite information environment for the establishment, initiation, and completion of a wide range of business processes between trading partners. PIPs exist in seven "clusters" that include partner product and service review; product information; order management; inventory management; marketing information management; service and support; and manufacturing. The semantic content of PIP specifications is represented in document type definitions. Each business process includes a schema of the information transferred (e.g., in a quote request, the `GlobalPayment MethodCode`, `contractIdentifier`. `ProprietaryDocumentIdentifier` and `estimatedAvailabilityDate`. `Date Period` are each defined) and provides a choreography as the business process proceeds from initiation to completion.

The extensible business reporting language (XBRL) is an important markup language (based on XML) for the exchange of business performance data. XBRL is being standardized by XBRL International, an international consortium of more than 200 organizations and corporations. Whilst the primary rationale for XBRL was to provide a means for representing the financial and non-financial information typically found in a corporate quarterly or annual report, XBRL has been used in a variety of regulatory and other information exchange environments. Whilst the business processes established in RosettaNet are sufficiently structured and well defined to be incorporated directly into the RosettaNet technical specifications, financial reporting is more fluid and subject to variation at the international, regional, and entity level.

The XBRL specification establishes a framework for the establishment of reporting ontologies, known in the XBRL community as taxonomies, rather than attempting to predefine all reporting constructs. The taxonomies provide the metadata necessary to provide semantic value to facts reported by a reporting entity. XBRL is based upon three primary XML specifications: XML Schema, XML Namespaces, and XLink. Indeed, the XBRL community is arguably the most significant user of the XLink specification. XBRL taxonomies are, at their most essential, a simple XML Schema containing a flat list of the elements in the taxonomy. The elements described in the schema may take on the datatypes as defined XML Schema and the XBRL specification marks out several datatypes that have been defined especially for business reporting. The implementation of the monetary data type in the XBRL specification, for example, requires instance documents to report both the quantum and the reporting currency of any monetary item.

Most performance reporting applications require more than just a listing of elements within a particular knowledge domain. Descriptions of the taxonomy element and the nature of the mathematical and semantic relationship of one element of the taxonomy to another are all matters which application designers may wish to incorporate into the taxonomy. These elements of the XBRL ontology are bestowed in a set of so-called "linkbases." XBRL linkbases employ XLink to provide enhanced metadata and to impose a node structure on the elements defined in the XML Schema-based taxonomy. The XBRL specification defines the role of presentation, references, calculation, label, and definition linkbases in linkbases. Traversal of the arcs within the linkbase is optional – in other words, an application consuming an XBRL instance document may not need to associate the predefined label of an element with the element tag and will not therefore need to process the label linkbase to retrieve the label. Other applications will need to report the name associated with a given taxonomy element and will traverse the arc to retrieve the label.

The XBRL specification is silent on many important elements that are necessary to construct a complete reporting environment, including registration of taxonomies, transmission, signing, or choreography. The XBRL consortium leaves these issues to the designers of particular reporting applications.

E-commerce provided significant importance to the development of standard markup languages based on XML. ebXML (electronic business using extensible markup language) is an ambitious endeavor to construct a suite of XML-based specifications designed to facilitate electronic business over the Internet. ebXML was originally developed by OASIS (Organization for the Advancement of Structured Information Standards) and the United Nations/ECE agency CEFACT, with technical development now primarily resident at OASIS. Taking a significantly more ambitious approach to electronic business than taken by RosettaNet, ebXML aims to bring two or more trading partners together in a wide range of business transactions. Aspects of this exchange process include registration of trading partners, description of products and services, catalogues of business processes, mechanisms for the discovery of trading partners and products and services, and the establishment, undertaking, and conclusion of trading relations between trading partners. Semantic structure of the various information

exchanges is enforced in XML Schema and DTD frameworks. These knowledge schemas control the format of, for example, a trading entity's collaboration protocol profile (CPP), which is a document that allows a trading entity to describe its "business processes" and "business service interface" requirements. These profiles are managed in a repository. Information is exchanged between the firm and the registry using a set of controlled terms. ebXML uses the extensible nature of the XML suite of specifications to enable a highly flexible set of interactions, ranging from an entity that may only want to discover potential trading partners, through to discovery not only of trading partners but also of the detailed products and services offered by those partners, and development of an agreement for the purchase and delivery of those products and services and completion of the requirements of that agreement.

Bibliography

Bosak, J. (1997). XML, Java, and the future of the web. www.ibiblio.org/pub/sun-info/standards/xml/why/xmlapps.html.

Flynn, P. (ed.) The XML FAQ. www.ucc.ie/xml/.

Index

Note: Headwords are in bold type

Printed and bound by CPI Group (UK) Ltd, Croydon, CR0 4YY

23/04/2025

14660954-0004